DIANE RAVITCH

SIMON & SCHUSTER
New York • London
Toronto • Sydney • Singapore

LEFT BACK

*A Century
of Failed
School
Reforms*

SIMON & SCHUSTER
Rockefeller Center
1230 Avenue of the Americas
New York, NY 10020

SIMON & SCHUSTER and colophon are registered trademarks
of Simon & Schuster Inc.

Designed by Deirdre C. Amthor

Manufactured in the United States of America

10 9 8 7 6 5 4 3 2 1

Library of Congress Cataloging-in-Publication Data

Ravitch, Diane.
    Left back : a century of failed school reforms / Diane Ravitch.
        p. cm.
    Includes bibliographical references and index.
        1. Education—United States—History—20th century.   2. Educational
change—United States—History—20th century.   3. Public schools—United
States—History—20th century.   I. Title.

LA216.R28   2000
370'.973—dc21   00-038067

ISBN 0-684-84417-6

For Mary

Contents

LEFT
BACK

Introduction

For most of the twentieth century, Americans have argued about their public schools, some claiming that they are not as good as they used to be, others that they are not as good as they ought to be. Some think the schools should go "back to basics"; others insist that the schools should break free of the basics. Some want higher standards; others want schools where students pursue their own interests without any external pressures. Some think that the schools must liberate themselves from the dead hand of tradition, others that the schools are plagued by too many faddish reforms.

Each generation supposes that its complaints are unprecedented. Critics of the schools in the 1980s looked back to the 1950s as a halcyon era; critics in the 1950s looked back on their own Depression-era schooling as a high-water mark. But those who seek the "good old days" will be disappointed, for in fact there never was a Golden Age. It is impossible to find a period in the twentieth century in which education reformers, parents, and the citizenry were satisfied with the schools.

As that century drew to a close, American schools were once again at the center of acrimonious debates about their quality, their methods, and even their purpose. The schools were expected to do something they had never done before: educate all children to high standards. This demand for better academic performance unleashed arguments about the meaning of standards, how to set them, and how to measure whether they have been met.

Critics pointed to low scores on national and international tests; to the widespread practice of social promotion and grade inflation; to the large numbers of teachers who had received degrees in pedagogy, but not in the academic subjects they were teaching; to the high rates of remediation necessary in college; and to the low academic expectations that had become ingrained in many American schools. School districts in different parts of the country were rocked by disputes about the curriculum, standards of achievement, and classroom methods. Bitter debates broke out about how to teach reading and mathematics, how much emphasis to place on multiculturalism in history and literature, how to measure students' performance, and whether to hold students accountable for their work in school and teachers accountable for their pupils' progress.

Though American educators, parents, and policy makers living through these disputes in the 1980s and 1990s doubtless thought they were pioneers, in fact these issues have a long history. They have been debated for the past century. The great educational issues of the twentieth century in the United States centered on the questions of who was to be educated and what they were to learn: What are schools for and what should they aim to do? What is it that schools must do? As the stakes attached to education grew higher, parents' anxiety about their children's schooling grew as well; as the cost of education escalated, public officials insisted on surer evidence that the schools were succeeding in their most important tasks.

History helps us understand these issues. We cannot understand where we are and where we are heading without knowing where we have been. We live now with decisions and policies that were made long ago. Before we attempt to reform present practices, we must try to learn why those decisions were made and to understand the consequences of past policies. History doesn't tell us the answers to our questions, but it helps to inform us so that we might make better decisions in the future.

The aim of this book is to trace the origins of America's seemingly permanent debate about school standards, curricula, and methods. In particular, it recounts the story of unrelenting attacks on the academic mission of the schools. As enrollments in school increased in the early twentieth century, there was a decided split between those who believed that a liberal education (that is, an academic curriculum) should be given to all students and those who wanted such studies taught only to the college-bound elite. The latter group, based primarily in the schools of education, identified itself with the new progressive education movement and dominated the education profession in its formative years.

Thinking they could bridge the gap between school and society and make the schools socially useful, pedagogical theorists sought alternatives to the academic curriculum for non-college-bound students. Curricular differentiation meant an academic education for some, a nonacademic education for others; this approach affected those children—mainly the poor, immigrants, and racial minorities—who were pushed into undemanding vocational, industrial, or general programs by bureaucrats and guidance counselors who thought they were incapable of learning much more. Such policies, packaged in rhetoric about democracy and "meeting the needs of the individual child," encouraged racial and social stratification in American schools. This book will argue that this stratification not only was profoundly undemocratic but was harmful, both to the children involved and to American society.

As used in this book, the term "academic curriculum" does not refer to the formalistic methods, rote recitations, and student passivity about which all reasonable educators and parents have justly complained. Nor does it refer only to teaching basic skills. It refers instead to the systematic study of language and literature, science and mathematics, history, the arts, and foreign languages; these studies, commonly described today as a "liberal education," convey important knowledge and skills, cultivate aesthetic imagination, and teach students to think critically and reflectively about the world in which they live.

Certainly the college-bound need these studies. But so too do those who do not plan to go to college, for they may never have another chance to get instruction about the organizing principles of society and nature, about the varieties of human experience. Even if they choose not to enroll in a university, they too need the knowledge and skills that will enrich their lives as citizens, individuals, and members of a community.

The conventional story of the twentieth century told by historians of education is about the heroic advance of the progressive education movement, how it vanquished oppressive traditionalism in the classroom, briefly dominated American schools, then lost its vitality and withered away in the mid-1950s. The paradigm for this telling of the story is Lawrence A. Cremin's magisterial work *The Transformation of the School: Progressivism in American Education, 1876–1957.*[1] This is not the story told in this book. The progressive education movement did not disappear in the 1950s; at the very time Cremin thought he was writing its obituary, the movement was at a low ebb, but it sprang back to life in the early 1960s. More troubling, it sprang back to life with anti-intellectualism at the forefront.

In Cremin's important book, anti-intellectualism appears as an occasional, unfortunate by-product of the progressive education movement for much of the century. However, this book argues that anti-intellectualism was an inescapable consequence of important strains of educational progressivism, particularly the versions of progressivism that had the most influence on American public education. Cremin and other historians of progressivism give short shrift to the movement's critics, such as William Torrey Harris, William Chandler Bagley, and Isaac Kandel; in this book they are treated as major figures in American education whose ideas were balanced and sound, if not often heeded, and whose philosophy remains central to the reconstruction of American education today.

Why does this argument about the past matter today? As we shall see, whenever the academic curriculum was diluted or minimized, large numbers of children were pushed through the school system without benefit of a genuine education. As the academic curriculum lost its importance as the central focus of the public school system, the schools lost their anchor, their sense of mission, their intense moral commitment to the intellectual development of each child. Once that happened, education reform movements would come and go with surprising rapidity, almost randomly, each leaving its mark behind in the schools. Over time, as this happened, educators forgot how to say "no," even to the loopier notions of what schools were for. Every perceived need, interest, concern, problem, or issue found a place in the curriculum or provided a rationale for adding new specialists to the school's staff. Once the hierarchy of educational values was shattered, once schools lost their compass, hawkers of new wares could market their stock to the schools. Every purveyor of social reform could find a willing customer in the schools because all needs were presumed equal in importance, and there was no longer any general consensus on the central purpose of schooling.

Today, as the schools compete for children's time and attention with television, movies, the Internet, and other mass media, those who run them must know what schools alone can do. The schools must reassert their primary responsibility for the development of young people's intelligence and character. Schools must do far more than teach children "how to learn" and "how to look things up"; they must teach them what knowledge has most value, how to use that knowledge, how to organize what they know, how to understand the relationship between past and present, how to tell the difference between accurate information and propaganda, and how to turn information into understanding. If youngsters are set free from serious studies, unencumbered by the significant ideas and controversies of American and world history, untouched by the great poets and novelists of the world, unaware of the workings of science, they will turn to other sources for information and stimulation. Children today swim in a sea of images shaped by the popular culture, electronic media, and commercial advertising. Everything becomes trivia, everything is packaged to fit the terms of celebrity and sensationalism, famous for a minute or two, then gone.

If we are to have a chance of reclaiming our schools as centers of learning, we must understand how they came to be the way they are. At the opening of the twenty-first century, Americans find themselves in search of traditions that nourish and ideas that make sense of a world that is changing swiftly. One of the great virtues of the academic tradition is that it organizes human knowledge and makes it comprehensible to the learner. It aims to make a chaotic world coherent. It gives intellectual strength to those who want to understand social experience and the nature of the physical world. Despite sustained efforts to diminish it, the academic tradition survives; it survives because knowledge builds on knowledge, and we cannot dispense with the systematic study of human knowledge without risking mass ignorance. It survives because it retains the power to enlighten and liberate those who seek knowledge. Now, as parents, educators, policy makers, and other citizens seek high standards, it is time to renew the academic tradition for the children of the twenty-first century.

1

The Educational Ladder

*In the closing years of the nineteenth century, Americans prided them-*selves on their free public schools. Most children attended the public schools, and Americans felt a patriotic attachment to them. Unlike Europe, which was burdened with rigid class barriers, in America it was believed that the public school could enable any youngster to rise above the most humble origins and make good on the nation's promise of equal opportunity for all. Oscar D. Robinson, the principal of the high school in Albany, New York, declared that "the famous simile of the educational ladder, with its foot in the gutter and its top in the university, is in this favored country no poetic fancy, but portrays in vivid language a fact many times verified in the knowledge of every intelligent adult."[1]

The schools were expected to make social equality a reality by giving students an equal chance to develop their mental powers to the fullest. William A. Mowry, the school superintendent in Providence, Rhode Island, believed that the schools would abolish caste in America: "Your bootblack to-day may be your lawyer to-morrow, and the railsplitter or the tanner or the humble schoolmaster at twenty years of age may become the chief magistrate of fifty millions of free people before he is fifty." What was most important was not learning a trade but learning intelligence and virtue. As people became more intelligent and broad-minded, he believed, the community would improve. He declared, "Let the doors of the school-house, the 'brain factory,' be open to all the children; and the child once started on the career of learning, let him not find those doors ever closed against him."[2]

This was the American dream, the promise of the public school to open wide the doors of opportunity to all who were willing to learn and study. The schools would work their democratic magic by disseminating knowledge to all who sought it.

Americans were especially proud of their common schools, the schools that included grades one through eight. By 1890, 95 percent of children between the ages of five and thirteen were enrolled in school for at least a few months of the year. Less than 5 percent of adolescents went to high school, and even fewer entered college.[3] Beyond the age of thirteen, there were large gaps in opportunities to attend school. Race, poverty, and location certainly narrowed access to schooling. Neither a high school diploma nor a college degree, however, was required to get a good job or to succeed in business. The growing economy had plenty of jobs, especially for those who had gained the literacy that was supplied by the common schools; only those who planned to enter the learned professions (law, medicine, the ministry) found it necessary to go to college.

At century's end, there was no American educational "system." There were thousands of district schools, hundreds of colleges and universities, and scores of normal schools that trained teachers. The federal bureau of education, headed by a U.S. commissioner of education, had no control over local schools; its sole function was to collect information about the condition and progress of education. Education was very much a local matter, controlled by lay school boards made up of businessmen, civic leaders, and parents. State education agencies were weak, small, and insignificant; each state had a department of education, but its few employees had little or no power over local school districts. Even big-city school districts had few supervisors. The public schools of Baltimore, for example, had 1,200 teachers in 1890 but only two superintendents for the entire school district.

Despite local control, the American public school was remarkably similar across regions. Everywhere the goals were few and simple: Children learned not only the basics of reading, 'riting, and 'rithmetic, but also the basics of good behavior. Principals and teachers considered character and intelligence to be of equal value, and neither was possible without "disciplining the will," which required prompt, unquestioning obedience to the teacher and the school rules.

The common schools emphasized reading, writing, speaking, spelling, penmanship, grammar, arithmetic, patriotism, a clear moral code, and strict discipline, enforced when necessary by corporal punishment. The values they sought to instill were honesty, industry, patriotism, responsibility, respect for adults, and courtesy. The schools were vital community institutions, reflecting the mores of parents and churches; events at the local school, such as spelling bees, musical exhibitions, and speaking contests, were often important community events.

When the muckraker Dr. Joseph Mayer Rice visited public schools in thirty-six cities in 1892, he complained bitterly about the quality of education that he saw. In New York City, the school he visited was "the most dehumanizing institution that I have ever laid eyes upon, each child being treated as if he possessed a memory and the faculty of speech, but no individuality, no sensibilities, no soul." Recitation by classes "in concert" was common. In Baltimore, the children added long columns of numbers, singing "in perfect rhythm," "one and one are two; two and one are three; three and one are four," and so on. In Boston, the children sang together, "N-a-m-e, n-a-m-e, name; *e* at the end of the word makes the *a* say its own name, *e* at the end of the word makes the *a* say its own name; h-e-r-e, here; h-e-r-e; *e* at the end of the word makes the *e* say its own name, *e* at the end of the word makes the *e* say its own name." In Cincinnati, children were singing and spelling words. In Saint Louis, teachers cut students off with remarks such as "Speak when you are spoken to" and "Don't talk, listen," and continually reminded students, "Don't lean against the wall" and "Keep your toes on the line."[4]

Teachers seldom had much pedagogical training, so they relied mainly on time-tested methods of recitation from textbooks. Regardless of locale, textbooks were similar, as competitive publishing houses copied one another's best-selling books. The publishers hoped for a national market for their textbooks and knew that their products would be judged by members of local school boards, for whom continuity and tradition counted more than innovation. The school reading books were usually published as a series of four to six graduated texts; the first one or two taught reading, and the rest were compilations of good literature, usually selected to illustrate ethical and moral precepts.

The stories, poems, speeches, allusions, aphorisms, and fables in the readers introduced American children to a common literary tradition. The celebrated McGuffey Readers contained excerpts from writers such as Shakespeare, Hawthorne, and Dickens. First published in 1836, the McGuffey series dominated the textbook market in the latter half of the nineteenth century, eventually selling more than 120 million books. They were handed down from student to student and read out loud over the family dining table. When Theodore Roosevelt lambasted critics as "Meddlesome Matties," a generation of Americans recognized the allusion to a familiar story in McGuffey's. Other popular textbooks contained many of the same poems and speeches, making cultural touchstones of such pieces as Robert Southey's "The Battle of Blenheim," Henry Wadsworth Longfellow's "The Village Blacksmith" and "Paul Revere's Ride," John Greenleaf Whittier's "The Barefoot Boy," and Marc Antony's oration in Shakespeare's *Julius Caesar.*

The reading textbooks of the common schools emphasized the importance of proper elocution and public speaking; they encouraged students to read out loud. Public speaking was considered excellent preparation for the duties of life in a democratic society, such as participating in local politics and community lyceums. In daily lessons, boys and girls learned to pronounce words and syllables with accuracy and care. Tongue-twisting exercises taught elocution:

The sun shines on the shop signs.
She sells sea shells. Shall he sell sea shells?
Six gray geese and eight gray ganders.
Round the rough and rugged rocks the ragged rascal ran.
The old cold scold sold a school coal-scuttle.

Then there was the classic tale of Peter Piper, which amply exercised the lips and tongue:

Peter Piper picked a peck of pickled peppers;
Did Peter Piper pick a peck of pickled peppers?
If Peter Piper picked a peck of pickled peppers,
Where's the peck of pickled peppers Peter Piper picked?

The school readers and history textbooks favored patriotic selections. Children recited the stirring words of Patrick Henry, George Washington, Daniel Webster, Abraham Lincoln, and other noted Americans. Rote memorization was common, especially in learning history and geography. This method had mixed results. With the rote method, children amassed a solid store of facts that they could use to understand more complex material, but they also might memorize words, phrases, even lengthy passages without understanding their meaning.

The history books taught facts and patriotism. In the textbooks, the greatest national events were the Revolutionary War and the Civil War. Children studied the justice of the American cause in the former and the perfidy of the Southern states in the latter (unless they attended school in the South, where textbooks portrayed the Southern cause sympathetically). The textbooks described American history as a stirring story that demonstrated the importance of liberty, independence, and resistance to tyranny.

Literary readers echoed the same themes of courage and patriotism. Students often memorized and recited pieces such as Whittier's "Barbara Frietchie," "The Debate Between Hayne and Webster," Alfred, Lord Tennyson's "The Charge of the Light Brigade," and Lincoln's Gettysburg Address.

Geography lessons taught pride of country and often racial pride (and racism) as well; racial stereotyping was commonplace in the geography books. The facts of geography were of great importance, including such matters as the height of important mountains and the names of continents, oceans, and rivers. Geography was often taught by chants and rhymes, which was referred to as "singing geography." One popular chant consisted of the name of the state, the name of its capital city, and the name of the river where it was located. One popular chant began

> Maine, Augusta, on the Kennebec,
> New Hampshire, Concord, on the Merrimac,

and went on to include each of the states. The schoolhouse would often ring with geography chants. Some teachers used music to teach the alphabet and the multiplication tables as well, with students marching up and down the aisles of the classroom singing (to the tune of "Yankee Doodle Dandy"), "Five times five is twenty-five and five times six is thirty . . ."[5]

In mathematics, teachers "drilled" students in "mental arithmetic," requiring them to solve mathematical problems "in their head," without a pen or pencil. Children were expected to stand in front of the class and answer such problems as:

> How many square inches in a piece of paper six inches long and four inches wide?
>
> Reduce to their lowest terms: $\frac{12}{16}$, $\frac{24}{36}$, $\frac{16}{28}$, $\frac{28}{49}$, $\frac{32}{36}$.
>
> Henry paid $\frac{1}{4}$ of all his money for a knife, $\frac{1}{8}$ for a ball, and $\frac{1}{8}$ for a necktie: what part of his money had he left?
>
> A harness was sold for $\frac{3}{4}$ of $\frac{4}{5}$ of what it cost. What was the loss per cent?[6]

Educators thought of these exercises as a valuable form of mental gymnastics. For many children, though, they were surely mental drudgery.

The common school was dedicated to correct spelling, and spelling lessons were conducted every day. Competition was keen, and sometimes public exhibitions were held for parents and the community. Some teachers divided their class into teams, which competed with each other. Or a teacher would line up the entire class and give spelling words to the child at the head of the line; when that child missed a word, the next in line would "go to the head of the class." Schools competed with each other, and sometimes entire communities would participate in the spelling bee, showing off the prowess of the best spellers.

The aim of the common school was clear: to promote sufficient learning and self-discipline so that people in a democratic society could be good citizens, read the newspapers, get a job, make their way in an individualistic and competitive society, and contribute to their community's well-being.

THE MISSING RUNG OF THE LADDER

At the end of the nineteenth century, almost every community had an elementary school, but public high schools were sparse. By 1900, there were nearly one thousand colleges and universities (of widely varying quality, some no more advanced than high schools) scattered across the country. In between was a melange of public high schools, private academies, and preparatory departments of colleges. There could not be an educational ladder from "the gutter to the university" unless public high schools were as readily available as common schools.

Until the middle of the nineteenth century, most secondary education was supplied by thousands of small private academies. Most offered not only the classical curriculum of Latin, Greek, and mathematics, but also modern subjects such as history, science, and English, and practical subjects such as bookkeeping, surveying, and navigation.

As the economy changed from agrarian to industrial and commercial, and young people began to need more education, many cities—including New York, Chicago, New Orleans, Detroit, Saint Louis, San Francisco, and Dubuque—opened public high schools. These new schools existed in "every variety and quality" and usually offered both classical and modern studies.[7] Reluctant taxpayers grumbled and occasionally sued to block public funding for public secondary schools, and critics complained that they were elitist and unnecessary. Nonetheless, enrollments in the new public high schools soon eclipsed those in the private academies.[8]

Most towns viewed their new public high school as a source of community pride. In Nineveh, Indiana, the township high school was credited with raising "the standard of intelligence, of morality, of taste, and therefore, of life among the people. While a few in the township are opposed to higher education, the vast majority favor the school and would not do without it."[9] Of the high school's twenty-two pupils, half commuted from outlying farms. The curriculum consisted of Latin (including two books of Caesar and three of Virgil), mathematics, English literature, history, geology, physics, rhetoric, geography, and civil government. This was not an atypical high school. Every high school worthy of its name offered Latin and mathematics, the mainstays of the classical curriculum.

The people of Nineveh, Indiana, may have been happy with their high school, but the leaders of American education regularly debated what high schools should teach and to whom. As secondary enrollments steadily grew, ardent advocates of different persuasions contended over the future direction of the high schools, over whether they should educate students for college or for work, what they should teach, and whether they should have a required program for all.

It was an era of wrenching social and economic change, of rapid industrialization, high immigration, and increasing urbanization. It was a period in which social reformers sought strategies to combat the ill effects of these changes, especially in the cities, where living conditions for the poor were abysmal. Among intellectual leaders, Charles Darwin's theories of evolution challenged established truths in virtually every field of thought. Political and social reformers were convinced that the old order was dying and a new, dynamic, progressive order was being born.

UTILITY OR KNOWLEDGE?

As Americans debated the future direction of education, discussion veered between two poles of thought, as represented by the ideas of Herbert Spencer and Lester Frank Ward. Each of them articulated an influential worldview. To one side was education for utility, to the other was knowledge for general intelligence.

26

In the 1850s, the English philosopher Herbert Spencer asked, "What knowledge is of most worth?" and concluded that the purpose of education was "to prepare us for complete living." Every study must be judged by whether it had "practical value" and would be "useful in later life." Classical education had no intrinsic value, he wrote, and survived only as "the badge marking a certain social position."[10] The knowledge that was of most worth, he believed, was knowledge for self-preservation: gaining a livelihood, being a parent, carrying out one's civic duties, and producing and enjoying art. Spencer believed that the best way to attain useful knowledge was by studying science, which in the mid–nineteenth century was not taught by most schools and colleges. In education, he asserted, utility was the measure of all things.

In the United States, Spencer's prestige was immense. Historian Henry Steele Commager observed that "It requires an effort of the imagination, now, to appreciate the dominion that Spencer exercised over American thought in the quarter century or so after the Civil War and, in some quarters, down to the eve of the First World War."[11] Much of Spencer's popularity was due to his exposition of social Darwinism. The doctrine of "survival of the fittest," he claimed, justified laissez-faire government. In an age of individualism, Spencer's justifications for social Darwinism struck a resonant chord, but so too did his emphasis on utility in education among a practical people who were already inclined to doubt the value of book learning. Historian Lawrence A. Cremin described Spencer's book on education as "probably the most widely read in America."[12] His utilitarian ideas were later embraced by the progressive education movement, which ignored Spencer's opposition to state-supported public education.

Spencer's laissez-faire philosophy was opposed by the remarkable polymath Lester Frank Ward. Ward has been called "the philosopher, the protagonist, even the architect, of the modern welfare state."[13] Born in the Midwest in 1842, he attended public schools for a few years, then taught himself Latin, Greek, German, mathematics, French, botany, geology, and paleontology, served in the Civil War, and worked for the federal Bureau of Standards, the U.S. Geological Survey, and other government agencies. In his spare time, he earned degrees in law and medicine. By dint of his own reading and experience, he became an accomplished scientist, a founder of the field of sociology, and the first president of the American Sociological Society.

Ward believed that the government should take an active role in improving social welfare. He challenged those like Spencer (and his American disciple, William Graham Sumner of Yale University) who believed that the laws of nature required laissez-faire policies. Writing in 1884, Ward maintained that "the laissez faire doctrine is a gospel of inaction, the scientific creed is struck with sterility, the policy of resigning all into the hands of Nature is a surrender." [14]

Ward mocked advocates of laissez-faire by pointing out:

When a well-clothed philosopher on a bitter winter's night sits in a warm room well lighted for his purpose and writes on paper with pen and ink in the arbitrary characters of a highly developed language the statement that civilization is the result of natural laws, and that man's duty is to let nature alone so that untrammeled it may work out a higher civilization, he simply ignores every circumstance of his existence and deliberately closes his eyes to every fact within the range of his faculties.

If such a theory were correct, said Ward, "There would have been no civilization, and our philosopher would have remained a troglodyte." [15]

Ward insisted that the fundamental difference between man and other animals is that "the environment transforms the animal, while man transforms the environment." [16] All inventions, all art, all practical advances, all civilization are the fruits of intelligence, not nature; by the application of intelligence, human institutions are capable of changing the physical and social world. Government, Ward argued, is a human invention, and government should be consciously used to improve intelligence and social conditions.

A passionate egalitarian, Ward believed that the most important source of inequality was the unequal distribution of knowledge. "I know of no other problem of applied sociology that society can solve until this one is solved," he wrote.[17] Unlike Spencer, Ward insisted that "state education is far better for the pupil" than private education. He wrote in *Dynamic Sociology* (1883), "The lowest *gamin* of the streets here meets the most pampered son of opulence on a footing of strict equality. Nothing counts but merit itself. Pupils take their places according to what they are, not what they are called."[18]

The main purpose of education, Ward argued, was to equalize society by diffusing knowledge and what he called "directive intelligence" to all. He literally believed that knowledge was power.[19] He considered education "the great panacea" and insisted that access to knowledge was the key to all social progress. He wrote, "There is no need to search for talent. It exists already, and everywhere. The thing that is rare is opportunity, not ability." The greatest advances in civilization had been created, he held, by men who had had opportunities for education and the leisure to think. With unyielding optimism, Ward maintained that "the potential giants of the intellectual world may now be the hewers of wood and drawers of water. On the theory of equality, which I would defend, the number of individuals of exceptional usefulness will be proportionate to the number possessing the opportunity to develop their powers."[20] Those who stood to benefit from education were not a fixed percentage of the population, as many believed. Ward felt that the entire population would gain if there were more and better educational opportunity.

Throughout his career, Ward defended "intellectual egalitarianism." He insisted that not only all classes but all races were equally capable of learning and employing the social achievements of mankind. Against both popular and scholarly opinion, he argued that "the lower classes of society are the intellectual equals of the upper classes." The difference in intelligence between those at the bottom and those at the top, he held, was due not to any difference in intellect but to differences in knowledge and education. The main job of formal education, he held, was to ensure that "the heritage of the past shall be transmitted to all its members alike," not just to those who are deemed to be part of the most intelligent class.[21] All children, he contended, should have the right to the accumulated knowledge of the past: the information, intelligence, and power that come from studying humankind's inheritance of arts and sciences.

Apostles of Liberal Education

The two most influential educators in the 1890s were Charles W. Eliot, president of Harvard University, and William Torrey Harris, U.S. commissioner of education. As vigorous proponents of liberal education, they believed that the primary purpose of education was to improve society by improving the intelligence of individuals. They insisted that schools in a democratic society should aim to develop the intelligence of all children fully, regardless of their parents' social status or their probable occupation. Both asserted that the same quality of education should be available to all children. Together they represented the mainstream consensus about American education at the approach of a new century.

Eliot, though prominent in higher education, took a keen interest in the schools. After graduating from Harvard in 1853, he taught mathematics and chemistry at Harvard, served on the Boston Primary School Committee, and studied European school systems. In the spring of 1869, he attracted wide attention with articles in *The Atlantic Monthly* advocating "the new education." Criticizing the narrow classical curriculum of ancient languages and mathematics in American colleges, he called for the addition of modern studies such as science, modern foreign languages, and English literature. That same year, he was appointed president of Harvard University. A strong advocate of both higher standards and electives, he raised the university's admission requirements and eliminated required subjects.

In the late 1880s, Eliot became a national leader in discussions about schooling, which was an unconventional role for the president of Harvard University. Aware of the poor quality of many high schools, he referred to them as "the gap between the elementary schools and the colleges."[22] He knew that the rural population—three quarters of the American people—had little access to secondary schools; that only one state (Massachusetts) required districts to establish high schools; and that more than 80 percent of colleges and universities reluctantly maintained their own preparatory schools to compensate for inadequate high schools. Eliot insisted that more and better schools and common standards were needed.

Eliot urged educators to shorten the grammar school course by eliminating redundant work in arithmetic and grammar while introducing natural sciences such as botany, zoology, and geology, as well as physics, algebra, geometry, and foreign languages. Eliot opposed lock-step recitations and memory drills, especially the customary practice of memorizing geographic facts and grammatical rules. He wanted students actively involved in laboratory demonstrations, where they would be expected to observe, weigh, measure, and do fieldwork.

Many educators thought that these advanced studies were beyond the reach of many children, but Eliot insisted that "We shall not know till we have tried what proportion of children are incapable of pursuing algebra, geometry, physics, and some foreign language by the time they are fourteen years of age." He noted disapprovingly that "we Americans habitually underestimate the capacity of pupils at almost every stage of education" in comparison to Europeans, and consequently many capable students never got the chance to study advanced subjects.[23]

Eliot opposed uniformity in education. Recognizing that children differ in many ways, he suggested that the public schools should "promote pupils not by battalions, but in the most irregular and individual way possible." A good model, he thought, was the country district school "in which among forty or fifty pupils there are always ten or a dozen distinct classes at different stages and advancing at different rates of progress."[24] The uniformly low expectations of the current program, he said, actually denied children of the poor equal access with children of the rich to the best education of which they were capable.

Eliot believed that a convention of experts should be able to agree on the best way of teaching every subject and which topics should be studied.[25] Once these determinations were made, he expected, there would be clear teaching standards for every subject, even though not all children would study the same subjects or move at the same pace while studying them.

It was not subject matter, however, that was important to Eliot; rather, it was mental power, the power to think, reason, observe, and describe. The object of education, he frequently said, was to gain mental discipline, what educators in the late twentieth century would call "critical thinking skills." To develop the power of observation, he held, "it does not matter what subject the child studies, so that he study something thoroughly in an observational method." It was unimportant to Eliot "whether the student write an historical narrative, or a translation from Xenophon, or a laboratory note-book, or an account of a case of hypnotism or typhoid fever, or a law-brief, or a thesis on comparative religion; the subject-matter is comparatively indifferent."[26] No matter what was taught, what mattered most to Eliot was the development of clear thinking.

In the 1890s, Eliot was a spokesman for liberal education. He believed that the essential purpose of education was to improve the power to think and reason well, and that all youngsters should develop these capacities. As the mass of people gained these powers, he thought, society as a whole would benefit.

W. T. Harris: Egalitarian Traditionalist

The other great advocate of liberal education during this era was William Torrey Harris. Unlike Eliot, who endorsed mental discipline (the training of the mind) as an end in itself, Harris believed that certain academic subjects were the indispensable foundation of a liberal education. Born in Connecticut in 1835, Harris left Yale without graduating because of his dissatisfaction with the classical curriculum (Latin, Greek, and mathematics) and his eagerness to study "the three 'moderns'—modern science, modern literature, and modern history."[27]

When he was twenty-two, Harris moved to Saint Louis, where he became an elementary school teacher. Eleven years later, he was named superintendent of schools. At the time, he was also a leading Hegelian scholar and founder of *The Journal of Speculative Philosophy.* In 1880, he moved to Concord, Massachusetts, to work with Bronson Alcott on philosophical matters. In 1889, President Benjamin Harrison appointed him U.S. commissioner of education, and he served in this office until 1906.

For most of the twentieth century, generations of students of education learned nothing of Harris's ideas or contributions, because he scorned the fashionable pedagogical bandwagons of his time. Today, he is usually and unjustly referred to as a "conservative" whose work as an educator confirmed the status quo.[28] As historian Herbert M. Kliebard has noted, Harris "earned a reputation as a conservative in educational policy" because of his "lukewarm reaction" to his fellow pedagogues' enthusiasms such as manual training, child study, and specialized vocational training. This unjust reputation was cemented by historian Merle Curti's derogatory treatment of Harris in 1935. Writing in the depths of the Great Depression, Curti found Harris wanting because he had criticized socialism. Because Harris was out of step with Curti's progressive views, Curti concluded that his educational ideas were as deficient (i.e., conservative) as his economic ones.[29]

In his own era, however, Harris was a reformer, an advocate of modern subjects, and a tireless crusader for universal public education. As superintendent of schools in Saint Louis and later as U.S. commissioner of education, Harris struggled against taxpayers' opposition to public high schools and new subjects. In his reports to the public, Harris argued unceasingly that the purpose of education was to give the individual the accumulated wisdom of the human race, and that this was a public purpose fully deserving the support of the entire community.

Like his friend Lester Frank Ward, Harris maintained that public education benefitted the public. Under his leadership, the Saint Louis public schools added science, art, music, and drawing to their curriculum and made kindergarten a regular part of the school system. Harris denounced excessive reliance on rote memorization, claiming that it produces "arrested development (a sort of mental paralysis)" and causes the mind to lose "its appetite for higher methods and wider generalizations."[30] As U.S. commissioner of education, he encouraged colleges to broaden their entrance requirements to include modern subjects, not just the time-honored classical curriculum.[31]

Being a Hegelian, Harris regularly delivered extended disquisitions on the relationships among the state, civil society, the family, and the individual. His reports as superintendent in Saint Louis were unlike any written by other school superintendents before or since. In addition to the customary statistics about the school system's needs, he often reflected on the purpose of public education. In his annual report of 1872, for example, he explained that the right kind of moral education could not be obtained from private tutors, because only in public schools did pupils learn the disciplined behavior necessary for life in a civilized community.[32]

His praise for the liberating power of good habits, discipline, and self-control did not endear Harris to later generations of progressive educators, who believed that the child needed to be liberated, not reined in by artificial conventions and external authority. Harris thought that "a system which proposes to let the individual work out his education entirely by himself . . . is the greatest possible mistake. Rousseau's doctrine of a return to nature must also seem to me the greatest heresy in educational doctrine."[33]

Harris held that schooling strengthens both the individual and the community by enabling the individual to "live over in himself the lives of his fellowmen without having actually to make all the original experiments and suffer all the temporary defeats and disappointments" of others. "The lowest savage" learns the traditions of his own tribe and learns from hearsay, he said, "but it is incomparably more useful to be able, by means of books and the printed page, to have access to the observations of all men who have observed and reflected in all times and all places." Other institutions—the family, the church, the state, and the industrial community—also educate, but only the school gives individuals the inestimable power of reading and writing, which opens to them the ability to learn from others, to "climb the heights of achievement" for the rest of their lives. The habits and self-control taught in school, Harris claimed, teach "directive power," by which he meant a combination of ingenuity, initiative, persistence, and the ability to work with others (Lester Frank Ward called this "directive intelligence").[34] Directive power strengthens the individual and, in doing so, promotes social and economic progress.

Harris defined the essentials of the curriculum as the five windows of the soul: "Illiterate man is shut up in the dark tower of ignorance, and the school undertakes to illuminate and emancipate him by opening windows on five sides (for this tower is a pentagon). It teaches arithmetic, geography, history, grammar, and literature."[35] He held that "arithmetic quantifies . . . geography [in which he included the sciences] localizes.

. . . Grammar fixes and defines speech. . . . History deals with human progress. . . . Reading . . . includes the mastery of literature."[36] To Harris, these were the five essential ingredients of knowledge in the common school curriculum.

The process of education adds to "the child's experience the experience of the human race. His own experience is necessarily one-sided and shallow; that of the race is thousands of years deep, and it is rounded to fullness. Such deep and rounded experience is what we call wisdom." Unlike other institutions in society, the special purpose of the school, he argued, is that it teaches students how to acquire, preserve, and communicate intelligence. Once the conventionalities of learning have been mastered, "the youth has acquired the art of intellectual self-help; he can of his own effort open the door and enter the treasure-house of literature and science. Whatever his fellow men have done and recorded, he can now learn by sufficient diligence of his own."[37] The goal of education, as Harris saw it, is freedom, self-dependence, self-activity, and directive power. The educated person with a trained mind and a disciplined will would be prepared to solve the practical problems of daily life.

Harris frequently heard complaints about the expense of providing education to the children of common laborers. He contended that good education must be for all children, not just the children of the prosperous. It wasn't right, the critics said, to make children aspire beyond their "station" in life, to which Harris replied, "The critics of our educational system are never done with telling us that its results are to make the rising generation discontented with its lot. As if this were a defect rather than the greatest glory of an educational system!" Unlike many of his peers, Harris understood that the age of industrialism had introduced a constant "shifting of vocations" and that the best preparation for any youngster was not a trade but "versatile intelligence," which would enable an individual to learn to operate new machines and invent new ones.[38]

Harris defended the teaching of Latin in public schools as egalitarian. In America, he maintained, "The children of poor people have the same opportunities here that the children of rich people have to improve their condition and to obtain directive power if they make the same outlay of industry and intellectual preparation."[39] He believed that the American public would reject a school system that provided one kind of education for the children of laboring people and a different kind for the children of the rich and powerful. Such inequality, he held, would be completely unacceptable in the United States.

Harris defended classical studies on unusual grounds. Traditionalists talked about mental discipline, and educational progressives wanted school to be more practical and more like everyday life, but Harris spoke of the value of "self-alienation." He believed that education should involve "a period of estrangement from the common and familiar. The pupil must be led out of his immediateness and separated in spirit from his naturalness, in order that he may be able to return from his self-estrangement to the world that lies nearest to him and consciously seize and master it." Without a period of self-alienation, the student would remain "merely instinctive and implicit." To create self-alienation, Harris suggested that the student needed to be removed from his familiar surroundings and allowed to "breathe the atmosphere of the far-off and distant world of antiquity for several years of his life."[40]

His concept of self-alienation explains the fascination that many young children develop for learning about dinosaurs or lost civilizations, which are remote from their own lives. What Harris called self-alienation is the learned ability to step away from one's immediate experience and view it with critical perspective.

A strong proponent of intellectual development, Harris was an outspoken critic of manual training, which was a highly acclaimed innovation in the 1880s. Advocates of manual training wanted to introduce practical studies into the high school, such as woodworking, metalworking, and patternmaking.[41] Harris set such activities on a par with games of "marbles, quoits, base-ball [or] jack-straws." Such learning, he said, may be educative, but "it is not properly school education." Harris drew a sharp distinction between the casual learning that children pick up spontaneously and the purposeful education that teaches them to comprehend beyond what they can see and touch: "Man elevates himself above the brute creation by his ability to withdraw his attention from the external world of the senses and give attention to energies, forces, producing causes, principles. He can look from the particular to the general. . . . He can see in a cause its possible consequences."[42]

The great power of education, Harris suggested, was not gained by repeatedly performing an action, such as sawing wood or welding two pieces of iron. No, its great power derived from the ability to think, reason, and generalize. For Harris, the use of intellect was man's quintessential power, hardly to be compared to the mundane task of learning how to use a few tools. Intellect grows not from manual labor, he argued, but from active engagement with language, literature, science, mathematics, and history. Not only did manual training lack intellectual value, said Harris, it had no vocational value either, since only 8 percent of the nation's laborers worked in wood or metal.

Despite Harris's low regard for manual training, the movement was not to be denied. It became one of many movements that periodically swept through American education, as zealous education reformers, businessmen, and philanthropists searched for a panacea to make education useful to employers and more attractive to students. The promoters of manual training were certain that working with hand tools was just the right preparation for the new industrial age, and Harris appeared to be an old fogy.

Interest in manual and vocational training soared: Baltimore opened the first public manual training high school in 1884. Other cities added manual training courses to their high schools. Private manual training schools were launched in Saint Louis, Toledo, Cleveland, Cincinnati, New Orleans, New York, and Cambridge, Massachusetts, many with business support.[43] Many cities added courses in industrial trades such as carpentry, plumbing, bricklaying, metal and machine work, sewing, and cooking to prepare young people for jobs. Business leaders hailed industrial and technical education, expecting that it would contribute to the nation's industrial growth and perhaps to their own corporate growth as well.

The popular enthusiasm for manual training may have annoyed Harris, but it was merely a mote in his eye. A far larger issue was what to do about the connection between the high schools and the colleges. On this question, Harris and Eliot were in agreement. Both disliked the overly prescriptive nature of college entrance requirements, especially the insistence by many colleges that students must study Greek and Latin to be admitted. Neither man was an enemy of the classics, but they wanted American colleges to admit students who had not studied the classical curriculum. Together, they found a way to influence the growth of the curriculum in the nation's thoroughly decentralized schools.

THE DEBATE ABOUT EDUCATING BLACK CHILDREN

As white educators were struggling to define the program of the public high school, black educators were struggling to expand access to publicly supported elementary schools for black children. Only a third of black children in 1890 attended any school at all, and few had any access to high school.[44]

The African-American population was concentrated in the rural South, where educational opportunities were meager for blacks and whites alike, and where white hostility to the education of blacks was intense. In the late nineteenth century, barely a generation after the abolition of slavery, most southern blacks were poorly educated, trapped in grinding poverty as sharecroppers or tenant farmers, and politically disenfranchised. Southern legislatures adopted Black Codes to curtail the rights of blacks and to preserve whites' control of the social and political order. The development of schools for black children in the South relied on the framework established by the Reconstruction-era Freedmen's Bureau, as well as missionaries, churches, northern foundations, and local people of both races; public funds for black primary education were provided reluctantly and inequitably.

The most prominent African-American leader at the turn of the century was Booker T. Washington. Born into slavery, Washington was educated at Hampton Institute at Virginia, which was known for its philosophy of industrial, vocational, and moral training. In 1881, Hampton's president, General S. C. Armstrong, selected Washington to lead a new state-chartered normal school for blacks in Tuskegee, Alabama. Though only twenty-five, Washington proved fully equal to the task, not only establishing Tuskegee as a major institution but eventually winning recognition as the nation's best-known spokesman for black Americans.

Washington was a masterful fund-raiser who maintained good relations with northern white philanthropists, enlightened white southerners, and other black leaders. Tuskegee emphasized industrial education, teacher training, and character building; its students learned certain skilled trades, farming, and homemaking skills, as well as personal hygiene and manners. Its curriculum was in the mainstream of progressive education, providing the type of practical education allegedly suited to students' needs and the needs of their communities. In his history of black education in the South, James D. Anderson assailed the Hampton-Tuskegee model of industrial education; he maintained that it was designed as second-class education to keep blacks in low-skilled jobs and preserve the racial caste system.[45]

In 1895, Washington delivered a major address at the Cotton States and International Exposition in Atlanta. Directing his remarks to southern whites, he reassured them that blacks intended to work hard, downplay their grievances, and acknowledge that "there is as much dignity in tilling a field as in writing a poem. It is at the bottom of life we must begin, and not at the top." He pledged that whites could count on black workers to be "patient, faithful, law-abiding, and unresentful," and to "stand by you with a devotion that no foreigner can approach. . . . In all things that are purely social we can be as separate as the fingers, yet one as the hand in all things essential to mutual progress." Washington sought to allay southern whites' concerns about the willingness of blacks to accept their role at the bottom of the social order. A reporter who was present that day wrote that at the end of the speech, "Most of the Negroes in the audience were crying, perhaps without knowing just why."[46]

Both whites and blacks applauded Washington, but the African-American intellectual W. E. B. Du Bois several years later deplored his message of deference. Du Bois, who graduated from Fisk University, received a doctorate at Harvard, and was a founder of the National Association for the Advancement of Colored People, attacked Washington's Atlanta speech as a surrender of the black population's civil and political rights.

Washington's program, he charged, "practically accepts the alleged inferiority of the Negro races." Du Bois was outraged because Washington had not objected to racial prejudice and the denial of black suffrage; had counseled submission to civic inequality; and had deprecated the value of black higher education, which would limit the numbers of black teachers and handicap blacks' education at every level. Du Bois deplored Washington's failure to proclaim that "manly self-respect is worth more than lands and houses, and that a people who voluntarily surrender such respect, or cease striving for it, are not worth civilizing."[47]

Du Bois questioned whether industrial education was the best strategy for the black population. To rely wholly on industrial education, he warned, would be a mistake, for it would preclude the education of future leaders, who would require a liberal education. He insisted that "the Negro race, like all races, is going to be saved by its exceptional men," whom he called the "Talented Tenth." Du Bois asked, "Can the masses of the Negro people be in any possible way more quickly raised than by the effort and example of this aristocracy of talent and character? Was there ever a nation on God's fair earth civilized from the bottom upward? Never; it is, ever was and ever will be from the top downward that culture filters."[48]

To have a Talented Tenth, he wrote, the best of the younger generation must go to college and university, there to gain the intelligence, knowledge, and culture that are transmitted from generation to generation. The Talented Tenth, he believed, would supply the leaders and teachers of future generations. Du Bois could not imagine a successful system of common schools nor even good trade and industrial schools without an adequate supply of well-educated teachers, as well as teachers of teachers.

Thus, while white educators were debating whether the educational ladder should be open to all students and for how long a common education should be offered, black educators were worrying about how to secure the very lowest rungs on the ladder for black children and debated which educational strategy (industrial education or liberal education or a combination of both) was likeliest to improve the prospects for blacks' advancement.

The Committee of Ten

In the 1890s, educators often complained about the absence of any organized system for college admissions. Nearly half the nation's colleges had either low entrance requirements or none at all. Many colleges accepted only those students who passed their own examinations, while others accepted all applicants from certain preapproved schools. High school principals and headmasters groused about "domination" by the colleges, whose requirements determined what they taught. Colleges that gave their own examinations often had maddeningly explicit requirements for prospective students, such as testing students' ability to translate certain passages from Homer or Herodotus. Principals objected to preparing boys and girls differently for twelve to fifteen colleges, each with its own requirements in foreign language, science, history, and literature, particularly when only a handful of them were preparing for any college at all.[49] Educators wanted a predictable *system* of education, instead of the informal, haphazard situation that had evolved over the years. Like the practitioners of other nascent professions at the time, educators sought order and stability.

In an age marked by the development of systems and organization, the schools seemed helter-skelter, lacking uniformity or standards. What should be taught? To whom? At what age? For how long? What were the best methods? What subjects should be required for college entrance? Should "modern" subjects such as history and science be accepted for college admission? Should students be admitted to college who had not studied the ancient languages? Should there be different treatment, even different curricula, for the great majority of students who were not college-bound? Should high schools offer manual training and commercial subjects?

In the absence of any general agreement about these nettlesome issues, each school and local district arrived at its own answers. In 1892, the leading organization of professional educators, the National Education Association, responded to the debate by doing what had never been done before: it created a national committee, the Committee of Ten, to study the issues and offer constructive proposals. Never before had a national body been established to make recommendations to the nation's thousands of school districts and hundreds of colleges. At a time when other professions were trying to organize themselves, it seemed perfectly reasonable that professional educators would assert that their expert judgment was superior to the hodgepodge created by the uncoordinated actions of thousands of individual schools, school boards, and colleges.[50]

The Committee of Ten, the nation's first blue-ribbon commission to study the schools, brought together the nation's two best-known proponents of liberal education, Harvard President Charles W. Eliot and U.S. Commissioner of Education Harris. Eliot was chairman of the committee, which included four other college presidents, three high school principals, and a college professor. Both Eliot and Harris were well known among educators as reformers and proponents of the modern subjects.

The Committee of Ten published its report in 1893. For years afterward, its recommendations were hotly debated. The high schools, said the committee, should be committed to academic excellence for all students in a democratic society. They should foster the continuous intellectual growth of their pupils through study of the major academic disciplines. The report urged that young people should go as far in school as their talents and interests would take them.

The Committee of Ten assumed that every child would benefit by receiving a liberal education of the highest quality. Its most controversial recommendation was that all children should receive an academic education, differentiated only by which foreign languages were learned. The committee noted that it was "a very general custom in American high schools and academies to make up separate courses of study for pupils of supposed different destinations." It opposed this kind of differentiation, declaring that "every subject which is taught at all in a secondary school should be taught in the same way and to the same extent to every pupil so long as he pursues it, no matter what the probable destination of the pupil may be, or at what point his education is to cease." It recognized that not all pupils would "pursue every subject for the same number of years; but so long as they do pursue it, they should all be treated alike."[51]

The Committee of Ten insisted that the secondary schools of the United States "do not exist for the purpose of preparing boys and girls for colleges." Only a tiny proportion of high school graduates would ever go to college. The main purpose of the high school was to prepare all its students for "the duties of life," whether they planned to go to college, went to work immediately after graduation, or left high school without graduating.[52]

The report of the Ten was a reform document. It urged colleges to admit students who had not studied the classical languages. It supported new subjects such as history, the sciences, and modern foreign languages as coequals with Latin, Greek, and mathematics. It recommended active teaching methods instead of rote memorization. It endorsed the democratic idea that all students should receive a liberal education.

The report represented a melding of the objectives of liberal education (i.e., a curriculum of rich content) and mental discipline (i.e., the training of the mind). The members of the committee agreed that a person with a well-trained mind would be well prepared for any path in life. But the Committee of Ten did not say that any subject at all was equally valuable for mental discipline; a well-educated person must have a mind that was not only well trained but well furnished with knowledge. It left decisions about manual training and commercial subjects to individual high schools.

Almost immediately, the report came under fire from opposite directions. On one side were the traditionalists, who saw the report as an insult to their own field. Classicists were outraged by the committee's suggestion that colleges admit students who had not studied Latin; Greek professors complained bitterly that Greek was being downplayed. Other traditionalists were disturbed by the proposal that the modern subjects—science, history, and modern foreign language—should be considered equal in value to the classical subjects.

The cry went up among classicists that the report of the Ten supported "equivalence" among all studies for mental discipline and college admission, regardless of their inherent value. Since so many classicists had made the mistake of justifying the ancient languages solely on the basis of their value for mental training, they correctly saw that "equivalence" threatened their very survival. If English or German or chemistry were as good for mental discipline as Latin, why would anyone study Latin?

Attacking from the other extreme were critics who objected to the report's support for academic education for all students, even those who did not plan to go to college. These critics claimed that the Committee of Ten was dominated by college men, that it had neglected practical studies such as manual training, and that its proposed programs were too difficult for most students. They complained that the report would lead to the overeducation of those who were bound for the labor force and that it was the work of aristocrats who wanted to impose a narrow college preparatory curriculum on everyone.

One Massachusetts educator, W. R. Butler, scoffed at the idea of offering the same kind of education to all high school students. Students, he wrote, are of widely varying capacities: this "procrustean bed . . . will necessitate more stretching and cutting off of legs than the pedagogical world has ever before known." To those who contended that the high school should offer all students the chance to qualify for college, he replied that "in other countries the choice of courses must be made almost at the beginning of school life, while we in America allow a postponement of the choice for eight or nine years." Butler saw no good reason to offer the same kind of education to both kinds of student: "No builder thinks of laying the same foundation for a cottage as for a ten-story block." Besides, he observed, most high school students and high school graduates were girls, and "the higher education of girls is of doubtful utility to the race."[53]

James H. Baker, a member of the Committee of Ten (and a former high school principal), had a different objection. He opposed the implication that "the choice of subjects in secondary schools may be a matter of comparative indifference." He insisted that "Power comes through knowledge; we can not conceive of observation and memory in the abstract." He wanted a stronger statement about the value of certain subjects, otherwise "we might well consider the study of Egyptian hiero-glyphics as valuable as that of physics, and choctaw as important as Latin."[54]

Six months after the report's release, Charles Eliot responded to critics who had charged that college men who knew nothing about the schools were trying to dominate the high school. Eliot maintained that educational reform had an essential unity, regardless of the age of the students. Certain principles, he said, were paramount whether one was concerned about college-age youths or kindergartners.

First, it is important to direct instruction to individuals, not to groups or classes; the best education recognizes that each student learns "at his own rate of speed." At whatever age, he said, "we must learn to see straight and clear; to compare and infer; to make an accurate record; to remember; to express our thought with precision; and to hold fast lofty ideals." These were the elements of mental discipline to which Eliot was unswervingly loyal. Eliot reiterated his well-known support for students' choice of studies, although he contended that "school pro-grammes should always contain fair representations of the four main divisions of knowledge—language, history, natural science, and mathe-matics; but this does not mean that every child up to fourteen must study the same things in the same proportions and to the same extent."[55] He looked forward to the day when American teachers, like American pro-fessors, would become masters of their subject so that they could teach it expertly to children of all ages and capacities.

Nothing Eliot said could satisfy G. Stanley Hall, president of Clark University in Massachusetts, who was the report's most caustic critic. Hall was relentless in his efforts to tarnish the report. Renowned at the turn of the century as the founder of the child study movement, Hall de-rided the proposal that every subject "should be taught in the same way and to the same extent to every pupil so long as he pursues it." Calling this "a masterpiece of college policy," Hall declared that "this principle does not apply to the great army of incapables, shading down to those who should be in schools for dullards or subnormal children, for whose mental development heredity decrees a slow pace and early arrest, and for whom by general consent both studies and methods must be different."[56] This was demagoguery on Hall's part, since the numbers of children who were incapable of benefiting from an academic curriculum were certainly not a "great army."

Hall challenged the report's claim that "all subjects are of equal educational value if taught equally well." This implied, he said, that "shorthand, Greek, agriculture, mathematics, sewing and surveying, elocution and drawing, the humanities and science, pure and applied knowledge, and all the newest as well as the oldest branches, if taught alike well, have equal educational worth. . . . I can recall no fallacy that so completely evicts content and enthrones form." Of course, the report had recommended only the humanities and sciences, not shorthand, sewing, and other nonacademic subjects. Hall's coup de grâce was his charge that the report asserted that "fitting for college is essentially the same as fitting for life," for this was the image that stuck. The report, which did assert that a good solid liberal education was the best way to prepare for "the duties of life," now stood accused of wanting to push all children into what Hall described as a "sedentary, clerical, bookish, and noetic" education, with the attendant evils of coaching, cramming, and examinations.[57]

Having ridiculed the report, Hall wrote admiringly of European school systems, where students received different educations on the basis of career choices made before they reached their teens. Hall's allegations of elitism were especially ironic because the Committee of Ten had emphasized that all children—*especially those who were not going to college*—should have the benefit of a liberal education.

In 1905, Eliot tried one last time to refute Hall's attacks. In a democratic society, he reasoned, "the classification of pupils, according to their so-called probable destinations, should be postponed to the latest possible time of life." While Europeans were accustomed to classifying children early in their lives as "future peasants, mechanics, tradespeople, merchants, and professional people," and giving them an education appropriate to their future role, this was not the American approach: "In a democratic society like ours, these early determinations of the career should be avoided as long as possible, particularly in public schools." The American public, he predicted, would object to having its children "sorted before their teens into clerks, watchmakers, lithographers, telegraph operators, masons, teamsters, farm laborers, and so forth and treated differently in their schools according to these prophecies of their appropriate life careers. Who are to make these prophecies? Can parents? Can teachers? Can university presidents, or even professional students of childhood and adolescence?" Eliot insisted that "the individual child in a democratic society had a right to do his own prophesying about his own career, guided by his own ambitions and his own capacities." As for Hall's claim that the population included a "great army of incapables," Eliot replied that "any school superintendent or principal who should construct his programs with the incapables chiefly in mind would be a person professionally demented."[58]

THE LEGACY OF THE COMMITTEE OF TEN

The report of the Committee of Ten was influential for a decade or so after it was issued. Colleges increasingly accepted modern academic subjects for admission, and high school enrollments in Latin rose. Some states, cities, and schools tried to align their curricula to the report's recommendations. The public schools, however, did not remove the distinctions between students who were preparing for college and those who were not; as historian Edward A. Krug notes, the schools added modern academic subjects to what was required for college preparation, and "the idea of a college-preparatory curriculum became as rigidly fixed from this point of view as it had ever been with reference to Greek."[59]

One of the most significant legacies of the Committee of Ten, at least indirectly, was the establishment in 1900 of the College Entrance Examination Board, which was created to offer a common examination for many different colleges. The College Board achieved what Eliot had been seeking, which was to set uniform standards for each academic subject, while allowing schools maximum flexibility about what to teach and relieving colleges of the burden of administering their own entrance examinations. Each year, the College Board consulted with teachers and college professors and issued a syllabus to help students get ready for the examinations. High schools no longer had to prepare students for different entry requirements at different colleges.

The Committee of Ten showed the power of reform by commission. Its example spurred a frenzy of professional activity as educational leaders discovered a potent tool for organizing themselves, seeking public support, and asserting the claims of their expertise. Hardly was the ink dry on the Ten's report when new commissions and committees were established to promote education reform, including a committee of five, a committee of seven, a committee of twelve and a committee of fifteen.

In time, as the progressive education movement came to prominence, the Committee of Ten report became an object of scorn. Progressive educators considered it a misguided elitist effort to impose a college preparatory curriculum on everyone. The Ten, said the critics, had ignored individual differences and social needs. Its report was reactionary, old-fashioned, elitist. It was a relic, consigned to the dustbin of history by a rising tide of contempt for the academic curriculum.

The negative reactions to the Committee of Ten report gave rise to myths about the American public high school in the late nineteenth century that proved useful to foes of the academic curriculum. The high school of this era, reformers said again and again, had been an aristocratic institution, devoted solely to those who were preparing for college; its curriculum had been determined by the colleges; most students had been compelled to take Latin and Greek to enter college; most of its students had gone to college; it had ignored the needs of non-college-bound students. None of this was true. In the 1890s, most high school students—indeed, most high school graduates—did not go to college.[60]

Public high schools at the turn of the century were not devoted solely to academic studies. They commonly offered nonacademic courses such as bookkeeping, music, art, drawing, manual training, and surveying. Isaac L. Kandel, a scholar noted for his international studies of education, found that the nineteenth-century American high school was characterized by "remarkable flexibility" of curriculum as compared to European secondary schools and that "it was rather difficult to understand this charge, which was admittedly very widely accepted."[61]

Historians David L. Angus and Jeffrey E. Mirel concluded that the high schools of the late nineteenth century, far from being rigidly traditional, had offered a variety of courses for students who planned to go to work: commercial courses, normal training for future teachers, surveying, manual training, mechanical drawing, and electives in art, music, and physical education. In reality, there had been great variation among high schools, and no two of them had been alike.[62]

Another version of this myth depicts late-nineteenth-century public high schools as "schools that taught Greek to the college-bound."[63] In fact, in 1890 only 3 percent of high school students studied Greek, and by 1910 Greek enrollments fell to less than 1 percent and few public high schools even offered it.[64]

Latin was a different story. Evidently students, their parents, or their teachers valued the study of Latin, and students took it even when it was not required. In his study of secondary schools at the turn of the century, Theodore R. Sizer described Latin as "one of the most popular courses in the curriculum, even for children who had no thought of going on to college. Its appeal was not only that it supposedly refined the taste and disciplined the mind. . . . Its appeal was in its tradition of culture, its symbolic mantle of refinement."[65]

In 1890, about one third of all secondary students took Latin. The Committee of Ten may have encouraged even more Latin study, because by 1900, fully 50 percent of all high school students were taking Latin. Even a decade later, despite the fact that the high school enrollment had doubled from 1890 to 1900 and doubled again by 1910, Latin enrollments remained at 50 percent (with more girls than boys enrolled). To the extent that Latin enrollments serve as a gauge, the academic curriculum seems to have reached a high-water mark in the years from 1900 to 1910. And this was so even though the overwhelming majority of high school students were *not* preparing to enter college.

As the century opened, American education seemed to be firmly committed to the ideals of liberal education. There seemed to be a broad consensus among educators and parents that the purpose of schooling was to improve a youngster's ability to think and reason well through studying certain essential subjects. Behind this consensus was an implicit understanding that access to education was a democratic right and that the role of the school in a democratic society was to provide not just the three R's but access to the knowledge and thinking power necessary for every citizen. The promise of liberal education was that all children would study the same knowledge that had once been available only to elites. Opponents of liberal education, however, rose like dragons' teeth from the soil in the following decades, never understanding the promise, never seeing why children of workers and farmers needed the kind of education once deemed appropriate only for the elite.

2

A Fork in the Road

At the turn of the century, there were two paths American education could take. One was the Committee of Ten's common academic curriculum that would have all high school students—not just the college-bound few—study history and literature, science and mathematics, language and the arts. The other was the differentiated curriculum, which divided students according to their likely future occupations, offering practical studies for the vast majority and an academic curriculum only for a small minority.

Education reformers dismissed the Committee of Ten's proposal of a solid liberal education for all youngsters as the last gasp of the reactionary old order. Reformers agreed that the new century required a new education, but they did not agree on what that new education should be. When Harvard's Charles W. Eliot wrote about the "new education" in 1869, he meant introducing science into the schools. By the turn of the century, the "new education" had come to mean manual training, industrial education, vocational education, commercial studies, domestic science, agricultural studies, and other occupational studies.

Criticism of the academic curriculum came mainly from two sources: business leaders, who wanted economy and efficiency in the schools, and progressive educators in the nation's new colleges of education, who wanted the school curriculum to be more closely aligned to the needs of society in the industrial age. The business community was primarily interested in securing low taxes and well-trained workers. Progressive educators wanted socially efficient schools that would serve society by training students for jobs.

With the establishment of colleges of education in most major universities at the turn of the century, authority in American education began to shift from school superintendents to the professors at institutions such as Columbia's Teachers College, Stanford, the University of Chicago, and Harvard. School superintendents, who had once tried to impress each other with their learning, boasted instead of their prowess as efficient managers of the educational system. Professors of pedagogy saw themselves as reformers of a deeply conservative field that needed to be liberated from tradition and guided by modern science.

In colleges of education, the professors of psychology, sociology, administration, and methods outnumbered "subject matter specialists." Since the pedagogical profession arose as a protest against the academic tradition, it was not surprising that few adherents of that tradition joined its ranks. The imbalance favoring the new fields on pedagogical faculties accounts for a Teachers College legend that stated that the three professors who taught mathematics, history, and Latin "habitually marched along arm-in-arm down Riverside Drive in New York City singing:

We are the scholars of Teachers College,
The only scholars of Teachers College." [1]

Teachers College, the premier pedagogical institution in the nation, began as an alternative to the academic tradition. It traced its origins to the Kitchen Garden Association, incorporated in 1880 to teach "the domestic industrial arts among the laboring classes," that is, to train young girls to work in domestic service as cooks and housemaids. Four years later, hoping to attract boys as students, the institution changed its name to the Industrial Education Association and added classes in carpentry and manual training to its curriculum of sewing, cooking, drawing, and domestic service. According to James Earl Russell, later the dean of Teachers College, children "clamored for admission to its classes." [2]

In 1887, under the leadership of the energetic Nicholas Murray But-ler (who was later president of Columbia University), the institution de-cided to specialize in teacher training. It was once again rechristened, this time the New York College for the Training of Teachers, and began offering courses in the history of education, pedagogy, industrial arts, and natural science. That year, at the behest of its philanthropic bene-factors, the college adopted a statement of principles stressing the value of "formal discipline" and "development of the intellectual faculties," doctrines that the college's faculty devoted much energy to debunking in the decades ahead. In 1889, a final name change produced Teachers College, which in 1893 became the pedagogy department of Columbia University.

Opened during the formative years of the progressive movement in politics and education, the pedagogical departments of American uni-versities became seedbeds of progressive education. American educa-tion had problems, and the pedagogical schools had answers. It became the mission of the new pedagogical science to refute the assumptions of traditional education, demonstrate the inutility of teaching academic subjects, and encourage schools to replace traditional subjects with practical studies.

→ → ← ←

The progressive movement in education emerged in the 1890s, at the same time as the larger Progressive movement in politics. In the three decades before 1920, the Progressive movement in politics espoused a broad-based array of reforms. It galvanized political campaigns to ex-pand participation in the political process, regulate monopolies, improve the living conditions of the urban poor, introduce equitable taxation, and reform municipal politics. Among its best-known figures were the social worker Jane Addams at Hull House in Chicago and muckraking journal-ists such as Ida Tarbell and Jacob Riis, who exposed greed and corrup-tion in American life. Historians have long debated whether political progressivism was a single reform movement or a series of overlapping reform movements; whether its leaders were upper-middle-class Protes-tant reformers trying to restore the moral values of the preindustrial era;

and whether some Progressive reforms were intended to reduce the power of urban political machines controlled by immigrants. The legacy of progressivism is complicated by the facts that some Progressives were linked to anti-immigrant causes such as nativism, immigration restriction, and eugenics and that Progressives were divided over women's suffrage.[3]

In education, the progressive movement had numerous, related aims: It sought to make the schools more practical and realistic. It sought to introduce humane methods of teaching, recognition that students learn in different ways, and attention to the health of children. It sought to commit the schools more to social welfare than to academic studies. The progressive education movement wanted to make education into a profession. It wanted to curb the influence of laymen, especially in poor and immigrant neighborhoods, in decision making about the schools. Toward these ends, progressive reformers created centralized school bureaucracies and civil service systems in urban districts that minimized lay participation in education policy.

Progressive education was clearly a complex series of related movements, and historians have debated its coherence, as well as its influence. Herbert M. Kliebard argued that the term "progressive education" covered such a broad range of different, even contradictory, ideas that it was a meaningless term. Other historians, notably Lawrence A. Cremin, saw congruence among the different strands of progressive education. David L. Angus and Jeffrey E. Mirel concluded that progressive reformers shared certain underlying principles and values, including their beliefs that nineteenth-century high schools were "bastions of elite, college preparatory training"; that the high school could become "democratic" only by expanding its curriculum to include practical, vocational studies; that programs should be designed to meet the "needs" of students; and that professional educators, not lay boards of education, should decide how to group students and how to determine their "needs."[4]

Progressive education reformers wanted the public schools to make a significant contribution to the emerging industrial order. They pressed the schools to adjust to the rapidly changing society and to cast aside outmoded assumptions, one of which was the idea that the academic curriculum was appropriate for all children. Progressive educators argued that the bookish curriculum blocked social progress and that it was unfitted to the hordes of immigrant children crowding into the urban schools. These children, the reformers said, needed training for jobs in the industrial economy, not algebra and literature.

Crusaders for educational change attacked the high school curriculum as rigid and elitist, falsely implying that all students were involuntarily compelled to study the classical curriculum of Latin, Greek, and algebra. In the early years of the twentieth century, the classical curriculum was available as one option among many in the high schools. The reformers overstated their case for the sake of achieving maximum effect; they began by attacking stultifying classroom methods and ended by attacking the academic subjects themselves. Education reformers denounced the academic curriculum as if it were the classical curriculum, heaping as much scorn on history, modern foreign languages, and literature as they had previously reserved for the ancient languages. They continued to denounce the classical curriculum long after Greek had disappeared and Latin was available only as an elective.

The goal of many educational reformers was not to make the academic curriculum accessible to more students but to devise a practical curriculum for those who would soon be in the workforce, especially students who were poor, foreign-born, and nonwhite. The dramatic increase in immigrant children in the nation's schools provided a rationale that seemed to link social reform and school reform. Because the children were "different," because many did not come from English-speaking homes, it was argued that they needed a curriculum different from the one available to the children of affluent, native-born families. Not for them the "old limited book-subject curriculum"; the experts in the new schools of pedagogy said these children needed industrial education, vocational education, nature study, sewing, cooking, and manual training.[5]

The arrival of millions of new immigrants had a large impact on the nation's schools, particularly those in the urban centers. In the first decade of the century, the majority of students in most large cities were either immigrants or the children of immigrants. A congressional study in 1908 found that 71.5 percent of the children in the New York City public schools had foreign-born fathers, as did 67.3 percent of the children in Chicago, 63.5 percent in Boston, 59.6 percent in Cleveland, 59 percent in Providence, 58.9 percent in Newark, and 57.8 percent in San Francisco.[6]

Many of these children came from desperately poor families and lived in crowded, malodorous slums, where public services were meager or nonexistent. Many public school systems introduced medical inspections; dental clinics; evening and summer classes; vocational courses; and special classes for the physically and mentally handicapped. Some public schools remained open for community use after school and adult education in the evenings. These were valuable innovations because the schools supplied medical and social services that were greatly needed and deeply appreciated by immigrant families.

But the reformers saw these changes as half measures. The newly immigrated children required a different kind of education, they said, because so many had come from countries in southern and eastern Europe "where general education is not common and where the Anglo-Saxon conception of law, order, government, and public and private decency do not prevail."[7]

Immigrant children, it was widely believed, lacked the intellect for academic studies. In contrast to earlier arrivals from England, Germany, and other northern European countries, these immigrants allegedly were incapable of intellectual work. Their "powers" were "fundamentally manual," and they were suited for manual labor and industrial occupations, where they would serve society best by performing the roles fitted to their meager talents.[8] Some suggested that it was not only unrealistic but possibly socially dangerous to offer an academic curriculum to all students, since only a small number would need it for college. James Earl Russell of Teachers College wondered, "How can a nation endure that deliberately seeks to rouse ambitions and aspirations in the oncoming generations which in the nature of events cannot possibly be fulfilled? If the chief object of government be to promote civic order and social stability, how can we justify our practice in schooling the masses in precisely the same manner as we do those who are to be our leaders?"[9]

The new experts in the education world insisted that a school that offered the same academic curriculum to all students was "antidemocratic" and "aristocratic," while a school with differentiated educational programs was democratic. "Equality of opportunity" was redefined to mean that only a minority should continue to get an academic education, while the great majority—the children of the masses—would get vocational or industrial training.

※　※　※　※

Progressive education did not begin with the intention of creating different educational programs for children from different social classes. Its primary purpose, as defined by its leading spokesman, John Dewey, was to make the schools an instrument of social reform. Dewey was internationally known as a major philosopher and the father of progressive education. Born in 1859 in Burlington, Vermont, he entered the University of Vermont at age fifteen; after graduation, he taught high school in Oil City, Pennsylvania, for two years. He earned his doctorate in philosophy at Johns Hopkins, then taught at the Universities of Michigan and Minnesota before assuming the chairmanship of the combined departments of psychology, philosophy, and pedagogy at the new University of Chicago in 1894. Two years later, in 1896, Dewey and his wife, Alice, opened a "laboratory school" at the university to experiment with new methods and approaches. The school lasted until 1904, when Dewey moved to Columbia University.

In 1897, Dewey summarized the main themes of progressive education. He held that the advance of education depended on the application of the social sciences, particularly psychology, to education. The school, he said, "must represent present life—life as real and vital to the child as that which he carries on in the home, in the neighborhood, or on the playground." The best way to correlate school subjects was to focus not on science, literature, history, or geography but on "the child's own social activities." He recommended that education should be conceived of as "a continuing reconstruction of experience," meaning that children should understand what they learned as it applied in real life. Whatever was presented in school, he said, should be guided by a child's ability to understand it. These recommendations were a reasonable corrective to the common practice of teaching by recitation and memory work without regard to students' understanding.[10]

The school, said Dewey, was a fundamental lever of social progress and social reform. He told the parents at his school that it was not enough to seek only the education that was best for their own child: "What the best and wisest parent wants for his own child, that must the community want for all of its children. Any other ideal for our schools is narrow and unlovely; acted upon, it destroys our democracy. All that society has accomplished for itself is put, through the agency of the school, at the disposal of its future members."[11]

Dewey recalled a time when the household had been the active center of the community, when members of the household had had responsible roles to play in raising food, shearing sheep, spinning wool, dipping candles, and making furniture; in that era, character building and discipline had been taught by "the obligation to do something, to produce something, in the world." He had experienced a pastoral childhood in a small town in Vermont, when children like himself had learned by doing important jobs around the home. With the advance of the new industrial era and the rise of cities, the simple agrarian past that Dewey had known as a child was rapidly receding into history. In his Laboratory School, Dewey wanted to create an "active community life, instead of a place set apart in which to learn lessons . . . a miniature community, an embryonic society," where "occupations are made the articulating centers of school life." There children would perform constructive work that needed to be done and would gain scientific insight into the materials and processes of man's historic development.[12]

Dewey wanted schools to concentrate on problems and processes rather than academic subjects. In a traditional school, children might study science by memorizing the technical names for different plants and their parts. In Dewey's school, children would plant seeds, observe how they grew, and consider the soil and climatic conditions that affected plant life. Either way, they would learn biology, but the learning gained through experience, wrote Dewey, was far more valuable than that obtained by memorizing names.[13]

Dewey's writings encouraged those who thought that education could be made into a science; those who wanted to create child-centered schools based on the interests of children rather than subject matter; those who believed that learning by doing was more valuable than learning from books; those who expected vocational and industrial education to train poor and minority children for their future jobs; and those who wanted the schools to serve as an instrument to improve society. These disparate, sometimes discordant, ideas had been discussed for years, but Dewey's intellectual eminence certified them as the dominant doctrines in the new professional schools of pedagogy.

Those who hoped to create a "new education" were inspired by Dewey's ideas. But the "new education" was interpreted very differently in private and public settings. In private progressive schools, which enrolled the children of well-to-do families, the "new education" was child-centered, meaning that children's interests and activities were the basis of the curriculum. In big public school systems, however, the "new education" meant vocational and industrial education to train the children of the masses for work in farms, shops, factories, and homes. Such curriculum changes appeared to be socially efficient. They were identified with progress, reform, and modernity in an age when these qualities were revered.

Dewey was naive about how his ideas could be implemented in the public schools. In one of his famous lectures, he chided those who favored a course in zoology over a course in laundry work; he said that either could be narrow and confining, and either might "be so utilized as to give understanding and illumination—one of natural life, the other of social facts and relationships." This was true in theory, but in practice the children who were studying zoology were probably learning the principles of science, while the children in the laundry work course were surely training for unskilled work. In the reality of American public education, students in a course in laundry work were not gaining "understanding and illumination" and were not learning about "social facts and relationships." They were simply learning to wash and press clothes.[14]

The progressive education movement was inspired by Dewey's writings but was not always strictly loyal to Dewey's intentions. The movement encompassed four significant ideas. Taken together, these ideas undermined the premise that all children should study a solid academic curriculum. Indeed, they raised doubts about the value of a solid academic education for *anyone*.

- First was the idea that education might become a science and that the methods and ends of education could be measured with precision and determined scientifically. This was the basis of the mental testing movement.
- Second was the idea that the methods and ends of education could be derived from the innate needs and nature of the child. This was the basis of the child-centered movement.
- Third was the idea that the methods and ends of education could be determined by assessing the needs of society and then fitting children for their role in society. This was the basis of the social efficiency movement.
- Fourth was the idea that the methods and ends of education could be changed in ways that would reform society. Proponents of this idea expected that the schools could change the social order, either by freeing children's creative spirit or conversely by indoctrinating them for life in a planned society. The first version was the faith of the child-centered movement and the second was the basis of the social reconstruction movement.

At different times in the first four decades of the twentieth century, each of these camps claimed the sanction of modern psychology, sociology, and science. Eventually, however, the camps began to war with one another, as there were contradictions among their views that made them incompatible. But in the formative years of the progressive education movement, the advocates of these ideas agreed that their common enemy was the traditional academic curriculum.

In their rebellion against the academic tradition, many advocates of progressive education envisioned a future in which schools would offer what both society and students needed, instead of what they considered "useless" cultural courses. In the education reformers' view, the academic program justified its elevated status only by appeals to tradition and snobbery. In a nation where practicality was valued far more than intellectual pursuits, the progressives' demands for vocational and practical studies found a responsive audience among business leaders and social reformers, especially those who wanted to think of themselves as modern and up to date.

Social and educational reformers agreed on the importance of breaking down the barriers that separated the schools from society. The old way, as Dewey had written, was to look at the school in terms of "the progress made by the individual child of our acquaintance"; the new way was to view the schools "as part and parcel of the whole social evolution." Dewey's writings provided coherence to the burgeoning progressive education movement. Dewey lauded schools that introduced manual training, shop work, sewing, and cooking, because such activities made school real and vital to children, rather than a place set apart for "lessons having an abstract and remote reference to some possible living to be done in the future." [15] Dewey wanted the schools not to make students into cooks, seamstresses, or carpenters but to use the occupations to provide insight into how society evolved and how it functioned. In the public schools, however, many of those who promulgated the "new education" simply wanted the schools to train better cooks, seamstresses, and carpenters.

ATTACKING MENTAL DISCIPLINE

Whatever their cause, reformers knew that they had to dethrone the academic curriculum and that they would not succeed unless they were able to break the tenacious hold of the doctrine of mental discipline. Most parents and educators believed in that doctrine, even when they didn't know what it was called, because they assumed that the purpose of education was to "train" the mind and "discipline" the will. Mental discipline was based on faculty psychology, which held that the mind was composed of specific "faculties" or powers, such as reasoning, memory, will, observation, judgment, and imagination, and that these powers could be trained and strengthened by vigorous effort, regardless of what was being studied.

According to one popular saying, it didn't matter what children studied as long as they didn't like it; doing unpleasant things was supposed to train the will. Mental discipline, it was believed, was the fruit of hard work. With appropriate study and memorization, students could develop their reasoning powers, their willpower, and their capacity to judge and observe. Latin was believed to be unusually valuable for mental gymnastics. Parents and teachers alike believed that Latin "trained the mind" and encouraged logical thinking. Latin was justified primarily for its value for mental discipline and only secondarily as a means of reading great works of literature in the original language. Many youngsters struggled through Caesar or Ovid without any appreciation of the literary quality of what they were reading, but with the hope that they were learning to think clearly. The newer, practical studies made no claims to either training the mind or strengthening the faculties. The girls who learned to sew and the boys who learned to saw wood gained useful skills, but no one claimed that their mental faculties had been improved because they could sew or saw.

Mental discipline was objectionable not only to progressive educators, but also to liberal educators who believed that knowledge and understanding were of far greater importance than the alleged power gained from mental gymnastics. James H. Baker, a dissenting member of the Committee of Ten, had argued that "mere form, mere power, without content, means nothing. Power is power through knowledge. The very world in which we are to use our power is the world which we must first understand in order to use it. The present is understood, not by the power to read history, but by what history contains." Jacob Schurman, president of Cornell University and editor of *School Review,* similarly rejected "that popular psychology which defines education merely as the training of mental faculties. As though the materials of instruction were a matter of indifference! . . . No, education is not merely a training of mental powers. It is a process of nutrition. Mind grows by what it feeds on." [16]

It was unfortunate both for the ancient languages and for the academic curriculum as a whole that their defenders chose to justify them primarily for their value in training the mind, for they were left defenseless when experimental studies undercut the validity of mental discipline. Based on these studies, educational psychologists insisted that certain faculties, such as memory and reasoning, could not be trained to function more efficiently. These psychologists sought to demonstrate that training in one activity did not transfer to other uses, either in other subjects or outside the school. This turned out to be a crucial issue in the history of education in the twentieth century.

The first attempt to test the validity of mental discipline was recorded by the eminent Harvard psychologist William James, who conducted a trial of his own memory. He wanted to see "whether a certain amount of daily training in learning poetry by heart will shorten the time it takes to learn an entirely different kind of poetry." During an eight-day period, he memorized 158 lines of Victor Hugo's poem "Satyr" at the rate of one line every fifty seconds; then, over a thirty-eight-day period, he memorized the first book of *Paradise Lost*. When he returned to the Hugo poem, it took him fifty-seven seconds to memorize each line, which indicated that he had gained nothing in speed or efficiency from his earlier memory feats. While James thought that one's memory might be improved by various methods, he doubted that the faculty of memory could be strengthened merely by training. He referred to his self-test in a footnote in his monumental work *The Principles of Psychology*.[17]

James allocated only a footnote to his whimsical experiment because he did not take seriously the idea that education could become a science. In his celebrated lectures to teachers in 1898, he had warned, "You make a great, a very great mistake, if you think that psychology, being the science of the mind's laws, is something from which you can deduce definite programmes and schemes and methods of instruction for immediate schoolroom use."[18]

Other educational psychologists, however, were intent on proving that training in one study did not transfer to any other studies. That effort was undertaken in 1901 by psychologist Edward L. Thorndike. After earning his doctorate in psychology in 1898 for studies of animal behavior, Thorndike went on to become a founder of the field of educational psychology and a leading figure in the progressive education movement. Thorndike formulated "laws of learning" that were based on the observed connection between stimulus and response and on whether the response was rewarded or punished, whether it produced satisfaction or annoyance. His behaviorism led him to conclude that school studies were effective only for specific, particular purposes, not for general improvement.[19]

To other progressive educators, Thorndike's empirical studies were a refreshing change from the customary appeals to metaphysical or traditional sources of authority. He was quickly recruited to the faculty of the young Teachers College, Columbia University, in New York City, where he became a major figure in the mental testing movement.

Thorndike and his colleague Robert S. Woodworth conducted several experiments to determine whether training one mental function would improve any other mental function. In one instance, subjects were asked to estimate the length of various lines or to estimate weights. In another, subjects were instructed to select certain letter combinations (e.g., the letters *e* and *s*) or words or geometric figures. They also tested the influence of memorizing "on the general ability to memorize." From their various experiments, the authors found that "the amount of improvement gotten by training in an allied function is small." They concluded that "It is misleading to speak of sense discrimination, attention, memory, observation, accuracy, quickness, etc., as multitudinous separate individual functions are referred to by any one of these words. These functions may have little in common. There is no reason to suppose that any general change occurs corresponding to the words 'improvement of the attention,' or 'of the power of observation,' or 'of accuracy.' " The alleged benefits of mental discipline, they held, were "mythological, not real entities." Rather than seeing the mind as a collection of separate functions (or "faculties"), they maintained that "the mind is, on the contrary, on its dynamic side a machine for making particular reactions to particular situations."[20]

With these studies, Thorndike and Woodworth attacked some of the most fundamental assumptions in education, casting doubt not only on the value of mental training but also on the possibility of transfer of training from one activity to another. Although few classroom teachers were likely to have read these studies in *The Psychological Review,* the Thorndike-Woodworth studies had a dramatic effect among pedagogical professors, who greeted them as proof that the theory of mental discipline had been decisively "exploded." Parents and other members of the public continued to talk about "training the mind," but educationists believed that this had been revealed as a myth.

The issue of transfer of training became crucial to the viability of the academic curriculum, and the implications for the schools were mind-boggling. Some educational psychologists, citing Thorndike and Woodworth, insisted that nothing learned in one situation could be applied to any other, so that all training must be specific to the task at hand. Seen in this light, nothing taught in school had any value or utility except to satisfy college admission requirements or to prepare those who planned to teach the same subject in the future or those who might have an occupational purpose for learning subjects such as algebra, chemistry, history, or German.

Pedagogues quickly realized that Thorndike's experiments had undermined the rationale for the traditional curriculum and that it was up to them to create a new education, one that would train students for the real world of work. Frederic Burk, president of the San Francisco State Normal School, spoke for many other progressive educators when he dismissed the disciplinary value of academic studies as "traditional nonsense" and asked, "What is the product of four years in Latin? What is the output of algebra? What is the value of the narrow and prescribed course in literature?"[21] Instead of such useless studies, he insisted, "the pupil's energy shall be centred upon the mastery of those things which existing world life requires of its active and productive journeymen; anything less is insufficient, and anything of a different character is irrelevant."[22]

In 1914, Thorndike acknowledged that transfer sometimes occurred, but in limited situations in which "a change in one function alters any other only in so far as the two functions have as factors identical elements." This was known in the pedagogical literature as Thorndike's theory of identical elements. So, for example, "improvement in addition will alter one's ability in multiplication because addition is absolutely identical with a part of multiplication." Thorndike confidently asserted that scientific research had made obsolete the once-customary claims about "training of the reason, of the powers of observation, comparison and synthesis" or "training the faculties of perception and generalization" or "disciplining the senses." At the same time, he chastised those who had been tempted by "the experimental results . . . to proceed too far toward the absurd conclusion that all practice is utterly specific in its effects."[23]

Despite Thorndike's qualification, his work continued to serve as ammunition for attacks on the academic curriculum. To many educators, the disinterested voice of science had confirmed the uselessness of the academic curriculum, except for those students who needed to meet college entrance requirements. In the early decades of the century, science had a dazzling allure because it appeared to provide an impartial means of settling disputed matters. And now, at last, Thorndike had shown that there was a *science of education,* capable of resolving the nettlesome issues that were endlessly being debated by school boards and educators. The nature of the high school curriculum had been controversial since the mid–nineteenth century. Now pedagogical science would decide which youngsters should study Latin, geometry, English, bookkeeping, cooking, sewing, or woodworking, and which subjects should be removed from the curriculum.

Thorndike revisited the issue again in the 1920s, administering intelligence tests to nearly nine thousand high school students. He concluded that it didn't matter what students studied because the smartest ones always learned the most anyway. He wrote:

> If our inquiry had been carried out by a psychologist from Mars, who knew nothing of theories of mental discipline, and simply tried to answer the question, "What are the amounts of influence of sex, race, age, amounts of ability, and studies taken, upon the gain made during the year in power to think, or intellect, or whatever our stock intelligence tests measure," he might even dismiss "studies taken" with the comment, "The differences are so small and the unreliabilities are relatively so large that this factor seems unimportant." The one causal factor which he would be sure was at work would be the intellect already exis-

tent. Those who have the most to begin with gain the most during the year. Whatever studies they take will seem to produce large gains in intellect.[24]

Thorndike advised that no particular school subject made any large differences on student achievement: "When the good thinkers studied Greek and Latin, these studies seemed to make good thinking. Now that the good thinkers study Physics and Trigonometry, these seem to make good thinkers. If the abler pupils should all study Physical Education and Dramatic Art, these subjects would seem to make good thinkers."[25]

Thorndike had faith in the scientific value of measurement, and he developed intelligence tests, aptitude tests, and every other kind of mental test. Only such a faith, detached from any cultural values, could make possible the assumption that studies such as Latin and geometry had been decisively invalidated by laboratory experiments in which students memorized nonsense syllables or underlined meaningless letter combinations. After Thorndike, it was considered hopelessly reactionary or ignorant to appeal to the "training value" of any subject. It became customary to say instead, "You train what you train" and "You learn what you learn." Latin, in short, was good only for learning Latin, not for improving one's reasoning powers or self-discipline. The boy who intended to be a farmer should study agriculture, not geometry or English literature; the girl who expected to be a secretary should study typing and bookkeeping, perhaps household arts, but certainly not physics or algebra.

Progressive educators were heartened by Thorndike's critiques of the traditional academic curriculum. His experimental studies encouraged those who wanted to base the curriculum on vocational concerns, as well as those who thought that the curriculum should reflect children's immediate interests.

In Defense of Mental Discipline

Not everyone accepted Thorndike's conclusions. Alexander Meiklejohn, a philosopher who later became president of Amherst College, ridiculed

Thorndike's studies for denying the possibility of general education and allowing only for specific training:

> What will you say of a theory that the training of the mind is so specific that each particular act gives facility only for the performing again of that same act just as it was before? Think of learning to drive a nail with a yellow hammer, and then realize your helplessness if, in time of need, you should borrow your neighbor's hammer and find it painted red. Nay, further think of learning to use a hammer at all if at each other stroke the nail has gone further into the wood, and the sun has gone lower in the sky, and the temperature of your body has risen from the exercise, and in fact, everything on earth and under the earth has changed so far as to give each new stroke a new particularity all of its own, and thus has cut it off from all possibility of influence upon or influence from its fellows.[26]

For several decades, education psychologists debated the likelihood of "transfer of training." Some studies confirmed Thorndike's findings, others refuted them. Perhaps because of Thorndike's reputation, or perhaps because his theory gave pedagogues a scientific stick with which to beat the academic curriculum, the refutations were usually ignored.[27]

One of the sharpest responses to Thorndike came in 1928 from a graduate student, Pedro Orata, whose brilliant doctoral dissertation contended that Thorndike's experiments had been profoundly misleading; that the efforts to replicate them had been inconclusive; that they tested only "mechanical habits," which were of little value; and that Thorndike's theory supported an apprenticeship system, not a democratic system of education. Orata pointed out that psychologists who had trained students to understand "meanings, concepts, and principles or generalizations" had demonstrated considerable transfer of training. When students understood what they were learning, why they were learning, and why it had implications outside the classroom, they were likely to transfer what they had learned to new situations. Transfer of training occurs, Orata pointed out, when teachers make it a goal of instruction.[28]

Thorndike's experiments had been focused too narrowly on habit formation and drill, Orata complained, excluding any role for logical thinking and concept formation. His emphasis on the specialized nature of mental functions had made no provision "for disinterested study, for the acquisition of knowledge for its own sake," or for gauging the ways in which studies of literature, science, and the arts taught important intangibles such as open-mindedness and appreciation of other cultures.[29] Despite his critics, however, Thorndike's views continued to have enormous currency; he was, after all, a towering figure in his field. His claims were embedded in pedagogical textbooks, most especially his own, and were taught to generations of teachers and administrators.

In the late 1950s, Walter B. Kolesnik of the University of Wisconsin surveyed hundreds of studies of transfer of training and concluded that "it is now generally accepted as a sound principle that under certain conditions and to a certain extent transfer can and does take place. Except for some psychologists and educationists, perhaps, no one has ever seriously doubted this." Kolesnik noted that "the very notion of formal education" assumes that what is taught in school will prepare students for new and unexpected situations. Kolesnik observed, "Indeed, if the knowledge, skills and ideals acquired in the classroom could not be carried over and made to function outside the classroom, it is doubtful that the time, money and energy being expended on schooling could be justified."[30] After reviewing this controversy, historian Richard Hofstadter concluded that the "misuse of experimental evidence" by opponents of mental training "constitutes a major scandal in the history of educational thought."[31]

Romantic Pedagogy Versus the Academic Curriculum

Another educator who aspired to wed science and pedagogy was G. Stanley Hall. Born in 1846 in Massachusetts, Hall studied at Williams College and Union Theological Seminary, where he lost his religious faith. In 1878, Hall was the first American to earn a doctorate in psychology, at Harvard. A man of seemingly boundless intellectual energy, Hall also studied philosophy, theology, biology, physics, anthropology, and physiology. He taught psychology at Johns Hopkins University, where one of his students was John Dewey.

A prolific writer and lecturer, Hall founded major publications and organizations. He was an enthusiastic herald of Darwinian theory and zealously attempted to apply evolutionary biology to studies of the mind. An enthusiastic exponent of "natural education," Hall blended the romanticism of Jean-Jacques Rousseau's *Émile* with his own interpretations of evolutionary science and genetic psychology. His main contribution to American education was his leadership of the child study movement, which—like Thorndike's experiments—was used by critics to diminish the status of the academic curriculum and provide an intellectual rationale for the child-centered school.

The premise of the child study movement was entirely sensible: that educators and parents needed to pay attention to children's health and well-being. But to Hall, children's health and well-being were almost always jeopardized by traditional school studies. Hall encouraged legions of volunteers in the child study movement to collect data about children's development; he counseled them that education should be based on a child's own nature and needs, not on subjects that existed outside the child's immediate experience. Teachers were wrong, he warned, to think that their primary responsibility was "perfecting the art of imparting knowledge," when *they* should be learning from the child: "Too often the ideal of knowledge for its own sake is held up. This is narrow and selfish, and antagonistic to evolution, for it places the interests of the individual before those of the race." Scientifically trained educators, he held, exhibited "a willingness to fit the school to the child, rather than the child to the school."[32]

Today many of Hall's supposedly scientific claims would be considered crackpot. Like Mr. Casaubon in George Eliot's *Middlemarch,* Hall dreamed that he could find the keys to eternal questions about human nature and destiny. He believed that he had found the keys in Darwinism, genetics, heredity, instincts, and the unconscious. He endorsed the notion that ontogeny recapitulates phylogeny, meaning that each individual experiences the same cultural stages of growth as the history of man. From infancy to maturity, he believed, the individual relived the age of prehistoric man, advanced to a savage stage, and eventually became civilized.

Hall first received wide attention as a result of his 1883 article "The Contents of Children's Minds," in which he reported what children entering primary school in Boston knew. Questioned by experienced kindergarten teachers, these little children were ignorant of many things, such as what a beehive, a crow, a bluebird, an ant, a squirrel, a snail, a robin, an island, or a beach was; nor did they know the origin of leather or cotton or woolen things, what bricks were made of, or what a triangle was. Why five-year-old children should know all of these ill-assorted things was not clear. Hall sensibly suggested that teachers should teach with objects, and parents should teach their children about the natural world. But he then leaped to a romantic assertion: "Alas for the teacher who does not learn more from his children than he can ever hope to teach them!" If children arrived in school, as he concluded after studying the contents of children's minds, with "next to nothing of pedagogic value," one would expect that the teachers would have much more to teach them than the other way around.[33]

After assuming the presidency of Clark University in 1888, Hall became the leader of the child study movement. This movement appeared to be an exemplary application of modern science to education. With Hall at the helm, child study became a crusade, with thousands of devoted followers organized in hundreds of "mothers' clubs" across the nation.[34] Child study organizations were also formed in other nations, and many universities developed child study programs. In 1894, the prestigious National Education Association—the same body that had sponsored the Committee of Ten—created a Department of Child Study. Volunteer teachers and mothers administered Hall's questionnaires to children and gathered information about their games, toys, habits, fears, interests, collections, physical development, and health; children were asked to "tap, press a dynamometer, count lines, put a needle through a small hole . . . [and] name their favorite story"; their weight and height were measured, and their vision, hearing, and speech were tested.[35]

71

Some educators thought the findings of child study produced trivia. O. T. Corson, commissioner of education in Ohio, declared, "To be told that a careful and scientific investigation has revealed the wonderful fact that Santa Claus appears to have a strong hold upon the hearts of boys and girls of all ages makes us tremble at the dense ignorance in which we have all been living." [36]

Hall portrayed traditional schooling as an unfortunate, often harmful intrusion into a child's natural life. Long after Hall's speculations about instinct and heredity were forgotten, American education and culture in the twentieth century continued to reverberate with echoes of Hall's romanticism, naturalism, and mysticism. Educational radicals of various eras have been inspired by Hall's romantic views of the child. Writing in 1885, Hall declared that "the new education . . . holds that there is one thing in nature, and one alone, fit to inspire all true men and women with more awe and reverence than Kant's starry heavens, and that is the soul and the body of the healthy young child." [37]

Hall ridiculed the proposition that all children should receive the same kind of education. Pointing to European school systems, he recommended different school programs for the college-bound and for others, starting at the age of eight. He vilified the academic curriculum. Learning to read was not especially important, he said; in fact, "it would not be a serious loss, if a child never learned to read. Charlemagne could not read, and he had quite an influence upon the world's history and was a fairly brainy man." Learning to write was "not of great educational value." Typewriting and telegraphy were more useful than writing, and "a system of gesture is as valuable." Learning foreign languages interfered with young people's ability to master English, as did grammar (which he described as "more or less of a school-made artifact and an alien yoke"). [38]

Nor did Hall see much use in studying arithmetic or geography, particularly when compared to training for the trades or manual training in activities such as woodwork, cooking, sewing, and drawing. In no event, Hall believed, should children learn to read, write, spell, or do number work before the age of eight. [39] Nothing that the school might ever do, said Hall, could ever compare in importance to the child's heredity, which was fixed by his genes. [40]

In 1901, Hall described his ideal school to the annual meeting of the National Education Association. Hall spoke of "health, growth, and heredity, a pound of which is worth a ton of instruction," implying that instruction was not worth much. His ideal school expressed his naturalistic, romantic view of children:

> The guardians of the young should strive first of all to keep out of nature's way, and to prevent harm, and should merit the proud title of defenders of the happiness and rights of children. They should feel profoundly that childhood, as it comes fresh from the hand of God, is not corrupt, but illustrates the survival of the most consummate thing in the world; they should be convinced that there is nothing else so worthy of love, reverence, and service as the body and soul of the growing child. . . . We must overcome the fetichism of the alphabet, of the multiplication table, of grammars, of scales, and of bibliolatry.[41]

It was not so very long ago, he pointed out, that the great men of the world could "neither read nor write," and "even the blessed mother of our Lord knew nothing of letters." Then he carried his thought to its logical conclusion:

> Nay, more: there are many who ought not to be educated, and who would be better in mind, body, and morals if they knew no school. What shall it profit a child to gain the world of knowledge and lose his own health? Cramming and over-schooling have impaired many a feeble mind, for which, as the proverb says, nothing is so dangerous as ideas too large for it. We are coming to understand the vanity of mere scholarship and erudition, and to know that even ignorance may be a wholesome poultice for weakly souls.[42]

Strange to hear praise of illiteracy from this master pedant, who liberally sprinkled foreign phrases and obscure Latinate words throughout his writings!

Believing as he did that biology was destiny, Hall admired woman as an intuitive, feeling instrument of reproduction. Woman, he wrote, was "at the top of the human curve from which the higher super-man of the future is to evolve. . . . Her whole soul, conscious and unconscious, is best conceived as a magnificent organ of heredity, and to its laws all her psychic activities, if unperverted, are true." Hall cited numerous studies to show that women's reproductive system was endangered by too much study, too much thinking, and the stress of competing with men. Hall worried that "modern woman . . . is in danger of declining from her orbit; that she is coming to lack just confidence and pride in her sex as such, and is just now in danger of lapsing to mannish ways, methods and ideals, until her original divinity may become obscured."[43] Women who strayed too far from their biologically defined nature, he suggested, were jeopardizing the future of the race.

Hall often inveighed against the study of Latin. In 1902, he told the annual meeting of the National Education Association that other modern nations were getting rid of it. He pointed to Booker T. Washington, who "says the two chief desires of the colored youth during all the reconstruction period were to hold office and to study Latin, and that his life-work for his race has been directed against these two evils." The rising enrollments in Latin, Hall said, were "calamitous," because Latin was actually harmful to students: "Most high-school Latinists do not go on to college. Beginnings that leave abandoned tracks in the brain because there is no relation to after-life are evil." His ideal high school would emphasize literature and oratory, science and industrial training.[44] Hall pointed to the Hampton Institute, where black youths were taught trades and occupations, as a model for the kind of training that all youth needed.

Hall frequently warned educators and parents of the conflict between the "needs of the growing child" and traditional studies. What must the schools do? "Public education must get into a new vital relation to what children love to do, are curious to know, and the things they most want."[45] Hall did not recognize the possibility that teachers might awaken in children new interests to love, new ideas to be curious about, and new pursuits to explore.

In 1901, at a meeting of the New England Association of Colleges and Secondary Schools, Hall described his views of the proper relationship between schooling and the "nature and needs of adolescents," and Eliot attempted to refute him. Eliot criticized Hall's claim that boyhood was the ideal stage for "drill." Eliot did not believe that any period of human life should be devoted to drill: "Drilling is a highly mechanical process, intended to produce a mechanical end. It is at its best in a factory. Is a factory the kind of place which we think appropriate to boys and girls?" To Hall's complaints about Latin and other academic subjects, Eliot said he saw no reason to tell students that they "had better not take Latin." It seems, said Eliot, that Hall did not approve of anything the high schools taught: "What remains? What shall the child do? . . . Shall we advise the pupils in our high schools not to study Latin, or English, or physics, or algebra, or French, or German?"

Eliot defended the principle that high school programs should not differentiate between students who planned to go to college and those who did not. It was a principle that he believed in, "root and branch," and he explained that:

In the first place . . . thousands of high-school pupils do not know whether they are going to college or not; therefore, postpone as late as possible that fateful decision, postpone as late as possible the forking of the ways in the high school. Carry to the college or scientific school every child that can be led that way, and put no obstacle in the way till the latest possible moment, no obstacle created by a too early choice between diverging roads . . . the training of a youth from fourteen to eighteen should be one and the same, whether he is going into college or . . . going to earn his living.[46]

Unfortunately, events and the moving ideas of the day were not running in Eliot's direction. And before the decade was out, even Eliot would fall into step with the times.

The Crusade for Social Efficiency

*Nineteenth-century educators believed that the best way to improve so-*ciety was to offer a sound education to as many children as possible. They believed that well-educated individuals would become responsible citizens and would improve society by dint of their intelligence and character.

Progressive educators of the early twentieth century rejected that view as hopelessly conservative, even reactionary. Forward-looking educators aligned themselves with the dynamic new social sciences, which promised to reveal the secrets of individual and social development. Educational psychologists believed that they could turn education into a precise science; educational sociologists described ways in which schools could best serve society; and professors of educational administration claimed that they could apply the tenets of scientific management to schooling. The new university-based experts of education maintained that existing practices in the schools, particularly the expectation that all students must study an academic curriculum, were unscientific and inefficient, based on nothing more than custom and tradition.

What, then, should be the objectives of education? Progressive educators admired Herbert Spencer's emphasis on *utility* as the ultimate measure of educational value. There was, to be sure, a large irony in Spencer's influence on progressive educators because he was an outspoken proponent of social Darwinism, popularly interpreted as "survival of the fittest," which counseled against efforts at social reform; he was also a steadfast opponent of public education. Nevertheless, his strictures on utility resonated among progressive educators who shared none of his other views.

Progressive educators demanded that every academic subject had to prove its value. What was it good for? Did it have a purpose outside the classroom? Did it serve a function in adult life? They concluded that academic subjects that did not meet the test of immediate utility were irrelevant for the great majority of youths who planned to work or become homemakers after they left school.

Progressive educators who wanted to dispense with everything but the useful were encouraged by leaders of the new social sciences. Speaking to the National Education Association in 1896, sociologist Albion Small of the University of Chicago lambasted the traditional curriculum. He said that youngsters were educated best by reality, not by subject matter, and that the purpose of education was the adaptation of the individual to his society. Sociology, he said, demands that the child's studies be relevant to his life. For example, he regretted that he knew so much about the British Constitution and virtually nothing about the government of his local community. Instead of teaching about the history and government of faraway places, he recommended, instruction should be based on the life of the individual: "The child should begin to study economics,—literally, the law of the household,—he should learn the civics and ethics and history of the household, in the practice of normal household relations. The economy and politics and ethics and history of the school, and then of the parent's shop, and then of the neighboring factory, and later of the whole town, are the best educational material that the sociologist can recommend."[47] Small's proposal was a reasonably accurate prediction of social studies, which would not come into formal existence for another twenty years.

Small asserted that "sociology demands of educators, finally, that they shall not rate themselves as leaders of children but as makers of society."[48] Many progressive educators, frustrated with the slow pace of social reform, were eager to see themselves as "makers of society." How much more exalted it was to be considered a maker of society rather than merely a teacher of English or geography. In Small's rhetoric lay the seeds of social engineering, which appealed to those who sought a larger role for themselves and their profession as social reformers and "makers of society."

THE INDUSTRIAL EDUCATION MOVEMENT

In the early years of the new century, educators saw the possibility of making the school the leading edge of social reform. Some, thinking that they were following John Dewey's lead, got swept up in the national enthusiasm for industrial education. The event that launched the industrial education movement was the report of the Massachusetts Commission on Industrial and Technical Education in 1906.

The commission recommended the introduction of industrial and vocational education into the public schools, as well as the establishment of industrial schools that were completely separate from the regular school system. It claimed that the "old-fashioned type" of schooling caused large numbers of children to leave school early, unprepared for the labor market. Despite the fact that public schools already offered vocational and commercial studies, the commission complained that the public schools were "too exclusively literary in their spirit, scope and methods." Most children needed "industrial intelligence" to prepare them for "productive efficiency" in employment. The benefits of industrial education would flow to the child, who would be ready for work; to the employer, who would be able to hire trained labor; and to the nation, which would enjoy "the highest technical success." The commission explained that "the latest philosophy of education re-enforces the demands of productive industry by showing that which fits a child for his place in the world as a producer tends to his own highest development physically, intellectually, and morally."[49] Instead of a "literary" education, the commission recommended that the vast majority of children should be trained in school for jobs in industry.

In the same year, 1906, the director of manual training in the New York City public schools and a professor of manual training at Teachers College, Columbia University, organized the National Society for the Promotion of Industrial Education. This organization enlisted industrialists, labor leaders, social workers, and other educators to support legislation and funding for the cause. In 1913, one educator likened the rapid spread of the industrial education movement to a "mental epidemic" not unlike religious revivals or Klondike gold fever.[50] Historian Sol Cohen wrote later of this period that "Bankers, businessmen, industrialists, philanthropists, social workers, educators, all jumped on the bandwagon. Few movements in the history of American education have taken so sudden and so powerful a hold on the minds of school reformers."[51]

In 1907, with reformers acclaiming industrial education as the key to social progress, President Theodore Roosevelt declared, "Our school system is gravely defective in so far as it puts a premium upon mere literary training and tends therefore to train the boy away from the farm and the workshop. Nothing is more needed than the best type of industrial school, the school for mechanical industries in the city, the school for practically teaching agriculture in the country."[52]

Many educators agreed, and annual meetings of the National Education Association rang with oratory in praise of the practical and the useful, anything that trained children for work in the home, the shop, or the factory. In 1903, the NEA had joined the social efficiency crusade by creating a Commission on Economy of Time in Education. After churning out studies for a decade, the commission concluded that too much time was wasted in the name of culture that would be better spent in vocational and industrial education. The best way to make the schools efficient, it said, was to be sure that they adjusted young people to meet society's needs.

This conclusion was supported by most sociologists, who agreed that the aims of the school should be utilitarian, not cultural or spiritual; cultural studies such as literature and foreign language, sociologists found, contained "a selfishly unsocial factor." Committee member Henry Suzzallo, a professor of philosophy of education at Teachers College, advised that "The selection of a course of study is always primarily a sociological matter; and every activity, traditional or innovative, should be eliminated when no relatively important social sanction can be found for it." The unique role of the school, he wrote, was "to distribute men and women to those tasks in life where their abilities will count most and their defects least."[53] It was not socially efficient for individuals to pursue the education they themselves wanted. Such decisions should be based on the needs of society.

The belief that sociological principles could determine which group should be educated and what they should learn fueled the industrial education movement. High school enrollments soared in the early decades of the century, and educators wanted to see continued growth. Education experts predicted that the children of the masses, as they reached high school, would be sure to reject the academic curriculum as irrelevant to their lives. According to the sociological analysis, most of these youngsters needed training for industrial occupations, and few were intellectually capable of mastering academic courses. Nicholas Murray Butler, a founder of Teachers College and president of Columbia University, said that the purpose of vocational education was to adapt "the larger proportion of the population to their environment."[54] The job of the modern school was to prepare children to fit into society, to train them for the industrial or manual occupation that awaited them.

Faced with the choice between a liberal education for all and a differentiated curriculum based on social class, educators began a stampede toward a differentiated curriculum. The authoritative voice of social science, and most especially of sociology, advised that the essential purpose of the schools was to adapt the populace to meet the needs of society. In 1901, sociologist Edward A. Ross, a disciple of Lester Frank Ward, explained that free public schooling was "an engine of social control." It was the job of the schools, he wrote, "to collect little plastic lumps of human dough from private households and shape them on the social kneading-board. . . . And so it happens that the role of the schoolmaster in the social economy is just beginning." Ward had imagined that the purpose of schooling was to redistribute knowledge, believing as he did that "the lower classes of society are the intellectual equals of the upper classes."[55]

Ross labored under no such illusions. He saw the schools as "an economical system of police." He knew that to acknowledge as much "shocks the public and chills teachers. But now and then the cat is let out of the bag." Ross predicted that the disestablishment of religion would be followed by the establishment of the school as the guarantor of social order. The new education, he predicted, "will be realistic, and its starting-point will be the facts of personal and social life." The ultimate goal of the powerful, centralized, state-controlled educational system, he prophesied, would be "to perfect an education in the interests of society."[56]

The rise of educational sociology and the success of the industrial education movement radically changed public discussion of educational goals. By 1910, educators were busily engaged in creating courses differentiated by the future occupation of each child; the school curriculum would vary, depending on whether the child was likely to become a farmer, housewife, clerk, factory worker, salesman, or mechanic. The social efficiency movement took hold at the very time that record numbers of high school students were enrolling in Latin and other academic subjects. As school systems put differentiated courses into place, educational experts advised that only a few students should prepare for the learned professions, and many schools began to use "vocational guidance" to direct their students into the appropriate programs. Within only a few years, discussions among educators about how to teach all children the great ideas and art of the ages faded away, seeming slightly antique, and were replaced by discussions of social efficiency.

SOCIAL EFFICIENCY VERSUS THE ACADEMIC CURRICULUM

If Edward L. Thorndike was the foremost practitioner of educational psychology and G. Stanley Hall dominated the field of child study, David Snedden was the leading representative of the social efficiency movement. A California schoolmaster and superintendent, Snedden made his mark as a founder of the field of educational sociology.

As a young teacher, Snedden admired the educational writings of Herbert Spencer, and as a student at Stanford, he absorbed the social control doctrines of his teacher, Edward A. Ross. After receiving his doctorate from Teachers College in 1907, Snedden was appointed commissioner of education for the state of Massachusetts in 1909 and served for six years. In 1916, he accepted a chair at Teachers College as professor of vocational education and educational sociology, where he was one of the nation's most prominent advocates of vocational education.[57]

Throughout his career, Snedden viewed education through the lens of social control doctrine. He believed that the needs of society determined the needs of individuals and that the primary aim of education was to adjust individuals or groups to carry out their social roles. Snedden advocated several interrelated ideas:

- First, he insisted that different groups, as defined by their likely occupation, required different kinds of education. A differentiated curriculum was democratic and socially efficient, he felt, because it supplied appropriate education for girls, the college-bound, and youngsters destined for certain occupations.
- Second, he believed that most students, after the age of twelve and not later than fourteen, should be in a vocational program, preparing for a specific job or occupation.
- Third, he derided academic studies as useless, elitist, and of little value to a democratic society, except for the few students who had a specific occupational reason for studying them.
- Fourth, he believed that his own views reflected modern scientific thinking. He considered those who disagreed with him to be ignorant of modern science or "wrapped up in the cocoons of blind faiths, untested beliefs, hardened customs."[58]

In 1900, at the outset of his career, Snedden described the education he believed to be appropriate for "the rank and file of society," those "who will follow, not lead." He prophesied that the public school would increasingly take on the duties of the home and the church, as well as specifically training students for work. Snedden's caricature of the traditional school became a staple of progressive attacks for years to come: it was "repressive," "monarchical," "barren and repellant," founded entirely on the classics and completely out of touch with American democracy. The educational system itself, he said, was causing massive school leaving because it had "developed under the conditions of autocracy." It demanded "unquestioning submission to authority" and required the student to respond like an "automaton."

The new education, he predicted, would rely on the "aptitudes and preferences" of students to gain their cooperation. Snedden had no desire to weaken authority; he sought "only a change in the motives leading to submission to it." Only tradition, he argued, decreed that girls should "master mathematics and physical science" and that boys and girls should study English literature, "which was produced under times and conditions so different from those of the present day." There was no reason, he said, to provide the same education to the college-bound and to the boys and girls of "the rank and file."[59]

Snedden offered no evidence for his claim that youngsters were dropping out because of the curriculum, rather than because of their need to earn money. The dramatic increases in high school enrollments at this time should have suggested that the schools were teaching skills and knowledge that growing numbers of students wanted and needed. Snedden's harsh portrayal of the schools as elitist institutions devoted solely to the classical curriculum bore little resemblance to the relatively new public high schools that had grown up in the late nineteenth century to offer a common academic curriculum, as well as commercial courses such as bookkeeping, typing, and surveying.

As commissioner of education in Massachusetts and later as a prominent professor at Columbia's Teachers College, Snedden insisted that only practical studies could produce "the socialized and efficient individual." He saw social benefit in teaching penmanship, civics, and vocational education but maintained that almost every other school subject survived only because of custom. Algebra, he believed, had no utility, and speculations about its value "are on the same basis as those of our forebears, who guessed about the flatness of the earth, the location of the soul in the body, or night air as a cause of disease." Latin and Greek were utterly without social value, and he doubted the utility of grammar, arithmetic, and geometry. He complained that most liberal studies in high schools did not "function" at all: "Of what cultural or civic value for girls is most algebra, as now studied? Latin? French? Ancient history, or even medieval and modern history? Physics? Classical English literature? On the basis of what tokens of enduring interests, cultural ideals, well-informed minds, elevated tastes, persisting devotion to the 'enterprise of learning,' can it be contended that any of these studies are 'functional' for all or some boys?" No study, he insisted, could be "regarded as an end in itself."[60] As for art, he claimed that our civilization had reached a stage where the "general social need for art of good quality" was no longer vital and compelling, and its only future in our society was to "divert and entertain."[61]

Snedden had the courage of his convictions. In 1914, he told the

New England History Teachers' Association that there was no reason to believe that the study of history teaches judgment, reasoning power, culture, social efficiency, or even good citizenship. The only justification for teaching history that Snedden could imagine was equipping students with "ideals of right social action" or training them for citizenship, which he defined as "submission to established political order [and] cooperative maintenance of the same." He opposed the chronological teaching of history, as he opposed the logical organization of any subject matter, and insisted that the only history worth teaching was about present social institutions. Any history that was not related to the present, he asserted, was simply " 'the cold storage' theory of education," nothing more than facts packed away into students' mental storehouse for possible future use.[62]

Snedden thought that the idea of learning for its own sake was a luxury, which had no place in the public schools. At the same meeting, George L. Burr, a historian at Cornell University, replied to Snedden that history taught "imagination, sympathy, insight, [and] judgment" and that it was the best training "for life and action." Burr complained that the only history Snedden would approve was "history with the history left out." Unpersuaded, Snedden continued to inveigh against history and in favor of social education, whose purpose was to teach correct attitudes and social responsibility.[63]

In the closing days of World War I, Snedden argued that mathematics was not necessary for all students, and he referred casually to "the dead hand of mathematics" and the "mummified study" of algebra. Charles N. Moore, a mathematics professor at the University of Cincinnati, pointed out in reply to Snedden that many young men had failed to qualify as artillery officers because of their ignorance of mathematics. Moore wrote caustically, "I have felt for some time that some of the ill-advised agitators in the educational world who have been advocating sweeping changes in our school curricula without offering any valid reasons in support of their claim, were, perhaps unconsciously, perpetrating an injustice on the youth of our land who are entitled to the best available education."[64]

Unmoved, Snedden responded that "girls did not, as a rule, become artillery officers, or navigators, nor did they aspire to follow the peaceful pursuits of the civil or electrical engineer, machinist or architect." Nor, in fact, did most boys. He insisted that only "those rare elect spirits who can or will follow the mathematics-using vocations" should study the subject.[65]

Snedden's uncompromising commitment to differentiation was both his most distinctive cause and, in time, his undoing. Unlike John Dewey and most other progressive educators, Snedden believed that public vocational schools should be separate from regular public schools. He wanted special schools for such vocations as "tailoring, jewelry salesmanship, poultry farming, coal cutting, stationary engine firing, waiting on table (hotel), cutting (in shoe factory), automobile repair, teaching of French in secondary school, mule spinning, power machine operating (for ready made clothing), raisin grape growing, general farming suited to Minnesota, linotype composition, railway telegraphy, autogenous welding, street car motor driving, and a hundred others."[66]

Snedden's advocacy of curricular differentiation based on pupils' occupational destination (and gender) rapidly entered the mainstream of educational thought, as did his disparagement of learning for its own sake; his views concurred with those of industrialists and people who thought of themselves as practical. But his stubborn insistence on separate vocational schools eventually pushed him to the margins of progressive education, even among vocational educators, because the leadership of the profession opposed what came to be called "dual administration." Dewey believed that separate vocational schools were inherently undemocratic and would narrow both general education and vocational education.[67] School officials feared that separate schools would weaken professional control of public education. They preferred comprehensive high schools, where academic and nonacademic studies coexisted. In 1924, H. Gordon Hullfish, a leading progressive educator, chastised Snedden for trying to separate vocation and culture (thus violating a fundamental Deweyan principle) and declared that Snedden was not "the expected educational Moses."[68]

Snedden's large contribution to American education was not the separate vocational schools that he favored but his fervent advocacy of the use of sociological criteria to assign children to different curriculum tracks. Social efficiency, he believed, decreed that schools should classify and train the children of the rank and file to meet the needs of society. At times he inadvertently acknowledged that the demand for vocational studies did not emanate from the public, as when he noted, "If many parents, whether wisely or mistakenly, insisted that their children have opportunity, or be required, to study drawing or Latin or Spanish or cube root, it was only human that moderately prepared, incurious, harried teachers and principals should say, 'We will try to give the people what they think they want.' "[69] Snedden was everlastingly certain that the public was misinformed and that it was up to scientifically trained educational experts like himself, not parents or teachers, to decide the objectives of education.

Charles W. Eliot's Defection

The new era of social efficiency seemed to have unstoppable momentum; it even made a convert of Charles W. Eliot, who for many years had defended the principle of a common academic curriculum. In 1908, he changed sides when he addressed the National Society for the Promotion of Industrial Education, an organization committed to the proposition that the academic curriculum was too bookish for those who needed industrial training and vocational guidance. Only three years earlier, Eliot had argued eloquently that the educational ladder should remain open to all American children for as long as possible; that "the classification of pupils, according to their so-called probable destinations, should be postponed to the latest possible time of life"; and that individuals had a right to make their own decisions about their studies and careers.[70]

But three critical years had passed, in which professional and public opinion had shifted seismically. Once again abreast of his times, Eliot noted that many children would be "obliged to leave the regular public school system by the time they are fourteen, or even earlier" and that they needed guidance. In 1908, he asked, "How shall the decision be made that certain children will go into industrial schools, others into the ordinary high schools, and others again into the mechanic arts high schools? Where is that decision to be made? It must be a choice, or a selection. Here we come upon a new function for the teachers in our elementary schools. . . . The teachers of the elementary schools ought to sort the pupils and sort them by their evident or probable destinies."[71]

It seemed an eminently sensible recommendation, and no one noticed that he had abandoned many years of advocating against such guidance and differentiation based on probable destinies.

3

The Age of the Experts

In 1918, the superintendent of schools in Topeka, Kansas, hardly a hotbed of educational radicalism, declared that "the large objective in modern education is to socialize the school." What he meant was that everything taught in school should have utility and that students should work in groups, not alone. The good school, he said, was socially efficient; there should be no more teaching of knowledge or culture for its own sake. The goal of education was to serve society as efficiently as possible.[1]

The superintendent had caught the wave of reform. An innocent bystander might understandably be confused by the proliferation of school reform movements in this era, but all of them shared certain characteristics. One was the discrediting of the ideal of the educational ladder, the notion that all children should have an education that was both liberal and general. Another was a shift of educational authority from parents, teachers, and school leaders to the scientific experts in the new schools of education. A third was the claim, advanced by the same experts, that a democratic education was synonymous with a differentiated curriculum.

In the new educational order, the experts advised school authorities to make their schools efficient by dividing up students into appropriate programs. Every teacher and school official knew that most youngsters left school at the end of eighth grade, sometimes even sooner, to go to work, and that large numbers of immigrant children had difficulty keeping up in school, usually because of their poor command of English. The problem of "laggards in the schools"—students who were far behind others of the same age—persuaded many progressive reformers that the curriculum of the schools had to change, that the slow progress of many students was caused by the academic curriculum.

The differentiated curriculum was supposed to give each group of students the program they needed. Only a small number of students would continue to get an academic education, not because it had any inherent value but because it was necessary for college admission. The other students—the overwhelming majority—were to be sorted into programs to prepare for their likely future in the workforce or the home. Using intelligence tests, school officials would predict which students should enroll in college preparatory courses and make sure that the majority were directed to vocational programs that "met their needs."

By discrediting the generally understood and broadly accepted definition of schooling for intellectual growth, pedagogical experts such as Edward L. Thorndike, G. Stanley Hall, and David Snedden cleared the way for the new education based on utility. From Thorndike's research came the mental testing movement, which facilitated the assignment of children into academic and vocational curriculum tracks. From Hall's advocacy came the child study movement, child-centered schools, and demands to eliminate all academic pressures (such as homework) that allegedly injured children's health. From Snedden and other professors of educational administration and educational sociology came the social efficiency movement, which held that children should get the education appropriate to their future roles as workers or homemakers.

The experts also cleared the way for two of the worst manifestations of anti-intellectualism. First, the loss of education's historic rationale meant that the definition of education itself was up for grabs, available for capture by any idea, fad, or movement that was advanced by pedagogical experts, popular sentiment, or employers. Second, the notion that education should be determined by the child's future occupation turned democratic rhetoric upside down: in the old way of thinking, equal opportunity meant that all children should have access to the same quality of education; in the new way of thinking, equal opportunity meant that a banker's children would get a very different education from a coal miner's children, and all would be fitted to occupy the status of their parents.

THE NEW ROLE OF THE SCHOOLS

Educators wanted to be "modern." But what did it mean to be modern? For those influenced by the ideas of G. Stanley Hall, modern education meant a "natural" education, one that removed all stress and strain from the growing child, leaving plenty of time for play (a great admirer of Sigmund Freud and his controversial sexual theories, Hall invited him to America in 1909 to receive an honorary degree from Clark University and give a celebrated series of lectures).[2]

Influenced by Hall's ideas about natural education, Edward Bok, editor of *The Ladies' Home Journal,* mounted a campaign in 1900 alleging that the mental health of American children was being destroyed. Bok charged that there was "A National Crime at the Feet of American Parents." What was this terrible national crime? Homework. Homework was ruining American childhood. Bok insisted that no child should be sent to school before the age of seven and that no child under the age of fifteen should be "given any home study whatever by his teachers." Nor should any child under fifteen go to school for more than four hours each day. All this cramming and book learning, he asserted, were evil, and American parents must not stand by "as their child is being permanently crippled by a cramming system of education."[3]

For progressive educators such as Junius Meriam, director of the University Elementary School at the University of Missouri, modern education meant eliminating any "isolated subjects of an abstract nature," which included "practically all the content of our curriculum." To demand that a boy "learn the principles of percentage and the geography of Australia because, perchance, he may have use for that information in adult life" was "a serious injustice." Drawing on the ideas of both Dewey and Hall, Meriam designed a child-centered school where adult purposes and subject matter virtually disappeared. Children care only "to live in the immediate present," he wrote, and whatever is taught must meet the "real, present needs of the pupils." At Meriam's school, the first three years were devoted to "the playing of wholesome games, the observation of anything interesting and profitable to children, and the making of things useful and ornamental."[4]

For those in public education, especially in the big cities, modern education meant a differentiated curriculum in which children were placed in markedly different programs. Many cities proved that they were up to date by creating vocational and technical high schools.

William H. Elson and Frank P. Bachman, the superintendent and deputy superintendent of public schools in Cleveland, insisted that differentiation should begin in the elementary school, which extended through the first eight grades. The elementary curriculum, they said, had to be reorganized in light of the fact that "The social order needs lawyers, doctors, preachers, teachers, men of science, of art, and office-holders, but it takes but 4 per cent of the breadwinners of our country to do all the professional work of society." In addition, only 1 percent were likely to be employed as managers. The remaining 95 percent of the youngsters in Cleveland's schools were destined to be "industrial and commercial workers," and the program of the public schools should reflect their different occupational destinations.[5]

How would the schools know which children were likely to go to college and which to work in industry? One way of classifying children was by their home environment: "It is obvious that the educational needs of the child in a district where the streets are well paved and clean, where the homes are spacious and surrounded by lawns and trees, where the language of the child's playfellows is pure, and where life in general is permeated with the spirit and ideals of America—it is obvious that the educational needs of such a child are radically different from those of the child who lives in a foreign and tenement section." Elson and Bachman rejected the traditional idea of equality of opportunity, which implied the same course of instruction for all in the eight years of elementary school. This, they believed, was a false notion of equality because the academic curriculum was suited only to children "of strong mental capacity . . . of bookish tastes and inclined to the professions." They proposed a common course of study for the first four grades, then a separation of children into two tracks, one preparing for high school, the other for work. For those students over the age of thirteen who were not interested in "bookish things," there should be a special school devoted to industrial and commercial subjects.[6]

Cleveland's problem was common to many other school districts, especially those where enrollments grew each year with the addition of large numbers of foreign-born children. Educators' responses to this problem were determined by their fundamental beliefs about the value of education. If educators believed that the job of the school was to keep open the ladder of opportunity from the kindergarten to the university, their goal was to figure out how to teach mathematics and science, history and literature, language and art to children from every kind of neighborhood and home, varying instruction when necessary to help children learn. If, however, educators believed that the job of the school was to provide a different path for the children who were not likely to go to college, their task was to place them in the right program. The latter approach allowed the academic track to remain "literary" and "bookish" for the few, while most other children were directed into vocational programs.

One response to this dilemma was the invention of the junior high school, which spread rapidly after 1910. Its advocates believed that the common elementary course should be only six years, followed by three years in which students would be "guided" to the right curriculum for their future occupation. The main effect of the establishment of junior high schools was to reduce the number of years of common schooling from eight to six.

In 1915, the annual meeting of the National Education Association's Department of Superintendence approved a resolution in support of the "tendency to establish, beginning with the seventh grade, differentiated courses of study aimed more completely to prepare the child for his possible future activities." In support of the resolution, U.S. Commissioner of Education Philander P. Claxton said that differentiated curricula would enable large numbers of children to divide their school years equally between school and work.[7]

The only voice raised in opposition to the junior high school was that of William C. Bagley, a psychologist at the school of education at the University of Illinois, who would soon become the foremost critic of progressive education. Bagley warned against early differentiation in the junior high school, which he saw as "a radical step away from our democratic institutions" that would promote social stratification along European lines. The purpose of the junior high school, Bagley charged, was to limit access to a common curriculum, which would mean "the ultimate disintegration of our 'educational-ladder' type of organization." Bagley wondered who was clamoring for this reorganization: "Not the 'working people,' one may be confident. What they wish for their children is the opportunity that liberal education implies. . . . Hitherto in our national life we have proceeded on the assumption that no one has the omniscience to pick out the future hewers of wood and drawers of water,—at least not when the candidates for these tasks are to be selected at the tender age of twelve."[8]

Progressive educators carried their attack on the academic curriculum to the popular press, where they appealed to popular anti-intellectualism. William Hughes Mearns, who later taught poetry and creative writing at the experimental Lincoln School at Teachers College, Columbia University, caricatured the cultural ideals of the traditional high school in *The Saturday Evening Post*. His title posed the question "Our Medieval High Schools: Shall We Educate Children for the Twelfth or the Twentieth Century?"

Mearns mocked the idea of learning for its own sake and the study of dead languages; it was the colleges, not long-suffering taxpayers, he said, who were imposing such dreary stuff on schoolchildren in the name of "culture." What is the use, he asked, "whether your graduate knows how to eliminate x and y if he is too dainty to paint a roof, or pound hot bolts, or stoke a stationary engine, or tie up a decent package?" Modern education, he told his readers, "signifies a study of individual needs and an attempt to fit that individual for what the best

wisdom of the moment considers his welfare." Professional pedagogues, of course, not parents or even teachers, had a monopoly on "the
best wisdom of the moment." Mearns pointed admiringly to the example
of Commissioner David Snedden in Massachusetts, who "is developing
boys educationally in work that looks marvelously like landscape gardening, housepainting, furniture making; and he claims there's culture
in it too!"[9]

The Saturday Evening Post published several similar articles, reiter-
ating the progressivist charge that the "narrow" academic curriculum
was forcing most youngsters to drop out of school. Never mind that enrollment in the high schools continued to surge every year, nearly dou-
bling between 1900 and 1910 and more than quadrupling between 1900
and 1920!

An article by William D. Lewis, the principal of the William Penn
High School in Philadelphia, caught the attention of President Theodore
Roosevelt and was expanded in 1914 into a book, *Democracy's High
School,* for which the president wrote a foreword. Lewis complained
about the inappropriateness of requiring youngsters to study the dead
languages, history, and algebra, requirements reflecting the "aristocratic" origins of the high schools. He asserted that "the schools are
organized to serve the progress of civilization by fitting our youth
for their part in the new order," not by forcing them into the narrow
Procrustean bed of the academic curriculum. Lewis demanded an
equal place in the curriculum for practical subjects such as agriculture,
business training, and manual arts. In "democracy's high school," girls
would learn the domestic sciences (cooking, dressmaking, household
budgeting, shopping) that would equip them either to make a living
as household workers or to be efficient wives and mothers. The modern
schools would also recognize that the boys "can't all be doctors,
lawyers, preachers, and teachers. They are crying out for equal opportunities—a thing very different from identical opportunities." Such
subjects as history, foreign languages, and literature, he wrote, were
nearly insuperable obstacles to all but a handful of students and thus the
prime cause of school failure for the ordinary boy and girl. He insisted
that the public was "paying the bills" and would surely not want to sup-

port a curriculum of "little practical value" that failed to serve "all the people."[10]

REDEFINING "DEMOCRACY" IN EDUCATION

*Slowly but surely, the meaning of "democracy" was redefined by pro-*gressive theorists. Instead of a ladder that stretched from kindergarten to the university and was open to all students, there would be many paths leading to different destinations: the future professional would prepare for college; the future farmer would study agriculture; the future housewife would study household management; the future clerk would study commercial subjects; the future industrial worker would study metalworking and woodworking; and so on.

Requiring all to take college preparatory studies, said the experts, was elitist; providing an "appropriate" education for every child was democratic. Thus were John Dewey's strictures about the democratic purposes of the school twisted into antidemocratic practices in the schools. In 1906, Dean James E. Russell of Teachers College, Columbia University, claimed that the new education would repair the error caused by the mistaken idea of the educational ladder: "The movement is only begun. The trend is unmistakably towards still further differentiation and still more complete adaptation to the needs of every-day life. . . . We boast of an educational ladder that reaches from the gutter to the university, and we see nothing amiss in making our elementary schools preparatory to the high school, and the high school preparatory to the college and university. In other words, that which few need all must take." Pointing with admiration to the highly selective European school systems, Russell wrote, "No other great nation that I know of thinks it worth while to train everybody for everything—and nothing!—and to do it at public expense."[11]

Ellwood P. Cubberley, a leader of the new progressive education movement, advocated the introduction of vocational education and expert professional management of public education. An Indianan, Cubberley was a teacher, a school superintendent, then a professor of education at Stanford University (and later its dean). He was convinced that American society had entered a period of cultural decline in which families, communities, and churches were being weakened by immigration, industrialization, and urbanization.[12]

In 1909, not long after completing his graduate education at Columbia's Teachers College, Cubberley predicted that "Our city schools will soon be forced to give up the exceedingly democratic idea that all are equal, and that our society is devoid of classes, as a few cities have already in large part done, and to begin a specialization of educational effort along many new lines in an attempt better to adapt the school to the needs of these many classes in the city life."[13] Modern schools, he felt sure, would soon recognize that only youngsters headed for the professions needed an academic curriculum; those who would be "common wage earners" needed vocational training.

Like many of his generation, Cubberley was alarmed by the arrival of large numbers of immigrants from southern and eastern Europe: "Illiterate, docile, lacking in self-reliance and initiative, and not possessing the Anglo-Teutonic conceptions of law, order, and government, their coming has served to dilute tremendously our national stock, and to corrupt our civic life." The role of the public schools, he said, was to break up these distinctive groups and amalgamate them into the general population.[14]

To allay any concern that vocational education would threaten liberal culture, Cubberley reassured an audience at the Harvard Teachers' Association in 1911 that *all* secondary education was vocational; the customary academic program was merely vocational training for the professions, and the great majority of students needed vocational training for their future work too. Much of the demand for the new vocational subjects, Cubberley acknowledged, came from business interests, and much of the resistance came from ultraconservative schoolmasters, who lacked "imagination, as well as any deep insight into democracy's problems and needs."[15]

Cubberley insisted that "the common man" was demanding vocational education for his children, but he did not have any actual examples of common men expressing this demand. He was sure, however, that common men wanted their children to receive an "efficient" education to prepare for jobs. If the claims of efficiency were not enough to persuade his audience, he warned that it was dangerous to overeducate the children of the masses:

> From a national point of view it is always dangerous to educate a boy, and to a certain extent also a girl, with no reference to vocational ends, and we may well pause and reflect when we see great numbers of our brighter young people saturating themselves today with a mass of knowledge that can have little application for the lives which most of them must inevitably lead. Disappointment and discontent are almost sure to be the result, and disappointment and discontent among its educated classes are not good for any nation.[16]

Cubberley was one of the major figures of progressive education; his books on education history and school administration were basic texts for generations of teachers and principals. In *Changing Conceptions of Education,* Cubberley portrayed the public school as a powerful tool that the state must use to assimilate immigrants and train workers for their place in the social order. He stated that the nation would be "increasingly dependent on education for guidance and progress," that the new era would be "paternalistic, perhaps even socialistic, in the matter of education," and that "each year the child is coming to belong more and more to the state, and less and less to the parent."[17]

Cubberley worried that too many teachers were still attached to antiquated academic ideals and too many entered teaching by passing subject matter examinations: "If our schools are to become more effective social institutions, our teachers must become more effective social workers. What teachers need, as much as anything else, is a knowledge of democracy's needs and problems." This they could learn only at a college of education, instructed by pedagogical experts who had deep insight into society. "Those teachers who enter the work wholly by examination have little opportunity ever to acquire this point of view, and the examination door should be closed as soon as financial conditions will permit," Cubberley opined. Of one thing he was sure: "The overeducated man is scarcely possible if an education adapted to his needs and station in life is given to him." [18]

Cubberley's *Public School Administration,* published in 1916, was the basic text for school administrators for many years. He laid out the principles for managing a complex bureaucracy and getting along with a board of education. When it came to curriculum, he authoritatively contrasted two approaches: One was "the knowledge curriculum," which he described in highly pejorative terms: "Facts, often of no particular importance in themselves, are taught, memorized, and tested for, to be forgotten as soon as the school-grade need for them has passed." The opposite of this dreary approach was "the development type of course," in which "knowledge is conceived of as life experience and inner conviction, and not as the memorization of the accumulated knowledge of the past." Using the latter approach, school would change from a place in which children prepare for life by learning traditional subjects to one in which children live life. [19]

The solution to the problem of individual differences among children, Cubberley held, was curricular differentiation. At the end of sixth grade, every student should be promoted into a different course of study, either academic, business, household arts, or vocational. Cubberley pointed admiringly to school districts such as Santa Barbara, California, and Newton, Massachusetts, which had successfully differentiated their curricula in accordance with students' vocational aspirations after sixth grade. By reading Cubberley, who was the leading expert on public school administration, aspiring principals and school superintendents learned that modern, up-to-date educators were replacing the obsolete "knowledge curriculum" with an array of vocational programs.

The progressives, who commanded the colleges of education in the universities, shared a remarkable hubris. They believed that they understood society as no one else did; unlike those who worked in the schools, they understood psychology—the principles of learning—and sociology—the dynamics of society. Given their supposedly superior understanding of industrial, social, economic, and educational conditions, they saw themselves as being empowered to remake the schools. A professor of education at the University of Missouri explained the error of the past: "A little over a century ago, the view became popular that education should emancipate the individual and develop his powers and capacities as an individual. . . . That this view is not the full truth is now evident, for we are beginning to see that individual development, regardless of social standards and social needs, may work in the very opposite direction from social harmony, social efficiency and social survival."[20] In other words, individuals must not be free to make decisions about their future; this important task must be put into the hands of experts who understand the needs of society.

The litany of complaints against the schools came at an odd time. Speaking in unison, the pedagogues complained that the schools would have to change to accommodate the tidal wave of ordinary youths who were unable to gain anything from the "bookish" and "aristocratic" academic curriculum. But even as their complaints rose in the years before World War I, high school enrollments were growing fast. In 1900, only 10.2 percent of youngsters aged fourteen to seventeen were in high school; that proportion increased to 14.3 percent in 1910 and to 31.2 percent in 1920. Enrollments grew rapidly, even though the curriculum was still dominated by academic subjects. Until World War I, enrollments in academic courses were at an all-time high, and progressive educators insisted on driving them down so that everyone would get an "appropriate" education.[21]

As high school enrollments soared, the word went out from the great centers of pedagogy at Teachers College, Harvard, Chicago, and Stanford to the hinterlands to guide youngsters into practical courses, not the useless academic subjects that they or their parents wanted. The hinterlands got the message. In a bulletin for parents and teachers, Professor William A. McKeever of the Kansas State Agricultural College lamented that many girls' schools were still offering courses in algebra, geometry, and trigonometry, even calculus:

This whole scheme seems wrong and foolish to me. Where does the trigonometry apply in a good woman's life? Will it contribute anything toward peace, happiness and contentment in the home? Will it bake any bread, sew on any buttons or rock any cradles? What has the girl as a result of her course in trigonometry? The answer is, trigonometry, and that quickly vanishes from her memory. But the girl who has been taught just how to make a dollar do a dollar's worth of service in supplying the necessities and the reasonable luxuries for her life—that girl has so much permanent culture.[22]

In the nation's pedagogical journals, writers never tired of telling one another why the academic curriculum should be dumped. Louis W. Rapeer, a professor at Pennsylvania State College, proposed the elimination of all non-English languages, algebra, and geometry from the curriculum, and he recommended that colleges abandon all entrance requirements except a high school diploma. He recited what had become a mantra among professors of education: that the purpose of academic studies was to "accentuate class distinctions and fit an aristocracy for awing and ruling the masses"; that academic subjects were a waste of time; and that learning to solve the ordinary problems of life was far more valuable to young Americans than studying academic subjects. He asked, "Why remain bound to the curricula of those who were without a social aim of education, without a knowledge of psychology, without subject matter outside the 'classics' and were 'hard up' for something to put into the high-school courses to fill up four years of time?" Nothing more than "blind imitation, mere tradition, and other-worldly aristocracy converged to bring about the anomalous situation today."[23]

Differentiation in the Public Schools

Spurred on by the endorsement of the experts, curricular differentiation spread rapidly into the public schools. Some schools really offered different curricula; others only claimed to do so. Professor Charles Hughes Johnston of the University of Illinois reported in 1914 that the public high school in Springfield, Massachusetts, ostensibly offered five choices but that "the unsupervised pupil election cards showed that only one curriculum was actually provided in practice. This curriculum was the 'college preparatory,' despite the fact that only 16 pupils out of a high-school enrollment of 883 went to any college." In other words, the pupils *elected* of their own choice to enroll in college preparatory courses, even though few intended to go to college.[24]

Professor Johnston could not understand this failure of supervision. More admirable to him was Newton, Massachusetts, where a progressive superintendent had installed fourteen distinct curricula, based on the pupils' "vocational needs and expectations." This example of "the most modern basis of curriculum building . . . automatically restricts vicious habits of election by students." When students were allowed to indulge their "vicious habits of election," they tended to choose inappropriate academic courses. To guide students to better choices, the Illinois State School Survey collected data to determine whether to provide public school training in the following occupations: "housewives, household servants, dressmakers, seamstresses, retail merchants, clerks, salesmen, saleswomen, carpenters, delivery boys, steam-railroad men, machinists, painters, bookkeepers, waiters, engineers (stationary), chauffeurs, printers, blacksmiths, masons, barbers, messenger boys, plumbers, street-railroad men, telephone operators, telegraphers, ironworkers, tailors, teachers (rural school), laundresses, nurses, factory girls."[25] Johnston singled out Los Angeles as a city that had made considerable progress: in 1906, it had offered only four curricula; by 1914, the fourteen thousand youngsters in its high schools could choose from forty-eight different curricula!

Johnston was editor of the journal *Educational Administration and Supervision* (of which David Snedden was a member of the editorial board). In an editorial in 1916, Johnston explained that some educators were "violently opposed" to curriculum differentiation, while others were ardent supporters of it. The opponents he called "absolutists" and the supporters he referred to as "experimentalists." The absolutists wanted to impose a single, uniform national curriculum on everyone; the experimentalists, clearly in step with modern pedagogical science, proposed to use psychology and vocational guidance to ensure that each child got the curriculum appropriate to his needs and future occupation.[26]

A new age had dawned, one in which utility was the watchword. A high school principal in New York City wrote in 1914 that "Every subject must present itself at the bar of competent opinion and plead for itself. One of the first questions asked will be, 'Does it function?' ... Latin, justify thy presence in a twentieth century American high school curriculum! What has the prevailing study of physics, of chemistry, and of biology to do with liberal education? These are the days of accounting. High school sciences, what report can you render? History, you too, are on the rack."[27]

By the second decade of the century, certain practices were identified as "modern," "scientific," "progressive," and "professional," including curricular differentiation, vocational guidance, intelligence testing, and the restructuring of school systems into highly centralized organizations controlled by a hierarchical bureaucracy. Every professional journal and professional organization expressed the same demands for efficiency and education reforms based on "modern science."

The School Survey Movement

But how to disseminate these practices to the schools? The din of criticism by progressive educators and like-minded journalists stirred groups of civic-minded citizens and business leaders to seek close scrutiny of the efficiency and cost-effectiveness of their public schools. A superintendent of schools or board of education would placate the critics by commissioning a survey of the school system by efficiency experts.

Who were the efficiency experts? They were educationists such as Ellwood P. Cubberley of Stanford, George Strayer of Teachers College, John Franklin Bobbitt of the University of Chicago, Edward C. Elliott of the University of Wisconsin, and Paul Hanus of Harvard. Between 1911 and 1930, nearly two hundred cities and states were surveyed by experts from the major schools of education. According to historians David Tyack and Elisabeth Hansot, "the surveyors were so closely linked as a group that when a member of the Portland Chamber of Commerce wrote to seven educators across the nation for nominations of people to do a survey of city schools, they nominated each other with astonishing regularity."[28]

The recommendations by the surveyors were remarkably similar. School districts, they said, needed more curricular differentiation, more group intelligence testing to decide which students belonged in which program, more vocational programs, more power to the superintendent, more administrative staff, and more money for facilities and salaries. School officials welcomed the surveys because they invariably proposed more power to the professionals, less lay interference, and more money. The surveyors usually attributed high levels of dropping out to the academic curriculum, even though youngsters were far more likely to leave school for economic reasons than because of a distaste for their studies. A state survey in Texas in 1924 blamed the "conservatism" of parents and colleges for "the absurd emphasis on ancient history, composition, and algebra."[29]

In 1915, Cubberley and four associates conducted a survey of the public schools of Salt Lake City. A few years earlier, critics had complained that the schools were inefficient and "instruction in the fundamental school subjects was not producing the best results."[30] Cubberley and his team, which included Lewis Terman, the Stanford expert on intelligence testing, visited the Salt Lake schools for three weeks and compiled a 346-page report.

The surveyors commended the city for its "excellent racial stock" (only a small proportion was foreign-born or nonwhite). The city had an excellent school system, with cheerful, optimistic teachers ("no burden seemed too great, no work so hard as to cause complaint . . . the fine professional attitude of the teaching force deserves the highest commendation") and happy children ("The children were free and natural in their movements, yet there was no disorder. Not a single instance of cross word or stubborn manner was noticed by any member of the survey staff"). The principals were excellent (seldom had the survey staff seen "greater professional zeal on the part of principals").[31]

Were there any problems? Well, yes; the efficiency experts administered a spelling test and discovered that there was a wide variation in spelling achievement (although so many children got a perfect score in spelling that it was difficult for the experts to interpret the results). They were upset to discover that better results were shown in third grade, where spelling was taught 150 minutes per week, than in fourth grade, where spelling was taught only 100 minutes each week. It might have seemed logical to conclude that the fourth grade should also be taught spelling for 150 minutes each week, but Cubberley and his team decided that this was "too high a price to pay for this superior record" and that not more than 75 minutes per week should be devoted to teaching spelling in *any* grade.[32]

In arithmetic, the Salt Lake City schools were also getting excellent results, but the surveyors proposed a reduction in the amount of time spent on arithmetic. So instead of assuring the citizens of Salt Lake City that the schools were doing a superb job of teaching the fundamental subjects, the surveyors advised the schools to reduce the amount of time allotted to spelling and arithmetic, even though concern about achievement in these subjects had been the original reason for the survey.[33]

The experts concluded that this apparently fine public school system needed major change, including intelligence testing for proper classification of students ("it is best not to trust the judgment of any person who is not a psychologist"); standardized achievement tests; separate junior high schools, where the prevocational needs of students could be ascertained and most would get "definite industrial training," such as woodworking, metalwork, gardening, buying, and selling (for boys) and cooking, sewing, and domestic science (for girls); and higher taxes to pay for the recommendations.[34]

Another major efficiency expert was John Franklin Bobbitt of the University of Chicago, a proponent of scientific management in education who presented himself as an "educational engineer." His scheme for instructional "cost accounting" made it possible to calculate and compare how much school districts were spending on different subjects per hour. Bobbitt did not have high regard for what he called "scholastic education." He complained that too much time was devoted to scholastic studies and not enough to functional education: "So much useful knowledge is now needed that there is no longer any necessity of including ancient, musty, useless studies merely for the intellectual gymnastics that they provide."[35]

In 1915, Bobbitt was hired to survey the public schools of San Antonio, Texas. The city already had an extensive program of vocational training in its schools; the white high school offered a four-year commercial course, as well as a course of "carpentry, joinery, furniture-making, wood-turning, pattern-making, foundry practice, forging, machine shop work, and mechanical drawing." There were also vocational schools, and vocational education began for black children as early as the third and fourth grades.[36]

Students at the segregated black high school were offered courses in "gardening, poultry raising, horticulture, floriculture, bench work with wood, iron work, forging, automobile operation and repair, cement construction, sewing, cooking, laundry work, manicuring and hairdressing" as well as cooking and catering. Bobbitt had to admit that San Antonio was certainly a progressive city.[37]

But, alas, not progressive enough. Bobbitt found to his dismay that students in the commercial course were compelled to study algebra and geometry, which he believed had no relationship to their future occupations: "To hoodwink a community into paying for such useless subjects is to obtain and to spend their money under false pretenses." Teaching these "useless subjects to commercial students," he said, was a waste of public funds. To make matters worse, commercial students were "forced" to take two years of science, which they certainly would not need when they became bookkeepers, stenographers, or clerks. It was another waste of the public's dollars.[38]

In almost every corner of the schools, Bobbitt found waste: Why were girls in domestic science studying physics and chemistry when what they really needed was "the physics of the household, the chemistry of the household, the bacteriology of the household"? Even more wasteful were the useless courses in algebra and geometry for girls: "A committee of intelligent women of the community who are not teachers but who are familiar with the fundamentals of household occupations should be asked to go through the arithmetic text now taught in the upper grades and to point out the matters . . . which could be omitted without loss from the work of the girls in their training for household occupations. The more such a committee of women could forget the arithmetical matters that they themselves studied in elementary school years ago, the better perhaps would be their judgments as to what is actually needed."[39]

How should a school district decide which vocations to teach? Bobbitt advised school districts to look at the local community and observe what kind of jobs were currently performed. No matter how much parents might want their children to have an academic education, there was no point in preparing them for professions in which they would never work. The chief responsibility of the school, he claimed, was to prepare those who would be farmers, laborers, clerks, and domestic workers. Based on census figures that showed the occupations of 1910, Bobbitt predicted that only 6 of every 100 boys would ever enter a profession. The other 94 percent needed vocational training. Among women who were employed, about 7 percent would be teachers, and the rest would work as "servants, cooks, waitresses, laundresses, saleswomen" or in other low-skilled occupations.[40]

Like others in the social efficiency wing of the progressive movement, Bobbitt could not imagine that the economy might change and need more highly educated people. He could not imagine that educated people might create new ideas, inventions, businesses, and technologies. He could see only the status quo, and his recommendations were intended to preserve that status quo by limiting opportunities for a liberal education to a very small number of boys and girls. He could not even imagine that boys and girls who would someday be farmers, housewives, or laborers would have any reason to learn history, literature, science, mathematics, or the arts for their intrinsic value.

As the survey movement rolled forward, adding city after city to its list of conquests, Professor Cubberley exulted in his 1916 textbook on public school administration about the importance of efficiency experts (like himself) and school surveys: "Wholly within the past decade one of the most significant movements in all of our educational history has arisen . . . it bids fair to change, in the course of time, the whole character of school administration . . . it means nothing less than the ultimate changing of school administration from guesswork to scientific accuracy . . . the substitution of professional experts for the old and successful practitioners." The school surveyors were in a position to exercise enormous power over the design of school systems, as well as the fate of millions of children.[41]

The survey movement certainly registered real gains for public education by making an authoritative case for better facilities, more attention to children's health, additional programs for children who needed extra attention, and higher taxes to pay for these improvements. But at the curriculum level, the level of addressing what should be studied and by whom, the survey movement was an instrument for disseminating a narrow, functional view of the purpose of schooling.

The experts' notion of social efficiency decreed that the schools should fit children into predetermined roles in an unchanging social order. None of the surveyors seemed to think there was anything to be said for teaching a love of literature or history to all students; none made the case that all citizens in a democracy need a broad and rich liberal education; none believed that all children should have the same opportunity for an intellectually stimulating education. No, the ideal path was one in which different groups of children went in different directions to different destinations: a few to college, the rest to occupations or household management.

The surveyors had a static notion of both the individual's capacity for development and society's needs. They did not see youngsters as people with curiosity and imagination that transcended their likely occupational role, nor could they imagine a future in which men and women, by improving their skills and knowledge, could change their occupations, indeed change society. Nor had they any sense of a dynamic society in which the nature of occupations was regularly redefined by technological change. The possibility of social change and social mobility was beyond their purview.

A DIFFERENT KIND OF EDUCATION
FOR BLACK CHILDREN

The new gospel of industrial education and curricular differentiation dealt a deadly blow to the aspirations of African Americans. A half century removed from slavery, 90 percent still lived in the South, and rampant racial prejudice had left southern blacks disenfranchised, ill educated, and powerless to fight for their rights at the ballot box or in the courts. What they did not need was an education that would fit them to their preordained roles in society and their likely destinations as domestic servants, farmhands, and blacksmiths. But those were the recommendations of a major federal survey published in 1917, titled *Negro Education.*

Negro Education was a two-volume report issued by the U.S. Bureau of Education and underwritten by the private Phelps-Stokes Fund. The project was led by Thomas Jesse Jones, who was considered one of the nation's leading experts on the nation's black population. Born in Wales and educated in the United States (he had a doctorate from Teachers College), Jones was a social worker who had taught "social studies" for eight years at the Hampton Institute, an industrial and trade school for African Americans and Indians in Virginia. During the 1910 census, he worked at the U.S. Census Bureau, where he was in charge of "Negro statistics"; he was then hired by the Bureau of Education as a "specialist in the education of racial groups."

Negro Education, published with the prestige and authority of the federal government, treated the education of the black population in the South as a problem to be solved by wise public policy and careful philanthropic investment. It made the case for increasing the funding of public schools for black children, while criticizing black educators and parents who wanted a precollegiate education for them. It advocated "modern," progressive solutions for southern black public schools, which meant a practical curriculum allegedly adapted to the needs of pupils and their communities. It treated racial segregation as legitimate and inevitable.[42]

After the Civil War, which had left its economy shattered, the South had been slow to build a public education system. When the Jones report was written, the southern states were building public schools for white children but had made only the barest provision for black children. Of black children aged six to fourteen, only 58 percent attended any school. Few black children remained in school beyond the fifth grade, and high schools for blacks were rare; about half of all black secondary students attended private schools funded by either northern foundations or religious organizations. There were 1,238 public high schools in the South for white children, but only 64 for black students, mainly in the cities (North Carolina and Louisiana had no public high school for blacks, and South Carolina had only one); in proportion to population, there were ten times as many white students as black students in public high schools.[43]

The first volume of Jones's report made several points: first, that the education available to black children in the South was abysmal in both quantity and quality; second, that the economic development of the South depended on appropriate education for all, both white and black; third, that an appropriate education (especially for black children) meant industrial education, manual training, agricultural education, instruction in hygiene, and other kinds of training to make them useful members of society; fourth, that too many schools and colleges for black students wasted time on useless academic studies; and fifth, that public and private institutions for black youngsters should cooperate not only with state education departments and private foundations, but also with the white majority who controlled the government and the public schools. The South, it noted, bore the heavy economic burden of maintaining a dual school system—different schools for each race—but the author did not suggest ending that system.

The second volume of the Jones report contained an exhaustive survey of private and public schools for black students in every southern state. It listed every school and its program and advised foundations whether the school was worthy of private support. Some private schools were listed as "important," others as "unimportant." Of 625 private schools for black children, Jones deemed only 266 to be important. Those that did not get Jones's blessing were unlikely to raise much money from philanthropists.[44]

The Jones report showed that black schools in the South were grossly inadequate and underfunded, compared to schools for white children. Lacking the right to vote, blacks were unrepresented on state and local school boards, and black public schools were "almost entirely dependent upon the local sentiment of the white school board." Unable to demand a fair share of public funds, black schools suffered from severe inequities. In counties where 50 percent or more of the school population was black, only $1.77 was spent per capita for black children, while six to twelve times as much was spent for white students. Many communities, lacking a school building for black children, borrowed a makeshift building from a church, lodge, or other benefactor. In the Deep South states, white teachers earned more than double the salaries of black teachers. Outside big cities in the border states, black children had less access to schools than whites. Many black schools were ill equipped, ramshackle, and filthy, yet it was "not uncommon to find pupils who walk 6 or 7 miles to attend school."[45]

Confronted with such clear evidence of inequality of educational opportunity, Thomas Jesse Jones might have declared that the dual system of education was wasteful and inefficient; he might have insisted on the right of black students to equal educational opportunity. But he did not intend to antagonize the white South or the northern philanthropists who supported hundreds of private schools for black children. Instead, he accepted racial segregation and emphasized the need for more funding, better collaboration between the races, and a different kind of instruction and curriculum in black schools.

Jones quoted approvingly a southern education group's recommendation that "economic and psychological differences" between the races necessitated different courses of study, different methods of teaching, and different curricula, something more in tune with the "needs of Negro youth" than an academic program. A strong advocate of industrial education, Jones wanted black schools in the South to resemble the Hampton Institute, where students "learn to do by doing." Jones observed that some black parents and "a large number of the colored leaders have been much more eager for the literary and collegiate type of school" than for the agricultural, mechanical, and industrial training that their children needed. He attributed their "distrust of any economic feature in their schools" to being out of touch "with the progressive educational movements of the day. . . . So far as the needed changes are in the direction of larger recognition of industrial and agricultural instruction, the opposition of the Negroes is based on a suspicion that the white people are urging a caste education which confines them to industrial pursuits." The primary need of Negro pupils, Jones maintained, was not knowledge of "the printed page," but "knowledge of gardening, small farming, and the simple industries required in farming communities."[46]

The federal report was illustrated with numerous photographs of black children learning to sew, garden, plow, cook, milk cows, lay bricks, harvest crops, and raise poultry. Jones believed that Negro children in the early elementary grades needed instruction in agriculture, manual training, "shuck mat work, simple sewing, patching and quilting for girls, repair of buildings and woodworking for boys." To Jones's consternation, virtually all the public and private high schools for black youths in the South persisted in emphasizing an academic curriculum, including Latin, which he considered wholly unsuitable and unprogressive. They apparently were completely unaware of modern trends in education that decreed a different kind of education for their young people.[47]

W. E. B. Du Bois, the renowned black scholar, excoriated the Jones report in 1918 in the NAACP's publication, *The Crisis,* which he edited. He described the report as a "dangerous," even "sinister," publication. It outraged Du Bois that Jones wanted to replace academic and higher education for Negroes with manual training, industrial education, and agricultural training. Even more dangerous, he warned, was Jones's insistence that black private schools in the South must "cooperate" with southern whites and that black private schools and colleges should willingly accept control by state education departments and northern foundations.

Particularly galling to Du Bois was Jones's proposal that private schools be placed under "community" authorities; he wrote that "if a plebiscite were taken tomorrow in the South, the popular vote of white people would shut every single Negro school by a large majority." He asked, why should the black private schools put themselves "into the hands of the same people who are doing so little for the public schools?" To cooperate with the white South, he feared, would mean "the surrender of the very foundations of self-respect." He was equally horrified by Jones's desire to unify the northern philanthropies that supported black education, since so many foundations deferred to the wishes of the white South (the Rockefeller family's General Education Board, he noted, was "spending more money today in helping Negroes learn how to can vegetables than in helping them to go through college"). Whoever "unified" the northern philanthropies would control the future destiny of black education in the South, and Du Bois knew that such control would further diminish the power of blacks over their own education. Such a move would turn African Americans into supplicants, allowing the philanthropists to decide "which Negro school is right or is wrong."[48]

Du Bois believed that Jones's recommendations would make "the higher training of Negroes practically difficult, if not impossible." If Jones had his way, said Du Bois, black students in elementary school would spend half their day in fields and shops. Such a program of industrial education would make it impossible for a black youth, no matter how gifted he might be, to go to either high school or college, which was "grossly unfair" both to the boy and to the race. The inevitable result of such a program would be to "deliberately shut the door of opportunity in the face of bright Negro students." Such schools, he concluded, would produce "servants and laborers and *not* educated men and women."

Du Bois agreed that the curriculum of the schools needed to be improved but did not accept the idea that intellectual development was unnecessary for Negro children: "The object of a school system is to carry the child as far as possible in its knowledge of the accumulated wisdom of the world." When the student was no longer able to continue his education, for whatever reason, then vocational training should follow, Du Bois believed. "Anyone who suggests by sneering at books and 'literary courses' that the great heritage of human thought ought to be displaced simply for the reason of teaching the technique of modern industry is pitifully wrong," he wrote, "and, if the comparison must be made, more wrong than the man who would sacrifice modern technique to the heritage of ancient thought."[49]

A FEW CRITICS DISAGREE

The constant attacks on the academic curriculum during the first two decades of the century encountered surprisingly little dissent. There were surely superintendents, principals, and teachers who understood that the academic curriculum was not the classical curriculum and that it was democratic, not elitist, to encourage all children to study history, literature, mathematics, sciences, arts, and foreign languages; nor did the introduction of vocational programs in high school preclude participation in the academic curriculum. There must have been many who continued to believe in the educational ladder that kept educational opportunity open to all for as long as possible. Progressives frequently denounced "conservative" or "reactionary" teachers and principals who disagreed with their prescriptions. But dissenters were relatively quiet, perhaps reluctant to be publicly identified as "absolutists," enemies of modern education, or defenders of an "aristocratic" tradition.

One superintendent who did speak out against the surveyors, efficiency experts, and faddists was William Henry Maxwell of New York City. Maxwell didn't have to prove his bona fides as an education reformer; an effective innovator, he had expanded the role of the public schools to include a wide array of after-school programs, facilities for children with disabilities, and adult education. At the annual meeting of the National Education Association in 1915, he blasted "time-wasting, energy-destroying statistical research" and singled out for particular reproach those "scientific" theorists such as John Franklin Bobbitt, who compared the educating of children to the manufacture of steel rails and other industrial products.[50]

Maxwell suggested that "our good friends, the statistical professors of education, would do well to try out their theories on the work of their college and university colleagues before applying them to the common schools. . . . When the university professors 'make good' in their own field, we shall welcome them into ours." Maxwell knew that children vary enormously in their ability and that their school performance was influenced by poverty and social conditions. Fearing that such realities might be turned into rationalizations for failure, he insisted that children from poor homes and poor districts could learn just as much as children from rich homes and districts.[51]

"Educational theorists," he complained in 1914, were known for their "arrogant unreasonableness" and lack of tolerance: "Unmindful of the lessons of educational history, regardless of the universal rules of logic, they proclaim the validity of untested theories and untried ideals, and denounce as traitors and malingerers all who do not agree with them." Every method has some kernel of good in it, he suggested, even the memoriter method, "now so universally condemned." Learning by heart, he said, requires "close and continuous concentration of mind; and, if there is any one intellectual habit of mind which, more than another, our children should acquire, which will stand them in good stead in every walk of life, it is the habit of concentration of mind." But the theorists could see nothing good in the method, and "it is the scorn of traditional method and the air of implicit confidence—almost of infallibility—in his own theories, that characterize the educational theorist." [52]

During his own long career, Maxwell had seen a parade of educational theorists with their panaceas, such as those who claimed that "vertical penmanship" was the answer to all problems, or that all children should be trained to be ambidextrous, or that recesses were a waste of time. Then came the theorists who insisted that penmanship, grammar, and spelling should be taught incidentally (" 'Burn the spelling books,' was the rallying cry"), without practice or effort: "It was so comfortable to imagine that, thru interesting reading and thru story-telling and thru counting the petals of flowers and the legs and ears of animals, and writing about them, children could learn arithmetic, and composition and grammar, and that those tiresome drills to which old-fogy teachers and superintendents pinned their faith could be neglected with impunity! Hence thousands of teachers followed this new will-o'-the-wisp. The results were most deplorable."

Maxwell reserved his sternest outrage for "the agitation with which the educational world is now seething for the introduction of industrial or trade teaching in the public schools," which "originated with the manufacturers," who wanted the state to absorb the cost of training workmen. Maxwell had already introduced vocational education into the New York City school system but firmly opposed giving "any narrow trade schooling" to children. He insisted that general education was the right and the "spiritual inheritance" of every child. Because the nation needs "men and not slaves," he wrote, "we must set reasonable bounds to the arrogant demands of manufacturing capitalists." [53]

Maxwell objected with equal vigor to the junior high school, where children chose an academic, commercial, or industrial course. He insisted that children of "tender years, only just verging on adolescence" were far too young to make a choice that would shape their entire lives. The typical elementary program, "with its eight-year course leading onward and upward in any and every direction, furnishing two-thirds of the ladder that leads directly from the gutter to the university, is the most characteristic and most successful American educational institution. Let us preserve it intact."[54]

Maxwell was in a decided minority. Despite his commitment to a common academic education for all, he bowed to political pressure and added public vocational and technical high schools to the public school system (ironically, a vocational-technical high school in New York City was named for him).[55] The profession's forums—its annual conventions and pedagogical journals—resounded with calls for more efficiency, more surveys, more curricular differentiation. Most schoolmen either agreed with the emerging trends or kept silent.

THE CLASSICISTS PROTEST

The only sustained dissent against the social efficiency movement came from a few classicists who recognized the threat not only to their own subjects but to the larger humanistic tradition. Most classicists, however—lulled by the extraordinary surge in Latin enrollments and dulled by years of sniping at Latin—treated these developments like an insignificant cloud on the horizon.[56]

Even as more and more students signed up for Latin, the number of broadsides against it increased. Two prominent educators, Abraham Flexner and Charles W. Eliot, joined forces against Latin and any other study that had no functional purpose. Eliot, known both as the chairman of the Committee of Ten and as an advocate of electives during his presidency of Harvard University, urged colleges to cease requiring Latin for admission; the highest purpose of education, he believed, was to train the senses and the powers of observation and reasoning. He was appar-

ently unaware that Professor Thorndike allegedly proved that such powers—or faculties—could not be trained.[57]

Flexner, a former teacher of the classics and headmaster of his own
private progressive school in Louisville, won national fame in 1910 for a
report on medical education that he wrote for the Carnegie Foundation;
in 1912, he became secretary of the powerful General Education Board,
funded by John D. Rockefeller. In 1916, he wrote a tract for the board
called *The Modern School*, making the case for a new, experimental
school that would eliminate useless studies that based their claim on
mental discipline—such as ancient languages and algebra—and offer
only those studies for which there was real purpose and need. Not that
these were new ideas, for a contemporary educationist noted that
Flexner's proposal had merely repeated the same "desirable reforms that
schoolmen had been urging for thirty years and more."[58]

As members of the General Education Board, Eliot and Flexner persuaded their colleagues to establish a laboratory school—the Lincoln
School at Teachers College, where children would learn through activities rather than lectures and memorization and where teachers would experiment with new methods and curricula. In 1919, Eliot accepted the
honorary presidency of the new Progressive Education Association, an
organization that shared few, if any, of the assumptions of Eliot's Committee of Ten.

Certainly there was irony in Eliot's transformation from the leadership of the Committee of Ten to a prominent role in the progressive education movement. But he had always believed that students should study
whatever interested them, so he was comfortable urging the elimination
of required subjects, and his belief that *how* children learn is more important than *what* they learn made him comfortable with the new progressivism and its preference for child-centered activities rather than a
set curriculum.

Classicist Paul Shorey of the University of Chicago was the leading
defender of Latin against its critics. For nearly a decade, Shorey argued
in print with detractors of the classics and warned that the classics were
only the first target in the pedagogues' campaign against the academic
curriculum. Shorey understood that for many professors of education,

Latin was a symbol of everything they despised about traditional education; utterly lacking any vocational purpose, it was the embodiment of the hated classical education, and as such it had to be extirpated from the public schools.

Writing in 1910, Shorey recognized that his cause was not a popular one; he knew that

> the man in the street has not changed his opinion of dead languages, and the great drift of American education and life toward absorption in the fascinating spectacle of the present has not been, perhaps cannot be, checked. . . . The majority still believe that modern civilization can find not only entertainment but also all the instruction and all the culture which it requires in the contemplation of moving pictures of itself, whether in the five-cent theater or the ten-cent magazine or the one-cent newspaper.

Yet he harbored the hope that thoughtful people were not agreed on the suppression of Latin and Greek: "They are observing with mixed feelings a Greekless generation of graduates and wondering what a Latinless generation will be like. . . . They recognize that a real education must be based on a serious, consecutive, progressive study of something definite, teachable, and hard."[59]

Shorey asserted that Greek and Latin were valuable for "development of the critical intelligence and the habit of exactness, and the maintenance of high standards of national taste and culture among the educated classes." He did not argue that they should be required of all students, nor even of all high school graduates; but he wanted these studies to survive and feared that his antagonists meant to banish them from the curriculum altogether, even for students who wanted to study them for their own intellectual satisfaction. Every civilization has its classics, he insisted, and through them the civilization transmits "a cultural, social, moral tradition."[60]

Shorey predicted that after the dead languages were ousted, every other academic subject would become targets for those who demanded only relevance and utility: "After Greek, Latin, and after Latin, all literary, historical, and philological study of French and German. Convert your departments into Berlitz schools of languages. It is that which you are educating the public to demand, and that is all your students will be capable of." The same, he warned, would happen in English, where only contemporary writers would be studied. Shorey contemplated with dismay the prospect of a society completely ignorant of the ideas and literature of the ancient world: "We are not saying that it is a great thing for our undergraduates to know a little classics. We are saying that it is a monstrous thing that they should not know any."[61]

Shorey responded energetically to Flexner's attacks on Latin in a 1917 article called "The Assault on Humanism" that attracted so much notice that it was quickly turned into a book. He derided the educationists' claims as nothing more than a pastiche of trivia, half-truths, and pseudoscience. He was particularly vexed by the constant invocation of "democracy," which he considered a shameless "appeal to prejudice." Why did he find the modernist agenda so threatening? Shorey wrote that he was not concerned about the survival of the sciences, which were not in danger; nor about the introduction of vocational training, which was a foregone conclusion; these were not issues for him. What he worried about was "the survival or the total oppression, in the comparatively small class of educated leaders who graduate from high schools and colleges, of the very conception of linguistic, literary, and critical discipline; of culture, taste, and standards; of the historic sense itself; of some trained faculty of appreciation and enjoyment of our rich heritage from the civilized past." The danger from the educationists, he concluded, went far beyond their effort to eliminate the ancient languages. He saw a larger and more insidious danger in their arguments against the entire academic curriculum:

The things which, for lack of better names, we try to suggest by culture, discipline, taste, standards, criticism, and the historic sense, they hate . . . the tendency of their policies is to stamp out and eradicate these things and inculcate exclusively their own tastes and ideals by controlling American education with the political efficiency of Prussian autocracy and in the fanatical intolerance of the French anticlericalists. Greek and Latin have become mere symbols and pretexts. They are as contemptuous of Dante, Shakespeare, Milton, Racine, Burke, John Stuart Mill, Tennyson, Alexander Hamilton, or Lowell, as of Homer, Sophocles, Virgil, or Horace.[62]

Shorey understood that his forebodings of cultural decline would not hold back the tide, would not forestall

a world of nothing but ragtime, chewing gum, chocolate sundaes, the wit of the colored Sunday supplements, best sellers, uncensored films, continuous vaudeville—the reverend William Sunday installed in every pulpit, and the racy American idiom of Shorty McCabe displacing in the schoolroom our glorious heritage of English speech one and indivisible, the language not only of Emerson, Longfellow, Lowell, Poe, Holmes and Howells, but of Hamilton, Jefferson, Webster, Lincoln, and Wilson.[63]

The educated people to whom Shorey appealed may have been moved by his arguments, but as far as they could tell, the academic purpose of the schools seemed secure; after all, fully 85 percent of all high school students were studying Latin, German, or French; mathematics, history, and the sciences were well established. Perhaps he was exaggerating. Perhaps it did not matter that the new schools of pedagogy had a single-minded devotion to utility and a bias against intellect. It was easy to discount the alarums of an angry, perhaps overwrought university classicist.

In fact, the educationists' campaign to drive down enrollments in the academic subjects and promote practical studies was beginning to take hold. An early indication of what was happening at ground level came in 1915 from an education professor in Missouri, who reported that the number of students in that state enrolling in agricultural science had climbed while enrollments in the other sciences had dropped from 64.4 percent to 49.2 percent. This was a welcome development, he held, because science was "failing to meet the popular demand for a practical usable education" and "there is no room in the secondary school for science for science's sake." Similarly, algebra, geometry, trigonometry, and Latin all registered declines, while "domestic science" (homemaking) and commercial subjects were all showing a healthy growth. Typically, the shifts were attributed to "popular demand" rather than to the policies promoted by educational leaders.[64]

The national figures for 1915 showed the same trends. Although the absolute numbers of students enrolling in subjects like Latin, French, German, Spanish, algebra, and geometry showed strong growth, the percentages enrolled steadily declined. As the numbers of high school students escalated rapidly, more and more of them were directed away from the academic curriculum. So, for example, Latin enrollments increased from 405,502 in 1910 to 503,985 in 1915, but the overall proportion of students enrolled in Latin fell from 49.6 percent to 39 percent. By 1923–24, Latin enrollments had soared to 940,000, but the proportion of high school students taking Latin had fallen to 27.5 percent.[65]

The World War I years were a turning point for all foreign language study, not just Latin. Because of anti-German sentiment during the war, the teaching of the German language was virtually wiped out, never to recover. Simultaneously, educational leaders were encouraging boys and girls to take utilitarian studies. Enrollments in foreign languages, which were of dubious utility for future housewives and plumbers, began a steady decline from this point, never to regain the proportions recorded in 1910.

Of course, the future of liberal education did not hinge on the fate of Latin; it is possible to visualize a solid liberal education that does not include Latin, even though Professor Shorey thought it unimaginable. But the potential conflict between utilitarian and liberal education was seldom offered for public debate, because educationists such as Snedden and Cubberley coyly insisted that *all* education was vocational, that even Latin was vocational education for certain professions.

LIBERAL VERSUS VOCATIONAL EDUCATION

The issue was squarely joined at a National Education Association meeting in Richmond, Virginia, in 1914, when David Snedden, then commissioner of education in Massachusetts, debated Professor William C. Bagley of the University of Illinois. Snedden reiterated his familiar proposal for large numbers of separate public schools to teach agricultural, commercial, industrial, and homemaking occupations to youngsters over fourteen. Bagley, like Snedden, was a well-known educationist who had made his reputation as a proponent of social efficiency.

But Bagley had become a renegade, a critic of the untested fads and reforms that were constantly raining down on the schools. In the debate, Bagley questioned the validity of the "science" and "research" that supported the progressives' attack on the academic curriculum. "We are hearing so often today these charges that the traditional methods and processes of teaching have been utterly futile that we are coming to take the statement as a fact without asking for the evidence," Bagley told the NEA meeting. "The evidence for these sweeping indictments has, so far as I know, never been presented." Bagley distinguished between vocational education, which was specific to certain occupations, and general education, which every individual needs. Part of general education was the basic knowledge, skills, habits, and ideals that should be the common property of all. But also part of the general education that everyone needs is liberal education, whose primary aim was to equip the individual to confront new situations:

It will furnish him with standards of value, thru which he can view his problems in their proper proportions—not distorted by local, selfish, sectional, or partisan points of view. It will rid his mind of the fallacy of the immediate; thru the study of history, it will give him a time-perspective upon his own life and upon the issues of his own generation which he must help to meet. Thru science, it will rid his mind of superstition and error—those soul-destroying and energy-destroying forces that reduce strong

121

men to the helplessness of infancy. Thru literature and art, it will reveal the finer and more subtle forces which dominate human motives and so often determine human conduct.[66]

Bagley knew that there were limits to the ability of schools to impart this kind of education to their students, but he insisted that educators must constantly strive to overcome these limits so that every individual would have access to a liberal education. How much liberalizing education could be given to every individual depended, Bagley believed, on how long a child stayed in school; how successfully the teacher could connect what was taught to the child's own motives and interests; how skillfully the school could stimulate the child to exert his own effort to learn; and how successfully the school could balance the need for both fundamental and vocational education. Bagley contended that the nation should emphasize liberal education for all students, for this was the kind of education that made a nation truly great.[67]

To denigrate liberal education as a leisure activity for the few instead of the right of all, Bagley said, "is a sin against the children of the land, and it is a crime against posterity." Bagley claimed that the American people were dedicated to "the theory that talent is distributed fairly evenly among the masses and that it is the special prerogative of no especial class or group. As a people, we are fairly firm in our faith that this latent talent may be trained to high efficiency in practically every case. We mean to keep open the door of opportunity at every level of the educational ladder. It is a costly process, but so are most other things that are precious and worth while."[68]

Bagley argued valiantly, but he was in the position of a man trying to stop an onrushing locomotive with words. Snedden accused Bagley of appealing to the vague, mystical aims that modern educators had long since rejected. For his refusal to join the progressive tide, Bagley got an unenviable and unwarranted reputation as an educational conservative.

In the same year as the Snedden-Bagley debate, the Commission on National Aid to Vocational Education declared that "vocational training is needed to democratize the education in this country" and that lack of vocational education denied most children equality of opportunity.[69] A great movement of progressive educational change was afoot, intended to fit workers for their future jobs while they were still in school. When the U.S. Congress passed the Smith-Hughes Act in 1917, establishing federal aid for vocational education (the first federal program of any kind for schooling), it was plain for all the world to see that men such as Bagley were out of touch.

The New Goals of a High School Education

Any doubts that social efficiency had become the reigning ideology of the education profession were dispelled in 1918 by publication of the "Cardinal Principles of Secondary Education." The product of the NEA's Commission on the Reorganization of Secondary Education (CRSE), this report appeared exactly twenty-five years after the Committee of Ten issued its findings. Both reports were sponsored by the prestigious National Education Association on behalf of the leaders of American education; both sought to redefine the curriculum of the high school.

But there the similarities ended. The dominant group in the Committee of Ten had been college presidents; the dominant group in the CRSE was professors of education. The chairman of the Committee of Ten had been Charles W. Eliot, president of Harvard University; the chairman of the CRSE was Clarence Kingsley, former social worker, former teacher of mathematics at the Brooklyn Manual Training High School, and—at the time of the report—supervisor of high schools in Massachusetts, appointed by Commissioner David Snedden. The main idea in the report of the Committee of Ten had been that every high school student should have a solid liberal education regardless of the student's ultimate occupation. The main idea in the CRSE report was that high schools should provide different curricula for different groups of students, depending on their likely occupation in the future.

The CRSE identified three reasons to change what was studied in high school: first, the schools had to respond to social and economic trends, particularly the mechanization of labor (implying the need for industrial education rather than academic studies); second, the high school enrollment had become larger and more diverse (implying that the new students were less capable than those who had traditionally gone to high school); and third, advances in educational theory, especially psychology, had made educators aware of the importance of "applying knowledge to the activities of life, rather than primarily in terms of the demands of any subject as a logically organized science" (implying that the subject matter curriculum was obsolete).[70]

Based on these assertions, the CRSE identified the main objectives of secondary education as: "1. Health. 2. Command of fundamental processes. 3. Worthy home membership. 4. Vocation. 5. Citizenship. 6. Worthy use of leisure. 7. Ethical character." All of these objectives were utilitarian, derived from analyses of the activities of adults. These "cardinal principles" reflected the leaders' belief that students should learn only what they actually needed to know. An early draft of the report neglected even to include "command of fundamental processes," which was the only objective that referred directly to academic skills.[71]

Why should high school education be dedicated to the development of these particular objectives? Because, said the committee, "the purpose of democracy is so to organize society that each member may develop his personality primarily through activities designed for the well-being of his fellow members and of society as a whole." There was no more talk about a ladder open to all, leading to the university; no more talk about developing the intellectual capacity of each individual or giving youngsters full access to the cultural heritage of the past. The point was to enable each individual "to find his place and use that place to shape both himself and society toward ever nobler ends."[72] Thus began a rhetorical tradition of inflated pedagogical language characterized by invocations of democracy and other lofty ends for whatever was proposed.

The committee might as well have said, "We have a lot of dumb kids coming into high school who don't need to learn algebra and chemistry, and we want to hold on to them for as long as possible before they quit to go to work. The schools should train youngsters to be effective workers for the nation's factories or to be good clerks or capable housewives. If some nevertheless insist on studying college preparatory subjects, that is their right." But that sort of straight talk was out of the question, because it had become the fashion in the education world to claim that every new idea was more progressive, more modern, and more democratic than whatever it superseded. Over the next forty years, the jargon of the profession became more impenetrable, but never less earnest in its claims to be more democratic than any alternative.

The CRSE endorsed junior high schools (still in their infancy), where children of twelve or thirteen could explore vocational choices. High schools, it said, should be comprehensive, divided into differentiated curricula based on vocations "such as agricultural, business, clerical, industrial, fine-arts, and household-arts curriculums." The Commission added that "Provision should be made also for those having distinctly academic interests and needs," as though the academic component of schooling had been an afterthought. This was social efficiency with a vengeance. Everyone could study English and social studies, but it was clear that the academic curriculum would be for the few and the majority would be guided into a vocational curriculum. The CRSE argued that the traditional curriculum was especially incongruous with the future responsibilities of girls as homemakers. Women's colleges such as Bryn Mawr, Wellesley, Smith, and Mount Holyoke insisted that young women were as capable of mastering academic studies as young men. But the CRSE insisted that every high school girl, even those who intended to go to college, should study "the household arts" to prepare for their "lifelong occupation."[73]

The driving purpose behind the seven objectives was socialization, teaching students to fit into society. The comprehensive high school would offer a curriculum for every interest; the traditional academic requirements for entry to high school would be eliminated so that every student would be admitted; and classroom methods would be adjusted to teach the correct attitudes for democratic living: "Among the means for developing attitudes and habits important in a democracy are the assignment of projects and problems to groups of pupils for cooperative solution and the socialized recitation whereby the class as a whole develops a sense of collective responsibility. Both of these devices give training in collective thinking."[74] The overriding goal was social efficiency, not the realization of individual desire for self-improvement.

The commission sought to legitimate curricular differentiation as

the basic pattern of American secondary education. Before issuing its report, the CRSE convened several committees to examine each school
subject in light of the seven cardinal principles. As historian Edward A.
Krug put it, "Social efficiency called upon the school subjects to prove
their right to exist. The so-called practical subjects, it was often assumed, did so by definition. Inevitably, then, the demand fell heavily on
those fields by this time identified as traditional or academic, namely, the
foreign languages, mathematics, history, English, and science."[75] Each
subject was called to the bar and asked to justify its place in the modern
comprehensive high school. None escaped unscathed.

The Committee on the Problem of Mathematics was headed by
Teachers College Professor William Heard Kilpatrick (who was already
famed for his advocacy of child-centered education and learning by
projects instead of subject matter). The Kilpatrick committee recommended that mathematics be tailored for four different groups: first, the
"general readers," who needed only ordinary arithmetic in their everyday lives; second, students preparing for certain trades (e.g., plumbers
or machinists), who needed a modest amount of mathematics, but certainly not algebra or geometry; third, the few students who wanted to
become engineers, who needed certain mathematical skills and knowledge for their jobs; and last, the "group of specializers," including students "who 'like' mathematics," for whom the existing mathematics
program seemed about right, although the committee proposed "even
for this group a far-reaching reorganization of practically all of secondary mathematics."[76]

The Kilpatrick report maintained that nothing should be taught in
mathematics unless its probable value could be shown. It aimed to supply "a grim pruning hook to the dead limbs of tradition."[77] Mathematicians objected to Kilpatrick's "grim pruning hook" and criticized the
report as an outrageous attack on their field (Kilpatrick dismissed them
as conservatives who thought that the problem of mathematics could be
solved by better training of teachers instead of wholesale reconstruction
of the curriculum). David Eugene Smith, who taught mathematics at
Teachers College, tried to persuade the commission not to release Kilpatrick's report, but U.S. Commissioner of Education Philander P. Clax-

ton, a good friend of Kilpatrick and a supporter of progressivism, came to Kilpatrick's rescue and published the report in 1920.[78]

Transforming History into Social Studies

No field was as profoundly affected by the deliberations of the CRSE as history. The CRSE created a new subject called "social studies," into which history was supposed to fit. History had been considered a modern subject by the Committee of Ten in 1893. By 1915, most high schools offered or required a four-year sequence in history that included ancient history, European history, English history, and American history. In addition, a course in civics was usually offered or required.[79] For the advocates of social efficiency, however, this pattern of historical studies would not do: it had no ostensible purpose, it was too academic, it was not utilitarian, it needed reorganization. History was no longer viewed as a modern subject because it lacked immediacy and utility.

The chairman of the Committee on Social Studies was Thomas Jesse Jones, the specialist on racial matters who had written the important 1917 federal report *Negro Education*. A well-known proponent of industrial and trade education, Jones was one of the first to coin the term "social studies." This new field was formed by the intersection of two congenial ideas: one was social efficiency, or teaching students the skills and attitudes necessary to fit into the social order; the other was "the new history," whose advocates believed that the content of history in the schools should be selected on the basis of "the pupil's own immediate interest" and "general social significance."[80] Proponents of social studies believed that pupils could not possibly be interested in history unless it was directly related to the present.

The trouble with history, it seemed, was that it frequently didn't have a social purpose at all; too often, it was geared toward satisfying the student's imagination or curiosity, which modern educators deemed socially useless. In its preliminary report, the Committee on Social Studies proclaimed that "good citizenship" would be the goal of social studies: "Facts, conditions, theories, and activities that do not contribute rather directly to the appreciation of methods of human betterment have no claim." Even civics, which was a study of government, had to change to a study of "social efforts to improve mankind. It is not so important that the pupil know how the President is elected as that he shall understand the duties of the health officer in his community." This was a false dichotomy, since all citizens in a democracy need to know how the president is elected. In the future, the study of history would be subject to

> the test of good citizenship. The old chronicler who recorded the deeds of kings and warriors and neglected the labors of the common man is dead. The great palaces and cathedrals and pyramids are often but the empty shells of a parasitic growth on the working group. The elaborate descriptions of these old tombs are but sounding brass and tinkling cymbals compared to the record of the joy and sorrows, the hopes and disappointments of the masses, who are infinitely more important than any arrangement of wood and stone and iron.[81]

The Committee on Social Studies stressed that social efficiency was "the keynote of modern education," and "instruction in all subjects should contribute to this end." In the future, social studies would be devoted to teaching students the right attitudes and adjusting them to the "present social environment and conditions."[82] The report urged a diminution of the time allotted to history, eliminating the study of dead civilizations to make way for new courses in social studies that devoted more attention to current events.

THE LEGACY OF THE CARDINAL PRINCIPLES

The CRSE report strongly endorsed social efficiency as the goal of American education and urged schools to initiate curricular differentiation at the conclusion of the sixth or seventh grade. Its conclusions showed the influence of a generation of education reformers who opposed teaching any subject matter as an end in itself and who preferred that schools adopt functional objectives such as vocation, health, and citizenship.

The release of the CRSE report was overshadowed by World War I, but the report was nonetheless a milestone in the history of American education. It quickly became famous among educators as "the seven cardinal principles," the seven objectives based on the needs of life. Assessing its place in history, Lawrence A. Cremin wrote that it launched "a pedagogical revolution" and introduced "a whole new age in American secondary education."[83] The report was a triumph for the anti-academicians in the schools of pedagogy, as well as for the ideology of social efficiency.

Its recommendations could not be implemented immediately because most current teachers had been educated in earlier times, when subject matter had been considered all-important. Nonetheless, the report represented a broad consensus about the future of American secondary education among educationists in the schools of education, state departments of education, and the U.S. Bureau of Education. It did not recommend the creation of hundreds of separate vocational schools, as David Snedden wanted, and it did preserve some flexibility among the proposed vocational tracks and curricula in the high school.

All that was needed to put the Cardinal Principles into effect was an efficient mechanism that would enable educators to decide quickly which children belonged in which program, which would be the future professionals, and which would be the hewers of wood and drawers of water. That crying need would be met by education psychologists, who were busily creating tests to classify children at an early age in the interest of social efficiency.

4

IQ Testing: "This Brutal Pessimism"

By the end of World War I, educational psychologists believed that they were on the verge of a major scientific breakthrough, the ability to measure the human mind. During the war, they had developed group intelligence tests for the Army that quickly assigned large numbers of recruits to different duties.

The psychologists believed that their intelligence tests accurately identified innate capacity; after the war, they perfected group intelligence tests that public schools could use for vocational guidance and to assign students to different curricula.

Mental testing was the linchpin of the scientific movement in education. In the first two decades of the twentieth century, educational psychologists produced both achievement tests and intelligence tests. Achievement tests aimed to determine what students had learned in school, while intelligence tests claimed to test what students were *capable* of learning. One tested *knowledge,* which could be taught and learned, while the other tested *mental power,* which most psychologists believed to be innate, inherited, and relatively constant over time.

Before World War I, Edward L. Thorndike of Columbia's Teachers College, along with other educational psychologists, had devised standard tests (or "standard scales") to measure students' performance in reading, arithmetic, spelling, handwriting, composition, geography, and every other school subject. In 1921, educational sociologist Ross Finney of the University of Minnesota observed, "At the present time scales and tests are used in all but unprogressive schools everywhere . . . their use is transferring many educational problems out of the realm of mere opinion and into the sphere of exact science."[1]

Most school districts adopted the new standardized tests because they were more objective than teacher-made tests, faster to administer and grade than essay examinations, and produced comparable results for different students and classes. Some critics warned that the "norm" on the new tests might be mistaken for a standard, when it was only a statistical average of those who had taken the test. But American schools accepted the new, mass-produced, "objective" tests because of their practical advantages. As American industry progressed by becoming more mechanized and standardized, so too did the schools incorporate the techniques of mass production.

Psychologists believed that their profession would play a pivotal role in shaping the society of the future along rational lines. Edward L. Thorndike, broadly recognized as one of the foremost leaders of progressive education, predicted that "Education is one form of human engineering and will profit by measurements of human nature and achievement as mechanical and electrical engineering have profited by using the foot-pound, calorie, volt, and ampere." He observed that just as science had been able to harness "the powers of wind and water, the energy of chemicals, and the vibrations of ether" for man's benefit, it now appeared that "man's own powers of intellect, character, and skill are no less amenable to understanding, control, and direction."[2]

Like others in his field, Thorndike considered intelligence to be hereditary and immutable: "Individuals differ by original nature in intelligence as in stature or eye color or countenance." Unlike many of his colleagues, who perceived intelligence as a single attribute, Thorndike recognized multiple intelligences, such as abstract intelligence, social intelligence, and mechanical intelligence. However, he did not consider these different intelligences to be equal in importance; those with abstract intelligence, he believed, were likelier to have high character. To those who feared that such views were undemocratic, Thorndike said that "in the long run, it has paid 'the masses' to be ruled by intelligence."[3]

THE EARLY DAYS OF IQ TESTING

The first intelligence tests were developed in Europe. In the mid-1880s, Francis Galton, a pioneering scientist and cousin of Charles Darwin, opened an "Anthropometric Laboratory" in London, where he administered tests of reaction time and sensory acuity to thousands of volunteers in an effort to create a eugenic screening device.

Eugenics was considered by its supporters to be the science of improving the human race by better breeding. Galton believed that talent and intelligence were inherited and that each race and nationality shared certain innate characteristics. An ardent eugenicist, he hoped that intelligence tests would identify superior persons and that the state would encourage them to marry and propagate an improved racial stock. Galton's tests, however, proved to be a dead end, because whatever qualities they identified bore little relationship to intellectual or academic achievement.[4]

Nonetheless, the idea of mental testing attracted many other researchers, most notably Alfred Binet of France. Unlike Galton, who tested large numbers of people in search of a single measure of innate intelligence, Binet created case studies of individuals; he believed that intelligence "was neither unitary nor simple of measurement, and that any attempt to measure it must take into account complexity and diversity of manifestation." And unlike many who followed in his footsteps, Binet was skeptical about the validity of precise statistical measures of intelligence. In 1905, on behalf of a French government commission seeking a means of identifying mentally deficient children, Binet and his colleague Théodore Simon devised the first effective intelligence test, which consisted of tasks of increasing difficulty that measured such mental functions as attention, memory, visual discrimination, imagination, and verbal fluency. Binet and Simon concluded that the fundamental characteristic of intelligence is judgment, "otherwise known as good sense, practical sense, initiative, or the faculty of adapting oneself."[5]

Binet rejected the idea that a child's test score was an absolute measure of innate intelligence because he believed not only that the test might err but also that the child's intelligence was "susceptible of development. With practice, enthusiasm, and especially with method one can succeed in increasing one's attention, memory, judgment, and in becoming literally more intelligent than one was before." Binet developed exercises that he called "mental orthopedics" to demonstrate that the intellectual level of any child, even a retarded one, could be definitely increased. In his 1909 book *Modern Ideas About Children,* Binet rebuked those who "assert that an individual's intelligence is a fixed quantity, a quantity which cannot be increased. We must protest and react against this brutal pessimism."[6]

→ → ← ←

Binet's work was translated into English by Henry Goddard, research director at the Training School for the Feebleminded in Vineland, New Jersey. Goddard, who had received his doctorate in psychology from Clark University, where he had studied under G. Stanley Hall, immediately saw the value of Binet's scale for classifying retarded children. Whereas Binet had seen the tests as a way of identifying children who needed extra help, Goddard perceived the tests as an effective way of measuring an innate, fixed quantity of intelligence. A strong believer in the heritability of intelligence, Goddard warned about the proliferation of feebleminded people and supported immigration restrictions (he also invented the word "moron," based on a Greek word for "foolish" or "stupid").

Goddard's starkly hereditarian views reached a large readership in his 1912 book *The Kallikak Family,* which purported to tell the story of two branches of one family—both descendants of a single man (the pseudonymous Martin Kallikak), who allegedly had fathered an illegitimate child by a feebleminded woman and subsequently had married a woman of good family. The illegitimate branch of the Kallikak family was afflicted with mental and moral disorders; the other was highly respectable. The quality of each branch over several generations, Goddard claimed, was determined by hereditary factors. The fate of the Kallikaks entered popular consciousness and, according to Stephen Jay Gould, "functioned as a primal myth of the eugenics movement for several decades."[7]

Like many other devotees of intelligence testing, Goddard was active in the eugenics movement. Inspired by Darwinian evolutionary ideas, the eugenics movement attracted many prominent scientists, social scientists, and reformers, who believed that the human racial stock might be scientifically improved, just as plant and animal stocks were improved, by careful selection of the best specimens and elimination of the weakest. Historians later saw the eugenics movement as "closely related to the other reform movements of the Progressive Era," drawing support from many of the same people. From approximately 1905 to 1930, enthusiasts of the eugenics movement included such people as birth control advocate Margaret Sanger; David Starr Jordan, president of Stanford University; the philanthropist Mrs. E. H. Harriman; and the psychologists Robert Yerkes of Harvard University, Walter McDougall of Harvard University, Edward L. Thorndike of Teachers College, Columbia University, and Lewis M. Terman of Stanford University. During the 1920s, however, the movement also attracted racists and nativists and eventually was discredited by the rise of Nazism in Germany.[8]

Many American eugenicists advocated policies to limit the propagation of the unfit, including sterilization and permanent institutionalization of the feebleminded; thirty states passed laws permitting sterilization of designated groups, such as the insane, the feebleminded, and criminals.

Lewis Terman, like Goddard, had studied at Clark University with G. Stanley Hall, who espoused the critical importance of biology and heredity. Terman rose to prominence in 1916 after he revised the Binet intelligence test; known as the Stanford-Binet intelligence test, it became the most widely used individual mental test for the next two decades. A former teacher and school principal, Terman saw the intelligence test as an instrument that would facilitate progressive reforms in education, especially identification of the feebleminded and the gifted, curricular differentiation, vocational guidance, and grouping based on students' ability. Terman expected that the schools eventually would employ intelligence tests rather than tests of students' knowledge to determine readiness for promotion.[9]

Like other testing experts of the era, Terman believed that intelligence tests accurately measured innate or "native" intelligence, which could be represented by a single score, which he called the "intelligence quotient" (IQ). The IQ was the ratio of mental age (determined by an IQ test) divided by chronological age, multiplied by 100. If a six-year-old, for example, recorded a mental age of eight years, his IQ would be 133, but the IQ of a twelve-year-old with a mental age of eight years would be only 67.

In his 1916 book on the measurement of intelligence, Terman maintained that low IQs (in the 70–80 range) were "very, very common among Spanish-Indian and Mexican families of the Southwest and also among negroes." He believed that "their dullness seems to be racial, or at least inherent in the family stocks from which they come . . . the whole question of racial differences in mental traits will have to be taken up anew and by experimental methods." Terman predicted that such investigations would demonstrate racial differences so large that they could not be closed "by any scheme of mental culture." Terman recommended segregation of such children in special classes that emphasized practical studies. He regretted that "There is no possibility at present of convincing society that they should not be allowed to reproduce, although from a eugenic point of view they constitute a grave problem because of their unusually prolific breeding."[10]

Terman was typical of the American psychologists who adapted Binet's techniques for assessing intelligence but embraced Galton's assumptions about the inherited and fixed nature of intelligence. Binet, who died in 1911 at the age of fifty-four, did not survive to challenge the "brutal pessimism" of his American interpreters.

PSYCHOLOGISTS AND THE ARMY TESTS

When the United States entered the First World War in 1917, the nation's psychologists offered to help the Army classify new recruits. This effort was led by Robert M. Yerkes of Harvard University, who was president of the American Psychological Association and chairman of the Psychology Committee of the National Research Council.

Yerkes and his colleagues developed two intelligence tests, the alpha test for literate recruits and the beta test for illiterate recruits. The alpha test included arithmetic problems, analogies, synonyms and antonyms, and information questions; in the beta test, an examiner gave oral directions and recruits responded to pictorial questions, such as incomplete drawings and comparisons of shapes. Administered to some 1.7 million men, the tests enabled the Army to classify large numbers of recruits quickly, to select tens of thousands for officer training, and to distribute men to different units on the basis of their intelligence scores.[11]

The wartime experiences of the psychologists forever changed the face of testing in the schools; in the 1920s, almost all of the psychologists who had participated in the Army mental testing program became leaders of the intelligence-testing movement. The group intelligence tests that had been introduced during the war were well suited for mass adoption in the schools and other institutions. They were cheaper and easier to administer than individual intelligence tests, and they provided group "norms," which facilitated assignment of children to different programs.

In the postwar years, no one was more instrumental in the development and marketing of intelligence tests to the schools than Lewis Terman of Stanford University. He was at the center of a powerful network of educational psychologists. He was elected president of the American Psychological Association in 1922; served on the editorial board of half a dozen major research journals; and edited a textbook series for World Book that enabled him to promote the careers of his students and colleagues. Valuable alliances formed, not only among like-minded psychologists but between professors of educational psychology and professors of educational administration, who shared a common vision about curricular differentiation, vocational guidance, and intelligence testing. Ellwood P. Cubberley, Terman's colleague at Stanford, edited a major textbook series for Houghton Mifflin, and between them they controlled many important platforms in the field of education.

Terman took the lead in bringing group intelligence testing to the schools. Before the war, many American cities had been using the Binet test to classify individual pupils by their mental ability, but the tests had not yet gained broad acceptance.[12] After the war, Terman and other psychologists promoted group intelligence testing as a valuable tool for solving thorny administrative problems caused by surging enrollments. Mental age, Terman explained, could be used to assign pupils to homogeneous groups for instruction.[13]

Terman popularized the concept of the IQ as a firm and constant basis for prediction: "The fact is that, apart from minor fluctuations due to temporary factors, and apart from occasional instances of arrest or deterioration due to acquired nervous disease, the feeble-minded remain feeble-minded, the dull remain dull, the average remain average, and the superior remain superior." Even ordinary teachers could administer the new tests, he suggested, either under the supervision of a trained psychologist or by careful study of books like his own. Terman believed that the mental tests were an accurate gauge of "original endowment," that they measured innate intelligence with the same certainty as assaying the amount of gold in "a given vein of quartz."[14]

Shortly after the war, the General Education Board of the Rockefeller Foundation made a grant of $25,000 to the National Research Council to convert the Army tests for use in the schools. A cadre of psychologists, led by Terman, Yerkes, Thorndike, and Guy M. Whipple of the University of Michigan oversaw the development of "National Intelligence Tests" in 1919–20 for students in grades three to eight. More than 400,000 copies of the test were sold within a year of its publication. By 1920, Terman was predicting that eventually there would be "a mental test for every child" and that schools would use these tests to sort and classify students into the appropriate curricula. By the mid-1920s, psychologists had created more than seventy-five different tests of mental ability for students of all ages, and each year some 4 million students took an intelligence test.[15]

In short order, testing became a major part of the educational publishing industry, and, as Stephen Jay Gould observes, "marketing companies dared not take a chance with tests not proven by their correlation with Terman's standard."[16] Since curriculum differentiation and homogeneous grouping were considered fundamental principles of modern, progressive education, mental testing was promptly accepted by school administrators as a scientific methodology that would enable them to identify individual differences and determine which students belonged in which program.

Terman's view of intelligence as constant and innate led him to draw clear implications for the schools. First, he argued that "the limits of a child's educability can be fairly accurately predicted by means of mental tests given in the first school year" and that "these limits can be determined accurately enough for all practical purposes by the end of the child's fifth or sixth year. This early, at least, vocational training and vocational guidance should begin." Second, he claimed that a school's program could not improve a child's IQ, but it could surely discourage gifted children by failing to challenge them and also discourage low-IQ children by failing to offer them suitable courses. Third, he believed that students who dropped out of high school were "in the main pupils of inferior ability" and that they left because "the high school offers little which can be done by pupils of much less than average intelligence," who, he estimated, made up about one third of all children.[17]

From these premises, Terman concluded that the schools must expand their offerings of vocational subjects and other studies of a "practical nature" for children of inferior intelligence. He insisted that differentiation of courses should begin in the sixth or seventh grade. This scheme was not undemocratic, he said. The school that differentiated courses for children of lesser abilities, he said, would actually come closer to the democratic ideal than one that tried to teach a common course of studies to all.[18]

Terman held that there were only two ways of solving the problem of individual differences, either by individualizing instruction or by making classes more homogeneous in ability. "It was only natural," Terman wrote, that individual instruction had prevailed as long as education "was for the selected few only. It was equally natural that with the growth of democratic ideals and the movement toward universal education the individual method should be replaced by group instruction." Most school districts found it easier and cheaper to sort classes into homogeneous groups, as recommended by Terman and his disciples, rather than attempt individualized instruction. Terman favored a division of children into five groups: the "gifted," the "bright," the "average," the "slow," and "special" pupils: "For each of these groups there should be a separate track and a specialized curriculum. . . . At every step in the child's progress the school should take account of his vocational possibilities."[19]

Children who scored below 70 could expect to perform unskilled labor; those from 70 to 80 were likely to become semiskilled labor; those from 80 to 100 were likely to be skilled or ordinary clerical labor; those from 100 to 115 would qualify for semiprofessional pursuits; while scores above 115 would "permit one to enter the professional or the larger fields of business." Terman stressed that "the road for transfers from track to track must always be kept open. A fixed and permanent grouping would not only be repugnant to American ideals of democracy, but also pedagogically unjustifiable." He anticipated that "frequent transfers from one educational track to another "would be imperative."[20]

Terman predicted that his five-track plan would become a standard feature of public school organization. He was particularly concerned about the education of gifted children, believing that they were likely to be overlooked unless there were special efforts to identify them (by IQ testing) and to place them in an enriched curriculum track. In an address to the National Education Association in 1923, he said, "I have no patience with those who condemn this plan as undemocratic. The abandonment of the single-track, pre-high school curriculum is in fact the first necessary step toward educational democracy. The single-track is a straight [*sic*] jacket which dwarfs the mental development of the inferior as well as the gifted." He lambasted the critics of mental tests as sentimentalists who denied the reality of individual differences.[21]

Intelligence testing fit neatly into the progressive educators' movement for curricular differentiation and facilitated their redefinition of educational democracy. After taking an intelligence test, each child could be assigned a score that expressed not only his native intelligence but also his capacity for future learning. This number could then be used to group students, define what they would learn, and determine their future vocation.

Some ability grouping was surely necessary and inevitable, given the wide gap between the most advanced and the least advanced students and the presence in the schools of large numbers of non-English-speaking children. What was not necessary, however, was the idea that the curriculum tracks should provide an essentially different *quality* of education, instead of a different *pace* of instruction and different methods. The decision to offer different educational programs, depending on children's IQ, repudiated the fundamental concept of the American common school idea, which was to provide the same curriculum to all children in the first eight years of their schooling.

By the logic of the IQ testing movement, the common school itself was antidemocratic.

The Political Uses of the Army Tests

*After World War I, even as the schools adopted group intelligence test-*ing, there was vigorous debate about the results of the mental tests the Army had administered during the war. Leading psychologists claimed that the average mental age of draftees had been only thirteen or fourteen. Intelligence, they said, was fixed and innate. Nativists and racists cited the Army test data to support their campaigns for restrictions on immigration and for a eugenics program. Their critics insisted that the test data had been deeply flawed and that the results had been misinterpreted.

Nativists said that the "new immigration" from countries in southern and eastern Europe lacked American ideals, came from backward societies, were likely to be carriers of foreign ideologies such as socialism and anarchism, and would dilute the American racial stock. Worse, these new immigrants lived in self-contained communities in congested neighborhoods and resisted efforts to assimilate them to American ways. The progressive sociologist Edward A. Ross, well known for his theory of social control, warned about the danger to American society of continued immigration from southern and eastern Europe and the Orient.[22]

But whatever complaint was lodged against the new immigration, the clincher in the argument for immigration restriction was the Army mental tests, which supposedly offered scientific proof of the mental superiority of the Nordic stock from northern European countries. One commentator complained, "We are being swamped with the offscourings of Europe. Those at the lower end of the intellectual scale have brought us their social customs, their language, their political ideals. They cannot assimilate our ideals. . . . They cannot become citizens in the highest meaning of that word. . . . We do not need the ignorant, the mentally feeble, the moron."[23]

In 1922, Lothrop Stoddard's eugenicist book, *The Revolt Against Civilization: The Menace of the Under Man,* used the Army test results and the writings of Yerkes, Terman, and other prominent psychologists as evidence that the American racial stock was being threatened by the addition of inferior racial groups from southern and eastern Europe. Like other advocates of eugenics, Stoddard claimed that his views were founded on the scientific principles of evolutionary biology rather than on sentimental ideas about natural equality. Modern biology, he wrote, had begun with Darwin, and it was Darwin who had established that *"evolution* proceeded by *heredity."* The Army tests, Stoddard declared, showed that nearly one half the population "will never develop mental capacity beyond the state represented by a normal twelve-year-old child."[24]

In 1922, the Army test results were analyzed in *The Atlantic Monthly* by Cornelia James Cannon, who concluded that nearly half the white draft could be considered "morons" and fully 22 percent were "inferior men." The "inferior men" included disproportionate numbers from Poland, Italy, and Russia: "They are persons who not only do not think, but are unable to think; who cannot help in the solution of our problems, but, instead, become a drag on the progress of civilization. In a crude society, they have a place, may even serve a use. In a society so complex as that which we are developing, they are a menace which may compass our destruction." Common school education, she felt, should be limited to very basic subjects, followed by "a pretty rigorous process of selection," so that society would not waste money on "second-rate men."[25] What was to be done for the masses of "inferior men"? She predicted that vocational guidance, based on mental testing, would match each individual with the right job. Democracy would be best served, she

141

claimed, by relying on men of "superior ability" and showering favors on them, for they would provide the science, art, philosophy, and leadership for everyone else.

In 1923, Yerkes offered his own interpretation of the Army mental tests in *The Atlantic Monthly,* claiming that he wanted to counter popular misconceptions about them. Actually, he did nothing to blunt the arguments of eugenicists, nativists, and racists; in fact, he reinforced them. His argument went like this: Most of his readers probably overestimated the intelligence of the general population because they tended to know only people like themselves; besides, the average thirteen-year-old is really fairly intelligent; perhaps the draft had not been an entirely representative sample because many men of low-grade intelligence had been screened out, and an even larger number of high-grade men had not been tested because they had been assigned to essential occupations or the officer corps. Most tellingly, he wrote, the overall results had been depressed by the inclusion of large numbers of foreign-born recruits, who were "markedly inferior in mental alertness to the native-born American." Yerkes claimed that the mental age of the average native-born white American was fourteen or fifteen, while that of the foreign-born was less than twelve years. He asserted that the intelligence tests had demonstrated significant differences not only between the races but among white "racial groups." He believed that the low scores of Negroes, Italians, and Poles accurately indicated their inferior intelligence as compared to that of immigrants from England and Scotland and native-born whites.[26]

Yerkes asserted his faith in the scientific measurement of intelligence: "Theoretically, man is just as measurable as a bar of steel or a humanly contrived machine"—more complicated, certainly, but just as subject to accurate measurement. Yerkes predicted that psychologists would be the social engineers of the future.[27]

The Army testing program, Yerkes believed, had demonstrated the importance of race in national destiny. He reaffirmed this belief in his introduction to a 1923 book by Carl C. Brigham, a professor of psychology at Princeton University and a colleague of Yerkes in the Army testing program. In *A Study of American Intelligence,* Brigham warned that the Army test data revealed the danger to the nation of continued immigration from southern and eastern Europe. Brigham, wrote Yerkes, "presents not theories or opinions but facts. It behooves us to consider their reliability and their meaning, for no one of us as a citizen can afford to ignore the menace of race deterioration or the evident relations of immigration to national progress and welfare."[28]

Brigham's book was published as a "companion volume" to Charles W. Gould's *America: A Family Matter,* a polemic advocating purebred races. Brigham thanked Gould for his assistance and added that he had relied on two other books, Madison Grant's *The Passing of the Great Race* and William Z. Ripley's *Races of Europe.*[29] Both these books were notoriously racist; Grant wrote, for example, "it has taken us fifty years to learn that speaking English, wearing good clothes, and going to school and to church, does not transform a negro into a white man. . . . We shall have a similar experience with the Polish Jew, whose dwarf stature, peculiar mentality, and ruthless concentration on self-interest are being engrafted upon the stock of the nation."[30] In 1918, Grant, described by later historians as "the nation's most influential racist," founded the Galton Society in New York City, whose members included, among others, Lothrop Stoddard ("the second most influential racist"), Edward L. Thorndike of Teachers College, and Henry F. Osborn of the American Museum of Natural History.[31]

Citing eugenicists, Brigham asserted the existence of three distinct European races: the Nordics, the Alpines, and the Mediterraneans. Eugenicists believed that Nordics—from northern European countries such as Sweden, Belgium, the Netherlands, and England—were far superior to Alpines from nations such as Romania, Russia, Poland, and Austria-Hungary, and Alpines were in turn superior to Mediterraneans from such ill-starred nations as Turkey, Portugal, Spain, Greece, and Italy. Germans, he estimated, were 40 percent Nordic and 60 percent Alpine; the French were a combination of all three racial types, 30 percent Nordic, 55 percent Alpine, and 15 percent Mediterranean; and people from Ireland were 30 percent Nordic and 70 percent Mediterranean.[32]

The centerpiece of Brigham's book was his compilation of charts and graphs comparing the Army intelligence test scores by national origin and race; these factors, he believed, were the primary determinants of intelligence. He dismissed the hand-wringing over the low test scores of the average recruit, saying that the psychologists' standards "are those that he gets, not those that he thinks he ought to get. Therefore, instead of deploring the fact that the average person has a 'mental age' of thirteen, we can simply say that the conversion of the results of the army test into the Stanford-Binet scale shows an average score of 13, and that this is the score to be expected from the average adult."[33]

Brigham detected a positive relationship between intelligence and years of schooling, but he nonetheless insisted that the tests were "genuine measures of intelligence," not just measures of years of schooling, because some recruits with *more* schooling had scored below others with *less* schooling. Native-born whites had higher scores than foreign-born whites, which he attributed to higher native intelligence. He acknowledged that the scores of the foreign-born increased in relation to their years of residence in the United States and that the gap narrowed significantly after ten years of residence and closed completely after twenty years of residence; after then, the scores of the foreign-born whites were actually slightly higher than those of native-born whites.

But he found a clever way of explaining this phenomenon. He flatly denied that schooling or other environmental factors had contributed to the higher scores of those immigrants who had lived in this country for ten to twenty years: "Instead of concluding that our curve indicates a growth of intelligence with increasing length of residence, we are forced to take the reverse of the picture and accept the hypothesis that the curve indicates a gradual deterioration in the class of immigrants examined in the army, who came to this country in each succeeding five-year period since 1902. . . . The fact that the average intelligence of the immigrants . . . becomes progressively lower with each succeeding period indicates that an explanation of this phenomenon might be found in a change in the character of immigration."[34] The "change in the character of immigration" referred to a steady decline in immigrants from mainly Nordic nations such as England, Scotland, and Sweden and a marked increase in immigration from non-Nordic nations such as Russia and Italy.

Brigham did not deny that the tests were affected by educational opportunity but insisted that race and national origin were determinative. He did not doubt the intellectual superiority of the Nordic group over all other racial groups. He derided "the theory that disregards all differences found between racial groups unless the groups have had the same educational and environmental opportunities." Psychologists had consistently found that children from families of higher social status scored higher on mental tests than children from lower-status families; was it possible that superior environment had increased the children's intelligence? Brigham disputed this possibility by quoting Terman, who wrote that "Practically all of the investigations which have been made of the influence of nature and nurture on mental performance agree in attributing far more to original endowment than to environment. Common observation would itself suggest that the social class to which the family belongs depends less on chance than on the parents' native qualities of intellect and character." [35]

Brigham's book was intended not to change education policy (which he insisted was impotent to influence intelligence) but to encourage immigration restriction and a policy of eugenics. The increasing flow into the United States of Alpines and Mediterraneans, he predicted, would lower the nation's overall intelligence. He also feared that future racial mixing among Nordics, Alpines, Mediterraneans, and Negroes would inevitably produce a less intelligent population. Presenting a facade of scientific neutrality, he concluded that the "steps that should be taken to preserve or increase our present intellectual capacity must of course be dictated by science and not by political expediency. Immigration should not only be restrictive but highly selective." But even if all immigration were ended, he wrote, the problem of racial mixing would still lead to a decline in American intelligence, and "this is the problem which must be met, and our manner of meeting it will determine the future course of our national life." [36]

Just as Brigham refused to credit education and acculturation for improving the intelligence of foreign-born recruits, Yerkes too discounted the value of education. Yerkes noted that the Army recruits with the least education got the lowest scores on the intelligence tests and that the individuals with the most education received the highest scores. Some, wrote Yerkes, might interpret this relationship to mean "that intellectual ability is largely the result of education. Indeed, it is quite commonly believed that intelligence increases with schooling. This, however, is flatly contradicted by results of research, for it turns out that the main reason that intelligence status improves with years of schooling is the elimination of the less capable pupil." Yerkes insisted that the purpose of the school was not to boost intelligence but to select and retain the most intelligent. He declared that not more than 50 percent of the population was capable of completing the work of "a first-rate high school," and not more than 10 percent was able to meet the requirements for a bachelor's degree in "a reputable college." Education,"instead of increasing our intellectual capacity, merely develops it and facilitates its use."[37]

As intelligence testing spread rapidly among the nation's schools, its major proponents—Yerkes, Brigham, and Terman—agreed that the tests measured innate intelligence; that intelligence is largely inherited; that an individual's IQ remains constant throughout his life, with only minor variations; and that knowing a student's IQ would enable school officials to predict "what manner of adult he will become." Terman acknowledged that some teachers found the prediction of their students' intelligence to be "actually repugnant." He ridiculed the qualms of skeptical teachers as nothing more than "deep-seated and blind faith that anything is possible for any child," which he said was akin to believing in miracles.[38]

CRITICS OF IQ TESTING

Initially, the bold claims of the mental testers met little challenge, in part because of the shield provided by the apparently inviolable mantle of science, whose technical language, arcane methods, and aura of objectivity kept outsiders at bay. But in 1922, the testers encountered a double-barreled assault by one of their own, William C. Bagley, a professor of educational psychology at Teachers College, and by a distinguished journalist, Walter Lippmann.

Bagley had played a public role eight years earlier, when he had defended liberal education in a debate with David Snedden, but as far as his colleagues knew, he was not a dissident or a troublemaker. In 1922, at the very time intelligence tests were being hailed by most educators as the acme of the scientific movement in education, Bagley blasted the tests, warning that they posed grave "educational and social dangers." He labeled the mental testers "educational determinists" and complained that the IQ tests encouraged "fatalistic inferences" about children. The testers, he observed, treated intelligence as an unchanging given, like the color of one's eyes, even though they had no common definition of what they were measuring. He was especially incensed that the testers accorded so little credit for a person's intelligence to education and considered even the most skillful teacher to be nothing more than "a sort of rubber stamp to certify that his pupils have a certain amount of native intelligence." Bagley predicted that the tests would be used to close the doors of educational opportunity to large numbers of people and that they would encourage educators to "neglect the broader education of mediocre and dull children, to let them be satisfied with a narrow specific training that will fit them only for routine work, and to reserve the high privileges for the 'gifted' children."[39]

Bagley warned that the misuse of IQ tests threatened democracy itself and that "if the determinist is right, then democracy is wrong." Bagley knew that the tests were being used by schools to assign students to different kinds of curricular programs. He argued that the role of the schools in a democracy is not to sort students for their future careers but to provide "a high level of trained and informed intelligence as a basis for collective judgment and collective action." Bagley insisted that schools must lift up the common man and improve his intelligence. He did not claim that teaching a common man the principle of gravity would make him the equal of Newton. But he did maintain

> that I have enabled this common man to participate in a very real measure in the experiences of one of the most gifted men of all time; I maintain that I have given him one control over his environment equal in a substantial way to that which this gifted man himself possessed; and I maintain that *in respect of this posses-*

sion I have made this common man the equal of all others who possess it. There are undoubtedly some men who could never grasp the principle in question, but I should wish to refine my teaching processes far more . . . before reaching any fatalistic conclusions as to where the line is to be drawn.[40]

Like Bagley's earlier critique of vocational education, his vigorous attack on intelligence testing expressed his conviction that education is powerful and that virtually anyone can become better informed and more intelligent if education aims to make him so. The new tests, he charged, rejected the promise of education and created a technology that would justify limitations on educational opportunity for many children.

Bagley argued that talented teachers "can do something even with morons. As I watch these teachers at their work it is not what they can not do that impresses me, it is rather the miracles that their consummate art enables them to perform." He had seen how teachers could reach even the slowest children: "I have seen dull eyes lighted with a momentary gleam of intelligence. It was a little light in a world of darkness. But grant that little light glowing with rapidly increasing intensity as we go up the intelligence scale, and my case is won."[41]

Bagley's polemic drew a withering response from the big gun himself, Lewis M. Terman. He accused Bagley of having "a sublime faith that anything is possible for any child" and of preferring to "believe in 'miracles,' " which Terman characterized as "Christian Science Psychology." Bagley's cardinal sin was that he "seems to deny any possibility of a science of education, for of course the essence of science is that it enables us to predict." Terman sneered that Bagley's vision was "blurred by the moist tears of sentiment" and that he was a naïf for believing in "the miracles that skillful teachers work with morons and on the ultimate illumination of the world by gleams of light struck from dull minds." Terman mocked Bagley for suggesting that all children should be educated as if there were no limits to what they could learn. Speaking for the testing fraternity, Terman admitted that he "pleads guilty of demanding new types of secondary education which would be better suited to inferior intellects than is the typical college preparatory curriculum."

Only a differentiated curriculum, he contended, would "keep the low I.Q.'s in school and insure that their time there would not be wasted."[42]

Bagley's 1922 exchange with Terman secured his reputation among professional pedagogues as a conservative who was out of step with the scientific movement in education. His reputation for "conservatism" only deepened in the 1930s, as he continued to defend liberal education and to argue that virtually all children should have the same access to a liberal education.

Later in 1922, Walter Lippmann blasted the intelligence testers in a series of articles in *The New Republic*. Deeply disturbed that the Army psychologists were giving fodder to the nativists, Lippmann set out to demolish their conclusions. He was incensed by the claim that the average mental age of Americans was fourteen; this statement, he wrote, is "not inaccurate. It is not incorrect. It is nonsense."[43]

He maintained that the psychologists had never agreed on "what intelligence means," but they had invented puzzles and problems to test this indefinable something. Since the psychologists were not even sure what they were measuring, he suggested that they should desist from making "large generalizations about the quality of human beings." The tests were a good tool for classifying people "from best to worst" on their capacity to solve certain arbitrarily selected puzzles, but he was not persuaded that they accurately measured intelligence.[44]

Lippmann recognized that the testers implied that education is impotent as compared to heredity. He argued that the purpose of a school was not to measure a child's capacities but to increase them. A child's "success in life must be a significant measure of the school's success in developing the capacities of the child. If a child fails in school and then fails in life, the school cannot sit back and say: you see how accurately I predicted this." The grave danger of the intelligence test in a mass system of education, he said, was that some educators "will stop when they have classified and forget that their duty is to educate." He could not imagine "a more contemptible proceeding than to confront a child with a set of puzzles, and after an hour's monkeying with them, proclaim to the child and his parents, that here is a C-individual. It would not only be a contemptible thing to do. It would be a crazy thing to do."[45]

Lippmann suspected that not far behind the testers' "will to believe" was "the will to power." If the testers really knew how to measure pure intelligence, they would become very powerful in society, deciding which children should go to college, which to the professions, and which to manual labor. If testers had this sort of power, they would "occupy a position of power which no intellectual has held since the collapse of theocracy. . . . What a future to dream about!" He insisted that the tests might have some value in the schools, but that only quacks claimed that they could isolate intelligence, unalloyed by training and knowledge.[46]

Terman replied to Lippmann as he had earlier to Bagley, with sarcasm. Perhaps, suggested Terman, "there ought to be a law passed forbidding the encroachment of statistical methods upon those fields which from time immemorial have been reserved for the play of sentiment and opinion." He ridiculed Lippmann's arguments as uninformed and ignorant, probably proceeding from an "emotional complex." He pointed out that the majority of psychologists in America, England, and Germany supported intelligence testing. Terman haughtily dismissed Lippmann as a naive idealist who refused to accept the reality that people differ in intelligence and that the average person is not especially intelligent.[47]

Terman's tone enraged Lippmann, who replied with a scornful blast. Lippmann noted in his reply that he did have "an emotional complex" about IQ testing. He wrote, "I hate the impudence of a claim that in fifty minutes you can judge and classify a human being's predestined fitness in life. I hate the pretentiousness of that claim. I hate the abuse of scientific method which it involves. I hate the sense of superiority which it creates, and the sense of inferiority which it imposes." Lippmann predicted that the field of intelligence testing, whatever its possible value, would become "the happy hunting ground of quacks and snobs if loose-minded men are allowed to occupy positions of leadership much longer."[48]

In the midst of the controversy, John Dewey felt compelled to speak out. He was widely recognized as the nation's most eminent philosopher as well as its undisputed titan of educational thought. A sharp, stern rebuke by Dewey might have caused his worshipful disciples in education to reassess the extravagant claims they were making for their testing programs. But Dewey was strangely oblique, choosing to criticize George B. Cutten, the new president of Colgate University, for saying that "only fifteen percent of the people have sufficient intelligence to get through college." Dewey said nothing about the psychologists whose published works were the source of Cutten's remarks.

Dewey took issue with any scheme for classification of pupils, which he said tended to produce mediocrity, not individuality.[49] He disagreed with "a procedure which under the title of science sinks the individual in a numerical class; judges him with reference to capacity to fit into a limited number of vocations ranked according to present business standards; assigns him to a predestined niche and thereby does whatever education can do to perpetuate the present order." He scoffed at the idea of racial superiority and inferiority, saying that such judgments were solely a reflection of the values of those who had created the standards. Unlike Lippmann and Bagley, however, he refrained from criticizing the psychologists at Stanford, Teachers College, Harvard, Michigan, and elsewhere who were then creating and disseminating the ideas and practices he abhorred. He named no names. He emphasized that his comments were "in no sense a hostile criticism of the scientific procedure of mental testing" but rather an effort to encourage the use of tests to help "in analysis of an individual."[50] Thus Dewey pulled his punches.

REASSESSMENT OF THE ARMY TESTS

*Even as the great debate about mental testing raged on, a Stanford grad-*uate student reanalyzed the Army test results and found that the group comparisons were flawed: they did not adequately consider the influence of social and economic factors on group scores. Herbert B. Alexander maintained that the hereditarian claims made by the developers of the Army tests were insupportable.

Alexander examined the rank order of the states according to the median scores of literate white recruits. States from the Far West and New England were at the top, while southern states were at the bottom. He then ranked the states according to their percentage of native-born whites, and it happened that the lowest-scoring southern states had the highest proportion of native-born whites of native parentage. This demonstrated, he said, "that the state with a large population recruited from southern and eastern Europe is not necessarily inferior to the state with a far greater proportion of North European stocks. The Southern states, for example, can trace almost their entire white population back to northern stocks established in this country before the influx of industrial workers from Italy, Austria-Hungary, and Russia. Yet these states are found at the bottom of the Alpha list." Alexander found that men from the states with the best schools ranked highest. He concluded that "where density of population, favorable economic conditions, and educational opportunities exist in conjunction, there will be found the better intelligence." The Army's intelligence test, he argued, appeared to be "a test of what *has* been learned rather than what *can* be learned."[51]

Using Alexander's research, Walter Lippmann returned to the offensive in 1923 with a scorching assault on Carl C. Brigham, the Princeton psychologist whose book *A Study of American Intelligence* claimed that scores on the Army tests were determined by heredity, not education or experience. Lippmann called Brigham and his colleagues "the Psychological Battalion of Death," practitioners of "a yellow science," because of their insistence that educational opportunity did not improve people's ability to use "language, numbers, geometrical figures, grammatical constructions, logical choices, and the like." The psychologists' unwarranted claims, he said, were "producing something like a panic, using misleading statistics to destroy confidence in the value and possibilities of education. . . . Even by their own measuring scale, education works. There is, then, no slightest reason for losing faith in the one human activity which amidst all the bewilderment of these times gives the most certain promise of a better world."[52]

William C. Bagley continued the ideological battle in the academic journals, where he criticized the testers' racial and biological determinism. Bagley's fundamental point was not that native intelligence was unimportant but that "nurture"—especially education—had a large effect on the development of intelligence. The greatest steps forward in human evolution, he said, such as the invention of writing and the printing press, had been "marked by improved methods of disseminating experience—*of letting more light into common minds!*" The nations that rank highest in civilization, he held, are those with the most nearly universal forms of popular education. Bagley warned that "the current teachings of educational determinism are dangerous because they proceed with a dogmatic disregard of the possibilities of insuring progress through environmental agencies. This disregard is so studied, so pointed, as to brand the determinist as thoroughly prejudiced."[53]

Bagley believed that the net effect of the determinists' activities was "to weaken public faith in universal education." To Terman's charge that he was an unscientific sentimentalist, Bagley replied:

> [I]f my scientific training failed to make me a scientist, it left, I think, as a faint deposit, a moderate ability to distinguish fairly clearly between a fact and an artifact, between a fact and an assumption, and between a law and an hypothesis. Some frank untangling of their 'evidence' on the basis of these distinctions, I venture to say, might well have been for the determinists a preliminary to the rather presumptuous assumption that, in the field of education, they and they alone are doing truly 'scientific' work.[54]

Bagley did not doubt that youngsters of genius would prevail in spite of all obstacles. But what would happen to the children of average intelligence unless the schools fostered their intellectual development? "To endow the masses with genius," he wrote, "is biologically impossible; but to endow the masses with the fruits of genius is both educationally possible and socially most profitable. The mental tests will help most if they aid the teacher in discharging this transcendent duty. They will render a gratuitous and disastrous disservice if they encourage in the teacher the conviction that the illumination of common minds is either an impossible or a relatively unimportant task."[55]

In 1924, Bagley chided Brigham for identifying himself "with that 'parlor' cult of ku-kluxism of which our radical pro-Nordic propagandists constitute the mother-klan. To recognize unrestricted immigration as an evil is one thing; to fan the fires of race-prejudice with alleged scientific findings is quite another." Bagley demonstrated that Brigham's assertions of Nordic superiority were not supported by the results of the Army tests, for virtually every group that registered higher intelligence scores had also had greater educational opportunities. Bagley found, for example, that the scores of literate northern blacks were higher than those of literate whites in Mississippi, Kentucky, and Arkansas. Since southern whites represented the purest Nordic stock in the country, Bagley concluded that Brigham would have to make a choice: either he would have to admit that schooling did affect the test scores, or "his theory of Nordic superiority is knocked into a cocked hat."[56]

Terman stubbornly refused to budge in the face of criticism. He doubted that any amount of education or training could overcome the "rather hard and fast limits to the possibilities of training." He proposed an experiment to settle the issue: Select two groups of six-year-old children, Group A, with an IQ between 115 and 120, and Group B, with an IQ between 80 and 85; select only children whose parents are English-speaking with exactly eight years of schooling; place the high-IQ group in the care of the least qualified teachers in classes of fifty, and place the low-IQ group in the care of superior teachers in classes of twenty-five; ensure that they get the same curriculum for twelve years; compare the groups after eight, twelve, and sixteen years. Terman was sure that the high-IQ group, notwithstanding its relative educational deficiency, would produce more college graduates, lawyers, doctors, and teachers than the low-IQ group. If intelligence were due mainly to heredity, he believed, the role of the schools would have to change and "the practical consequences would be well nigh incalculable. Eugenics would deserve to become a religion." Education would begin by testing the native ability of all pupils, then give them the kind of instruction that suited their level of ability. Schools would either offer completely individualized instruction or, more likely, would be organized into a three-track or five-track plan beginning in the first grade, each track with its own curriculum and methods.[57]

If well-reasoned critiques had sufficed to shape public policy, the determinist claims of Yerkes, Brigham, and Terman would have been discredited—or, at the very least, school officials would have viewed them with healthy skepticism. But after the Great War, the United States was swept by a tide of nativist, xenophobic fervor, and the determinists' interpretation of the Army test results confirmed the popular prejudices. This was not a time in which competing claims about immigrants were soberly weighed. Pressures for conformity bore especially hard against those of foreign birth, and radical groups such as socialists, Communists, and anarchists were targeted for suppression or deportation. Some states passed laws banning the teaching of foreign languages. Oregon passed a law requiring all children to attend public school, fearing that parochial schools might contaminate children with foreign influences.[58]

In an era when the popular mood demanded loyalty and 100 percent Americanism, the Lippmann-Bagley arguments had little impact. The popular understanding of the Army tests fed the crusade for limitations on immigration. In 1921 and 1924, Congress passed laws restricting future immigration on the basis of nationality quotas tied to the 1890 census, to reduce the number of new immigrants from southern and eastern Europe. These acts received broad bipartisan support, as well as endorsement by the American Federation of Labor.

IQ Testing in the Mainstream

Despite the debates of the 1920s, group intelligence testing became a routine feature in American public schools and even in many private schools. As early as 1922, the director of the Psychological Clinic of the Detroit public schools declared that "the adoption of the group method [of testing intelligence] is now an old story." The majority of educational psychologists endorsed intelligence testing, and their work was supported by such prestigious foundations as the Carnegie Foundation, the General Education Board, and the Commonwealth Fund, as well as the U.S. Bureau of Education. The school survey movement, which advised school districts across the nation about "best practices," recommended group intelligence testing as a progressive innovation that would promote administrative efficiency; future teachers and administrators who studied in the nation's schools of education read the textbooks on mental measurement written by Terman, Thorndike, and other leaders in the field. Publishing companies competed to market their IQ tests, and test developers such as Terman earned handsome royalties. When Terman was elected to the presidency of the American Psychological Association in 1922, he estimated that 50 to 65 percent of the organization's membership was engaged in test research and development. Not only were critics of the mental tests few in number, they were well outside the mainstream of educational psychology.[59]

It became axiomatic among professionals that modern school districts should test their students' intelligence. The U.S. Bureau of Education surveyed 215 cities in 1925 and reported that group intelligence tests were used to classify pupils into homogeneous groups by 64 percent of elementary schools, 56 percent of junior high schools, and 40 percent of high schools; the same survey found that intelligence tests were used more frequently than standardized achievement tests. The public schools employed the tests to predict which students were likely to go to college and which should be guided into vocational programs; the decision became a self-fulfilling prophecy, since only those in the college track took the courses that would prepare them for college.[60]

Intelligence testing was broadly recognized by progressive educators as the leading edge of the scientific movement in education. In 1924, Michael V. O'Shea, a progressive professor of education at the University of Wisconsin, wrote about the current state of scientific knowledge about children's needs and stressed the complementarity of progressive approaches to child development, including intelligence testing. In the same year, Eugene Randolph Smith, president of the Progressive Education Association and headmaster of the private Beaver Country Day School in Brookline, Massachusetts, praised intelligence tests as good indicators of a child's "natural mental ability" and "inborn capacity." Teachers who "prefer to trust their own judgment concerning pupils" instead of using intelligence tests revealed their ignorance, he noted.[61]

By the 1930s, intelligence testing reached the colleges; a survey in 1933 found that ninety-three colleges required applicants to take an intelligence test. Several states, including Ohio and Wisconsin, required all high school students to take an intelligence test to determine their fitness for higher education. The National Research Council sponsored an intelligence test for college freshmen that was offered annually by the American Council on Education (in 1935, the test was administered by 493 institutions to nearly 200,000 students).[62]

THE COLLEGE BOARD CHANGES ITS EXAMINATIONS

Even as intelligence testing advanced through American education, one significant holdout still affirmed the principle of examining what students *had learned,* rather than testing what they were *capable of learning:* the College Entrance Examination Board. Since its establishment in 1900 as a voluntary association of colleges and universities, the College Board had offered annual examinations in every academic subject. Critics frequently complained that the College Board's examinations unduly influenced the secondary school curriculum, even though the syllabus and reading lists for the examinations were regularly revised by high school teachers and college professors.

Ever sensitive to criticism, the College Board took note of the enthusiasm among schools and colleges for the new intelligence tests. Gradually its resolve eroded. In 1922, the College Board expressed "favorable interest" in the use of "general intelligence examinations" and appointed an advisory commission of psychological experts, including Brigham and Yerkes. Since its founding, the College Board had always relied on teachers and college professors, not psychologists, to write its subject matter examinations; the decision to turn to psychologists, particularly two who were so closely associated with intelligence testing, virtually guaranteed that the College Board's traditional written subject-specific examinations, which tested knowledge, would in time be replaced by a general intelligence test.

In 1926, the College Board introduced Brigham's "Scholastic Aptitude Test" on a trial basis. The Scholastic Aptitude Test was an intelligence test whose purpose was to ascertain not what students had learned but their aptitude for learning. In 1930, Brigham joined the staff of the

157

College Board to continue developing the SAT, a short-answer, multiple-choice test that measured linguistic and mathematical aptitudes. In 1941, at the outbreak of World War II, the College Board dropped the traditional college entrance examinations altogether and adopted the SAT as its sole measure of college "aptitude."[63]

REACTIONS AGAINST THE IQ CONCEPT

By the late 1920s, a growing number of scholars such as Franz Boas and Otto Klineberg asserted that intelligence was affected not only by heredity but also by culture and environment. In major universities, the proponents of nurture rather than nature became ascendant. The changed climate of opinion in the academic world produced some notable recantations.

In 1928, Henry Goddard, popularizer of the incorrigibly stupid Kallikak family, admitted that he had been wrong in claiming that the "feebleminded" could not benefit from education and training. In an address to the American Association for the Study of the Feebleminded, Goddard asserted that "Feeblemindedness (the moron) is *not incurable*" and that *"the problem of the moron is a problem of education and training.* Not that education and training will change his moronity or raise his intelligence level," but with the right kind of education, such persons could learn to manage their own affairs and become "happy and useful hewers of wood and drawers of water." With this recantation, he admitted that he had "gone over to the enemy."[64]

Two years later, Carl C. Brigham (by then a member of the staff at the College Board) corrected his earlier, nativist interpretation of the Army tests. He had been wrong, he wrote, when he had compared immigrant groups by combining different measures into a single score; consequently, his study "with its entire hypothetical superstructure of racial differences collapses completely." He further conceded that "tests in the vernacular must be used only with individuals having equal opportunities to acquire the vernacular of the test." He concluded that "comparative studies of various national and racial groups may not be made with existing tests" and acknowledged that "one of the most pretentious of these comparative racial studies—the writer's own—was without foundation."[65]

Brigham's remarkable retraction had limited value as a corrective to his inflammatory book *A Study of American Intelligence,* which had provided ammunition for proponents of immigration restriction. Seven crucial years had gone by before he disavowed his book, the legislation to restrict immigration had already passed, and many who had heard about the alarmist claims of Brigham's 1923 book never learned of his 1930 retraction. Further, as psychologist Lee J. Cronbach later pointed out, Brigham admitted error "on the largely irrelevant grounds that the Army tests were inhomogeneous; he bowed not at all to the professional consensus that ethnic comparisons themselves are meaningless."[66]

Terman continued his advocacy of intelligence testing throughout his career, becoming especially noted for his studies of gifted children. In his autobiography, *Trails to Psychology,* written in 1932, Terman wrote "That the major differences between children of high and low IQ, and the major differences in the intelligence test scores of certain races, as Negroes and whites, will never be fully accounted for on the environmental hypothesis." But next to this sentence, in his personal copy of the book, Terman wrote in the margin in 1951, "I am less sure of this now," and four years later he added, "And still less sure in 1955!"[67]

Yet Terman, one of the most influential figures in American education, never publicly renounced his strong support for hereditarianism and racial differences in intelligence. Henry Minton, his biographer, observed that Terman was astonished to discover that he was considered a conservative; he described himself as a political liberal, a civil libertarian, a New Dealer, and "a committed liberal throughout his adult life . . . he never lost faith in his belief that science was an instrument for social progress."[68]

THE LEGACY OF IQ TESTING IN THE SCHOOLS

In the many decades since the great debate about intelligence testing in the 1920s, it has become clear that aptitude tests may be useful for specific purposes: for example, for identifying children with learning problems who need special attention and children with superior intellectual capacities who need greater challenges. They measure mental facility with words, numbers, concepts, and problems; they do not measure wisdom, originality, creativity, or insight. What is not clear and may never be are the precise determinants of whatever qualities are measured by the tests. No testing experts believe that one's intelligence is completely determined by either heredity or environment; most believe that some combination of nature and nurture is involved; but there is no consensus about the relative emphasis attributable to these influences. Is it 60 percent nature and 40 percent nurture or the reverse? Is it 80 percent nurture and 20 percent nature or the reverse? Short of some investigative breakthrough that is not now available, perhaps not even imaginable, it is impossible to know with certainty to what extent a child's intelligence derives from genes or experiences.[69]

The lasting effects of the intelligence-testing movement on American schools were far more negative than positive. On the one hand, the tests gave hard-pressed administrators a tool that could quickly identify children whose mental functioning was at one extreme or the other and who needed unusual attention beyond what was available in the ordinary classroom. On the other, they provided a selection instrument that facilitated the ongoing progressive campaign to restrict the academic curriculum to the minority of students who were preparing for college.

Beginning in the 1920s, the most common use of the IQ test was to determine which students qualified to study an academic curriculum and which did not. School officials could scarcely be blamed for the use they made of the group intelligence tests. After all, the tests were commended to them in textbooks and pedagogical research journals as the best scientific tool available; their validity was attested to by the nation's most prominent professors of educational psychology and administration; and their availability in the schools was considered by pedagogical experts to be a mark of modern, progressive practice.

And there was the constant refrain from the intelligence testers that intelligence was innate and relatively constant; that education had little influence on a child's intelligence; that, as the eminent Professor Terman of Stanford University had written in his landmark study in 1919, "the dull remain dull, the average remain average, and the superior remain superior."[70]

The intelligence testers promoted fatalism, a rueful acceptance that achievement in school is the result of innate ability, not sustained effort by teachers and students. The cult of the IQ became an all-purpose rationale for students' lack of effort and for poor teaching: Why study hard in school if IQ determines outcomes? Why work hard to teach slow learners if their IQs predict that they cannot do well in school?

Nor did the leaders of the intelligence-testing movement offer reason to believe that education could improve a child's intelligence or change his life chances. As Bagley warned, the intelligence tests made it easy to decide which children would get a broad liberal education and which would be placed into a vocational track or into a watered-down general curriculum that led nowhere.

5

Instead of the Academic Curriculum

Progressive reformers believed that the scientific movement in educa-
tion had "exploded" the theory of mental discipline and demolished the
rationale for the academic curriculum. They agreed that the academic
curriculum was archaic, but they did not agree on what should replace it.
Before World War I, reformers championed industrial and vocational
education. After Congress passed the Smith-Hughes Vocational Education Act in 1917, subjects such as home economics, trade training, and
agriculture became a permanent, important part of the public school
curriculum.

Yet to the chagrin of educationists, the traditional academic curriculum was scarcely disturbed. Even the widespread adoption of mental
testing left much of the status quo intact. Students were still enrolling in
Latin, history, and algebra, even some who didn't expect to go to college. Progressive reformers who wanted to transform the role of the
school from academic to social were deeply frustrated by the schools'
resistance to change. Something more was needed to dislodge the reign
of the academic curriculum.

After World War I, progressive reform advanced on two fronts:
some educationists continued to demand a socially efficient curriculum
tied to the labor market, while others sought to extend the influence of
child-centered schooling from private to public schools.

162

Neither vocational education nor child-centered schooling had an immediate effect on the schools. Teachers who had been trained to teach Latin or chemistry resisted changes that not only repudiated their ideas about what schools were supposed to do but also threatened to abolish their jobs; parents frequently balked at reforms that ignored their views about what schools were supposed to do. Immigrant and African-American parents wanted their children to have the same kind of education that children from more favored circumstances got, not job training that might lock them into low-status occupations.

Encountering this resistance by teachers and parents, progressive educators confidently told one another that implementation of their reforms would be delayed by a cultural time lag, until they had changed public opinion or trained a new generation of teachers and administrators. In the 1920s and 1930s, the reformers never doubted that they—not parents, not local school boards, not teachers—should decide what should be taught in the nation's public schools, and to which group of children. They may have disagreed among themselves about tactics, but not about the need for dramatic change. They looked to the future with confidence, sure that any setbacks were temporary, that any critics were hopeless reactionaries, and that any resistance would inevitably yield to the unstoppable march of progress.

The Curriculum of Social Efficiency

John Franklin Bobbitt of the University of Chicago and W. W. Charters of the Carnegie Institute of Technology created the field of curriculum studies after World War I. Before Bobbitt and Charters, lay school boards and local educators decided what courses to offer. There was a striking homogeneity of offerings, since teachers and parents had a broadly shared understanding about what children should learn in school.

Virtually all communities wanted their children to learn reading, writing, arithmetic, history, geography, and nature study in the common schools, and they wanted the high schools to teach Latin, a modern foreign language or two, mathematics, literature, grammar, the sciences, ancient history, English history, American history, drawing, music, and practical courses such as bookkeeping and woodworking. Local school boards and educators had a keen sense of what their own communities expected.

But after the field of curriculum studies was established, curriculum experts insisted that curriculum making was a science and that it was too esoteric and complex to be entrusted to teachers and laymen. Only those who had studied the textbooks, read the research, taken the courses, and mastered the theories could be permitted to decide what children should learn.

The invention of the scientific curriculum expert represented an extraordinary shift of power away from teachers, parents, and local communities to professional experts. The most vital educational decisions would in the future be made by experts who spoke an arcane language of their own, incomprehensible to laymen. This shift redefined the meaning of democratic control of education. In modern school districts, control over curriculum was transferred from educators who had majored in English, history, or mathematics to trained curriculum specialists.

John Franklin Bobbitt was the first progressive educator to realize that "the curriculum" was a field of study that demanded expert, scientific leadership and that its practitioners must be trained and certified by other experts in the field. Bobbitt, as noted earlier, was also a leading voice of scientific management in education, an efficiency expert who surveyed city school systems and applied cost accounting to instruction, enabling administrators to compare the relative costs of different subjects; it was he who figured out how to convert the time of teachers and students into dollars and cents and insisted that everything taught must have a specific function.

In 1918, Bobbitt published *The Curriculum,* the first textbook on the theory of curriculum making; it became a standard text in teacher-training institutions. He set the problem of curriculum making at the center of a debate between two antagonistic schools of thought. On one side were the traditionalists, the advocates of culture who preferred knowledge for its own sake, for the joy of learning. On the other were the utilitarians, such as himself, who were concerned mainly with teaching whatever would be useful in a student's future work. "In an age of efficiency and economy," he wrote, the utilitarians "would seek definitely to eliminate the useless and the wasteful."[1]

Bobbitt saw no justification for teaching science or any other subject unless it had some functional value in real life. Science would be taught so that it could be used "by the farmers in their farming, by mechanics in their shops, and variously in the fields of manufacturing, mining, cooking, sanitation, etc." They would learn only the facts needed for their work. What was the point of wasting so much time and money on useless studies? He saw no purpose in learning about "the glory that was Greece and the splendour that was Rome," the epics of Homer or the dramas of Shakespeare. Why teach about ancient history and the literature of other ages? "These deal with a world that is dead, a civilization that is mouldered, with governments that are now obsolete, with manners and customs and languages that are altogether impracticable in this modern age." Better to have youngsters learn about current practical problems and read literature about present social issues in fields such as "commerce, industry, sanitation, civic relationships, and recreational life; not classics, but current literature."[2]

Bobbitt believed that a curriculum maker was an educational engineer who could establish precisely what students needed to learn in order to function effectively in life. The scientific curriculum maker would decide which "abilities, attitudes, habits, appreciations, and forms of knowledge" people needed. The objectives of the curriculum, he wrote, would be "numerous, definite, and particularized." The scientific curriculum maker could determine with precision what each social class would need to know for success in its future work, health, recreation, family, religious, and other social activities. Whatever students could not learn on their own is what a school should provide. So, for example, a curriculum expert who wanted to devise a good agricultural course would observe farmers at work, talk to them, read about farming, and ascertain what specific skills and knowledge farmers need to know.[3]

Moreover, Bobbitt believed that schools were agencies of social progress and that they must endeavor to overcome and prevent deficiencies in the social order. If agricultural production falls off, he thought, the schools must provide better agricultural education. If factory production is inefficient, the schools must teach industrial education. When studies show the cost of ill health, the schools must provide health education. If large numbers of men are unfit for military duty, the schools must give military training. When traffic accidents become common, the schools must offer safety training. Everything taught in school must have a purpose. Studies such as history and literature were merely leisure activities, he held, and not more than one in a thousand students had any real need to learn a foreign language. Knowing a foreign language contributed nothing to personal hygiene, vocational efficiency, or community sanitation. It was, he said, "too expensive a method to require the same of the other 999 in order that the one be accommodated."[4]

In 1923, W. W. Charters suggested that it was time to "frankly accept *usefulness* as our aim rather than *comprehensive knowledge*." Like other progressives, Charters thought of himself as a man of science, in step with Darwinian evolutionary theory and committed to social progress, able to see the world as it was, not as reverential tradition and obsolete custom decreed. In the old days, he wrote, teachers had adopted "the works of the masters" as textbooks for children; instead of determining what was "most useful to the young in coping with the humble problems of their lives," teachers had insisted on teaching the "brilliant products of genius" during the first twelve years of school, and organized subject matter had "attained positions of almost unassailable strength." Obviously, the curriculum specialist faced the monumental task of cracking the monopoly of the established disciplines that teachers unthinkingly adhered to.[5]

Charters developed a technique he called "activity analysis," which would specify what youngsters needed to know to prepare for adult life. In the history of twentieth-century pedagogy, Charters probably deserves credit (or, more likely, blame) for originating the practice of creating elaborate lists of aims and objectives for planning educational programs in public schools. A list could be generated by a "duty analysis," an "informational analysis," a "difficulty analysis," or an analysis of "methods of performing duties." Suppose, for example, that a youth planned to be a department store clerk, responsible for credit applications. A "job analysis" (which apparently was the same as a "duty analysis") produced the following activities for which he must be prepared:

1. Meets people who desire to open accounts.
2. Asks them for the information to fill out blank.
3. Writes form letters or telephones for references.
4. Fills out Mercantile Agency blanks.
5. Looks up rating in Dunn's, etc.
6. Files applications temporarily till references come in.
7. Makes notes of references on blanks and hands to Credit Chief, who passes on them.
8. Enters name, address, and number of applications in index.
9. Answers requests from other firms for references.[6]

After the activities were specified, it was possible to identify the "ideals" that the job applicant needed; in the case of a credit clerk, these would include: "friendliness"; "ability to question tactfully"; "discrimination in using blanks"; "spirit of 'follow-up'"; "ability to summarize references"; "copying skill"; and "keen judgment in answering credit questions."[7]

According to Charters, curriculum construction in public schools should begin by listing the major objectives of schooling, such as citizenship, morality, social efficiency, and growth. After that was done, the curriculum maker would create one list of ideals and another of activities related to the work in which the student planned to engage, now or in the future. Based on these many lists, the curriculum maker would then prepare study units ranked in relation to the interests of the pupils, their difficulty, and their utility.

Charters recast every school subject in terms of its relationship to activities that were useful in adult life. Unlike some of his progressive contemporaries, he did not suggest discarding school subjects altogether. He thought of academic subjects such as chemistry, history, geography, and physics as "organized information," perhaps valuable as electives, prepared "from the specialists' point of view by those who are interested in specialists' problems."[8]

Textbooks by Bobbitt and Charters became required reading for future teachers and administrators in their professional training. Both men also advised school districts. Bobbitt's *How to Make a Curriculum* (1924) described his involvement in revising the curriculum of the Los Angeles public schools. Bobbitt declared "that education is to prepare men and women for the activities of every kind which make up, or which ought to make up, well-rounded adult life; that it has no other purpose; that everything should be done with a view to this purpose; and that nothing should be included which does not serve this purpose." The most important task of the schools, he believed, was to find out what men and women do and to make sure that children learn these things.[9]

Like Charters's, Bobbitt's method for determining the curriculum was activity analysis. The curriculum maker must focus relentlessly upon the actual activities of mankind. Which activities were most important in deciding what to teach? Bobbitt's list (of course, a list) included ten activities, including health, vocation, citizenship, recreation, parenting, and social intercommunication.

Bobbitt recommended that the curriculum maker take each of these major activities and develop another list of specific abilities. "Maintenance of physical efficiency," for example, suggested thirty-nine abilities, including the "ability to care for the skin," the "ability to care for the hair and scalp," and the "ability to care properly for the feet." Under the rubric of "general mental efficiency," there was the distinct possibility that intellectual development might remain one of the purposes of schools. There was something mind-numbingly technical about Bobbitt's approach to learning. Even when he referred to "delight," "appreciation," and "interest," such terms were simply ticked off as a small part of a lengthy, dry list of functional objectives. The study of literature was assigned fifty objectives; dozens and dozens of objectives were attached to the new field of social studies. Bobbitt could not understand why anyone would want to study Latin. In his view, no one needed to speak it or understand it; no one needed to read it or write it. He dismissed the claim that Latin helped students to function better in English as groundless "special pleading."[10]

Bobbitt and Charters not only created a new professional field, they made social efficiency the measure of good curriculum practice. According to historian Edward A. Krug, few school systems were willing to engage in the tedious and burdensome process of activity analysis, but educators enthusiastically embraced the idea that curriculum making was a specialized science. If its objectives were described as social rather than academic, they were presumed to be "inherently scientific."[11] By implication, curriculum objectives that related to the growth of students' knowledge or aesthetic appreciation were not scientific.

Spurred on by practical businessmen, economy-minded school board members, and the leading voices in their profession, educators tried to justify their schools on grounds of social efficiency, not the intellectual or cultural development of students. Educators were constantly reminded that it was modern and scientific to ask what social purpose was served by academic subjects, not whether they had any cultural or aesthetic value. Bobbitt and Charters, the fathers of scientific curriculum making, cast a long shadow over American schools for the balance of the twentieth century. Long after their names had been forgotten, public school administrators were dutifully cobbling together elaborate lists of goals and objectives to justify their curricula.

JOHN DEWEY AND THE CHILD-CENTERED MOVEMENT

At the same time that Bobbitt and Charters were paving the way for the scientific study of curriculum, the movement to create a child-centered curriculum emerged. The idea that the curriculum should be based on the needs and interests of children had an even longer pedigree than the claims of social efficiency.

The seminal text of the child-centered movement was Rousseau's *Émile*. Since its publication in 1762, it has inspired educational reformers in Europe and the United States who sought alternatives to routinized and formal schooling. In this celebrated book, Rousseau describes his program for Émile, an imaginary pupil whom he will educate naturally, free from the oppressive influence of society. It was ironic that Rousseau became a hero to progressives in the United States who were building state systems of public education, because he was hostile to social institutions and insisted that the best teacher for a child was his own father ("A child will be better brought up by a wise father however limited, than by the cleverest teacher in the world.")[12] He was a champion of home schooling, not public education. There was irony, too, in Rousseau's role as an adviser on parenting because he had abandoned his own five illegitimate children.

Rousseau opposed teaching either habits or lessons; his pupil would learn by experience, and the role of the tutor was to "do nothing and let nothing be done," so that the child would learn whatever he needed to know without instruction, keeping "the mind inactive as long as possible." His pupil would never learn anything "by heart," nor would he learn to read until he needed to. "Reading is the greatest plague of childhood," wrote Rousseau. "Émile at the age of twelve will scarcely know what a book is." Rousseau's strategy for learning was to rely on his pupil's needs and interests: "If nothing is to be exacted from children by way of obedience it follows that they will only learn what they feel to be of actual and present advantage, either because they like it, or because it is of use to them. Otherwise, what motive would they have for learning? . . . Present interest: that is the great motive impulse, the only one that leads sure and far."[13]

Rousseau's belief in education as "natural development" was an important influence on the American progressive education movement. His mark can be seen in the child study movement and the writings of G. Stanley Hall. John Dewey cited *Émile* as a reminder that what is learned in school is "relatively superficial" compared to what is learned in the ordinary course of living. Rousseau, he wrote, "was almost the first to see that learning is a matter of necessity; it is a part of the process of self-preservation and growth. If we want, then, to find out how education takes place most successfully, let us go to the experiences of children where learning is a necessity, and not to the practices of schools where it is largely an adornment, a superfluity and even an unwelcome imposition." Like Rousseau, Dewey rejected the rote learning and formalism of the public schools, especially the common belief that what was taught should be disagreeable so as to teach children to exercise their willpower and self-discipline. Dewey did note, however, that "if Rousseau himself had ever tried to educate any real children," he would have had to set some sort of fixed program.[14]

The Dewey School in Chicago

The most influential model for child-centered schooling in the United States was the Laboratory School, founded by John Dewey and his wife, Alice, at the University of Chicago in 1896. Dewey wanted to demonstrate that it was possible to teach significant ideas by using projects and activities that appealed to children's interests and unleashed their intellectual energies. In an admiring profile of his friend Dewey, the journalist Max Eastman wrote in 1941 that Dewey was "the man who saved our children from dying of boredom as we almost did in school." Eastman summed up Dewey's educational philosophy in these pithy terms: "If you provide a sufficient variety of activities, and there's enough knowledge lying around, and the teacher understands the natural relation between knowledge and interested action, children can have fun getting educated and will love to go to school."[15]

Teachers at the Dewey school created projects and activities to enliven the studies that were taught by rote in more traditional schools. They wanted to show that the traditional subjects, so often taught without any imagination, could be turned into exciting learning experiences. Far from being hostile to subject matter, they continually experimented with different ways of involving their young students in learning about primitive life in the Bronze Age; Phoenician civilization; early Greek civilization; the voyages and adventures of Marco Polo, Prince Henry of Portugal, Columbus, and other explorers; English village life in the tenth century, the story of William the Conqueror and his conquest of England, and the Crusades; American colonial history; the European background of the colonies; Shakespeare's plays; science; mathematics; algebra and geometry; English, French, and even Latin.[16]

The Dewey school, which existed only from 1896 until 1904, when

171

Dewey left the University of Chicago and moved to Columbia University, was very likely one of the most exciting schools in American history. Free from the bureaucratic demands of urban public education and free to select its staff and pupils, the Dewey school was able to assemble an extraordinary staff and to experiment with materials and methods. Pupils were encouraged to initiate and direct their own work, and they frequently engaged in activities such as sewing, spinning, weaving, cooking, gardening, carpentry, building, dramatics, storytelling, and re-creating basic occupations. Children became involved in social activities in which they could explore, create, and find out for themselves. The teachers wanted children to have firsthand experience, but they did not neglect "the accumulated knowledge and past experience of the race." The school was supposed to be like a home, in which experienced adults lovingly guided children to develop their social, physical, and intellectual capacities.[17]

Many of Dewey's disciples drew the wrong lessons from the Dewey school. They seemed to think that the liberation of children from formal instruction was an end in itself. Dewey did not agree. In 1902, while in charge of his school, he insisted that there was no conflict between child and curriculum, between the child's experiences and subject matter. The relationship between the child and the curriculum was a continuum, he wrote, not an opposition: "[T]he child and the curriculum are simply two limits which define a single process. Just as two points define a straight line, so the present standpoint of the child and the facts and truths of studies define instruction. It is continuous reconstruction, moving from the child's present experience out into that represented by the organizing bodies of truth that we call studies."[18]

The various school studies, such as arithmetic, geography, language, and botany, said Dewey, "are themselves experience—they are that of the race. They embody the cumulative outcome of the efforts, the strivings, and successes of the human race generation after generation. They present this, not as a mere accumulation, not as a miscellaneous heap of separate bits of experience, but in some organized and systematized way."[19] Unfortunately, many of Dewey's disciples treated subject matter as an outmoded relic from an antediluvian past. Over the years,

Dewey was far too tolerant of fellow progressives who adored children but abhorred subject matter, and who loved random experiences and cared not at all for connecting children's experience to the cumulative experience of the human race.

The Dewey school developed its own intelligence tests, the same kinds of tests that Galton in England and Binet in France were experimenting with. Eventually, the school introduced ability grouping. At the close of its third year, Dewey reported that

> When the school was small, it was intended to mix up the children,—the older and the younger—to the end that the younger might learn unconsciously from the older. . . . As the school grew, it became necessary to abandon this policy and to group the children with reference to their common capabilities or store of knowledge. These groups are based not on ability to read, write, etc., but on the basis of community of interest, general intellectual capacity and mental alertness, and the ability to do certain kinds of work.[20]

This remarkable school was like a Roman candle in American education, casting a vivid light of pedagogical dreams and possibilities and then disappearing to become a legend. It was an exemplar of what might be done under ideal conditions, but it was never reproduced except in elite private schools and in a very small number of public schools, and then only for relatively brief periods of time under the direction of a charismatic leader. No ordinary public school could re-create the extraordinary circumstances of this school, advantaged as it was by the leadership of John Dewey, a remarkable staff, highly educated parents, and a network of supportive intellectuals. Nor could the Dewey school serve as a model for the typical public school system, which was bound by rules and regulations, as well as by bureaucracy, civil service, and unions. The experimental nature of the Dewey school, as well as its environment of constant reflection and adjustment, guaranteed that it could not be translated into a "program" for a large bureaucratic structure.

Almost everything about the school was exceptional, including John

Dewey. Its student body was not representative of the Chicago population. As shown in photographs, all the students were white, and they were the children of affluent, professional families. In its last three years, the Dewey school had 140 children, 23 teachers, and 10 assistants (graduate students at the university). Thus there was one teacher for every five to six students, a ratio that would have been impossible to reproduce in the public schools, either at that time (when public school teachers regularly had classes of fifty or more pupils) or any time since then. Unlike the regular public schools, where teachers were assigned on the basis of seniority, sometimes ill prepared, the teachers at the Dewey school were carefully selected and were "specialists by taste and training—experts along different lines." The school's director of instruction was Ella Flagg Young, an outstanding educator who had been a supervisor in the Chicago school system. In addition, the school attracted students and instructors from the university's Department of Pedagogy, which Dewey chaired, as well as the active interest of prominent scientists and social scientists from the university faculty.[21]

The Dewey school sought to balance individual growth, social goals, and knowledge. As progressive education evolved in the 1920s and 1930s, this balance was often forgotten; instead, individual growth and social goals were exalted, but efforts to teach history, literature, foreign language, science, and mathematics were frequently disparaged.[22]

Schools of Tomorrow

John Dewey consistently criticized traditional education and praised experimental education, even when it ventured to the extremes of permissiveness. Dewey sometimes chided progressive educators for going too far in following children's whims, but at other times he encouraged and lauded the very same behavior. In the popular and influential *Schools of Tomorrow,* published in 1915, Dewey (and his coauthor, his daughter Evelyn) praised child-centered schools and echoed Rousseau and G. Stanley Hall, invoking "reverence for childhood" and "natural growth" in opposition to "adult accomplishments" and "information in the form of symbols."[23]

The Deweys' choice of exemplary "schools of tomorrow" showed the hazards of trying to predict the future. One of their featured schools was Public School 26 in Indianapolis, a racially segregated school in which black children learned trades such as carpentry, tailoring, shoemaking, and cooking; if anything, this school demonstrated how industrial education, then popular with progressive educators and philanthropists, would restrict students' opportunities for higher education. The Deweys also devoted a chapter to the public schools in Gary, Indiana, where an innovative superintendent (a former student of John Dewey) had designed a "platoon" system, rotating groups of children among classrooms, shop work, playground, and auditorium to permit maximal use of the school facilities. When Dewey was writing in 1915, the Gary school system was a favorite of progressive reformers, and the platoon system was adopted in many cities. However, it eventually came to be seen as a system that valued scientific management and economy over good education.[24]

Most of the schools that Dewey identified as "schools of tomorrow" were private, child-centered schools populated—like the Dewey school—by white children from upper-middle-class families. For example, he warmly praised Marietta Pierce Johnson's Organic School in Fairhope, Alabama, which was, according to historian Lawrence A. Cremin, "easily the most child-centered of the early experimental schools."[25] The Organic School featured a completely natural education, free of rewards, punishments, tests, grades, promotions, prohibitions, commands, and other pressures. It emphasized freedom, self-initiative, and spontaneity. Formal studies such as reading, writing, spelling, and arithmetic were delayed as long as possible; Johnson would have preferred to wait until children were ten but acceded to parents' demands to begin teaching these skills at eight. She believed that if children waited to read until they were ready, they would be as adept as those who started earlier.

On a brief visit to the school, Dewey was deeply impressed, seeing it as an incarnation of Rousseauian pedagogy. The main activities of the children, instead of the usual curriculum, were exercise, nature study, music, storytelling, dramatics, and games. Dewey wrote admiringly of children running from activity to activity, following their spontaneous interests, learning only when they felt the need. In a statement that raises questions about Dewey's knowledge of conditions in the public schools of 1914, when large classes were the rule, Dewey declared that "Mrs. Johnson is trying an experiment under conditions which hold in public schools, and she believes that her methods are feasible for any public school system."[26]

The Deweys selected Junius L. Meriam's elementary school at the University of Missouri in Columbia as another "school of tomorrow." Meriam had started the school in 1905 as a laboratory for the university's school of education. Like Johnson, Meriam believed that the schools of the past had pressured children too much by forcing adult facts on them. In his school, children learned only "when they need to do so. The pupils do in this school about what they would do at home, but they learn to do it better." What would they be doing if they did not go to school? They were "playing outdoors, exercising their bodies by running, jumping, or throwing; they would be talking together in groups, discussing what they had seen or heard; they would be making things to use in their play: boats, beanbags, dolls, hammocks, or dresses; if they live in the country they would be watching animals or plants, making a garden, or trying to fish." Dewey believed that what the child learns out of school is more apt to be remembered because it is pleasurable and useful, and further, "these occupations are all closely connected with the business of living; and we send our children to school to learn this. What, then, could be more natural than making the school's curriculum of such material?"[27]

Meriam's school day had four periods, one each for play, stories, observation, and handwork. During the observation period, the children might learn about flowers, trees, and fruits; the weather; holidays; the local jewelry store; the grocery store; the bakery; the fire department; or houses in the neighborhood. When it was time for play, the children played mostly competitive games. Neither Meriam nor the Deweys wondered why competition, extrinsic goals, and genuine performance standards were valuable in games but should be banished from the rest of the curriculum; these factors stimulated the children to do their best in play but were treated as undue pressure when it was time to learn academic subjects.

Meriam believed that the purpose of elementary school was *"To help boys and girls do better in all those wholesome activities in which they normally engage"* (italics in the original). He vehemently rejected the possibility that schools should help children prepare for the next grade or adult responsibilities. How could traditional studies compare in vitality to the children's own interests? "The teacher's arbitrary assignment of the next ten pages in history, or nine problems in arithmetic, or certain descriptions of geography, cannot be felt by the pupil as a real problem and a personal problem."[28]

Curiously, Meriam's determination to avoid imposing adult standards on his students disappeared when it came to choosing books and stories. He did not want children to select their own books because he thought that most of them would make poor choices. He believed that children needed suggestions by their teachers and that it was the duty of teachers to make sure that their students read good literature. Meriam compiled extensive reading lists of fables, fairy tales, myths, legends, travel stories, books about nature, history, and biography, novels and humor, which included such renowned authors as Nathaniel Hawthorne, Sir Walter Scott, Rudyard Kipling, Robert Louis Stevenson, Louisa May Alcott, Charles Dickens, and James Fenimore Cooper. Where literature was concerned, Meriam was unwilling to trust children's interests; he directed them to the authors whom he considered best, even though his preference for high literary standards was inconsistent with the rest of his philosophy.[29]

In addition to Marietta Pierce Johnson's Organic School and Meriam's Elementary School, more than a dozen other private child-centered schools were founded by upper-middle-class parents in various parts of the country, including the Play School (later known as City and Country School) in New York City; the Walden School in New York City; Shady Hill in Cambridge, Massachusetts; the Park School in Baltimore; and the Lincoln School at Teachers College. In 1919, their leaders joined to form the Progressive Education Association as an advocacy group for child-centered practices.[30]

KILPATRICK AND THE PROJECT METHOD

In 1918, William Heard Kilpatrick of Teachers College at Columbia University published his essay on "The Project Method." Other progressive educators immediately hailed it as the quintessential statement of the child-centered school movement.

Born in 1871 in Georgia, Kilpatrick majored in mathematics at Mercer University in Macon, Georgia, where (like others of his generation) he studied Latin and Greek. After graduate study at Johns Hopkins, he became a teacher and principal in the public schools of Georgia. Then, after a few years as professor of mathematics and acting president at Mercer (from which he resigned after being accused of atheism), Kilpatrick went to study at Teachers College in New York City in 1907.

Although he had planned to return to the South, he found himself at an institution "pervaded with messianic zeal" to which students flocked from all over the world, not just to earn credits but "to build a profession." In 1911, he joined the faculty of Teachers College, teaching courses in history and philosophy of education; over the course of his long career, he was a phenomenal success, attracting more students than any other professor at the college. During his twenty-seven years on the faculty, he taught some 35,000 students and was known as "the million-dollar professor" because of the student fees he generated.[31]

Kilpatrick embraced Dewey's ideas, which so well expressed his own perspective, and aspired to be his chief exponent. Soon after joining the faculty, Kilpatrick wrote in his diary, "I feel in some measure that I am best qualified of those about here to interpret Dewey. His own lectures are frequently impenetrable to even intelligent students." Despite Dewey's gospel of learning by doing, the great philosopher taught by standing in front of his class and lecturing. Kilpatrick was so impressed by Dewey's thought that, according to his biographer, he "was now committed to the experimental method in all areas of living. From now on he would accept no absolute! No principle, no faith, no authority, no dogma was sacrosanct, beyond criticism and beyond the test of man's intelligence."[32]

Kilpatrick thought of the project as not just a method but a fundamental reinvention of education. The project was an activity undertaken by students that really interested them. Kilpatrick, in his dense pedagogical language, called it "whole-hearted purposeful activity proceeding in a social environment." What was a typical project? A girl making a dress; a boy producing a school newspaper; a class presenting a play; a group of boys organizing a baseball team. If students were told to do something by their teacher, they would not do it wholeheartedly, so such activities would not qualify as projects by Kilpatrick's definition. The students must have a genuine purpose of their own and must really want to see the project through to a conclusion in a "whole-hearted" way.[33]

Kilpatrick made large claims for the project method. Because it demanded initiative on the part of students, he said that it shaped character and personality. Because it required activity, not docility, he called it the educational method precisely suited to a democracy. Because it relied on children's own purposes, he said that it enlarged their "interest span." Furthermore, it fulfilled Dewey's demand that education should be "life itself" and not merely a preparation for future living; what could be "a better preparation for later life than practice in living now?"

Even better, Kilpatrick insisted, the project method fully utilized the behavioristic "laws of learning" that Thorndike was supposed to have discovered. In contrast to assignments by the teacher, the "purposeful act" at the heart of the project method motivates the student, who mobilizes his inner resources and learns happily, willingly, and energetically. In contrast to the "customary, set-task sit-alone-at-your-own-desk procedure," which promotes "selfish individualism," the project method builds moral character. Ideally, children would pursue projects in a group, under the teacher's expert guidance, and the pressure of social approval would encourage conformity to "the ideals necessary for approved social life."[34]

Kilpatrick's admirers praised the project method as the answer to the ills of American education. Here was a method that promised to solve virtually every problem. It would motivate students, enable them to take the lead in their self-education, promote democratic citizenship, teach character, and unleash creativity; and it was in accord with pedagogical science too! It gave high priority to children's interests and low priority to the curriculum. It did not matter whether the activity was connected to any part of the traditional academic curriculum. Kilpatrick's article was a sensation; tens of thousands of readers ordered reprints.

Child-centered schools such as Junius Meriam's Laboratory School and Marietta Pierce Johnson's Organic School had been using child-directed purposeful activities in a social context for many years. But as his essay received national and international attention, Kilpatrick's name became synonymous with the project method. He was the most influential teacher in the nation's leading college of education, and his ideas resonated through the college's remarkable alumni network. By 1921, according to Kilpatrick, Teachers College had trained one of every seven teachers and "at least three out of every four educational supervisors" in the United States, as well as many foreign educators who attained leadership roles when they returned to their home countries.[35]

In 1925, Kilpatrick elaborated on his ideas in a book titled *Foundations of Method,* which became a staple of teacher education courses across the nation. Written as if it were a conversation between teachers taking a course on pedagogical methods, Kilpatrick's book was even more hostile to organized subject matter than his article of 1918. Says one imaginary teacher, speaking in Kilpatrick's voice:

> As I see it, our schools have in the past chosen from the whole of life certain intellectualistic tools (skills and knowledge), have arranged these under the heads of reading, arithmetic, geography, and so on, and have taught these separately as if they would, when once acquired, recombine into the worthy life. This now seems to me to be very far from sufficient. Not only do these things not make up the whole of life; but we have so fixed attention upon the separate teaching of these as at times to starve the weightier matters of life and character. The only way to learn to live well is to practice living well.

At another point, Kilpatrick's imaginary teacher complains that the old way was to decide what children should learn, teach it to them, and then test them to see if they had learned it. This, it turns out, was all wrong, because it left out open-mindedness, critical thinking, concern for the common good, and other characteristics that could not be assigned or tested. Thus, the most important characteristics of a democratic citizen were being sacrificed to things such as reading, arithmetic, and geography, which could be assigned and tested.[36]

The starting point of curriculum construction, Kilpatrick asserted, was to learn what children were interested in and know how to stimulate these interests: "Most people get into trouble by choosing first what children should learn, then hunting about for the best way to teach it." Kilpatrick firmly opposed the idea of "sugar-coating" subject matter by trying to make it interesting. He insisted that the curriculum must begin with the child's interests, not with subject matter selected in advance. The starting point for teaching was not race experience, but child experience. Whatever is taught in school, he claimed, should be taught "when and because it was needed as a way-of-behaving right then and there."[37]

Although Kilpatrick had been trained in mathematics, he came to believe that the subject "had little in it to serve the needs and interests of children, or for that matter grownups." It was merely a game and a puzzle. He considered mathematical study to be "harmful rather than helpful" to the thinking needed for ordinary living, and he objected to teaching advanced mathematics to students who were not planning to go to college. In an address to university students in Florida, he said, "We have in the past taught algebra and geometry to too many, not too few. Algebra and mathematics based on algebra are essential to civilization, but practically useless to most citizens." Kilpatrick's admiring biographer Samuel Tenenbaum described a graduate class of more than six hundred teachers and administrators—presumably Kilpatrick's—voting that Greek, Latin, and mathematics "offered the least likely possibilities for educational growth," as compared to "dancing, dramatics, and doll playing."[38]

Kilpatrick's negative view of mathematics was not unique; he had the same antipathy toward all academic subjects, especially if they were set out in advance as something to be taught, learned, and tested. Education, he insisted, must be about "character and personality, not the acquisition of bookish information." Instead of subjects learned and material mastered, Kilpatrick sought *"activity leading to further activity"* (italics his) and "growth in richness of life and growth in control over experience. . . . If we can each day get him [the child] to do better than the day before, we can gradually build up a finer quality of living. The details of doing it are as infinite as there are children and situations that go on. What I should like to leave in reference to tomorrow is that your curriculum is the living. It is the living of children. It is the content of what they live."[39]

Kilpatrick's hostility to subject matter stood in contrast to the practice at the Dewey school in Chicago, where teachers planned carefully how to make history, mathematics, and science more interesting to students. Projects and activities were devised to achieve a curricular purpose. Yet Dewey never rebuked his disciple, never dissociated himself from Kilpatrick's view that how children learn is critically important but what they learn is irrelevant. Near the end of his long life, Dewey wrote a warm introduction to a biography of Kilpatrick, declaring that "progressive education and the work of Dr. Kilpatrick are virtually synonymous" and that "Dr. Kilpatrick has never fallen a victim to the one-sidedness of identifying progressive education with child-centered education." Dewey meant that Kilpatrick was equally concerned with children's interests and social reform; he did not mean that Kilpatrick saw any value in teaching subject matter, which was the customary criticism directed at child-centered education.[40]

Kilpatrick's ideas had a wide influence, for they offered practical applications of Dewey's philosophy and Thorndike's psychology. In the 1920s, they were taken as scientific justification for child-centered schools, most of which were private; in the 1930s, they were understood as the pedagogical underpinnings of a widespread campaign to eliminate academic subjects or merge them into new configurations in elementary, junior high, and high schools.

By the mid-1920s, progressive education was viewed by most educationists as the wave of the future, and child-centered schooling was its defining idea. The biggest obstacle to change, however, was the fact that parents and teachers did not understand the revolution that was under way. Child-centered schooling was well established in a small number of private schools but not yet in public schools. Education elites, however, urged its acceptance in public education. Even President Warren G. Harding's commissioner of education, John J. Tigert, praised the new methods associated with progressive education and complained about the conservatism of teachers who were blindly clinging to the practices that had predated the scientific movement in education.[41]

The Lincoln School

The single most influential showcase for progressive methods was the Lincoln School at Teachers College, established in 1917 by the Rockefeller Foundation's General Education Board as a laboratory school to determine whether children could be taught through firsthand experiences instead of abstract, "bookish training." Abraham Flexner, the founding father of the Lincoln School, persuaded the trustees of the General Education Board to endow the school on the hope that a model school, "quite modern in curriculum and discipline," would affect American education just as "one modest but sound institution," the Johns Hopkins Medical School, had influenced medical education (Flexner's 1910 report to the Carnegie Foundation on medical education had led to major reforms in medical colleges).

Each year, thousands of educators came to observe Lincoln's program of activities and projects. Teachers carefully recorded how children responded to different approaches and materials. The elementary grades featured topics that interested children and urged them to initiate their own activities. As topics developed, the teacher introduced elements of science, art, history, and other subjects; students learned skills such as reading and writing as they needed them to carry out their projects. In the junior high grades, academic subjects were merged or embedded in activities. Only the high school taught specific subject matter, because students needed to be prepared for college entrance requirements. Latin and Greek, however, were excluded from the curriculum at

Flexner's specific request, although he himself had taught the classical languages in a private school that he founded in Louisville and insisted that Greek had been his favorite study.[42]

Elementary children would build a play city of blocks and boxes, with houses, stores, a fire station, streets, automobiles, and so on. This activity would be accompanied by measuring, counting, dramatization, and painting, as well as science lessons about transportation, hygiene, and nature study. From the building of the city would come a study of how a city gets its food, leading to several weeks devoted to the study of farm life. A visit to a dairy farm would be followed by dozens of questions about cows and dairy farming. Students in the sixth grade studied "how man has made records or books through the ages," which involved field trips to museums and libraries, even a paper mill. Students learned about clay tablets, the Rosetta stone, wax tablets, and hieroglyphics; they learned about the illuminated manuscripts of the Middle Ages, the history of printing, and the technology of the printing press; they also learned about civilizations such as Egypt, Mesopotamia, China, Phoenicia, and the monks of the Middle Ages. The past was studied in lively ways, not ignored.[43]

Like the Dewey school at the University of Chicago, the Lincoln School was intended to be an experimental institution in which to try out new methods and materials. Like the Dewey school, it had a small number of students for each teacher. Unlike the Dewey school, its program of research and experimentation was munificently endowed by private funding for many years. It opened in 1917 with 116 students; a decade later, its enrollment was nearly 500 children in twelve grades. About one third of the students received scholarship assistance, but most students came from professional and socially elite families, including the Rockefellers, Vanderbilts, and Gimbels. Needless to say, the student body was not typical of the city's population: students at Lincoln scored, on average, more than one year higher on IQ tests than their public school counterparts. The teachers, too, were exceptionally talented and energetic, drawn not from a civil service list but from those who sought the challenge of working in an experimental school.

Despite progressive rhetoric about avoiding "bookish" learning, the students were constantly exposed to the best of high culture. In an English class for children aged twelve and thirteen, for example, students wrote plays based on their reading of Alexandre Dumas's *The Three Musketeers,* Charlotte Brontë's *Jane Eyre,* John Ruskin's *The King of the Golden River,* Henry Wadsworth Longfellow's "Evangeline," and Lewis Carroll's *Alice's Adventures in Wonderland.* The librarian of the school, Anne T. Eaton, insisted that students must exercise "individual choice," but their choice was limited to carefully screened books: "This chance for individual choice within the limits of the books which can be properly read, provides a better opportunity for promoting a taste for the best in literature than does the method of giving each one the same 'best thing' to read. The 'best thing' is not the same for all of us; one child may eagerly devour *Robinson Crusoe,* another of the same age may greatly prefer the *Arabian Nights,* or the same child may want *Robinson Crusoe* one week and the *Arabian Nights* the next."[44] The school compiled lists of books recommended by junior high school students, which included classic works by such writers as Charles Dickens, Arthur Conan Doyle, George Eliot, Rudyard Kipling, Herman Melville, Sir Walter Scott, Robert Louis Stevenson, and Jules Verne.

High school students took an "integrated" course in social studies, literature, and fine arts, taught by three teachers, which centered on six Greek cities. Students in the course were thoroughly immersed in Greek life and civilization, studying ancient Greece's sports, dress, myths, commerce, temples, customs, religion, food, government, and weapons. They read Homer, Aeschylus, Sophocles, and Pindar in English, and they learned about the Persian wars, the Peloponnesian wars, and the rise of Macedon. They visited museums, listened to phonograph recordings of Greek poems and dramas, made pottery, and occasionally listened to lectures.

B. J. R. Stolper, the English teacher who organized this course, also taught world literature in the high school, where students read Egyptian, Babylonian, Hindu, Hebrew, Chinese, and Greek masterpieces in translation; in the early 1930s, with political concerns at a high pitch, Stolper's students read such works as Plato's *Republic,* Thomas More's *Utopia,* Edward Bellamy's *Looking Backward,* Francis Bacon's *New At-*

lantis, and H. G. Wells's *Men like Gods* and compared their readings to developments in Fascist Italy, Nazi Germany, Soviet Russia, and the United States under the New Deal. Experimental though it was, the Lincoln School never abandoned the classics.[45]

According to historian Lawrence A. Cremin, "no single progressive school exerted greater or more lasting influence on the subsequent history of American education" than the Lincoln School. Educators across the nation sought out the school's course models, making it an informal but very effective national curriculum development center. The school's "units of work" were diffused to elementary schools in other cities and states; the Lincoln influence could be seen wherever small children worked informally in small groups on projects or used a reading center or science center, instead of sitting quietly at individual desks. The teacher-researchers at Lincoln wrote articles and books, delivered speeches at national conventions, consulted with other schools and districts, and aided the burgeoning curriculum revision movement.[46]

By 1930, Lincoln's energetic staff had given 2,800 talks to professional organizations across the nation and served as advisers to scores of school districts. School officials in Houston, Denver, Pittsburgh, Chicago, Baltimore, and Greenville, South Carolina, credited Lincoln staff for their reforms. In response to the urging of Lincoln educators, experimental schools were opened in Cleveland, Rochester, Denver, Chicago, and Saint Louis; these institutions collaborated with Lincoln and used many of its curriculum materials. In addition, Lincoln teachers taught summer courses for public school teachers; in 1921, for example, twenty-one Lincoln staff offered instruction in eleven different teacher-training programs.

Their greatest impact, however, was undoubtedly at Teachers College, where in the 1920s Lincoln staff taught more than two hundred different courses on subjects ranging from curriculum construction to teaching reading, mathematics, and science. As Lincoln teachers left to join institutions of higher education, they disseminated Lincoln's ideas; one organized a laboratory school at the University of Michigan, two at the University of California played a leading role in statewide curriculum reform, and a group established a program at Montclair (New Jersey) State Teachers College. By 1938, former teachers from Lincoln held positions in twenty university departments of education and ten normal schools.

The Lincoln School also spread its influence through the widely circulated books of its teacher-researchers. Lincoln teacher William Hughes Mearns demonstrated the value of creative writing, even for young children; Satis Coleman involved children in making musical instruments and playing music. Harold Rugg's twelve-volume social science textbooks for junior high school sold more than 600,000 copies and were used by schools in forty states; between 1920 and 1940, they were read by more than 5 million children. Although Rugg's textbooks were driven out of the public schools in the late 1930s by right-wing extremists who objected to Rugg's political views, his lasting (if dubious) contribution was the creation of the field of "social studies," which diminished the role of history and emphasized current events.

The public schools quickly absorbed the forms and processes developed at Lincoln, but few preserved the intellectual rigor that underlay most of Lincoln's projects and activities. Elementary school teachers and principals around the nation learned from Lincoln how to create activities and projects. The work at the Lincoln School inspired what was called "the activity movement" in elementary classrooms across the nation and curricular "integration" (merging different subjects into one course) in junior high schools and high schools. The common thread of both the activity movement and the integration movement was deemphasis of instruction, subject matter, and reading, which was a misinterpretation of Lincoln's model.

The lesson that some public school officials drew from the Lincoln example was that learning occurred naturally, while children were involved in interesting experiences and activities; they also gathered that there was no point in hurrying children to learn, nor was there much reason to teach spelling or punctuation. Surrounded by interesting materials and worthwhile activities, children would presumably be motivated to read and write when they were ready and would pick up the conventions of language without any direct instruction.

As for punctuation, the Lincoln example may have misled public schools. Lincoln conducted an experiment in teaching punctuation to two matched groups of seventh-graders: one group received drill (that is, conscious practice), the other did not. At the end of the experiment, the students who had been drilled had gained three times as much in punctuation skills as the group that had not been drilled. However, the school decided that since both groups were far above the national norm, further drill would not be "either wise or desirable."[47] This was an instance in which the high socioeconomic standing of Lincoln students rendered an experiment meaningless; what might have been an important finding for students at ordinary public schools was dismissed as unnecessary for the socially advantaged students at the Lincoln School. In all of the excitement about Lincoln's innovative work, little attention was given to the problem of reluctant learners; perhaps at Lincoln they did not exist. Not enough thought was given to the social gulf between the pupils at Lincoln, whose parents were affluent and well educated, and the great majority of children in the nation's public schools, whose parents were neither.

The Spread of
the Curriculum Revision Movement

By the mid-1920s, the new pedagogical trends began to make a significant impact on the nation's public schools. A curriculum revision movement got under way, concentrated in the cities. The best exemplars of the curriculum revision movement were featured in the 1926 yearbook of the National Society for the Study of Education, an organization that represented the nation's pedagogical leaders. The yearbook showcased the accomplishments of curriculum making, a field of study that had been virtually nonexistent a scant decade earlier, and it demonstrated the advance of progressive curricular practices. A large section of the massive yearbook was allocated to "private laboratory schools," such as the Lincoln School, the Beaver Country Day School in Brookline, Massachusetts, the City and Country School in New York City, the Walden School in New York City, and Marietta Pierce Johnson's Organic School in Fairhope, Alabama.

But the real news in the volume was the curriculum changes in the public schools. The yearbook offered "examples of progressive curriculum-construction" in several cities, including Detroit, Denver, Saint Louis, and Los Angeles. A survey of public elementary schools in 132 cities reported that "we are in a transition period of vigorous experimentation and change." A survey of the high schools concluded that the curriculum was rapidly changing, so much so that "if changes should proceed at the present rate for a single generation, the curriculum might easily assume a form which would make it almost unrecognizable." High schools were adding subjects much faster than they were dropping them, and "for every subject dropped, almost three were added." The subjects likeliest to disappear were ancient and modern foreign languages; the subjects most often added were "social science" (in place of history), commercial subjects, industrial arts, and home economics.[48]

The most thorough curriculum revision was implemented in Winnetka, Illinois, under the leadership of school superintendent Carleton Washburne. After Washburne's arrival in 1919, the Winnetka schools launched two major initiatives: one to determine what children needed to know to function successfully in contemporary society, the other to develop methods to help them learn what they needed to know.

To find out what children needed to know, Winnetka teachers carried out "an exhaustive study of the common allusions to persons and places in periodical literature, recognizing that in order to read intelligently a person must have familiarity with these persons and places." The principle employed was that "If a certain bit of knowledge or skill is necessary to practically every normal person, every child should have an opportunity to master it. There should not be excellent grasp for some, good for others, fair for others, and poor for still others—there should be real mastery for every child." Winnetka educators recognized that some children needed extra time to achieve mastery and might also need different methods or instructional materials. After they decided what knowledge and which skills children needed to learn, the staff then individualized instruction, so that each child could work at his or her own pace on "self-instructive, self-corrective practice materials."[49]

The Winnetka approach to education used the methods of progressive education—individualized instruction, group projects, creative activities, and motivation through students' interest—to reach the goals of traditional education: knowledgeable and skilled students. Instead of rejecting spelling, penmanship, phonics, grammar, and arithmetic as unimportant, Washburne and his teachers tried to figure out the best ways to teach them; they carefully tested and tabulated each pupil's progress. They developed new teaching materials and wrote new textbooks; they conducted research to see whether the pace of instruction was too fast or too slow. Washburne pursued a very practical course of action by asking: What do children need to know and be able to do to succeed in this society? How can we help every child learn those things? How should we change our methods and materials? How do we know if children are making progress?[50]

Unfortunately, Carleton Washburne's practical model of progressive methods wedded to traditional ends never won the acclaim it deserved. By all accounts, the public schools of Winnetka did a superb job of educating their students; yet their approach lacked the drama and flair that surrounded some of the nationally recognized private laboratory schools. Nor did Washburne command a national stage to the same extent as the gurus of the Teachers College faculty. Harold Rugg, one of progressivism's superstars, dismissed the Winnetka program as "tinkering with the school curriculum."[51]

The Winnetka approach was out of step with the reigning ideological passions of progressive education: it did not base the curriculum on activity analysis, as Bobbitt and Charters proposed; it did not base the curriculum on child interests, as Kilpatrick insisted; it did not liberate the child from social norms, as child-centered advocates wanted; it did not claim to be a program to reform society, as other progressives urged. It merely claimed to do a better job of educating children, individualizing instruction, and encouraging group projects and individual creativity. But that commonsense approach did not capture the hearts and minds of other progressives.

Harold Rugg and Curriculum Reform

*When it came to discerning the emerging trends in the progressive edu-*cation movement, no one was better than Harold Rugg. Rugg was a barometer of the movement; his enthusiasms both reflected and shaped the changing scene. Educated as a civil engineer at Dartmouth College, Rugg earned a doctorate in education at the University of Illinois with a dissertation on the teaching of mathematics (Bagley was his faculty sponsor). During the First World War, Rugg was one of the educational psychologists who developed the Army intelligence tests. In 1920, he joined the staff at the Lincoln School and the faculty at Teachers College. Although he began his career as a statistician and psychologist, expecting to contribute to the new science of education, at the Lincoln School Rugg shifted gears, committing himself to reconstructing the curriculum. He spent several years developing a new social studies curriculum intended to replace traditional courses in history, geography, and civics with a unified study of all the social sciences. As a result of his experiences at Lincoln, Rugg championed both child-centered education and social reform. He combined in his own person the often discordant tendencies in the progressive education movement and saw no contradiction between a curriculum that grew out of children's interests and an educational program that would reform society.

Rugg was a national leader in the curriculum field. As editor and chief writer of the 1926 yearbook of the National Society for the Study of Education, he assembled the dozen leading curriculum experts and somehow got everyone to agree on a consensus statement about what American children should be learning. The statement was bland enough for everyone to sign, even though it was written in progressivist language with numerous invocations of the needs of children and society but no reference at all to specific subjects such as science, mathematics, history, geography, or foreign languages, nor any suggestion that all children should have access to a common curriculum for six or eight years.

Each of the signatories penned a supplementary statement, and it was clear that the chasm between the extremes was wide indeed. At one end was Rugg, who declared passionately that "it is not refinement of existing 'subjects' that is most sorely needed; it is, rather, the radical reconstruction of the entire school curriculum." Rugg averred that this radical reconstruction must meld together a "comprehensive and scientific

191

study of society" and "the interests and doings of children." The goal, he argued, must be to close the gap between the curriculum and "the content of American life," to construct the curriculum "out of the very materials of American life—not from academic relics of Victorian precedents." He wanted the public school, through its curriculum, to become "a competent instrument for social improvement." Rugg cautioned that "the tasks of curriculum-making are manifold and difficult and can be carried on effectively only by professionally equipped specialists."[52] In other words, this complex business of determining the needs of society and children was not to be carried out by ordinary teachers and local school officials; it could be done properly only by professional specialists who had been trained in university programs.

At the opposite pole from Rugg was William C. Bagley, now well established in his role as the profession's leading dissident, arguing that what was needed was not radical reconstruction but "a further refinement of materials and their better adaptation to the capacities of the learner." Bagley insisted that the job of American schools was to educate all children well and that this would happen only when there were better methods, better materials, and better-prepared teachers. He warned against radical changes, which he believed were virtually doomed to fail: "As in biological evolution, the chances that a variation will mean real improvement become smaller the more extreme is the change." He urged that "wherever possible, radical proposals should be subjected to controlled experimental tests before being put into effect on a wide scale." It was precisely these kinds of utterances that kept Bagley in hot water with his colleagues at Teachers College. Bagley pointed out that the most important "complicating factor" in curriculum planning was the mobility of the American people; many people would not spend their adult lives in the same community where they had been schooled. Given this fact, he proposed that the school curriculum should not be based on the "needs of the local community" but should aim to provide a curriculum, at least in the elementary school, "that will be the nucleus of a common culture for the children of the nation."[53]

Bagley could not resist chiding his fellow curriculum makers by reminding them that the general public "has a very high regard for literacy, both numerical and linguistic" and that it expected the elementary schools to teach the basics well. The general public continued to hold a "firm faith in certain one-time virtues now generally discredited in our profession—notably 'thoroughness' and 'discipline' (both mental and moral)." The public, in other words, "finds it difficult to understand many of the current proposals for educational reform. . . . If there is a recognizable public demand, it is not at all for what the profession regards as 'progressive' reform. It is rather for simplification and for an emphasis upon materials and processes in which the profession has pretty largely lost its faith." And here was the nub of a huge problem: "In no other country are the professional students of education so influential. In no other country is school practice so quickly responsive to the suggestions emanating from this group. We may stigmatize our schools as 'static,' 'reactionary,' 'slow to change,'—reluctant to adopt what we, in our wisdom, prescribe. But compared with other countries, ours is the educational expert's paradise."[54]

Bagley clearly was an exile in this experts' paradise. He continually wrote and said things that few of his peers agreed with. He did not share their enthusiasms. He understood that a yawning gap was opening between the theories of the progressive educators and the expectations of the American public. Although appeals to democracy had become a mantra among educationists, Bagley failed to understand how the profession could embark on programs that had so little public support. He kept reminding his colleagues that the public schools belonged to the public and that what the public wanted for its children should not be dismissed out of hand. He too thought that the schools should improve society. But he did not believe that his colleagues' proposals would produce either good teachers or good schools.

Bagley's warnings persuaded none of his peers. The child-centered movement continued to roll relentlessly forward, buoyed by the enthusiasm of professional leaders such as Kilpatrick and Rugg and by faith that child-centered schools were in the vanguard of educational reform.

→ → ← ←

Already recognized as one of the leading figures in American education, Harold Rugg proclaimed in 1928 that the child-centered school—the

193

school that put its faith in radical change, not tinkering or evolution—embodied the "true Educational Revolution." In their book *The Child-Centered School,* Rugg and coauthor Ann Shumaker waxed ecstatic about the new education, and their contrast between the new schools and the "conventional school" portrayed Manichean opposites. The new schools were based on "Freedom, not restraint. Pupil initiative, not teacher initiative. The active, not the passive, school . . . [and] child interest as the orienting center of the school program" rather than school subjects. The old education, they charged, had been puritanical, imitative, and conformist; the new education would unleash creativity, self-expression, and originality. The old education had been dedicated to discipline and logical organization of subject matter, while the new education was boldly inspired by "the concept of Self." The teachers in the child-centered schools were "artist-philosophers," "enthusiastic rebels," and "fiery individualists," while the teacher in a conventional school was a domineering taskmaster, "a blind, helpless cog in the great machine of enforced mass education."[55] Advocates of the child-centered school believed that they were in step with the latest Freudian theories, introducing new ideas about child rearing that would liberate children from anxiety-provoking discipline and punishment. The dichotomy was sharp: on one side lay freedom and blissful activity; on the other, a joyless regime of order and control.

The new schools excelled in the arts. They were far in advance of traditional schools in incorporating arts and crafts into the daily life of the school, not as an add-on but as the center of the curriculum. Rugg and Shumaker elaborated upon the importance of rhythm in these schools, devoting two chapters to "the rhythmic basis of life," the incorporation of rhythm into almost every kind of study, and the relationship between rhythm and individuality. Instead of subject matter, the child-centered schools used "activities," "units of work," and "centers of interest," and whatever was taught was supposed to spring from children's interests and to promote experiences and doing.

Rugg and Shumaker recognized significant shortcomings in the child-centered schools. Because these schools prized spontaneity, they abhorred the idea of a planned curriculum; little or no attention was paid to what children were supposed to learn, so that "seemingly only by accident do basic epochs and movements of history get included in the course of study." Having rejected the "subject-matter-set-out-to-be-learned" that was typical of the old education, many of the new schools strenuously avoided any sort of intellectual development or intellectual rigor. Having discarded the old regime's slogan of "knowledge for knowledge's sake," they seemed to have adopted a slogan of "activity for activity's sake." Rugg and Shumaker complained that the child-centered schools were "too often conspicuous examples of following the path of least resistance." The authors counseled the new schools to make sure that their students mastered essential knowledge and skills. They even advised the child-centered schools to overcome their hatred of drill and practice; after all, they said, the development of skill in any activity requires repetition.[56]

Despite the "apparent anarchy" in some child-centered classrooms, Rugg and Shumaker concluded that "their defects sink into insignificance compared to the revolutionary contribution of the new schools." This handful of schools, "alone in the midst of a great mechanized system of a million teachers, recognized the inadequacy of the philosophy of subject-matter-set-out-to-be-learned, discarded the concept of knowledge for knowledge's sake, and explored vigorously the concept of freedom." These schools, predicted Rugg and Shumaker, provided an ideal "that will orient and redirect next-step applications in town and city systems." The richest promise of the new schools, they concluded, was that public school teachers everywhere could bring about "a similar revolution" in their own schools.[57]

Rugg later admitted that many of the new child-centered schools had been chaotic: "In rebelling against the regimentation of children they went too far in the other direction, defining freedom as complete 'absence of restraint.' . . . In some cases liberty was extended to license. In their first years most of the new schools were too garrulous, noisy and not too clean. While they were active, alive, and experimental, the fine balance of freedom and control which makes for child initiative, regard for order and for other personalities, was lacking in many of them." Many failed to balance "discipline and initiative. . . . Indeed, the original Dewey Laboratory School had such a reputation for disorderliness, it led to a thoroughgoing misinterpretation of Dewey's theories."[58]

But Rugg did not understand why a reputation for disorderliness, indiscipline, and license might repel some parents. Passionately devoted to self-expression and creative freedom, he tended to consider those who did not share his views to be backward Puritans. Like many other progressives, he believed that the public schools clung to subject matter and traditional methods only because they were controlled by conservative, business-dominated boards that did not represent public opinion; if such boards were elected, he believed, it was only because the public was not truly educated. He could see no reason for subject-centered schools other than unthinking conformity to obsolete tradition.

How did he reconcile his relentless advocacy of child-centered schools with the public's apparent preference for orderly, subject-centered schools? He did not discern in himself a certain intellectual arrogance and condescension toward the benighted mass of people who did not see the world as he did. His engineering background led him to believe that he could identify the correct answers to problems through careful analysis. Those who failed to see the light, he felt, needed to be educated. Once they learned what he knew, they would see that he was right. The great mass of people suffered from cultural lag; they simply didn't yet understand what the experts did. With more time and education, they would understand, and once they understood, they would give their consent.

Curriculum Revision in the Public Schools

Harold Rugg had good reason to feel encouraged about the future direction of education. By the mid-1920s, progressive principles of curriculum making were winning adherents in small and large districts across the country.

After taking a summer course with Rugg at Teachers College, the superintendent of schools in Burlington, Iowa, invited Rugg, Kilpatrick, and other professors to help revamp the district's curriculum. Based on their recommendations, separate subjects were eliminated from the curriculum, which was reorganized into four activity units: Language Activities, Health and Happiness, Social Science (Living Together), and Mathematics and Construction. The Health and Happiness unit included hygiene, natural science, art, music, and inspirational literature, all of which were to be taught with the goal of "healthy, happy living." In a typical fourth-grade project, students considered what it takes to make a happy home; having determined that a happy home must have "right-acting people, clean and attractive surroundings, including interior and exterior decorations," the students designed, built, and decorated a model home. After revising the curriculum in Burlington, the superintendent left to become headmaster of a private progressive school.[59]

Denver launched an extensive curriculum revision project under the leadership of Superintendent Jesse Newlon. Teachers were involved in every phase of the work, guided by specialists from university schools of education. The teachers studied the theory of curriculum construction, read the work of leading thinkers, and learned about various experiments. Eventually Denver teachers reached the point, wrote Newlon and his deputy Archie L. Threlkeld, where they were ready to consider what should be taught "from the point of view of the pupils' needs." Educators had to decide which subjects were most useful to students and eliminate those that did not have immediate value in the student's life. The content of and methods of teaching home economics classes, for example, were determined by surveying which activities girls participated in at home. Commercial courses were revised after studying practices in Denver offices. A three-year course in social studies, organized around problems rather than subjects, was adopted for the junior high schools. Latin survived, because of tradition, college entrance requirements, and public opinion, even though the curriculum revisers did not see its purpose. Superintendent Newlon recognized that curriculum revision would be slowed in a public school system by "the force of tradition and of public opinion," as well as by conservative teachers who were out of sympathy with "modern thought" in education. In 1927, Newlon left public education to become head of the Lincoln School at Teachers College.[60]

More and more elementary schools were adopting the principles of child-centered schools, where the program consisted of units and activities derived from children's interests, instead of subject matter. In the high schools, most public schools offered differentiated curricula, specifically to provide an array of vocational programs for students of widely differing abilities. By 1923–24, Los Angeles offered students a choice among eighteen different curricula, including agricultural, accounting, secretarial, mechanic arts, printing, building industry, automobile industry, and salesmanship. In Newton, Massachusetts, there were fifteen, including classical, clerical, electricity, printing, and household arts. Saint Louis had thirteen; Joliet, Illinois, had sixteen; New Orleans had ten.[61]

Progressives often complained that the traditional subject matter curriculum continued to dominate the public schools, especially the high schools, but their own ideas advanced steadily. Bobbitt and Charters had established curriculum making as a profession; every school of education established a curriculum department to train specialists, and school districts and states began to hire their own curriculum directors and revise their curricula. Growing numbers of public school systems were implementing activity programs in their elementary schools. Among the nation's educational leadership, not only in the colleges of education but also in the states and even the U.S. Bureau of Education, there was a broadly shared consensus that the solutions to the problems of American education had been discovered and all that was needed for their complete success was to win over (or outlast) conservative teachers, administrators, and parents. Time was on the reformers' side.

CRITICAL VOICES

Not all progressive educators were comfortable with the flow of events, however. In a 1930 symposium on "The New Education, Ten Years After," in *The New Republic,* Boyd H. Bode of Ohio State University remarked querulously that "To the casual observer, American education is a confusing and not altogether edifying spectacle. It is productive of endless fads and panaceas; it is pretentiously scientific and at the same time pathetically conventional; it is scornful of the past, yet painfully inarticulate when it speaks of the future." Bode noted that the common bond between practitioners of the "scientific method" in education (such as Bobbitt and Charters) and the champions of child-centered schools was their rejection of traditional education. But the weakness of the new educational movements, he pointed out, "is that they have no program to offer as a substitute for the one they seek to replace. . . . The lack of concern for the scientific organization of subject matter that is shown by the newer movements in education is an ominous fact. It tends to justify the suspicion that they seek to achieve the ends of education by a kind of magic." Bode worried that the new educational movement had no guiding philosophy, no program, no sense of direction other than to oust the old education.[62]

Criticism came from another unexpected quarter: John Dewey. Even as the champions of "free expression for the child" multiplied, Dewey ridiculed their ideas. Noting that schools tended to veer between extremes of external imposition and "development from within," Dewey criticized both but directed his harshest comments to his own followers:

> There is a present tendency in so-called advanced schools of thought . . . to say, in effect, let us surround pupils with certain materials, tools, appliances, etc., and then let pupils respond to these things according to their own desires. Above all, let us not suggest any end or plan to the students; let us not suggest to them what they shall do, for that is an unwarranted trespass upon their sacred intellectual individuality. . . . Now such a method is really stupid. For it attempts the impossible, which is always stupid; and it misconceives the conditions of independent thinking.[63]

Dewey pointed out that it was the responsibility of experienced adults to guide children in their learning, not to insulate them from adult guidance. Surely, he wrote, the teacher has as much right to make suggestions to the child as does a head carpenter who lets apprentices know what they are expected to do.

In 1928, John Dewey warned the Progressive Education Association that the time had come for progressive education to advance the science of education or risk irrelevance. He observed that "if they do not *intellectually* organize their own work, while they may do much in making the lives of children committed to them more joyous and more vital, they contribute only incidental scraps to the science of education." Dewey recognized that the experimental school valued improvisation, "yet if it permits improvisation to dictate its course, the result is a jerky, discontinuous movement which works against the possibility of making any important contribution to educational subject-matter." Noting with disapproval that progressive schools were often hostile to planning, organization, and subject matter, he suggested that "much of the energy that sometimes goes to thinking about individual children might better be devoted to discovering some worthwhile activity and to arranging the conditions under which it can be carried forward."[64]

Rebuking those who idealized "learning by doing," Dewey pointed out that "Bare doing, no matter how active, is not enough." Nor was it enough to surround children with wonderful materials and tools and let them do whatever they wanted. How would children know what to do? If they merely acted on a chance idea, its interest would soon be exhausted; but if they acted on an idea that had been carefully prepared and developed by the teacher, then it would be likely to be fruitful and lead to further learning. The teacher, he insisted, was the person with "riper and fuller experience" and greater insight, who "has not only the right but the duty to suggest lines of activity" without being afraid of adult imposition. Dewey insisted that the progressive schools had a responsibility to develop "definite and organized bodies of knowledge" about how to educate children.[65]

The best progressive schools, whether private (like the Lincoln School and the Dalton School in New York City) or public (like the Winnetka schools), tried to promote children's understanding of science, history, geography, mathematics, art, and other traditional subjects. Progressive education was most successful when its leaders realized that they needed unusually well-educated teachers and carefully planned projects that would lead to deeper understanding of subject matter; when it foundered, it was because its leaders eschewed planning and subject matter, believing that spontaneity and children's interests were both means and ends. As progressive ideas were popularized and broadly disseminated throughout the nation's public schools, the problems Dewey described were magnified. And it must be said that Dewey himself, especially in his book *Schools of Tomorrow,* had confused his followers by praising schools in which spontaneity and planlessness were considered virtues. At this fateful moment, the onset of the Great Depression captured the attention of progressive leaders, substantially diminishing their attention to the orderly development of subject matter appropriate to progressive schools. With the future of the nation hanging in the balance, certain progressive educators decided that it was up to them to reconstruct society.

6

On the Social Frontier

In the 1920s, well before the Great Depression began, intellectuals were highly critical of American society. They looked with contempt at a society that seemed self-absorbed, narrow-minded, puritanical, repressed, materialistic, indifferent to poverty, and easily swayed by religious evangelists. The national mood was conservative, at times reactionary, and indifferent to political and social reform. The great American public was intrigued by motorcars, radio, talking pictures, jazz, celebrities, baseball, and other diversions. All this seemed petty and superficial to avant-garde intellectuals, who were alternately fascinated by experimentation in the arts and psychoanalysis and outraged by such things as government roundups of radicals, the revival of the Ku Klux Klan, the Scopes trial, and the Sacco-Vanzetti trial. The educated elites disparaged those whom H. L. Mencken described as the "booboisie."

In education, too, the intellectual leadership was alienated from the main currents of American society but had the solace of knowing that the progressive education movement had not only survived the war but was thriving. Indeed, their pedagogical ideas were rapidly gaining credibility in the public schools, where progressive education was commonly referred to as "the new education" or simply "modern education."

Progressive education always contained complex currents under its broad umbrella, but none so dissonant as the simultaneous calls for child-centered schools and schools that would reform society. In the 1920s, William Heard Kilpatrick and Harold Rugg were the most prominent champions of the child-centered school, offering it as a model for changing American society. But other progressives wondered whether such schools—liberating as they might be for individual children—could ever change American society.

The child-centered schools were inherently individualistic, and it required a leap of faith to believe that they could eventually reform society. There was always tension within the progressive education movement over its conflicting aims: Were the schools supposed to reflect present-day society, to be more realistic and better attuned to current needs? Were they supposed to prepare children to fit in to present-day society? Were they supposed to change society and teach children to criticize the status quo? Or were they supposed to make learning joyful? Could they meet all these different purposes simultaneously?

John Dewey always saw social reform as the overriding goal of educational reform, so in the 1920s and 1930s he was frequently skeptical of his disciples' excessive concern for individualism and spontaneity. Dewey insisted that education was about not only teaching skills and knowledge to children but developing a better society. It was up to educators "to shape the experiences of the young so that instead of reproducing current habits, better habits shall be formed, and thus the future adult society [will] be an improvement on their own."[1]

When the country plunged into a grinding economic depression in 1929, prominent progressive educators urged the schools to take a leading role in planning and creating a new social order. They believed that they could remake society by remaking the schools. They tried to integrate child-centered education with social reform. Perceiving the academic curriculum as a symbol of a corrupt and dying social order, they advocated replacement of academic studies by projects, real-life problems, activities, and socially useful experiences. Child-centered schools prided themselves on their individualism and freedom from external directives, but those pressing for social reform wanted collective planning and controls. These conflicting imperatives created a difficult balancing act for progressive educators that nevertheless had one constant theme, namely that the academic curriculum and subject matter were obstacles to social reform.

In 1927, the progressive leaders at Teachers College started an informal group that met regularly over dinner to discuss social, political, and economic problems and consider how education might promote change. With Kilpatrick as its leader, the group attracted the most liberal members of the faculty, including Harold Rugg, George S. Counts, R. Bruce Raup, Jesse Newlon, and Goodwin Watson. Dewey, Counts, and Rugg were interested in socialism and believed that capitalism was blocking the full potential of technology to solve social and economic problems. Rugg described this group of men as "frontier thinkers."

The Kilpatrick discussion group met regularly during some of the most tumultuous years in American history, as the country went precipitously from prosperity into a deep and wrenching economic depression. The group agreed that American society and its economy were being hampered by heedless individualism and self-seeking business entrepreneurs; that collectivism must replace individualism; that the profit motive was destructive; and that the economy should be planned and controlled by government agencies. In effect, they projected their views of the ideal progressive school onto society. The ideal society, it seemed, would function like the ideal progressive school, without competition, rewards, or individual striving for recognition. To a man, the progressive educators despised the phrase "rugged individualism," which Herbert Hoover had used in 1928; ever after, the phrase was anathema among progressive educators, symbolizing the selfish competitiveness of capitalist society.[2]

In the late 1920s, several members of the discussion group visited the Soviet Union, where they saw at first hand the world's most important experiment in social planning and collective action. Although the members of the discussion group were not Communists, they admired the Soviet Union, and the glowing reports they brought back increased their determination to advocate radical changes in American education and American society.

PROGRESSIVES IN THE SOVIET UNION

John Dewey, recognized as America's greatest living philosopher, made the trip in 1928, when he was nearly seventy. Dewey was deeply moved by what he saw. The Bolshevik Revolution, he observed, had released "an outburst of vitality, courage, [and] confidence in life" on a scale that was significant not only for Russia but for the world. He tried to refute any negative assumptions about the revolution. He claimed that the shops were owned by independent cooperatives, not the government, and that the Bolsheviks were carefully preserving enough churches to satisfy the needs of worshipers. All in all, he was impressed by the safe and orderly character of life in the new Russia, "in spite of secret police, inquisitions, arrests and deportation of *Nepmen* and *Kulaks*, [and] exiling of party opponents."[3]

Like so many other travelers to the Soviet Union both then and later, Dewey saw what he wanted to see, particularly the things that confirmed his vision for his own society. He believed that the gains of the revolution were being secured by educators in the nation's classrooms, that its leaders were animated by a spirit of community, and that it aimed to raise the aesthetic cultivation of the people. Propaganda was everywhere, but he justified it because it was employed not for private gain but for the good of humanity. The revolution impressed him as heroic, "evincing a faith in human nature which is democratic beyond the ambitions of the democracies of the past."[4]

Dewey thought that the best way of understanding the Bolshevik Revolution was by examining the changes in Soviet education, rather than in political and industrial conditions. It was education, after all, that was charged with creating a collective mentality and popular cultural institutions. Dewey admired "the marvelous development of progressive educational ideas and practice under the fostering care of the Bolshevik government." When meeting Soviet educators, including Commissar Anatoly Lunacharsky, the pedagogy professor Albert Pinkevich, and an important reformer, S. T. Schatzsky, he was heartened to learn that Soviet educators had successfully broken down the barriers between school and society about which he had written so often and so fruitlessly. Soviet educators, he wrote, realized that the goals of the progressive school were undermined by "the egoistic and private ideals and methods inculcated by the institution of private property, profit and acquisitive possession." Soviet educators, he enthused, had discovered that school and society must work together to foster a collective ideology.[5]

Dewey expressed guarded admiration for the Soviets' efforts to dismantle the traditional family, which Marxists considered "exclusive and isolating in effect and hence as hostile to a truly communal life." The authorities, he said, were deliberately taking advantage of crowded living quarters to create new social combinations broader than the family. An unsentimental observer, he noted, would recognize that an interesting sociological experiment was under way to determine how valid traditional family ties were and to what extent the family was actually "a breeder of non-social interests."[6]

What was especially exciting to Dewey was that Soviet educators were committed to the project method. Unlike the United States, where the project method was established only in private progressive schools and a small number of public schools, the Bolsheviks had placed the authority of the state behind it. Dewey exulted that for the first time in history an entire educational system was officially committed to connecting school and society. Faced with the concrete realization of his theories, he was thrilled:

> I can only pay my tribute to the liberating effect of active participation in social life upon the attitude of the students. Those whom I met had a vitality and a kind of confidence in life—not to be confused with mere self-confidence—that afforded one of the most stimulating experiences of my life. . . . All that I had ever, on theoretical grounds, believed as to the extent to which the dull and dispirited attitude of the average school is due to isolation of school from life was more than confirmed by what I saw of the opposite in Russian schools.[7]

Dewey wondered whether good schooling was even possible in a capitalist society, where it was necessary to shield children from the baneful effects of their acquisitive society. The greatest obstacle to linking school and society, he thought, was "personal competition and desire for private profit in our economic life." In such a society, he observed, "in important respects school activities should be protected from social contacts and connections, instead of being organized to create them. The Russian educational situation is enough to convert one to the idea that only in a society based upon the cooperative principle can the ideals of educational reformers be adequately carried into operation."[8]

The Soviets had discovered the way to make the schools into agencies of social reform, said Dewey. Soviet teachers familiarized themselves with the detailed economic plans of the central government. Then, instead of encouraging students to pursue their own interests (which Soviet educators considered "trivial"), Soviet teachers directed their students to engage in socially useful projects, working on problems of sanitation and hygiene, assisting in the campaign against illiteracy, helping "ignorant adults to understand the policies of local soviets," "engaging in Communist propaganda," and helping in economic development activities. In the Soviet Union, schools and society were as one; the school, in effect, had become an arm of the state, sharing its purposes and carrying out its aims.[9]

Dewey insisted that "the most significant aspect of the change in Russia is psychological and moral, rather than political." He expected that political and economic problems would fall into place once the psychological problems were solved. He wrongly imagined that the emerging society would be managed by voluntary cooperative groups, rather than by the iron hand of dictatorship. This flawed analysis led him to conclude that the success of the revolution would depend on having the right kind of education, and it allowed him to ignore the egregious, persistent violations of civil liberties and democratic rights that already characterized the Soviet regime.

Sometimes Dewey's innocence was comical. When he met Lenin's widow, Nadezhda Krupskaya, an official in the Ministry of Education, he was surprised that she was "strangely silent upon matters of school organization and administration." He seemed unaware that the great man's widow was a political appointee. Dewey's colleague George Counts later identified Krupskaya as "head of the Department of Political Education in the Commissariat of Education"; she was concerned with shaping political attitudes and producing propaganda, not with education.[10]

Despite his extravagant praise for the Soviet experiment, Dewey allowed that "for selfish reasons I prefer seeing it tried in Russia rather than in my own country." Yet he was certain that Russia would provide important lessons for the rest of the world. He saw the experiment as a contest between opposites, with the individualistic capitalist "fanatic" pitted against the Marxist "fanatic." He claimed not to be on either side, but as usual when he set up his famous dualisms, he made his own preferences clear. The individualistic philosophy, he wrote, caused men to resign themselves to the evils of the status quo, believing that human nature and the economic order were fixed. But "the Marxian philosophy gave men faith and courage to challenge the regime."[11]

Dewey made it plain that he had no sympathy for the individualistic capitalistic system. Accustomed to a society in which intellectuals sat on the sidelines and complained, feeling impotent and unappreciated, Dewey admitted, "It is hard not to feel a certain envy for the intellectual and educational workers in Russia; not, indeed, for their material and economic status, but because a unified religious social faith brings with it such simplification and integration of life." Dewey asserted that a teacher's status was considerably enhanced by becoming a partner of the state: "An educator from a bourgeois country may well envy the added dignity that comes to the function of the teacher when he is taken into partnership in plans for the social development of his country. Such an one can hardly avoid asking himself whether this partnership is possible only in a country where industry is a public function rather than a private undertaking."[12]

Dewey's message to fellow progressives was clear: Something remarkable was happening in Russia. Educators were leading the way in creating a new cooperative social order. The revolution was replacing the old selfish values of individualism with new collective values of sharing and caring. The capitalist struggle for profit had been discarded in favor of a workers' republic, which liberated idealists to build a just community for all.

This was almost too good to be true; the Soviets seemed to be doing on a national scale what progressive educators were talking about over dinner, far from the centers of power. Nonetheless, Dewey's account posed a daunting question for American progressive educators: What was the good of connecting school and society when society was controlled by greedy capitalists? The most hopeful idea that Dewey imparted was that education was the key to social transformation, for he wrote repeatedly that the most significant aspect of the Russian Revolution was not political or economic but psychological, moral, and intellectual. Perhaps, he implied, even in a capitalist society, visionary educators could show the way to a better social order.

In 1929, William Heard Kilpatrick visited Moscow, where he discovered that his books were read in all the teacher-training institutes and the project method was widely used. The three R's were not taught directly but were learned, much to Kilpatrick's approval, "incidentally from tasks at hand." [13]

He visited a fourth-grade classroom that was working on the problem "How can we increase the yield per acre?" Another group of students studied "the problem of disposing of disintegrating carcasses of animals left frozen on the roadside, both for the salvage of fertilizer and leather and for better sanitation." Kilpatrick observed that "no school system in history has been more thoroughly and consistently made to work into the social and political program of the state. . . . Down to the smallest detail in the school curriculum, every item is planned to further the Soviet plan of society." He met many of the same progressive educators that Dewey had met; one of them, the reformer Schatzsky, who was in charge of a large number of village schools, promised Kilpatrick that within two years, all of his schools would be "one hundred percent on the project method." [14] Another, Professor Albert Pinkevich, subsequently lectured at Teachers College about the Soviet education system, at Kilpatrick's invitation.

Unknown to Kilpatrick, though, the system of progressive schools, along with the leading progressive educators, was being eliminated by

Soviet officials. Commissar Lunacharsky, the principal architect of Soviet progressive education, was removed by authorities shortly after Dewey's visit. In the mid-1930s the reformer Schatzsky committed suicide. Professor Pinkevich was arrested in the regime's mass purges of intellectuals and died in a forced-labor camp.[15]

Much as he admired what he saw in the Soviet Union, Kilpatrick recognized that the Soviet system of education was deeply flawed. When he visited China on the same international tour, he advised Chinese educators to study the Soviet example but not to adopt it. Its primary purpose was indoctrination, not education, he said, and he doubted that children were learning to think for themselves or to act on their own freely chosen purposes.[16]

George Counts, another member of the Kilpatrick discussion group, made several pilgrimages to the Soviet Union. Counts, a prairie populist born on a farm near Baldwin, Kansas, in 1889, graduated from Baker University in Baldwin (where he majored in the classics), then earned a doctorate in education at the University of Chicago. He began his career with a study of the teaching of mathematics but was soon drawn to educational sociology. In the 1920s, Counts published studies showing that most high school students were disproportionately drawn from the upper middle class and school board members tended to be from the higher echelons of business and the professions. Soon after he joined Teachers College in 1927, he became allied with the most progressive faculty members.

Counts visited the Soviet Union in 1927 and again in 1929. On his second trip, he shipped a Ford sedan to Russia and toured the countryside on his own. Beginning his trip in Leningrad in July 1929, Counts drove some six thousand miles over a period of three months, later writing a delightful account of his experiences in *A Ford Crosses Soviet Russia*.

Undeterred by the inconveniences of travel in a largely undeveloped country, Counts enthusiastically reported that he had witnessed "the growth of a new social order in the Soviet Union." He described "a bold adventure in social planning" marked not only by ambitious industrialization projects but by "the quality of the Soviet leadership, the social position of the workers, the active ferment of ideas, the vitality of the younger generation, and the development of new attitudes toward life." All who were involved in "the building of the new social order seem on the whole to possess in extreme measure the qualities of courage and devotion." The young leaders Counts met "feel themselves engaged in a work of sublime importance. . . . They do not appear to feel, as do the more intelligent of my own countrymen, that they face an unknown future to which they must adapt themselves." Rather, they viewed uncertainty as weakness, believing that "the strong mold the future to their will. Thus through the Five-Year Plan and other plans to follow they *know* that they can fashion society according to their own desires."[17]

Counts was smitten. He was a firsthand witness of what he considered "the greatest social experiment of history." This great experiment was far preferable, he thought, to the planless, selfish individualism in his own country. Over the next several years, Counts became the most forceful advocate for radical ideas in American education. He also translated a book on Soviet pedagogy by Albert Pinkevich (the same educator who had befriended Dewey and Kilpatrick) and a children's primer that enthusiastically explained the Five-Year Plan (and was selected by the Book-of-the-Month Club). During this same period, Counts published a withering critique of the United States, bemoaning its conservatism, its worship of individual success, its insistence on separation between education and politics, and its opposition to centralized social planning. Counts complained that Americans tended to reject social planning as utopian. His countrymen believed that all such planning was

certain to fail because the modern social order is so complex and dynamic that no man or group of men has sufficient wisdom to bring the vast range of its processes under orderly control. . . . The Americans contend, moreover, that if men had sufficient wisdom to plan on such a gigantic scale, they would lack the necessary moral integrity. Those to whom the task would be delegated could not be trusted to employ their power in the interests of the whole of society. . . . The American people therefore prefer to place their faith in the irrational rather than in the rational forces of society.[18]

Drawing on his trips to and studies of the Soviet Union, Counts asserted that large-scale social planning did work. He insisted that the Soviet Union was embarking on a carefully conceived social and economic plan designed for the good of society by highly intelligent, idealistic leaders. Education, he noted, was the key to building the new social order. By contrast, the United States seemed to be drifting, its leaders mouthing platitudes, its people cynical and fearful about the future.

Counts's major work of this period, *The Soviet Challenge to America* (1931), was written at the very time when the capitalist economic system appeared to be collapsing. He argued that the Soviet Union's goal of surpassing America was by no means far-fetched. Having passed through rigorous trials, he wrote, the Soviet Union was now moving "from victory to victory, to a position of unsurpassed power among the nations of the earth." He contrasted the Soviet Union's Five-Year Plan for economic development, launched in 1928, with events in the United States, where the "evolution of institutions proceeds for the most part without plan or design, as a sort of by-product of the selfish competition of individuals, groups, and enterprises for private gain." Unlike in the Soviet Union, where planners controlled every phase of the economy, the American people lacked the machinery to control their vast economic structure and were reduced to "wondering and guessing what will happen." While the Soviets were calibrating their economic development, the depressed American economy "seems as helpless as a canoe in a typhoon." [19]

Counts naively believed that Soviet society was ruled by the State Planning Commission and the system of public education, not the Communist Party, the Red Army, or even the secret police (a predecessor of the KGB, known then as the GPU, which Counts referred to as the "Gay-Pay-OO," as pronounced in Russian). He candidly acknowledged the undemocratic features of Soviet rule but justified them on grounds of the necessity of protecting the revolution. He observed that the country was ruled by "the dictatorship of the proletariat," which in turn was closely controlled by the Communist Party. He knew that the Party had never hesitated to use extreme measures against its enemies but rejected the idea that it ruled by violence.

The power of the Communist Party, he asserted, rested on its intense idealism, rigid discipline, and excellent "system of reporting," which kept the Party well informed about public opinion. It did not trouble Counts that certain categories of people—such as merchants, priests, private employers, traders, landholding peasants, and anyone associated with the old regime—were not permitted to join the Party or to vote. After all, how could the revolution survive if its enemies were allowed to influence decisions? Such people were "pariahs," and their lot was a hard one, he acknowledged, but their numbers were "rapidly dwindling"; eventually they would disappear altogether. Counts insisted that Joseph Stalin was not a dictator; he believed that the "Party line" emerged from the deliberations of many thousands of small units of the Party and that even Stalin had to obey the mandate of "mass opinion" or risk losing his job. Similarly, he defended the "Gay-Pay-OO," the secret police whose very name struck terror "in the hearts of persons opposed to Bolshevik rule"; it served its purpose well, he maintained, by supporting the revolutionary cause against its enemies.[20]

Counts was impressed by the system of public education, which embraced not only schools but also book publishing, magazines, newspapers, the cinema, museums, art, and theater. The state controlled all of these agencies so as to shape the knowledge, habits, and attitudes of the people. Counts was not at all bothered by censorship and propaganda, because they enabled the government to eliminate undesirable influences. Furthermore, government control compelled the public press "to throw practically its entire weight on the side of building the new society." Nor was it problematic to him that the state controlled scientific research, because this guaranteed that research would be coordinated (instead of competitive) and that new findings would be freely shared for the benefit of society.[21]

Like Dewey, Counts thought that the fate of the Russian Revolution would be determined by changes in the educational system, not by political power. He was impressed that educators were helping to formulate plans for the new social order and carried out these plans in their classrooms. This close coordination between education and social planning guaranteed that the schools would remain in close touch with reality. He declared that "The union of education and social planning may well prove to be the most significant achievement of the Russian revolution." While Soviet schools emphasized activity, he observed approvingly, it was not the aimless activity so characteristic of American progressive schools: "it is activity with a purpose; it is activity with a strongly collectivistic bias; it is activity devoted to the promotion of the welfare of the surrounding community; it is, in a word, to a very large degree, *socially useful labor.*"[22]

Even more impressive to Counts than the practical advantages of the new social order was its stirring idealism. In the United States, the schools promoted individual success, but in the Soviet Union, "individual success is completely subordinated to the ideal of serving the state and through the state the working class." Through centralization of authority and complete ideological direction of education, Counts noted, "the Communists have thus fashioned the most powerful instrument of agitation, propaganda, and education known to history." In America, the only stimulus to patriotism was the prospect of war, but in the Soviet Union, patriotism was identified with the goals of the Five-Year Plan, such as building factories, organizing farm communes, improving the harvest, making labor efficient, and rationalizing industry.[23]

Because of his firsthand experience and extensive knowledge of what was happening in the Soviet Union, Counts came to be regarded as an expert on both Soviet education and Soviet economics. In 1931, Counts reported that the successes of the Five-Year Plan "were so marked as to become almost embarrassing." During the winter of 1929–30, the campaign for collectivization took on the features of a mob movement, he said, under the slogan "The Liquidation of the Kulak as a Class." He expressed hardly a murmur about the mass arrests and ruthless murders of tens of thousands of *kulak*s, whose only crime was that they were landholding peasants. The Five-Year Plan, he boldly declared, was a "brilliant and heroic success." Dismissing critics for demanding that the revolution "be conducted according to the very latest rules of parlor etiquette," he predicted that "the full significance of the ideas which it generated can scarcely be fully realized in less than a century."[24]

DARE THE SCHOOLS BUILD A NEW SOCIAL ORDER?

Counts's enthusiasm for the Soviet system must be seen in the context of the deepening economic crisis in the United States, which led many to conclude that capitalism was finished. After the stock market crash of October 1929, economic conditions steadily worsened. Unemployment rose from 4 million in 1930 to 8 million in 1931 and to 12 million in 1932, when nearly one quarter of the workforce was out of a job. Banks closed, wages fell, families lost their farms, their savings, their homes. In the cities, the hungry lined up for bread and soup, while the unemployed sold apples. States, cities, and counties were unable to support adequate public services, and public employees were laid off at the very time that the need for public services soared. In the absence of coordinated public programs to help the hungry and homeless, many children and adults suffered from malnutrition and disease. As the Depression deepened, growing numbers of economists concluded that laissez-faire economics had plainly failed and that public authorities should take control of economic and social planning to rationalize production and distribution, allocation of capital, and the distribution of income. In the terrifying days of the early 1930s, there was a widespread sense that the nation was drifting dangerously close to the brink of economic and social chaos and that any plan was better than none at all.[25]

It was at this juncture—with the economy in a tailspin, with millions of workers unemployed and families scrounging for scraps for their next meal—that George Counts was invited to address the Progressive Education Association at its annual meeting in Baltimore in early 1932. The combination of speaker and audience promised to be interesting, since Counts favored social planning and the PEA had a long-standing commitment to child-centered schooling and to Rousseauian principles such as "Freedom to Develop Naturally" and "The Teacher a Guide, Not a Taskmaster." The membership of the PEA was largely drawn from child-centered schools that emphasized activities, spontaneity, and freedom from curricula planned in advance.

Counts challenged the PEA and asked its members, "Dare progressive education be progressive?" He called on his audience to jettison capitalism, support the creation of a socialized economy, and overcome their groundless fear of indoctrination.

Counts accused the progressive education movement of having no "theory of social welfare unless it be that of anarchy or extreme individualism." He derided its views as those of

> the liberal-minded upper middle class who provide most of the children for the Progressive schools—persons who are fairly well off . . . who pride themselves on their open mindedness and tolerance, who favor in a mild sort of way fairly liberal programs of social reconstruction, who are full of good will . . . but who, in spite of all their good qualities, have no deep and abiding loyalties, who possess no convictions for which they would sacrifice over-much, who would find it hard to live without their customary material comforts.

The parents of children in progressive schools did not want their children to mingle with the children of the poor or children of other races, he charged. Nor did they want them to be exposed to radical social doctrines. Counts insisted:

> If Progressive Education is to be genuinely progressive, it must emancipate itself from the influence of this class, face squarely and courageously every social issue, come to grips with life in all of its stark reality, establish an organic relation with the community, develop a realistic and comprehensive theory of welfare, fashion a compelling and challenging vision of human destiny, and become somewhat less frightened than it is today at the bogeys of imposition and indoctrination. In a word, Progressive Education cannot build its program out of the interests of the children; it cannot place its trust in a child-centered school.[26]

Counts prophesied that modern technology would make it possible to launch an age of plenty if only educators were willing to abandon individualism, competition, and capitalism and build "a new tradition in American life." What did it matter if his vision required indoctrination? Indoctrination, he noted, goes on all the time anyway. Educators must take the lead in shaping a vision of a new socialized economy, "because men must have something for which to live." Counts told his audience that they must choose between futility or committing themselves to building a new social order.[27]

The delegates reacted to Counts's proposal with stunned silence. According to contemporary accounts, small groups "met spontaneously and carried earnest discussions far into the night and the following day." The next day's program was canceled to make time for discussion. The leaders of progressive schools seemed ready to accept Counts's challenge, but they could not agree on what to do. One proposed that "admission to progressive schools shall be based entirely upon the personal attributes of the child, regardless of race, color or class" and that "competition shall be eliminated (it corresponds to the profit motive in industry)." Another suggested that better teacher training was needed. Yet another recommended spending more on rural education. Several insisted that progressive educators should avoid indoctrination and instead teach students to question whatever they were taught. About the only point of consensus was a decision to appoint a committee to study social and economic problems.[28]

In the months that followed, Counts took his message to other major organizations, including the National Education Association. The requests for reprints were so numerous that in April 1932 his speeches were published as a book titled *Dare the Schools Build a New Social Order?* Even more radical in tone than Counts's original speech, the book forthrightly called for elimination of capitalism, property rights, private profits, and competition, and establishment of collective ownership of natural resources, capital, and the means of production and distribution.[29]

Counts's bold question stirred heated debates within the education profession. For most of the 1930s, Counts and his progressive colleagues produced a steady stream of articles and books and even a journal—*The Social Frontier*—calling on schools to take a leading role in building a new social order. But the debate went far beyond the colleges of education. Even the National Education Association, which represented the nation's presumably conservative school superintendents, climbed aboard the bandwagon. At the NEA's annual meeting in 1932, an official asked, "What agency shall take the lead in creating a new social order?" Surely, he said, it must be the NEA, which would "assume the leadership and point the way . . . the educators of America propose to assume major responsibility for building such a social order."[30]

OTHER PROGRESSIVES RESPOND

Progressive educational leaders seized upon the issues raised by Counts to advocate not only reconstruction of society but the reconstruction of the public schools, especially the replacement of academic subjects by projects and cooperative activities. Virtually every prominent progressive in the 1930s agreed that the traditional academic curriculum reflected the failed capitalist economic order and that a radical change in the social order required equally sweeping changes in the schools.

In 1933, these themes were sounded in *The Educational Frontier,* a book written collectively by leading progressive educators. Historian Lawrence A. Cremin later described this book as "the characteristic progressive statement of the decade." It laid out the conventional wisdom of progressive educators: competitive individualism had failed and must be replaced by collectivism and cooperation; grades, honors, and competition in school appealed to the same selfishness as the profit motive and must be abandoned; educators must take responsibility for shaping children's social, moral, and cultural values; children must engage in activities that expand their social and political consciousness; educators have a special responsibility to teach children "the ability and desire to think collectively."[31]

Employing oblique language, the authors of *The Educational Frontier* urged schools to engage in political education. Schools were advised to give their students the appropriate political "orientation," which would eventually become "integrated" into the students' outlook on life. In this way, the schools would help to build a new social order. Schools should involve their students in activities that would teach them about economic, political, and social conditions: "Airports may be visited, ice-cream plants studied, factories surveyed, municipal officers interviewed, printing plants looked over, and other similar community-discovering activities carried on." But such visits were not to be merely diverting field trips; the point was to "reveal those factors that breed actual insecurity in the present as man struggles in the grasp of individualistic concepts." As students learned about local economic activities, their teachers were supposed to help them understand the necessity for "intelligent planning and social control."[32]

Certain lessons, it was suggested, would "orient" students by demonstrating the evils of the existing economic system. Students might examine, for instance, the local housing situation: "as the teacher directs this orientation, he will see to it that certain basic factors intrude. Individuals living in the better residential sections may be maintaining their status there through the ownership of houses in slum districts. Furthermore, these owners may take advantage of their control of these houses and refuse to provide minimum opportunities for decent living." Students would learn that these property owners might have political connections that allow them to ignore housing regulations. Through this orientation, the student would learn about the ills of a profit-motivated economy. Or students might study the dairy industry, in which case they would examine the causes of milk price wars and discover the "effects of this competition upon both the home to which the milk goes and the farm from which it comes. And in this picture, the racketeer may be expected to show his head." In this way, students would learn about the evil results of competition in a market economy. The authors suggested that students should work at the polls at election time to learn about the evils of the political situation, which could not be corrected merely by voting.[33]

Even putting out a school newspaper would open up the opportunity to teach students how regular newspapers were affected by "a profit motive; how news gets colored; how editorials ignore facts; how work is done in line with pressure from above, or from without; how positions are lost when the ethics of the profession are adhered to too closely." As students came to understand the evils of the profit system and the benefits of social planning, the school would contribute to "the immediate reconstruction of the social situation."[34]

Even as progressives argued for educational reconstruction, they kept up a relentless attack on academic subject matter. References to subject matter were always derisive, as though the very idea of teaching algebra, chemistry, or history were archaic: "The school, even if forced to start with subject-matter, will find that its point of interest is increasingly an intelligently formulated scheme of social action and decreasingly an orderly parade of compartmentalized knowledge." The successful progressive school was one that had "escaped the tentacles of subjects." The schools must abandon their attempt "to present the same organization of knowledge to all students" and allow students to pursue their own interests. Some might become interested in chemistry after studying the local water supply, others in physics after surveying different methods of refrigeration in the local community; still others might pursue their own idiosyncratic interests.[35]

That academic subject matter would soon disappear seemed certain to progressive educators. There was less agreement about whether schools should consciously indoctrinate their students for participation in the new social order. Some thought that indoctrination was inevitable; others thought not. Most agreed that teaching the appropriate "orientation" toward social and political issues was not indoctrination. John Dewey expressed the progressive consensus when he wrote that "education cannot be neutral and indifferent as to the kind of social organization which exists . . . education must operate in view of a deliberately preferred social order."[36]

→ → ← ←

It was odd that the Russian Revolution inspired educators to want to build a new social order through the schools, because the schools in Russia had not created the Russian Revolution; nor did any of the progressive educators wonder how their own social ideals had been forged, since all of them were products of a subject-centered, traditional education.

Nonetheless they shared the faith that progressive education would lead the way in building a new, collectivist social order. In the early 1930s, few in the education profession questioned whether schools should lead a campaign for social reform or whether they should engage in the political education of their charges. Any educator who said his goal was to teach young people to master academic subjects risked being seen as a reactionary. At a time when the Depression had reduced tax revenues for schools, causing layoffs and salary reductions, workaday teachers were too preoccupied with their precarious situation to contribute to this heated debate about the role of the schools in social change.

The eminent historian Charles Beard, a close friend of George Counts, wrestled with the dilemma that Counts had posed and straddled it. In a 1932 report for the American Historical Association called "A Charter for the Social Sciences," Beard warned that it was best not to overestimate the capacity of the schools to solve critical problems of democracy; for most problems, "even the wisest statesmen have no certain solution." The schools, he said, have "no access to super-wisdom. If they do, the educators might well take over the government of the country." Yet Beard also concluded that a teacher must select what to emphasize, based on a "more or less logical picture of an ideal social order to be preserved or realized." He agreed that neutrality was nearly impossible; choices would be necessary. In the politicized atmosphere of the early 1930s, when educational leaders were heatedly debating the ethics of indoctrination, Beard's report was widely viewed as support for indoctrination by teachers of social studies, although he gave equally strong endorsement to the teaching of patriotism and freedom of opinion.[37]

➔ ➔ ← ←

When the Progressive Education Association's Committee on Social and Economic Problems reported back in 1933 in response to Counts's challenge to build a new social order, it delivered a militant statement that split the organization down the middle. Written primarily by Counts, "A Call to the Teachers of the Nation" bristled with fire-breathing Marxist oratory about the class struggle; it urged teachers to "speak out and take their stand" against reactionary capitalist elites: "In America today God is served through mammon; the general good is made a by-product of the pursuit of private gain; self-interest is clothed in the garment of civic virtue; science is converted into a tool of privilege; production is made to tyrannize over consumption; the fruits of technology contribute to the debasement of culture; justice is bought and sold in the marketplace; racketeers justify their behavior in terms of business ethics; powerful barons of finance extol the ways of democracy." The report proposed that teachers adopt a philosophy, "take up boldly the challenge of the present . . . and transfer the democratic tradition from individualistic to collectivist economic foundations." Teachers, the report said, "owe nothing to the present economic system, except to improve it; they owe nothing to any privileged caste, except to strip it of its privileges." It called on teachers to "unite in a powerful organization, militantly devoted to the building of a better social order" and financially supported by the Progressive Education Association.[38]

The members of the Progressive Education Association were not willing to commit the organization to building a new social order along Marxist lines; they certainly did not want to finance a militant teachers' group. They worried that the PEA would be damaged by the report's radical views, causing it to lose members and damaging its relations with local school boards. Others, especially those from the PEA's child-centered schools, did not understand why the PEA should endorse any social philosophy, particularly one that was so negative. Opponents of the report, led by Carleton Washburne of the Winnetka public school system, persuaded the 1933 PEA convention to disavow the report. It was eventually published in pamphlet form as *A Call to Teachers of the Nation,* but without the PEA's endorsement. Historian C. A. Bowers later wrote that it was "one of the most extreme and utopian statements to be made by any group during the Depression."[39]

In a withering critique, historian James Truslow Adams, whose work was much admired by progressives, said that it was completely unrealistic to expect teachers to know how to organize society: "One is staggered at the ease with which such a problem is stated for hard-worked teachers to solve. It may well be questioned whether any one, or any group, here and now in 1933 can solve these problems." Taking issue with the report, Adams maintained that the teachers' job was not to indoctrinate their students but to help them become well informed, free from prejudice and emotion, and able to use intellectual tools.[40]

The preeminent African-American scholar W. E. B. Du Bois thought that it was unrealistic to expect the schools to reform society. Speaking to a convention of black school teachers in Georgia in 1935, Du Bois told his audience that there was only one way for the schools to cure society's ills, and that was by making people intelligent. To do this,

> the school has again but one way, and that is, first and last, to teach them to read, write and count. And if the school fails to do that, and tries beyond that to do something for which a school is not adapted, it not only fails in its own function, but it fails in all other attempted functions. Because no school as such can organise industry, or settle the matter of wage and income, can found homes or furnish parents, can establish justice or make a civilised world.[41]

Kilpatrick and Rugg, both of whom were already nationally and internationally famed for their advocacy of the child-centered movement, joined Counts's crusade to reconstruct the social order through the schools. In the past, they had regularly criticized the subject-centered curriculum and called on schools to respond to children's interests and needs; the national economic crisis of the early 1930s gave them new reasons to attack traditional academic studies. But they had to resolve a puzzling intellectual problem: If a school based its curriculum on the interests of students, how could it reconstruct the social order unless the children wanted to?

A few months after Counts issued his radical challenge, Kilpatrick analyzed "the social crisis" by comparing the capitalist system to the traditional classroom. The traditional classroom stressed extrinsic motives and individual success, just like the capitalist system, he said. In the progressive classroom, children worked because they wanted to, not because of rewards or competition. Kilpatrick believed that American society needed "a new philosophy of life" that would result from a "new adult education" conducted by carefully selected leaders. In the new society, the traditional school would disappear and a good society would emerge. The first step in building a new society would be to get rid of academic subjects and use the schools to analyze life's problems.[42]

Until the Depression, Kilpatrick had asserted that the curriculum should follow the interests of children; he could not imagine any child who was sincerely interested in science, history, or literature, nor did it seem possible to him that such studies might equip young people to deal with the problems of life. Instead of such abstract studies, he believed, youths needed "to share with their elders in actual social activities." Ideally, the entire population would study and work together, making responsible decisions, building social attitudes, and thinking critically; in the ideal society, he predicted, life itself would take the place of the traditional school. Were schools even necessary? Kilpatrick observed, "Whether there will be in that distant day an actual school separately existing from the social process the writer would hardly care to hazard a venture." Until that day arrived, however, schools could devote most of the day to "socially useful activities." Students should be mainly engaged in projects, group work, and field trips, all of which would build "valuable social attitudes" and "direct knowledge of affairs." If the conventional subjects were neglected, Kilpatrick asserted, it would be "no great loss."[43]

HAROLD RUGG AND THE GREAT TECHNOLOGY

*In 1933, Harold Rugg thought he had found a way of integrating the nat-*uralness of child-centered schools and the requirements of collective social planning. Trained as an engineer, he proclaimed that man now stood on the verge of what he called "the Great Technology," an era that could produce an earthly economic paradise. This paradise would come to pass, however, only if there were a centrally controlled economy, designed and controlled by technological experts.

How would educators fit into the creation of the Great Technology?

The social engineers would plan and design the new society, and the educational engineers would produce the mass understanding that would be needed for the new order to succeed. Rugg contended that social progress required the consent of the people, but elections did not actually produce that consent because most people were not informed and did not vote. Democratic government did not really exist because "true consent can be given only by people who understand their conditions," and it was up to educators to create that understanding. Therefore, educators must lead a massive campaign of adult education to create a new climate of opinion and develop the consent of the people for a new economic and social system. The way to create this new climate of opinion, he held, was to employ high-powered sales techniques to win over the minds of the "thinking minority" of 25 million or so with high IQs.[44]

Where did child-centered schools fit into his scheme? Rugg believed that once a new social order was established, schools would be "schools of living instead of schools for literacy." Instead of a "bookish" education, children would participate in the work, play, and social life of the community. Subject-centered schooling, which he considered "thoroughly authoritarian," even "Fascist," would disappear. The fundamental error of American education, Rugg believed, was the survival of its "scholastic, literary education designed for an elite." Rugg maintained that if the nation's schools had been created by "garden-variety, run-of-the-mill Americans, *who had neither been subjected to a scholastic education, nor knew of the existence of one,* the schools of our time would have been very different from these formal schools of literacy" (italics in the original). Rugg recommended education without schooling, of a sort that he thought must have existed "before the days of machines and great cities." He imagined a Garden of Eden, when education had been centered around the family and the community, when children had learned what they needed to know: "the boys, working with their elders in the fields, shops, stores, offices, the girls helping their mothers as self-sustaining producers in the homes and the neighborhood activities. . . . Skills would have been learned as the product of natural and direct education, ranging from the simple chores of the household to the more specialized trade skills of shop, market, office, and governing bodies."[45] In such a scheme, built directly on learning from everyday life, the school would disappear. This vision recalls Rousseau's ideas about natural education, free of any artificial constraints. In this romantic, nostalgic, pastoral vision, all learning is easy and informal as the school of life replaces the school of formal literacy.

KANDEL'S CRITIQUE

Not everyone at Teachers College admired the new radicalism. Isaac L. Kandel, a leading scholar of international education, ridiculed the idea that the school should be expected to build a new social order. Kandel found it richly amusing that the latest slogans called for collectivism and social planning to replace selfish individualism. This new movement for collectivism, he pointed out, came from the very same people who had been "the most vociferous advocates of individualism, the new freedom, the child-centered school, and the sanctity of the child's ego—in a word, of laissez faire in education." For nearly two decades, progressive educators had "consistently refused to define goals or ends in advance, and [had] relied on the magic of growth, self-expression, and development from within." Now these educators had become leaders of the movement for social reconstruction through the school.[46]

It was ironic, he said, that the same progressive educators who had stoutly opposed any planned curriculum now took it upon themselves to advocate a centrally planned society. Almost overnight the advocates of individualism had become convinced that

> the cult of selfish, self-centered interests and purposes have been responsible for the crisis which is upon us. . . . The cynic may be pardoned if he seeks to prick the bubble of the new enthusiasm for social reconstruction by posing a few questions. What is the difference between individual selfishness and a philosophy which has been preaching the gospel of individual satisfactions as the mainspring of education and conduct, and which has made that which works synonymous with truth? . . .

Those who are loudest in denouncing the profit motive and the competitive spirit are fortunately able to forget that they ever propagated the theory that every child has the inherent right to ask, *"Cui bono?"*[47]

Kandel noted that it was the progressives, not their critics, who had propagated rampant individualism in education; it was they who had embraced a philosophy of hedonism, "the pain-pleasure or annoyance-satisfaction theory of education which has dominated educational thought for the past twenty years." Ideals and convictions had no place in their philosophy, nor did discipline and effort. Having discarded tradition and standards, they offered no moral or social purposes to put in their place. Kandel hoped that the progressives had at last recognized the inadequacy of their laissez-faire principles, had at last discovered that "individual whims, caprices, needs, satisfactions, and annoyances" could not serve as the basis of education. He hoped that they understood that "through education men should become better informed, more intelligent about affairs, guided by a scientific attitude, imbued with convictions and ideals to motivate sound conduct," but he suspected that they intended no such thing and that their plans for social reconstruction through the schools, based on untried theories and lacking public consent, were "mere nonsense."[48]

THE AHA REPORT

*While Rugg, Kilpatrick, and other progressives were trying to find con*nections between the activities of the child-centered school and a mass program of collective social reform, Counts advanced his quest for a new social order on another front. From 1931 to 1934, at the height of his radicalism, Counts served as research director for a major study by the American Historical Association.

Launched in 1926 with ample funding to examine the place of history and other social sciences in the schools, the study soon lost its raison d'être. The committee, which included prominent progressive educators and historians, decided that increased secondary enrollments made it impossible to propose a history program, which (they assumed) was appropriate only for the "self-selected few seeking culture." It was an article of faith among progressive educators that children should study only whatever was of immediate interest to them, and the historians (with their own elitist traditions) agreed that the masses lacked the intellectual capacity to study history. So in 1929, the group retitled itself the Commission on the Social Studies; its chairman claimed that "the select few with academic ambitions" had become a small and insignificant proportion of the high school enrollment, that history was far beyond the competence of the average student, and that as a subject it was of little value in fitting students for "effective participation in society."[49]

By the time its final report was issued in 1934, the commission, although still sponsored by the American Historical Association, had little to say about history in the schools and a great deal to say about "the condition and prospects of the American people as a part of Western civilization now merging into a world order." The fiery rhetoric of George Counts could be discerned in the report. Its most famous statement was "[I]n the United States as in other countries, the age of individualism and laissez faire in economy and government is closing and . . . a new age of collectivism is emerging." Although uncertain about the precise form of the new economy, the AHA commission agreed that the next stage would be "a consciously integrated society in which individual economic actions and individual property rights will be altered and abridged." It proposed that the public schools teach new values and understandings to the American people to ease the transition to the new collective economy: the "efficient functioning of the emerging economy and the full utilization of its potentialities require profound changes in the attitudes and outlook of the American people, especially the rising generation—a complete and frank recognition that the old order is passing, that the new order is emerging, and that knowledge of realities and capacity to co-operate are indispensable." The commission warned that if American education continued to emphasize individualism, "it will increase the accompanying social tensions." But if it adopted a philosophy "which harmonizes with the facts of a closely integrated society, it will ease the strains of the transition taking place in actuality."[50] In short, the commission lent its prestige to indoctrination for a new, collective social order. A choice would have to be made, the report sternly warned. Those who did not actively support the transition to collectivism were on the wrong side of history. When the report was issued, four of the sixteen members of the commission declined to sign it.

The report was released by a prestigious organization and endorsed by leading historians and educators; at the time, its radical prescriptions seemed unexceptional, even praiseworthy. One critic, however, perceived its antidemocratic overtones. Boyd H. Bode, whose role in history was to be a progressive educator who criticized other progressivists' extremism, wrote a scathing commentary: "The cynic who said that teaching is the art of taking advantage of defenseless childhood will find confirmation for his pessimistic view in the recent Report of the Commission on the Teaching of the Social Studies." The report, he said, endorsed a particular set of policies, including social planning, redistribution of wealth, and curtailment of private property, and encouraged educators to put these ideas across to unwitting children. Bode found this deeply objectionable and antidemocratic. The student, he said, was the forgotten man. He wondered, "Does it not seem reasonable to suppose that he should have some voice in determining what he is to believe and how he is to act? All our educational reformers seem to be agreed that the pupil himself is not to be trusted, but that his thinking is to be done for him."[51] The issue raised by the AHA report, he said, was whether educators could trust the intelligence of the average person or must—in what was surely an undemocratic fashion—guide them to predetermined conclusions.

DEBATING *The Social Frontier*

As the Depression deepened and the ideological struggle over the future of American schools intensified, the social reconstructionists at Teachers College established a new journal, *The Social Frontier,* to advocate the building of a new social order. Counts agreed to serve as its editor, and the first issue appeared in October 1934. Its lead editorial laid out the familiar themes: American society was in the midst of an epochal transition from an agricultural age to an industrial era; the old anarchic individualism would have to be replaced by social planning; in the new order, unprecedented prosperity would be possible; and educators must prepare the minds of the rising generation to make this historic social reconstruction possible. "In a word," wrote the editorialist, echoing the AHA report (Counts probably wrote both the editorial and the AHA report), "for the American people the age of individualism in economy is closing and an age of collectivism is opening. Here is the central and dominating reality in the present epoch." The purpose of the new magazine was to provide a forum for "educational workers" who agreed on the need for social reconstruction, to attract others to the cause, and to forge their voices "into a mighty instrument of group consensus, harmonious expression, and collective action."[52]

The Social Frontier offered a lively debating ground for progressives, radicals, socialists, liberals, Communists, and even an occasional conservative. Its circulation never exceeded ten thousand, but it was the most significant forum for politically minded educators in the 1930s. Its pages regularly deplored restrictions on academic freedom and the economic effects of the Depression on the schools, in particular budget cuts, layoffs, and reduction of teachers' salaries in many districts.

But the consistent theme of *The Social Frontier* was the need for a planned, collectivist social order. One member of the journal's board of contributors, Broadus Mitchell, an economist at Johns Hopkins University, excoriated the New Deal for propping up capitalism; he called on teachers, "above all others, to become propagandists" against the economic system and to stir discontent "into the mind of the millions."[53] Kilpatrick railed against the "profit motive" for degrading workers, corrupting politics, and destroying the character of the American people. Men (and children in school), he insisted, should work for inherent satisfaction, not for extrinsic rewards.[54]

The historian Merle Curti reminded his readers that our nation's founders (referring to Washington and Jefferson) had subscribed to "the right of revolution by violence."[55] The editors of *The Social Frontier* were chagrined by the Roosevelt administration's apparent deference to the existing economic order; in language recalling Counts's description of the all-encompassing Soviet education system, an editorial asked, "Dare a President harness the press, the radio, the cinema, the public educational system to the star of a new, economically secure and culturally free social order? What would have stopped Roosevelt with his marvelous political equipment and his ingratiating personality from exercising effective leadership in this direction at a time when great masses of the American people were desperately ready for almost anything?"[56] Another editorial asserted that "an economy based on private property in the means of production and private profits" could not possibly preserve freedom of thought and expression: "History has pronounced this verdict."[57]

Prominent educators debated the ethics of indoctrination, and the editors invited the views of critics, including Harry D. Gideonse, an economist at the University of Chicago, who disparaged the journal's editors as "an attractive group of able young men [who] are bartering the moral freedom of the school for a mess of ill-digested collectivist pottage."[58]

John Dewey held that teachers could not evade their responsibility to make a choice about their role in social change: "Drifting is merely a cowardly mode of choice." He disingenuously claimed that he would not tell anyone "with which of the antagonistic tendencies of our own time they should align themselves—although I have my own convictions on that subject. . . . If a teacher is conservative and wishes to throw in his lot with forces that seem to me reactionary and that will in the end, from my point of view, increase present chaos, at all events let him do it intelligently."[59] Boyd Bode insisted that the only tolerable indoctrination in a democratic society was "indoctrination in the belief or attitude that the individual has the right to a choice of beliefs," even beliefs not shared by progressives, for anything less demonstrated a lack of faith in the intelligence of the common man.[60]

Jesse Newlon, director of the Lincoln School at Teachers College and former superintendent of the Denver public schools, declared that "every educational leader should shoulder responsibility for molding the public mind. He cannot intelligently discharge this responsibility by inaction or by attempting to assume a neutral role. . . . The neutral educational leader is always active for the status quo and the vested interests. He throws the weight of his influence on the side of conservatism and reaction."[61]

While progressive educators debated various schemes to reconstruct the social order along collectivist lines and the desirability of indoctrination, the Hearst press ran regular feature stories on "Red" influence in the schools and on university campuses. The clash of radicalism in the universities and alarmism in the press produced a predictable result. In October 1935, *The Social Frontier* reported that twenty-two states had enacted legislation requiring teachers to sign loyalty oaths.[62]

The radical progressives' efforts to persuade teachers to become advocates for collectivism ran aground on a variety of real-world shoals. First, teachers were not free to indoctrinate their students, even if they wanted to (and there is no reason to think they did). Unlike university teachers, who enjoyed a large degree of academic freedom and tenure, teachers could be fired almost at will by their principal or local school board.

Second, as Counts himself had complained before the Depression, the public schools generally reflected and transmitted the values of the local community, and those values tended to be patriotic and civic-minded, not radical and experimental. Most people, he ruefully observed, believed that the American social system was fundamentally sound, and "in spite of the demands of educational theorists that the school should serve as an agency of continuous social reconstruction, the forces of formal education tend to throw their weight on the side of social conformity."[63]

Third, the radical progressives found little support outside their own institutions for their belief that the public schools should build a new social order. Even a friendly academic such as Charles Beard doubted that educators were the group best qualified to reconstruct society.

Fourth, the radical progressives lacked a popular base for their program. Most Americans continued to have faith in the resilience of the political system, believed in the traditional idea of improving society one person at a time, trusted the Roosevelt administration to take action against the Depression, and did not expect the schools to reconstruct society.

THE DISSENTERS SPEAK OUT

Charles H. Judd, head of the Department of Education at the University of Chicago, was one of the few prominent educators to challenge the progressives' radical proposals openly. In 1934, as the demand for social reconstruction was in full cry, Judd wrote:

> Inspired by the idea that schools must contribute in some way to social reform, certain radicals have gone so far as to advocate that teachers assume the role of leaders and direct the reorganization of the economic and political systems. These extremists have misconceived the function of the schools. The duty of education is to prepare people to make intelligent judgments on social problems. A people properly educated will act on questions of public policy through the constituted channels of local, state, and national government. It is not proper for the educational system to attempt to control the policies of the state and the nation. Education trains minds to operate with clarity and independence.

Knowing that he risked being branded a conservative, Judd nonetheless complained about "writers who would turn the schools into instruments of propaganda for a vague doctrine which they call 'collectivism' but which they fail to define clearly."[64]

The progressives' newfound devotion to the collective will had its dark side, as did the readiness of some progressives to support indoctrination for a new social order. A historian of the Depression era, Richard H. Pells, observed that many of the radical progressives' propositions "often sounded ominously manipulative and repressive." They had

233

mounted a powerful campaign, he suggested, for intellectual conformity (in the guise of democratic thinking), for obedience (in the guise of idealism), and for smoother adjustment of the individual to the status quo (in the guise of socialization). "By teaching men to suppress their egos for the betterment of society, education for the future could also be a way of reconciling people to the present," he wrote. In what was surely a paradox, he said, leading progressives such as Dewey and Counts had equated "freedom with order, human aspiration with social control, liberation of the self with security for everyone." Their insistence on putting the group first had serious risks for the individual. Absent a revolution, then, the progressive emphasis on collective behavior might prepare children to conform to the demands of advertisers, the marketplace, mass media, popular opinion, or any other powerful social pressure.[65]

The progressives averted their eyes or possibly rolled them when one of their most persistent critics, William C. Bagley, announced with undisguised pleasure in 1933 that the Soviet Union had abandoned progressive education. In an article titled "The Soviets Proceed to the Liquidation of American Educational Theory," Bagley had a good laugh at the progressives' expense when he reported that Soviet educational authorities had issued a decree in 1931 sweeping away everything that Dewey, Counts, and Kilpatrick had praised. The decree restored classroom recitations, textbooks, discipline, and compulsory examinations. Wrote Bagley, "Now if all this does not constitute as nearly complete an 'about face' as modern education records, our American educational pilgrims to the land of the Soviets have been giving us false reports." Bagley knew that for progressive theorists, Russia was the Mecca to which they flocked to see their ideas put into practice on a wide scale. The Soviets had abolished progressive education, Bagley thought, because they wanted able, competent men and women, which progressive education could not supply. "Our dominant educational theory," he complained, "has too long been committed by a limited psychology and an essentially opportunistic philosophy to a debilitating hedonism."[66] This might be useful for teaching animals and very young children, he noted, but would ultimately prove wholly inadequate for the education of a strong and vigorous people.

The Effects of the Soviet Purges

No amount of criticism from carpers such as Bagley could have per-
suaded the radical progressives to abandon their views, because they
firmly believed in the concept of cultural lag, which permitted them to
belittle critics and popular opinion as uninformed and retrograde. But
the campaign for collectivism eventually collapsed because of events in
the Soviet Union. Progressive educators could ignore critics, but they
could not long ignore the purges in the Soviet Union of professionals,
government officials, scientists, intellectuals, and artists, including
every educator known to Dewey, Counts, and Kilpatrick.

As word of the Moscow show trials and systematic political repression seeped out in the mid-1930s, the progressives reconsidered their un-
stinting praise for the Soviet Union. In 1937, at the advanced age of
seventy-eight, John Dewey led an investigation of Soviet charges of treason against Leon Trotsky; the Dewey Commission concluded that Trotsky was not guilty of the charges and that the Moscow trials were
"frame-ups." Dewey, who was a socialist, decided that "the great lesson
to be derived from these amazing revelations is the complete breakdown
of revolutionary Marxianism." He acknowledged that the recent events
in the Soviet Union had "been a bitter disillusionment for me personally,"
because he had "looked upon the Soviet Union as a social laboratory in
which significant experiments could be carried out." The other great lesson, he said, was the importance of peaceful, democratic methods of economic and political reform, rather than violence and dictatorship.[67]

In a remarkably short period of time, *The Social Frontier* did an
abrupt about-face. As late as January 1936, its editors had called for a
"united front" between liberals and Marxists, faithfully echoing the
Communist Party line of the day. But by mid-1936, the journal began
perceptibly to back away from such radical rhetoric. Invocations of
"class struggle," once a staple on the editorial menu, were replaced by a
decided tilt toward liberalism; Kilpatrick wrote a stinging critique of
"high Marxism," and Jesse H. Newlon defended the incrementalism of
the Roosevelt administration.[68]

Most startling, however, was George Counts's change of heart. Counts, after all, was the man who, more than any other, had hailed the Soviet Union's ideals and methods. Counts had challenged progressive educators to indoctrinate their pupils for a new collectivist social order. More than any other progressive, Counts had written off the American economic and social system.

But at some point in late 1936 or 1937, shaken by the purges, Counts decided that the American democratic-liberal tradition was worth fighting for. In 1938, he denounced the Soviet government as "a rigid dictatorship" that had seized political power, ruthlessly obliterated dissent, and "molded the entire cultural apparatus to its purposes." Counts still wanted a new social order, and he still raged against the "economic aristocracy," but he turned decisively against Communist methods, both in the Soviet Union and at Teachers College.[69]

In 1939, Counts was outraged by the disruptive tactics of a Communist faction at Teachers College (whose members were never identified), which had attempted to "bait" the administration and provoke class struggle ("the administration and board of trustees being the 'exploiters,' the faculty members and employees the 'exploited' "). Liberal members of the faculty, including Counts, passed a resolution at a faculty meeting denouncing the Communists and their "anonymous, ill-considered, and irresponsible attacks on institutions and individuals." Counts was elected national president of the American Federation of Teachers on a platform pledging to eliminate Communist influence from the union (he established a tradition within the union of being both anti-Communist and social democratic, a tradition later carried on by Albert Shanker).[70]

By 1941, reflecting on what he had learned, Counts held that his political goals had not changed but that he had come to realize that "Means and ends cannot be separated. The use of undemocratic means to achieve democratic ends, wherever and whenever democratic means are available, can only lead to disaster." The "canons of the democratic process," he said, require not only freedom of speech and press but also "a measure of honesty, fair-mindedness, restraint and even scientific spirit. . . . Democracy, to be successful, must rest upon the integrity of the individual. It requires the wide acceptance and practice of the so-called 'bourgeois virtues.' " He concluded that "the forces of democracy cannot cooperate or form a united front with any totalitarian movement or party, however loudly it may announce its devotion to the cause of democracy. Any claim it may make to the standards of democracy is spurious and fraudulent. In particular does this mean that the Communist party, as an instrument of popular advance, is completely repudiated. My experience convinces me that it poisons everything that it touches."[71] For the rest of his life, Counts was an outspoken anti-Communist and critic of Soviet totalitarianism.

In recoiling from his infatuation with the Soviet experiment, Counts turned against state control of the public schools. He decided that the state should have no authority over details of curriculum, methods of instruction, or the social doctrine to be inculcated. State control of the schools, he worried, would end in totalitarianism, as it had in the Soviet Union.

Counts was particularly fearful about "the encroachments of the federal government" and the possibility of a centrally controlled education system, fearing that any such machinery would result in "the political regimentation of the national mind." He preferred to place control of educational policy in the organized teaching profession (i.e., the teachers' unions), hoping that the profession could be trusted to put the best interests of students over the class interests of the profession: "The schools are not run to give employment to teachers nor to establish the rule of pedagogues. About this there should be no mistake. The guiding consideration must always be the welfare of children and society."[72]

Yet even after abandoning the Soviet Union as their model, progressive educators still clung to the ideas that the schools had a specific responsibility to direct social change and that the intellectual development of children was no longer the major goal of education. But most Americans would probably have said that the schools make society more democratic, as Lester Frank Ward had argued, by diffusing knowledge as broadly as possible throughout the population, thereby narrowing the gaps between those of different social classes and races.

7

The Public Schools Respond

What were the nation's superintendents, principals, and teachers to make of the theories and demands that rained down upon them in the 1930s? The education journals, the textbooks, the courses that were required of administrators for advanced degrees, the summer teacher-training institutes: all agreed that whatever was taught should be determined by the needs and interests of children, not by academic subjects, and that the schools had a special responsibility for changing society. The pedagogical textbooks of the 1930s reported on the new Gestalt psychology, which supported the idea of educating "the whole child" through seamless "organismic" experiences (that is, through "life situations" instead of subject matter). Popular interpretations of Freudian theory warned that children's psychological development would be harmed by discipline and any sort of correction. It became a cliché to say, "We teach children, not subject matter."[1]

Over the course of the decade, schools responded to the new theories by revising their curriculum. In the elementary schools, the activity movement changed what was taught and how it was to be taught. The teaching of reading and history in the early grades reflected the influence of child-centered methods. In the high schools, officials expanded the availability of nonacademic courses and often reduced the proportion of students who took academic programs. An extraordinary consensus de-

238

veloped among pedagogical theorists and high-level policy makers about the changes needed in the schools. This consensus had a large effect, particularly on the education of low-income and black students, for whom an academic education was allegedly inappropriate.

School officials surely wanted to be "up to date" and "modern," but these theories and demands came at an especially difficult time for the public schools, whose biggest problem was surging enrollments. Between 1880 and 1940, high school enrollment soared. In 1920, it stood at 2.2 million, doubled to 4.4 million by 1930, then reached 6.6 million by 1940. Youngsters and their parents realized that the changing economy required more knowledge, skills, literacy, and numeracy; the basic skills taught in the common schools were no longer sufficient.

The first necessity, of course, was building new schools and hiring additional teachers for this vast horde of new students, some of whom were in high school because the Depression had pushed them out of the labor market. A second pressing problem for school officials was figuring out what to do with their new students, especially those who probably didn't want to be there at all.

With the latter problem, progressive educators provided ready assistance, for they had been creating programs for youngsters from different kinds of backgrounds for many years. By the mid-1930s, it would have been difficult to find a school that did not reflect the pervasive effects of progressive reforms. School officials routinely tested students to determine their IQ and aptitudes; they used this information to decide whether students belonged in one of several vocational curricula or in the academic curriculum, which was becoming known as the college preparatory track; many schools continued to offer Latin, but only for the small minority of students who needed it to meet college entrance requirements.

Such changes, however, had become so completely conventional that they no longer sufficed to demonstrate that a school system was in step with the latest thinking. To keep abreast of modern pedagogical science, state and local superintendents did what their peers around the country were doing: they revised the curriculum to make it less academic and more like "real life."

In the 1920s, a few cities and school districts revised their curriculum. In the 1930s, the curriculum revision movement spread to nearly forty states and large numbers of school districts. By the middle of the decade, curriculum revision programs had been established in 70 percent of cities with populations greater than 25,000 and in nearly half the towns with populations from 5,000 to 25,000.[2] Experts asserted that reorganized schools could train wise consumers, stabilize family life, prepare future workers, reduce crime, and improve society—but only if the schools diminished their concern for "mastery of knowledge" and concentrated instead on "pressing issues of present living."[3]

Curriculum revision typically began after an administrator attended a professional conference or took a course at a school of education, where he discovered that his school or district or state was out of step with modern thinking. He would return home and inform his teachers that they were going to work cooperatively to revise the curriculum, based on the latest findings of educational science. Professional consultants would lead the process, using techniques of group dynamics to engineer consent for a new philosophy of education that emphasized socialization (changing student attitudes and behavior) instead of intellectual development. The teachers were assigned to study groups, where they read the works of John Dewey, William Heard Kilpatrick, Harold Rugg, and other well-known education theorists. The study groups would conduct a survey of the needs of the community, the city, or the state and ask whether the schools were meeting the most pressing needs. Since most communities, cities, and states had serious problems of unemployment, health, housing, sanitation, and poverty, teachers would invariably answer that the schools were not meeting those needs. In response to these findings, the curriculum would be revised to address the needs of the community or society.

In every district, regardless of the nature of the community, regardless of whether it was rural, urban, or suburban, regardless of the local economy, the deliberations produced nearly identical conclusions. Although there may have been exceptions, there are no reports of curriculum revision in which teachers decided that the theorists were wrong. In the records of that era, there is no indication that any school districts went through the process of curriculum revision and then decided to make sure that there was a solid academic curriculum for all students. Or that vocational choices should be deferred until youngsters were in high school. Or that what was good enough for professionals' children should be equally provided for the children of farmers and workers.

Every curriculum revision project of the era echoed the rhetoric of progressive educators, declaring its intention to "meet the needs of the whole child" and achieve "democracy in education." Educators agreed that the curriculum must be dynamic; that education was a continuous reconstruction of experience; that education had to embrace the total life experience of the child; that the goal of education was effective living for all; that instruction had to shift from subject matter to the child's experience; that college preparatory studies were narrow and aristocratic; that promotion and failure were anachronistic concepts; that marks and other extrinsic rewards were undemocratic.[4]

Virginia was one of the first states to embark on a statewide revision of its entire elementary and secondary school curriculum. In 1931, Sidney B. Hall, its new state superintendent and a former professor of education, declared that discoveries in educational science had been so fundamental and so well documented in the previous twenty years that the state's curriculum had to be revised to shift the emphasis "from the subject to the child." The state hired curriculum specialists to direct teachers' study of writings by "frontier thinkers." The guiding principles of curriculum revision were "the ideals of a democratic society" (an ironic claim since no reference was made to the state's undemocratic system of racial segregation in schools and society) and recognition that "all learning comes from experience."[5]

The Virginia revision was called a "core curriculum" because it eliminated distinct subjects, combined different academic subjects, and emphasized the "social implications of each field." Classroom activities from the first to twelfth grades were based not on subject matter but on the "major functions of social life," such as "Protection and Conservation of Life, Property, and Natural Resources"; "Production of Goods and Services and Distribution of the Returns of Production"; "Consumption of Goods and Services"; "Expression of Aesthetic Impulses"; and "Expression of Religious Impulses." These themes produced units such as "How does a changing culture affect the church as an agency of social control?" "How can modern means of transportation and communication be utilized to enhance the social welfare of nations and people?" Virginia's "social functions" approach was reproduced in pedagogical textbooks and adopted by other states and many cities.[6]

It is not clear why anyone thought that these ponderous topics would be more interesting to children than the study of history, geography, mathematics, literature, and science.

THE ACTIVITY MOVEMENT

The curriculum revision movement paved the way for the activity movement in elementary schools. Many elementary school teachers were comfortable blending different subjects because they had long been responsible for teaching a variety of subjects in their classrooms; the idea of correlating history, geography, and literature around a "center of interest," such as Indian life or the adventures of Robinson Crusoe, was standard practice in these grades.[7] At the high school level, however, teachers reacted skeptically to interdisciplinary studies because they were likely to have been educated to teach a specific subject—English, history, mathematics, or science—and were therefore less willing to merge their subject with another teacher's.

The activity movement drew its inspiration directly from Kilpatrick's writings about the project method and the importance of activities initiated by pupils and built on children's interests. In the 1920s, a small number of public elementary schools around the nation began to introduce "units of work," projects, and activities. In the new elementary school, each classroom had a reading corner and a "center of interest" for science (a place set aside with science-related materials). Pupils had free time to explore activities that interested them, such as building a house or a city made of big wooden blocks. Teachers planned projects related to themes that they believed were interesting to children, such as the study of boats or pets.

Ann Arbor, Michigan, turned its elementary schools into activity schools in which pupil experience rather than subject matter was emphasized. The transformation was led by Edith Bader, a progressive supervisor who had studied at Teachers College in the early 1920s. Bader rejected the philosophy that "knowledge is power" and that schools should transmit the social heritage; instead she thought that schools should concentrate on children's immediate needs and on their learning experiences. She believed in joint teacher-pupil planning of the day's activities. Under her leadership, academic subjects were integrated, textbooks were eliminated, and even reading classes were discontinued for a time because reading was taught in "situations" rather than in specific classes. Teachers were not always pleased with the new regime; a colleague later observed that under Bader "teachers were free to do what they wanted in the classroom, but they were not free to use a textbook."[8]

An important victory for the progressive movement occurred in California in 1930, when the state's Curriculum Commission—charged with setting minimum standards for elementary and secondary schools—endorsed the child-centered school as the model for the state's elementary schools. Citing the work of Dewey, Rugg, and Kilpatrick, the commission urged elementary schools to focus their teaching on activities based on children's interests.

Echoing Kilpatrick's theories, the California commission wrote that an activity program must give children the opportunity to "continually purpose [*sic*] and act in situations of meaning to them; in which they live fully, richly, happily, now, and so have the best possible preparation for living successfully after they leave school."[9] Do not worry about subject matter or discipline, said the commission; if children are pursuing their interests in a wholehearted way, they will learn habits of self-control and seek out information as they need it.

One suggested activity was "The Making of a Pet Park" by first- and second-grade children, an activity developed by the Demonstration School at the University of California at Los Angeles. The children would measure and lay out the park; build appropriate housing for rabbits, chickens, ducks, pigeons, and sheep; draw pictures of the animals; make posters for fund-raising; sing songs related to animals; take care of the animals; and write reports about what they were doing. Whatever the activity, it had to be "closely related to the child's life so as to lead him to want to carry it through." The activity program was already functioning in many schools across the state; the report cited children in Stockton building a "Raggedy Ann House," children in San Diego building a playhouse, children at the Auburn Union Grammar School learning about chickens.[10]

When used by teachers who saw activities as a *better way* of teaching subject matter rather than as a way of *avoiding* it—as means to an end rather than ends in themselves—the activity program was valuable. But in the hands of teachers who lacked subject matter knowledge, the activities became ends in themselves. The model for the activity program was the Lincoln School at Teachers College, Columbia University, which was staffed by well-educated, handpicked teachers. As new elementary teachers who received less education in subject matter entered the schools, however, it became increasingly difficult for them to connect pupils' activities to such fields of knowledge as science, history, geography, art, and literature, because the teachers themselves had little or no education in these fields. When they were no longer expected to teach subject matter, they had little reason to study it, and they studied pedagogy instead.

By 1930, the activity movement had grown into a formidable force in the nation's elementary schools, and curriculum leaders decided to compile a special yearbook to assay its status and prospects. The first problem they faced was that there was little agreement about what the movement was. A survey of experts and practitioners produced forty-two definitions. One group declared that the essential ingredient of the movement was that students themselves decided what and how to learn. Some believed that reading and learning multiplication tables should be considered legitimate activities, but others disagreed. Kilpatrick, whose theories had inspired the movement, boiled down the various definitions to mean "actual child living as nearly complete and natural as school conditions will permit." He approved only activities that were natural, not a curriculum set out in advance.[11]

Alice V. Keliher, a supervisor of elementary schools in Hartford,

Connecticut, claimed that the activity movement was a response to the new Gestalt psychology, which emphasized "the reactions of the *organism* to the *total situation*." Keliher explained that the new psychology of learning required a change in testing. No longer should educators be concerned with measuring what students had learned; instead, they should study children's development: "When education was primarily concerned with reading skill, arithmetical ability, and knowledge of geographical facts, tests of these abilities were relevant and acceptable. Now, when education must become synonymous with 'development,' such tests are no longer relevant to the basic purposes of education."[12]

Boyd H. Bode, a progressive who could usually be counted on to criticize the foibles of progressive education, worried that the activity movement had become incoherent. He said that it was implicitly promoting "phobias that have developed against 'imposition' by the teacher, against 'subjects,' and against the introduction of 'described' situations." In its present formlessness, it appeared that "the Activity Movement can lay claim to everything in sight and that this 'Movement' has contributed nothing but an empty name to our already overburdened professional vocabulary." Bode thought there was little danger that elementary school children would be harmed by the movement's confusion of means and ends, but he predicted that its lack of clear aims and its inability to "appreciate the permanent values in traditional education, particularly with respect to 'logical organization of subject matter' " would very likely prove an embarrassment when the movement reached the high schools.[13]

William C. Bagley, the best-known critic of progressivism, was skeptical about the activity movement. He was willing to acknowledge its value as a "supplement to a program of systematic and sequential learnings." But if the intention was to substitute aimless experiences for such learnings, it was "pitiably inadequate." He believed that "the freedom of the immature child to choose what he or she will or will not learn is utterly insignificant in comparison with freedom from want, fear, fraud, and superstition—a type of freedom which is won only by a systematic and effortful mastery of the lessons that man has learned as he has traversed his rough road upward from the savage and the brute." The theory behind the movement, he said, failed to recognize that "one of the factors differentiating mankind from other animal species is the ability to work systematically and persistently in the face of immediate desire or impulse or interest." Furthermore, the theory "denies the plain biological significance of the period of immaturity—namely, the inescapable need of the human offspring for control, guidance, instruction, and discipline as a basis for the responsibilities of adulthood." As a parting shot, Bagley declared, "I can conceive of no set of assumptions, which when made the sole basis of an educational program and carried out consistently, would more certainly intensify individualism and enthrone a glorified hedonism."[14]

Even John Dewey, whose name was considered sacred by everyone associated with the activity movement, agreed that not all kinds of activity were of equal value. Activity was surely better than "quiescence and passive absorption," but activity could also be "boisterous, rowdy, thoughtless, blindly emotional, passionate, mechanical, and perfunctory, swallowed up in doing what others are doing, or the opposite." He noted that "when children are asked in an overt way what they want or what they would like to do, they are usually forced into a purely artificial state and the result is the deliberate creation of an undesirable habit. It is the business of the educator to study the tendencies of the young so as to be more consciously aware than are the children themselves what the latter need and want. Any other course transfers the responsibility of the teacher to those taught."[15]

As one would expect, the activity movement was warmly defended by Kilpatrick, its spiritual father. The best education, he insisted, was "intelligent living," and he proposed that "to secure education it were better . . . to forget education and instead to center attention upon life and its intelligent bettering. If we do so forget education, so lose it in fostering the life process, we shall find it more surely by far than if we continue the ordinary school deception that education is to be got by seeking it directly, as somehow outside of living itself and mainly as a preparation for living later to come." The virtue of the activity program, he held, was that it was the same as "life" and "living." Kilpatrick disagreed with those who feared neglect of the social heritage: "Only one committed to subject-matter-set-out-to-be-learned could so claim or think. The child lives and moves and has his being in the all-surrounding and pervasive social heritage. Every act of study will involve it. Under competent guidance he will get all of it that a varied life will call for, more and better it seems safe to claim than in the traditional way." To Bagley's fear that the activity program "makes for hedonism and selfish individualism," Kilpatrick replied that this could be asserted only by someone who believed "the exploded theory that man naturally acts for self and pleasure only." [16]

THE ACTIVITY MOVEMENT IN PRACTICE

In the 1930s, the activity movement spread rapidly into many of the nation's elementary schools. It was not only modern and scientific, but it was much more fun for children to learn while engaged in playful activities. The New York State Education Department promoted the activity curriculum in public schools across the state, making a special effort to institute it in rural schools. According to Helen Hay Heyl, a supervisor from the State Education Department, the New York approach emphasized "gradual integration of subjects," substitution of "child-planning" for "teacher-planning," and a shift toward activities "more on the basis of the child's interests and needs and less on the basis of subject-matter-set-up-to-be-learned." In the Los Angeles schools, the activity curriculum aimed to promote "a happy and successful group life" by allowing all children to participate in "good living" and interesting experiences. In Carteret County, North Carolina, the elementary schools switched to activities, units of work, and projects as their daily program. [17]

Although Kilpatrick thought that the activity movement would put an end to "subject-matter-set-out-to-be-learned," most public schools that adopted activity programs reserved part of the day for "drill" in the basics of reading, spelling, mathematics, and writing.

In the late 1920s, an activity program was introduced into the elementary schools of Montclair, New Jersey, where school officials were very enthusiastic about it. However, principal Albert L. Hartman reported that activities by themselves were not adequate to ensure that children learned basic skills; after two years, the children in fourth grade "were very deficient in their ability to read, spell, and write." It was necessary to set aside part of the day for skill instruction. "In our experience," said Hartman, "the bright pupils and a few of average ability acquire the skills of reading, writing, and arithmetic with a minimum of help" but most average and below-average pupils continued to need "specific practice in the skills and certain knowledges."[18]

The assistant superintendent of schools in Battle Creek, Michigan, Dessalee Ryan Dudley, was also enthusiastic about the potential of the activity methods for enlivening the classroom and motivating students. Students who were studying trains, for example, might engage in "building trains, playing train, drawing trains, and in other means of expression." Yet she too warned that "too frequently the term 'activity' covers a mere making of things out of which no learnings of real value emerge." Wise teachers, she said, were not willing to leave to chance their students' growth in "basic and sequential knowledge and skills." The activity curriculum would remain for them a "valuable guide and not a taskmaster."[19]

In Houston, School Superintendent E. E. Oberholtzer reported that teachers in activity classrooms spent between 35 and 42 percent of the day on drill, even when they were told that they were not required to do so, as compared to traditional classrooms, where 65 percent of the day was devoted to drill. He found that the students in activity classrooms read more, had higher levels of interest, and achieved at least as much as students in traditional classrooms. Like many other school districts, Houston utilized some features of the activity program while maintaining systematic teaching of basic skills.[20]

Maude McBroom, the principal of the University Elementary School at the University of Iowa, was an ardent supporter of the activity program but admitted frankly that such schools were problematic. Far from being an *easier* way to educate children, she noted, an activity program demanded more space, more equipment, more planning, more resources, more supplies, and better-educated teachers than a conventional program did.

She acknowledged that children too often became accustomed to mediocre standards of workmanship particularly when they engaged in projects far beyond their ability. They also wasted time on superficial activities. After getting accustomed to "active doing," they were unwilling to engage in work that was not immediately satisfying. When classes were as large as thirty, most children became passive observers. Selfish children became more selfish, timid children became more timid. Too often, "inaccurate and 'half-baked' ideas were permitted to go unchallenged and were accepted as the truth." McBroom concluded that teachers had gone overboard in their desire to have children do "less memorizing and more imagining." No one, she said, "has ever done any imagining worthy of the name who did not have a vast store of memorized facts and thoroughly understood experiences out of which to build his imaginings."[21]

THE ACTIVITY PROGRAM IN NEW YORK CITY

New York City launched the most ambitious trial of the activity program, placing it in sixty-nine public elementary schools with 75,000 students and nearly 2,500 teachers in 1935. These schools were regularly evaluated and compared to an equal number of traditional schools; at the end of six years, the Board of Education recommended the program's gradual adoption in all elementary schools.

The experimental classes promoted creative work in the arts; dramatic experiences (e.g., playing store, staging puppet shows); construction activities; teaching current events and becoming involved in community activities; student self-government; and efforts to discover the "interests, aptitudes, and talents of each individual." Children were encouraged to "do the kind of work they can do best and to enjoy the kind of experience they like best as long as they do not interfere with others. . . . Situations in which everybody in the class is doing the same thing at the same time should be more and more infrequent." In the experimental classes, emphasis shifted from acquiring information to acquiring "desirable attitudes and beliefs." Tests were created to measure "emotional adjustment and social adjustment," "social beliefs and attitudes," even the pupils' "happiness." Tests assessed whether students agreed with "progressive" or "reactionary" views on controversial issues.[22]

In 1941, Benjamin Fine of *The New York Times* hailed the New York City program as "one of the most significant experiments in the history of American education." Describing the children in activity schools as "happy guinea pigs," Fine asserted that revolutionary changes were introduced in their classrooms.

> Instead of studying their reading, 'riting and 'rithmetic in the sedate traditional way, the children played and frolicked all day long. Gone were the agonizing hours spent on long division, on bounding the State of Maine, on grammar and composition. . . . Their classrooms ran over with hammers, saws, nails, coiled snakes in glass jars, packing boxes, posters and similar unorthodox objects—enough to give a disciplined schoolma'am of the conventional order apoplexy.

Fine concluded that "the Royal Road to Learning" had been discovered and the biggest obstacle ahead was teaching the new methods to the nation's teachers.[23]

The results of the six-year experiment in New York City were mixed. As the experiment neared its end, John J. Loftus, the Board of Education official who supervised both the program and its evaluation, acknowledged that no definition of "activity program" had been agreed upon, so it was not clear what was being evaluated and how consistent "it" was from school to school. In addition, there had been "an incredible turnover of pupils, teachers, and supervisors" (for example, 45 of the principals in the study's 69 experimental schools had changed during the six years of the study). Because of pupil turnover, the activity schools set aside an hour a day for "drills and skills." The activity program was hampered by budget cuts that eliminated teachers of art, music, and health. In the traditional schools, 93 percent of the children's day was devoted to projects involving the entire class, compared to 84 percent in activity schools. The activity schools spent more time on arts and crafts; the traditional schools spent more time on reading and penmanship. Otherwise the differences between them in how time was spent and what the children learned were small.[24]

Historians have cast doubt on how successfully the activity program was implemented after it was supposedly adopted for the entire school system. Many schools did not change their practices; the overwhelming majority of teachers in traditional schools and even one-third of those in activity schools preferred traditional methods. Historian Larry Cuban maintained that the New York City public school system adopted "the progressives' vocabulary" but instruction changed little; the "connective tissue of instruction—classroom architecture, class size, report cards, rules, the evaluation process, and supervision," he held, determined "prevailing teaching practices." Recalling his own experiences as a student in a well-regarded New York City public elementary school from 1944 to 1946, historian Arthur Zilversmit remembered an old-fashioned school building, seats and desks bolted to the classroom floor, and a "repressive" atmosphere. The official rhetoric may have changed, he wrote, but the reality for students did not.[25]

Perhaps the lesson to be drawn from New York City's large-scale experiment is that, even with the best of intentions, revolutionary changes tend to merge with whatever precedes them. At the outset of the experiment, those in charge said that "education's biggest problem is whether to make traditional schools better traditional schools or whether to transform them into some type of 'progressive' or activity schools."[26] Long after the experiment was a forgotten footnote in history, it appeared that the only change in schooling that endures is evolutionary, building on the strengths of teachers and acknowledging the aspirations of those who send their children to learn.

The activity program was never quite the same in any two classrooms. Whether it was a good program or not depended on the quality and ingenuity of teachers. When the teachers were as gifted as those in the Lincoln School, the activity movement engaged children in stimulating projects, which helped them learn reading, science, mathematics, and history. In the hands of less skillful teachers, the activity movement kept children busy on aimless projects without teaching them the knowledge and skills that they needed. Without question, the activity movement changed elementary education for the better. Also without doubt, the nation's experienced public school educators recognized that the activity movement would succeed only if teachers continued to teach children the knowledge and skills that they were unlikely to pick up on their own.

Changes in the Content of Readers

As the activity movement entered the mainstream of elementary education, it left a mixed legacy. The shift to activities, projects, and experiences meant that school was more enjoyable for children. But the activity movement disseminated some of the most dubious practices associated with progressive education, especially those related to the teaching of reading and history.

In teaching reading, progressive educators warned against oral reading and "too early attention to the alphabet, phonics, or any other kind of analysis of words." Reading experts insisted that silent reading was superior to oral reading, because it was faster and produced greater comprehension and was used more often by adults. The abandonment of oral reading changed the daily life of the public schools because "reading out loud" by pupils and teachers was a common practice.[27]

Some educators insisted that it was literally harmful for adults to read to children. Eugene Smith, headmaster of the private Beaver Country Day School and president of the Progressive Education Association, advised parents not to read to their children because it "lessens the amount the child will read to himself" and "makes it easier to get information through the ear than through the eye." He described a bright child who was seriously handicapped because her father had read to her for years "and in so doing had trained her ear as a source of information, while her eye, having no such practice, was almost helpless as an avenue for learning." In the modern method, said Smith, the child was "taught to form a mental picture of an entire word or phrase" instead of recognizing the letters or their sounds. Smith called this "the picture method," but it was more often referred to as the "whole-word" method or "look-say."[28]

The "whole-word" method of reading was used by William S. Gray in his phenomenally successful Elson Readers, better known as the "Dick and Jane" series, introduced in 1930. The "Dick and Jane" readers and others like them contained simple stories about children, home life, animals, and toys. In line with the progressive educators' emphasis on children's interests, reading reformers insisted that reading methods should be as natural as possible and that the content of readers should be connected to children's point of view. "Natural," in this context, meant that children should learn to recognize whole words rather than sound out unfamiliar ones. The "whole-word," "look-say" method became associated with child-centered education, and progressives considered phonics to be obsolete. Look-say readers employed a simple vocabulary with a small number of words that could be quickly recognized. The language of the Dick and Jane readers was simple and repetitive, with colorful illustrations. In little time, the young child could read "Come, Dick. Come and see. Come, come. Come and see. Come and see Spot. Look, Spot. Oh, look. Look and see. Oh, see."[29]

For many years before 1920, the primary purpose of school readers (after children had learned to read) was to develop a taste for good literature. The McGuffey Readers, read by tens of millions of American children in the latter half of the nineteenth century, contained classic poems, speeches, and stories by well-known American and British authors. Other readers competed to replace McGuffey by creating even better assemblages of literary gems. Among the best schoolbooks of this era were the "Heart of Oak" reading books, edited by Charles Eliot Norton, which included Mother Goose rhymes, fables, legends, fairy tales, classic short stories, and poetry. Assuming that his books would be read both at school and at home, Norton gave precedence to "the best literature, the virtue of which has been approved by long consent. . . . Every competent teacher will already be possessed of much which they contain; but the worth of the masterpieces of any art increases with use and familiarity of association. They grow fresher by custom; and the love of them deepens in proportion to the time we have known them, and to the memories with which they have become invested."[30]

The most popular selections included Abraham Lincoln's Gettysburg Address, Henry Wadsworth Longfellow's "The Village Blacksmith," Washington Irving's "Rip Van Winkle," Robert Browning's "The Pied Piper of Hamelin," William Wordsworth's "Daffodils," Walt Whitman's "O Captain, My Captain," Alfred, Lord Tennyson's "The Charge of the Light Brigade," and Ralph Waldo Emerson's "Concord Hymn." The readers frequently included excerpts from Daniel Defoe's *Robinson Crusoe* and Benjamin Franklin's *Autobiography*. The authors whose work appeared most often were Aesop, Shakespeare, Longfellow, Robert Louis Stevenson, Tennyson, Charles Dickens, Nathaniel Hawthorne, John Greenleaf Whittier, Hans Christian Andersen, and the Brothers Grimm. Textbook editors extolled the importance of introducing young Americans to good literature written by American and European writers.[31]

Pedagogical experts, however, insisted that children's stories should be more realistic. A professor of education at Syracuse University complained in 1923 that the readers contained too much that was "untrue to life." He insisted that children "may be bored by stories that seem to them to be entirely impossible. . . . In the stories boys of ten or twelve do things that are impossible for the reader to do, and out of such material may easily grow a feeling of self-depreciation, [*sic*], or excessive daydreaming." Especially offensive were stories in which "great things happen over-night. . . . Vergil's [*sic*] Aeneid and ancient mythology are full of this idea of suddenness, an unnatural way of bringing things to pass. It is no wonder that the products of our schools are often referred to as 'impatient youths' and that they become discouraged if they can not reform a city over night, or change the political complexion of a state in a day."[32]

Many of the new readers in the 1920s and 1930s were prepared by professors of reading who valued a limited vocabulary more than literary merit. A study in 1931 noted that "a great change has been made in the reading material in the last five or six years." There was a dramatic decrease in fables, poetry, and folklore and an equally dramatic increase in the space provided for "information" pieces, selections about "children's experience," and "objective tests."[33]

When the public got hints of these changes, it did not approve. In the fall of 1929, the Teachers College library mounted a display of "modern" textbooks that replaced traditional fairy tales with content based on "modern theories of child psychology." Two faculty members told *The New York Times* that the "utterly ridiculous" old stories, with their "mawkish sentiment" and talking animals, had to go. Most typical of the modern trend, the *Times* noted, was "the story of junior's pajamas. Instead of having the pajamas walk off by themselves or fly about the room as in the old stories, this tale opens with a description of colored men picking cotton on the plantations and mentions in turn all the necessary operations before the cotton becomes junior's new pajamas." With sublime indifference to the racial and social implications of the new story, the faculty members offered it as an illustration of how cotton becomes clothing. In response to this story, hostile public reaction ignited what was briefly known as "the Mother Goose controversy at Teachers College." The editor of the college's journal jokingly protested that Teachers College had been unfairly accused of "sacrilege, heresy, and treason," and the faculty "so far as is known" had no wish to "put an end to Mother Goose."[34]

By the late 1930s, the content of second-grade readers had changed significantly, compared to twenty years earlier. There was a sharp decline in folk and fairy tales, poems, legends, and myths, and an equally large increase in social studies material, animal stories, and "realistic" stories. Literary selections had dropped from 80 percent of the content in 1920 to 40 percent by 1935 and in some readers made up less than 2 percent. Noting that "the greatest change in primary readers in twenty years has been the decreasing amount of literary or traditional type of material," researcher Agnes G. Gunderson predicted that within the next decade traditional literature would disappear from second-grade readers entirely. She suggested that, in the future, it would be the responsibility of parents and librarians to "provide for all children this traditional literature which in the past has been a part of every child's literary background. It would be sad indeed were a child to complete the primary school without having made the acquaintance of Lucky Hans, Espen the Cinder Lad, Little Half Chick, the Elves and the Shoemaker, the Easter Rabbit, and many other characters in folklore who are to the child what Shakespeare's characters are to the adult."[35]

Sad it was, but not everyone thought so. By 1940, William S. Gray announced with satisfaction that "the problem of teaching pupils to read has been clearly differentiated from the traditional effort to cultivate appreciation for classic literature." Gray claimed with assurance that the new-style readers, such as his own "Dick and Jane" series, "are increasingly of such quality that they tend by their very nature to cultivate a preference for artistic forms of writing." Actually, the new reading textbooks for the early grades were so pedestrian that it was hard to imagine how they could "cultivate a preference for artistic forms of writing."[36]

THE FATE OF HISTORY IN THE ELEMENTARY GRADES

*Just as the activity movement reduced classic literature in the elemen*tary grades, it also led to the gradual removal of history and mythology from the early years. Before the 1930s, children in first, second, and third grades learned legends and stories about heroic historical figures. There was a good deal of playacting, and teachers prided themselves on their ability as storytellers. Most young children read Greek and Roman myths, as well as myths and legends from around the world. The third grade in the Philadelphia public schools, for example, studied "heroes of legend and history," including "Joseph; Moses; David; Ulysses; Alexander; Horatius; Cincinnatus; Siegfried; Arthur; Roland; Alfred the Great; Richard the Lion Hearted; Robert Bruce; William Tell; Joan of Arc; Peter the Great; Florence Nightingale." Such stories and historical literature were found in every school's curriculum, and most districts also taught civics or "home geography." In home geography, children learned about home, school, community life, occupations, and industries, as well as nature study, the seasons, and the weather.[37]

The activity movement's emphasis on the present doomed history in the early grades. The champions of social studies considered the study of historical stories, myths, and heroes to be an evasion of social responsibility. John A. Hockett, a former Lincoln School teacher who became a leader in curriculum reform in California after he joined the faculty at the University of California at Berkeley, condemned schools that encouraged "day-dreaming" and that "refuse[d] to deal realistically with the conditions and problems of the world." In his view, the goal of social studies in the elementary school was to socialize the student by using co-operative activities and discouraging "out-moded" individualism. These activities should be centered on "home, family, neighborhood, school, and community," he said, and on the present, not the past.[38]

The revised Virginia social studies standards set a new pattern for the nation, expanding home geography into the entire elementary school social studies program and eliminating any history. In the first three grades, children studied " 'me' and my family, my school, my community." Children were expected to engage in "socially useful labor" and also, with adults, "to attack the problem of raising the standard of living, of increasing the amount of food, shelter, clothing, recreation, and education of the members of their own families and their local communities."[39]

The chief consultant on the social studies in Virginia was Paul R. Hanna, a researcher at the Lincoln School (and later dean of education at Stanford University). Hanna criticized "romanticism," which occurred when children "learn to escape from this suffering world" by "reliving the days of old when knights were bold and rode through the land in search of great adventure" and when "they draw and paint the symbols of heraldry, dance the festivals of historic peasant folk . . . become courageous, sea-faring men of the north countries, construct small models of picturesque boats and again sail unknown seas to find new lands. Or these pupils imagine themselves to be Athenians or Romans living in the Golden Age of art, architecture, or philosophy. And many of them become pantalooned Dutch children, clumping along in wooden shoes and raising beds of tulips." He did not doubt that children lived "a happy life for the few hours they spend in school—dancing, singing, painting, reading, writing, dramatizing, modelling," but all of this was artificial, and "the children in such a curriculum do not face the realities of the world in which they live—they escape, they retreat to a romantic realm of the yesterday."[40] This kind of romantic education, Hanna insisted, bolstered the status quo. He and other progressive educators believed that social reconstruction began by requiring children in the first, second, and third grades to learn about their family, home, school, and community life.

In the 1930s, in state after state, district after district, the social studies curriculum in the early grades slowly changed. History, myth, and legend, the great stories that had linked earlier generations, began to disappear. By 1937, a national survey of curriculum trends reported that the early elementary grades were increasingly organized around "socially real situations" and "the major activities of child life," such as the farm, the city, the post office, milk, clothing, food, and pets.[41] First-graders studied home and family; second-graders studied their neighborhood; third-graders studied their community. The textbook industry readily accepted this simple format, which provided a predictable framework for its products. This sequence remained in place in American public schools for the rest of the twentieth century, firmly institutionalized in state curricula, textbooks, and the guidelines of the National Council for the Social Studies. Generations of teachers assumed that this approach—known as "expanding environments" or "expanding horizons"—was grounded in research, but it was not. Rather, it was the product of a period in which pedagogical leaders chose socialization over intellectual enrichment and rejected stories of what happened "long ago and far away."

THE "INTEGRATION" MOVEMENT IN SECONDARY SCHOOLS

While the activity movement swept the elementary schools during the 1930s, junior high and high schools were influenced by the curricular integration movement. This pedagogical movement extended the premises of the activity movement into the upper grades and sought to replace subject matter with student experiences, socially significant studies, and "life situations."

The curricular integration movement was initiated by the Lincoln School after the arrival of Jesse H. Newlon, who left the Denver public schools to become Lincoln's director in 1927. Newlon campaigned relentlessly for a new social philosophy of education, "adjusted to meet the needs of all individuals." At a 1931 meeting of the NEA, Newlon asked, "Why should millions be droning over subjectmatter [*sic*] utterly without value to them?" American education, he maintained, represented "the ideology of a social order that has long since passed away." He said, "It is far more important that the farmer understand agricultural economics than a Latin conjugation, that he learn something of landscape gardening than how to demonstrate the *pons asinorum,* and it is more important that all youth understand the causes of the last war and the conditions making for the next one than that all should know how to solve a quadratic equation."[42]

Why Newlon thought that these were mutually exclusive alternatives was not clear, but he seemed to have an abiding hostility to the academic curriculum. He complained that the "academically-minded teacher, interested primarily in subjectmatter as the end of education, constitutes one of the greatest barriers to integrated, socially effective schools." Integration, as practiced at the Lincoln School, meant that learning would no longer be "in the sole sense of acquiring book knowledge and mastery of skills but as including every aspect of the individual's development—physical, intellectual, aesthetic, emotional, social, ethical; in short, the total personality."[43] Like the activity movement, the integration movement made socialization of the student, not transmission of knowledge, the primary goal of schooling.

The curriculum director of the Lincoln School, L. Thomas Hopkins, was the leading theorist of the integration movement. An entire issue of the *Teachers College Record* was devoted to "Integrated Education in Lincoln School." Hopkins described a "great battle of educational ideas," which he believed had already ended with a victory for his side:

> When someone in the year 2000 writes the history of American education for the twentieth century, the decade between the close of the World War and the financial and economic collapse which heralded the great depression will stand out as of peculiar importance. It was in these years that the great battle of educational ideas took place. The death struggle between two opposing types of curriculum practice was fought and decided. On the one side was the large group of educators who championed the

subject curriculum; on the other was the small group of educators who advocated the experience curriculum. A decision was rendered in 1929.[44]

Inspired by the events of the Depression, he said, educators looked hard at what they were doing and began to abandon the subject curriculum from the kindergarten to the liberal arts college. Consequently, the movement toward the experience curriculum, which began in 1931, "has in this year, 1937, almost reached a tidal wave."

Hopkins traced the outlines of this epochal struggle of ideas. The subject curriculum, he said, was taught by authoritarian methods and controlled entirely by the teacher, who employed a variety of strategies to motivate students to accept abstract learning. The experience curriculum relied not on the teacher's authority but on joint planning between pupils and teachers. Its main ideas, he wrote (in characteristically brain-numbing pedagogical jargon), were that

> education is the reconstruction of the present life and living of the individual. This is a never-ending, continuous process. It is achieved through all experiences of the individual, both in and outside of the school. It goes on wherever the child is alert to the situation in which he is taking part or to the experience in which he may be engaged. Since improvement of life and living constitutes the curriculum, the experiences cannot be set out and organized in advance of the life of the individuals who will participate in it.[45]

The experience curriculum was the heart and soul of progressive education; it was living, good living, democratic living. It was interaction with situations involving children's needs, purposes, interests, problems. It was not planned in advance. It was not organized into topics or lesson plans but "selected on the spot by pupils and teachers who compose the particular learning group."[46] Such conditions might be met, with a great deal of effort, at the private Lincoln School, with its carefully selected staff and students; but they were a nearly impossible and constantly receding ideal for the nation's public schools.

An integrated (or as Hopkins preferred to say, an "integrating") person was well adjusted to his environment and to society. A person who was not integrating, he warned, would question the group's goals and would likely be "rejected by certain persons" and by "certain groups." This nonintegrating person would constantly be in difficulty with others because of his tendency to "resist attempts to enforce conformity upon him through dominance." Since the world was growing ever more interdependent and "consequently more and more functions need to be performed group-wise," the schools would have to equip individuals for participation in group life.[47] In other words, they would have to teach students to conform to the group.

CURRICULUM CHANGE AND SOCIAL ADJUSTMENT

At this point in the evolution of progressive ideology, an important shift occurred: the radical, free-spirited individualism associated with the child-centered schools of the 1920s disappeared, replaced by calls to "adjust" the individual to the requirements of collective society. The shift occurred quietly. The political mood of the Depression had put an end to the celebration of nonconformity; even Harold Rugg, who had championed freethinking progressive schools in the 1920s, endorsed the collectivist ethos of the social reconstructionists.

It was a short step from the radical idea that the schools should build a new, collectivist social order—which the public schools had plainly rejected—to the distinctly nonradical idea that the schools should teach students to conform to the group. "Rugged individualism" was a remnant, reformers agreed, of the failed capitalism of the past. The new social order required students to be cooperative group members. This was a concept that even conservative school superintendents could comprehend, for it called upon the public schools to adjust students to the needs of society. The key to this shift from individualism to cooperative group living was clear: it required a de-emphasis of the academic curriculum, which stood in opposition to child-centered schools, social reconstructionism, and social conformism.

Whatever integration was, it had wide influence, if one can believe a

1935 study by a professor at the University of Texas who estimated that 80 percent of American schools had been affected by the integration movement to some extent. In practice, integration was almost any effort to replace academic subject matter with experiences tied to either pupil interests or community problems, or both. In one version, integration was called "fusion"; activities connected with a current or local problem took the place of academic studies. In social studies, fusion meant "the elimination of the separate subjects of history, geography, civics, economics, sociology, and the like," and in science it meant "the abandonment of the separate subjects of biology, physics, chemistry, zoology, physiology, and botany." A 1933 study identified more than fifty cities where junior high schools practiced "fusion" in the social studies. The Lincoln School's L. Thomas Hopkins considered even fusion to be inadequate, because "the subject-matter is still set-out-to-be-learned although the current problem is used to make it slightly more enticing."[48]

Another form of integration, the "broad-fields curriculum," grouped academic subjects into large categories, such as social studies, language arts, and vocational arts. In 1933, the North-Central Association of Colleges and Secondary Schools, a major accrediting agency for high schools and colleges, adopted four "broad-fields" objectives for secondary education: health, leisure, social relationships, and vocations. In the following decades, the "broad fields" approach was installed in public schools across the country, as social studies replaced history and language arts replaced English language and literature. (Hopkins faulted "broad fields" because it did not leave pupils free to "follow their own interests, determine their own goals, select their own means, and organize and evaluate the results of their own experiences."[49])

The Core Curriculum and "Social Living"

A step beyond even the broad-fields curriculum was the core curriculum. In the late twentieth century, the term "core curriculum" was used to describe the essential academic subjects that formed the "core" of the curriculum. But as conceptualized in the 1930s, the core curriculum de-emphasized academic subjects and centered on practical problems of "social living." All of the other curricular patterns were built around various subjects. The core curriculum in the 1930s was supposed to get rid of academic subjects altogether and put students' experiences and problems in their place, although in practice this seldom happened except in guidance classes.

In 1934, the NEA's Department of Secondary School Principals, which presumably spoke for the nation's high school leaders, endorsed the idea of replacing subject matter courses such as science and history with "fundamental categories of genuine student experiences," thereby reorganizing the curriculum to "start with the student rather than with items of subject matter." Some high schools were actually moving in this direction and gained national attention for their efforts.[50]

Certain prosperous suburban school districts outside New York City, Chicago, and Los Angeles reorganized their secondary curriculum along the recommended lines. Roslyn, New York, for example, experimented with variations on the core curriculum, such as a merger of English, social studies, and general science; Latin, English, and social science; English, science, and "general business practices"; or even mathematics, shop, and home economics. In one core class, which met daily for three hours, ninth-graders studied their own homes, made maps and scale drawings, and learned about family life, "costs of operating and financing homes, furnishing of fuel, light and power, cost and operation of appliances, budgeting for and purchasing of proper foods, nefarious advertising and adulteration of foods." In 1937, hundreds of Roslyn parents complained that their children couldn't read and that they preferred a more traditional form of education. One parent was incensed when a class spent an entire day "learning how to make nut bread," even though the superintendent had explained that baking nut bread was a very good way to teach mathematics. The parents' objections were investigated by progressive bureaucrats in the State Education Department, who assured the parents of Roslyn students that their children were doing as well as could be expected in light of their group IQ.[51]

Denver also energetically introduced core curricula in its high schools. According to an account by a spokesman for the Denver public schools, the Manual Training High School created a core program that met two hours daily to study the "common problems of youth." The students' first problem was getting to know the school; they then moved on to problems of health, appearance, conduct, and "friendly adjustment to others." In the art class, they learned how to select clothing. The science teacher helped them learn "how to think" and how to "use such words as data, assumptions, evidence, proof, fallacy, and conclusions," but they didn't seem to learn any science. Emphasis was also placed on leisure activities and preparation for vocational choices, as well as how to be good consumers, how to select a marriage partner, and how to make a home attractive. At East High School in Denver, the required core program included units on "personal development, adjustment to the school program, family relations, consumer education, the effective use of the radio, and the like"; all other studies were elective. By 1938, the curriculum director for the Denver public schools reported that the new core program featured "a real break with the traditional subject-matter of high school courses . . . a break from the study of subject-matter set out to be learned in order that it may be used in the future to the study of subject-matter that pupils find essential in meeting their everyday problems of living."[52]

In 1937, the Evanston, Illinois, Township High School created an experimental core curriculum program, in collaboration with the Northwestern University school of education, based upon "the real interests and needs of children." The purpose of the new program was to replace the traditional academic subjects, which "often warp the developing personalities of boys and girls" with studies of "community living." The youngsters' activities were centered around the following themes:

1. Understanding the Community Setting
2. Protecting Life and Health
3. Making a Home
4. Getting a Living
5. Expressing Religious Impulses
6. Satisfying the Desire for Beauty
7. Securing an Education

8. Cooperating in Social and Civic Action
9. Engaging in Recreation
10. Improving Material Conditions

The staff insisted that it would not set out a detailed course of study in advance. Nor would there be any prior determination about the exact sequence of what was to be taught or learned; instead, teachers and pupils would decide on their own what they wanted to study and would spontaneously develop their own plans as they saw fit. Not until later in their high school years would students in the experimental program take academic subjects and then only if they had the desire and ability to do so.[53]

In Holton, Kansas, a small town of 3,000, the dire conditions associated with the Depression facilitated the reorganization of the curriculum. The head of the English Department in the high school had been trying to replace formal courses in literature and composition with "functional work," with less attention to "correct forms and structures." When a statewide fiscal crisis in 1933 caused the school to lose two English teachers, the department head recognized a blessing in disguise: he assigned some English classes to a home economics teacher and a physical education teacher, neither of whom had "preconceived ideas concerning how English should be taught." This innovative department head proceeded to eliminate grammar, composition, and literature in the seventh and eighth grades and instituted a core curriculum in which children studied their homes and home community, with particular attention to building materials such as metals, woods, and masonry, as well as landscaping and grounds. Eventually, the classes produced a housing survey of Holton, which the staff considered far more valuable than the traditional study of English.[54]

Not only were traditional subjects merged in the core curriculum, but some were converted to practical activities. In Goldsboro, North Carolina, a high school class in physics was turned into a shop class, where the students made diving helmets and built radios; two farm boys made "fence chargers for the electrical fencing of pastures." Trigonometry was turned into surveying and mechanical drawing. In homemaking, the girls figured out how to equip the girls' restroom, which "led to the improvement of the general personal appearance of all the girls in school." Students in Business Training filed book cards in the library, while students in Manual Training built library furniture. Presumably there was a track for the college-bound, but the teachers who wrote about the high school forgot to mention it.[55]

In Los Angeles, the Abraham Lincoln High School "vitalized" its curriculum, replacing traditional academic studies with a required program of health, science, and "social living." For four years, all 2,500 students were required to study both science and health for one hour each day, and social living for two hours. Social living—a combination of English, social studies, and the arts—aimed to teach the student "to understand appreciatively his own self, to develop normal mental attitudes, controlled emotional reactions, sound social manners, the habits of clear thinking, the power of adaptability, and the freedom to express himself creatively." The actual content of the social living course varied according to the "mental endowment" of each group of students, with superior students getting college preparation, while others received watered-down instruction adjusted to their needs and abilities. The principal wrote, "We are eager . . . to keep the retarded but socially mature students happy and in an environment in which they can best develop, and in order to safeguard them from restless dissatisfaction our program gives the same name to all subjects whether they be planned for a recommended group of high mental endowment or for a 'special-certificate' group of pupils." Since every student was in a program supposedly tied to his needs and interests, promotion from grade to grade was automatic, and failure was abolished.[56]

In Evansville, Indiana, in the 1930s, the public school system created an "integrating-experience curriculum" for Lincoln High School, a school of nearly five hundred black youngsters, in connection with the opening of a nearby low-income federal housing project. The school designed its entire course of study around the concept of housing. Students learned about the history of the housing project, the administration of the project, health and safety issues, home management, electricity, plumbing, care of furniture, home mechanics, budgeting, and "housing in literature."[57]

Harold Spears, director of research and secondary education in Evansville, insisted that the modern, democratic school must provide different opportunities, standards, and expectations for different children, because of their individual differences. *"Equality* of educational opportunity calls for just such adjustments, and was never supposed to have been *identity* of educational opportunity," he wrote. This meant that one child might spend a major share of his time in the machine shop while another would spend most of his time in music classes. It was time, Spears insisted, for the school "to accept these differences among youth, to relinquish its faith in certain minimum essentials and cultural aspects of the older program," and to drop the idea of common standards and expectations.[58]

The core curriculum that focused on the needs, problems, and interests of youth was almost always described as a great advance for the principles of democracy, although the connection between "democracy" and "social living" was difficult to perceive. Most often, students learned how to fit into the status quo, rather than about universal values from which the status quo could be questioned.

The core curriculum in Tulsa, for example, was supposed "to develop a fundamental faith in the American ideal of democracy and to become a positive force in the process of its achievement." The core program was devoted to topics such as "home and family life," "man and his environmental setting," and "living in the community." All seventh-graders were required to take the core course, which took up the entire school day; in eighth grade, it consumed five sixths of the day, and in twelfth grade, one sixth of the day. "Specialized interests," that is, *academic subjects,* were electives. Junior high school students worked on problems such as "How can a family spend their leisure time?" In recognition of the possibility of war in Europe, the children were asked, "Why do people in the various parts of the world live differently?," which led to the study of "How do people in Oklahoma live?" In Tulsa high schools, a local educator reported, "subject-matter boundaries have more or less broken down and the children speak of their class as social relations rather than English, social studies, science, and home economics, or they are more likely to identify the class by the problem on which they are then engaged."[59] In such trivial ways were these young Americans prepared in school to understand a world on the brink of catastrophic conflict.

The undemocratic implications of the core curriculum could be seen in sharp focus at Wells High School in Chicago, which served nearly three thousand students from families that were mainly low-income and foreign-born. Most of the youngsters were "normal in mental ability but possessed serious reading deficiencies." Despite their poor academic preparation, many of these students chose to study such subjects as foreign languages and algebra. Instead of helping them gain the skills they needed to succeed, the staff designed a core course for "nonacademic pupils," giving primary attention to "activities necessary for effective everyday living," vocational guidance, and socialization.

The new core curriculum at Wells High School merged social studies, English, general science, music, drawing, and physical education into a single core curriculum, which then was devoted to studies such as "the school," "the home," "the local community," "consumer activities," and "work in relation to everyday living." Soon after the introduction of the core curriculum, the school's college preparatory curriculum was completely eliminated. Consequently, Wells High School no longer prepared *any* of its students for entry to college. The school's principal noted with pride that "the reorganization program has been officially evaluated by standardizing agencies as 'purposeful,' 'based on sound educational principles,' and 'serving the community with a high degree of success.' "[60]

The principal of McKinley High School, the largest in Hawaii, noted that progressive programs had been easily adopted for the simple reason that most parents of students in the school could not speak English and were unable to question changes in the curriculum: "This has made it possible for the school leaders to make certain innovations here which might have been stoutly resisted as 'fads' in a mainland community." Writing in 1933, the principal observed that Hawaii had an unusual problem caused by the arrival in the 1920s of thousands of plantation workers from the Philippines whose children "showed little desire to enter plantation work," preferring instead to enter "white-collar" jobs or go to college. At the same time, the cost of education was spiraling upward, which distressed business leaders and politicians, who complained that the younger generation refused to work on the plantations because of the academic program in the public schools: "Insistent demands were made on all sides [though not by students or their parents] that the public school program be made more 'practical.' "[61]

The remedy, the principal wrote, was curriculum revision to align the work of the schools with the practical needs of life. Junior high schools were introduced in 1920. An activity program began in the elementary schools in Honolulu in 1927, then was implemented in schools throughout Hawaii. In 1928, social promotion was initiated in the public schools, which unsurprisingly led to a sharp drop in failures (if almost everyone is promoted by age rather than achievement, almost no one will fail). The high school curriculum was reorganized into "core studies," merging English and social studies so as to deal with "the real problems" of boys and girls, such as "What Is Personality? How Can We Develop a Good Personality?" and "How Can I Spend My Leisure Time More Wisely?" The changes in the public schools of Hawaii, imposed on uncomprehending students and parents, were described by the principal as "a living object lesson in democracy," but in retrospect they seem more like a class-biased, racist effort to restrict educational and social opportunities.[62]

In 1939, the superintendent of schools in Norris, Tennessee, described his philosophy, which echoed the conventional wisdom:

The curriculum should be centered around basic areas of human activity. These basic areas should be outgrowths of the needs and interests of the participants. . . .

There should be core fields of instruction adjusted to the needs and interests of individuals rather than a definite number of separate subjects.

Integration, rather than specialization, in the main should be followed. . . .

Subject matter should be used as it applies to real life situations, not as having virtue in itself. . . .

> The curriculum should be society-centered rather than sub-
> ject-centered. . . .
>
> Marks, honor rolls, contests, and other forms of rivalry and
> competition should be eliminated as far as possible.[63]

Students in Norris were required to participate in health, recreation, and physical education classes. Academic subjects such as English, social studies, mathematics, science, the arts, and homemaking were melded into a core curriculum that addressed social and personal problems. Students who wanted to go to college were permitted to elect Latin, French, and mathematics.

This trend toward "vitalizing" the curriculum and developing nonacademic core courses put a premium on social utility. Socially useful activities were functional activities. Academic subjects were generally considered to be neither socially useful nor practical. Many schools that revised their curriculum experienced a decrease in the number of students enrolled in college preparatory courses. Some school officials actively sought this result on the ground that an academic program was suitable only for the few who planned to go to college.

After curriculum revision in Hackensack, New Jersey, school officials reported with satisfaction that enrollment in the college preparatory course in high school had dropped from 30 percent to 15 percent. After the curriculum in Westwood, California, was revised, all students were offered a "Basic Course" devoted to the problems of social living, but courses such as chemistry and physics were reserved for the college-bound.[64]

After the curriculum of an Alabama high school was revised, its principal reported that his school had "moved from a narrow academic college preparatory program to one that is largely vocational" and lamented the fact that 30 percent of students still insisted on enrolling in academic courses, even though only 10 percent intended to go to college. The principal, claiming to have converted his teachers to the new philosophy, boasted that "the backbone of the whole business is the vocational training. The pupils must leave us ready and willing to work, able to pay their own way and to earn their living. The day has passed when it suffices for the applicant for work to say, 'I have a high school diploma.' Any graduate can say that. We want ours to be able to say in addition, 'I can cook your meals.' 'I can type your letters.' 'I can repair your automobile.' 'I can paint your house.' 'I can tend your garden.' " The school's motto was "Call us when you need workers."[65]

High schools in Oakland, California, adopted an approach called "the individual-needs or group-needs basis." A school official in Oakland lauded this approach because of its total absence of any subject matter and likened it to the teaching methods normally found only "in the nursery school and the early pre-primary and primary years," where the teacher ministers to students' needs. University High School required tenth-graders to take a Personal Management course, for which English credit was granted, but the course actually had no subject matter at all. In the same school was a course called Leisure Activities, in which non-college-bound students could learn recreational skills, and another course called Special Interests, where college-bound students could work on projects that met their needs without regard to subject matter. Three other high schools in Oakland offered a course in Personal Planning for the 90 percent of students who did not plan to attend college. Academic courses survived, though only because of "college entrance requirements, vocational standards, social and civic mores, etc." [66]

The academic curriculum, it seemed, stood in the way of all that was socially desirable. Apparently the best way of attacking the problems of youth and the ills of American society was to make sure that as few youngsters as possible studied foreign languages, history, advanced mathematics, or any science unrelated to the practical necessities of daily living.

Even rural communities felt the effects of this thinking. Breathitt County, Kentucky, located in the southern Appalachian region, suffered extreme poverty, high unemployment, poor housing, and inadequate schools. The University of Kentucky responded to Breathitt's social and economic ills with a program to revise its school curriculum, adding projects, activities, guidance, and vocational courses. As a result of the changes, the high school eliminated "all foreign languages, all mathematics beyond elementary algebra, commercial geography, psychology, a textbook course in agriculture, and some old-type courses in history dealing wholly with a period remote in time and application." [67]

Black Education and Social Adjustment

When confronted with the dilemma of black youths, who faced bleak prospects in a society where racial discrimination and segregation were common, progressive advocates of social adjustment urged them to accept society as it was instead of agitating for social change.

Writing in *The Journal of Negro Education,* Harl R. Douglass of the University of Colorado insisted that the greatest need of Negro youths—like white youths—was to be "adjusted" to society. They must learn to be healthy, emotionally stable, and psychologically adjusted. Education must seek to make the black youth "a cooperating member of a democratic society," to engage in a productive occupation so that he does not become dependent, and to "further the general social good rather than conflict with it." Like the federal report on Negro education in 1917, Douglass recommended "practical" education for the realities of life rather than a bookish education for black students. The high school curriculum for black youngsters, he complained, was "largely of a non-functional academic type offering meagre training in health, vocation, leisure, worthy home membership or citizenship, but apparently aimed at, if at anything, the acquisition of a cheap type of superficial erudition."[68]

Douglass expressed his puzzlement with "the unreasonable tendency for Negro adolescents and their parents to favor this linguistic-mathematical-historical-date type" of schooling even though it would not prepare them to adjust to society. Rather than pursuing this allegedly misguided "cultural" education, Douglass recommended that black youngsters have vocational training. He criticized black leaders who complained about racial discrimination and said that they should devote themselves instead to preparing the black youth "to fit into the framework of society as he will find it."[69] If Douglass and like-minded progressives had succeeded in their campaign for social adjustment, there would not have been a cadre of dissatisfied black leaders in law, medicine, education, and the ministry, prepared to challenge and overturn the status quo.

Meeting the Needs of Youth

In the late 1930s, the Progressive Education Association—an advocacy group for child-centered education in public and private schools— launched a new campaign to persuade school officials that the academic curriculum conflicted with "the needs of youth." Several major PEA publications contended that the nation's high schools should concentrate on their students' personal, emotional, and social problems rather than academic studies.

Writing for the PEA's Commission on Human Relations, Katharine Whiteside Taylor in *Do Adolescents Need Parents?* claimed that traditional high schools had "neglected the adolescent's nature and needs in favor of the preoccupations of advanced scholars." Taylor pointed out that "forward-looking" high schools were devoted to "the wholesome development of the individual as the goal of all education" and were concerned about adolescents' "personality problems." In view of the expertise of the modern school, wrote Taylor, parents might well wonder if they were needed at all. Yes, she assured parents, they were still needed, but mainly to befriend their children and not to be judgmental. To grow to maturity, she maintained, young people need to develop a friendly relationship with their parents, to acquire the capacity for "mate love and for vocational effectiveness, and [to] . . . evolve a scheme of values that makes life meaningful for them." High school students had "the need to conform," and the school must help them make friends, look attractive, prepare for family life and vocations, and achieve social success.[70]

Among the pressing needs of young people Taylor identified were "How can I get to be popular?" "How can you win friends among both boys and girls and keep them?" "How can I be *sure* to get a boy friend (girl friend) and afterwards how do you go about keeping him (her)?" Girls wanted to know "Do boys like finger-nail polish? Make-up?" Boys worried about such issues as "Is it all right to date a girl who is taller than you?" "Do girls like a fellow to be dolled up or to look like a he-man?" Clothes, complexion, and physical appearance topped teenagers' list of "needs," not their intellectual development or academic competence.[71]

The Progressive Education Association's Commission on the Secondary School Curriculum pressed to make "the needs of youth" the central purpose of the secondary curriculum. Its research director, Caroline B. Zachry, had earned her undergraduate and graduate degrees at Teachers College, where her adviser had been William Heard Kilpatrick. The many publications of this commission confidently asserted that schools must actively shape students' attitudes, feelings, values, and personality, as well as their psychological and sexual development; just as consistently, they portrayed the academic curriculum as a relic that no longer served any useful purpose and that impaired students' personal development.

A major summary of the commission's work, *Reorganizing Secondary Education,* referred disparagingly to intellectual development as "narrow," "sterile," "impotent," "passive," and "limited in meaning except for the purposes of 'scholarship.' " Written in the depths of the Depression by a team of authors (including Zachry), the book argued that the collapse of the economy had radically altered the purpose of the high school, which in the past had prepared young people for either college or occupations. Because of declining economic opportunity, "the bright" could no longer count on going to college, and the "not-bright" could no longer hope for a skilled job. Therefore, the high school would have to "seek new goals and objectives," to offer a new kind of education that prepared neither for college nor for a vocation but for personal and social growth. The curriculum must take into account students' "wants, wishes, inclinations, and desires . . . problems, feelings, aspirations, foreseen and desired achievements. The student must not be required to make up lacks that he himself does not recognize." If students did not feel the need to learn mathematics, science, or a foreign language, they should not be expected to do so. The authors warned ominously that "unless the school discovers some way to help these young people find and accept new roles and new status, new relationships with others, new missions in life, democracy may disappear." The PEA Commission suggested that the transformation of the high school from an academic institution to a custodial institution based on the "needs of youth" was essential to preserving "the living tradition of democracy in American life."[72]

In her book *Emotion and Conduct in Adolescence,* Zachry maintained that high schools must focus on the social and personal problems of adolescents. She had little to say about academic subjects but a great deal to say about how adolescents felt about such things as changes in their bodies, preparation for sexual relations, and relationships with parents and peers. Having been an English teacher at the Lincoln School, Zachry understood that nearly all academic subjects had potential relevance for the growing adolescent. But her central theme was that the schools must help adolescents as they met the "tasks of life adjustment" so that they could be "fit and happy member[s] of contemporary society." She wanted schools to guide their students' personality development, personal and social relationships, vocational preparation, acceptance of appropriate sex roles, participation in civic life, and readiness for marriage and family life.[73]

The PEA tried to show how every academic subject could be converted to meet the "needs of youth." For example, *Science in General Education* maintained that science teaching should center on practical problems that young people were likely to encounter in their daily lives, especially problems of health, homemaking, sex, sanitation, living conditions, and understanding how familiar machines work. Studies such as chemistry and physics, it was suggested, relied too much on "mental discipline" and were organized according to "logical unity, internal consistency, and the maximum possibility of deduction," instead of dealing with "problems or issues of practical interest." Reorganized science courses would emphasize students' "pressing questions," such as "How may I keep in good health?" and "Do my religious views conflict with the teaching of science?" Or the sciences might be integrated into a core curriculum along with social studies, English, and mathematics to address broad themes such as "Problems of Social Living" or "The Progress of Man Through the Ages."[74]

The point of these curricular reorganizations was to replace logically organized academic subject matter with contemporary social issues, exchanges of opinion, or useful information. The social studies program proposed by the PEA, for example, replaced history with studies of personal relationships and current events. This change was justified by the "changing character of the school population." Translated into plain language, this meant that certain forms of knowledge, such as history and chemistry, were too difficult to offer to the children of the masses, too far beyond their limited intellectual ken. It was ironic that the decision to provide curricular differentiation was called a victory for democratic values. Far from being democratic, this curricular differentiation restricted access to the academic curriculum; it turned the academic curriculum into elite knowledge for the college-bound, while excluding the large majority of students from gaining deep knowledge of scientific, social, and economic principles, from preparing for higher education or the professions, and from developing the ability to make an original contribution to the advancement of knowledge. At the very moment when science and technology were about to transform modern life, and at the very time when the world was entering a prolonged period of political and military crisis, expert educators were insisting that most students needed a curriculum that limited their access to knowledge and narrowed their understanding to the practical problems of daily life.[75]

Aside from the antidemocratic implications of such reorganization, the "needs of youth" ideology also had the substantial defect of hubris. The many publications that advanced these ideas displayed a specious claim to expertise. The guidance experts asserted that they knew how to "adjust" youngsters' personality; knew better than their parents how to turn them into the right sort of persons, with the correct ideas, values, appreciations, attitudes, behaviors, and feelings; could, if only the curriculum were revised, shape a society infinitely better than the one that existed. Certainly it was appropriate for the schools to assume custodial responsibility for children who were neglected by their parents or who needed special care; but under what theory should government-run schools in a democratic society claim the power to probe, shape, and control the most intimate feelings and attitudes of their students?

The "John Jones Letter"

The Progressive Education Association was not alone in its demands for a curriculum based on "the needs of youth." Prestigious national commissions churned out numerous reports during these years, making the same arguments. Perhaps strangest of all in this barrage of attacks on the academic curriculum was the "John Jones Letter."

This letter first appeared in 1936 in an article by Lloyd N. Morrisett, then assistant superintendent of public schools in Yonkers, New York. The article was published in a small education journal called *The Clearing House*. Presented as "a letter from an alumnus to his high school principal," it was addressed to "Mr. John B. Blank, Principal, Central High School." Allegedly a graduate of the class of 1930, "Jones" complained that he was "completely disillusioned. . . . I want to know, dear principal, why you and your teachers did not tell and teach me about life and the hard, critical, practical world into which you sent me. Why did you have me spend so much time on dry, uninteresting subject matter and so little on genuine life problems?" The high school, he bitterly recalled, had done nothing to prepare him for married life or parenthood. When he was out of work, he found no demand "for factoring or geometrical demonstrations; for translations of Caesar or Cicero, or for my knowledge of Goldsmith, Shelley, Keats, Wordsworth, and Browning. My history did not function." What had he gained, he asked, by learning to read and write essays when people in the real world wanted only to read "success fiction, harmless puzzles, action-compelling editorials, community gossip, wisecracks and humor?"[76]

What did he think he should have learned instead? "I wish I had been taught more about family relationships, child care, getting along with people, interpreting the news, news writing, paying off a small mortgage, household mechanics, politics, local government, the chemistry of food, carpentry, how to budget and live within the budget," wrote the alleged graduate. He wished too that someone had taught him "how to grow a garden, how to paint a house, how to get a job, how to be vigorous and healthy, how to be interesting to others, how to be popular, how to be thrifty, how to resist high pressure salesmanship, how to buy economically and intelligently, and the danger of buying on the installment plan." Bereft of this miscellany, "Jones" felt ignorant of "life as it is really lived." In Morrisett's article, the letter was used to explain why Yonkers had revised its secondary school curriculum to make it "vital," "functional," and "more closely related to life." Morrisett claimed that the new Yonkers curriculum was devoted to "solving the problems of life," with special attention to health, economic competence, and getting along with others.[77]

Although the John Jones letter was meant as an allegory, it took on a life of its own. Historian Edward A. Krug recounted the long afterlife of the letter, which so perfectly captured the spirit of the progressive crusade against the academic curriculum. The letter was quoted two years later in an article by the principal of a high school in Los Angeles, who described it as "the words of an actual high school student." A pedagogical magazine, *School Executive,* claimed in 1940 that John Jones had graduated from a Washington, D.C., high school but later retracted the claim. A major textbook reprinted the letter in 1941; it was quoted in a nationally syndicated article as late as 1970. Not to be outdone by the John Jones letter, *Progressive Education* ran a letter in 1938 by "a high school student" who claimed to speak for "the youth of today": "Our time in school is squandered on the details of war, generals, dead kings and queens, dead and unused languages, mythology, portions of philosophy, economics and a literature that is hopelessly out of date." What did the "youth of today" really want to know? How to care for their bodies, how to have a happy marriage, how to rear children. "Why not have a course in personality in high school? This should be a course in which boys and girls are taught to dance, talk interestingly, dress with good taste, and get along with each other. . . . Why not also teach us how to swim, dive, ride horseback, play golf, ski, play tennis and other outdoor games?"[78]

Voices of the Mainstream

*The views expressed in the "Jones" letter and its imitators were not con-*fined to the extremist fringe of progressive education. The nation's major professional education organizations shared them. In 1937, Harl R. Douglass's *Secondary Education for Youth in Modern America,* a report to the American Youth Commission of the American Council on Education, declared that the academic curriculum was irrelevant to the needs of large numbers of high school students. The "great mass of the populace" should not be expected to study the classics, the arts, or advanced mathematics. Most students needed education attuned to "primitive instincts for physical and practical activity, the more familiar pursuits of the masses—the home and its furnishings, nature, sports, games, the radio, and social activities." The curriculum did not need to include subjects "merely because they have made significant contributions to civilization." Only a small number of experts actually needed to be trained in these subjects.[79]

Similar antidemocratic themes were expressed in a 1938 report called *The Purposes of Education in American Democracy,* issued by the National Education Association's Educational Policies Commission and written by its longtime executive secretary, William G. Carr. Carr held that the major objectives of education were "self-realization," "human relationship," "economic efficiency," and "civic responsibility." Too much emphasis, he observed, was placed on the teaching of grammar and the classics in English: "Whatever may be the merits of such exercises as a preparation for a career as an author, the great majority of American boys and girls will profit more by a wide-ranging program of reading for enjoyment and fact-gathering." Carr urged a reduction in the number of youngsters studying advanced mathematics, advanced science, and foreign languages, as well as an emphasis on everyday uses of mathematics and science.[80]

In 1939, the National Association of Secondary School Principals published B. L. Dodds's *That All May Learn,* which might as well have been titled *That All May Learn Only Whatever Is Useful.* A professor of education at Purdue University, Dodds thought that it was ridiculous for high schools to offer an academic curriculum to "the new fifty percent," the youngsters of low intelligence who stayed in high school because there were no jobs. He claimed to be concerned about the "educationally neglected," but he was equally contemptuous of students at both extremes of ability. It was not "the educationally neglected" who were "abnormal"; on the contrary, "the academic person who can happily devote a lifetime to the pursuit of work dealing largely in abstract symbols of experience as reported through writing could with far more justification be considered abnormal."[81]

Dodds complained that the academic curriculum had encouraged unrealistic ambitions and made too many "unselected" youths aspire to enter managerial and professional jobs for which they were not suited and which were not available in any case. Too much time, money, and effort, he felt, were being expended trying to teach the academic subjects to the "educationally neglected." Only those who needed to know mathematics and science should learn those subjects. Nor did many people need a high level of reading comprehension; most needed only enough to use as an "essential tool" for reading newspapers and magazines. There was no point in trying to teach the classics to ordinary students, nor did they need many writing skills for "the small amount of writing they will have to do." Their curriculum should be based on their needs and interests, giving particular attention to problems such as how to dress, how to make friends with the opposite sex, and how to get a job.[82]

In 1940 the American Youth Commission, a distinguished panel of public officials and private citizens, published a report called *What the High Schools Ought to Teach*. Historian Edward A. Krug called it "the most anti-academic" of any of the major reports of this era. Once again came the assertion that the changing pupil population required a total reorganization of the curriculum; that what had been appropriate for a select few in the past was no longer appropriate for "the great majority of those now in secondary schools"; and that the academic curriculum was the enemy of the young. This was what the high schools ought to teach: reading; work experience; social studies centered on contemporary problems; and a course about personal problems, such as health and family life. As for English, too much time was wasted on grammar and literature. Algebra and geometry were "stumbling blocks" that could easily be dropped. Foreign languages should give way to practical experiences. History courses should center on inventions and democratic ideals; the rest could be eliminated. As for natural sciences, they relied too much on facts; they would have to prove their value to survive. The report called attention to the "vicious aspects of the ninth grade," when students were required to study unappealing subjects such as English composition, algebra, science, history, and possibly a foreign language.[83]

These reports assumed that schools existed to provide only what students needed to get along in daily life, not to transmit knowledge, develop appreciation for the great artistic and cultural achievements of humanity, or promote intellectual development, especially among those who did not plan to go to college. All shared the hereditarian assumption that schools could not expand the intellectual horizons of students and should not even try. All accepted the determinist calculation that schools were unable to inspire new interests in their students. All sought to limit the education of average students.

THE PROBLEM OF COLLEGE ADMISSION REQUIREMENTS

The survival of the academic curriculum in secondary schools rested in equal measure on tradition, which was under constant assault by pedagogical experts, and college entrance requirements, which shaped the program of students who wanted to attend selective colleges. The Progressive Education Association set out to break down college admission requirements. In 1932, it began a long-term project, known as the Eight-Year Study, to demonstrate that such requirements were unnecessary.

The PEA persuaded "practically all accredited colleges and universities" to waive the traditional entrance requirements for graduates of thirty high schools, both public and private, beginning with the class entering in 1936. Their admission to higher education would depend not on taking certain required courses and examinations but on the recommendation of their principal and their school record, including activities and interests, as well as tests of scholastic aptitude and achievement administered in school. Researchers carefully followed the progress of the class in college and concluded that on both academic and nonacademic measures they performed as well as or better than students in a control group who had met the conventional entrance criteria.[84]

This study was supposed to show that students would do just as well in college without the straitjacket of entrance requirements. It certainly demonstrated that students who were selected by their principal and who had a record of good performance and test scores in high school, were likely to succeed in the best colleges. In light of the highly selective population of students able to afford higher education in the mid-1930s, the generalizability of this experiment was questionable. The Ivy League colleges were not persuaded to drop their requirements for admission, but the study was cited for many years as "proof" that college entrance requirements were unnecessary.

→ → ← ←

Most schools continued to offer the traditional academic curriculum to the college-bound. Despite the Progressive Education Association's Eight-Year Study, college entrance requirements were still the strongest shield for the academic curriculum. But by 1940, after more than a generation of constant criticism, educators had come to think of the academic studies in the high school as the college-preparatory curriculum, not suitable for future farmers, clerks, housewives, barbers, secretaries, and factory workers.

How much of a difference did the reforms of the 1930s make?

Surely the elementary schools were more joyful places, yet there was no good reason to pose a dichotomy between children's well-being and the thoughtful study of school subjects. Nor was it reasonable to insist (as Kilpatrick had) that a planned curriculum was an inappropriate burden on schools and teachers; learning can be joyful even when planned in advance. And good schools, whether traditional or progressive in their pedagogy, attend to the health and needs of individual children.

Progressive reformers pressured public high schools to serve as custodial institutions that met miscellaneous socio-personal needs, kept idle youth off the streets, provided a range of nonacademic curricula, and deemphasized the importance of the academic curriculum for all but the college-bound.

The high school that adopted these progressive reforms became, in the words of a major sociological study in 1944, "an enormous, complicated machine for sorting and ticketing and routing children through life," a conveyor belt that inspected young people and then directed them to different destinations, some to the outside world, some to college, others to different vocations. Because this sorting process was linked closely to race and social class, historians Davd L. Angus and Jeffrey E.

282

Mirel observe that it had the effect of "sharpening rather than eliminating divisions along class and racial lines."[85]

High schools are essentially conservative institutions, staffed mainly by teachers who are educated to teach specific subjects, so their curricula and practices responded slowly to the reformers' demands to diminish their intellectual goals, but did move in that direction as reports from many districts indicated.

The strong allegiance of parents and teachers to the academic curriculum slowed the implementation of radical changes even after superintendents announced them. Teachers knew that they had to go along, join study groups, and give outward signs of compliance to their supervisors. But they could always close the classroom door and teach the subject they knew best. What they could not do, however, was to revive subjects that were dropped from the curriculum altogether.

8

Dissidents and Critics

Preoccupied with economic crisis at home and ominous military events abroad during the 1930s, the public paid scant attention to the transformation of the schools. Occasional press reports heralded the steady advance of the progressive education movement. In 1938, Eunice Fuller Barnard, the education writer for *The New York Times,* noted its "meteoric rise," crediting it with an unbroken string of successes. Children in joyful progressive schools, she wrote, learned as much and as well as those in grim traditional classes; honors were "constantly heaped upon" its "prophets," John Dewey and William Heard Kilpatrick; the Progressive Education Association received large research grants from conservative foundations; and few public school officials were willing to oppose the movement. The critics of the movement, said Barnard, were "grumblers" who demanded a return to the hard path of the three R's.[1]

The reality, however, was more complicated. The general public did not understand the debate going on within the profession, and progressive educators did not understand that some of their ideas would prove unacceptable to the public. Debates among educators about theory and practice, couched in obscure pedagogical language, were difficult for laypeople to understand. The progressives' successes encouraged them to ignore those who disagreed with them; their refusal to heed their critics eventually proved costly to the movement.

THE LEADER OF THE OPPOSITION

William C. Bagley was the profession's most prominent dissident. His impeccable credentials as an educator made his criticisms doubly galling to his progressive colleagues. Others could be disdained as know-nothings; not Bagley. He knew what they knew, yet he disagreed profoundly with their remedies.

Born in Detroit in 1872, Bagley graduated from the Michigan Agricultural College, where students were required to do farm labor two hours each weekday. Although he had intended to make a career in agricultural science, he graduated in the midst of an economic depression in 1893, and the only job he could find was teaching in a one-room rural school. Concluding that more was known "about the raising of pigs than about the minds of children," he decided to study psychology at the University of Wisconsin and Cornell University. He wanted to help develop a science of education that would be as certain and predictable as any of the physical sciences.[2]

After Bagley finished his graduate studies, he worked as an elementary school principal in Saint Louis, then as a school superintendent in Montana, where he also taught psychology at the state teachers' college. He then spent nine years as a professor of education at the University of Illinois, published several books, and was a founder of the *Journal of Educational Psychology* and president of the National Society for the Study of Education. As a prominent figure in the new profession, he was an unlikely candidate to become controversial.

As early as 1907, Bagley lamented "the waves of fads and reforms that sweep through the educational system at periodic intervals," and he chastised reformers who would "leave teacher and pupil to work out each his own salvation in the chaos of confusion and disorder." The purpose of schooling, he maintained, was to prepare children for civilized social life. Youngsters needed to acquire a fund of knowledge and such ideals as "industry, accuracy, carefulness, steadfastness, patriotism, culture, cleanliness, truth, self-sacrifice, social service, and personal honor."[3]

Throughout his career, Bagley adhered to a few bedrock principles. He believed that the public schools should provide a common curriculum grounded in the liberal arts and sciences—at least for the first eight grades—so that all youngsters could gain the knowledge, skills, habits, and ideals that were necessary to participate in American society. He believed that the common school in a democratic society should not decide whom to educate. And he believed that the knowledge built up by the human race over many centuries was a precious heritage that must be taught to each succeeding generation in order for progress to continue. To achieve these goals, he believed, every classroom should have a well-educated, cultured teacher. In 1914, acting on these principles, Bagley spoke out against the vocational education movement. A year later, he opposed the establishment of junior high schools, because they were designed to sort children into industrial and vocational programs at the end of sixth grade.

Bagley's able defense of liberal education attracted the attention of James Earl Russell, the dean of Teachers College, Columbia University, who invited him to lead its Department of Teacher Education in 1918.[4] By the time Bagley joined the Teachers College faculty, he had abandoned hope that education could ever become an exact science. This was the very time, however, when most of his professional colleagues were actively promoting mental testing as the leading edge of the scientific movement in education. Again defying the professional consensus, Bagley attacked intelligence testing, forecasting that IQ tests would encourage sorting of children for different kinds of education instead of promoting the education of all.

Because of his opposition to curricular differentiation and intelligence testing, Bagley got a reputation among his fellow educationists as a conservative who was hostile to modern, scientific education. His stubborn insistence that all children should have a liberal education, regardless of their IQ or future occupation, at least through the first eight grades, caused many of his professional associates to brand him a reactionary. Philip W. L. Cox, a progressive educator at New York University, referred to Bagley in 1933 as "our great polemic" who "has stood resolutely in opposition to almost every innovation that has attempted to enter the public schools." Cox accused Bagley of giving encouragement to "intrenched administrators and teachers who merely wish to protect what is traditional." Bagley replied that he had fought persistently to put "a competent and cultured teacher into every American classroom." If that should ever happen, he predicted, it would do more for American education than all the other innovations lumped together.[5]

Although Bagley often disagreed with progressive educators about methods and curriculum, his views on other issues were consistently egalitarian and politically progressive. In 1938, when nearly half the states had passed loyalty oaths for teachers, Bagley defended academic freedom, insisting that "there are occasions, when, with or without support or the prospect of support, one must stand firm—alone, if necessary, with one's back against the wall." He consistently supported federal aid for education to promote equality of educational opportunity, long before it was a popular cause. The nation had a direct interest in having a literate and informed population, he believed; ignorance was "a menace to national welfare." He expected that the improvement of education would contribute to social progress by reducing not only illiteracy but crime, corruption, drunkenness, divorce, and poverty.[6]

Unlike his progressive colleagues, Bagley advocated a common national curriculum in basic subjects such as arithmetic, history, geography, and science. He described the curriculum revision movement of the 1930s, where each school system had written its own curriculum, as "curriculum chaos." The progressive idea that every community had to have its own curriculum, he said, was not only silly but tragic; in a democracy, he said, the people need a fund of common knowledge so that they can discuss common problems in terms that are widely understood. And besides, wrote Bagley, there was another important reason for a common national curriculum, and that was that "the American people simply will not 'stay put.' " Because of the high mobility of the population, it made little sense for every school district to have its own curriculum and even less for every school or teacher to write a new curriculum.[7]

When progressive theorists such as Harold Rugg and William Heard Kilpatrick urged that schooling be based on children's interests, Bagley vigorously dissented. His last major book, *Education and Emergent Man,* challenged the central doctrines of progressive education, especially the claim that the only knowledge of value was that which was useful for everyday life. Bagley contended that while knowledge for immediate use is valuable, knowledge for understanding and interpretation of significance may be even more important. Only a fraction of what one needs to know, he said, can be learned by participating in activities and solving immediate problems. A broadly educated person also needs a large fund of background knowledge drawn from the systematic and sequential study of history, geography, science, mathematics, literature, and the arts. He wrote, "One who has lived vicariously through the great episodes of human history; one who has come to understand natural phenomena through the recorded findings of scientific investigation; one who has appreciated vicariously the shades and tints of human nature that Shakespeare was the first to detect;—such a one will have an outlook on the world that an untutored person could not have."[8]

To Bagley, the progressives' concept of childhood was naive and their contempt for subject matter misguided. "What do you think of a theory," Bagley asked an audience in 1934, "which holds that, in the absence of an immediate 'real-life' problem or purpose as a motivating stimulus to learning, ignorance becomes a virtue?" Yet Bagley recognized the powerful emotional appeal of progressive pedagogy:

If you wish to be applauded at an educational convention, vociferate sentiment[al] platitudes about the sacred rights of the child, specifying particularly his right to happiness gained through freedom. You are likely to get an extra "hand" if you shed a few verbal tears over the cruelty of examinations and homework, while if with eloquent condemnation you deftly bring into every other sentence one of the favorite stereotypes of abuse, such as Latin, mathematics (geometry, especially), grammar, the traditional curriculum, compartmentalization, "chunks of subject matter" to be memorized, discipline, formal discipline, and the like, you may be fairly certain of an ovation.[9]

For fully a generation, he charged, progressive educators had led a propaganda campaign that had lowered standards. They had opposed examinations, assignments planned in advance by the teacher, and efforts to retain students who failed in their work. Progressives had persuaded hundreds of school systems to promote their pupils without regard to their achievement. By eliminating the problem of children being "left back," they had created a new problem: children who were essentially illiterate were being "piled up" in the junior and senior high schools. Such misguided policies, said Bagley, not only contributed to illiteracy but were grossly unjust to children, who surely should have the right to competent instruction.

Bagley insisted on a balance between interest and effort. Not everything in the classroom could be fun. He knew from his own experience as a teacher that some children would choose the path of least resistance if allowed to. If everything were based solely on appeal to students' interests, they would learn to respond only to pleasure and self-gratification, never learning self-discipline and the value of effort. There was a good deal to be said, in his view, for teaching children to complete difficult tasks. The reward for doing so would be the self-confidence that comes from conquering challenges.

Progressive theory was not new at all, said Bagley, which accounted for its success. It restated two powerful American frontier traditions: anti-intellectualism and utilitarianism. He likened the progressives' hostility to "bookish" learning to long-standing frontier attitudes. The "narrow utilitarianism" of progressivism, he warned, would equip the individual to learn what was needed for the present moment but leave him unprepared to cope with new situations. From academic studies, he maintained, students learned general principles of action as well as important habits and ideals, such as persistence and the ability to concentrate.[10]

Bagley disagreed with William Heard Kilpatrick, who regularly invoked Thorndike's "laws of learning" regarding the connection between stimulus and response to support his pedagogical claims. Kilpatrick said that the child was likelier to learn when the purpose in learning was his own (the Law of Readiness) and when the results were satisfying, not annoying (the Law of Effect). A boy who wants to make a kite will do so joyfully, Kilpatrick noted, but a boy who is told to make a kite by his teacher will comply reluctantly and will gain less skill and knowledge from his actions. Bagley observed with amusement that "the study of the learning process by the experimental method has been on the whole disappointing. The 'laws' which seem at a given time to be well established have an irritating habit of collapsing as evidence accumulates." He admitted his own error in once having believed that education might become a science. He had come to believe that teaching was "a fine art, not a technological art" and that what teachers needed most was insight, a sensitiveness to learners' difficulties, and a keen appreciation for the social heritage of knowledge and ideals. Lest there be any doubt on this point, he noted that there had been great teachers long before anyone had studied the technology of teaching. He suggested this contrast:

> If I were seriously ill and in desperate need of a physician, and if by some miracle I could secure either Hippocrates, the Father of Medicine, or a young doctor fresh from the Johns Hopkins School of Medicine, with his equipment comprising the latest developments in the technologies and techniques of medicine, I should, of course, take the young doctor. On the other hand, if I were commissioned to find a teacher for a group of adolescent boys and if, by some miracle, I could secure either Socrates or the latest Ph.D. from Teachers College, with his equipment of the latest technologies and techniques of teaching, with all due respect to the College that employs me and to my students, I am fairly certain that I would jump at the chance to get Socrates.[11]

Bagley insisted that there were no shortcuts to improvement of the schools. No country in the world, he said, had witnessed so many educational reforms in the past generation as the United States: "It has been one nostrum after another. We have tried to improve the educational system by shuffling school grades into new divisions with new names; by adopting, one after another, different 'methods' of teaching; by trying this and then that and then another pattern of organizing curricular materials." To make matters worse, the schools had developed a huge top-heavy bureaucracy, with the teacher at the bottom of the heap. None of this made much difference, he said. The fundamental factor in education was the quality of classroom teachers.[12]

THE DISSIDENT ÉMIGRÉ

Another notable antiprogressive was Michael J. Demiashkevich, who was born in Mohilev, Russia, in 1891. He earned degrees at the Imperial Historico-Philological and Imperial Archaeological institutes in Saint Petersburg, worked at the Soviet Ministry of Education after the revolution, and emigrated to the United States in 1923 because of his opposition to communism. Supported by scholarships, he earned his doctorate in educational philosophy at Teachers College in 1926.

Demiashkevich's dissertation, published as *The Activity School,* was supposedly a critical examination of activity schools in western Europe but in fact was an incisive critique of progressive ideology in the United States. Demiashkevich's work was striking because of his nonpedagogical style. His writings were laced with casual references to mythology, philosophy, ancient and medieval history, economics, science, and world literature. Other pedagogues quoted Dewey, Kilpatrick, and Rousseau; Demiashkevich quoted them, too, but was just as likely to quote Plutarch, Schiller, Shakespeare, Molière, Confucius, Sophocles, Wordsworth, and Goethe.

Doubtless because of his own painful experiences, Demiashkevich believed that education must prepare the individual for the stern test of living. He wrote, "Someone has said that it is the doom of man to have to gain the true knowledge of things, not unlike his bread, by the sweat of his brow." He appreciated self-discipline, restraint, effort, and duty but also the joy associated with learning from an inspiring teacher and the delight of reading a wonderful book. In his study of activity schools, he was particularly disturbed by "the campaign against 'bookishness,' which he found to be

so violent as almost to lead one to suspect that a "bookless" school is the unexpressed ideal of certain activists. They seem to overlook the fact that the printing press is the very *deus ex*

291

machina of intellectual democracy and very much so in relation to political and social democracy. Or they are forgetful of the truth that it has done for knowledge what steam has done for trade; reduced time and distance to their lowest terms in the intellectual commerce of men.[13]

Throughout history, Demiashkevich observed, despots had been openly bibliophobic, understanding the democratizing power of books and literacy. Demiashkevich could not understand why progressive educators failed to see the beauty and power of books. He insisted that the school in a democratic society "must be more bookish than the conventional public compulsory school has been." The traditional public school, he insisted, did not give books the respect that they deserved as instruments for children's intellectual freedom. He loved learning and could not see why others were not equally excited by its joys. The philosophical principle he recommended for the school was borrowed from Auguste Comte: "The principle, Love; the basis, Order; the end, Progress."[14]

After two years of study in Europe, Demiashkevich joined the faculty of the George Peabody College for Teachers in Nashville, Tennessee, where he continued his philosophical critique of progressive theory and practice. In 1933, he criticized those who believed that everything in the world was constantly changing, calling them neo-Heracliteans, like the ancient philosopher Heraclitus, who had taught that change was the only constant in the world. In a real school, he held, the neo-Heraclitean method results in "an exaggerated degree of pedagogical chaos characterized by the absence of emphasis upon sustained, consecutive and robust programs of study as well as by the anathema put on direct teaching and directed learning." He called this "organized pedagogical anarchy" and said that it was known as the "curriculumless curriculum." Under such a regime, a good teacher was relegated "to the role of an educational chambermaid entitled to appear on the floor only when called forth by one or several pupils."[15]

Demiashkevich wanted the schools to "introduce students to the highest standards of accurate and fertile thinking, through direct or indirect contacts with the best minds of humanity, and in that way to put them on solid ground for the critical judgment of their own thinking and that of others." Students must be able to capitalize on accumulated human experience, to learn efficiently what others have learned slowly and painfully. It was antidemocratic, he wrote, to allow students to remain ignorant of accumulated human experience and knowledge.[16]

What students needed, he said, was mastery of systematic knowledge and the habits of effort that would make that mastery possible. He accused progressive educators, specifically those who promoted the project method and the child-centered school, of subverting these goals. Demiashkevich defended memory work, which was routinely denounced by progressive educators as "rote memorization" unworthy of any teacher or student. To the contrary, Demiashkevich insisted that memory was "one of the most important and valuable possessions of man" and should be developed as fully as possible. Learning required effort and craftsmanship, not just play. Making mud pies and dressing dolls were fine kindergarten activities, but "the kindergarten must not be permitted to extend its domination over the secondary school and the college."[17] Views such as these were not calculated to win friends and influence professional colleagues in the highly charged atmosphere of the 1930s.

Demiashkevich's magnum opus, *An Introduction to the Philosophy of Education,* was published in 1935. He described two competing conceptions of education. One was the "essentialist," which aimed to transmit the social heritage and prepare individuals to survive in a difficult world. The other, which he called "individualist-pragmatist" (that is, progressive education), sought to assist individuals toward a happy and fulfilled life by developing their interests and aptitudes. Each had its dangers: the former might turn into exaggerated uniformity, the latter into exaggerated hedonism.

But for this refugee from the Russian Revolution, there was no real choice between the alternatives. He was convinced that progressive education was behavioristic, materialistic, and empty of any spiritual moorings. By contrast, essentialism connected the teaching of sequential subject matter and the teaching of character. Thoughtful study of mathematical and natural sciences, he argued, would protect students against false evidence and inoculate them against "crises of credulity, unreflecting enthusiasm, and fanaticism." The humanities (languages, literature, history, art, and philosophy) were a source of intellectual and moral development. These studies, he believed, would help the student develop "a heart capable of possessing wealth without becoming its slave, a mind capable of using machinery without becoming its victim, and will prevent him from becoming a tool of the tools created by man himself." From the sciences, students would gain knowledge, but from the humanities they would gain wisdom and sympathy.[18]

Demiashkevich contrasted essentialism, with its clear standards and belief in moral responsibility for one's actions, with progressivism, which approved of whatever was useful or instrumental for the moment. The philosophy of progressive education, he asserted, lacked any stable, permanent criterion of values. When progressives were asked how to measure students' progress, they would refer to the growth of the learner. But, said Demiashkevich, the doctrine of growth was "an empty slogan unless it means development in a desirable direction; in other words, development towards the attainment of a standard."[19]

The sharpest critique of progressive education from any source, *An Introduction to the Philosophy of Education* was widely reviewed. Yet this book, which should have established him as a major philosopher of education, had a fatal flaw: he did not accept the American commitment to egalitarian, popular education. He recommended that children should be sorted on the basis of their scholastic achievement after only four years of elementary schooling (progressives were willing to grant six years of common schooling before the selection began; Bagley insisted on eight). Demiashkevich envisioned rigorous education for an intellectual elite to prepare them for "Periclean" leadership of democratic society. Providing postelementary education "freely to all in non-selective public schools in non-classified groups, hazardously formed on the basis of the pupils' chronological age," he held, would "irresistibly degenerate . . . into wasteful lowering of standards in education." If this happened, he predicted, "the gifted and keen children" in public schools would be "thrown in with poorly endowed, incurious, and unwilling pupils whom the teachers must try to occupy in some worth-while manner." Such policies, he warned, would turn the public high schools into custodial institutions and the colleges into grade schools and high schools.[20]

He was right in one sense but profoundly wrong in another. He correctly described the effects of the lowering of standards, the neglect of gifted children, and the pressure on high schools to entertain bored students instead of educating them. He also accurately predicted the burden that remedial education would eventually impose on American colleges and universities when social promotion became commonplace and high school graduation standards disappeared. But he was disastrously wrong in his belief that American public education should pursue a policy of educational stratification on behalf of an elite. Ironically, such an outcome was already resulting from the laissez-faire programs introduced under the aegis of progressive education, as students were directed (and directed themselves) into different curriculum programs. By the 1930s, the majority of high school students were already sorted into vocational, commercial, agricultural, and other nonacademic curricula. In most high schools, only a minority of students studied the so-called college preparatory curriculum. This policy of voluntary stratification worked because it was called progressive, in that it supposedly met the differing needs of different students. Had it been called elitist, it might have caused a public backlash.

Demiashkevich had far too little faith in the possibility of educating the majority of youngsters in the very studies that he valued. It may have been true that only a fortunate few would be able to master the rigorous classical education he proposed, but a far larger proportion than he anticipated were capable of learning mathematics, the sciences, history, literature, and a foreign language if given the chance. Democracy requires an educated public, not just an educated elite. On this critical issue, the key difference between Demiashkevich and his progressive adversaries was that he openly advocated selection to produce an elite, and they tacitly promulgated selective practices for elite students but disguised them by using democratic rhetoric.

The Essentialist Committee

On February 26, 1938, in Atlantic City, New Jersey, during the annual meeting of the American Association of School Administrators, Bagley,

Demiashkevich, and five other educators organized the Essentialist Committee for the Advancement of American Education. Borrowing the term "essentialism" from Demiashkevich's book, the committee issued a statement calling for rigorous standards of achievement and a common curriculum to ensure a high level of shared culture across American society.

The essentialists criticized progressive education for championing "interest, freedom, immediate needs, personal experience, psychological organization, and pupil-initiative." They asserted that they wanted to restore discipline, effort, academic subjects, teacher-directed classrooms, and "the ideal of good workmanship for its own sake." The statement did not reflect Demiashkevich's views about the need to educate an elite for leadership. Instead, it expressed Bagley's insistence that "a democratic society has a vital, collective stake in the informed intelligence of every individual citizen."[21]

The essentialists were promptly rebuked. Although they were careful to praise John Dewey and to claim that his followers had distorted his teachings, Dewey himself told a *New York Times* reporter that "the [essentialist] movement is apparently an imitation of the fundamentalist movement, and may perhaps draw support from that quarter as well as from reactionaries in politics and economics." William Heard Kilpatrick, Dewey's chief disciple, told the same reporter, "The essentialists represent the same sort of reactionary trend that always springs up when a doctrine is gaining headway in the country. The astonishing thing is not the fact of the reaction but that it is so small and on the whole comes from such inconspicuous people." *Newsweek,* observing that "it seems unlikely that [essentialism] will do much to halt the steady growth of the modern method," summed up "Dr. Dewey's progressivism" in a single sentence: "His followers believe children learn best by their own experience: give the student opportunity for expanding interests, and his mind will follow spontaneously; confront him with new situations and he will solve them for himself; uninhibited curiosity, rather than any code of rewards or punishments, gives the pupil his maximum incentive." *Time* magazine showcased the contretemps by putting a picture of the president of the Progressive Education Association on its cover. Progressivism, said *Time,* had established strongholds in the suburbs of New York, Chicago, and Los Angeles and was "transforming such major public school systems as those of Denver, San Francisco, Los Angeles, New York City, Detroit. No U.S. school has completely escaped its influence."[22]

This first organized effort to check the advance of progressive education had turned into a public relations fiasco. The essentialist committee was not a large or an unusually distinguished group, but it did not deserve to be disparaged by Dewey and Kilpatrick as "fundamentalists" and "reactionaries." A prominent progressive at the University of Michigan assailed the essentialists as "a fascist menace" and "enemies of progress." The name-calling helped to marginalize the essentialists' efforts, as did their own ineptitude at making their case to the press: they let their adversaries define them, and they probably lacked an executive summary or even a few pithy quotes for reporters. All they could offer was a wordy statement about standards.[23]

Demiashkevich wanted to create regional associations of the committee, but Bagley preferred to limit appeals to other educators, and he would not permit any public fund-raising. At the time of the essentialist controversy, Bagley was sixty-four and approaching retirement at Teachers College; Demiashkevich was forty-six, presumably with the energy to lead the long battle ahead. But Demiashkevich was overwhelmed by constant rejection and his own demons. He had lived in exile for many years, separated from his family in the Soviet Union. He was unhappy about the working conditions at Peabody, where his salary was low, and he had little time for research and writing. His efforts to find a position at a major university came to naught, despite his impressive record of scholarship. His educational ideas were held in contempt by leaders of the profession. The political climate in the United States of "the popular front," which encouraged warm feelings toward the Soviet Union, outraged him. Overworked and despairing, he became depressed and had difficulty working. Hoping to recover his mental and physical health, he went to his vacation house in Maine. In August 1938, he committed suicide there.[24]

The essentialist committee continued to meet for a time, and Bagley continued to argue the case for essentialism in professional journals that never reached a lay public. Overshadowed by the Second World War, the essentialists disappeared from public view. Bagley's death in 1946 robbed the cause of its last prominent spokesman. When Kilpatrick read of Bagley's death in *The New York Times,* he wrote in his diary, "He has long been a hurtful reactionary, the most respectable vocal of all. . . . His going marks the end of an era. No one who professes to know education will henceforth stand forth in opposition as he did."[25]

Hutchins and the Great Books

Bagley annoyed progressive educators, but Robert Maynard Hutchins drove them into a rage. He excoriated the aimlessness of American education, both at the college level and in high schools. His earnest advocacy of the "Great Books" received an amazingly positive reception from the public and put him in opposition to the nation's leading pedagogues. Brilliant, handsome, and witty, Hutchins was a skillful speaker and writer, a media star whose comments were frequently quoted in the daily press and news magazines. Named dean of the Yale Law School at the age of twenty-eight, Hutchins was selected as president of the University of Chicago in 1929, when he was only thirty. The "boy wonder" promptly reorganized the university to strengthen general education for undergraduates.

One of his first actions as president of the university was to invite Mortimer Adler, who had just received his doctorate in psychology at Columbia University, to come to Chicago; Adler arrived in the fall of 1930. Having met when Hutchins was dean at Yale Law School, the two proceeded to become the Don Quixote and Sancho Panza of American education, tilting at the huge windmill of the education establishment on behalf of the "Great Books."

They were an oddly matched pair: the elegant, patrician Hutchins, descendant of Protestant ministers who traced their lineage to the Puritans, and the ungainly, abrasive Adler, son of German Jewish immigrants, high school dropout, and relentless autodidact (Adler was probably the only person ever to earn a doctorate without having previously received a high school diploma, a bachelor's degree, or a master's degree). Adler had managed to insult or irritate most of his professors, but Hutchins was charmed by his freewheeling intellect.

Adler had taught a Great Books course for several years at Columbia and had organized adult discussion groups in the New York City area. He persuaded Hutchins that a liberal education was unthinkable without a grounding in the Great Books, which Hutchins himself lacked. Hutchins claimed that he "had arrived at the age of thirty . . . with some knowledge of the Bible, of Shakespeare, of *Faust,* of one dialogue of Plato, and of the opinions of many semiliterate and a few literate judges, and that was about all." Adler warned him that the "sole reading matter of university presidents was the telephone book" and suggested that unless he "did something drastic," he would close his career "a wholly uneducated man."[26]

In part to advance his own education, but also to test Adler's theories about liberal education, Hutchins joined with Adler to teach a weekly freshman honors seminar devoted to systematic study of the classic books of Western civilization. The reading list spanned the centuries from Homer to Freud and included works by philosophers, theologians, scientists, novelists, poets, historians, and social theorists. Contemporary works were excluded from their seminar, since none could be considered "classic" until it had passed the test of time. The course proved popular, as did the professors' methods of Socratic dialogue and oral examinations conducted by external examiners. Hutchins and Adler eventually taught "Great Books of the Western World" to students in the college, the university's high school, the humanities division, the Department of Education, the law school, and the Extension Division, and even to laymen at the University Club in downtown Chicago.

As he pursued his self-education, Hutchins became persuaded that the classics were the heart and soul of a liberal education, a necessary means of entering into what he called "the great conversation" among generations of thinkers in the Western world. He concluded that every educated person should read and understand the classics and relate them to modern scholarship and contemporary issues. As a proponent of the

Great Books, Hutchins emerged on the national stage as a major critic of American education, with his own clear and controversial proposals for reform.

In the mid-1930s, Hutchins began to speak out against the triviality and mediocrity of American education. He wanted to abolish the customary "painful accumulation of credits" and put into its place clear goals for students and "a system of general examinations to be taken by the student when he is ready to take them, and given, if possible, by external examiners." He thought students should demonstrate what they knew and could do, not how long they had been "incarcerated." Future teachers, he argued, should have a good general education that included not only mastery of the theory of learning but also the intellectual content of the subject matter they intended to teach. A "good general education" did not include vocational education, he said; any employer could teach machine work in a couple of weeks.[27]

Hutchins disapproved of the objectives of progressive education. It was wrong, he asserted, to "adjust" students to their environment; this was nothing more than preparation for the status quo. Nor did he approve of preparing youngsters for a collectivist social order. No one, he noted, could say with any certainty what the social order of the future should be, and it was mere conceit to design a course of study based on one's own political and economic opinions. Nor did he agree that the shaping of personality or character should be the object of education: "If we place personality and character before us as the aim of education, we shall get neither personality, character, nor education." Character, he said (paraphrasing Woodrow Wilson), was a by-product of "hard work well done." Worse, the resources that ought to go into intellectual training would be "lavished on athletics, social life, and student guidance, a kind of coddling, nursing, and pampering of students that is quite unknown anywhere else in the world."[28]

Hutchins insisted that the object of general education should be "the training of the mind." Such a program would "facilitate social change and make it more intelligent. The educational system cannot bring about social change. It cannot work out and impose on the country a blueprint of the social order desired by the teachers colleges." The kind of educational program that was needed, he argued, would teach students to appreciate the importance of ideas, to understand history, the fine arts, and literature, and to grasp the principles of science. This was his vision of what American education might be if teachers were truly well educated.[29]

Hutchins's critique of the schools was closely linked to his critique of higher education. In 1936, he denounced American higher education for its efforts to be all things to all people. The American university, he said, had become a vast "service-station," constantly seeking to serve changing needs. Its surrender to vocationalism, he charged, had produced the strange phenomenon of "an anti-intellectual university." The central aim of education, he declared, must be "the cultivation of the intellect for its own sake." Hutchins contended that the best preparation for most professions was a good education and on-the-job experience.[30]

But what was "a good education"? In Hutchins's view, a good education was a general education that supplied "a common stock of fundamental ideas," enabling students and professors in different departments and divisions to understand one another. General education, he wrote, was "education for everybody, whether he goes on to the university or not. It will be useful to him in the university; it will be equally useful if he never goes there." A general education might not help the individual make money or get ahead. But it would cultivate his intellect and equip him to operate well in any field of endeavor.[31]

In a sharp rebuke to progressive education, to its desire to fit education to each student and each locality, Hutchins declared that education should "draw out the elements of our common human nature. These elements are the same in any time or place. The notion of educating a man to live in any particular time or place, to adjust him to any particular environment, is therefore foreign to a true conception of education." In a statement guaranteed to raise the hackles of pragmatists and relativists, Hutchins asserted, "Education implies teaching. Teaching implies knowledge. Knowledge is truth. The truth is everywhere the same. Hence education should be everywhere the same."[32]

Hutchins recognized that the world is constantly in flux and that great advances in science and technology were revolutionizing daily life. But he complained that a mistaken notion of progress "has thrown the classics and the liberal arts out of the curriculum, overemphasized the empirical sciences, and made education the servant of any contemporary movements in society, no matter how superficial." The true purpose of education, he maintained, was cultivating the intellect, pursuing wisdom, teaching students how to reason. He ridiculed the progressives' notion that it was the responsibility of formal education to give experiences; that was the job of the home, the church, the state, the mass media, "the boy next door," and life. Only the school and college could supply intellectual discipline, and if they abandoned this responsibility, no other agency would do it.[33]

Hutchins decried the child-centered school as "an aimless, trial-and-error process" that turned teachers into "nothing but chaperons." The child-centered school was, he said, a child's version of the elective system that Charles Eliot had introduced at Harvard, which amounted to "a denial that there was content to education. Since there was no content to education, we might as well let students follow their own bent. . . . This overlooks the fact that the aim of education is to connect man with man, to connect the present with the past, and to advance the thinking of the race. If this is the aim of education, it cannot be left to the sporadic, spontaneous interests of children or even of undergraduates."[34]

His vision for education reform involved a four-year course, beginning in the last two years of high school and including the first two years of college. The reading in this course would be composed of classics: "A classic is a book that is contemporary in every age. That is why it is a classic. . . . How can we call a man educated who has never read any of the great books in the western world?" Students, he knew, had read *about* Cicero, John Locke, Descartes, Galileo, and Adam Smith in their textbooks. They might even have read brief excerpts from their writings. None of this, though, was an adequate substitute for carefully reading original works, which would not only develop standards of taste and criticism but would enable students as adults to "think and act intelligently about the thought and movements of contemporary life." Merely reading the classics was not enough, however; students must also learn "the arts of reading, writing, thinking, and speaking, together with mathematics, the best exemplar of the processes of human reason."[35]

Did Hutchins expect that his proposed reforms might be widely adopted? He anticipated three objections. One was that students might not like the course of study. He discounted this as irrelevant, but in any event not true, since he believed that students would like it because it was coherent and free of triviality. A second likely objection was that the course of study would be too difficult. He countered that it could be mastered by any student who could read or who could be taught to read. The third and most significant objection, which he expected would be fatal, was that professors and teachers would refuse to teach the course. Few had read the Great Books, few were willing to change their habits, and most were likely to train their successors as they had been trained. He knew that nothing less than an "evangelistic movement" or the establishment of a new college could reclaim general education from its swamp of triviality, anti-intellectualism, and utilitarianism.[36]

Everything that Hutchins advocated was rank heresy to progressive educators. Unthinkable, his claim that the fundamental purpose of education was intellectual training. Outrageous, his belief that certain studies "discipline" the mind and "develop" the faculties. Didn't he know that Thorndike had proven that there was no such thing as intellectual discipline? Didn't he understand that you learn what you learn and you train what you train, and that sewing was more valuable than Latin? Didn't he know that students would learn best if they engaged in life situations and solved meaningful problems of daily life? And then there was his absurd claim on behalf of obsolete books that no one read anymore, books written centuries ago that had no bearing on the needs of youths or contemporary social problems.

The charismatic president of the University of Chicago could not easily be dismissed or ignored, however. His heresies had to be answered, and the rebuke was delivered by John Dewey himself in 1936 and 1937.

Dewey attacked Hutchins's proposed study of the classics as an effort to divorce learning from contemporary life. It was contrary to Dewey's lifelong efforts to close the gap between school and society. Even more distressing to Dewey was Hutchins's belief in fixed and authoritative principles, eternal truths. As a pragmatist devoted to scientific method, Dewey abhorred absolutes (other than an absolute aversion to

303

fixed truths), whether derived from philosophy or religion. Dewey claimed that Hutchins's proposal was authoritarian because it appealed to "the existence of ultimate first principles." Astonishingly, Dewey went so far as to imply that Hutchins was ideologically linked with the jackbooted thugs who were then brutalizing Europe: "I would not intimate that the author has any sympathy with fascism. But basically his idea as to the proper course to be taken is akin to the distrust of freedom and the consequent appeal to *some* fixed authority that is now overrunning the world."[37]

William Heard Kilpatrick was equally horrified by Hutchins's views. He fulminated that Hutchins was an authoritarian whose ideas were out of step with "every intellectual advance of the last 300 years." Worse, said Kilpatrick, "Dr. Hutchins stands near to Hitler. When you have a professed absolute, then you have to have some authority to give it content, and there the dictator comes in."[38]

Hutchins was a strange choice for the labels Dewey and Kilpatrick attempted to fasten on him. In 1932, he had publicly supported Norman Thomas, the Socialist candidate in the presidential campaign (in the same year, Dewey had tried to organize a radical third party and turned to Thomas only after his own efforts failed). Hutchins, moreover, courageously defended academic freedom whenever one of his faculty was under attack. When put to the test, as he was in 1935 when the Illinois State Senate investigated Communist influence at the University of Chicago, Hutchins vigorously defended his faculty and the principles of academic freedom. He considered such principles "fixed and authoritative" (yet another "absolute" principle).[39]

Mortimer Adler jumped into the fray on Hutchins's behalf, but with ill effect. Adler convinced other educators that he and Hutchins were trying to impose authoritarian values—if not derived from Aristotle, then certainly from Thomas Aquinas. The pugnacious Adler happily fed the fury of progressives by describing himself as a "Thomist," even though he was not Catholic. He seemed to relish insulting his audience, as he did when he first arrived at the University of Chicago and told a gathering of eminent social scientists that their methods were flawed. Adler later wrote that in 1938 and 1939, he and Hutchins had been in a chronic mood of "unrelieved despair" because of the hostile reception accorded to Hutchins's proposals by other educators. Both realized that their grand scheme to introduce the Great Books for mass consumption was hopeless, and Hutchins considered leaving Chicago.[40]

Adler then made matters worse. In the fall of 1940, he participated in a national Conference on Science, Philosophy, and Religion at the Jewish Theological Seminary in New York City. Speaking to two hundred professors, Adler denounced them for rejecting Hutchins's ideas and insisted upon the demonstrability of God's existence. Adler totally outraged his audience by declaring that "The most serious threat to democracy is the positivism of its professors, which dominates every aspect of modern education and is the central corruption of modern culture. Democracy has much more to fear from the mentality of its teachers than from the nihilism of Hitler." The philosopher Sidney Hook, a professor at New York University and disciple of John Dewey, blasted Adler for his assertions and his use of "calculated insults under the guise of plain speaking."[41] With war on the horizon and nerves on edge, Adler's intemperate address confirmed the suspicions of those who thought that Hutchins and Adler had dangerous authoritarian motives.

Although the academic and pedagogical world scorned Hutchins and his ideas, he nonetheless had an enviable level of popular renown as a writer for popular journals such as *The Saturday Evening Post*. His candor and clarity attracted a large public following but won him few friends in the academy. His 1943 book, *Education for Freedom,* inspired the Mutual Broadcasting System to broadcast the Great Books on national radio.

This was too much for his critics. Many of the same professors who had been insulted by Adler in 1940 called another national conference in 1944 and gave it the incredible title "The Authoritarian Attempt to Capture Education." It was not the Nazis that the conference organizers had in mind, but Hutchins. The lead speaker warned, "Above the drone of the fighter planes, the shriek of the bombs, and the roar of the heavy shells, the hoarse voice of reaction rises over the earth." The conference devoted special attention to education "in the belief that certain organized movements in education constitute a threat to the scientific spirit and democratic faith." [42] Opposing Hutchins, it seemed, was part of the fight against fascism and totalitarianism.

At that meeting, Dewey attacked Hutchins as a reactionary who was engaged in a "definite campaign to make the scientific attitude the scapegoat for present evils, while a return to the beliefs and practices of a pre-scientific and pre-technological age is urged as the road to our salvation." He claimed that Hutchins, by asserting the primacy of the Great Books, wanted to return to "the medieval pre-scientific doctrine of a supernatural foundation and outlook in all social and moral subjects." Dewey criticized Hutchins's belief that intellectual development should be the central aim of education and condemned him as an elitist who wanted to restore the values of the feudal age. [43]

But Dewey completely misrepresented Hutchins's proposals. Hutchins wanted everyone to have an intellectual education, followed by on-the-job training; Dewey insisted that Hutchins wanted different types of education for different classes, which he called "social and moral quackery" and "a denial of democracy." At the same time, Dewey ignored the reality of separate vocational tracks instituted by his fellow progressives, which did offer different types of education for the children of different classes. Dewey preferred to believe in his nonexistent ideal of a liberalized vocational education, rather than confront the reality of narrow training for existing jobs. [44]

Other speakers flayed Hutchins for the effrontery of recommending the Great Books, averring that this amounted to indoctrination. Arthur E. Murphy, a professor of philosophy at the University of Illinois, excoriated Hutchins for trying to erect a standard of "established truth" with "100 great books." Murphy insisted that Hutchins was trying to impose the Great Books as "present gospel for an erring world," a guide to settling all disputed questions now and forevermore. Of course, Hutchins had said no such thing. But Murphy neatly accounted for the fact that Hutchins had never made such claims by saying that it was part of his clever campaign never to admit explicitly that this sort of indoctrination was his goal. [45]

Reflecting on the rage that Hutchins inspired, historian Edward A. Krug asked, "Why should books, especially 'great' ones, have given so much offense to the community of modern pedagogy? . . . The answer may well be the degree to which books symbolize academic education and become offensive to those with the anti-academic point of view." Krug concluded that Hutchins had attracted so much vitriol because he was advocating "a mainly literary education," and "the reading of books, great or otherwise, for their intrinsic and internal values could win neither acceptance nor toleration in the pedagogical scheme of things in the United States of the late 1930s." To progressive leaders, Krug observed, Hutchins was "a most dangerous heretic. To take part in the numerous burnings of President Hutchins had become an act of pedagogical faith."[46]

SELF-CRITICISM BY DEWEY AND BODE

*Even though Hutchins infuriated progressive educators, he also com-*pelled some to take a closer look at their own flaws. So intense was the reaction of pedagogues to Hutchins that the two leading progressive philosophers of education wrote books to counter his influence. In 1938, John Dewey and Boyd Bode each published a book ritualistically denouncing Hutchins but acknowledging that progressive education would have to engage in self-examination.

In *Experience and Education,* Dewey called upon the progressive education movement to set its house in order. Failure to do so, he warned, would encourage reactionary forces that wanted to "return to the logic of ultimate first principles expressed in the logic of Aristotle and St. Thomas" and to "the intellectual methods and ideals that arose centuries before scientific method was developed." Everyone understood that he was referring to Hutchins. To head off such an "emotional appeal," Dewey urged progressive educators to stop catering to the whims of students and to recognize the importance of organized subject matter.[47]

Dewey had heard that some teachers were afraid even to make suggestions to students about what they were expected to do. He had heard of children who were surrounded with objects and left on their own, with no direction from a teacher. This situation he found unacceptable. The weakest point in progressive schools, he admitted, was their selection and organization of intellectual subject matter. While he did not want all progressive schools to have a single course of study, he wanted progressive teachers to recognize that "No experience is educative that does not tend both to knowledge of more facts" and to a more orderly arrangement of facts. He warned that "Failure to give constant attention to development of intellectual content of experiences and to obtain ever-increasing organization of facts and ideas may in the end merely strengthen the tendency toward a reactionary return to intellectual and moral authoritarianism.[48]

Experience and Education has typically been seen as Dewey's most important effort to disavow the laissez-faire individualism and radical romanticism that frequently embarrassed progressive education. Having quoted Rousseau approvingly in the past, Dewey now disassociated himself from the undisciplined, planless kind of schooling that characterized many progressive schools. Dewey made clear that he saw little value in schools that had no curriculum planned in advance and that allowed children unlimited freedom (he wrote that the person whose conduct is governed by "immediate whim and caprice . . . has at most only the illusion of freedom"). Not for him the progressive school where children plaintively ask, "Do I have to do what I want to do today?"[49]

Valuable as *Experience and Education* was, Dewey failed to acknowledge the forms in which progressive education was influencing the public schools in the late 1930s. Dewey made the same arguments against excessive student freedom in 1938 that he had made a decade earlier, when he had seen that private progressive schools were going overboard in their celebration of child liberation. But he offered no reproof for public schools that offered different curricula for different youngsters, based on their likely occupation, nor did he chastise public schools that were institutionalizing social conformism and anti-intellectualism in required courses such as "social living" and "basic living." Since these intellectually vacuous courses were clothed in the rhetoric of collective social improvement, their defects may have been harder to detect than the extremes of individualism. Progressive education was always multifarious and hard to define. The excessively permissive version that Dewey criticized in 1938 was an easy target for caricature. The version that he did not criticize—which turned principals and teachers into social engineers responsible for their students' personality development and social adjustment—had far greater staying power in the public schools.

With the perspective of time, it is striking to recognize that John Dewey was locked in dualisms, the famous "either-ors" that he so often wrote about. He frequently described opposing tendencies in education (school and society, the child and the curriculum, interest and effort, experience and education) and claimed that he wanted to reconcile these dualisms. However, he never presented them as equally compelling alternatives, so it was scarcely surprising that his followers unfailingly chose society, not the school; the child, not the curriculum; interest, not effort; experience, not subject matter. In *Experience and Education,* Dewey described traditional education in a highly pejorative fashion, with frequent references to its brutality and dogmatism, its reliance on methods of coercion, its "strait-jacket and chain-gang procedures." Was this a description of the schools he had known in the 1880s and 1890s? Possibly. Was it an accurate description of typical public schools in the 1930s? Not likely. Yet throughout this book, his last major work on education, Dewey returned again and again to "eithers" and "ors," presenting traditional and progressive education as polar opposites, between which there was no real overlap and little possibility of convergence or evolution.[50]

In this influential 1938 book, Dewey concluded that the fundamental issue was not "of new versus old education nor of progressive against traditional education" but of what deserved to be called education at all. This disclaimer was not persuasive, however, because Dewey disparaged traditional education at every turn while identifying progressive education, correctly designed, as the only hope for the future. It was precisely this sort of dualistic thinking—which Dewey reinforced—that created a wall of antagonism between traditionalists and progressives, as well as stereotypical thinking on both sides.[51]

Boyd H. Bode was the progressive education movement's most perceptive in-house critic. He too rejected Hutchins's ideas. But he acknowledged that the flaws of progressive education were self-inflicted.

His *Progressive Education at the Crossroads* (1938) was a searing indictment of the inadequacies of progressive education. He respectfully cited the work of Dewey, Kilpatrick, and Rugg while showing how their ideas had become inane doctrines.

The greatest weakness of progressive education, Bode wrote, was its failure to liberate itself from Rousseau, which had led to "a superstitious reverence for childhood." Schools that centered their program on the "needs of children" had become trapped in anti-intellectualism, he argued, preferring improvisation to long-range planning, emphasizing the here and now, expecting pupils to plan their own activities, and joining in tirades against academic subjects. The result was "an unhealthy attitude towards children, an attitude which suggests that there is no such thing as a normal child, and that we must be everlastingly exploring his insides." Bode decried his fellow progressives' dedication to children's "interests," saying that the "purpose of sound education is precisely to emancipate the pupil from dependence on immediate interests. A person cannot remain a baby all his life."[52]

The movement's fascination with children's "needs" was foolish, he wrote, because it was so easy to conflate "needs" and "desires." The "hankering of an old soak for another drink, for example, or the yearning of a small boy to punch his playmate's nose" might be needs but should not be recognized as such by any reputable educational program. Bode observed that "It is high time to realize that examining a youngster to ascertain his needs is different from examining him, say, for adenoids." It was high time to stop attacking academic subjects, he said, because they represent educational values "which we neglect at our own peril."[53] Bode predicted that progressive education would founder and die unless it formulated a clear program of education connected both to democracy and to the maximum development of intelligence.

OUTSIDERS SPEAK OUT

Outside the profession a few critical observers noticed what was happening in the schools during the 1930s, and they did not like what they saw.

In 1933, the literary critic Howard Mumford Jones complained in *Scribner's* that American education was ineffective because it was wedded to method, not content. He worried that the rank utilitarianism of educators was contributing to "the steadily diminishing function of general ideas in the life of the American people" and that this loss of interest in ideas was contributing to a cheapening of American politics and culture.[54]

Education, Jones complained, had become "an intricate machine managed by educational 'experts.' " The elementary schools, he observed, had "wholly adopted the philosophy of the specific," and children were expected to learn only what was visually attractive, amusing, and emotionally appealing. In the upper grades, he wrote, "No one who has not kept up with the vast output of educational 'theory' can be aware how intellectual content for its own sake is disappearing from the curriculum." Jones knew of one school system where eighth-grade arithmetic was optional but physical training was required. "Fed on this soft food," he said, "the high-school graduate who enters college naturally exhibits that interest in the immediate, the practical, the 'do-able' which has led to overemphasis upon vocational instruction, 'practical' courses, and laboratory techniques."[55]

The educationists' insistence on practical experience and their abhorrence of abstract thinking robbed children of intellectual power, Jones believed: "The 'interest' of 'the child' has been consulted, but not his future; and in the name of a free development of meaningful experiences they have in fact substituted an adolescent wish-fulfillment for that rigorous discipline which alone will permit modern man to survive." Jones agreed that there was much in the old curriculum that was wasteful and that public schools had become more cheerful places. But he doubted that "cheeriness is proof of progress toward the control of our complicated civilization—toward that mastery of the past, that education in fundamental significances, that intellectual rigor which America so desperately needs."[56]

A similar complaint was voiced in *The Atlantic Monthly* in 1934 by scholar Carl Joachim Friedrich. Friedrich visited the Lincoln School in New York City with a wealthy woman who kept telling him with pride that her children were "happy." Friedrich horrified his friend by telling

311

her that the children there were being trained for a life of leisure in "a golden pastoral age." His own children, he said, would have to work for a living in a very competitive world, a world that would favor those with intellectual self-discipline. It was paradoxical, he thought, that people who considered themselves progressive would organize a school that would "hinder rather than help the development of children destined to carry on our progressive industrial society."[57]

In 1940, Walter Lippmann, one of the nation's most widely respected commentators on public affairs, charged that schools and universities no longer taught the classical and religious studies of the Western tradition; that these studies had been supplanted by eclectic electives; and that consequently "there is no common faith, no common body of principle, no common body of knowledge, no common moral and intellectual discipline." The graduates of these institutions, he said, were "expected to form a civilized community. They are expected to govern themselves. They are expected to have a social conscience. They are expected to arrive by discussion at common purposes." Instead of transmitting a common cultural heritage, education had become "egoist, careerist, specialist and asocial." What enables people to know more than their ancestors, Lippmann pointed out, is that "they start with a knowledge of what their ancestors have already learned." To study every problem with "an open and empty mind, without preconception, without knowing what has already been learned about it, must condemn men to a chronic childishness." Lippmann insisted that society could be progressive only by conserving its traditions.[58]

→ → ← ←

The frontier thinkers' demands for collectivism and socialism were inevitably followed by a counterreaction during the volatile years of the Depression. In 1934, Elizabeth Dilling's self-published *Red Network: A "Who's Who" and Handbook of Radicalism for Patriots* named 460 organizations and 1,300 individuals as having "knowingly or unknowingly" contributed to the growth of "the Red movement in the United States." Among them were not only Communists but socialists, liberals, liberal anti-Communists, and organizations supporting civil rights, civil liberties, and trade unions. On her list were the leading frontier thinkers, such as John Dewey, William Heard Kilpatrick, Harold Rugg, and George Counts. Dilling was a concert harpist and housewife from the Midwest who had visited the Soviet Union in 1931 and returned to lecture and write against the Communist menace.

Patriotic organizations such as the Daughters of the American Revolution and the American Legion were alarmed by growing signs of radicalism. The Hearst press took up the anti-Communist cause, paying close attention to leftist professors. Several state legislatures had enacted loyalty oaths for teachers during the 1920s, and another dozen states adopted such laws in the 1930s. In 1935, Congress passed a "little Red rider" to the District of Columbia's school appropriation bill, stipulating that no pay could go to anyone teaching or advocating communism (the rider was repealed in 1937). In 1938, the House of Representatives approved funding for its Committee on Un-American Activities to investigate subversive activities by fascists and Communists. Several state legislatures created committees to investigate subversive activities in their schools and colleges.[59]

Harold Rugg's series of social science textbooks became the target for Red-hunting vigilantes in 1940. Originally developed at the Lincoln School, the Rugg texts were read by millions of students in some five thousand schools. In 1940, the Rugg textbooks became highly controversial after the publication of vituperative articles in two prominent journals. Writing in *Nation's Business,* Augustin G. Rudd charged that Rugg and his textbooks were responsible for the growth of Communist youth organizations in the United States. Illustrated with a lurid drawing of a textbook festooned with the Soviet hammer and sickle, the article accused Rugg of trying to foment discontent against the nation's political and economic system. Later the same year, Augustin Rudd became the leader of a group called Guardians of American Education, which forged links to other right-wing extremist groups and continued the anti-Communist campaign in education after World War II.[60]

A few months later, O. K. Armstrong charged that the field of social science had been taken over by "radical and communistic textbook writers" whose motto was "Catch 'em young!" In an article called "Treason in the Textbooks" in *The American Legion Magazine,* Armstrong listed three dozen "subversive" social science textbooks, most written by Rugg. Armstrong was shocked when his son came home from school and asked, "Daddy, was George Washington a big business man?" On investigating, he discovered that his son was in a class called "Democratic Living" that undermined "faith in the American way of life." American institutions, he warned, were at risk because of the "frontier thinkers," whose works intended to persuade youth that the American system had failed.[61]

The articles attacking Rugg's writings and textbooks were libelous exaggerations. Rugg and his colleagues were certainly critical of capitalism and admiring of social planning and collectivism, but they were not subversives or Communists. By 1940, when the attacks began, the frontier thinkers had already retreated from the radical views they had held in the early 1930s. Rugg had moderated his views; Counts was leading the fight against Communist efforts to control the American Federation of Teachers; and Dewey had led the public defense of Leon Trotsky against Soviet charges.

The anti-intellectualism of the Right provoked an outburst of censorship and hysteria. The irresponsible charges by Rudd and Armstrong caused public schools across the nation to withdraw Rugg's textbooks. They were burned in a school library furnace in Bradner, Ohio, and banned elsewhere, including San Francisco and Binghamton, New York. Only Englewood, New Jersey, retained them after a public battle.[62] The persistent efforts by the radical Right to smear progressive education with the ludicrous charge of "un-Americanism" made it difficult for others to criticize progressive education, for fear of allying themselves with the radical Right and its political agenda.

KANDEL'S CRITIQUE

Of all those who criticized progressive education in the 1930s and early 1940s, the one whose work did the most to skewer progressive ideology was Bagley's colleague at Teachers College, Isaac L. Kandel. Bagley's critique was too pedagogical, too involved in issues of instruction. Hutchins's advocacy of the Great Books, though it delighted the public and outraged progressives, was too far removed from the realities of public education. Kandel, however, perceptively attacked the central ideas of progressive education as not only shallow and superficial but socially regressive.

Kandel was born in 1881 to English parents who were on a business trip in Romania. He earned his bachelor's degree in classics at Victoria University in Manchester, England, and a master's degree in education at the University of Manchester. After teaching German and classics for a few years, he came to Teachers College, Columbia University, in 1908 to pursue further graduate studies. The first Jew ever appointed to the faculty of Teachers College, he taught history and philosophy of education and achieved international distinction in the field of comparative education. In his four decades at Teachers College, Kandel published scores of books and hundreds of articles; he had an international reputation as a brilliant and fair-minded scholar.[63]

In 1929, Kandel wrote favorably about John Dewey and his educational ideas, predicting that his reputation would endure because of his recognition that "education is not synonymous with book-learning but implies teaching how to live." Thus, when he began to write critically about progressive education in the early 1930s, his views could not easily be dismissed as those of a reactionary or a hide-bound traditionalist. He was committed to education reform, which he understood to mean adequate funding, well-educated teachers, a well-designed curriculum, and equal educational opportunity. Kandel was appalled by the zeal of his progressive colleagues. His apostasy was punished in petty ways; for example, he was not invited to join the faculty panel that taught the celebrated course on Education and Society at Teachers College. Despite the fact that he was eminently qualified, the prominent progressives who controlled the course excluded him.[64]

In 1932, Kandel observed in an article called "Our Adolescent Education" that progressive leaders were impervious to criticism. If anyone compared American education with the standards achieved in Europe, he

would be told that the European system was highly selective and aristocratic. If he complained about low standards and about the numbers of
poorly prepared students who were entering college, he would be condemned for undermining the principle of equality of opportunity. No
matter how the criticism was framed, the result would be the same, which
was that anyone who found shortcomings in our system of education
"comes as near to blasphemy as to discuss evolution in Tennessee."[65]

The chief weaknesses of the American high school, Kandel complained, were its vague aims, its unwillingness to establish priorities
among subjects, and its hiring of teachers who had no preparation to
teach any subject or group of subjects. With high schools simultaneously
striving to cater to individual needs and to avoid commitment to a central
core of subjects, the curriculum had become flooded with courses in vocational and trivial subjects, and "the standard subjects were gradually
beginning to be elbowed out."[66]

The high school "accepted the obligation of meeting the needs of the
individual but hesitates to impose any intellectual obligations on him unless he accepts them himself as 'satisfying.' " In light of the pressure to
please the student, he noted, "effort, hard work, discipline, strenuous intellectual activity have become taboo." Current educational psychology
and philosophy, he observed, were aligned with a native tradition of anti-
intellectualism. It seemed that everything taught in school must bring instant gratification and leave nothing for the individual to figure out for
himself. Kandel observed that the one experiment that had never been
tried was to see what could be accomplished by a well-educated group of
teachers who took their responsibility to impart a liberal education to
their students seriously: "Education is not a commodity which can be
handed out over the counter as in a department store or a cafeteria, nor
can the selection of its constituent elements be left wholly to the learner;
society has as much interest in the character of the education given in its
schools as has the individual." Americans had always had a profound
faith in education, but unless education was given a richer content, he
feared, all that would be left of this ideal would be "faith in keeping the
younger generation in school."[67]

During the 1930s, Kandel examined the slogans and shibboleths of his progressive colleagues with considerable erudition and, on occasion, sarcasm. His closest friend on the faculty was Bagley, and the two of them certainly must have felt like outsiders in the midst of the nation's most renowned center of progressive educational theory. Kandel was noted for a certain mordant wit, and on one occasion he wrote a note to Dean William Russell: "The New York Times discovered recently that a member of the Teachers College faculty had 'nothing to say'; some of his colleagues have known that for some time." This was followed by doggerel:

WE COME FROM TEACHERS COLLEGE,
THE HOME OF KILPATRICK AND DEWEY.
WE TRY TO DISSEMINATE KNOWLEDGE,
BUT THE REACTION OF MANY IS "PHOOEY!" [68]

In 1933, when his colleagues were debating the merits of the activity movement and the schools' part in building a new social order, Kandel thought that their preoccupations were too absurd to merit a serious discussion, so he wrote a parody he called "Alice in Cloud-Cuckoo-Land." Up in the clouds, far detached from reality, Alice communes with the birds about "shared intelligence," group decision-making, a new social order, units of work, and self-expression. All the birds agree that an authoritarian, coerced education is terrible. "How about breaking up the subjects and using them whenever we want them and as we need them?" asks the cuckoo. "Good idea," says Alice, "and we won't call them subjects any more; let's call them units of work and then school will be a happy place for everybody." After much silly chatter and a happy exchange of slogans ("Society is a function of education; education is a function of society; if education is a function of society and society is a function of education, then is a function of society education?"), Alice wakes up to find that it is time to prepare her lessons for the next day "in arithmetic, science, English, history, and geography!" [69]

To those who opposed standards, Kandel held up the example of "one part of our educational system, secondary and higher, in which there is no compromise with standards, in which there is rigid selection both of instructors and students, in which there is no soft pedagogy, and in which training and sacrifice of the individual for common ends are accepted without question. I refer, of course, to the organization of athletics."[70] If ever American schools became as rigorous and well planned as their athletic programs, he suggested, they would be reinvigorated.

In 1940, Kandel defended a scheme for national teacher testing. The American Council on Education developed a test for would-be teachers in 1939, in the depth of the Depression, when teaching jobs were highly prized and there were more applicants than positions. The test was first offered in the spring of 1940 in twenty centers, including cities such as Philadelphia, Pittsburgh, Providence, Atlanta, and Boston. The examinations lasted from ten to twelve hours, and all candidates had to demonstrate their command of English expression, reasoning, quantitative skills, history, literature, science, fine arts, and current issues. In addition, candidates were tested on the history and philosophy of education, educational psychology, and teaching methods. Those who hoped to teach in high school also took tests in the academic subjects they wanted to teach.[71]

The National Teacher Examinations quickly came under fire from critics, who feared that states might rely more on test results than on credentials from schools of education. The critics, who were professors of education, claimed that the new examinations would introduce undesirable uniformity and would place too much emphasis on teachers' factual knowledge rather than their personality. Ben D. Wood, the director of the project, contended that "To abandon examinations of intelligence, general culture, and professional information because they do not also measure personality, moral character, interest in children, and other important factors that determine teaching ability, would be as illogical as to abandon the use of the clinical thermometer and stethoscope because they do not measure a thousand other important diagnostic factors."[72]

In defense of the tests, Kandel charged that the critics were asserting "the teacher's right to be ignorant." Kandel considered the examinations to be comparable to those offered to future doctors and lawyers. It was no secret, he noted, that thousands of high school teachers were teaching subjects they had never studied. Instead of trying to correct this situation, the critics were attacking the subject organization of the high school curriculum. Critics of the examinations, he held, reflected an old American tradition that all a teacher needed to know was how to teach. Kandel, however, thought that it was inconceivable that a teacher could be both ignorant and effective as a teacher:

> Even the most radical Progressive aims at a reorientation and reshuffling of the content that is to be used for educational purposes; even a child-centered school implies that pupils have their interests and problems which are to be enriched and solved through content of some kind; even an integrated curriculum must integrate something . . . and even a general education must have some content. Behind classroom procedures there must be a fund of something on which the teacher and pupils must draw; that fund all teachers must have; how they draw on that fund may vary with the current fashion, but "the what" can not be discarded in favor of "the how."[73]

School officials liked the National Teacher Examinations as long as teachers were abundant. The mobilization for World War II, however, created a teacher shortage. When the supply of teachers dried up, school districts no longer cared how well their teachers scored on an examination.

Even in the midst of the war, Kandel hammered away at the progressive education movement. In his 1943 classic, *The Cult of Uncertainty,* he charged that progressive education had become a hollow doctrine, empty of any intellectual vitality or moral purpose. Progressivism, wrote Kandel, celebrated change for its own sake, blithely tossing away tradition and experience, leaving only a legacy of "nihilism and anti-intellectualism." In its slavish adherence to tired dogmas, it had become as formal and ritual-bound as traditional education had ever been, but without the cultural moorings that might redeem the latter.[74]

Kandel was angry, not just at the pretensions of the theorists but at their failure to confront the alarming deficiencies in American education. It was intolerable, he wrote, that in a country that annually spent more for education than any other country in the world, there were 10 million people over the age of twenty-five with less than four years of schooling; that large numbers of men had been rejected by the military draft because of functional illiteracy; that educational opportunity was dependent upon accidents of birth; that teachers were paid abysmally low wages; and that so many teachers were poorly educated. Kandel fumed at the frontier thinkers in education, who were too busy fantasizing about grand social reforms to deal with the immediate problems in American education.[75]

What the progressives had wrought in education, Kandel charged, was curricular chaos. It didn't matter what a pupil studied, as long as he was entertained. The educational system counted time spent in class, he said, but had no priorities, no values, no traditions, no commitment to enduring ideas or to students' intellectual development. Particularly abhorrent to Kandel was the undisguised anti-intellectualism of progressive educators. Not far beneath the veneer of the child-centered school was contempt for knowledge and book learning. If the momentary interests of the child and the problems of the local community were more valuable than books, Kandel wondered, why should society establish schools? Why bother with adult education if people learned best through experiences in the local community?

Societies create schools, Kandel wrote, to perpetuate themselves and to teach intellectual and moral discipline to their young. Teachers should help children understand society and gain access to its tools—its books, techniques, customs, mores, and institutions. In all of this, he said, there must be purpose and planning. Values and knowledge do not unfold on their own, nor can children discover fields of knowledge such as mathematics and history by their own experiences and activities.

For educators to leave children free to figure out what they need to learn would be equivalent, he suggested, to a nutritionist refusing to teach students the knowledge accumulated by the field of nutrition. He preferred to "prejudice the garden toward roses" by careful nurture and tending, rather than letting the weeds overrun it. The school, he argued, is a social institution with the obligation to select thoughtfully those experiences that will develop the child into an intelligent member of the community.[76]

Kandel recognized that the commercial mass media were beginning to establish a national culture. It was the role of the schools, he argued, to counteract their influence by consciously raising students' standards of taste and appreciation instead of leaving them to cultivate their own. A great deal of attention had been directed to vocational training to prepare students to earn a living, but too little to ensuring that everyone would be able "to share the culture of the world." By insisting that the curriculum must be geared to whatever was immediately satisfying or useful, progressive educators were making their students subservient to the mass media, failing to equip them with meanings and values with which to insist on better fare.[77]

In contrast to the cult of uncertainty, Kandel affirmed that the schools had a clear mission: to promote common understandings, common knowledge, common values, and a common language of discourse, all of which were necessary for participation of equals in a democratic society. Good schools, he said, would foster the full development of each individual child, prepare students for citizenship, and cultivate interests of lifelong value. There was much to be gained, he believed, by studying the accumulated wisdom of the centuries, and it was the job of the schools to transmit this priceless heritage to their students.

9

The Great Meltdown

By the end of World War II, progressivism was the reigning ideology of American education. Educators at every level of public education spoke the same pedagogical language and claimed to be implementing the very programs that progressive educators had been advocating for decades. The evidence was everywhere: in textbooks for future teachers and administrators, in reports by august national commissions, in policy statements of leading professional organizations, and in publications of state education departments and the U.S. Office of Education. The works of Dewey, Kilpatrick, and Rugg enjoyed near-canonical status in the nation's education schools.[1]

The heated pedagogical debates of the 1930s disappeared, replaced by a solid professional consensus in the 1940s. The conventional wisdom decreed that subject matter and the academic curriculum were outmoded; that the curriculum should never be prescribed by city or state officials but jointly planned by teachers and pupils; that it should be based on students' interests and needs, not on the logical organization of subjects; that experiences and activities were more valuable to students than reading and study; that schools should offer different programs to different groups of students, depending on whether they were preparing for work or college; that students should be promoted every year, regardless of their performance; and that professional educators should think of themselves as social engineers, empowered to decide what was best for students and the rest of society.

This functional philosophy presumably fitted the practical, anti-intellectual strain in the American temper, yet it frequently encountered staunch resistance from teachers and parents. In the late 1940s and 1950s, this resistance grew into a loud public protest against the professional consensus.

Education for *All* American Youth

After World War II, the nation's educational leadership was optimistic, even though public education suffered from critical shortages of qualified teachers, poor salaries, overcrowded schools, and a backlog of deferred maintenance from the Depression and war years. The leaders had good reason for their optimism: in the middle of the war, they had defeated the federal government's attempts to challenge their exclusive control of tax-supported public education.

During the Depression, the Roosevelt administration had created two federal agencies—the Civilian Conservation Corps (CCC) and the National Youth Administration (NYA)—which had provided jobs, income, vocational training, and education to millions of unemployed youth. Established in 1933, the CCC eventually employed about 2.5 million young people at modest wages to work on public service projects in the nation's parks and forests; many learned to read and even earned high school diplomas while in the Corps. The NYA was created in 1935 as a relief program that eventually reached nearly 2 million young people. It provided work-study jobs in schools and universities, enabling many to remain enrolled. The NYA also underwrote jobs for unemployed youngsters in public libraries, museums, nursery schools, recreation programs, and community centers.

The federal government purposely kept the management of these programs out of the hands of the public school establishment, which complained repeatedly that these federal agencies were getting money that ought to go to the public schools and were violating the sacred principle of local and state control of education.

In 1942 and 1943, as the war economy solved the problem of youth unemployment, the National Education Association persuaded Congress to shut down the CCC and the NYA. The abolition of these two agencies guaranteed that public high schools would again enjoy a monopoly over the education and training of young people. Education professionals saw this brief intrusion by the federal government as a warning for the future. Never again would they be caught off guard by some other government agency that claimed to do a better job of training nonacademic youngsters. Never again would they allow anyone to say that the schools were too academic, too remote from the real world.[2]

Determined to prove that they were up to the task of taking care of unmotivated and even out-of-school youths (many of whom had been reached by the CCC and NYA), education leaders planned for postwar reconstruction of the nation's education system. In 1944, the NEA's prestigious Educational Policies Commission published *Education for All American Youth,* with the endorsement of the American Association of School Administrators and the National Association of Secondary School Principals. This report outlined the education establishment's vision for the future. It portrayed the public school as the fulcrum of social planning, designed to meet all the needs of all children and youth, as well as the needs of their communities. The report treated the once-central academic curriculum as an antique inheritance of dubious value, to be quietly set aside in favor of "the imperative educational needs of youth," such as gaining job skills, learning about family life, and becoming good citizens.

Education for All American Youth redefined the role of the public school. In the future, the main purpose of the public school would be career guidance; it would test students for their abilities and then direct them either to vocational training or to a college preparatory program. College entry would no longer depend on students' credits and grades, nor even on their completion of certain required courses. Instead, it would be based on tests of students' aptitude and intelligence and the recommendations of the high school.

In the school of the future, the educators predicted, there would be no required curriculum for college preparation. All studies would be utilitarian; nothing would be studied simply to gain knowledge for its own sake. In such a school, there would be "no aristocracy of 'subjects.' . . . Mathematics and mechanics, art and agriculture, history and home-making are all peers." Students would pay primary attention to vocation, consumer problems, citizenship, personal issues, and family life; knowledge about science, mathematics, literature, and history would be picked up on an incidental, as-needed basis.

The public school of the future would be a custodial institution for the community's children, keeping them busy and preparing them for the existing social order. The courses in family life were expected to teach youngsters how to form happy families. The vocational programs would train youngsters for the workplace and supply the needs of the labor market. Consumer economics would teach young people how to make wise purchases and not waste their money on gambling, carnivals, and other frivolities. In this expansive view of the public school, there was no social or economic problem that was beyond its capacity to solve, nothing it could not be expected to do—except teach academic subjects to the majority of its students.[3]

The report recommended a four-year high school course called "common learnings," combining everything that all students needed to know into a single course. All students would meet for two or more hours daily in "common learnings," which would merge the study of citizenship, family life, health, consumer economics, science, English, literature, and the arts. If youngsters studied housing, for example, they would learn about home furnishings, the planning of housing developments, the scientific principles of household equipment, housing in history, the design of houses, and so on. Subjects such as physics, chemistry, history, and algebra would be available as electives for those who wanted to learn them, but most students were expected to spend their time on more useful studies. "Common learnings" was another name for the integrated core curriculum that progressive educators had begun promoting in the 1930s; it anticipated and resembled the life adjustment movement of the late 1940s. Its main purpose was to diminish traditional subject matter in the high school and to make "the needs of youth" the organizing principle of the curriculum.[4]

While the report claimed to be a visionary statement, it was silent on the most important moral and social issue facing American education: racial segregation. This was not surprising, since the president of the National Association of Secondary-School Principals—which supported and publicized the report—was the state high school supervisor for Mississippi. Educators were well aware of the legal battle against racially segregated schools. The National Association for the Advancement of Colored People had won a major Supreme Court decision in 1938 requiring the admission of a black student to the segregated law school at the all-white University of Missouri. No crystal ball was necessary to see that civil rights lawyers would eventually challenge the segregated school systems of the South in court.

Nonetheless, the Educational Policies Commission accepted racial segregation as the norm. For all its bluster about boldly facing the future, the report timidly proposed that "education should be planned for *all* youth, so that economic, geographical, social, occupational, and racial limitations may have full understanding and consideration." There was nothing here about *removing* limitations, just making sure that these limitations received "understanding and consideration."[5]

The recommendations of *Education for All American Youth* were far removed from the Dewey school of 1900, where children had explored the life and times of ancient Greeks and Phoenician seafarers, and equally remote from the Lincoln School of the 1920s, where teachers had sought to improve the teaching of history, mathematics, science, the arts, and literature. Before World War II, progressive education had been a vigorous, argumentative movement in which various factions had contended for their various visions of schooling. Its leaders had criticized traditional education, but they themselves had been educated in the classics. By the end of the war, however, progressive education had become calcified, the property of professors of education who spoke and wrote in an obscure jargon understood only by their colleagues and students. Having set aside the earlier ideal of child-centered schooling that liberated individualism and creativity as well as the ideal of leading a socialist revolution through the schools, all that remained was the belief that the schools should adjust children to fit into their society.

THE LIFE ADJUSTMENT MOVEMENT

In the first four decades of the century, progressive education had many fractious components, including the vocational education movement, the social efficiency movement, the mental measurement movement, the child-centered movement, the activity movement, the curriculum revision movement, the mental hygiene movement, and the social reconstruction movement. The common denominator in all these movements was their antipathy to the academic curriculum; less clear was what their supporters wanted to put in its place. After World War II, these different emphases melded into a strange amalgam called the life adjustment movement.

This was the postwar form of progressive education as reinterpreted by bureaucrats at the state and federal levels, and it was unabashedly anti-intellectual. It drew on almost every element of the progressive tradition because it advocated vocational education, social efficiency, testing, activities, and curriculum revision; it claimed to meet the needs of youth by teaching students about their own personal and social problems. The life adjustment movement pointedly neglected, however, any concern for students' intellectual growth. What survived from the social and political agitation of the 1930s was a consensus that educators must be social engineers; but—unlike the education movements of the 1930s—the life adjustment movement of the postwar era avowed no intention to change the social order; rather, it aimed to adjust young people to it.

Life adjustment education made its debut in 1945 at a conference convened by the U.S. Office of Education to discuss vocational education. The conferees expected that there would be massive youth unemployment when the troops returned home from the war. No one seemed to have any solutions, and when the chairman of the meeting called on Charles A. Prosser, a veteran vocational educator, to summarize the conference, he offered what was quickly referred to as "an historic resolution." He worried that the schools were still too devoted to an academic curriculum. He thought that the schools should prepare 20 percent of young people for college and another 20 percent for skilled occupations but declared, "We do not believe that the remaining 60 percent of our youth of secondary school age will receive the life adjustment education they need and to which they are entitled as American citizens—unless and until the administrators of public education with the assistance of vocational education leaders formulate a similar program for this group."[6] Prosser called on the U.S. commissioner of education to convene regional conferences to figure out how to educate the 60 percent of students who needed life adjustment education.

The "Prosser Resolution" was adopted unanimously by an enthusiastic conference. The U.S. Office of Education promptly initiated a national crusade for life adjustment education in American schools. This federal agency, whose role in the past had been limited to collecting statistics and issuing reports, treated life adjustment education as its new mission. In 1946, it organized regional conferences in New York City; Chicago; Cheyenne, Wyoming; Sacramento; and Birmingham, Alabama, to discuss the meaning and implementation of the Prosser Resolution. In 1947, the U.S. commissioner of education appointed a National Commission on Life Adjustment Education, which included representatives from school districts, states, and the entire alphabet soup of education organizations. The commissioner convened a national conference each year to report on progress and in 1950 appointed a second national commission to promote the concept. Life adjustment education attracted enthusiastic partisans—vocational educators, social workers, and administrators from states and school districts—because it promised to transform the schools into multipurpose social service agencies.

The author of the historic resolution, Charles Prosser, addressed the first national conference on life adjustment education in 1947. For nearly four decades, he had been a staunch advocate for industrial education, first as secretary of the National Society for the Promotion of Industrial Education—where he lobbied successfully for passage of the federal Smith-Hughes Vocational Education Act in 1917—then as director of the Dunwoody Institute, a technical training institution in Minneapolis. All those years, he had argued that it was useless to study ancient history, foreign languages, classic literature, advanced mathematics, or physics unless one intended to teach it (he never explained to whom one was supposed to teach a subject if hardly anyone was expected to study it). He saw no point in studying anything that lacked immediate utility. Now, as his lifework reached its apogee, he told the national conference:

> Never in all the history of education has there been such a meeting as this one. . . . Never was there such a meeting where people were so sincere in their belief that this was the golden opportunity to do something that would give to *all* American youth their educational heritage so long denied. What you have planned is worth fighting for—it is worth dying for. . . . I am proud to have lived long enough to see my fellow schoolmen design a plan which will aid in achieving for every youth an education truly adjusted to life.[7]

The regional and national conferences were expected to define life adjustment education. They agreed that "Life adjustment education is designed to equip all American Youth to live democratically with satisfaction to themselves and profit to society as home members, workers, and citizens." It included home and family living education, vocational education, and guidance, and it de-emphasized learning from books and academic subjects. Experts in life adjustment education advised that the teaching of mathematics, for example, should concentrate on practical problems such as consumer buying, installment buying, insurance, taxation, and home budgeting, while courses in algebra, geometry, trigonometry, and solid geometry should be strictly elective, available only to carefully selected students. Any course that involved logical or symbolic thinking should be limited to the college-bound.[8]

Life adjustment education was based on the assumption that 60 percent of the nation's youth lacked the brains for either college *or* skilled occupations. Harl R. Douglass, dean of the College of Education at the

University of Colorado and a prominent advocate for the movement, claimed that this group actually accounted for *more than* 60 percent of the nation's young people. This large majority, he argued, was destined to become unskilled or semiskilled workers or the wives of laborers, and they did not need an academic education. What they needed was a functional program emphasizing the problems of "home, shop, store, citizenship, health, etc."[9]

Similarly, the National Commission on Life Adjustment Education cited a study in New Jersey that had found that only 2.8 percent of workers in Trenton required a college education; another 30 percent were technicians, clerks, or skilled workers. The remaining two thirds were semiskilled workers and laborers. This last group was the target of life adjustment education, for they were "the repetitive workers in the mass production scheme. They do the same operations over and over again and gain increased ability through repetition." They did not need job training in school because their work was so routine that it could easily be learned on the job. Their schooling would be devoted to courses that dealt with the daily problems of living.[10]

Prosser and his allies believed that academic education was wasted on these students, who were headed for jobs that required no brainpower. The schools, they felt, should forgo teaching them history, literature, foreign languages, or mathematics and concentrate on helping them become better workers, housewives, family members, and citizens. These students, said life adjustment educators, came from low-income homes with poor cultural environments. They were far behind in school, were unmotivated, and had poor grades and low test scores. Despite these handicaps, when they could be persuaded to go to school, they "wanted to be identified with the group regularly served by the school," that is, the students who did well. To avoid stigmatizing these youngsters, the leaders of the life adjustment movement decided that the program of non-academic studies should not be available only for the educationally neglected; indeed, it was the education best suited to meet the imperative needs of *all* American youth. So what had begun as an effort directed at high school students who were unmotivated and indifferent to academic studies turned into a movement to reconstruct the curriculum for everyone.[11]

Surely some significant portion of this alleged 60 percent and of the 20 percent who were directed to vocational studies had the intellectual capacity to benefit from the same quality of education that was regularly available to the upper 20 percent who were presumed to be college-bound. It should have been possible to improve methods and materials so that the traditional studies would be valuable to more than a minority of high school students. But the august members of the regional and national commissions decided against making any effort to raise the aspirations and intellectual functioning of the large majority of students and instead agreed to lower *everyone's* aspirations.

The life adjustment educators dramatically underestimated the proportion of the student body who would go to college, however. In 1944, Prosser proclaimed that only 20 percent had the capacity to prepare for college, a judgment based on historic rates of college attendance. But Prosser was a poor prophet: a decade after he launched the life adjustment movement, nearly one third of seventeen- and eighteen-year-old youths were entering college, and the number continued to grow each year.[12] Like John Franklin Bobbitt, Ellwood P. Cubberley, and other progressives in the 1920s, the life adjustment educators envisioned a static society, one in which the occupations of the present would remain unchanged. They proposed to adjust young people to a world that was already passing instead of providing them with an education that would equip them with the skills and knowledge needed to deal with an unpredictable future. Far from being progressive, their views were regressive as well as undemocratic.

→ → ← ←

In the late 1940s, Prosser's lifelong dream of life adjustment education for *all* American youths won the allegiance of large numbers of educational leaders. The bandwagon was crowded, not only with education professors but with federal, state, and local officials as well. Education organizations saw life adjustment education as the logical consequence of every progressive report since the Cardinal Principles of Secondary Education in 1918. Part of what carried the phenomenon forward was a habit of intellectual conformity in the education profession. The leaders also feared that if the high schools did not endorse a program of life adjustment education for non-college-bound young people, the federal government would create an agency like the Civilian Conservation Corps or the National Youth Administration to do the job. Even *Education for All American Youth* had raised the specter that the federal government would initiate a "National Board for Youth Service" unless the public schools moved quickly to offer vocational training, health education, citizenship training, and family life education to the great majority of students who presumably were repelled by the traditional curriculum.[13]

The primary rationale for life adjustment education, in the eyes of its proponents, was that it would enable the high schools to hold on to a greater proportion of young people until graduation. Without life adjustment education, they warned, large numbers of young people would leave school without graduating. The evidence for this claim was dubious, as the high school graduation rate had soared from 29 percent of seventeen-year-old youngsters in 1930 to 50.8 percent in 1940, even as progressive educators complained that the curriculum in the typical public high school was still too "traditional." Never before in American history—nor in the history of any other country—had half of all eligible youths earned a high school diploma. High school enrollment had zoomed, too; in 1930, 50.7 percent of youngsters aged fourteen to seventeen were in high school, and by 1940 the proportion reached 72.6 percent.[14] Despite these unprecedented increases, federal officials complained that "only" 73 percent were enrolled in high school in 1940 and that this was "not consonant with American ideals of equality of opportunity." These officials readily admitted that the most frequent reason that young people did not stay in high school was that they needed to earn money, a need that had been addressed directly by the New Deal youth agencies, which had given students part-time public sector jobs. But instead of recognizing that the need to earn money was an important cause of school leaving, educators mounted a crusade to change the curriculum.

In support of this crusade, the U.S. Office of Education released a steady stream of publications advocating life adjustment education. It energetically promoted the core program, in which different subjects (especially history, English, social problems, consumer education, and family living) were blended together into a daily two-hour block of time. In one publication, federal officials declared that "most boys and girls are headed for jobs that require little training" and that the high schools should not encourage false illusions by fostering "the myth of white collar superiority." The federal agency pointed out that there were relatively few physicians, architects, and lawyers, as compared to large numbers of chauffeurs, clerks, salesmen, mechanics, elevator operators, cashiers, filling station attendants, receptionists, and streetcar conductors. The schools were doing a terrible disservice to students, officials claimed, by offering them a curriculum that raised their aspirations. Instead of teaching the traditional curriculum, which "inspires glamorous hopes that may not be justified," schools should prepare adolescents for reality by teaching them about finding a job, being popular, and getting along with the opposite sex. The U.S. Office of Education urged schools to lower their students' career expectations and discourage their interest in academic studies.[15]

What was supposed to be of real value to the vast majority of adolescents was studying their own needs. A research literature grew that claimed to identify the specific needs of young people that schools should address, such as "How can I become more attractive and popular? Am I normal? Is God a person? How can I develop self-confidence? What should I do about people who are gossiping about me? . . . What causes pimples? Why can't I have dates like other students? . . . Am I expected to 'pet' on a date? . . . Should I choose my own clothes? . . . Why do I have to wear long stockings in winter when other girls wear socks? . . . Why do we have to study Latin (algebra, grammar, etc.)? . . . Why do our teachers seem so old?"[16] Educators developed elaborate checklists of adolescent concerns and found that high school students worried about getting along with their brothers and sisters, making arrangements to drive the family car, being underweight or overweight, poor posture, poor complexion, ill-fitting shoes, and not getting enough sleep. The traditional academic curriculum did not speak to those needs. It might teach them how to think clearly, it might teach them about the achievements of humanity, it might prod them to think about the causes of war, but it would not teach them how to behave on a date, what to do about acne, or what kind of socks to wear in the winter.

For a decade after the Prosser resolution, there was a great flurry of activity. At least twenty-nine states actively promoted life adjustment education, and thirteen (Colorado, Connecticut, Delaware, Iowa, Kansas, Massachusetts, Mississippi, Missouri, North Carolina, North Dakota, Oregon, West Virginia, and Wyoming) appointed statewide life adjustment education commissions (California did not need one, because of its well-established leadership in the field). Federal officials identified school districts that were showcases for life adjustment education, including Ann Arbor, Michigan; Forest Hills, New York; Hornell, New York; Spencer, New York; Washington, D.C.; Springfield, Missouri; Philadelphia; Pittsburgh; New Britain, Connecticut; Midland, Michigan; Rockville, Maryland; Ashland, Virginia; Amarillo, Texas; Bloomfield, New Jersey; Coffeyville, Kansas; Peoria; Saint Paul, Minnesota; Tulsa; and Wilmington, Delaware.[17]

In 1949, a national survey showed that the campaign to reduce the academic curriculum was gaining a foothold in the public schools. Federal officials asked schools whether they had adopted a core course that meets "for at least six periods a week and combines subjects which cut across major areas of the curriculum." An estimated 833—or 11.3 percent—of the nation's high schools with an enrollment over 500 claimed they had established such a program, as had 20 percent of the junior high schools of that size. Schools where the enrollment was less than 500 were far less likely to have a program in "common learnings," "basic living," or "social living." Seven states—California, Maryland, Michigan, Minnesota, Missouri, New York, and Pennsylvania—accounted for nearly two thirds of the schools with such programs.[18]

Reformers interpreted these figures as evidence that curricular integration in the public schools was slowly but surely replacing the subject matter curriculum. Harl R. Douglass, a leader of the life adjustment education movement, thought that the trends were irreversible: "Gradually, but certainly, schoolbook learning is giving way to healthy all-round growth through school related experiences." Douglass labeled as obsolete the idea that the curriculum was a "fixed body of subject matter, a different portion of which was to be mastered each year by the pupils as they passed from grade to grade"; equally obsolete was the notion that educational psychologists should be concerned with measuring and improving students' mastery of subject matter.[19] Such views were commonplace in pedagogical textbooks and education journals in the 1940s and 1950s. There was, however, a growing gap between the profession and the public, which had never consented to minimizing the academic role of the schools.

→ → ← ←

The case for changing the curriculum had been the same since the beginning of the twentieth century: Society is changing, and the schools must change too; the family and the community have become weaker, and the schools must now do what the family and community used to do; the best way of addressing the social and economic problems of society is to change the curriculum so that young people can solve these problems themselves (by studying social living, family life, and consumer education); the traditional curriculum of academic subjects is undemocratic, appropriate only for a minority of students and surviving for no reason other than college entrance requirements; a democratic society must have democratic classrooms, where the curriculum flows from the interests and needs of students and teaching methods do not rely on teacher authority.

With this credo, education reformers in schools of education and state education departments enjoyed a keen sense of mission, but they faced a familiar obstacle: How to persuade principals and teachers in the nation's public schools to follow their lead? The fundamental problem of curriculum change, they realized, was how to make it stick, how to make changes that would survive the skepticism and even hostility of recalcitrant teachers and parents. Though progressivism seemed triumphant, its advocates worried that their victory was hollow. They frequently saw evidence of reversion to traditional practices and feared that their advances were only temporary.

The elites of the profession agreed with striking unanimity that schools should be transformed into agencies that would meet youths' personal and social needs, but most high schools still clung stubbornly to subject matter, even when they offered multiple curricula. Reformers knew that the changes they favored had been slowed or even blocked by parents who insisted that their children learn academic subjects and by teachers who paid only lip service to the new ideas. Stories circulated about teachers who had saved their spelling books long after they had supposedly been banished or who closed their classroom door and taught history or literature that was not relevant to pupils' needs or contemporary issues. Ann Arbor, Michigan, eliminated textbooks from its elementary schools in the 1930s, but teachers' resistance compelled the school system to bring them back in the early 1940s.[20] Such practices seemed reactionary to progressive educators, who had long believed that social progress depended on implementation of their ideas and that traditional education was equivalent to fundamentalism in religion and politics.

What to do about the backsliders and footdraggers? Resistance to change, reformers recognized, came from many parts of the school and community. Most high school teachers actually blocked curriculum reorganization, complained Harold Alberty, a progressive professor of education at Ohio State University. They were all too complacent, he said, having been taught by subject matter specialists in college and believing that their job was to teach mastery of the cultural heritage to their students. Persuading teachers to go along with curriculum reform was never easy. After an administrator introduced a new program with directives, publicity, bulletins, and conferences, a few teachers would be interested, but many were apathetic and some even hostile. Skeptical teachers would pretend to comply, but they were only going through the motions. In Texas, for example, the elementary school curriculum was revised in the mid-1930s, and teachers were expected to use five core themes instead of subject matter. In 1943, however, the State Department of Education invited elementary teachers across the state to submit diaries describing "A Typical Child's Day in My Class or School," and most teachers were still teaching separate subjects on a daily basis.[21]

Something had to be done to convert the skeptical. Reformers turned to the new field of social psychology, with its techniques of human engineering, to find ways of persuading individuals to conform to group norms. Specialists advised state and local school leaders how to use group dynamics to build consensus among teachers. Getting teachers to abandon their traditional ideas and adopt progressive ideas was known as "the change process." The change process involved organizing group discussions run by trained leaders; encouraging group members to express their feelings freely; guiding the group to a consensus about the need for change; and building a sense of group solidarity. Techniques such as role playing, the specialists suggested, helped to develop participation and the group's "we-feeling." Individualism should be discouraged, as it would create too many problems. Carefully planned exercises in which all staff members identified common problems and eventually came to share common goals would produce group thinking. The successful group would adopt common norms and values, which subtly pressured dissident individuals to conform.[22]

Kenneth D. Benne and Bozidar Muntyan of the College of Education at the University of Illinois prepared a study guide to help Illinois school officials utilize group dynamics. On the basis of psychological research, they understood that individuals behave differently when they become members of a group because they tend to seek the approval of that group. Benne and Muntyan recognized that group dynamics could be used to prod teachers to accept new ways of thinking. They anticipated questions about undemocratic manipulation of "those who are being led to change their ways." Benne and Muntyan insisted that it was the " 'democratic right' of leadership to induce educational workers to change their ways and their beliefs." The leaders were doing these things not merely because of their own preferences but because they understood the "maladjustments" between school and society. Those who did not understand these maladjustments would require "re-education," using "processes of social engineering which employ methods of collectively planned change."[23]

Benne described the group leaders as "democratic social engineers" and "change agents" who were trained to guide social change. Benne insisted that "democratic methodology" must be "anti-individualistic," because "individualism tends to threaten rather than to promote the values of individuality." Participation in group processes elevated collective judgment over private judgments. Benne recognized that others might question the ethics of social engineering, but he believed these social processes were necessary to advance democratic ideas and values.[24] The social engineers thought of the public schools as an instrument with which to change society, not as schools that belonged to the public. They discussed how to shape public opinion, never considering the possibility of heeding it.

→ → ← ←

Hollis Caswell, dean of Columbia's Teachers College and a nationally recognized expert on curriculum reform, insisted that citywide or statewide curriculum standards, which specified what students were expected to learn, were outmoded. Modern school systems, he wrote, were moving away from a systemwide curriculum organized around subjects such as mathematics, science, and English. Such a program was neither desirable nor consistent with modern ideas about the curriculum. Caswell urged school systems to build their curricula around pupils' interests and integrated subjects from different fields.[25] Teachers and principals who believed in the value of teaching subjects, who thought that external standards would promote higher levels of achievement, or who saw the utility of common academic standards for a mobile student population were out of step with modern professional thinking. Authoritative pedagogues, such as Caswell, sought to convince such people that their ideas had been thoroughly discredited by modern, scientific research.

The biggest obstacle to curriculum change, Caswell reported, was getting teachers to abandon their traditional ways of teaching. Caswell recalled his participation as a consultant to the Virginia curriculum revision project in 1930. Teacher participation had been extensive, the new materials had been excellent, but a survey had soon revealed that the program had not affected classroom practice. Caswell observed that reformers had been naive to think that all they needed to do was to write a new course of study, which would then be mandated by the state or local school board. They had done this in state after state, district after district, only to see teachers revert to traditional ways of teaching subject matter. He and other progressives began to realize that just as students needed to "experience" whatever they learned, so teachers must participate in every aspect of curriculum change because "the primary means of changing the curriculum is through changing teachers."[26]

Alice Miel, Caswell's colleague at Teachers College, pointed out in her study *Changing the Curriculum: A Social Process* that curriculum change required changing people, not just writing paper plans: "To change the curriculum of the school . . . means bringing about changes in people—in their desires, beliefs, and attitudes, in their knowledge and skill." Miel noted that one of the best ways of supporting deliberate social change was by "capitalizing upon dissatisfaction. Men do not change their social arrangements so long as they are perfectly satisfied with them." The wise administrator should size up the teachers and adults in the community and "attempt to determine at what stage of readiness for change they are." Some would be dissatisfied, others satisfied.[27]

Miel divided the complacent into two groups: In one group were subject matter teachers who feared that curriculum change threatened their jobs and parents who wanted their children to go to college. In the other were people who were naive about social realities, ignorant about principles of human development, and uninformed about "the increasing ineffectiveness of the traditional curriculum."[28]

Miel proposed three "methods of arousing dissatisfaction," all of which would undercut support for the academic curriculum. One involved the study of local social conditions by teachers, parents, and local community members, which would lead them to recognize that the school curriculum should address local problems. A second method was to study human development, which would lead to curriculum change adapted to principles of growth and mental hygiene. A third was to engage teachers, parents, and members of the local community in "group problem-solving," which, under "skillful, evocative leadership" would move rapidly from trivial problems to recognition of the need for curriculum change.[29]

Citing Miel's definition of curriculum change as a social process, Caswell recommended ways in which school districts could persuade teachers of the need for curriculum change. All these approaches aimed to socialize teachers and occasionally parents and community members by engaging them in group activities. A district could set up staff development programs (also called in-service education) for teachers. It could hire outside consultants from colleges of education to offer "an impartial point of view" to staff members, parents, and lay community members. It could establish study groups and community surveys to learn about unmet needs in the community. One of the most popular ideas for advancing curriculum change was a workshop in which teachers would discuss their common problems. Reformers believed that curriculum would change on "a broken front," which meant that a small number of exceptional teachers and schools would lead the way and their example would influence others.[30]

One sure consequence of using the social process to change the curriculum was the creation of a large number of committees. In school districts that embarked on curriculum reform, teachers were constantly involved in committee work: committees at every school; committees for the elementary and secondary school divisions; committees to coordinate different schools; committees for core programs; committees for subjects; committees for planning; committees for health and audio-visual education; even a committee of committees. There was in-service education for teachers, curriculum work after school, consultants from the local school of education who managed study groups, workshops, and conferences. The social process was relentlessly time-consuming for teachers at a time when teacher shortages were acute and teachers' salaries lagged far behind those of comparable professionals.

What did all of this activity produce? In 1950, Hollis Caswell tallied up the victories: Battle Creek, Michigan, had halved the percentage of students enrolled in the college preparatory curriculum, while simultaneously introducing a health program and a tenth-grade course in "basic living." Denver, which had been a pioneer of curriculum revision in the 1920s, had tossed out the course of study prepared by teachers then and replaced it with a firm commitment to cooperative planning of curricula by teachers and pupils. Kingsport, Tennessee, had abandoned its "highly traditional curriculum with an academic emphasis at the high school level," whose chief goal had been "subject-matter achievement." Many committee meetings, study groups, and consultants later, the Kingsport schools also dropped the study of mythology and Hebrew history from the elementary curriculum; replaced the separate study of history and geography with a course in social studies; substituted narrative reports for letter grades; mixed slow and fast learners in the same classes; and agreed to keep on revising the curriculum continuously.[31]

In Alameda County, California, a course in world problems that "had degenerated into chronological history" was dropped "to make room for something 'more important,' " namely, driver education. Here, instead of learning about history, students could truly "penetrate democratic living" by gaining direct experience with an automobile. This shift outraged "those whose vision is limited to the dictum that 'history is good for you,' " but wise educators understood that using a "purposeful tool" (the automobile) in a real "learning situation" (driving) was far likelier to teach responsibility, appreciation for the rights of others, and critical thinking than the study of history.[32]

The public schools in Minneapolis initiated a "common learnings" program in one senior and two junior high schools in 1945 and set about persuading teachers and parents to support it. There were summer workshops for teachers at the local college of education; afternoon teachers' conferences; meetings of parents; and surveys of parents' opinions. In 1950, "common learnings" was adopted across the system. The two-hour daily program combined English and social studies into a single course. It emphasized the personal and social problems of students rather than subject matter. Chronological history was dropped, as was classic literature. "Common learnings" was devoted to studying problems "meaningful to youth" and building "the right attitudes." Instead of a course of study, the curriculum was planned by teachers and pupils together.[33]

Within a year of the program's adoption, there was a large uprising against it by parents, who formed a Parents Council to voice their objections. This group was led not by the right-wing zealots who had attacked the Rugg textbooks in the late 1930s but by professors from academic departments (not the college of education) at the University of Minnesota. Some eight hundred persons attended a mass meeting called by the Parents Council. Their spokesman was Robert Penn Warren, a Pulitzer Prize–winning novelist, who complained about the lowering of standards in the "Common Learnings" program and criticized the "patronizing attitude" of progressive educators, their "condescending democracy on the one hand and their smug authoritarianism on the other." The Minneapolis Board of Education bowed to community pressure and made the controversial program optional; the superintendent resigned. But progressive educators learned nothing from the contretemps in Minneapolis; they saw it only as an attack on modern education by a "militant minority."[34] They did not understand how educated people could disagree with them.

In 1950, Harvard sociologist David Riesman criticized the new face of progressive education in his classic work *The Lonely Crowd*. Americans, he wrote, were changing from "inner-directed" to "other-directed," from people with an internalized set of principles to people guided chiefly by what others thought of them. In the past, the schools' emphasis on intellectual ability had shaped "the inner-directed character. It affirms to the child that what matters is what he can accomplish, not how nice is his smile or how cooperative his attitude." Progressive education, Riesman observed, had begun as an effort to free children from excessive discipline; "today, however, progressive education is often no longer progressive; as people have become more other-directed, educational methods that were once liberating may even tend to thwart individuality rather than to advance and protect it."[35]

Riesman wrote that teachers were now being told to pay more attention to their students' social and psychological development than to their intellectual prowess. They had become responsible for the socialization of students' friendships, tastes, interests, even their fantasies, realms that teachers of an older generation would not have touched. Children were implicitly told that what mattered was not their hard work but their adjustment to the group. Progressive education, Riesman noted, facilitated "the breakdown of walls between teacher and pupil; and this in turn helps to break down walls between student and student, permitting that rapid circulation of tastes which is a prelude to other-directed socialization." Intellectual growth had become unimportant, he said, supplanted by attention to popularity and friendliness.[36]

An Abundance of Critics

*By midcentury, the public schools had become agencies dedicated to so-*cializing students, teaching them proper attitudes and behaviors, and encouraging conformity to the norms of social life and the workplace. Educators at the national, state, and local levels who subscribed to life adjustment education thought that the schools were meeting the needs of their students and of democratic society admirably.

The leaders of American education in the late 1940s and early 1950s were so assured of their purpose that they were caught completely unawares when the grumbling of dissident parents and school board members grew into a loud roar. There was simply no precedent in the history of American education for the tidal wave of protest that broke over the public schools during this period. Almost overnight, there was a deluge of books and articles criticizing the public schools and singling out progressive education as the source of their defects. At the very time when educators shared a strong consensus about progressive ideas and practices, progressive education became an object of public ridicule.

There were several different groups of unrelated critics. First and most numerous were critics who charged that the schools had abandoned their primary function of developing the knowledge and intelligence of the young. These critics—scholars, school board members, and journalists—held that the schools had lost sight of their central purpose while trying to meet their students' diverse social and personal needs.

Others complained that the public schools, imbued with the spirit of pragmatism, had become too secular, thus undercutting the nation's moral and spiritual fiber.[37] In addition, there were superpatriotic zealots who tried to identify progressive education with communism. In the prosecutorial spirit of Senator Joseph McCarthy, these extremists blamed progressive education for juvenile delinquency, demanded censorship of textbooks, and maligned administrators, teachers, and school board members.[38]

After World War II, Americans had good reason to be concerned about the education of their children. The economy was changing rapidly, and there was a growing demand for well-educated people in the professions, in white-collar jobs, and in technical work. Parents worried about whether their children would have the education to succeed in an increasingly competitive economy. They wanted their children to be educated, not adjusted. Education had become an increasingly important qualification for access to jobs and opportunity, in ways that it had never been before the war. Anxious to protect their children from the economic and social turmoil their own generation had experienced, parents did not want to take risks with their children's education.

When the great outpouring of criticism began, educators treated all critics as if they were connected to the irresponsible extremists who had made groundless accusations about subversives in the schools (in Pasadena, California, right-wing forces had ousted the school superintendent). Particularly unpersuasive were the educators' efforts to discredit the critics of anti-intellectualism. Among the leading critics of the schools' academic quality were Mortimer Smith, a school board member in Connecticut; Harry J. Fuller, a botanist at the University of Illinois; Albert Lynd, a school board member in Massachusetts; and Arthur Bestor, Jr., a historian at the University of Illinois.

Unlike the ill-fated essentialists of the late 1930s, these critics could not be ignored, because they wrote for the public.

Mortimer Smith attacked John Dewey's pragmatism, saying that it had removed all intellectual and moral standards from the schools, leaving only "a vast bubbling confusion . . . in which hairdressing and embalming are just as important, if not a little more so, than history and philosophy."[39]

Harry J. Fuller lambasted the education professors who asserted that education should satisfy or reduce students' needs, most of which they could, in fact, manage on their own. He asked, "How many students have a need to read and study *Hamlet,* or Wordsworth's sonnet "Composed upon Westminster Bridge," or Matthew Arnold's "Dover Beach," or Willa Cather's *Death Comes for the Archbishop,* or Lincoln's Address at Gettysburg, or to learn something of the awesome wheeling of the heavenly bodies or the intricate, unending biological cycles of our world?"[40]

Albert Lynd excoriated educationists for arrogantly imposing their own ideas about the curriculum without consulting parents and local communities. He argued that " 'Democracy' is a ritual word in the New Education, but has any community ever been consulted about educational theory in any meaningful way? . . . If we must have one dominant philosophical influence upon the reform of our schools, who voted for Dewey?"[41]

Arthur Bestor charged that progressive education had turned into "regressive education," having "severed all real connection with the great world of science and learning." Bestor opined that

One can search history and biography in vain for evidence that men or women have ever accomplished anything original, creative, or significant by virtue of narrowly conceived vocational training or of educational programs that aimed merely at "life adjustment." The West was not settled by men and women who had taken courses in "How to be a pioneer." . . . I for one do not believe that the American people have lost all common sense and native wit so that now they have to be taught in school to blow their noses and button their pants.[42]

A common complaint among the academic critics was that the schools of education required the study of education but did not require future teachers and administrators to be well educated. They claimed that education professors had taken control of the public school system and were beyond the reach of the democratic process, despite their frequent paeans to "democratic living." Lynd complained that "the Education bureaucracy" had relieved citizens of making the basic decisions about the aims and methods of schooling in their communities.[43] Bestor described "an interlocking directorate of professional educationists" that included professors of education, school administrators, and bureaucrats in state and federal education agencies. This powerful network, he asserted, excluded scholars connected to any intellectual discipline and laymen who represented the public.[44]

Long accustomed to dismissing criticism of their philosophy and methods, the spokesmen for American education did not know how to respond to such challenges. They preferred to disparage all critics as "enemies of the public schools." Complaints about the teaching of basic skills, they said, were a sure sign of an attack on public education, as was any criticism of modern education. In the face of the manifold attacks on the schools, the profession launched a counterattack on its enemies. The National Education Association described the critics as subversives who wanted to destroy public education, disgruntled teachers who were not abreast of the latest methods, unreasonable parents who blamed the schools for their children's shortcomings, and racketeers who were out to make money by assailing the schools.[45]

James B. Conant, the president of Harvard University, who had been a member of the NEA's Educational Policies Commission when it had issued *Education for All American Youth*, told the annual meeting of the American Association of School Administrators in 1952 that anyone who criticized the public schools should be asked two questions: "Would you like to increase the number and scope of private schools?" and "Do you look forward to the day when tax money will directly or indirectly assist these schools?" Another speaker at the same meeting declared that many of the attacks on the public schools had been initiated by " 'hirelings' of organizations whose motives are suspect." Those who support these "paid troublemakers," he said, "are among the emotionally least stable members of the community."[46]

Albert Lynd, one of the prominent academic critics, replied to Conant in his book *Quackery in the Public Schools*. Lynd said that he would not like to increase the number and scope of private schools but would like to increase the number and scope of better public schools. He added, "I should greatly prefer that the public schools provide for more children the quality of education provided by the very private schools to which Mr. Conant sent his own children, before he was moved to lecture the rest of us on our duty to send children to the public schools." His own children, Lynd wrote, had in aggregate spent four years in private schools and seventeen years in public schools, while he had served as a member of the local school board in Sharon, Massachusetts, supporting new school construction and higher teachers' salaries. Nor did he look forward to the day when tax money would support private schools. Lynd charged that the public schools' defenders were questioning the motives of their critics in an attempt to deflect attention from the anti-intellectual practices in the schools.[47]

Bestor, who had attended the progressive Lincoln School from 1922 to 1926 and later served on the faculty of Columbia University's Teachers College, insisted that progressive education had strayed from its original purposes. In its early days, he wrote, progressives contributed to the improvement of public education through careful experiments in the teaching of academic subjects. He recalled that the faculty at the Lincoln School "believed thoroughly in the intellectual purposes that had always been central in education as a whole. . . . Adequate preparation for college was not a separate goal; it was the natural consequence of a sound secondary school program based on the great intellectual disciplines." However, when professional educationists had lost interest in improving traditional instruction and began to revise the curriculum, progressive education had turned into "regressive education."[48]

The academic critics outraged the defenders of public education. Archibald W. Anderson, editor of the journal *Progressive Education,* drew a distinction between them and "constructive" critics who were "honest and sincere." The constructive critics, he said, were "willing to work with the schools, and generally favor the same lines of progress as the educators." But critics such as Bestor and Lynd were guilty of "inherent academic conservatism. The group defined by this trait is for the most part composed of business and professional people who have had a traditional academic education at the secondary and college level, and of some professors of academic subjects in colleges and universities."[49] These critics, he alleged, were elitist because they cared only about the college preparatory function of the high school. Their criticisms gave ammunition to the enemies of public schools and of democracy.

Anderson betrayed his own bias by his negative characterization of the academic critics. Smith, Lynd, and Bestor had complained not about what was taught to college preparatory students, but about what was customarily taught (or not taught) to most students. The critics insisted that the overwhelming majority of children were being denied a liberal education, while Anderson—accepting the well-established progressive tradition of curricular differentiation—insisted on referring to liberal education as "the college preparatory function."[50]

One of Bestor's choice targets was a speech given by A. H. Lauchner, a junior high school principal in Urbana, Illinois, to the annual convention of the nation's high school principals in 1951 on the question, "How Can the Junior High School Curriculum Be Improved?" Lauchner derided the importance of reading, writing, and arithmetic and insisted that they were not a necessity for all students. The biggest problem facing the schools, he asserted, was selling the public and classroom teachers on new ideas about education. It was basically a public relations problem, and "it will not be easy. Through the years we've built a sort of halo around reading, writing, and arithmetic. We've said they were for everybody . . . rich and poor, brilliant and not-so-mentally-endowed, ones who liked them and those who failed to go for them. Teacher has said that these were something 'everyone should learn.' The principal has remarked, 'All educated people know how to write, spell, and read.' " But, he said, these subjects were not for all children, and as soon as the public understands that "not every child has to read, figure, write, and spell . . . that many of them either cannot or will not master these chores," then there would be progress toward improving the junior high curriculum.[51]

Such improvement of the junior high curriculum was inevitable, Lauchner declared:

Between this day and that a lot of selling must take place. But it's coming. We shall some day accept the thought that it is just as illogical to assume that every boy must be able to read as it is that each one must be able to perform on a violin, that it is no more reasonable to require that each girl shall spell well than it is that each one shall bake a good cherry pie. . . . When I visit a school that worries and frets constantly because "so many of the children cannot read," I find myself asking the question if these teachers know that thousands of youngsters never will be able to read.[52]

Lauchner was also ready to jettison history, geography, and algebra as other subjects that were consuming far too much time. He pointed to several programs that he admired: the "social living" course in Long Beach, California, which combined grammar, literature, reading, writing, spelling, library work, citizenship, and history; the "common learnings" course in Minneapolis, where social studies and language arts courses reflected students' needs and interests; the "core curriculum" in Battle Creek, Michigan; the "home-room-centered curriculum" in Baltimore; the "general education" program in Denver, where the three "R's" were "human Relationships, Responsibility, and Rectitude"; the "unified studies" in Elizabeth, New Jersey, where different subjects were integrated and correlated. Even better, he said, were "auditorium classes" in Dubuque, Iowa, and Rockford, Illinois, where students "meet in groups, weigh matters of interest to school and community, determine courses of action, appoint committees, and work at problems."

Lauchner's candid remarks reflected the spirit of a long line of national commissions since the 1930s, as well as the declarations of the life adjustment movement. Lauchner said nothing different from the conventional wisdom shared by educators who considered themselves to be up to date. George H. Henry, the principal of a high school in Dover, Delaware, wrote in *Harper's* in 1946 that "at least a third of the entire secondary school population" was incapable of learning to read and write and that as a result of their presence, high school education in the United States had "virtually collapsed." These youngsters were not mentally handicapped, nor were they poor, Henry asserted; they were simply "non-verbal." Other educators, said Henry, had agreed to keep secret the awful fact that anywhere from a third to a half of all high school students were not capable of profiting from a liberal education.[53]

Critics and defenders of progressive education debated whether students were learning more or less than in the past. The critics insisted that standards in the public schools had fallen and that students could not read, write, spell, or do anything else as well as their parents. Defenders of the public schools insisted that they were actually doing a better job of teaching the basic skills than ever before. In fact, everyone in this debate relied on anecdotal reports, forceful assertions, or dubious evidence. There were no objective data on which anyone could rely, since there was no test that had been consistently administered to representative national samples of students over the decades. No one could say with certainty whether students were performing better or worse than in the past.

What was incontestable, however, was that enrollments in academic subjects in the high schools had declined at the same time as overall enrollments were soaring. Enrollment in physics had declined from 19 percent of high school students in 1900 to 6.3 percent in 1934 to 4.6 percent in 1955. Enrollment in geometry had dropped from 27 percent in 1900 to 17 percent in 1934 to 11.4 percent in 1955. The foreign languages had also experienced a sharp attrition. From 1900 until the late 1920s, a majority of high school students had studied Latin, French, German, or Spanish. In 1910, for example, 83 percent of all students had enrolled in foreign language classes. By 1955, however, foreign language enrollments had dropped to 20.6 percent of high school students. In 1922, ancient and medieval history had attracted one third of all students—some 700,000; by the 1940s, these subjects had nearly disappeared, having dropped to a mere 81,000 students, or 1.5 percent of enrollment.[54]

Progressive educators had a ready answer to the enrollment declines. It was a scientific fact, they asserted, that talent was distributed across a normal curve, the bell curve. They insisted that the expansion of enrollment had meant a lowering of the average ability of students because only a fixed and small proportion of students were capable of taking academic courses. Furthermore, they pointed out, while the percentage of students in academic courses had dropped, the absolute number of students was actually higher because of the phenomenal growth of high school enrollments. So, they argued, it didn't matter if the *percentage* studying physics, geometry, foreign languages had fallen precipitously, because the actual *numbers* studying these subjects were larger than ever.

This defense was manifestly untrue and relied on antidemocratic assumptions. Even though high school enrollments had grown by nearly 50 percent between 1934 and 1955, the absolute numbers of students taking any foreign language had fallen since 1934, as had the absolute number of students taking geometry. In 1934, nearly 900,000 students were studying a modern foreign language, and some 700,000 were taking Latin; by 1955, the number enrolled in a modern foreign language was unchanged (even though the student population had soared), and the number taking Latin had dropped to 454,000. Nor was there any good explanation for the decline in algebra enrollments from 35 percent in 1928 to 25 percent in 1955, other than the educators' dogmatic belief that only a small minority of American students was intelligent enough to study any academic subject beyond introductory courses.[55]

The absolute number of students studying some subjects, such as algebra, had indeed risen over the decades, yet the proportionate growth was very far below the twelvefold increase in high school enrollments during the first half of the twentieth century. There was merit to the educators' claim that the broadening of the enrollment in high school had reduced the demand for traditional academic courses. Certainly, some students were staying in high school who did not want to study chemistry, physics, geometry, trigonometry, or French. But there was no evidence to support the educators' assertion that a *majority* of high school students were incapable of studying any part of the academic curriculum. Such thinking was based on nothing more than the belief of intelligence testers and life adjustment educators that most students were not bright enough to study an academic curriculum. Yet the policy of steering students away from academic subjects prevailed in American high schools in the 1950s. This trend was regularly described by educational leaders as the democratization of the high school.

Harl R. Douglass, a leading progressive educator, pointed out with satisfaction that enrollments in French, Latin, geometry, physics, and algebra had dropped from 1934 to 1949, while they had increased in general mathematics, general science, home economics, problems of democracy, physical education, and American history (the U.S. history courses were more likely to be social studies courses than chronological history, which was disfavored by life adjusters). Douglass saw these trends as heartening evidence that the life adjustment movement was transforming the high schools, because students were learning about real-life problems instead of academic subjects (which he called "the sacred-cow curriculum"[56]).

Douglass reported that the standard high school curriculum in most high schools emphasized "broad preparation for life" rather than vocational education or preparation for college. In the typical high school of the early 1950s, students could choose among several different curricula: a college preparatory curriculum (which included mathematics, science, and two years of Spanish or French); a stenographic curriculum (which included typing, shorthand, and physical education); a business curriculum (which included English, social studies, and business mathematics); a general curriculum (which contained no foreign language, little mathematics, and three years of science); an industrial arts curriculum (which was long on "general" courses and mechanical drawing); and a domestic arts curriculum (which had no academic studies). The only subjects common to these different curricula were three years of English and one year of American history. Everything else was elective, and the only students who were expected to take a foreign language and advanced courses were those hoping to enter a selective college.[57]

Many high schools—especially those in rural and small communities—did not even offer important academic subjects. In 1954, 56 percent of the nation's high schools did not offer any modern foreign language. Such courses were available in fewer than 25 percent of the high schools in Indiana, Alabama, Minnesota, Missouri, Montana, Kentucky, Kansas, Mississippi, Arkansas, Oklahoma, Nebraska, Iowa, South Dakota, North Dakota, and Wisconsin. Nearly one quarter of the nation's high schools (with 11 percent of its students) offered neither physics nor chemistry. About one third of all high schools offered no intermediate algebra, plane geometry, or trigonometry; 11 percent of high school seniors attended these schools.[58]

THE NEA REPLIES TO THE CRITICS

In defense of public education against its critics, the National Education Association came up with an ingenious set of arguments. Were the public schools unduly influenced by progressive education? No, but progressive education was more effective than traditional education. Had the curriculum of the public schools been watered down by life adjustment education? Of course not, but life adjustment education had been a great success in reducing the dropout rate and increasing the range of electives in the curriculum. Whatever the charge was, the NEA denied it while affirming the superiority of whatever was being attacked by the critics. Had there been a decline in academic enrollments? It was true that the percentage of students enrolled in foreign languages and in most advanced courses in mathematics and science had declined. But this was "understandable," because there were now many electives to choose from, and the school was still doing a good job of preparing those students who went to college.[59]

The NEA correctly claimed that life adjustment education was not a new idea but was entirely consistent with the Cardinal Principles of Secondary Education, issued in 1918, and the many pronouncements of the NEA's Educational Policies Commission in the 1930s and 1940s. Those who wrote these reports believed that a finite minority of students were capable of profiting from a real academic education. The majority, they insisted, should be prepared for the everyday problems of earning a living, staying healthy, and using their leisure time well, but they did not need to study classic literature, foreign language, history, or any advanced courses in science and mathematics.

THE READING WARS

For several years, the debate raged about the condition of public education. In 1955, just when educators thought that the storm of public criticism was about to blow over, Rudolf Flesch's *Why Johnny Can't Read* reached the national best-seller lists, where it remained for more than thirty weeks. Serialized in many newspapers, Flesch's book struck a nerve, especially among parents who were not convinced that the new teaching methods were effective in teaching basic skills. Progressive educators cited studies to prove the superiority of classrooms without textbooks, homework, or lesson plans, but they were unable to allay these concerns.

Flesch charged that the systematic neglect of phonics had caused a national crisis in literacy; that "look-say" readers such as the widely used "Dick and Jane" series were based on a flawed theory that required children to memorize words and guess unknown words instead of sounding them out; and that the look-say or whole-word method had swept the textbook market despite the fact that it had no support in research.[60]

Like the other education jeremiads of the 1950s, Flesch's book blamed the literacy crisis on the education professors. Each of the major commercial primers, he noted, had been written by a leading authority in the field of reading, all of whom disdained phonics. Since the late 1920s, Flesch argued, the look-say method had been the only approach endorsed by the reading experts. This method was unsuccessful, Flesch maintained, because it did not teach students the alphabet or the sounds of letters, leaving them unable to decipher unfamiliar words. The look-say primers simply taught children to memorize easy words that were repeated again and again.

Flesch complained that "reading isn't taught at all. Books are put in front of the children and they are told to guess at the words or wait until Teacher tells them. But they are *not* taught to read." Because of their meager vocabulary, the stories in the look-say readers were "artificial sequences of words—meaningless, stupid, totally uninteresting to a six-year-old child or anyone else." In a typical excerpt from *Fun with Dick and Jane,* children read: "Oh, oh! Come, come! Look, look! You will see. You will see." Such language, Flesch observed, "is word-method-reader idiom, a language to be found solely and exclusively in the books" used in American classrooms, adding, "It is *not* the language used in telling a story, making a narrative interesting, or conveying information intelligibly."[61]

Flesch's polemic set off a national debate about literacy. The book was favorably reviewed in the general press but almost unanimously rejected by reviewers in education journals, who insisted that Flesch was unqualified, irresponsible, and just plain wrong. Because of its popularity, Flesch's book had a swift and large effect on the teaching of reading.

Several publishers issued new reading textbooks that featured phonics. Reading professionals warned that a return to phonics would be disastrous, that it would lead to dull and dispirited classrooms dominated by rote memorization of meaningless sounds.

In 1961, the Carnegie Corporation of New York commissioned Jeanne S. Chall of the Harvard Graduate School of Education to review the controversy and settle the debate about reading once and for all. Chall spent three years visiting hundreds of classrooms, analyzing research studies, and examining textbooks; she interviewed textbook authors, reading specialists, and teachers. She did not agree with Flesch that there was one and only one successful method for teaching beginning readers. No method had completely solved the problems of teaching reading; some methods were better than others; but none was a panacea.[62]

Comparing the effectiveness of reading methods turned out to be extraordinarily tricky because each approach contained elements of the other. Chall found that "every school that introduces a new method still retains a good deal of the old one." Schools that had recently adopted phonics programs still used the look-say readers, and teachers tended to rely on the methods with which they were most familiar. She observed that in the 1930s, phonics had survived in a hostile environment because some teachers had "got[ten] out their old phonics charts, *closed the doors,* and hoped the supervisor or principal would not enter unannounced." But teachers who had been trained since the 1930s had never learned phonics and were likely to fall back on what they knew best, which was the look-say method.[63]

Chall found that from 1930 until the early 1960s, there had been a pervasive professional consensus on the one best way to teach reading. This consensus de-emphasized the use of phonics and concentrated on reading whole words, sentences, and stories closely geared to children's experiences and interests. It stressed silent reading rather than oral reading (oral reading was associated with phonics because it demonstrated a child's knowledge of the sounds of letters and syllables). Children were encouraged to identify words "at sight" by referring to pictures and context clues; the sight vocabulary was carefully controlled and repeated often in the primers. While phonics was not necessarily banned, it was relegated to a minor role in learning to read.[64]

This orthodoxy, Chall discovered, was not supported by research. In reviewing reading research from 1912 to 1965, Chall identified two primary approaches: one stressed the importance of "breaking the code" of language, the other the meaning of language. Phonics programs had a code emphasis, while look-say or whole-word programs had a meaning emphasis. Studies of beginning readers over the decades had clearly supported code breaking, Chall concluded. Early decoding, she found, not only produced better word recognition and spelling but also made it easier for the child eventually to read with understanding. The code-emphasis method, she wrote, was especially effective for children of lower socioeconomic status, who were not likely to live in homes surrounded with books or with adults who could help them learn to read. For a beginning reader, she found, knowledge of letters and sounds had more influence on reading achievement than the child's tested "mental ability" or IQ.[65]

→ → ← ←

"The great debate" about teaching reading did not begin with Rudolf Flesch in 1955, nor—unfortunately—was it resolved by Chall's painstaking analysis. American educators, and European educators before them, had been trying for generations to find methods that would be more natural than the time-honored practice of reciting isolated, meaningless syllables. Reading reformers in the nineteenth century had believed that children would find it far more interesting and pleasurable to memorize words and read short sentences and stories without having to bother to learn the names of the letters.

Horace Mann, the great mid-nineteenth-century school reformer, had condemned the alphabet method, claiming that it was repulsive and soul-deadening to children. He described the letters of the alphabet as "skeleton-shaped, bloodless, ghostly apparitions." It was no wonder, he said, that children looked so frightened when compelled to learn the alphabet. Teaching the alphabet was entirely illogical, he held: "When we wish to give to a child the idea of a new animal, we do not present successively the different parts of it,—an eye, an ear, the nose, the mouth, the body, or a leg; but we present the whole animal, as one object."[66] Mann believed that children's earliest books should teach whole words, skipping the alphabet and the sounds of the letters. Other reformers agreed, and many nineteenth-century school readers did feature the word method.

By the 1890s, the alphabet method had virtually died out. By then, most schools were using a combination of the word method and phonetic methods. When Joseph Mayer Rice visited schools in thirty-six cities in 1892, most teachers were using the word method (and most, he said, were teaching in a dry, mechanical fashion). William A. Mowry, a veteran New England educator, wrote in 1908 that children were being taught to recognize words, not letters, and "the alphabet takes care of itself. No time is lost in learning it."[67]

Progressive educators recoiled against any sort of linguistic or phonetic analysis in the classroom. The word method appealed to them because it seemed to be a "natural" way of learning, a way of avoiding the tedious drill required to teach the sounds of letters. The historian of reading Mitford M. Mathews claimed that "there is no question but that the one man most responsible for the triumph of the word method was Colonel Francis Parker."[68] Parker was a pioneer progressive educator. As superintendent of the Quincy, Massachusetts, schools in the 1870s, Parker had eliminated not only the set curriculum but spellers, readers, and grammar textbooks; children learned words and sentences, not the alphabet.

John Dewey, an admirer of Parker, believed that children should not learn to read or write until they were at least eight. In 1898, Dewey advanced the bizarre idea that the need for reading and writing was decreasing as society became more advanced. He argued that the proliferation of various modes of communication, such as newspapers, magazines, libraries, and literary clubs, made the acquisition of reading and writing in school less important than in the past, when reading "was practically the sole avenue to knowledge." The significance of reading and writing, he averred, had "shrunk proportionately as the imminent intellectual life of society has quickened and multiplied." These linguistic skills had become "more or less arbitrary tasks which must be submitted to because one is going to that mysterious thing called a school." Too much emphasis on literacy in the early grades, he warned, caused "undue nervous strain . . . a sad record of injured nervous systems and of muscular disorders and distortions." Teaching children of six and seven to read was dangerous because it "cripples rather than furthers later intellectual development."[69]

G. Stanley Hall of Clark University agreed that children should not learn to read before the age of eight and gave his blessing to the word method. He wrote in 1911 that "Nearly all reading methods now start from the word and sentence rather than from the letter." However, Hall did not put too much stock in reading methods as such, as this superpedagogue thought that reading itself was vastly overvalued:

Very many men have lived and died and been great, even the leaders of their age, without any acquaintance with letters. The knowledge which illiterates acquire is probably on the whole more personal, direct, environmental and probably a much larger proportion of it practical. Moreover, they escape much eyestrain and mental excitement, and, other things being equal, are probably more active and less sedentary. It is possible, despite the stigma our bepedagogued age puts upon this disability, for those who are under it not only to lead a useful, happy, virtuous life, but to be really well educated in many other ways. Illiterates escape certain temptations, such as vacuous and vicious reading.[70]

The word method appealed to partisans of the "new education" because it fit comfortably with the theories of spontaneity, experience, and incidental learning so admired by Parker, Dewey, and other progressives. Progressives insisted that they taught the "whole child," and they valued a reading method that taught whole words and sentences, rather than singling out sounds and letters. During the 1920s, when reading research became a growth industry, the experts concurred that reading books should consist of simple words and phrases that could be recognized "by sight." By 1930, teaching children to read with letters and sounds was considered obsolete in colleges of education, not the sort of thing that modern educators did.

When the U.S. Office of Education took up the campaign for life adjustment education in the late 1940s and early 1950s, it warned parents against using phonics and teaching children to read "too soon." According to the federal agency, "scientific studies" had shown that successful readers learned to read by guessing the meaning of words based on their appearance—their length and shape; parents were advised not to let their children learn to read before they were six. The Office of Education described the modern elementary classroom as one where learning occurred spontaneously. The teacher never actually taught reading, spelling, mathematics, or any other subject. Without prompting, children moved happily from one delightful activity to the next. They explored the materials in the classroom, worked enthusiastically on projects, asked questions of visitors, solved problems that caught their attention, read when they wanted to know something, and planned together with the teacher whatever they wanted to learn about. In this natural, noncompetitive, progressive classroom, the teacher remained in the background, facilitating but never instructing.[71]

This was the ideal that progressive leaders had shared for decades, but somehow, despite efforts by school districts to "sell" it, the public had never gone along. As the success of Rudolf Flesch's book revealed, parents worried whether the schools had gone overboard in one direction and whether their children were learning to read. Many of the progressive theories and programs were incomprehensible to the public. People who were paying taxes to support schools did not want to hear that 60 percent of their community's children lacked the brains either to get into college or qualify for a skilled job; nor did they want to be told that one third of their children would never learn to read or write because they were "nonverbal." Nor did they see the rationale for promoting children to the next grade if they had not mastered the work of the previous grade. Nor could they understand why so many schools were trying to replace traditional academic studies with electives and practical programs.

While some of these issues may have been hard for parents to fathom, most people had opinions about reading, and they disagreed with the experts. Why weren't schools teaching the alphabet? Hadn't children always learned their "ABCs"? Why weren't they teaching children that letters have sounds? The answers did not make sense to large numbers of parents, and the public was not cowed by invocations of "modern science."

Reading specialists claimed that it was "natural" to learn whole words rather than letters and sounds, but nonspecialists wondered what was natural about learning to read. Historian Mitford Mathews pointed out that reading was "one of the most unnatural activities in which man has ever engaged. Nature has never taught anyone to read and never will. . . . Words are not like tadpoles or flowers or horses. Words are man-made." If reading was natural, why did anyone need to be taught? Why was there so much illiteracy in backward nations, where teachers were scarce? If learning occurred naturally, why maintain schools at all? Why pay teachers more to get advanced degrees? If learning is best when children are having real experiences, why not let them work in homes, shops, fields, and factories, instead of placing them in schools with teachers? Even ordinary people without pedagogical credentials could see that communities well endowed with schools had higher rates of literacy than communities with few or no schools.[72]

And the public was exceedingly fond of the alphabet, even though pedagogical leaders claimed that the schools relied too much on abstractions and symbols. Far more convincing was Jeanne Chall's speculation that early knowledge of the alphabet might be an important step in a child's intellectual development. She wrote: "The child who can identify or reproduce a letter engages in symbolic representation . . . while the child who is working with a picture of an actual object engages in iconic representation. When the child engages in symbolic representation, he is already practicing a higher form of intellectual behavior. Perhaps early mastery of this first step contributes to building the abstract attitude so necessary in our highly scientific and automated world."[73]

The response to Chall's work was almost immediate. In the late 1960s, most reading textbooks for the early grades adopted her recommendations by emphasizing the teaching of the alphabetic code. The great debate about reading, however, was not over. Opponents of the code method were only temporarily in retreat; they made their comeback in the 1980s as the whole language movement.

The Brief *Sputnik* Era

The 1950s was a horrible decade for progressive educators. Progressive education became a stereotype, the butt of jokes and vitriol. First came the great flood of books and articles attacking progressive ideas and practices. Then, in 1955, the Progressive Education Association closed its doors, followed two years later by its publication, *Progressive Education*. Since the late 1930s, the organization had struggled unsuccessfully to formulate a credo, raise money, and recruit members. It had changed its name to the American Education Fellowship in 1944, then reverted back to the original name in 1953—all to no avail, for no cosmetic changes sufficed to resuscitate the PEA or its journal.

Having shaped the nation's educational agenda and dominated the nation's schools of education for most of the twentieth century, the progressive education movement expired from intellectual exhaustion. Its leaders were no longer the stars of American education but the workhorses of the pedagogical faculty; its ideas were no longer fresh and exciting but hackneyed phrases grown stale from repetition. Historian Lawrence A. Cremin observed that the history of the PEA in its last dozen years was "a rather sad tale of manifestos and revised manifestos, of little by way of program, of few members," and of fruitless ideological debates.[74] The PEA's demise was ironic, because progressive ideas, practices, and rhetoric were deeply ingrained in American schools.

In October 1957, two years after the organization's collapse, the Soviet Union launched *Sputnik,* the first space satellite. The press treated *Sputnik* as a major humiliation for the United States, as well as a dangerous threat to the nation's security. *Sputnik* became an instant metaphor for the poor quality of U.S. schools. President Dwight D. Eisenhower, according to a historian of the period, was "puzzled by the panic over *Sputnik*," but ultimately bowed to political pressure to pump new funding into defense and education.[75] Congress responded to the perceived crisis by passing the 1958 National Defense Education Act, which provided fellowships, grants, and loans for students in higher education to study mathematics, science, and foreign languages, as well as funding school construction. Overnight, a clamor arose for higher academic standards and greater attention to mathematics, science, and foreign languages in the schools. Those who had criticized the schools for their lack of rigor felt vindicated.

Admiral Hyman Rickover, known as the father of the nuclear-powered submarine, attracted national attention with his charge that the nation was hobbled in its competition with the Russians for technological supremacy by a school system that failed to prepare young people with a rigorous education. Unlike progressive educators, who for two generations had argued that schools should be more like "real life," Rickover argued in 1959 in his book *Education and Freedom* that "life in a modern industrial state demands a great deal more 'book learning' of everyone who wants to make a good living for himself and his family." He dismissed the modern school's emphasis on trivial concerns of youth: "Today's big problems for young people are not how to choose the proper tie, or how to be socially popular—these are minor problems which any mother can teach her children with little difficulty. . . . The schools must now . . . concentrate on bringing the intellectual powers of each child to the highest possible level. Even the average child now needs almost as good an education as the average middle- and upper-class child used to get in the college-preparatory schools."[76] Rickover pleaded for greater public investment in education, especially higher salaries for teachers in fields such as mathematics and the sciences, where shortages were greatest. He maintained that advanced countries provided excellent education for *all* their children.

Salvation was soon on the way for beleaguered educators. Just when the chorus of critics calling for higher academic standards reached a crescendo, James B. Conant rode to the rescue of the status quo. In 1957, the Carnegie Corporation of New York invited Conant, on his retirement as ambassador to the Federal Republic of Germany, to examine the problems of the American high school. A former president of Harvard, Conant had long been interested in the public schools, and his views were already well-formed. Conant told friends that he "intended to devote a year to sharpening my prejudices about secondary education and a subsequent year peddling said prejudices all around the United States."[77] As a member of the NEA's Educational Policies Commission, he had been part of the grand consensus of the 1940s that saw the school as a social mechanism that would "meet the needs" of youth by supplying the vast majority with vocational and life adjustment skills and a small fraction with college preparatory studies. The book that Conant wrote at the behest of the Carnegie Corporation in 1959, *The American High School Today,* was the whitewash the educational establishment had been hoping for.

Refuting the impassioned critics of the 1950s, Conant praised the nation's public high schools and concluded that no basic changes were necessary. His strongest recommendation was that small high schools should be eliminated so that no high school would have a graduating class of fewer than one hundred students. This meant reducing the number of high schools in the United States from 21,000 to 9,000. Conant strongly preferred large, comprehensive high schools that offered multiple curricula: a strong academic program for the minority who were academically gifted and an array of vocational and general courses for the large majority who were not. Conant belittled the small high schools that tried to provide an academic program for all their students. Such high schools, he held, wasted the time of students who were uninterested in academics, as well as of the top quarter of the class, who did not get the specialized attention they deserved.[78]

Every high school, he said, needed to have a good counseling staff to ensure that students were guided into the right program. In his vision, all students would take a basic required program of four years of English, three or four years of social studies, one year of science, and one year of math. Everything else would be elective, and it would be up to the guidance staff, using tests of aptitude and intelligence, to make sure that students chose the appropriate electives. Conant endorsed social promotion in the required courses, and he advised colleges and universities not to raise their entrance requirements in ways that might strengthen the academic side of the high school curriculum. These proposals surely made administrators happy because they reflected what was already common practice.[79]

Only 15 percent of high school students, Conant claimed, had the mental ability to take rigorous courses in mathematics, science, and foreign language. Perhaps another 10 to 20 percent might stretch to take an academic program as well. But the remaining 65 to 75 percent of students, he believed, should take courses to learn marketable skills. Conant almost obsessively insisted that the schools must stand firm against parents who wanted their children to take academic courses even though they were not "academically talented." Repeatedly, he warned that "ambitious parents" might attempt to get their children enrolled in advanced mathematics, physics, and foreign languages but that school officials must resist their entreaties. Counselors would have to be prepared to persuade "overambitious parents" that their child was not "academically talented." To withstand "unreasonable parental pressures," schools would have to insist upon *"policy"*—that is, a consistent bureaucratic defense of what was done and not done—and make sure that they offered a full panoply of nonacademic electives.[80]

Highly praised by reviewers, Conant's book reached the top of the nation's best-seller lists. It inspired news stories across the nation and prompted *Time* magazine to put Conant on its cover with an adulatory story. *The American High School Today* was treated in the press as an objective evaluation by a disinterested and distinguished outsider, rather than as an endorsement of current practice by someone who had long been an inside player in the education establishment. Conant never mentioned the critics who had dominated media attention for the previous decade, nor the words "progressive education." From Conant came the Olympian judgment that large comprehensive high schools were best because they made it possible to provide differentiated curricula both for the talented minority and for the large majority who needed something other than academic courses.

Conant's proposals put strong pressure on state and local officials to get rid of small high schools because they could not offer a full array of academic, vocational, and general courses. Conant's report was welcomed by educators because its message was reassuring: Any changes needed were minor and would conform to the basic philosophical premises that had ruled American education for more than a generation.

10

The Sixties

In the 1960s, American society was shaken by seismic social, cultural, and political changes. This was all the more shocking because it followed the relatively placid era of the 1950s, when social problems had seemed solvable and ideological conflicts appeared to have abated. In 1960, John F. Kennedy was elected to the presidency, promising to make the federal government an active sponsor of social change. The next dozen years were characterized by turmoil and cataclysmic events. President Kennedy, his brother Senator Robert F. Kennedy, and civil rights leader Martin Luther King, Jr., were assassinated. Reaction against the war in Vietnam provoked massive antiwar protests, a radical student movement, a countercultural youth movement, and violent clashes between radical students and police.

At the same time, the struggle for black civil rights led to protest demonstrations, bloody encounters between civil rights activists and southern police, racist murders, and devastating urban riots. The civil rights movement saw the public schools as the one institution crucial to the prospects for black children; it aimed first to dismantle the dual system of racially segregated schools in the South, then to strike down racially discriminatory practices in northern and western schools.

In the midst of these upheavals, Kennedy's successor, President

Lyndon Johnson, persuaded Congress to endorse ambitious social programs, including the Head Start program in 1964 and federal aid to education in 1965, and the Supreme Court issued a series of far-reaching decisions to secure minority rights. The era popularly known as "the sixties" did not really end until the mid-1970s, with the resignation of Richard M. Nixon as president, the conclusion of the Vietnam War, and the ebbing of domestic turmoil. The cultural reverberations of the sixties were felt in school and society for many years afterward.

The nation's schools were at the center of many of the social upheavals of this era. As the children of the postwar baby boom came of age, the schools grew rapidly to accommodate the surge in enrollments. Long familiar with issues of growth, educators knew how to cope with the baby boom: more money, more classrooms, more teachers. They were uncertain, however, about how to respond to the civil rights movement, which put them into the middle of a political cross fire between white and black communities and between the federal judiciary and local political structures. At this crucial moment, with the schools trying (often reluctantly) to comply with the demands of the civil rights movement and with court decisions, along came pressures from the radical and countercultural movements to change the curriculum and the very nature of schooling. The confluence of events left the schools morally battered and uncertain about their authority, unsure whether they had any control over their students' behavior and over what the students learned.

THE LEGACY OF THE FIFTIES

The 1960s began with no hint of the troubles ahead for the schools and society. Educators enjoyed a keen sense of success. They had come closer to providing universal access to high school education than any generation before them. In 1900, it was a rare youngster—only about 6 of every 100—who earned a high school diploma. After World War II, young people stayed in school longer to take advantage of new economic opportunities for high school graduates. By 1960, an astonishing 70 percent of the age group received a high school diploma.[1]

The 1950s was a time of unprecedented prosperity, which spurred the growth of a large middle class, new suburbs, and a popular culture shaped by television, advertising, and child-centered parenting. The middle-class children of the 1950s, unlike their parents, had never experienced depression or war; whatever their fears about the atomic bomb, these children were sheltered from the disasters that older generations had known. But the complacency of postwar America was profoundly unsettling to many social scientists and journalists, who criticized the materialism of American society, the conformity and consumerism that were stimulated by television and advertising, and the apathy of the young (certainly a contrast to the political activism of the 1930s, when most of the academics involved had been college students).

In the 1940s and 1950s, the schools offered no obstacles to the values of the consumer society. By embracing life adjustment education, they taught youngsters to go along and get along. This philosophy emphasized the importance of finding a job, adjusting to the demands of society, dressing correctly, and fitting in with the crowd. Such lessons prepared youngsters to conform to the group, like what their peers liked, and buy what they bought. That was the recipe for social success.

In high school, youngsters were routinely assigned to different programs—academic, vocational, or general—based on their IQ test scores and grades. Those in the academic program received an excellent education, but most of their classmates got job training or undemanding, low-level courses. Educators believed that they were "meeting the needs" of their students by supplying differentiated curricula. They had done this for years with great success. The practice of assigning youngsters to varied curriculum tracks satisfied different political constituencies as well: conservatives thought that it was inefficient to offer an academic education to all children (their own excepted), while liberals believed that this was an appropriate response to the differing needs and abilities of individual children (as long as their own children were in the academic track).

Social critics such as Paul Goodman and Edgar Z. Friedenberg had written doleful polemics about the hopelessness of American youth and the soul-deadening conformism of American high schools in the 1950s, but the students themselves were maddeningly complacent. When sociologist James Coleman surveyed ten high schools in northern Illinois in the late 1950s, he discovered an adolescent society devoted to superficial, consumerist concerns, mirroring many of the least attractive attitudes of the adult society. Coleman was deeply disturbed by this adolescent world, particularly since American society seemed to have transferred responsibility for education from the family to the school.[2]

More than half a century earlier, John Dewey had seen that the school was replacing the family and had perceived this as a positive opportunity for educators to shape a better future. What had actually happened, Coleman observed, was far different: instead of living in a world shaped by caring and idealistic adults, teenagers were living in their own society, seeking approval from one another rather than from adults, and participating in a subculture with its own language, symbols, and values. With more money to spend, adolescents had become an important market for popular music, movies, and advertising. Instead of influencing them to become intellectually alert and politically concerned citizens, the schools facilitated the isolation of youth from adult influence.

What were the values of the adolescent society? Coleman found that adolescents were anti-intellectual and materialistic. What counted most among them was not brains but athletic prowess, physical attractiveness, and popularity. Neither the leading boys nor the leading girls wanted to be remembered as exceptional scholars. If a girl wanted to be popular and admired, it was better not to be seen as "a brain" by other students. "Brainy" girls were actually penalized and excluded from social networks. Coleman observed that the adolescent subculture exerted "a rather strong deterrent to academic achievement." The students who got the highest grades were not necessarily those of the highest intelligence but rather those who were willing to work hard "at a relatively unrewarded activity."[3]

Despite their materialism and disdain for their studies, the teenagers whom Coleman surveyed were good, well-behaved kids. Nearly 70 percent of the boys and 77 percent of the girls never smoked cigarettes; 70

percent of the boys and 87 percent of the girls did not drink beer; 81 percent of the boys and 88 percent of the girls never drank liquor. Coleman did not even ask about drug use, which in the late 1950s was much rarer than smoking or drinking. When asked what was necessary "in order to be popular in the group," almost 90 percent of the girls responded, "Have a good reputation." Having "a good reputation" meant not being sexually "wild" or promiscuous. A double standard operated openly, discouraging girls—but not boys—from promiscuous behavior. This code, supported by both boys and girls, protected girls from the boys' sexual demands.[4]

American college students were just as placid as younger American teenagers. Reviewing numerous surveys of campus attitudes, political scientist Philip E. Jacob found the same values and norms at campuses across the country, whether they were state universities, denominational colleges, Ivy League colleges, or commuter colleges. Collegians were "*gloriously contented* both in regard to their present day-to-day activity and their outlook for the future," he said. They were "supremely confident that their destinies [were] within their own control rather than in the grip of external circumstances." Most were "unabashedly *self-centered.* . . . They cheerfully expect to conform to the economic status quo and to receive ample rewards for dutiful and productive effort." They wanted to live in a society free of any racial or ethnic discrimination but had no plans to help bring it about, "merely to accept it as it comes." They praised the moral virtues but accepted cheating as a common practice in college. They were dutiful citizens but had little interest in influencing public policy. They were devoted to the idea of a college education, but only a minority seemed to care about the intellectual dimensions of their education. Most wanted little more than vocational preparation and social experience from their higher education. These were the values of school and society. They were remarkably Panglossian, holding a contented view that "all's for the best in this best of all possible worlds."[5]

Sociologist Gerald Grant portrayed the students of the 1950s in his 1988 book about a pseudonymous American high school he called "Hamilton High." Its students were "neatly groomed and clean-cut," and most were white. Located in a small northeastern city, the school was a tightly knit community; students, teachers, administrators, and parents shared the same values. Teachers were respected and enjoyed a clear sense of authority. Discipline and morale were high, and the school's rules about behavior and dress were mostly implicit. The school emphasized a traditional academic curriculum, students worked hard to strengthen their academic record, and 85 percent of its graduates went on to some form of postsecondary education. Students and teachers had tremendous school pride and believed that the world was orderly, predictable, and right.[6]

The youths of the 1950s came to be known as "the silent generation" because of their conformist attitudes and their lack of interest in political issues. They did not appear to be likely recruits for the youth movements of the 1960s. Surely some part of the rebellion of radical students in the 1960s was directed at the apathy and conformity of their older siblings and families. Certainly the leaders of the youth rebellion in the 1960s were not representative of the generation that was in high school and college in the late 1950s.

The Crisis of African-American Schooling

While white middle-class students in the 1950s looked forward to social advancement and material comfort, black Americans stirred restlessly, dissatisfied with their lesser place in the American social order.

Civil rights organizations won a steady stream of court cases against racially discriminatory laws and practices. Their greatest victory was the U.S. Supreme Court's 1954 *Brown v. Board of Education* decision, which spelled the beginning of the end of state-imposed racial segregation, not only in public schools but in all other public institutions.

In 1955, the campaign to remove racial restrictions from the nation's laws and institutions developed a popular base when the eloquent Dr. Martin Luther King, Jr., led a mass protest against racial segregation in Montgomery, Alabama. Initially led by black clergy in the South, the civil rights movement expanded its ranks in 1962, when black college students sat down at a whites-only lunch counter in Greensboro, North

Carolina, and refused to leave when they were denied service. Hundreds and eventually thousands of black and white college students engaged in similar peaceful protests against the racial caste system that separated American citizens on the basis of their color.

At the time of the *Brown* decision, more than 10 million children, including 3.4 million African Americans, were enrolled in public schools that were racially segregated by law in seventeen states and the District of Columbia (four other states permitted districts to segregate students by race). In the immediate aftermath of the *Brown* decision, the states bordering the South (Maryland, Delaware, West Virginia, Kentucky, Missouri—and, with some reluctance, Oklahoma) agreed to comply with the Supreme Court's decision.[7]

However, the white leaders of the eleven states of the Deep South hoped they could ignore the Court's ruling against *de jure* school segregation just as they had ignored the *Plessy v. Ferguson* decision of 1896, which had endorsed racially "separate but equal" facilities. For nearly sixty years, the federal courts had looked the other way as southern and border states had operated separate and grossly unequal schools; many governors and state legislators thought that the *Brown* decision would be as toothless as the *Plessy* ruling had been.

Over the next decade, as it became clear that the federal courts would not back away from the *Brown* decision, the states of the Deep South avoided desegregation by engaging in legal maneuvers, intimidation, and "massive resistance" against court orders. Despite President Dwight D. Eisenhower's despatch of federal troops to enforce a court order to desegregate the public schools in Little Rock, Arkansas, in 1958, the southern strategy was working: ten years after the *Brown* decision, only 9.3 percent of black students (315,841) were attending school with white students in the formerly segregated jurisdictions. In the eleven states of the Deep South, only 1.18 percent of black students (34,118) were—none at all in Mississippi and only a handful in South Carolina, Alabama, Georgia, and Arkansas.[8]

Racial segregation institutionalized white supremacy. Combined with a long-standing and successful effort in the southern states to prevent blacks from voting and gaining any political power, racial segregation preserved a caste system based solely on color. Segregation daily reminded blacks of their subservience to the dominant white political structure, and it rewarded poor, ignorant whites solely for their skin color. In the South, racial segregation was a well-established part of daily life in schools, colleges, hotels, restaurants, transportation, recreation, movie theaters, drinking fountains, and other public and private facilities.

In the public schools, racial segregation and discrimination imposed massive educational disadvantage on the black population. Those who were in greatest need of education, the black children whose forebears had been illiterate slaves, were consigned to the least adequate schools. In the southern states that maintained a dual school system for whites and blacks, the black schools had a shorter school year, shabby buildings, teachers with less education and lower salaries, and inadequate supplies. Already burdened by grinding poverty and political powerlessness, most black southerners were trapped at the bottom of the social and economic ladder by inferior schools, which generated a sense of hopelessness about the future.

Despite the significant disadvantages imposed by school segregation, some segregated black schools managed to nurture talent and excellence among their students. Dunbar High School in Washington, D.C., for example, was legendary for its excellent teachers and high standards. A small number of segregated black schools (such as Wayne County Training School in Jesup, Georgia; Douglass High School in Bristol, Virginia; Dunbar High School in Okmulgee, Oklahoma; Langston High School in Johnson City, Tennessee; and J. C. Corbin High School in Pine Bluff, Arkansas) produced a disproportionate number of high-achieving African-American professionals. The Caswell County Training School in rural North Carolina created a keen sense of community solidarity on behalf of African-American children, encouraging "their highest potential." These public schools, many of which had started as church-affiliated schools, maintained a strong academic tradition and developed business and professional leadership for their local communities, as well as for the civil rights movement.[9]

Many white southern leaders considered education to be dangerous and undesirable for blacks, in that it might give them ambitions beyond laboring in the fields and even encourage them to challenge segregation. Limitations on educational opportunity for black students sharply restricted blacks' educational attainment. As late as 1930, nearly 40 percent of black youths in the South lived in counties that did not have a four-year secondary school for blacks. In 1940, when nearly 80 percent of the black population lived in the South, 41.8 percent of blacks in the United States over the age of twenty-five had less than five years of elementary education, compared to 10.9 percent of whites. Only 7.7 percent of blacks over twenty-five had finished four years of high school, compared to 26.1 percent of whites. Only 1.3 percent of blacks over twenty-five had finished college, compared to 4.9 percent of whites. Blacks between twenty-five and twenty-nine had higher educational attainment than older blacks, but the gap between the races remained huge: 27 percent of this younger group had less than five years of schooling, compared to 3.4 percent of whites. Only 12.3 percent had completed four years of high school, compared to 41.2 percent of whites, and only 1.6 percent of blacks had graduated from college, compared to 6.4 percent of whites.[10]

During the 1940s and 1950s, the southern states pumped money into black schools, hoping to avoid desegregation by proving that their dual system really was equal as well as separate. But the rush to equalize spending followed several decades of purposeful and malign neglect of black schooling, during which ignorance had been cultivated and sustained by public policy.

Segregation facilitated unequal spending on black and white schools. Because blacks were largely excluded from voting in the South, particularly in rural areas and small towns, they could not participate in the political process. White officials could thus safely ignore the needs of black pupils when public funds were allocated to schools. The South was the poorest region in the United States and spent far less on its schools than the rest of the nation did. Southern school officials did their best to provide a decent education for white children but did so at the expense of black children: in 1940, white public schools in the South typically received three dollars or more for every dollar spent on black public schools. Often the imbalance was even more lopsided: Mississippi, for instance, spent $52.01 per white child but only $7.36 per black child.[11]

In Louisiana, where the state spent $77.11 per white child and $20.49 per black child, and where half the black children and one quarter of the white children left school before fifth grade, the state legislature commissioned a school survey in the late 1930s. It was not the purpose of the survey to highlight the contrast between white and black education but to call attention to the need for better public schools for children of both races. Nonetheless, the survey included a stark portrayal of the lives and schooling of blacks in rural Louisiana in 1940, written by Charles S. Johnson, a prominent black sociologist at Fisk University. Johnson, who later became the president of Fisk, had been educated at the University of Chicago.

The typical black family, Johnson wrote, consisted of mother, father, and at least six children. They lived in a two- or three-room frame cabin near cotton or cane fields. The cabin had no indoor plumbing. The parents were sharecroppers, and during the cropping season everyone worked in the fields. Those too young to work in the fields stayed home from school to take care of the babies. The house had a radio but no books, no newspapers, no piano or Victrola; the furnishings consisted of three beds, a small table, and a few chairs. The mother and father had the equivalent of a fourth-grade education; they could read and write "feebly." Most children dropped out of school around the fifth grade. "From such homes a large proportion of the Negro children come," Johnson reported.[12]

The schools were typically either one- or two-teacher schools (at the time of the survey, about two thirds of the black schools in Louisiana were one-teacher schools and only 8 percent had more than three teachers). The buildings were mainly dilapidated, the equipment was meager, and many of the teachers were poorly educated. The teacher in the typical one-teacher rural school was barely literate, herself the product of an inadequate education; she was also a very poor teacher, unable to move beyond empty and mechanical activities and memorization of meaningless, disconnected facts. Johnson complained of "a vicious circle in which the child leaves a home setting of cultural backwardness to attend a school that is only another facet of this setting. He receives instruction from a teacher who comes from the same level of incompetence and he returns home without having glimpsed very far beyond the folk pattern which conditions his behavior and his thinking."[13]

Such was the condition of schools for black children in the Deep South in 1940 on the eve of the great migration from South to North. The black children of rural Louisiana, like those in the rural schools of other Deep South states, were woefully uneducated, as were their parents. These children and their families, Johnson pointed out, were isolated from the mainstream of American culture, and their underfunded, ragtag schools did little to help them make the transition to the larger culture.

Despite their lack of education, African Americans were not content with the meager prospects available to them. During World War II and in the postwar years, many left behind the hard life they had known on the land and sought jobs and better lives in the North and in cities. The result was an extraordinary internal migration. Between 1940 and 1960, over three million blacks left the South and moved North. During these years the proportion of blacks living on farms dropped from 35 percent to 8 percent, and the proportion living in cities grew from 49 percent to 73 percent. During the 1940s alone, more than one third of all young blacks aged twenty to twenty-four in Deep South states moved north.[14]

African Americans who moved to urban areas, whether in the north or south, settled in predominantly black neighborhoods, where housing was crowded and substandard, and their children usually attended predominantly black schools, which were also crowded and substandard. Coming as they did from families that had attained no more than a primary school education, these children needed intensive instruction in the skills and knowledge that were required for economic and social advancement. Unfortunately, many of their white teachers were racist, sharing the general belief of educators and the public that racial differences in intelligence were innate, real, and fixed.

To make matters worse, the black migration coincided with the heyday of life adjustment education in the public schools. The smoothly running administrative machinery in urban schools tested the black newcomers for their IQs and their achievement to determine their abilities. When it was found that their scores on these tests were low—which was hardly surprising in view of their parents' low educational attainment and their own limited exposure to books and literacy—black children were disproportionately assigned to nonacademic programs and to classes for slow, defective, and retarded students. Dedicated to the idea of social adjustment rather than social advancement, the schools in the 1940s and 1950s prepared children to fit into society as it then was. Education for social adjustment was the worst possible program for black children, who needed to prepare to break through social barriers, not conform to them.

Since one of the key principles of life adjustment education was to train each student for the specific job he was likely to hold, the public schools had the burden of adjusting black students to the bleak reality of limited opportunity. Most professions were closed to blacks, and the major labor unions barred blacks from entering the skilled trades. The use of IQ tests to place students into different curriculum tracks made the administrative task of the schools easier. But instead of getting the intensive instruction in literacy and numeracy they needed, black students were all too often placed in educational programs where little was taught to them and they were effectively prepared for the low-status jobs as unskilled laborers and domestic servants that were open to them. This was social adjustment in its meanest sense.[15]

The burgeoning of the civil rights movement in the late 1950s and the first half of the 1960s offered a promise of changing this squalid arrangement. In cities across the North, the Midwest, and the South, civil rights organizations demanded racial integration to improve the education of black youths. But at the same time, the populations of cities and their schools were shifting dramatically: whites were leaving the cities for the suburbs as blacks moved in, and nonwhite children became a majority of the enrollment in most big-city school systems. As demographic changes made the goal of integration ever more elusive, protest activity became more fervid, and black leaders became more militant in the face of inadequate responses by school boards to their demands for integration.[16]

Into this maelstrom stepped James B. Conant, the former president of Harvard University, who was nationally recognized as a spokesman for progressive reform. In 1961, Conant warned in his best-selling book *Slums and Suburbs,* "We are allowing social dynamite to accumulate in our large cities," where large numbers of young black men were out of school and out of work. What could the schools do? He maintained that *"to a considerable degree what a school should do and can do is determined by the status and ambitions of the families being served"* (Conant's italics). He recognized that schools in affluent suburbs were preparing the majority of their students for college but recommended that schools in the cities should concentrate on preparing their students for the job market with practical vocational training. He strongly believed that *"the educational experiences of youth should fit their subsequent employment."* [17]

This was the classic progressive doctrine of curricular differentiation, loudly espoused in the early twentieth century by efficiency experts such as John Franklin Bobbitt and W. W. Charters and in the 1930s and 1940s by the prestigious national commissions on which Conant had served. How should these youths be prepared? Conant maintained that "It does no good to prepare boys and girls for nonexistent jobs." Given the pervasiveness of employment discrimination, the number of jobs that black youngsters could prepare for would necessarily be limited. Should children in poor neighborhoods get the same quality of education as children in rich suburbs? Conant did not think so; parents in poor neighborhoods, black or white, he believed, had to be "realistic" and recognize that their children needed a different kind of education from children in higher-income communities. This was the very issue that had been debated since the report of the Committee of Ten in 1893, which had recommended that all students be given the same quality of education regardless of their likely future occupations. Without referring to the decades-long debate, which seemed to have been settled long ago, Conant sided with the critics of the Committee of Ten, asserting that those who were not going to college should be trained for a specific job, not liberally educated.[18]

In 1964, Conant was sharply criticized by *Fortune* journalist Charles E. Silberman in *Crisis in Black and White.* Conant's recommendations, he warned, "would condemn Negroes to be hewers of wood and drawers of water in a society that needs fewer and fewer such people. Negro youngsters need precisely the same kind of education that white young-sters need." Silberman recognized that the changing economy would place a high premium on knowledge and that the average person was likely to change his job and his occupation many times. In such a world, vocational training for a specific job was not only "wildly impractical" but actually destructive of students' future opportunities. What both white and black youngsters needed, Silberman believed, was the intel-lectual discipline to apply existing knowledge to new situations. The most important of all vocational skills was literacy, he said, and the most important mission of the schools was to teach black children to read and write in the early grades.[19]

Silberman had been influenced by the work of psychologist Kenneth B. Clark, whose research had been cited by the U.S. Supreme Court in the *Brown v. Board of Education* decision of 1954. In the early 1960s, Clark had directed a major study of the conditions of young people in Harlem. He believed in racial integration but feared that forced assign-ment of students to schools for purposes of racial balance would cause whites to flee, making segregation worse. He insisted that black children were not innately incapable of learning but had been systematically de-prived of good education "in such a way as to compel poor performance from Negro children—a performance that could be reversed with quality education." Unless firm steps were taken immediately, he predicted, the public school system in the urban North would become "predominantly a segregated system. . . . It will, in addition, become a school system of low academic standards, providing a second-class education for under-classed children and thereby a chief contributor to the perpetuation of the 'social dynamite' which is the cumulative pathology of the ghetto." Meaningful desegregation would occur "only if all of the schools in the system are raised to the highest standards, so that the quality of educa-tion does not vary according to income or the social status of the neigh-borhood. The goals of integration and quality education must be sought together; they are interdependent. One is not possible without the other."[20]

Public education in Harlem, Clark wrote, was characterized by "inefficiency, inferiority, and massive deterioration." The schools had disproportionate numbers of substitute and inexperienced teachers; discipline problems among students were endemic, as was physical brutality by teachers toward students. One teacher told Clark's team, "The children are not taught anything; they are just slapped around and nobody bothers to do anything about it." The longer students in Harlem remained in school, the worse their academic achievement was in comparison to other children in the city. Clark complained, "Little is expected of them; they are rewarded for mediocre performance, and consequently accomplish increasingly less than pupils at their grade level should accomplish." Fewer than half the students in Harlem who started high school received a diploma; of those who did, few were prepared for any job, and fewer still were prepared to attend college. Most of the dropouts were far behind in reading and mathematics. Clark concluded that they were failing because their teachers did not believe they were capable of learning. By expecting so little, the schools were "presently damaging the children they exist to help."[21]

Clark lashed out at the nest of related assumptions that had dominated educational thinking and policy since the 1930s. The idea that "each child should be educated in terms of his own needs and capacities," he said, allowed teachers to have lower expectations for black children, whose capacities they doubted. He challenged the belief that children from working-class backgrounds need "a different type of education from that provided for children from middle-class families," which encouraged schools to supply an education of lesser value to children from working-class families. The belief that one cannot expect much from children whose families don't have books in the home rationalized the failure of children from poor families, he said. He challenged the use of IQ tests to predict a child's ability to learn, saying they should be used instead to determine what a child *needs* to learn.[22]

Clark derided what he called "the cult of 'cultural deprivation'" among educators and social scientists. Those who attributed the academic failure of black children to the environmental disadvantages of their family or neighborhood, he said, were merely finding a polite way of saying that those children could not be expected to learn to read or do arithmetic in the elementary grades. He considered such determinism to be indistinguishable from earlier, discredited notions about the biological bases of academic failure.[23]

Low expectations became a self-fulfilling prophecy, Clark insisted. Black children were not learning because they were not being taught effectively, and they were not being taught effectively because their teachers "do not believe that they can learn, do not expect that they can learn, and do not act toward them in ways which help them to learn." Most teachers and administrators interviewed for Clark's project talked of lowering standards to meet the low intellectual levels of the children, a strategy that Clark condemned as a shift from teaching to custodial care.[24]

Clark believed that New York City's Board of Education should establish rigorous standards for those who taught in ghetto schools, where children's needs were greatest. They should be the system's best teachers, its master teachers, who would be paid more for their superior skills and readiness to tackle challenging responsibilities, and who would work within a "system of accountability" that rewarded excellent teaching and banished inferior and mediocre teaching. With highly competent teachers who believed in the children's capacity to learn and with the opportunity for intensive tutorials, Clark predicted, poor black children would learn. He insisted that black children as well as black teachers

> must be held to the same high standards of academic performance as their white counterparts. . . . Negro students cannot be excused for shoddy performance *because* they are Negro. To do so makes more rigid and intolerable the pathology, injustices, and distinctions of racism. There can be no double standards in education, no easy alibi. Schools are institutions designed to compensate for "cultural deprivation." If this were not true there would be no need for schools.[25]

Recognizing the impossibility of immediate integration, at least in the major cities where the black population was concentrated, Clark advocated a campaign for excellence in ghetto schools, arguing that it was best "to save as many Negro children as possible now." He knew that years of discrimination, bigotry, and blighted hopes had produced frustration and rage within the black community. Recognizing that militant leaders were getting involved in school issues, Clark warned against "inflexible emotional postures. Heroics and dramatic words and gestures, over-simplified either-or thinking, and devil-hunting might dominate headlines; but they cannot solve the fundamental problems of obtaining high-quality education in the public schools."[26]

Clark's cautions were ignored as angry activists turned from demanding integration to demanding black control of black schools. As cries of "black power" rang out on the barricades, violence and disorder in urban schools increased. In his history of the Detroit public schools, Jeffrey E. Mirel noted that the period from 1969 to 1971 had been marked by a dramatic increase of violence in the schools. A high-level administrator in Detroit reported that "there is growing concern among school staff, pupils and parents about order and personal security in the school environment. This concern is based on substantial evidence of physical assaults by students and non-students on both students and teaching staff members, the high rate of thefts and vandalism against school property, and a significant amount of drug and narcotic traffic in and around school buildings."[27]

In this crisis-ridden atmosphere, the difficult, painstaking, long-term job of improving the education of black children was replaced by political struggles for control of the black schools, which, even when successful, did not improve the quality of these schools. As Clark had feared, "heroics and dramatic words and gestures," a sort of street theater, obscured the pursuit of specific actions to secure better teachers, acquire better materials, establish better curricula, use more effective teaching methods, set higher expectations, and put in place the other ingredients that are essential elements of good education.

THE COUNTERCULTURE IN THE SCHOOLS

In the mid-1960s, tumultuous events began to occur with such rapidity as to create a sense of relentless social crisis. American society seemed literally to be falling apart amid civil rights protests, antiwar demonstrations, campus upheavals, black separatist demands, and zany countercultural happenings.

In 1964, on the University of California's Berkeley campus, student radicals demonstrated against university regulations governing their right to assemble, and their protest eventually escalated into a national movement against the war in Vietnam. Beginning in 1965 in the Watts section of Los Angeles, the nation's cities endured four consecutive summers of violent disorders that took a heavy toll of life and property, mainly in black neighborhoods. Whether in poor black neighborhoods or on elite university campuses, clashes between police and protesters became a frequent occurrence in the last half of the 1960s.

On campus and in cities, the so-called Age of Aquarius (as it was dubbed in the popular rock musical *Hair*) dawned, with the appearance of large numbers of hippies, heralds of a free-spirited and rebellious counterculture, calling for liberation from adult strictures, conventional behavior and dress, and middle-class manners and mores, especially those related to sex and drugs. Tradition and authority seemed to crumble as the nation's popular culture absorbed the anarchic, flamboyant styles of rebellious youths.

All these cultural movements and political shocks collided at the very time that American schools were presented with a major new challenge. In the early 1960s, in response to the public outcry following the 1957 launch of *Sputnik,* the federal government had funded major efforts to improve mathematics and science curricula, especially for college-bound students. But in 1963 and 1964, the post-*Sputnik* enthusiasm for academic improvement abruptly ended, replaced as the leading national topic by the "urban crisis." Armed with the powers contained in the Civil Rights Act of 1964 and the funds contained in the 1965 Elementary and Secondary Education Act, the federal government, with the support of the federal courts, began to impose desegregation plans on recalcitrant southern districts.

Ready or not, American schools were confronted with the necessity of educating black children from a wide variety of backgrounds, many of whose parents had been denied a decent education. In the past, the schools had absorbed this diversity of backgrounds by dividing children into groups and directing the highest-quality instruction to those with the highest test scores; the group at the bottom, it was assumed, would eventually drop out. This time-tested approach was untenable in the era of integration, however, because it would have consigned the majority of black children to the lowest educational track and foreclosed their opportunity to prepare for higher education. Some federal courts even prohibited tracking as racially suspect because of its segregating effect.

As never before, the schools needed a clear strategy to raise achievement and expectations. They needed to determine which methods and materials were most effective and to ascertain that teachers were well educated and well prepared to teach their students. They needed thoughtful, carefully constructed programs to help the students who were most in need of a good education. Even under the best of circumstances, the schools in the big cities, where a large proportion of black families resided, were not likely to change the social order, but they could at least ensure that their students were literate, numerate, and fully prepared for further education, gainful employment, and the responsibilities of citizenship.

→ → ← ←

At this crucial moment, the zeitgeist in American education swung wildly toward the liberationist, pseudorevolutionary consciousness that was roiling the rest of the culture. The idea of improving performance by intensifying instruction seemed faintly ridiculous and decidedly uncool in the new age of student rebellion. Black and white militants talked glibly about "revolution," but the only real revolution was one of personal style—of hair, dress, and behavior—not of the political system. Activated by the war in Vietnam and resistance to the military draft, a radical student movement emerged on many college campuses, particularly those that were most elite and permissive, such as Berkeley, Columbia, Cornell, and Harvard.

College student militants demonstrated, boycotted, picketed, occupied administrative offices, closed down classes, disrupted public speakers whose views were unacceptable to them, and issued "nonnegotiable" demands to block military-related research or military recruiting on campus, or even, in the case of Columbia University, to stop the construction of a university gym on public parkland that abutted the Harlem community. On other campuses, such as San Francisco State College and Cornell University, militant black students engaged in disruptive tactics to dramatize their demands for black studies departments, more black faculty, and more black students.

Violence and threats of violence became commonplace. Students' causes expanded beyond war and racism to include demands for a greater role in university decision making and the right to choose their own courses and design their own curricula, preferably those that were "relevant" to their interests. Meeting "the needs of youth" was back in fashion. "Relevance" became both a slogan and a goal, to which many campuses responded by creating courses on revolution, youth movements, rock poetry, popular culture, and other topics intended to satisfy the student rebels.

During this era, the word "requirements" became anathema. College graduation requirements were reduced, and college entrance requirements, especially the foreign language requirement, tumbled; this, in turn, removed one of the most important incentives for studying a foreign language in high school. The demand for relevance in the curriculum encouraged students to turn inward and pursue their own interests; the necessity of appealing to students' interests also spurred schools and colleges to "market" courses with alluring titles as if students were consumers in a vast educational marketplace.

In Gerald Grant's book about the pseudonymous (but real) "Hamilton High," the placid and coherent school community of the 1950s was destroyed by the turbulence of the 1960s. After taking small steps to increase racial integration, the school was convulsed with riots and violence from 1968 to 1971. Discipline dissolved, respect for teachers evaporated, racial separatism increased, many white middle-class students left the school, and administrators had to devote most of their time to disciplining unruly students. After three students who rampaged through the school library were given only a mild rebuke, teachers became reluctant to enforce any code of behavior. As students asserted their legal rights to behave as they wished, teachers withdrew, locked their classroom doors to keep out intruders, and "were unwilling to confront students."[28] In a school that had once prided itself on its keen sense of community, adult authority collapsed: students played their radios in class, cut classes, insulted teachers, littered the halls with trash, and threatened (with the backing of their parents) to sue teachers who tried to maintain academic or behavioral standards.

Fearful of litigation, the adults at "Hamilton High" retreated to "a purely legal, technical view" of their role, "which for many boiled down to a responsibility to house students, to keep the peace, to avoid engagement or demands in the way of either moral or intellectual standards." Students' use of drugs, alcohol, and tobacco grew, as did their abusive behavior toward teachers and fellow students. The school responded to these changes with a policy of "let the students decide," which amounted to an abdication of adult responsibility for students' conduct. The school added new specialists to its staff, not only for security but for counseling and various social services. To placate student demands for autonomy, the school liberalized its curriculum with numerous nonacademic electives, such as "Parenting Today," "How to Fix Your Bachelor Pad," and "Scuba Diving." The students responded by tracking themselves; the best students took the best courses, and others avoided the demanding ones. Counselors were nonjudgmental, seeing themselves as facilitators who helped students make choices and specialized in therapeutic strategies without recourse to values or issues of right and wrong. As the school became more bureaucratic and teachers distanced themselves from their authority as adults, the school lost any sense of shared expectations. It grew "more democratic" and more individualistic but was also "more bureaucratic, more adversarial, and officially value neutral."[29]

The upheavals of the era changed the public schools in important ways. Confronted with violence, disciplinary problems, and litigation, school officials backed away from acting *in loco parentis*. In an effort to reduce conflict, academic demands were minimized. Students were increasingly left to fend for themselves, without adult guidance. The withdrawal of adults from their responsibility for instructing their students had implications both for students' behavior and for the academic coherence of the schools.

THE PEDAGOGICAL LIBERATION MOVEMENT

A. S. Neill's Summerhill, *published in 1960, was a surprise best-seller* and one of the most influential books of the era. It was an account of the ultraprogressive school in England that Neill directed, and it inspired many imitators in the United States. *Summerhill* was the perfect book for the age of individualism and student freedom.

Neill believed above all in freedom for youth. No student in his school was ever compelled to learn anything against his will. He also believed in abolishing adult authority. Further, he was completely permissive in his attitude toward children's sexual activities (so long as no one got pregnant, embarrassed the school, or caused it financial difficulties). Neill spoke to the soul of radical youths and their adult supporters when he wrote, *"I believe that to impose anything by authority is wrong. The child should not do anything until he comes to the opinion—his own opinion—that it should be done.* The curse of humanity is the external compulsion, whether it comes from the Pope or the state or the teacher or the parent. It is fascism in toto"[30] (italics in original).

Neill had written other books about his school, but none had gained notice in the United States. When his American publisher first offered *Summerhill* for sale in 1960, not a single bookseller placed an advance order. By 1970, however, *Summerhill* was selling an amazing 200,000 copies a year and was required reading in at least six hundred university courses. (Surely it was ironic that Neill's paean to student freedom was *required* reading in American universities.) The book aroused intense emotions; some readers claimed that it had changed their lives, but one woman returned the book to the publisher, saying that "her husband had told her that either she or the book must get out of the house." Max Rafferty, the conservative state superintendent of education in California, averred that he would "as soon enroll a child of mine in a brothel as in Summerhill."[31]

Neill founded Summerhill in 1921 in Suffolk, England, as a boarding school for children from the early grades through high school. Its students, who usually numbered from forty-five to seventy, were drawn from relatively affluent families who shared Neill's laissez-faire educational philosophy. The school embodied the extreme child-centeredness that was popular among some American progressives in the early decades of the century. Summerhill was a school where the children's interests, wishes, and whims reigned supreme. Neill believed that children who were free of any compulsion would educate themselves when ready to do so and that they would be healthier than children who were made to study what he called useless subjects.

Echoing Rousseau, Neill wrote that "a child is innately wise and realistic. If left to himself without adult suggestion of any kind, he will develop as far as he is capable of developing." Neill renounced "all discipline, all direction, all suggestion, all moral training, all religious instruction." When children arrived at Summerhill, it was up to them to ask for lessons. If they did not want any lessons, they were left undisturbed to play all day, if that was what they wanted, for months or even years (Neill proudly described one student who had spent twelve years at Summerhill without ever attending a single lesson). Neill hated examinations, prizes, and marks, and he was contemptuous of books, which he considered "the least important apparatus in a school." Summerhill had no special teaching methods, Neill wrote, "because we do not consider that teaching in itself matters very much. Whether a school has or has not a special method for teaching long division is of no significance, for long division is of no importance except to those who *want* to learn it. And the child who *wants* to learn long division *will* learn it no matter how it is taught." [32]

Summerhill appealed to radical progressives not only because it tapped their deeply ingrained belief in the overweening importance of child-centered education but because Neill championed radical egalitarianism and sexual liberation. Neill boasted that he had eliminated his own authority as director of the school. Decisions at Summerhill were taken at meetings in which Neill's vote counted for no more than the vote of a six-year-old child. He emphasized that he and the children were equals, with neither able to make the rules. But of course the children did make the rules, because the children outnumbered the adults. When Neill tried to limit cigarette smoking to students over the age of twelve, for example, the students outvoted him and abolished the age limit. On the subject of sex, Neill was vociferous on behalf of "the child's right to masturbate." He was convinced that the cause of most of the world's miseries was sexual repression. Consequently, he was almost obsessive about the necessity of breaking down children's inhibitions against masturbation, and he overlooked sexual liaisons between students and even between students and teachers. He maintained that unfettered heterosexual play was "the royal road" to a healthy adult sex life and suggested that prohibiting such play caused homosexuality, promiscuity, sadism, anxiety, and hate.[33]

Neill ridiculed the idea that "every child should learn mathematics, history, geography, some science, a little art, and certainly literature." Too much emphasis on learning, he warned, killed creativity. It was not cramming or rote memory he objected to but any effort to instruct children before they asked to be instructed. If a child didn't want to learn history or mathematics, he asked, so what? Girls at Summerhill often avoided studying mathematics or physics, preferring to do needlework; later on in life such girls would be dressmakers or designers, he said: "It is an absurd curriculum that makes a prospective dressmaker study quadratic equations or Boyle's Law."[34]

Summerhill turned out to be the star of a bumper crop of radical critiques of the public schools that were published during the 1960s and early 1970s. In the first wave, the leading books were John Holt's *How Children Fail* (1964), Jonathan Kozol's *Death at an Early Age* (1967), Herbert Kohl's *36 Children* (1967), and James Herndon's *The Way It Spozed to Be* (1968). Like *Summerhill,* these books quickly became required reading for students of education.

John Holt, who taught in a private progressive school in Colorado, criticized almost everything that was usually done in school, including tests, grades, and a curriculum that described what children were expected to learn. Forcing children to find "the right answer," he insisted, made them fearful. The ideal learner was a baby, like his seventeen-month-old niece, who learned by experience and experimentation, without external rewards or penalties. Holt sounded like the child-centered progressives of the 1920s when he wrote that "knowledge which is not genuinely discovered by children will very likely prove useless and will be soon forgotten." Describing children as "subject peoples," he said that school was their jail and teachers were their jailers.[35]

Educators, Holt argued, should not decide what knowledge was essential for children to learn. Having a set curriculum based on some adult notion of what might be needed in the future, he declared, was "absurd and harmful nonsense. We will not begin to have true education or real learning in our schools until we sweep this nonsense out of the way. Schools should be a place where children learn what they most want to know, instead of what we think they ought to know." Real learning would not occur unless the school was "a great smorgasbord of intellectual, artistic, creative, and athletic activities, from which each child could take whatever he wanted, and as much as he wanted, or as little." All of this was familiar stuff to those who knew about the child-centered progressivism of the 1920s, but to a new generation of radicals it sounded fresh and exciting.[36]

Unlike Holt, who taught affluent children, Kozol, Kohl, and Herndon taught in urban public schools, where their students were mostly black and poor. Each reported that his students were badly educated and had been spiritually or physically abused by racist teachers and by an insensitive, bureaucratic school system. Kozol won the National Book Award for his account of the brutality inflicted on poor black children by the Boston public schools; some children had been caned, he said, and almost all had suffered the educational retardation caused by constant turnover of indifferent, unqualified teachers. Kohl taught in Harlem; setting aside the dull prescribed curriculum and the bland, outdated textbooks, he engaged the children in projects, science experiments, and writing their own novels. Herndon wrote a comical account of his year as a teacher. Uncertain what to teach his junior high school students (many of whom were far behind in reading), he believed that the kids should do whatever they wanted to do. When an experienced black teacher chastised him because he did not expect the children to use proper language or to behave correctly, he was sure that he knew more and cared more about his students than she did.

The many radical critiques written during this period made clear that the public schools in poor neighborhoods lacked the tools and perhaps even the will to educate the children assigned to them. All agreed that low expectations were endemic. There was a mismatch between the children and the schools; if the schools were going to educate the children, they would have to change. The poorest schools had the fewest resources and the least experienced, least qualified teachers; the children who most needed intensive instruction and intellectual nurturing were least likely to get it. Certainly they needed ample resources, and certainly they should have had the best-qualified teachers, not a steady stream of greenhorns, substitutes, and burnt-out cases.

Yet something else was amiss. Big-city schools had become routinized bureaucratic systems that worked as mechanically as progressives such as Edward L. Thorndike, David Snedden, W. W. Charters, John Franklin Bobbitt, Ellwood P. Cubberley, and Lewis Terman had hoped, testing children for their ability and sorting them into predetermined niches. For years, the system worked just as planned, sending appropriate proportions of children to colleges, farms, factories, offices, shops, domestic service, and homemaking. What the system was not designed to do was to take children who did very poorly on the tests and raise them to higher levels of knowledge and skill. Many children, by dint of their own aspirations or their teachers' extraordinary dedication, broke free of the system's low expectations. But the system itself was static, assigning low-performing children to programs in which little was expected of them and there was no intellectual challenge.

⇥ ⇥ ⇤ ⇤

The radical critics of the 1960s were legitimately angry at the appalling condition of urban schools for black children, but their rage turned into a rejection of virtually all manifestations of formal education: textbooks and tests, marks and grading, curricula and lesson plans, and knowledge itself. In the age of the counterculture and the student revolution, the answer to most problems was freedom, freedom to "do one's own thing," freedom from intrusive adult authority. In the 1920s and 1930s, progressives had talked about choosing experience over knowledge and liberating the schools from the knowledge curriculum; their ideological children unwittingly pursued the same goals.

In 1969, in their book *Teaching as a Subversive Activity,* Neil Postman and Charles Weingartner recommended a series of steps that would have disrupted the transfer of knowledge from generation to generation. Every class should be an elective, they proposed, and all subjects and requirements should be abolished. They recommended that teachers should be assigned to teach subjects they had never studied ("Have 'English' teachers 'teach' Math, Math teachers English, Social Studies teachers Science, Science teachers Art and so on"; "Transfer all the elementary-school teachers to high school and vice versa"). Postman and Weingartner complained that the biggest obstacle to good education was teachers' desire to "get something they think they know into the heads of people who don't know it."[37]

Such ideas could only worsen the plight of poor children, who in fact needed more opportunity to learn, more adult attention, more structure, better curricula, better materials, and better-prepared teachers to help them acquire knowledge and skills. Nonetheless, according to the radical critics, freedom was the answer. And their prescriptions grew increasingly extreme. Thus the proposals for freedom *in* the schools and freedom *from* the schools began to roll out, first from writers and social critics, then from professors of pedagogy, and eventually from the schools themselves.

Some radical critics saw the nature of schooling itself as the primary problem. Carl Rogers, a psychoanalyst, contended that schools should ignore traditional learning and concentrate instead on "personal growth" through "encounter groups" and "sensitivity training." In a claim that was widely parroted by those eager to jettison all academic requirements, Rogers maintained that the world was changing so fast that the knowledge and skills of the past were obsolete; therefore students needed to learn only "the *processes* by which new problems are met." He asserted that students needed to learn how to solve problems but did not need to study the origins of problems or how people had solved them in the past. In his ideal system, teachers would not teach but would be "facilitators" of "self-directed learning." All this would come about by engaging teachers, administrators, students, even parents in therapeutic group experiences where they could share their innermost feelings. Rogers wanted to turn the schools into group therapy sessions.[38]

Tinkering and reform would not do, said the radical critics. The schools would have to change so drastically that they could create a new kind of person and thus a new kind of society. In the 1930s, when radical educators had wanted to build a new social order, they had recognized that there was a conflict between their desires for child-centered schools and for schools that could reconstruct society. When, in 1932, George Counts had dared progressive educators to build a new social order, he had rejected the extreme individualism of the child-centered schools, knowing that they lacked the collective discipline to build a new social order. The progressive educators of the 1960s seemed unaware that these issues had been debated a generation earlier and asserted their quasi-religious belief that unfettered student freedom must necessarily produce a better society. Inspired by *Summerhill,* the critics expected that children left free to choose would always make wise choices and that in time the world would be a far, far better place, where racism, war, and hatred no longer existed.

One might question their idealistic concept of human nature or even the practical problem of finding teachers to realize their Rousseauistic vision. One might even wonder why the critics seldom asked whether parents wanted their children to attend schools like Summerhill. But on one issue, there should be no doubt: an educational philosophy of "do your own thing" was the worst possible prescription for poor children, because it left to their own devices the very children who were most in need of purposeful instruction. Poor children in classrooms where teachers "facilitated" instead of teaching were at a terrific disadvantage as compared to privileged children who came from homes where educated parents read to them, took them to museums, surrounded them with books, and supplied whatever the school was not teaching. There were no such protections for poor kids. If the school did not make the effort to educate them, no one else was likely to. The radical idea that poor kids should be left free to learn or not was a large gamble with their lives (the gamblers were upper-middle-class graduates of prestigious universities). This laissez-faire approach to education was an abandonment of the fundamental promise of public education to provide social equality.

The radical critique of the schools blossomed into a dynamic movement, founded on the proposition that the public school system was a vast machine of oppression, a tool of an unjust and corrupt society, and that new institutions would have to be created to liberate children from school and society. Since the early part of the century, there had been Summerhill-style schools in the private sector, their numbers waxing and waning with the persistence and fortunes of their founders. In the late 1960s, such schools, now called "free schools" and "community schools," multiplied. One advocate estimated that 20 to 30 new schools had been founded each year in 1967 and 1968, 60 to 80 in 1969, more than 150 in 1970, and more than 200 in 1971–72.[39]

One of the earliest free schools, the Children's Community School in Ann Arbor, Michigan, was specifically modeled on Summerhill. Its teachers, led by Bill Ayers, a member of the revolutionary fringe of the radical Students for a Democratic Society, believed that children should not learn to read until they "asked" someone to teach them. Modeled on Summerhill's, this was not a successful strategy. The biographer of Diana Oughton, another teacher at the Children's Community School, noted that "The single most important failing of the school, and the one on which it foundered in the end, was the fact that no one learned to read there." (Oughton died making terrorist bombs in the basement of a town house in New York City in 1970.) The severest critics of the school were the black parents, who wanted their children to learn academic subjects and "to rise in American society, not remake it."[40]

By the early 1970s, as free schools proliferated, the number of children enrolled in them was miniscule, only about one tenth of 1 percent of the nation's students. Nonetheless, these schools had a large impact on American education. Prodded by the example of the private free school movement, large public school systems opened public alternative high schools, which were generally smaller and more open to experimentation than regular high schools. One celebrated alternative high school was Philadelphia's Parkway Program, a "school without walls" that had no building of its own and sent its students to learn in community institutions and businesses. Instead of shocking the establishment, the Parkway Program served as a model for other cities and featured the U.S. commissioner of education as its graduation speaker in 1970.[41]

The Open Education Movement

Public schools responded to the torrent of criticism that washed over them in the late 1960s by embracing the open education movement, which was innovative yet pleasingly familiar, exactly the tonic they needed to overcome their despair. The open education movement was a spectacular phenomenon. Never before had an education reform movement risen to national prominence almost overnight, won the enthusiastic support of education leaders, dominated the national discussion, then disappeared within a few years. While the twentieth century had seen the coming and going of many educational fads, this one had a brilliant beginning and an unusually short life cycle.

The movement took off in 1967 after the publication of a series of articles by Joseph Featherstone in *The New Republic,* which created a sensation among educational leaders. Featherstone described British activity-centered infant schools as "a profound and sweeping revolution in English primary education." In the British primary schools, the routine of the day "is left completely up to the teacher, and the teacher, in turn, leaves options open to the children." The classrooms were well equipped with activity areas and tables for artwork, sand and water play, and reading, as well as a play corner. Teachers in the infant schools believed that "in a rich environment young children can learn a great deal by themselves and that most often their own choices reflect their needs."[42] The British infant schools fit neatly with the American progressive tradition, for they were modeled on the activity movement that had influenced many American elementary schools in the 1920s and 1930s.

Unfortunately, many American converts to open education did not realize that the schools lauded by Featherstone enrolled children between the ages of five and seven and that they were not necessarily an appropriate model for youngsters of every age. Educators who had been raised on the tenets of progressive education hailed "open education" as the best approach for every stage of schooling. Its hallmarks were familiar to American progressives. An open school emphasized projects, activities, and student initiative. Its teachers were "facilitators" of learning, not transmitters of knowledge. Students did not have to sit in classrooms but could gather to learn in the school's halls or corridors, or anywhere in the surrounding community. Affective (or emotional) learning was prized more than cognitive (or intellectual) learning. Multi-age groupings and individualized instruction were typical. Classrooms were arranged by activity centers, not by desks facing the teacher. A certain noise level was admired as a sign of active learning. These practices came right out of the child-centered progressive movement of the 1920s and 1930s.

In 1970, journalist Charles E. Silberman's best-selling *Crisis in the Classroom* propelled open education into the public eye as the answer to the problems of American education. More than that, he wrote, open education was a social panacea, an antidote to the collapse of "meaning and purpose in our lives." Only six years earlier, Silberman had written that intellectual discipline must be the lever of racial equality in American schools. Keenly responsive to cultural trends, he now decided that what American schools most needed was freedom from intellectual discipline. Funded by the Carnegie Corporation of New York, Silberman castigated the public schools as "grim, joyless places" and averred that the central problem of American education was its "mindlessness," its "slavish adherence to the timetable and lesson plan." The nation's "oppressive" public schools, Silberman wrote, should be replaced by the informal education found in the British infant schools. For high schools, he proposed student freedom to decide what courses to take, which courses should be offered, how to be evaluated, how to spend large blocs of unscheduled time, and how to dress.[43]

Although Silberman's encomium to student freedom was generally received with adulatory praise, some reviewers were skeptical. James Koerner, a critic of American education, said that, contra Silberman's claims, large numbers of American elementary schools were as informal and free as any schools in England ("Far from being obsessed with what in the trade is called the cognitive at the expense of the affective, they are regarded by many people, especially parents, as entirely too permissive and undirected.") He objected to Silberman's effort to inflict his preferred model of progressivism "on a widespread scale on parents who have no choice in the matter." No one would object if such schools were voluntary, wrote Koerner, but "Silberman's prescription admits of nothing so modest. He has seen the future and it works. He makes clear that nothing short of an overhaul of the whole educational system will do."[44]

Even more scathing was sociologist Amitai Etzioni, who said that Silberman had offered an impractical and misguided utopian vision. "No society could function," he maintained, "if all its members acted as selfishly as those who seek to maximize their freedoms." Challenging Silberman's optimistic view of human nature, Etzioni argued that children do not naturally educate themselves but need systematic encouragement and guidance, whether they come from permissive, privileged homes or from poor, disadvantaged ones. Nor did he think it reasonable to expect that children from so many divergent starting points would all benefit from precisely the same school structure.[45]

But there was no stopping this bandwagon. By 1970, the open education movement had become a full-blown crusade with hordes of avid followers. State education departments, federal agencies, schools of education, magazines, foundations, and schools enlisted in the cause of freedom for the student. Teams of American educators crossed the Atlantic to observe the revolution in British infant schools. The state commissioners of education in New York and Vermont declared themselves in favor of the movement (and the latter eventually became the chancellor of the New York City schools). Numerous books and articles extolling open education were published in the early 1970s. Across the nation, school officials established open classrooms, knocked down the walls between classrooms (which was another way of interpreting the meaning of "open" education), or designed new school buildings without walls. In high schools, the requirements for graduation were reduced, course electives were expanded, and traditional subjects were broken up into "minicourses."

→ → ← ←

Despite the seeming triumph of open education, some radical writers concluded that the schools could not be reformed because the *very idea* of "school" *was* the problem. Prominent among such freethinkers were George Leonard and Ivan Illich.

In 1968, Leonard, a journalist at *Look* magazine, published a best-selling book, *Education and Ecstasy,* in which he condemned the usual villains: grades, tests, competition, honors, and "right answers." Schools, he argued, were designed to squelch learning and create "a generation of joyless drudges." The true aim of education was "freedom, self-expression, and the ecstatic moment." He fantasized a campus in 2001 where children would be free to come "when and if they please," and "to go and do *anything* they wish that does not hurt someone else." The school of the future, he said, would consist of a series of "learning environments," fabulous domes that utilized sensory bombardment, computers, brain-wave analysis, mind-expanding activities, and other strategies to make learning "ecstatic." Leonard envisaged education from the perspective of the human potential movement, with its interest in self-awareness, meditation, brain-wave patterns, biofeedback, and encounter groups. These "affective" concerns, he believed, would soon replace the schools' traditional emphasis on the "cognitive" or "the old subject-matter entrapment." In fact, Leonard's school of the future seemed infinitely more threatening to individuals' personal freedom than the old-fashioned school where the teacher had had only a hickory stick, not the technological capacity for mind control.[46]

In 1971, Ivan Illich recommended the abolition of formal schooling in his book *Deschooling Society.* Universal schooling, he complained, was a government-funded scam that protected the jobs of bureaucrats and teachers. He endorsed economist Milton Friedman's proposal for school vouchers, with funds flowing directly to parents, who would then be able to purchase the schooling of their choice from any provider of education. Illich wanted to disestablish "the monopoly of the school." The more that government spent on schools, he insisted, the more destructive they were. He compared schools to jails or asylums, where the goal was mind-control and "behavioral modification," where students were indoctrinated with society's values and suffered "spiritual suicide," and where teachers acted as therapists and custodians.[47]

✦ ✦ ✦ ✦

Even as the radical critics of the schools spun out their apocalyptic and utopian visions of the future, the political climate shifted in the mid-1970s as the military draft ended and the Vietnam War wound down. The groundswell of enthusiasm for open education and other radical reforms dissipated in the face of a "back-to-basics" movement among parents and legislators alike.

If people who wrote books were responsible for the nation's educational system, the nation's public schools would probably have been eliminated or turned into versions of Summerhill. But no matter how successful their books and articles, education writers did not speak for the nation's parents or the American public in general. The public never endorsed the campaign for maximum student freedom; in a Gallup Poll of 1969, lack of discipline was named as the schools' leading problem. Some school districts created alternative schools in response to parents who wanted their children to attend a "fundamental" school that emphasized traditional academics, a dress code, and good behavior, but that was not enough to quell public demands for accountability. Most states established minimum competency tests in the basic skills in the mid- to late 1970s; nearly half of them required students to pass these tests to graduate from high school. Such tests focused schools on teaching the basic skills, hastening the demise of open education but doing nothing to raise standards beyond the minimums tested or to revive liberal learning in the schools.

The open education movement collapsed not only because of public opposition but because of its own internal flaws. Joseph Featherstone, whose articles had propelled the movement, worried as early as 1971 that it had turned into a fad. After visiting many open classrooms, he reported that "the best are as good as anything I've seen in England; the worst are a shambles."[48]

A cautionary note was sounded in 1972 by Roland S. Barth, a Massachusetts principal who was one of the most energetic proponents of open education. In his book *Open Education and the American School,* Barth described his own disastrous effort to introduce open education to two inner-city public schools with mainly black enrollments. Hired as instructional coordinator, he brought with him six teachers trained in the principles of open education. The teachers placed their desks at the rear of the classroom and organized learning centers for the children. The children were expected to select their own activities, while the teacher moved from group to group and child to child, offering encouragement. The children were supposed to exercise responsibility in leaving the classroom at will to use the bathroom or water fountain.

Within three months, however, the open education program had been abandoned. The teachers' desks were restored to the front of the classroom, the children's desks were in rows, and they were grouped by ability levels in reading and mathematics. The teachers assigned daily homework and issued hall passes for the bathroom and water fountain. The program succumbed to the resistance of both children and parents. The multitude of choices confused the children; the more options were available, the less they were able to follow through on any one of them and the more disruptive they became. Children "ganged up by tens and twenties outside the bathrooms and at the water fountains. A teacher would turn his back on a class, to find only three of twenty-five young-sters left in the room when he turned around again." The children de-manded "teacher-imposed order" and rejected teachers' attempts to shift the responsibility for learning to them.[49]

Barth admitted glumly that the children wanted stability and evi-dence of concern from their teachers: "The open classrooms and their teachers provided neither. . . . Children tested and abused every teacher who was attempting to run an unfamiliar classroom, until the teacher de-manded conventional order or was run out and another came to take his place."[50] The parents of the schools' black students were outraged when they visited classes, heard the noise level, and saw the children misbe-having without being corrected by the teachers. The parents feared that the experiment would deny their children the very education that had made the white teachers successful. They wanted their children to get the discipline, instruction, and structure that would make them as suc-cessful as their teachers. At the end of the year, the experiment in open education was terminated, along with all of the open educators.

In the introduction to Barth's sadder-but-wiser book, Featherstone wrote, "I'm growing wary of slogans like open education. So is Barth. I think they may do more harm than good. Currently I'm seeking to enlist everybody in favor of open, informal schooling into a movement whose one slogan will be a demand for decent schools." Featherstone added, "There ought to be more of a question about anybody's right to impose an educational program on the children of parents who find the program philosophically repugnant." This was a question that few proponents of open education had considered, because they assumed that everyone wanted or should want what they wanted.[51]

Donald A. Myers, part of a team that evaluated open classrooms in New York State, wrote in 1974 that "open education appears all but dead in America." It had died, he said, not only because it had not improved student achievement but because it had been oversold by yellow journalists and irresponsible evangelists. "The time has come in American education," he declared, "when teachers should stage a walkout when education evangelists" propose innovations that have not been validated by careful research over a long period of time. Instead of being paid and applauded, these hucksters should be sent packing and "should be thankful they are not jailed as would representatives of a pharmaceutical house for dispensing a drug before it had been tested." Myers disparaged those who wanted to dispense with any curriculum, to turn teachers into "unobtrusive valets," and to make learning into play. Why were so many American educators, he wondered, reluctant to acknowledge that "writing a sentence, speaking clearly, playing the piano, or learning inferential statistics, is simply difficult work?"[52]

Lisa Delpit, an African-American educator who had taught in inner-city Philadelphia in the early 1970s, worried about the effects of open education on poor children. Having imbibed the doctrines of open education in her undergraduate teacher-training courses, she created an informal classroom and watched as her black students lagged behind. Over her six years as a teacher, she found herself reluctantly becoming more traditional, more like the nuns who had educated her in Catholic school, and she observed a steady improvement in her students' skills. Then she went to graduate school, where she mastered the latest progressive teaching technique, the "writing process," which taught her not to correct her students' errors and not to teach skills but to concentrate on "fluency" (that is, just getting one's thoughts on paper). When she visited Philadelphia, a fellow black teacher railed about the inanity of the "writing process": "Our kids *are* fluent. What they need are the skills that will get them into college. . . . This is just another one of those racist ploys to keep our kids out. White kids learn how to write a decent sentence. Even if they don't teach them in school, their parents make sure they get what they need. But what about our kids? They don't get it at home and they spend all their time in school learning to be fluent." Delpit realized that the progressive white teachers thought they were freeing black students from a "racist educational system" by allowing them to express themselves without learning to read, write, or speak correctly. She realized that the students would not be able to enter the mainstream of society without these skills.[53]

The disappearance of open education as a movement, a rallying cry, and a slogan did not mean that American elementary classrooms reverted to rigid, formal practices. Most had been influenced by different varieties of progressive education since the 1920s. Most teachers had been trained in informal methods and knew nothing of "traditional" methods or rote learning. By the late 1970s, it would have been difficult—more likely impossible—to find either a college of education or a state department of education that favored formal methods. The traditional elementary classes in most American school districts were informal and already contained many, if not most, of the elements of open education. By the 1940s, activities, projects, and field trips had been incorporated into daily practice by most teachers, even those who considered themselves "traditional"; fixed rows of desks had long since been replaced by portable furniture. The valid practices of open education had long predated the movement and survived its demise.

The nation's high schools responded to the cultural upheavals and pedagogical turbulence of the late 1960s and early 1970s by cutting back graduation requirements, expanding electives, eliminating dress codes, and easing disciplinary rules. To placate students' demands for freedom, high schools reduced their behavioral expectations and their willingness to act *in loco parentis*. Teachers who had entered the classroom to avoid being drafted for military service in Vietnam were sympathetic to students' demands for freedom from dress rules and course requirements, even if the demands were voiced by only a handful of students. So were the new teachers who had studied the writings of the radical critics in their education courses and earned their degrees by passing examinations to demonstrate that they understood the critics' message. As teachers entered the classroom who had been college students during the time of campus upheavals, the education profession accepted the critics' claims that schools should not judge students, should not pressure them, and should allow them to decide what to study and how to behave. Slowly but surely, the schools withdrew from their responsibility to teach knowledge, good conduct, and appropriate behavior.

THE LEGACY OF THE SIXTIES

In 1975, the state of the nation's schools became a national political issue with the revelation in the press that scores on the Scholastic Aptitude Test (SAT) for college admission had fallen sharply since 1963–64. The College Entrance Examination Board, in charge of this important test for large numbers of college-bound students, appointed a blue-ribbon panel to investigate the decline. Its report in 1977 identified the likely causes of the score decline, including racial diversification of the test-taking pool (the assumption being that students who were not white were not as well prepared to meet the same standards as those who were), political upheavals (the war in Vietnam, political assassinations, and Watergate), as well as the influence of television and changes in the family (more divorces, more working mothers). But the panel noted that changes in the schools had also undermined academic achievement. An expansion of elective courses had been accompanied by a decline in enrollments in basic academic courses; between 1971 and 1973, for example, English enrollments had declined by 11 percent, as enrollments in electives had grown rapidly. To take another example, the number of schools in Massachusetts offering courses in filmmaking and mass media had increased, while the number offering junior-year courses in English and world history had fallen. In California, enrollments in basic

English and composition courses had plummeted in the early 1970s, while enrollments in electives had nearly doubled.[54]

The blue-ribbon panel observed ruefully that "Absenteeism formerly considered intolerable is now condoned. An 'A' or 'B' means a good deal less than it used to. Promotion from one grade to another has become almost automatic. Homework has apparently been cut about in half." Textbooks intended for the eleventh grade were being written at what had previously been considered a ninth- to tenth-grade vocabulary level, and the proportion of pictures in them had risen. Reviewing the evidence, the SAT panel concluded that "less thoughtful and critical reading is now being demanded and done" and that "careful writing has apparently about gone out of style." The high schools had reduced their requirements and lowered their expectations at the same time that the student body was becoming more diverse, with larger proportions of African-American and Hispanic students. This response was similar to the situation in the 1930s, when high schools had increased the number of nonacademic programs and curricula as the proportion of low-income white students had increased.[55]

The College Board's report was followed by equally gloomy commentaries on the state of foreign languages, mathematics, and science in the schools. In 1979, a commission appointed by President Jimmy Carter concluded that "Americans' incompetence in foreign languages is nothing short of scandalous, and it is becoming worse." High school enrollments in foreign languages had dropped sharply, from 24 percent in 1965 to only 15 percent in the late 1970s. Only one of every twenty high school students took as much as a second year of foreign language study. The near collapse of foreign language enrollments in high school followed the colleges' decision to cease requiring the subject for admission. In 1966, 34 percent of colleges had required foreign language study for admission, but a decade later only 8 percent did. In 1980, a presidential commission reviewing the condition of science and engineering education complained about "a general lowering of standards and expectations" in the schools, low enrollments in advanced mathematics and science courses, and the weakening of college entrance requirements.[56]

In 1983, Clifford Adelman, a researcher at the U.S. Department of

Education, analyzed the transcripts of high school graduates from 1964 to 1981. He concluded that during this period there had been a "systematic devaluation of academic (and some vocational) courses." High school students were spending less time in academic courses and more time in credit-bearing nonacademic courses. The curriculum had become "diffused and fragmented." Enrollments in the "general track" had jumped "from 12.0 percent in the late 1960s to 42.5 percent in the late 1970s," said Adelman, and the general track had become "the dominant student track in high school." Neither academic nor vocational, the general track consisted of courses such as driver education, general shop, remedial studies, consumer education, training for marriage and adulthood, health education, typing, and home economics.[57]

Another study by researchers at the U.S. Department of Education in 1984 compared high school graduates in the classes of 1972 and 1980. They found that over this eight-year period, test scores in verbal and mathematical skills had fallen, the amount of time spent on homework had declined, and grade inflation had increased. The percentage of seniors taking an academic curriculum had fallen from 46 percent in 1972 to 38 percent in 1980, and the percentage who had had to take remedial mathematics in high school had grown sevenfold during this period, from 4 to 30 percent. Nearly three quarters of the students thought their high school should have put more emphasis on basic academic subjects. But despite this array of negative indicators, the graduates of 1980 had "higher self-esteem" than their peers in 1972 and were more likely to believe that they had the ability to complete college.[58]

Taken together, it was a discouraging picture of a nation that had allowed electivism to dominate its high schools. In 1922, the federal government had counted some 175 different courses available in American high schools; by 1973, the number of courses available in high schools across the nation exceeded 2,100. Using their newfound freedom, high school students were opting out of rigorous courses and selecting easier alternatives. Highly motivated students continued to take advanced courses, but few others did. The egalitarian role of the high school was severely diminished, since the best students continued to be well prepared while the demands on and expectations of average and weak students were very low. As a result of the laissez-faire policies of the 1970s, American students were taking fewer courses, studying less, and learning less. During the 1970s, scores on standardized tests fell steadily, bottoming out in the early 1980s.[59]

The increase of permissive practices in school and at home accelerated other social trends that were even more ominous than the sinking test scores. The changes in "the adolescent society" that James Coleman had written about in 1961 were startling. He had observed then that adults were withdrawing from their responsibility for monitoring the character and civic behavior of young people, leaving them without adequate supervision and without any moral benchmarks. During the 1960s and 1970s, the rates of drug and alcohol use among teenagers soared, as did homicide deaths, suicide deaths, and out-of-wedlock births. During this period the schools experienced increasing difficulties in maintaining discipline, and students' disrespect for teachers became commonplace.[60]

Schools contributed to students' misbehavior by emphasizing students' rights but not their responsibilities. The dilution of academic and behavioral standards involved not just test scores but character issues. Many common practices in the schools—grade inflation, social promotion, lowered standards—taught students not to value hard work, personal effort, diligence, and perseverance. Allowing students to turn their assignments in late or not at all taught them that personal responsibility was unimportant. The reduction in homework not only shortened the amount of time that students spent reading, writing, and practicing their schoolwork but reduced the level of self-discipline that was expected of them. Such changes, while affecting all students, were especially pernicious for African-American students, who did not get the rigorous, high-quality education that they needed and that advocates such as W. E. B. Du Bois, William C. Bagley, Isaac Kandel, and Kenneth Clark had called for.

Changes in the curriculum in pursuit of relevance accentuated narcissistic themes. Social studies courses focused on immediate personal and social issues; chronological history and civic knowledge, which required students to think about worlds larger than their own acquaintance, were relegated to minor roles in social studies departments.

"Values clarification" courses, which encouraged students to make their own decisions about whether to use drugs or engage in other dangerous behaviors, proliferated. English became "English language arts," with more attention to self-expression and social issues than to classic literature. The study of heroes, once popular among students in search of models to emulate, fell into disfavor. In an effort to promote self-esteem and group identity, schools reduced their once-customary attention to the values of self-restraint, self-discipline, and humility.

All things considered, the hedonistic, individualistic, anarchic spirit of the sixties was good for neither the educational mission of the schools nor the intellect, health, and well-being of young people.

11

In Search of Standards

By the early 1980s, there was growing concern about the quality of the
nation's schools. The sustained assault on the academic curriculum in
the late 1960s and early 1970s had taken its toll. In 1980, the Gannett
newspaper chain sent investigative reporters into twenty-two schools in
nine states, where they discovered that academic credit was offered for
courses such as cheerleading, student government, and mass media. In
the average school, students had only three hours each day of instructional time; students spent most of their time, even in their academic
classes, on nonacademic activities. A teacher of "radio-TV" in Sacramento said, "Teachers need to get away from the attitude of teaching
specific subjects and start teaching values and learning abilities. The
kids will pick up knowledge on their own." In 1981, an editorial writer at
The Washington Post expressed concern that "American education is in a
fearsome decline . . . schools have been expecting less and students
have been learning less."[1]

In California in the early 1980s, the only statewide requirement for
high school graduation was two years of physical education. A study
conducted at Stanford University in 1983 found that high school students in California were assigned to four different tracks. The largest
proportion, 45 percent, was in the general track, where the typical student took courses such as typing, cultural awareness, homemaking, be-

ginning restaurant management, food for singles, exploring childhood, and clothing.[2] Researchers supported by the California Business Round-table concluded in 1982 that students' performance had declined because of lowered expectations: "Instruction is often aimed at the slowest learners, bright students are not challenged, and disadvantaged students and minorities are too often made to understand that little is expected of them." Remediation and grade inflation had increased; not only were the school day and school year getting shorter, but fewer than one fifth of high school seniors reported completing even a single homework assignment each week.[3]

In a study of three large comprehensive high schools in the late 1970s, Philip A. Cusick of Michigan State University described institutions in which learning was a minor goal, as compared to maintaining order and keeping students satisfied. While trying to cater to "the needs" of every student, teachers were free to teach whatever they wanted and students were left free to study whatever they wanted. Lacking any consensus about curriculum, the schools embarked "on an endless search for elective subjects to attract and interest students," such as "girl talk," "what's happening," "personal relations," and "man-to-man." In addition, graduation credits were conferred for activities such as yearbook, student council, band, and glee club. Faced with an array of alluring electives, motivated youth made reasonable choices, but students from disadvantaged families were short-changed. The schools, Cusick concluded, had "simply given up on any attempt to exert any moral authority relative to the student's education."[4]

In 1981, the Southern Regional Education Board (a voluntary organization of fourteen southern states) complained that the curriculum of the high schools had become fragmented during the 1960s, when educators had responded to demands for "relevance" by adding an array of trivial electives. In reaction to the excesses of that era, several southern states had adopted minimum competency tests in the 1970s, and the SREB warned about "the dangers of minimums becoming norms." The southern states pledged to raise standards for students and teachers and "to challenge all students to attain higher levels of achievement," not just minimum competence.[5]

The decline of Scholastic Aptitude Test (SAT) scores attracted intense press attention. After reaching a high point in 1963, average SAT scores had dropped steadily to a historic low in 1980. The average verbal score had fallen from a high of 478 in 1963 to the 420s in the late 1970s, where it remained for the balance of the century. The average math score had dropped from a high of 502 in 1963 to a low of 466 in 1980 and then began a slow rebound in the early 1980s, returning almost to its previous high level by the mid-1990s. The number of students who scored over 600 on the verbal portion of the SAT fell from 116,585 in 1972 to 66,292 in 1983, from 11.3 percent of all SAT test-takers to 6.9 percent of them; on the mathematics portion of the test, the number of high-scoring students dropped from 182,602 to 143,566 in the same years, from 17.9 percent of test-takers to 14.5 percent. Students' scores on most other national and state tests also fell in the 1970s. There were many likely reasons for the decline, including a weakening of families and communities and the distracting effects of television, but there was also the stubborn fact that students were not taking as many academic courses as they had before the mid-1960s. The test score declines appeared to parallel or follow course enrollment declines. In addition, studies found that the verbal difficulty of schoolbooks had dropped significantly over recent decades, so students encountered a smaller, easier vocabulary.[6]

More and more students were going to college, even though they were not taking the courses necessary to prepare for college-level studies. By 1982, 50 percent of high school graduates went to college immediately after graduation, but only 9 percent of them had taken four years of English, two years of a foreign language, and three years each of social studies, science, and mathematics.[7]

The old idea of the educational ladder had been revived, at least in form if not in reality. Students could get into college, but, lacking adequate literacy and numeracy, many enrolled in remedial courses or dropped out. Remediation in college had become commonplace: by 1983–84, most institutions of higher education offered remedial courses in reading, writing, and mathematics. Large numbers of students who entered college did not finish; between 1984 and 1987, nearly half of white students and two thirds of black students left college without earning a degree.[8]

For many students, the colleges were expected to do what the high schools had not done. Opening the doors of the college to unprepared students was a sham sort of democratization. Real democracy in education would have required the public schools to make sure that every high school graduate gained the literacy, numeracy, and other skills necessary for technical occupations and higher education. If there remained any commitment to sociologist Lester Frank Ward's claim that all people in a democracy required equal access to knowledge or to William C. Bagley's assertion that all young Americans were equally deserving of a liberal education, there was reason for grave concern about the rush to supply credentials instead of a solid education.

A Nation at Risk

In the early 1980s, there was a palpable sense that something had to be done to improve educational standards. The galvanizing event was the publication of *A Nation at Risk* in 1983. This was a report by the National Commission on Excellence in Education, whose members had been appointed by Terrell Bell, secretary of education in the Reagan administration. When Ronald Reagan had campaigned for the presidency in 1980, he had pledged to abolish the U.S. Department of Education, which had been established in the closing days of the Carter administration. Given President Reagan's disdain for a federal role in education, it was scarcely to be expected that his administration would be responsible for a report that redefined the politics of education for the rest of the twentieth century.

A Nation at Risk was a landmark of education reform literature. Countless previous reports by prestigious national commissions had been ignored by the national press and the general public. *A Nation at Risk* was different. Written in stirring language that the general public could understand, the report warned that the schools had not kept pace with the changes in society and the economy and that the nation would suffer if education were not dramatically improved for all children. It also asserted that lax academic standards were correlated with lax behavioral standards and that neither should be ignored.

411

A Nation at Risk was a call to action. "Our nation is at risk," the commission warned, and "the educational foundations of our society are presently being eroded by a rising tide of mediocrity that threatens our very future as a Nation and a people. . . . If an unfriendly foreign power had attempted to impose on America the mediocre educational performance that exists today, we might well have viewed it as an act of war."[9] The urgency of the report's rhetoric made legislators, school board members, parents, and the nation's press sit up and listen.

America could no longer rely for its future success on its natural resources and its isolation from the rest of the world, said the commission. Global interdependence meant that "knowledge, learning, information, and skilled intelligence are the new raw materials of international commerce. . . . Learning is the indispensable investment required for success" in the new information age. Those who were poorly educated faced bleak prospects in the emerging American economy; the strength of the nation's social fabric depended on improving education. The commission warned that

> individuals in our society who do not possess the levels of skill, literacy, and training essential to this new era will be effectively disenfranchised, not simply from the material rewards that accompany competent performance, but also from the chance to participate fully in our national life. A high level of shared education is essential to a free, democratic society and to the fostering of a common culture, especially in a country that prides itself on pluralism and individual freedom.[10]

In contrast to the national commissions in the 1930s and 1940s, *A Nation at Risk* did not propose differentiated education. It did not suggest that children should be sorted by their likely occupational futures, as had the NEA's Cardinal Principles in 1918. Instead, it took as given the promise that "All, regardless of race or class or economic status, are entitled to a fair chance and to the tools for developing their individual powers of mind and spirit to the utmost. This promise means that all children by virtue of their own efforts, competently guided, can hope to attain the mature and informed judgment needed to secure gainful employment, and to manage their own lives, thereby serving not only their own interests but also the progress of society itself."[11]

The commission held that four aspects of schooling needed to change: content, expectations, time, and teaching. The content of the high school program had been "homogenized, diluted, and diffused" and had turned into a "cafeteria-style curriculum in which the appetizers and desserts can easily be mistaken for the main courses." Students were faced with a "curricular smorgasbord, combined with extensive student choice" of studies. At the same time, expectations—meaning grades, examinations, graduation requirements, and college entrance requirements—had been considerably weakened by grade inflation, minimum competency examinations, and lowered requirements for high school graduation and college entry. No state required foreign language study for high school graduation, and most states required only one year each of science and mathematics. American students spent less time in academic studies than students in many other nations, where the school day and school year were longer; learning to cook or drive often garnered as much credit toward graduation as learning chemistry or history. The standards for teachers also needed to be sharply upgraded: many teachers had been drawn from the bottom quarter of college graduates, most teacher education programs were heavily weighted toward "methods" courses rather than academic subjects, teachers' salaries were too low, and half of all new teachers in mathematics and science were not qualified to teach these subjects.[12]

The commission recommended that all high school graduates study "the new basics": four years of English; three years each of mathematics, science, and social studies; and a half year of computer science. Those who were college-bound, it proposed, should also study a foreign language for at least two years.

Because there was widespread public concern about the schools, the report drew newspaper headlines across the nation. In direct response to *A Nation at Risk,* many states created task forces and commissions to appraise their graduation standards, curriculum, the length of their school day and year, and the qualifications and compensation of their teachers.[13]

Critics insisted that the commission had overstated the "crisis" and

413

that there had not been a decline in academic performance. In a sense, the critics may have been right. Considering the efforts of many decades to reduce the academic demands of the schools and to divert youngsters away from the academic curriculum, it would have been more accurate to describe the low expectations in the schools as a chronic, long-term condition rather than a "crisis."[14]

The good thing about militant reports such as *A Nation at Risk* is that they may wake up the public and stir a demand for change. The bad thing is that a report is only words, and words are often insufficient to overcome deeply ingrained practices. Even as the National Commission on Excellence in Education set out a compelling case for raising academic standards for all students, teacher education programs continued to stress pedagogy courses rather than academic skills and knowledge. For example, the Southern Regional Education Board reported in 1985 that graduates of teacher preparation programs in fourteen southern states were not receiving a solid liberal arts education. Future teachers—especially elementary teachers—were taking too many methods courses, too many low-level courses, and far fewer academic courses than graduates who majored in arts and sciences. Future elementary teachers were typically spending 65 percent more time in education courses than certification requirements demanded; 49 percent of their time was spent in education and physical education courses. One upper-level education course, the study wryly noted, was called "Lettering, Posters, and Displays in the School Program." Most future teachers never studied a foreign language, a physical science, or economics. Most future teachers completed mathematics courses that were either remedial or low-level courses designed specifically for teachers.[15]

Similarly, researchers at Arizona State University in 1984 noted that future teachers at that institution were disproportionately enrolled in pedagogy classes and low-level introductory courses. Half of future high school teachers majored either in physical education or home economics; all future elementary school teachers and special education teachers majored in pedagogy, and nearly half of them also took a minor in education. Because of this heavy concentration on pedagogy, future teachers got the equivalent of a three-semester college education in substantive subjects, which were mainly freshman-level courses. The authors, both members of the faculty at the university's school of education, complained that this heavy emphasis on pedagogy inevitably produced teachers who lacked in-depth knowledge of academic subjects.[16]

CAN SCHOOLS MAKE A DIFFERENCE?

The response to A Nation at Risk *revealed a major fault line in American* education: On one side were those who believed that the schools had little influence on children's ability to learn as compared to children's heredity, families, and social environment. On the other were those who believed that schools had the responsibility to educate *all* children regardless of their social circumstances or home life. This debate had raged throughout the twentieth century, appearing in different guises in different eras.

In 1966, the sociologist James S. Coleman had led a major federal study (*Equality of Educational Opportunity,* known afterward as "the Coleman report") that had concluded that the schools were relatively impotent in shaping children's life chances, as compared to the influence of their family and schoolmates. Coleman had maintained that the social composition of a school's student body was more significant for black achievement than a school's facilities or programs. For the next decade, Coleman advocated racial integration as "the most consistent mechanism for improving the quality of education of disadvantaged children," as long as these children were merged into a school where the majority were white, middle-class students. His study provided a powerful rationale for court-ordered busing to achieve racial balance. During the 1970s, most social scientists concurred that integration mattered but that otherwise "the schools don't make a difference," which implicitly devalued the importance of the curriculum and standards of learning.[17]

On the other side of the debate was a small number of educators who insisted that, under the right circumstances, schools could educate nearly all children to higher standards than had ever been achieved in the past, no matter what their race or social background. Psychologist John

B. Carroll of Harvard University had proposed in 1963 that almost any child could learn whatever a school expected if he spent enough time learning, if the task was clearly explained, and if the student persevered until he or she mastered the task. Differences in aptitude, Carroll had suggested, represented differences in "learning rates." With this insight, Carroll had repudiated the conventional wisdom in American education, which assumed that children's aptitudes were as fixed as their IQs.[18]

Carroll's work inspired Benjamin S. Bloom of the University of Chicago to develop a highly individualized program called "mastery learning." Bloom rejected the conventional view among educational psychologists that there were "good learners" and "poor learners." Like Carroll, he held that there were "faster learners" and "slower learners" and that the differences between them could be substantially narrowed if the slower learners received extra time and help. Children's capacity to learn was highly malleable, he argued in 1976, if they were helped before they fell behind their classmates. With "favorable learning conditions," students would become very similar in their ability and motivation to learn. Bloom proposed that schools cease sorting students based on their assumed future roles and instead take responsibility for developing the abilities of all children.[19]

Ronald Edmonds, a researcher and senior assistant to the chancellor of the New York City public schools, had maintained in 1980, "We can, whenever, and wherever we choose, successfully teach all children whose schooling is of interest to us. We already know more than we need to accomplish this task." Edmonds asserted that poor black children would learn if there was sufficient will to educate them. Based on his studies of successful schools in impoverished communities, he proposed that effective schools had a strong leader, high expectations for all students, an orderly environment, a relentless focus on basic academic skills, and regular testing to monitor pupils' progress. Edmonds disagreed with those who believed that school achievement was wholly determined by family background as well as those who believed that only racial balance could produce quality education. He warned, "Demographic desegregation must take a backseat to instructional reform or we will remain frustrated by a continuing and widening gap between white and black pupil performance in desegregated schools."[20] Edmonds seemed destined to play a large role in the national debate about education, but he died suddenly in 1983 at the age of forty-eight.

Despite the qualms of educators like Edmonds, the federal courts continued to order racial balancing of schools, even where there was no white middle-class majority, thus vitiating Coleman's original rationale about the value of integrating poor black children among advantaged white peers. In 1975, however, Coleman recanted his views on integration, concluding that court-ordered busing was causing white flight and leading to more racial segregation in urban districts. Although he was denounced by his former allies for betraying the cause of integration, Coleman accurately described the negative effects of mandatory racial balancing. In 1978, he argued that desegregation frequently depressed blacks' achievement. He admitted that little was known about the reasons for this:

> But we do know that in many cases desegregation was implemented with little attention to its possible effects in increasing disorder, conflict, absence from school—only with attention to having the right numbers of the right colored bodies at specified schools, in order to comply with a desegregation edict that addressed itself to numbers alone. And the school system . . . has only a limited amount of attention. If that attention is focused on compliance with a court's edict or HEW administrative orders, then it must be less focused on educational goals.[21]

In a major federal study of public and private schools in 1981, Coleman reversed himself on the crucial issue of whether schools make a difference. He found that private schools, particularly Catholic schools, promoted higher academic achievement, regardless of students' background, because they provided a common academic curriculum and high academic expectations. Once again Coleman was denounced, this time by defenders of the public schools, for seeming to favor private and sectarian schools over public ones. Actually, Coleman's change of mind was good news for public education, for he showed that schools can make a large difference for poor children and that the students who achieve the most are those who take academic courses, do their homework, and apply themselves to their schoolwork.[22]

PRESCRIPTIONS FOR CHANGE

The conditions that led to the writing of A Nation at Risk *in 1983* prompted others to propose new answers to the problems of the schools. Reformers in the mid-1980s agreed that the public schools had become overwhelmed by too many responsibilities and had lost their focus as educating institutions responsible for the development of young minds.

In the same year that *A Nation at Risk* appeared, Theodore R. Sizer published *Horace's Compromise,* which called for major changes in the schools. Sizer, a former headmaster of the elite Phillips Andover Academy and former dean of the Harvard Graduate School of Education, denounced the "mediocre sameness," the low expectations, and the dull routinization of the typical comprehensive American high school. Authority should be ceded to those who work in schools, he maintained, instead of bureaucratic overseers. Students should exhibit mastery of their school work, instead of taking machine-scored standardized tests. Students should choose the school whose purposes they shared, instead of being assigned by administrative fiat. Most consequentially, he insisted that schools should attend to teaching students to use their minds well and to think seriously about what they had learned.[23]

Sizer was quickly recognized as the leading voice of contemporary American progressivism. His philosophy mingled John Dewey's respect for intellectual endeavor and Robert Hutchins's concern for intellectual habits and demonstrations of mastery. He eschewed the earlier versions of progressivism that had produced IQ testing, industrial education, and trivial electives. Unlike the progressives of the 1920s, he did not make a fetish of children's interests or disparage the importance of basic skills.[24]

Sizer created an organization called the Coalition of Essential Schools to advocate his minimalist reform ideas ("less is more" was the slogan he urged on schools). Among the schools that joined Sizer's new coalition was Deborah Meier's Central Park East in New York City, a progressive school founded in 1974 to demonstrate that it was possible to develop intellectual competence in all children. By the year 2000, Sizer's network enlisted more than 1,200 schools.[25]

Another major reform proposal came from E. D. Hirsch, Jr., a professor of English at the University of Virginia. In his best-selling 1987 book *Cultural Literacy,* Hirsch urged schools to pay greater attention to teaching not just generic skills, but knowledge. Like Lester Frank Ward, William T. Harris, and William C. Bagley, Hirsch recognized that knowledge is power and that access to knowledge is crucial in a democracy. The more a person knows, the more he or she is able to learn; knowledge builds on prior knowledge. Hirsch insisted that cultural literacy—knowledge of "the basic information needed to thrive in the modern world"—was the most important path to opportunity for disadvantaged children, "the only reliable way of combating the social determinism that now condemns them to remain in the same social and educational condition as their parents." An explicit curriculum, he argued, would promote social justice by distributing knowledge to all children.[26]

Like Isaac Kandel, who thought that schools should help every individual "share the culture of the world," Hirsch argued that the decline of shared knowledge harmed poor children. Those who did not have access to knowledge would be impaired in education and in life, he maintained. With his colleagues, historian Joseph Kett and physicist James Trefil from the University of Virginia, Hirsch developed an explicit list of important names, dates, ideas, and allusions that all students should learn, while acknowledging that the basic list would evolve as society evolved. The authors intended the list to define "the basic vocabulary of our culture." It was subsequently expanded to become a dictionary of cultural literacy and a best-selling series for parents, organized grade by grade.[27]

Critics caricatured the list and derided the idea of teaching specific facts as trivia. Hirsch's goal, however, was remarkably similar to the lists that progressive educator Carleton Washburne had assembled in the 1920s to teach children what they needed to know to be conversant with the culture in which they lived. After the success of his book, Hirsch established a foundation to create schools to teach "core knowledge." By 2000, there were about one thousand of these schools across the nation.[28]

THE MULTICULTURAL MOVEMENT

*At the very time when the public expected progress toward higher stan-*dards, American education was plunged into divisive controversies about how schools should respond to the growing racial and ethnic diversity of their pupils. Changes in the nation's immigration policies in the late 1960s had substantially increased the proportion of children from Latin America and Asia in American public schools.[29] From 1989 until the mid-1990s, schools were besieged by rancorous disputes about whether their racial or ethnic composition should determine what was taught, whether children's self-esteem and test scores would rise if they studied the achievements of their ancestral group, and whether too much time was spent in class on the history and culture of Europe and Western civilization.

The main effect of public brawls about multiculturalism was to divert attention from the urgent need to improve the quality of teaching and learning, a subject that was never as newsworthy as confrontational battles over race and ethnicity. When adults argued about such matters as which group had the greatest ancient culture and which race or ethnic group could claim credit for which inventions, the educational needs of children took a backseat. Forgotten, too, was the commonsense understanding that ideas, inventions, art, science, technology, and knowledge are usually the result of extensive cultural exchanges, indifferent to geographical and ethnic boundaries, and seldom the product of a single cultural group.

The debate about multiculturalism in education was not new when it burst upon the national consciousness in the late 1980s. A generation earlier, the civil rights movement had demanded racially integrated textbooks. In 1965, the "Dick and Jane" reading series had introduced a black family into its previously white suburban world. The Detroit school system required publishers to produce classroom materials realistically portraying children of different racial groups. In the 1970s, hundreds of colleges and universities established programs in black studies, ethnic studies, and women's studies. During the same decade, major organizations, such as the National Education Association and the American Association of Colleges of Teacher Education, endorsed multicultural education in the schools.[30]

By the late 1970s, American history textbooks had changed significantly. In her book *America Revised: History Schoolbooks in the Twentieth Century,* journalist Frances FitzGerald noted that once-standard heroes such as Captain John Smith, Daniel Boone, and Wild Bill Hickok had "all but disappeared," while "Poor Columbus" was "a minor character now, a walk-on in the middle of American history." Military leaders had "faded away, as old soldiers do, giving place to social reformers such as William Lloyd Garrison and Jacob Riis." The history textbooks no longer portrayed American society as homogeneous and getting better all the time but as "a patchwork of rich and poor, old and young, men and women, blacks, whites, Hispanics, and Indians" with persistent social problems and no obvious answers.[31]

The great public battles over multiculturalism in the schools occurred at least a decade after multiculturalism was already firmly established in universities, school curricula, and textbooks. What happened in the late 1980s was a conflict between two opposing definitions of the idea. One was cultural pluralism, the generally accepted view that students should learn about the experiences of many different racial and ethnic groups in the United States and the rest of the world. The other was ethnocentrism (or particularism), the belief that children from non-European minority groups should be taught about the accomplishments of their own ethnic group. Ethnocentrism seemed to be new but was actually an inverted form of racism that reversed the color of favored groups from white to non-white. These were two nearly opposite definitions of "multiculturalism": One supported a common culture, while the other disparaged it. One was pluralist and integrationist, the other ethnocentric and separatist.

In the late 1980s, multiculturalism became a hotly debated issue because of events on opposite coasts, largely in connection with states' efforts to revise their history curriculum.

In California, Bill Honig, who took office as superintendent of public instruction in 1982, pledged to promote higher standards and a traditional curriculum in literature, history, the sciences, and mathematics for all students. Under his direction, grade-by-grade curriculum frameworks were published for every subject. Honig took particular interest in the creation of a new history–social science framework. In the early grades, myths, legends, and biographies replaced the customary social studies curriculum of "expanding environments" (home/family/community) that had been standard fare across the nation since the 1930s. The study of world history was expanded from one year to three. History in sixth grade would be devoted to ancient civilizations in Mesopotamia, Egypt, Africa, Greece, and Rome. This was probably the first time that ancient history had been taught to large numbers of children anywhere in the nation since the 1940s. Seventh-graders in California would be expected to study the medieval world in Europe, Africa, the Americas, and Asia, and tenth-graders would study the modern world.

The framework incorporated a multicultural perspective within the context of *e pluribus unum:* "We are strong because we are united in a pluralistic society of many races, cultures, and ethnic groups," the state's history framework said. "We have built a great nation because we have learned to live in peace with each other, respecting each other's right to be different and supporting each other as members of a common community."[32] The framework's goals were both knowledge and intergroup respect; it did not demonize the United States, Europeans, or white males. The framework was adopted by the State Board of Education in 1987 (which endorsed it again in 1997).

On the other coast in the same year, New York State adopted a new social studies curriculum that had been reviewed by scores of teachers and prominent scholars. Like the California document, the New York curriculum stressed racial and ethnic diversity in American and world history. In the normal course of events, not many people would even have noticed that the state had promulgated a new social studies curriculum. However, in 1987, Thomas Sobol, the state's new commissioner of education, appointed a committee representing different minority groups to review the State Education Department's hiring policies and the state's curriculum.

In 1989, two years after the new state social studies curriculum had been approved, the committee released a blistering critique titled "A Curriculum of Inclusion." It accused the state of damaging the self-esteem of children of color by teaching "Eurocentrism" and "white nationalism" in its social studies curriculum, reflecting "deep-seated pathologies of racial hatred." This document might have gone unnoticed but for inflammatory public statements by its primary author, Leonard Jeffries, Jr., of the African-American studies department at the City College of New York, who called whites "the ice people" and Africans "the sun people" and complained about the large influence of Jews in the movie industry and the slave trade.[33]

The storm over the "curriculum of inclusion" drew attention to the phenomenon of Afrocentrism—the belief that Africa should be at the center of the education of black students. Afrocentric theorists asserted that Greeks and Europeans had "stolen" African ideas and achievements; African-American students, they held, would have higher self-esteem and academic achievement if their studies reflected the Afrocentric perspective—not just in history but in other subjects as well. Many inner-city schools adopted Afrocentric materials called the Portland Baseline Essays (published by the Portland, Oregon, school system), which demonstrated an Afrocentric approach to the teaching of history, mathematics, science, and other subjects.[34]

From this point forward, multiculturalism became a hopelessly muddled subject as critics and supporters used the same term to mean different things. The proposition that students should learn about the cultural and scientific achievements of people from many different racial and ethnic groups had been broadly accepted before the rise of the multicultural movement. But it was a large leap from that commonplace view to the idea that students, both in school and in university, should engage in celebratory, uncritical appreciations of their own group (but only if their group was non-European or female).

In 1990, historian Arthur Schlesinger, Jr., who had worked in the White House under President John F. Kennedy, criticized "A Curriculum of Inclusion" for urging that the study of history should be used to raise children's self-esteem. Schlesinger urged, "Let us by all means teach women's history, black history, Hispanic history. But let us teach them as history, not as a means of promoting group self-esteem." When the New York commissioner of education appointed a second commission to revise the state's social studies curriculum, Schlesinger was invited to serve as a member.[35]

When the second report was released in 1991, it spoke in more moderate language than its predecessor, but Schlesinger again dissented forcefully from what he believed were its central assumptions: "that ethnicity is the defining experience for most Americans, that ethnic ties are permanent and indelible, that the division into ethnic groups establishes the basic structure of American society and that a main objective of public education should be the protection, strengthening, celebration and perpetuation of ethnic origins and identities." He warned, "I do not believe that we should magnify ethnic and racial themes at the expense of the unifying ideals that precariously hold our highly differentiated society together. The republic has survived and grown because it has maintained a balance between *pluribus* and *unum*. The report, it seems to me, is saturated with *pluribus* and neglectful of *unum*."[36]

The New York curriculum battle attracted extensive press coverage. Editorialists and columnists jumped into the fray, and *Time* magazine ran a cover story titled "Who Are We?" illustrated by a multiethnic fife-and-drum corps. Journalist Andrew Sullivan reported in *The New Republic* on an Afrocentric conference in Atlanta where one speaker had described Greek culture as "vomit," Leonard Jeffries, Jr., had denounced multicultural education as "mental genocide," and an Afrocentric educator from California had said, "The people in power want to maintain a myth: that our common culture is multicultural. . . . But the common culture of America is a system based on racism and hierarchy. . . . Inclusion is inclusion in somebody else's story."[37]

The press coverage demonstrated that the ideological battle was about far more than curriculum; it was about competing visions of American society. The advocates of a common culture sought not to merge or eliminate distinct cultures but to assert an overarching national identity based on common democratic principles that encompassed all citizens. The advocates of racial and ethnic distinctiveness vigorously opposed any effort to teach a common culture, fearing that it would weaken their racial and ethnic identities. The debate had resounded for generations in American history because of the diverse racial, national, and ethnic origins of the population. In each generation, its resolution has depended on a common commitment to *e pluribus unum* and an implicit agreement to honor the legitimate claims of both sides of the equation.

Some black writers defended the idea of a multicultural common culture. David Nicholson, an editor at *The Washington Post,* worried that the latest educational trend was a "dangerous step toward the tribalization of our society and the making of our schools into educational Bantustans." He recognized that the Afrocentric movement was "a result of the tremendous disappointment many blacks feel in the post-civil-rights era" but wondered "whose vision will prevail—that of the nationalists and the zealots, or that of more reasonable people who still believe in a common American culture and shared national values." [38]

Henry Louis Gates, Jr., professor of Afro-American Studies at Harvard University, wrote that "The challenge facing America will be the shaping of a truly common public culture, one responsive to the long-silenced cultures of color. If we relinquish the ideal of America as a plural nation, we've abandoned the very experiment America represents." Gates also denounced the virulent anti-Semitism in the Afrocentric movement, especially the distribution of the Nation of Islam's scurrilous anti-Semitic tract accusing Jews of having played a major role in the slave trade. Orlando Patterson, a sociologist at Harvard University, warned that celebrations of multiculturalism might have the paradoxical effect of minimizing the large African-American contributions to America's common culture. African-Americans, he insisted, had most to gain by cherishing the common culture that they themselves "did so much to fashion." [39]

The controversy over multiculturalism and Afrocentrism was bitter and protracted in the public arena, but not in the schools, where the principles of inclusive multiculturalism were already widely accepted. The major issue in public schools across the nation was not whether to adopt multiculturalism but what form it would take. Teachers and administrators agreed that it was a good idea to add more materials about non-

European cultures in response to the growing numbers of children who traced their origins to Africa, Latin America, or Asia. The public schools had long since learned to adapt and bend when faced with controversy, and most public schools comfortably incorporated celebrations of new ethnic holidays, new heroes, and new customs into their curricula and calendar. That was the benign face of multiculturalism in the schools. Less well known were the baneful effects of multiculturalism (in combination with demands for gender equity) on publishers, who altered textbooks to include balanced representation of ethnic groups and genders, dropping classic selections that violated these guidelines. Similarly, publishers of standardized tests deleted questions that referred to sex roles, religion, death, the supernatural, evolution, criminal behavior, or any other subject that might give offense to anyone, whether from the political left or right. The resulting self-censorship by publishers of texts and tests impoverished the language and literature available to students.[40]

The Self-Esteem Movement

Behind the uproar about multiculturalism were two big facts and one big theory. Fact one was that the population was indeed changing, and educators wanted the schools to be more welcoming to children from diverse cultural backgrounds and to acknowledge the cultural riches of the civilizations of Africa, Asia, and Latin America. Fact two was that the achievement of African-American and Hispanic-American pupils continued to lag far behind that of European-American and Asian-American pupils. The big theory that many seized upon to resolve the yawning achievement gap was that low-performing students would achieve more if they had higher self-esteem and that the schools could promote higher self-esteem by encouraging children to feel good about their racial or ethnic identity. In short order, this theory evolved into a generalized belief that the schools should help all children develop higher self-esteem.

Since the 1930s, guidance professionals had maintained that students' mental health and personality adjustment depended on their sense of self-esteem. Many educators also held it as an article of faith that too much emphasis on academic achievement might impair students' self-esteem. By the 1980s, self-esteem was touted in professional literature as both a means and an end of education. Anything that might encourage higher academic standards—such as grades, standards, deadlines, homework, correction of grammar or spelling—was potentially a threat to students' self-esteem. These beliefs echoed the "needs of youth" movement of the 1930s.

Critics of the self-esteem movement maintained that children gained self-esteem by successfully meeting new challenges and that youngsters who lacked literacy and numeracy were unlikely to have a genuine sense of self-esteem, no matter how often they were encouraged to feel good about themselves. In 1985, psychologist Barbara Lerner wrote in *The American Educator,* the publication of the American Federation of Teachers, that too many teachers relied on the belief that self-esteem was "the master key to learning." She said that the ideology of *"feel-good-now* self-esteem" produced students who were narcissistic and egotistical and responded only to the pleasure principle. When students received ample praise, regardless of how much or how little they worked in school or how well or how poorly they behaved, they never learned to persevere in the face of obstacles or to tolerate frustration. Lerner contrasted *"feel-good-now* self-esteem" with *"earned* self-esteem," which was the result of productive effort, self-criticism, and perseverance.[41]

The AFT magazine reprinted Lerner's essay in 1996. Its editor wrote, "Well-intentioned and misguided notions about self-esteem have become, if anything, even more deeply embedded in the culture of many, many schools . . . and constitute one of the most serious threats to the movement to raise academic and disciplinary standards and improve the learning opportunities and life chances of our nation's children."[42]

The therapeutic view of self-esteem became embedded in the structure of the rudderless, multi-purpose comprehensive high school. In 1985, a major study described the American high school as "the shopping mall high school." High schools, said the authors, had become like educational malls, offering a vast array of courses in "a neutral environment where a do-your-own-thing attitude prevails. High schools take few stands on what is educationally or morally important."[43] In the "shopping mall high school," students were left on their own, free to study what they wanted and to do as much or as little work as they wished.

The consumer-oriented high school described in this study succeeded by accommodating demands, not by making them; learning and mastery, for example, were "just one among many consumer choices." Teachers were committed to the proposition that students should feel successful even when their schoolwork was poor. The authors noted, "Many teachers seem preoccupied by the psychological costs of failure and the therapeutic benefits of success." Consequently many of them "believe more in the value of self-esteem than in the value of what they teach. Mastery and success are like ships that pass in the night." Convinced that students were unable or unwilling to learn, teachers turned to "therapeutic ideals as their only tool. What such sympathy usually means in practice is the wholesale replacement of academic goals by therapeutic ones of self-esteem and feelings of success."[44]

The ideology of therapeutic self-esteem became a public issue in 1987, when Assemblyman John Vasconcellos persuaded the California legislature to create a Task Force to Promote Self-Esteem. Frequently ridiculed by nationally syndicated cartoonist Garry Trudeau, the task force published its report in 1990. Vasconcellos identified low self-esteem as the "root cause" of the nation's social problems, including educational failure, crime, violence, welfare dependency, substance abuse, teenage pregnancy, and child abuse. He predicted the eventual development of a "social vaccine" to raise self-esteem.[45]

Yet the research commissioned by the task force virtually demolished the rationale for direct teaching of self-esteem. Summing up the findings, Neil J. Smelser of the University of California at Berkeley pointed out that "one of the most disappointing aspects of every chapter in this volume . . . is how low the associations between self-esteem and its consequences are in research to date." Such associations, he reported, were "mixed, insignificant, or absent." Self-esteem proved to be difficult to define or measure, and it was equally difficult to establish a causal relationship between self-esteem and either negative or positive behaviors. Students with high achievement tended to have high self-esteem, but the latter may not have caused the former; it was equally plausible that students' self-esteem grew because they learned more.[46] In light of these findings, it appeared that improving students' academic skills might be the best way to raise *both* their self-esteem and their academic achievement.

Not until the mid-1990s did the tide of academic and public opinion turn against self-esteem as a cure-all for social, psychological, and educational ills. In 1995, psychologist William Damon of Brown University scathingly criticized the relentless "self-esteem boosting" that had become commonplace in the schools. His own daughter came home one day from kindergarten with an index card saying, "I'm terrific." Children were sure to distrust adults who dispensed such empty flattery, he argued. Children do not need false assurances, Damon insisted, but patient help to develop character and competence. They need guidance to learn valuable skills and knowledge from adults whose judgment they respect. "Like happiness," he advised, "self-esteem is a goal that cannot be pursued directly or for its own sake."[47]

In 1998, a team of social scientists challenged the widespread belief among educators that low self-esteem caused violent and aggressive behavior. They noted that aggressors such as playground bullies, members of street gangs, and "master race" ideologues "often think very highly of themselves." Those who have a "grandiose self-image" are likely to respond aggressively to criticism. Persons who are urged to think that they are "the greatest," in the absence of any concrete accomplishments, may develop narcissistic attitudes based on nothing but the desire to feel superior.[48] Stable self-esteem, as Damon had argued, is well founded in objective reality and the result of having done something to feel proud of, not of repeating slogans in praise of oneself.

THE STANDARDS MOVEMENT

In the 1980s and 1990s, globalization was transforming the American economy. The collapse of the Soviet Union and the end of the Cold War in 1989, coupled with the rapid development of new technologies, promoted international trade and communications. The number of low-wage jobs for unskilled workers declined as factories moved to Third World countries, where wage scales were far lower than in the United States. New technologies eliminated some unskilled jobs altogether and put a premium on well-educated workers who understood mathematics, science, and technology and were prepared both to exercise individual initiative and to work in teams.

Employers complained about the cost of teaching basic skills to entry-level workers, and governors and legislators worried about the cost and quality of education. International tests regularly showed American high school students ranking below average in mathematics and science. Employers had come to consider a high school diploma to be a measure of seat time rather than reliable evidence of a good education, and higher education was increasingly expected to do the work of the schools.

Eager to improve the quality of education, governors, state legislators, and business leaders pressed for higher standards in the schools. They were egged on not only by their desire to attract new industries and jobs to their states but also by the impressive educational achievements of Asian nations, which demonstrated what might be achieved by good schools and supportive parents. Harold Stevenson of the University of Michigan produced a widely noted series of studies showing that the successful Asian nations had clear educational standards that were understood by teachers, students, and parents. Asian students performed better in school than American students, Stevenson found, because they (and their parents) believed that effort—not innate ability—mattered. That belief encouraged students to work hard in school.[49]

During the early 1990s, the person who influenced the nation's discussion of school quality more than anyone else was Albert Shanker, president of the American Federation of Teachers. In the decade before his death in 1997, Shanker tirelessly advocated the need for higher academic standards. The fact that Shanker led a union of nearly a million teachers gave him unusual credibility. He frequently used his weekly column-length advertisement in the Sunday *New York Times* to argue that students' achievement in American schools was far too low. He insisted that "our current system is devastatingly bad for all our youngsters. We are not producing a top group that is equivalent to that of other industrialized nations, and our bottom group is in terrible shape. We are crippling our youngsters because we're giving them the wrong message." The "wrong message," said Shanker, was that they could get a diploma merely by staying in school long enough. He believed that schools needed high standards as well as rigorous tests that had real consequences or "stakes" for students, such as getting into college or a good job-training program.[50]

In 1989, when President George Bush invited the nation's governors to an education summit in Charlottesville, Virginia, Shanker urged them to begin creating a national system of standards and assessments. He said that standards should be clear but not excessively detailed and that they should be assessed with what Shanker called "good tests, instead of the idiotic, low-level multiple-choice tests we now use." With realistic evaluations, he wrote, a community would be able to compare its children's performance to those in the next county or state and would have "a real basis for a system of parental choice [among public schools] and even for deciding which schools are so deficient they should be put out of business."[51]

Shanker often pointed out that other nations required high school students to pass examinations in more than one subject to qualify for college. These tests provided powerful incentives to study because students knew that their efforts would count toward reaching a valued goal. "Without stakes," he insisted, "nobody has to take education seriously." In this country, he observed, students knew that nothing in school counted, because they would get a diploma even if they exerted little effort. Shanker wanted explicit content standards that would spell out what "*all* students are taught at least through elementary school."[52] Some form of ability grouping would be necessary in high school, he believed, to acknowledge that some students planned to go to college and others wanted technical careers. He warned that any attempt to create a single graduation standard for all students would result in a universally low standard.

431

The National Goals

At the 1989 education summit, the nation's governors agreed to adopt six national goals for the year 2000. Governor Bill Clinton of Arkansas took the lead among the governors in drafting the goals. Two of the goals targeted higher academic achievement for all students, while the others defined targets for the high school graduation rate, school readiness for young children, adult literacy, and reducing substance abuse and violence in schools. This implied a major shift in priorities for American education, which had long been accustomed to keeping all children in school as long as possible without setting any real standards of achievement. To sustain public pressure for higher academic achievement, in 1991 and 1992 the Department of Education (in collaboration with other federal agencies, such as the National Endowment for the Humanities and the National Science Foundation) awarded grants to organizations of scholars and teachers to develop voluntary national standards in seven school subjects (science, history, geography, the arts, civics, foreign languages, and English [the National Council of Teachers of Mathematics had already promulgated its own standards]).

The voluntary national standards were supposed to describe what children should be expected to learn in different grades in every major academic subject. These standards were intended to create a coherent framework of academic expectations that could be used by teacher educators, textbook publishers, and test developers. The organizations that received the federal awards were supposed to identify clearly and succinctly what students should know and be able to do; their recommendations would not be mandatory but would be available to help states shape their own standards. When the federal grants were made, it was widely anticipated that Congress would create some sort of national board to evaluate the voluntary national standards and that this board would oversee an iterative process to review and revise the draft national standards. Even after President Bush lost his bid for reelection to Governor Clinton in 1992, there appeared to be bipartisan agreement on these issues because the new president had pledged in his campaign to establish a system of national standards and tests.[53]

Clinton's first major education legislation, called Goals 2000, was enacted in 1994. The program provided funds for states to develop standards and assessments, and it authorized a new federal board to certify national and state standards. The funds were distributed to the states, and almost every state began developing academic standards. However, President Clinton did not appoint anyone to the federal board, and when Republicans gained control of Congress in 1994, they abolished it. Consequently, there was no organization to evaluate the drafts prepared by the groups that had been funded to write voluntary national standards, nor was there any other formal public review process. The proposed national standards began to appear in print at the same time that most states were writing their own academic standards, which gave large influence to the groups that wrote the voluntary national standards without providing for any process of review.

Officials in the Bush administration expected that the voluntary national standards would describe the most important knowledge and skills in each field. However, the leaders of some of the federally funded projects wanted to revolutionize their field, not merely to identify the essential ideas that students should learn at different grade levels. To the extent that the standards projects tried to make a revolution, they encountered widespread public opposition. The abortive effort to create national standards revealed the deep fissures within academic fields, as well as the wide gap between avant-garde thinkers in the academic world and the general public.

The History Standards

*The first of the federal projects to become public was the history stan*dards. Their original goal was to restore historical content as the central element of the field of social studies. The uproar that followed their release damaged the prospects for setting coherent national academic standards in the United States. The standards were prepared by the National Center for History in the Schools at the University of California in Los Angeles. Two weeks before their official release in the fall of 1994, Lynne V. Cheney, the former chairman of the National Endowment for the Humanities, blasted them as politically biased in *The Wall Street Journal.*

Cheney attacked the standards for their negativism toward the United States and the West in general. She pointed out that the American history standards mentioned Senator Joseph McCarthy and McCarthyism nineteen times, the Ku Klux Klan seventeen times, and Harriet Tubman six times but omitted Paul Revere, Robert E. Lee, Thomas Alva Edison, Alexander Graham Bell, and the Wright brothers. Cheney's article set off a heated debate about history in the schools among editorialists, historians, talk-show hosts on radio and television, and elected officials.[54]

Gary Nash, a UCLA historian who had directed the development of the standards, dismissed Cheney's criticisms. He said that his group's goal "was to bring about nothing short of a new American revolution in history education . . . we want to bury rote learning and the emphasis on dates, facts, places, events and one damn thing after another." His organization sought to "let children out of the prison of facts and dates and make them active learners," involved in mock trials and classroom debates. Nash stressed the importance of teaching about ordinary people rather than heroes: "Every kid who went to Washington on spring break went to the Library of Congress and saw that inscription, 'History is the biography of great men.' Isn't that a very disabling notion in a democracy where we believe that active, knowledgeable, engaged citizens hold the fate of the republic in their hands?"[55]

Everyone, it seemed, had an opinion about the history standards. Advocates and critics argued on the nation's editorial pages. Conservative talk-show host Rush Limbaugh said they should be "flushed down the toilet." But they were endorsed by leading newspapers, including *The New York Times,* the *San Francisco Chronicle,* the *St. Louis Post-Dispatch,* and the *Los Angeles Times,* and defended by notable historians.[56]

Criticism of the standards, however, was relentless, and it came not just from conservative firebrands. *Time* noted that the document was "so insistent on resurrecting neglected voices that it becomes guilty of what might be called disproportionate revisionism." Columnist Charles Krauthammer complained that the standards were characterized not only by "ethnic cheerleading and the denigration of American achievements" but by "the denigration of learning itself," which he charged was an inevitable result of Nash's desire to free children from "the prison of facts." Without such mundane things as names and dates, said Krauthammer, it was hard to imagine that children would know much history, no matter how many activities they engaged in.[57]

In January 1995, as the public controversy raged, the U.S. Senate passed a resolution condemning the history standards by a vote of 99 to 1. The lone dissenter, a senator from Louisiana, wanted an even stronger condemnation. Albert Shanker endorsed the Senate vote. He concluded that the standards were unnecessarily "grim" in their treatment of American history: "Telling the truth about our warts does not mean ignoring our successes in securing rights and freedoms for our citizens—or trivializing important battles we have fought on behalf of our ideals." Shanker did not agree that active learning conflicted with the acquisition of facts: "The problem with many youngsters today is not that they don't have opinions but that they don't have facts on which to base their opinions."[58]

Secretary of Education Richard Riley disowned the national history standards in a statement asserting "This was not our grant. This is not my idea of good standards. This is not my view of how history should be taught in America's classrooms. . . . We have to acknowledge both the peaks and valleys in our past and recognize the contributions of all Americans, regardless of their station in life. But the message must be a positive one. Our schools should teach our students to be proud to be Americans."[59]

A number of prominent historians disagreed sharply with the standards. John Patrick Diggins of the City University of New York argued that the standards misled students by concentrating on social issues and neglecting the nature of power in history. Sheldon M. Stern, historian at the John F. Kennedy Library in Boston, charged that the standards encouraged an attitude of self-righteousness and cynicism among students by judging events solely from the point of view of the present. This made it difficult for them to appreciate "how hard our predecessors fought" for the freedoms and rights that were now taken for granted.[60]

Walter A. McDougall of the University of Pennsylvania complained that the American history standards had wrongly represented the nation's history as a struggle of minorities and women against white males. He summarized the standards sarcastically: "If Europeans braved the unknown to discover a new world, it was to kill and oppress. If colonists carved a new nation out of the woods, it was to displace Native Americans and impose private property. If the 'Founding Fathers' (the term has been banished) invoked human rights, it was to deny them to others. If businessmen built the most prosperous nation in history, it was to rape the environment and keep workers in misery." McDougall concluded that the standards accurately reflected what the historical profession wanted children to learn: "Indeed, they reflect what our children are *already* taught in schools across the country, and are sure to influence future authors of textbooks as well." The only embarrassment to liberal academics, he asserted, was that their "quiet conquest of America's schoolrooms" had been revealed by the controversy.[61]

After the Senate's vote of censure, the Washington-based Council for Basic Education set up review panels of historians to evaluate the history standards. The panels concluded that most of the problems stemmed from the project's hundreds of teaching examples, many of which presented "a disproportionately pessimistic and misrepresentative picture of the American past." Some of the teaching examples asked loaded questions, used prejudicial language, or encouraged students to reach "facile moral judgments" about complex issues. The panels found that the standards gave inadequate attention to science, medicine, and technology and tended to portray technological changes only in terms of their negative social impact. In the American history standards, twentieth-century Democratic presidents were described positively, while Republican presidents were described negatively. The world history panel discounted the charge that the standards denigrated Western civilization but noted prejudicial language in which Europeans had "invaded" other countries, while similar actions by non-Europeans were neutrally described as "expansion."[62]

On the basis of the panels' recommendations, the standards were substantially revised. Thousands of copies of both versions were sold to teachers and school districts. Most states, however, having seen the controversy engendered by the history standards, continued to adopt minimal and vague social studies standards, with only cursory attention to history. California, Virginia, Texas, and Massachusetts adopted standards for history, and in none of these four states did the national standards have a decisive influence.

What persisted after the controversy died down were questions about how national standards could ever be devised without running into an ideological minefield. The process itself had been deeply flawed because the standards had been produced without any field testing or any authoritative public body to evaluate them. With the exception of the history standards, the first draft was the only draft. What was required, if ever the nation were to venture again into the forging of national standards, was a long-term, iterative process, building on careful field testing of any proposed standards in whole districts and states.[63]

The English Standards

Despite their political problems, the history standards were rigorous and substantive. The same could not be said for the English standards, which were an unmitigated disaster. These "standards" were so lacking in content and actual standards that in 1994 the Department of Education cut off the project's funding.

Pressing forward without additional federal support, the International Reading Association and the National Council of Teachers of English published their standards for "English Language Arts" in 1996. This document buzzed with fashionable pedagogical concepts but lacked any concrete reference to the importance of accurate language usage, correct spelling and grammar, great contemporary or classic literature, or what students at any grade level should actually know and be able to do.[64]

The document proposed that students should "develop an understanding of and respect for diversity in language use, patterns, and dialects," meaning that English teachers should not judge the ways in which students speak or write English. "In other words," observed J. Martin Rochester of the University of Missouri, "the standards statement essentially says we should not hold students to any standards!" Dick Feagler, a columnist for the Cleveland *Plain Dealer,* observed that "English is a second language for members of the National Council of Teachers of English. Their primary language is gobbledygook."[65] *The New York Times* opined that the standard writers had gotten lost in "pedagogical molasses," instead of producing "a clear, candid case for greater competence in standard English." Albert Shanker agreed, saying that "No one reading the English standards is likely to believe that a passionate concern with English language and literature is the driving force behind them."[66]

Despite the barrage of critical responses to their convoluted prose and devotion to process, in the late 1990s the national English standards strongly influenced states' English language arts standards. As in history, the national standards accurately reflected the state of the field in higher education; relativism, deconstructionism, and postmodernism dominated English departments in the academy. It was not surprising, then, that the leaders of this field did not acknowledge the importance of conventions of correct usage and the varieties of imaginative literature that most Americans thought to be central aspects of the national language.

The NCTM Standards

*The national standards that seemed likeliest to succeed were those de-*veloped without federal funding by the National Council of Teachers of Mathematics. Released in 1989, the NCTM standards were intended to regain the ground lost after the failure of the "new math" of the 1960s and the "back-to-basics" movement in the mid-1970s.

The new math of the 1960s was the fruit of the mathematics profession's efforts to change the teaching of the subject in the schools; it was widely disseminated to the schools by the National Science Foundation, with funding inspired by the launch of *Sputnik* in 1957. The new math stressed the conceptual nature of mathematics rather than computation, introducing in the early grades topics such as numeration in bases other than 10. According to Bruce R. Vogeli, professor of mathematical education at Columbia's Teachers College, 1967 marked "the high tide of new mathematics in American elementary schools." By that year, no textbooks could be marketed that were not aligned with the "new math" and "no school was truly progressive that was not involved in some way with the new mathematics."[67]

The new math met its downfall, however, when test scores in schools that had adopted its methods dropped sharply. Then, in 1973, mathematician Morris Kline's *Why Johnny Can't Add: The Failure of the New Math* contributed to a parent and teacher rebellion against the conceptual methods.[68] The reaction against the new math produced a "back-to-basics" movement, which insisted that children should be taught the computational skills—adding, subtracting, multiplying, and dividing—that allegedly had been neglected.

Recoiling from both the abstractness of the "new math" and the rote drilling that was associated with "the basics," the NCTM organized in support of a curriculum that focused on real-world problems and that also reduced the amount of time spent on computation, drill, and memory work. In the early 1990s, the federal government treated the NCTM standards as a model for its own efforts to encourage each subject field to write standards.

Like the new math of the 1960s, the NCTM standards were an immediate success; every mass-produced mathematics textbook claimed to have adopted them, and they were quickly incorporated into the math curricula of most states. Intended to encourage critical thinking and problem solving, the NCTM standards put a premium on student-led activities, mathematical games, working with manipulatives (e.g., blocks and sticks), using calculators, and group learning, and discounted the importance of correct answers. Rote learning was out, and computation was also downgraded because students in every grade were expected to use calculators at all times. Unfortunately, the NCTM standards had not been field-tested and thus there was no evidence of their effectiveness.

For several years after their release in 1989, it seemed that the NCTM standards would completely dominate and transform mathematics education; after all, the national organization that represented mathematics teachers and professors of mathematics education endorsed them. Their most controversial recommendation was that basic skills had been rendered obsolete by calculators.[69] The NCTM had some inkling that trouble might lie ahead when it commissioned a survey of opinion about some of its precepts; for example, overwhelming majorities of math supervisors (87 percent) and education professors (83 percent) agreed that students "best learn to solve complex mathematics problems when they are given these problems even before they know all the basic skills they might need," but only 23 percent of high school principals and 41 percent of PTA members concurred.[70]

Signs of dissidence were ignored in the early 1990s, however, and then came a counterrevolution. The revolt against the NCTM methods began in 1995, organized by a group of irate parents in California, led by mathematicians and engineers. Calling themselves Mathematically Correct, they used the Internet to find like-minded mathematicians, teachers, and parents. One of these parents was Marianne M. Jennings, a professor at Arizona State University, who wrote a vivid critique of her teenage daughter's algebra textbook, an 812-page full-color tome replete with Dogon art from Africa, poetry, maps of South America, and warnings about pollution and endangered species; Jennings called this approach "rain-forest algebra." In 1997, a barrage of negative articles appeared in the national press, attacking the NCTM standards for deemphasizing basic skills—adding, subtracting, multiplying, and dividing—and for having recommended the use of calculators in the elementary grades to handle these tasks. Calling NCTM math "fuzzy math" and "the new new math," critics insisted that students could not learn higher-order skills if they did not first possess basic skills. The standards were faulted for belittling "right answers" in a field where right answers not only exist but are absolutely necessary in real-world applications of science, engineering, and medicine.[71]

What had gone wrong? The profession was well organized and shared a strong consensus around its product. But the NCTM lost the public relations battle when it de-emphasized basic skills; once that was communicated to the public, its other strategies, no matter how worthy, sounded like pedagogic jargon. Moreover, the NCTM standards were at heart a pedagogy, a way of teaching, rather than what most people would recognize as standards. Standards customarily involve a progression of accomplishments or competencies that are to be demonstrated at defined times in children's schooling. The NCTM standards gave no concrete description of what should be taught or the sequence of topics. Instead, they consisted of nebulous goals that were admirable but difficult to implement, such as valuing mathematics, becoming confident problem solvers, reasoning and communicating mathematically, and developing appreciation for the power of mathematics.

The NCTM standards achieved their greatest—albeit temporary—success in California, where they were the reference point for revision of the state curriculum in 1992. Mathematically Correct, however, persuaded the State Board of Education to adopt a different set of math standards in 1997. Unlike the NCTM standards, which were profusely illustrated with examples of how to teach, the new California standards described what students would be expected to learn in each grade, leaving teachers free to select their method, whether it involved NCTM pedagogy or something else.[72]

THE CONSTRUCTIVIST MOVEMENT

The underlying approach of the NCTM standards was solidly grounded in the familiar principle of progressive education that learning should be student-centered, not teacher-led, and dependent on students' activities rather than teachers' direction. The new theories of the 1980s were similar to the pedagogical thinking of the 1920s and 1930s but were called "constructivism," rather than progressivism. By the mid-1980s, constructivism had become the dominant idea among educational theorists, who frequently quoted John Dewey and the Swiss psychologist Jean Piaget to argue that students would be motivated to learn only if they were active learners, constructing their own knowledge through their own discoveries.

The central claim of constructivism was clearly correct: Students are not merely blank tapes or photographic film that record sensory impressions. All learning is digested by the learner and understood in relation to what the learner already knows. Good teachers use a variety of methods, including activities, experiences, and projects. As enthusiasm for constructivism grew, however, some enthusiasts went to an extreme, proclaiming that children should construct essentially all their knowledge. Wiser heads understood that students could not invent the world anew, rediscover basic principles of math and science, or "construct knowledge" without prior knowledge and good instruction. Some education researchers—such as Lauren B. Resnick of the University of Pittsburgh—recognized that "learning requires knowledge" and that "cognitive science does not suggest that educators get out of the way so that children can do their natural work." [73]

In the usual way of American education, however, where enthusiasm often outstrips evidence and fads tend to have a long shelf life, constructivism was hailed as a pedagogical breakthrough and treated as the holy grail of pedagogy. Paul Cobb of Vanderbilt University noted that constructivism had become "something akin to a secular religion," invariably accompanied by a "mantra-like slogan that 'students construct their own knowledge.' " Publications about constructivism increased rapidly, and at the 1993 meeting of the American Educational Research Association, more than a score of panels were devoted to the topic. [74]

Constructivist educators insisted that children were not empty vessels to be filled up with knowledge but "active builders of knowledge—little scientists who are constantly creating and testing their own theories of the world." It became axiomatic among constructivists that "knowledge is not transmitted directly from one knower to another, but is actively built up by the learner." This meant that teachers must never lecture or "tell," that any memorization was intolerable, that instruction was a discredited form of behaviorism, and that up-to-date teachers viewed themselves as "facilitators" of learning. Surely a middle ground was needed, one where students could actively solve problems at the same time as they mastered basic skills and gained new knowledge under the guidance of capable teachers. [75]

THE WHOLE-LANGUAGE MOVEMENT

Pedagogical theories of constructivism were at the root of national de-
bates about reading during the 1980s and 1990s. The great debate about
teaching reading, as Jeanne Chall of Harvard University had called it,
seemed never to end. Phonics or whole word? Phonics or "look-say"?
When Chall assessed the controversy in 1967, it appeared that the evidence was clear and the debate was over. She had concluded that most
children needed to learn how to "decode," that is, to learn the relationship between letters and their sounds, and they also needed to read good
children's literature in the elementary grades. Either method alone was
insufficient for most children.

In the 1980s and 1990s, the debate flared up again with the appearance of the "whole-language" approach to reading. The new movement
began with the writings of Frank Smith of the University of Victoria in
British Columbia and Kenneth Goodman of the University of Arizona.
Both believed that learning to read should be as easy and natural as
learning to speak; both were critical of instruction that emphasized
phonics or any other linguistic skills. Smith wrote that "the effort to read
through decoding is largely futile and unnecessary" and that most children learned to read "despite exposure to phonics."[76]

Like the "whole-word" methods of the 1920s, the whole-language
approach proposed that children read literature connected to their interests rather than textbooks and that they read for meaning and pleasure
rather than study the mechanics of language. Whole language was a rebellion against drill, workbooks, textbooks, and the other paraphernalia
associated with phonics that, overdone, could deaden students' interest
in reading.

What is whole language? Kenneth Goodman defined it as an alternative to any sort of linguistic analysis: "Whole language learning builds
around whole learners learning whole language in whole situations."
Any practices that "chop language into bits and pieces," he wrote, are
not whole. Surround children with a rich environment, have lots of opportunities for them to read and write, and children will learn to read

without direct instruction about the sounds that letters represent. Whole-language learning involved student-centered activities, "authentic" reading experiences, integration of reading and writing, and freeing teachers from skills instruction. It was distinguished by what it opposed, which was instruction about language, time spent on phonics, and concern for accurate spelling and punctuation. Goodman wrote that children would read when they had a need to communicate and that "language learning is easy when it's whole, real, and relevant; when it makes sense and is functional; when it's encountered in the context of its use; when the learner chooses to use it."[77]

According to Goodman, whole-language teachers "reject negative, elitist, racist views of linguistic purity that would limit children to arbitrary 'proper' language. Instead, they view their role as helping children to expand on the marvelous language they already use." Goodman described the teaching of phonics as "a flat-earth view of the world, since it rejects modern science about reading and writing and how they develop." He maintained that "if they are lucky enough not to have been taught phonics in isolation," children discover strategies to figure out what they want to know from print. Good readers "guess or make hypotheses about what will occur in the text." They use "invented spelling" and eventually learn conventional spelling without any prodding by the teacher; they read by figuring out words in their context. Reading, he wrote, is "a psycholinguistic guessing game." At the heart of the theory was the idea that "literacy develops in response to personal/social needs," and when children want to read, they will learn to do so.[78]

Enthusiasm for whole language, with its emphasis on children's literature and the joys of learning, was an understandable reaction against an overemphasis on drill and workbooks in the 1970s; it had a ready appeal to those who identified with child-centered methods and disliked the formalistic demands of phonics instruction. In the 1980s, whole language built up a large and dedicated following in schools of education and in professional organizations such as the International Reading Association and the National Council of Teachers of English. It confirmed those who had always believed that schools should teach "the whole child" and pay less attention to subject matter and linguistic skills such as syntax, grammar, and spelling. The rhetoric of whole language was reminiscent of Rousseau and of early-twentieth-century progressive educators such as Junius Meriam, director of the laboratory school at the University of Missouri, who had organized his curriculum around the premise that children learn only when they needed to do so, and Marietta Pierce Johnson of the Organic School at Fairhope, Alabama, who had wanted children to have a completely "natural" education, free of pressure and artifice. The nation's schools of education, long committed to progressive educational ideas, provided a ready audience for a theory that said that children are naturally motivated to learn and that they need to be insulated from instruction, textbooks, tests, and anything else that might interfere with their natural desire to learn.

Nothing, it seemed, could slow the whole-language movement, not even a 1985 report from the National Academy of Education (called *Becoming a Nation of Readers*), which said that "on the average, children who are taught phonics get off to a better start in learning to read than children who are not taught phonics." The Academy's report, the work of a panel of distinguished scholars, drew a rebuttal from the Commission on Reading of the National Council of Teachers of English, which strongly supported child-centered whole-language programs. Commission member Kenneth Goodman lambasted the National Academy of Education's report as "a political document" that advanced the agenda of "the Far Right." Ever since the publication of Rudolf Flesch's bestselling *Why Johnny Can't Read,* conservative parent groups had championed phonics, and Goodman dismissed the National Academy's report as an unwitting contribution to the far-right cause.[79]

Among reading professionals, the battle lines were drawn, with whole language on one side, and phonics-first-then-literature on the other. The larger public remained generally ignorant of the new phenomenon called whole language.

Bill Honig, the superintendent of public instruction in California, misunderstood how wide the gulf between these opposing philosophies really was. Honig had promised to establish a rigorous, traditional education for all children. When California adopted guidelines for teaching English in 1987, Honig did not realize that the state's document was

445

widely perceived as a great victory for whole language. A decade later, he complained that he had been trying to promote literature, but "the whole-language movement hijacked what we were doing."[80] Even though the term "whole language" never appeared in the state guidelines, the document endorsed the methods and ideology of whole language. It proclaimed, "We are in the midst of a revolution—a quiet, intellectual revolution spinning out dramatic insights into how the brain works, how we acquire language, and how we construct meaning in our lives. Psycholinguistics, language acquisition theory, and research in composition and literacy unite to present new challenges for students and teachers." This was the rhetoric of whole language, for it was Frank Smith and Kenneth Goodman who described whole language as psycholinguistics, the conjunction of psychology and linguistics, and they were the leaders of this revolution. Among whole-language reformers, the California English-Language Arts framework of 1987 was viewed as a milestone.[81]

For a time, it seemed that whole language would sweep the reading field and reduce the opposition to a footnote in the history of education. In 1988, 2,500 teachers, supervisors, and teacher educators showed up for a conference on whole language sponsored by the New York State Education Department. A consultant to the Vermont Department of Education estimated that 85 percent of the state's kindergarten teachers had adopted whole language. Developers of textbooks and instructional materials estimated that their products were aligned with this hot new trend in reading. Whole-language proponents could point to California's adoption of new textbooks that minimized skill instruction as evidence of their influence.[82]

Yet the increasingly visible success of whole language soon led to a counterreaction. By 1990, *Education Week,* the leading journal in education, declared that a "full-scale war" had broken out between adherents of whole language and those of phonics. The director of the NCTE's commission on reading said that teaching the mechanics of reading would actually interfere with children's ability to read. The best way to teach reading, she insisted, was to let children read whole texts, "even if they can't read all the words."[83]

A congressionally mandated study of reading methods in 1990 by Marilyn Jager Adams, a cognitive psychologist, called for an end to the "fruitless debate" and attempted—as Jeanne Chall had more than two decades earlier—to bridge the differences between the two approaches. Her research review showed consistently better results for students who started with "systematic code instruction" and concluded that good teachers combine the best features of both approaches. Adams's study was rejected by whole-language advocates, who insisted that test scores were unimportant as long as children were enjoying reading and learning to think critically.[84]

Kenneth Goodman continued to charge that critics of whole language were allies of "the far right," which he claimed wanted to undermine public education. Goodman criticized Chall, by then an emeritus professor of reading at Harvard, for allowing "the far right" to use her work "as a starting point in constructing their conspiracy theories." The detractors of whole language, said Goodman, were not afraid that it would fail; instead, they were "afraid it would work too well. They don't want people to be too widely literate, to have easy access to information that may empower them." Frank Smith, the other leader of whole language, claimed that phonics survived because it appealed to the "insensitive mechanical pedagogue" and to mean-spirited people who wanted to control children.[85]

Not many educators identified with the "far right" or thought of themselves as "insensitive mechanical pedagogues," so they were understandably drawn to whole language, which claimed to favor child-centered methods, "teacher empowerment," and the joys of learning.

But in 1996, whole language received an unexpected setback. The U.S. Department of Education released state-by-state reading scores on the federally funded National Assessment of Educational Progress (NAEP), which revealed that California's reading scores were near the bottom in the nation. Since 1970, the NAEP had regularly tested samples of American students in different subject areas. In 1992, the first year of state-by-state testing, California had been fourth from last in reading scores (ahead of Mississippi, the District of Columbia, and Guam). In 1994, California slipped behind Mississippi.[86]

Whether whole language was the cause of poor reading performance in California was not established, but the national press immediately drew a straight line between the rise of whole language in California and the decline of reading skills there. *Newsweek* reported that "most research backs the need for lots of phonics, the sooner the better" and that the most successful schools combine "the best of phonics and whole language." *Time* reviewed the controversy and concluded that the evidence supporting "explicit, systematic phonics instruction" was "so strong that if the subject under discussion were, say, the treatment of the mumps, there would be no discussion." Joan Beck of the *Chicago Tribune* described her own daughter's experience learning to read and observed that whole language was "a cruel mind game to encourage children to read printed words without telling them how."[87]

The release of California's reading scores prompted a flurry of official responses. The State Board of Education adopted a new English-Language Arts curriculum in 1997 that required both phonics and literature in the earliest grades. In view of that state's large share of the national textbook market, its decision influenced other jurisdictions across the nation. After leaving office in 1993, Bill Honig, the California state superintendent who had unknowingly sponsored the English language arts guidelines that launched whole language across the state, devoted himself to promoting "a balanced approach" to reading. A balanced approach, he held, included both explicit instruction in phonics and whole-language activities.[88]

Jeanne Chall had warned in 1967 that schools should not go overboard in teaching phonics. She had recommended phonics "only as a *beginning* reading method—a method to start the child on" in the first two grades, followed by a quick transition to reading good stories. She had predicted that if schools made a fetish of phonics, then "We will be confronted in ten or twenty years with another best seller: *Why Robert Can't Read*. The culprit in this angry book will be the 'prevailing' linguistic, systematic-phonics. . . . The suggested cure will be a 'natural' approach—one that teaches whole words and emphasizes reading for meaning and appreciation at the very beginning." She had described with canny accuracy the rise of the whole-language movement.[89]

Cynics might well have concluded that the great debate about teaching reading would never end and that one cycle would soon follow another, long into the future. But Americans felt a particular urgency about literacy. As the economy changed, it was obvious that those with poor reading skills would have diminished opportunities in modern society. The warning signals were clear: according to the National Assessment of Educational Progress, nearly 40 percent of fourth-grade students were "below basic" in reading in the 1990s. Students with such low scores were not able to demonstrate an understanding of what they had read or make simple inferences about the ideas in the text. Poor reading scores were most prevalent among poor and minority children. In 1998, 64 percent of black children and 60 percent of Hispanic children were "below basic" in reading in fourth grade, compared with 27 percent of whites.[90]

In the late 1990s a consensus began to emerge about how to teach reading. First came a spate of studies funded by the National Institute of Child Health and Human Development (part of the National Institutes of Health), which reconfirmed the earlier work of Chall and Adams about the importance of *both* phonemic awareness and reading comprehension. Then came a major report by the National Research Council, which convened a distinguished group of reading researchers. The panel concluded that beginning readers needed "explicit instruction and practice that lead to an appreciation that spoken words are made up of smaller units of sounds." In addition, it said, they needed "familiarity with spelling-sound correspondences and common spelling conventions and their use in identifying printed words, 'sight' recognition of frequent words, and independent reading, including reading aloud."[91] In short, good reading instruction incorporated the best practices of the different approaches.

It appeared that the great debate about reading instruction had ended. Not only was the research compelling, but a dozen major education organizations, including teachers, administrators, and teacher educators, joined to support the balanced approach to teaching reading. But the ideological battles that had raged throughout the twentieth century had not run out of steam. In December 1999, the annual meeting of the National Council of Teachers of English passed a resolution opposing phonics instruction. In particular, it took issue with the American Federation of Teachers for disseminating a booklet that explained the value of phonics instruction. The National Council of Teachers of English was the same organization that had produced the much-criticized English standards.[92]

After so many years, so many words, and so many heated battles, there appeared to be a solid consensus that both phonics and comprehension were necessary components of learning to read. Yet only a foolish optimist would predict that this consensus would end decades of squabbling about how to teach reading.

The Powerful Middle Ground

Throughout the curriculum wars of the 1990s, the message was clear: both extremes were wrong. In history, children need big thematic concepts, but they also need a solid grounding in factual knowledge, a secure scaffolding of dates, names, and events on which to build the big concepts. Important facts—such as the name, context, and date of the *Brown v. Board of Education* decision—represent important concepts, not merely isolated facts. In mathematics, children need to engage in active problem solving, and they also need to master the basic skills of adding, subtracting, multiplying, and dividing in order to become successful problem solvers. In English, children need to learn the skills of correct language usage as well as have opportunities to read excellent classic and contemporary literary works and write their own compositions. In science, which largely avoided the pedagogical battles that rocked other fields (but still had to fend off efforts to inject religious beliefs into the curriculum), the same principle holds true: both skills and knowledge are necessary in order for children to benefit from hands-on projects, field trips, and other activities. Teachers must use their knowledge and experience to instruct their students, not stand aside and allow them to construct their own knowledge. Teachers, in other words, must be *teachers,* not "facilitators."

In the debates about standards, the concept of knowledge was constantly under attack. Efforts to define which knowledge should be taught and tested opened up schisms among academics, who made their reputations (and living) by arguing whether knowledge was real, valid, particular, universal, relevant, or the privileged property of some elite group. Schools and the writers of state standards avoided such battles by focusing only on skills and bypassing any definition of what knowledge was important for students to master. In the early decades of the century, progressives had derided the knowledge taught in school as useless or aristocratic; late-twentieth-century critics called it arbitrary or trivial. The counter-argument, however, remains valid: Knowledge is power, and those who have it control the debate and ultimately control the levers of power in society. A democratic system of education, as Lester Frank Ward wrote a century earlier, disseminates knowledge as broadly as possible throughout society.

In the 1990s, despite the din of ideological combat, most states engaged in setting academic standards, assessing what students knew, and developing strategies to improve learning, especially for those who had fallen behind. Students of all racial backgrounds responded to the new demands by taking more advanced academic courses in subjects such as science and mathematics; the proportion of high school graduates who enrolled in an academic (as opposed to a general or vocational) program grew from 42 percent in 1982 to 69 percent by 1994.[93]

In the curriculum wars of the 1990s, the outcome was decisively influenced by one individual and two very different organizations, which interacted to inject a healthy dose of common sense into public discourse about education. Albert Shanker's courageous voice insistently reminded the nation that American teachers want higher standards, reasonable standards, and good behavior in the classroom.

One organization that made a decisive difference in public discussion was the National Assessment of Educational Progress (NAEP), the federally funded testing program that since 1970 had issued regular reports on student achievement in major academic subjects. NAEP was the only consistent national barometer of educational performance and a constant reminder of the need for improved achievement. NAEP kept

451

public attention focused squarely on important academic subjects: reading, writing, mathematics, science, and history.

The other important contributor to the national debate about education was Public Agenda, a nonpartisan private research group that conducted public opinion surveys about education starting in 1994. Public Agenda unfailingly showed that large majorities of the public agreed with those—such as Kenneth Clark, Ronald Edmonds, and Albert Shanker—who said that students would learn if the expectations of them were high and they were taught in an orderly atmosphere. Moreover, the public wanted youngsters to learn good work habits and the value of effort. Even students said that they would take their schoolwork more seriously if their schools asked more of them. Parents, regardless of race, wanted schools to focus on academic achievement and to make sure that their children had mastered the basics and that "all kids can speak and write standard English, with proper pronunciation and grammar." In its surveys, Public Agenda found that the public was of one mind about the importance of using correct English and "expecting students to be neat, on time, and polite."[94] In the midst of seemingly perpetual controversies, debates, and counterclaims about what works in the classroom and how children should be educated, the public knew what it wanted the schools to do.

Conclusion

At Century's End

If there is a lesson to be learned from the river of ink that was spilled in the education disputes of the twentieth century, it is that anything in education that is labeled a "movement" should be avoided like the plague. What American education most needs is not more nostrums and enthusiasms but more attention to fundamental, time-tested truths. It is a fundamental truth that children need well-educated teachers who are eclectic in their methods and willing to use different strategies depending on what works best for which children. It is another fundamental truth that adults must take responsibility for children and help them develop as good persons with worthy ideals.

Massive changes in curricula and pedagogy should be based on solid research and careful field-tested demonstration before they are imposed on entire school districts and states. There has been no shortage of innovation in American education; what is needed before broad implementation of any innovation is clear evidence of its effectiveness. Schools must be flexible enough to try new instructional methods and organizational patterns, and intelligent enough to gauge their success over time in accomplishing their primary mission: educating children.

The End of Utopianism

*What was only a dream at the beginning of the twentieth century—uni-*versal education—had become reality by century's end. This was no small accomplishment, and most Americans agreed that full access to education for people of all ages was a cornerstone of a democratic society. Yet the utopianism that had once been associated with universal education had dissipated. By century's end, elementary and secondary schools were readily available to all young people, and higher education was accessible for nearly all who wanted it, but serious problems persisted. Few believed anymore that schools alone could remedy the great ills of social and economic life or eliminate poverty.[1] They could surely change children's lives by giving them the opportunity to learn, which is a crucial ingredient in self-improvement. But their capacity to effect large-scale social and economic changes is inherently limited by the specifics of their mission and their institutional nature.

Moreover, in the closing years of the century it was obvious that the quality of schooling had not kept pace with its quantity. Students were staying in school longer than ever, but were they learning more than ever? Few thought so, nor did available evidence suggest that they were. More students were going on to college than ever before, but nearly a third of them found it necessary to take remedial courses in reading, writing, or mathematics. When so many first-year college students had not mastered the skills that were supposedly taught in secondary schools (or even earlier), it made a mockery of the "educational ladder" that idealistic educators had advocated at the beginning of the twentieth century.

What of the expectation that universal education would uplift the quality of American culture, refine popular taste, and strengthen appreciation for the arts and literature? It was difficult to credit the schools with such accomplishments when popular culture—the world outside the schools' walls—was growing increasingly vulgar and tawdry and the authority of teachers and schools in the lives of children was growing ever more tenuous.

Yet despite the dampening of utopian expectations, the schools remained society's best hope for teaching the rising generation the knowledge and skills that had slowly accumulated over time, transmitting to them the cultural and scientific heritage of humankind, and purposefully developing the knowledge, self-discipline, and thoughtfulness that a democratic citizenry requires.

CHILDREN ON THEIR OWN

John Dewey's belief that the schools were the most effective agency of social reform was turned inside out in the late twentieth century. Increasingly, schools were blamed for social changes that were beyond their control. At the very time that American women entered the labor force in large numbers, the schools lost their power to act *in loco parentis* because of the erosion of adult authority, fear of litigation, the decline of the neighborhood school, the lessening of community cohesion, and the loss of conviction within the education profession that schools should teach children the difference between right and wrong. As parents withdrew from their responsibilities, the schools lacked the capacity to take their place.

These circumstances combined to free young people from adult supervision and community constraints, leaving them to hang out at malls, watch television, roam the Internet, work part-time after school to satisfy the material wants stimulated by television, or get into trouble with drugs or alcohol during long hours on their own. For many children, no one was acting *in loco parentis*.

The schools were not responsible for the diminished authority of teachers and principals, nor were they able to counter the growing role of courts and the federal government in educational decision making. As schools tried to comply with decisions by distant officials and policy makers, as they absorbed new federal and state programs for targeted groups of students, as bureaucratic red tape grew more tangled, as they employed more specialists, it became ever more difficult for them to maintain their focus on teaching and learning or even to perceive teaching and learning as being their primary responsibilities. By the late twentieth century, a principal was being defined not as a "head teacher" but as a manager of personnel and community relations. The superintendent, who once might have pointed to a scholar-practitioner such as William T. Harris as a model, had become a manager of labor relations, strategic planning, budgeting, legislation, and political relationships, with little time to think about instruction or the intellectual coherence of the curriculum.

Large social, economic, and technological changes had undermined the family, made people more mobile and communities less stable, and turned adolescents into consumers whose dollars were ardently pursued by savvy advertisers. None of these changes promoted the well-being of children. The social supports that surrounded them were increasingly fragile, and fewer adults were likely to know them well, take a personal interest in them, or intervene to guide them. The rapid spread of the Internet in the 1990s added yet another avenue through which unknown people—seeking profits, power, or self-gratification—could influence children without the mediation of parents or teachers.

In the early 1980s, the eminent sociologist James S. Coleman had predicted the emergence of a social structure in which no one would be responsible for children, in which busy parents would view their daughters and sons as burdens and treat them with indifference. The exodus from city to suburb, he forecast, meant that many people would work far from their homes. As the home ceased to be the center of social life and became "psychologically barren," he said, women would join their husbands in the labor force. Children would remain behind, cared for by hired help or state agencies or given the latchkey to an empty home. Abandoned to their own devices and lacking responsible adult supervision, children would learn how to behave from other children and from television and movies. Under such circumstances, they would absorb myriad random cues about how to conduct themselves rather than being systematically imbued with consistent norms. Yet consistency of norms was a critical element in the socialization of children, Coleman explained, because norms "establish within the child a sense of what is 'right' and what is 'wrong.' If that content is inconsistent, and the norms conflict with one another, the child has a less fully developed sense of what is right and what is wrong."[2]

By century's end, it was painfully clear that Coleman had accurately foreseen the ebbing of the values of the old social structure (family, neighborhood, and community) and their replacement by the permissive ones of the new social structure, which were being shaped haphazardly by image makers in New York and Hollywood, by the television and movie industry, and by computer game makers, none of whom had children's best interests at heart. The new values were usually at sharp odds with the old ones, treating favorably—as Coleman had predicted—the very "activities or styles of behavior which community norms disapprove," making parents feel embattled and helpless, and confusing children about right and wrong.

THE TRIUMPH OF JAMES B. CONANT

Even as parents and teachers lost authority in the lives of children, schools grew larger and less likely to have a personal connection with their students. This can be traced in large measure to the pervasive influence of James B. Conant, who in 1959 had advocated the elimination of small schools and the creation of comprehensive high schools. Conant claimed that the small high school with a common curriculum was antiquated, and he urged the schools to become large enough for curricular differentiation. It was a direction that planners in the 1950s and 1960s welcomed, for World War II had given credibility to large-scale social planning and educational leaders were partial to such planning, which put professionals in control and minimized lay interference. The small school was irrational and inefficient, said Conant. The large school made it possible to offer several specialized programs within a single institution to meet the varied needs of students with widely different interests, from advanced academic courses to vocational courses to remedial courses.

Educational planners followed Conant's advice. As enrollments boomed in the 1950s and 1960s, small schools and districts were consolidated into larger units. The number of school districts declined from 101,000 at the end of World War II to about 15,000 by 1990. Total enrollments more than doubled in these years, yet the number of public

457

schools declined from 185,000 to 81,000. Large schools became the norm, not the exception. By 1996, nearly half of all American high school students attended a high school with an enrollment of more than 1,500 students, and 70 percent attended a high school larger than 1,000 students.[3]

Perhaps this would have happened even if Conant had not written his best-selling book *The American High School Today.* Many of the schools that closed were one-teacher schools, and they were likely to go the way of the horse and buggy in any event. Americans were already inclined to think that bigger was better, and bigger schools meant more diversity of curriculum, more electives, more interaction with different teachers and students, all of which were supposed to make the schools more modern and progressive.

Conant's advocacy put small schools on the defensive. Consequently, there was little consideration of what was lost when small schools of 500 students were consolidated into big, comprehensive schools. Bigness brought anonymity, bureaucracy, loss of contact between students and teachers, and a fraying of the bonds of community. In large high schools of more than 1,000 students, "the adolescent society" described by James S. Coleman in 1961 asserted its preference for superficial, consumerist values, such as physical appearance, dress, and athletic prowess and its disdain for intellectual and academic pursuits. Large schools may have worked well enough when adult authority was intact and educators set the tone, but they became dysfunctional when adult authority dissipated in the late 1960s and early 1970s.

In the 1990s, a reaction began to set in against the stultifying anomie and curricular incoherence of large public schools and the bureaucratic indifference of so many public school systems. The reaction against bigness contributed to enthusiasm for magnet schools, minischools, schools within schools, and urban small schools where enrollments seldom exceeded 500, a number that allowed the adults in a school to get to know almost every student. In that decade, nearly forty states passed laws to allow the creation of charter schools, which are public schools independent of local district administrators. In pursuit of alternatives to the existing public school system, some parents schooled their children at home; others sought public funds to subsidize the cost of nonpublic schools (in the late 1990s, state legislatures in Wisconsin, Ohio, and Florida approved public subsidies for some low-income children to attend nonpublic schools). Some parents were attracted to alternative schools and charter schools because they were more progressive than the regular public schools, others because they offered the solid academic curriculum that educators such as William T. Harris, William C. Bagley, and E. D. Hirsch, Jr., had advocated and that was often not available in the regular public schools.

A Lost Sense of Purpose

Throughout the twentieth century, progressives claimed that the schools had the power and responsibility to reconstruct society. They took their cue from John Dewey, who in 1897 had proclaimed that the school was the primary means of social reform and the teacher was "the prophet of the true God and the usherer in of the true kingdom of God."[4]

This messianic belief in the school and the teacher actually worked to the disadvantage of both, because it raised unrealistic expectations. It also put the schools squarely into the political arena, thereby encouraging ideologues of every stripe to try to impose their social, religious, cultural, and political agendas on the schools. What was sacrificed over the decades in which the schools were treated as vehicles for job training, social planning, political reform, social sorting, personality adjustment, and social efficiency was a clear definition of what schools can realistically and appropriately accomplish for children and for society.

The century-long effort to diminish the intellectual purposes of the schools had harmful consequences, especially for children from disadvantaged backgrounds. Time and again, experts urged the schools to deemphasize reading, writing, history, mathematics, and science; to drop foreign languages; to replace history with social studies; to eliminate high-quality literature and substitute for it uninspired scraps from textbooks; and to teach only what was useful and immediately functional. Such changes tended to have the least impact on children from privileged homes, whose schools continued to prepare them for college regardless of changing pedagogical fashions and whose parents shared with them the fruits of their own education.

The children most harmed by such practices were those who could not count on the protection of educated parents. While youngsters from poor and modest circumstances had greatest need for the intellectual stimulation that schools were supposed to provide, they were the targets of such "reforms" as curricular differentiation and industrial education, which purposely limited their prospects for intellectual development. The attacks on the academic tradition, by restricting its availability to those who were already advantaged and diminishing access to knowledge, undermined the democratic promise of public education.

Without firm adherence to the goal of intellectual development, the schools lost their sense of purpose. By succumbing to the demands for industrial education in the early years of the century, they subjugated their programs to the needs of industry. In their attempts to be "socially efficient," educational leaders told themselves that they were responsible for guiding social change, forgetting that they were responsible for improving the lives of many individual children, each of whom was precious to someone. The widespread use of mental testing served to propagate the belief that students' innate ability counted for more than their disciplined effort. The testers persuaded principals, teachers, and parents that the tests could accurately and conclusively identify children's native capacities, thus relieving schools of their responsibility to teach all children and to awaken new interests by varying methods and materials.

Intellectual development was further undermined by the child-centered advocates of the 1920s, who tried to eliminate an orderly curriculum and external standards and to make schools as much like "living" as possible, free of lessons, tests, marks, competition, textbooks, and lectures. Their conscious effort to build curricula around children's interests instead of intellectually challenging studies implied not only anti-intellectualism but a huge disadvantage for children of poor and immigrant families, because (as Dewey noted) children's interests are conditioned by what they already know and have previously been exposed to.

The disparagement of academic studies by advocates of custodialism, mental hygiene, and social reconstruction in the 1930s and by life adjustment educators in the 1940s and 1950s further downgraded intellectual growth and academic learning, seeking to make them only a minor part of schooling. In their efforts to turn the schools into mass agencies for social adjustment, the life adjustment educators promoted conformity, trivialized the curriculum, and displayed their contempt for students' intellectual development.

The 1960s brought the era of "relevance" to the schools, borrowing heavily (if unknowingly) from the anti-intellectual and anti-academic ideas of previous decades. Once again, the emphasis among theorists of education was on personal experiences, activities, and spontaneity. Requirements were replaced by electives, and students' interests replaced adults' decisions about what children needed to know. In the late 1970s, the reaction against the excesses of the 1960s produced the minimum competency movement, which expected far too little of students. The 1980s and 1990s saw a campaign among parents, legislators, governors, business leaders, and even presidents to strengthen curricula, raise graduation requirements, and set higher expectations for all children.

As late as the 1990s, however, there were still commentators who insisted that the schools should not even attempt to educate all children at a high level, that doing so was neither necessary nor wise because society did not need an overeducated workforce and might not have enough uneducated people to do menial work.[5] Similar objections were raised against efforts to create academically focused public charter schools; critics feared that such schools might fail to produce the low-wage workers that the economy presumably needed. Such worries echoed the anti-democratic views expressed in the early twentieth century by David Snedden, John Franklin Bobbitt, and W. W. Charters, who wanted the public schools to train children for their different niches in the occupational structure, not to "waste" the public's money by attempting to educate those who were unlikely to go to college and into the professions.

What if the critics were right and the economy did not really need so many well-educated people? Would it be a waste of time and money to try to educate everyone as if they were bound for college? After all, the

American economy performed exceptionally well in the past fifty years, despite life adjustment education and minimal standards.

It should be remembered that there are many more reasons to get a good education than preparing for gainful employment. Whether or not individuals get a better job with a better education, they will nonetheless find personal, lifelong value in their knowledge of history and literature, science and social science, art and mathematics. And democratic society itself is dependent on the judgments of a majority, which suggests that everyone benefits by disseminating reason, knowledge, and civic wisdom as broadly as possible.

Surely, the nation's economic success has relied in large part on broad access to schooling, a vigorous system of higher education, and a society-wide commitment to second chances for learning, as well as the immigration of highly educated people; improving education can only increase our national resources of skills and knowledge.

PROGRESSIVE AND TRADITIONAL EDUCATION

It is no simple matter to demarcate the divide between what is called progressive education and what is called traditional education. Neither term can be easily defined. The meaning of both terms has shifted over time, and there is a tendency to react to one or the other of them as "good" or "bad" depending on one's experiences and preferences. Both sides have had their virtues and defects, depending on circumstances.

At different times in the past century, a progressive educator was someone associated with the industrial education movement, the scientific movement in education, the curricular differentiation movement, the mental-testing movement, the child-centered school movement, the mental hygiene movement, or the life adjustment movement. At different times in the past century, a traditional educator was someone associated with a harsh regime of memorization and recitation, the "back-to-basics" movement, or a strong commitment to teaching all students the liberal arts and sciences.[6]

At their extremes, both sides can be faulted, the one for demeaning intellectual and academic standards, the other for caring more about sub-

462

ject matter than children. But at their best, both philosophies have made valuable and complementary contributions to American education. Progressive educators can justly take credit for emphasizing students' motivation and understanding and making the schools responsible for the health and general welfare of children. Traditionalists such as Harris, Bagley, and Hirsch must be credited for insisting upon the democratic responsibility of the school to promote the intellectual growth of all children. At their best, these traditions overlap and the differences between them become blurred because thoughtful educators, regardless of label, seek to develop their students' intellect and character.

Despite the heated controversies of the past century, there is surely an area of commonality between the best impulses of progressivism and traditionalism. There is a tradition within progressivism that respects intellectual development; this tradition was best exemplified in the work of private progressive schools such as the Dewey school and the Lincoln School, as well as the public schools of Winnetka under Carleton Washburne. Students at the experimental Dewey school were exposed to a liberal arts curriculum rich in literature, history, and opportunities to explore challenging ideas. Students at the Lincoln School were encouraged to read literary classics, create publications, debate historical issues, and conduct scientific experiments. In the public schools of Winnetka under Washburne's direction, teachers determined what students needed to know, then developed individualized programs so that every student would be able to achieve mastery of important knowledge and skills.

Although this intellectual heritage was not in the progressive mainstream during the heyday of the social radicalism of the 1930s, the life adjustment movement of the 1940s and 1950s, and the romantic rebellion of the 1960s, it did not die. In the latter years of the twentieth century, Theodore R. Sizer, Deborah Meier, and Howard Gardner became national leaders of an effort to reclaim the strain of progressivism that championed students' joy in learning without denying the importance of academic disciplines and to cleanse progressivism of its earlier associations with IQ testing, curricular differentiation, anti-intellectualism, and life adjustment education.

Whether intellectual progressivism of the sort advocated by educators such as Sizer, Meier, and Gardner could grow in a typical public school setting, however, was uncertain. At century's end, the typical public school was bureaucratically controlled, contained numerous inconsistent ad hoc programs, and lacked intellectual coherence. Intellectual progressivism in the late twentieth century tended to flourish best in private schools or in small public-sector alternative and charter schools.

Liberal traditionalists believed that knowledge is power and wanted the public schools to distribute that power as widely as possible throughout society. Lester Frank Ward, a proponent of intellectual egalitarianism, wanted all children to have access to what he called "directive intelligence." William T. Harris believed that educators should not merely identify children's "natural" abilities and interests, but teach them to appreciate and use the great heritage of ideas in the world. William C. Bagley advocated high standards and a common curriculum in major subjects for all children. Isaac Kandel warned that the schools, by failing to teach youngsters to share the developed culture of the world, were abandoning them to the entertainment devised by commercial mass media. Kenneth Clark and Ronald Edmonds believed that poor and minority children would learn if they received intensive instruction from dedicated teachers.

The most prominent advocate of liberal traditionalism in education in the late twentieth century was E. D. Hirsch, Jr., who argued for a culturally rich and explicit curriculum in the elementary grades; this was heretical to many in the education establishment. Hirsch's concern about curricular content was closely related to the earlier work of Carleton Washburne in the Winnetka schools. Hirsch was less concerned about pedagogy than Washburne and more concerned about the broad diffusion of knowledge to advance social justice. He understood that children could get excited by learning about dinosaurs, ancient Egypt, or modern China and that many teachers appreciated clear curriculum guidelines.

Neither intellectual progressivism nor liberal traditionalism was likely to take root in the public schools without a teaching staff of well-educated people. However, by century's end, such teachers were not abundantly available. In 1998, only 38 percent of public school teachers had majored in *any* academic field of study when they were undergraduates or graduate students; those with an academic major included only 22 percent of elementary school teachers, 44 percent of middle school teachers, and 66 percent of high school teachers.[7] Teachers who do not have a strong education themselves are not well prepared to inspire a love of learning in their students.

WHY SCHOOLS MATTER

Large social organizations cannot succeed unless they focus on what they do best. The same is true for schools. What is it that schools and only schools can and must do? They cannot be successful as schools unless nearly all of their pupils gain literacy and numeracy, as well as a good understanding of history and the sciences, literature, and a foreign language. They cannot be successful unless they teach children the importance of honesty, personal responsibility, intellectual curiosity, industry, kindness, empathy, and courage.

Schools must prepare youngsters to have the "versatile intelligence" of which William T. Harris wrote, the intelligence that allows individuals to learn new tasks and take charge of their lives. They must teach them to use symbolic language and abstract ideas. They must teach youngsters about the culture and world in which they live and about cultures that existed long ago and far away.

If schools know and affirm what they do well, they can liberate themselves from the fads and panaceas that have often been inflicted on them by pressure groups, legislators, and well-meaning enthusiasts. Schools cannot compete with the visual drama of television, the Internet, and the movies. But the mass media, random and impersonal as they are, cannot compete with teachers, who have the capacity to get to know youngsters, inspire them, and guide them to responsible maturity.

The three great errors demonstrated in these pages are, first, the belief that schools should be expected to solve all of society's problems; second, the belief that only a portion of children need access to a high-quality academic education; and third, the belief that schools should emphasize students' immediate experiences and minimize (or even ignore) the transmission of knowledge. The first of these assumptions leads to a loss of focus, diverting the schools from their most basic mission; the second contributes to low achievement and anti-democratic policies; the third deprives youngsters of the intellectual power that derives from learning about the experiences of others and prevents them from standing on the shoulders of giants in every field of thought and action.

Perhaps in the past it was possible to undereducate a significant portion of the population without causing serious harm to the nation. No longer. Education, today more than at any time in the past, is the key to successful participation in society. A boy or girl who cannot read, write, or use mathematics is locked out of every sort of educational opportunity. A man or woman without a good elementary and secondary education is virtually precluded from higher education, from many desirable careers, from full participation in our political system, and from enjoyment of civilization's great aesthetic treasures. The society that allows large numbers of its citizens to remain uneducated, ignorant, or semiliterate squanders its greatest asset, the intelligence of its people.

The disciplines taught in school are uniquely valuable, both for individuals and for society. A society that does not teach science to the general public fosters the proliferation of irrational claims and antiscientific belief systems. A society that turns its back on the teaching of history encourages mass amnesia, leaving the public ignorant of the important events and ideas of the human past and eroding the civic intelligence needed for the future. A democratic society that fails to teach the younger generation its principles of self-government puts these principles at risk. A society that does not teach youngsters to appreciate great works of literature and art permits a coarsening and degradation of its popular culture. A society that is racially and ethnically diverse requires, more than other societies, a conscious effort to build shared values and ideals among its citizenry. A society that tolerates anti-intellectualism in its schools can expect to have a dumbed-down culture that honors celebrity and sensation rather than knowledge and wisdom.

Schools will not be rendered obsolete by new technologies because their role as learning institutions has become even more important than in the past. Technology can supplement schooling but not replace it;

even the most advanced electronic technologies are incapable of turning their worlds of information into mature knowledge, a form of intellectual magic that requires skilled and educated teachers.

To be effective, schools must concentrate on their fundamental mission of teaching and learning. And they must do it for all children. That must be the overarching goal of schools in the twenty-first century.

Notes

Introduction

1. Lawrence A. Cremin, *The Transformation of the School: Progressivism in American Education, 1876–1957* (New York: Knopf, 1961).

Chapter 1: The Educational Ladder

1. Oscar D. Robinson, "Constants and Electives in the High School," *The School Review,* April 1901, p. 243.
2. W. A. Mowry, "The School Curriculum and Its Relations to Business Life," *Education,* November 1881, pp. 143, 149.
3. National Center for Education Statistics, *Digest of Education Statistics 1995* (Washington, D.C.: U.S. Department of Education, 1995), p. 68; National Center for Educational Statistics, *120 Years of American Education: A Statistical Portrait* (Washington, D.C.: U.S. Department of Education, 1993), pp. 11, 36, 55. Among black children from ages 5 to 19, only 32.9 percent were attending school in 1890, compared to 57.9 percent of white children, p. 14.
4. Joseph Mayer Rice, *The Public-School System of the United States* (New York: Century, 1893), pp. 31, 56, 100, 128.

5. Mark Sullivan, *Our Times: The United States, 1900–1925: America Finding Herself,* vol. 2 (New York: Scribner's, 1927), pp. 69–75, 83.

6. Ibid., pp. 120–122.

7. William J. Reese, *The Origins of the American High School* (New Haven, Conn.: Yale University Press, 1995), p. 93.

8. Isaac L. Kandel, *History of Secondary Education: A Study in the Development of Liberal Education* (Boston: Houghton Mifflin, 1930), p. 449. *120 Years of American Education: A Statistical Portrait,* pp. 36, 55, 76. By 1890, there were 202,963 students in 2,526 public high schools, compared to 94,931 students in 1,632 private high schools. 14.3 million children were enrolled in the common schools, but only a tiny number attended high school, and only 3.5 percent of seventeen-year-old youths actually graduated from high school. The majority of high school graduates were girls, and the majority of those who went to college were boys.

9. Fassett A. Cotton, "The Township High School in Indiana," *The School Review,* April 1904, p. 276.

10. Herbert Spencer, *Education: Intellectual, Moral and Physical* (New York: Burt, 1859), pp. 7–8, 16–17, 89–93.

11. Henry Steele Commager, ed., *Lester Ward and the Welfare State* (Indianapolis: Bobbs-Merrill, 1967), p. xviii.

12. Lawrence A. Cremin, *The Transformation of the School: Progressivism in American Education, 1876–1957* (New York: Knopf, 1961), p. 91.

13. Commager, *Lester Ward and the Welfare State,* p. xxii.

14. Lester Frank Ward, "Art Is the Antithesis of Nature," from *Mind,* 9 (October 1884), quoted in ibid., p. 73.

15. Ibid., pp. 78–79.

16. Lester Frank Ward, *Psychic Factors of Civilization* (Boston: Ginn, 1893), p. 257.

17. Lester Frank Ward, *Applied Sociology: A Treatise of the Conscious Improvement of Society by Society* (Boston: Ginn, 1906), p. 314.

18. Commager, *Lester Ward and the Welfare State,* p. 58; excerpted from Lester Frank Ward, *Dynamic Sociology, or Applied Social Science,* vol. 1 (New York: Appleton, 1883), pp. 590–591.

19. Ward, ibid., pp. 598–600.

20. Lester Frank Ward, "Broadening the Way to Success," *The Forum,* 2 (November 1886), pp. 345–350.

21. Ward, *Applied Sociology,* pp. 95–96. See also Lester Frank Ward, "Education and Progress," in Commager, *Lester Ward and the Welfare State,* pp. 409–415.

22. Charles W. Eliot, "The Gap Between the Elementary Schools and the Colleges," *National Educational Association Proceedings,* 1890, pp. 522–523.

23. Charles W. Eliot, "Shortening and Enriching the Grammar School Course," *National Educational Association Proceedings,* 1892, reprinted in *Charles W. Eliot and Popular Education,* ed. Edward A. Krug (New York: Teachers College Press, 1961), pp. 52–53.

24. Ibid., pp. 53–55.

25. Charles W. Eliot, "Undesirable and Desirable Uniformity in Schools," *National Educational Association Proceedings,* 1892, p. 89.

26. Charles W. Eliot, "Wherein Popular Education Has Failed," *The Forum,* 14 (December 1892), pp. 411–428, reprinted in Krug, *Charles W. Eliot and Popular Education,* pp. 68–71, 78.

27. William T. Harris, "How I Was Educated," *The Forum,* August 1886, p. 560. See also, K. F. Leidecker, *Yankee Teacher: The Life of William Torrey Harris* (New York: The Philosophical Library, 1946). For a recent essay on Harris, see William J. Reese, "The Philosopher King of St. Louis," *Curriculum and Consequences: Herbert M. Kliebard and the Promise of Schooling,* ed. Barry M. Franklin (New York: Teachers College Press, 2000), pp. 155–177.

28. Cremin, *The Transformation of the School,* pp. 15–19.

29. Herbert M. Kliebard, *The Struggle for the American Curriculum, 1893–1958* (Boston: Routledge, Kegan Paul, 1986), pp. 17–18; Merle Curti, *The Social Ideas of American Educators,* rev. ed. (New York: Pageant, 1959; first published 1935), pp. 310–347. The chapter on Harris is titled "William T. Harris, The Conservator."

30. W. T. Harris, "The Study of Arrested Development in Children As Produced by Injudicious School Methods," *Education,* April 1900, pp. 457–459.

31. Bureau of Education, *Report of the Commissioner of Education* (Washington, D.C.: U.S. Department of the Interior, 1891), pp. liv–lvii.

32. Board of Directors of the St. Louis Public Schools, *Seventeenth Annual Report of the Board of Directors of the St. Louis Public Schools* (Saint Louis, 1872), pp. 31–36. Among the specific duties that created moral training in a public school, he wrote, were punctuality ("the duty of obedience to the external requirement of time"); regularity (the discipline gained in calisthenics or vocal music, which teaches the self-control necessary "to free us from degrading slavery to our physical wants"); silence ("the basis for the culture of internality or reflection—the soil in which thought grows," by which he meant learning to think before speaking out); truth ("the basis of the duties of a man toward others"); justice (in which a child learns a sense of responsibility and replaces "I want" with "I ought"); and "Kindness or Love of Mankind," the highest of virtues, which grows only in a community that brings together people of all classes and condi-

tions and "subjects them to the same trials and the same standard of success."

33. William T. Harris, "The Pedagogical Creed of William T. Harris," in *Educational Creeds of the Nineteenth Century,* ed. Ossian H. Lang (New York: Kellogg, 1898), p. 37.

34. W. T. Harris, "How the School Strengthens the Individuality of the Pupils," *National Educational Association Proceedings,* 1902, pp. 118–125.

35. W. T. Harris, "What Shall the Public Schools Teach?" *The Forum,* 4 (February 1888), p. 575.

36. W. T. Harris, "Educational Values," Report of the St. Louis Public Schools for 1872–73, reprinted in *Annual Report of the Commissioner of Education* vol. I (Washington, D.C.: U.S. Office of Education, 1893–94), pp. 632–633.

37. W. T. Harris, "The Curriculum for Secondary Schools," *National Educational Association Proceedings,* 1894, pp. 500–502; W. T. Harris, "How the School Strengthens the Individuality of the Pupils," *National Educational Association Proceedings,* 1902, pp. 122–125.

38. W. T. Harris, "Does the Common School Educate Children Above the Station They Are Expected to Occupy in Life?" *Education,* May 1883, pp. 461–463, 475.

39. William T. Harris, "A Brief for Latin," *Educational Review,* April 1899, p. 316.

40. Harris, "Educational Values," pp. 622–623; reprinted from the report of the St. Louis public schools for 1872–73.

41. C. M. Woodward, "Manual Training in General Education," *Education,* July 1885, pp. 615–616.

42. W. T. Harris, "The Psychology of Manual Training," *National Educational Association Proceedings,* 1889, pp. 117–132; see also W. T. Harris, "The Psychology of Manual Training," *Education,* May 1889, pp. 571–582.

43. Cremin, *The Transformation of the School,* pp. 32–38.

44. *120 Years of American Education,* p. 14.

45. James D. Anderson, *The Education of Blacks in the South, 1860–1935* (Chapel Hill: University of North Carolina Press, 1988), pp. 79–109. See also Eric Anderson and Alfred A. Moss, Jr., *Dangerous Donations: Northern Philanthropy and Southern Black Education, 1902–1930* (Columbia, Mo.: University of Missouri Press, 1999), pp. 86–91, 200–210.

46. Booker T. Washington, "The Atlanta Exposition Address," *The American Reader,* ed. Diane Ravitch (New York: HarperCollins, 1991), pp. 185–186; Emma Lou Thornbrough, "Booker T. Washington," *Dictionary of American Negro Biography,* ed. Rayford W. Logan and Michael R. Winston (New York: Norton, 1982), p. 634.

47. William Edward Burghardt Du Bois, "Of Mr. Booker T. Washington and Others," *The Souls of Black Folk* (New York: Penguin, 1989, orig. pub. 1903), p. 43.

48. William Edward Burghardt Du Bois, "The Talented Tenth," ibid., pp. 518, 522.

49. William C. Collar, "The Action of the Colleges upon the Schools," *Educational Review,* December 1891, pp. 422–441.

50. David L. Angus and Jeffrey E. Mirel, *The Failed Promise of the American High School, 1890–1995* (New York: Teachers College Press, 1999), p. 9.

51. National Educational Association, *Report of the Committee on Secondary School Studies Appointed at the Meeting of the National Educational Association, July 9, 1892; with the Reports of the Conferences Arranged by This Committee, and Held December 28–30, 1892,* Document 205 (Washington, D.C.: U.S. Department of Interior, Bureau of Education, 1893), p. 17. The report is reprinted in Theodore R. Sizer, *Secondary Schools at the Turn of the Century* (New Haven: Yale University Press, 1964).

52. Ibid., p. 51.

53. W. R. Butler, "Should Preparatory and Non-Preparatory Pupils Receive Identical Treatment in High Schools?" *Educational Review,* December 1896, pp. 473–486.

54. James H. Baker, "Minority Report," in *Report of the Committee on Secondary School Studies,* p. 57.

55. Charles W. Eliot, "The Unity of Educational Reform," *Educational Review,* October 1894, pp. 212, 214, 217.

56. G. Stanley Hall, *Adolescence: Its Psychology and Its Relations to Physiology, Anthropology, Sociology, Sex, Crime, Religion and Education,* vol. 2 (New York: Appleton, 1904), p. 510.

57. Ibid., pp. 512–513.

58. Charles W. Eliot, "The Fundamental Assumptions in the Report of the Committee of Ten," *Educational Review,* November 1905, pp. 330–332.

59. Edward A. Krug, *The Shaping of the American High School, 1880–1920* (Madison: University of Wisconsin Press, 1964), p. 89.

60. Edward A. Krug, "Graduates of Secondary Schools in and Around 1900: Did Most of Them Go to College?" *The School Review,* 70, no. 3 (Autumn 1962), pp. 266–272.

61. Isaac L. Kandel, *The Dilemma of Democracy* (Cambridge, Mass.: Harvard University Press, 1934), pp. 26–27.

62. Angus and Mirel, *The Failed Promise,* p. 7.

63. David Wessel, "Scanning the Future, Economic Historian Plumbs Distant Past," *The Wall Street Journal,* February 13, 1996, p. 1.

64. John F. Latimer, *What's Happened to Our High Schools?* (Washington, D.C.: Public Affairs Press, 1958), p. 26.

65. Sizer, *Secondary Schools at the Turn of the Century,* pp. 2–3.

Chapter 2: A Fork in the Road

1. Lawrence A. Cremin, David A. Shannon, and Mary Evelyn Townsend, *A History of Teachers College, Columbia University* (New York: Columbia University Press, 1954), p. 53.

2. James Earl Russell, *Founding Teachers College* (New York: Teachers College Bureau of Publications, 1937), pp. 4–6. See also Lawrence A. Cremin, *The Transformation of the School: Progressivism in American Education, 1876–1957* (New York: Knopf, 1961), pp. 170–172.

3. Richard Hofstadter, *The Age of Reform: From Bryan to F.D.R.* (New York: Knopf, 1955); Peter G. Filene, "An Obituary for 'the Progressive Movement,' " *American Quarterly,* Spring 1970, pp. 20–34.

4. Herbert M. Kliebard, *The Struggle for the American Curriculum, 1893–1958* (Boston: Routledge & Kegan Paul, 1986), p. xi; Cremin, *The Transformation of the School,* pp. vii–x; David L. Angus and Jeffrey E. Mirel, *The Failed Promise of the American High School, 1890–1995* (New York: Teachers College Press, 1999), p. 13.

5. Ellwood P. Cubberley, *Public Education in the United States: A Study and Interpretation of American Educational History* (Boston: Houghton Mifflin, 1919), p. 358.

6. U.S. Immigration Commission, *The Children of Immigrants in Schools,* vol. 1 (Washington, D.C.: U.S. Government Printing Office, 1911), pp. 14–15.

7. Cubberley, *Public Education in the United States,* p. 357.

8. Robert A. Woods and Albert J. Kennedy, *The Settlement Horizon* (New York: Russell Sage Foundation, 1922), pp. 136–137, quoted in Sol Cohen, "The Industrial Education Movement, 1906–17," *American Quarterly,* Spring 1968, p. 100.

9. James E. Russell, "The Trend in American Education," *Educational Review,* June 1906, p. 39.

10. John Dewey, "My Pedagogic Creed," *The School Journal,* January 16, 1897, pp. 77–80; reprinted in *Dewey on Education,* ed. Martin S. Dworkin (New York: Teachers College Press, 1959), pp. 19–32.

11. John Dewey, "The School and Society," ibid., p. 34.

12. Ibid., pp. 36, 39, 41.

13. Ibid., p. 83.

14. John Dewey, *The Way Out of Educational Confusion* (Cambridge, Mass.: Harvard University Press, 1931), p. 21.

15. John Dewey, "The School and Society," pp. 33–35, 41–42.

16. James H. Baker, "Review of the Report of the Committee of Ten," *National Education Association Proceedings,* 1894, p. 653; J. C. Schurman, "The Report on Secondary School Studies," *School Review,* 2 (1894), p. 93; see also B. A. Hinsdale, "The Dogma of Formal Discipline," *Educational Review,* September 1894, pp. 128–142.

17. William James, *The Principles of Psychology,* vol. 1 (New York: Holt, 1890), pp. 666–667.

18. William James, *Talks to Teachers on Psychology* (New York: Holt, 1899), p. 7.

19. Edward L. Thorndike, *The Principles of Teaching Based on Psychology* (New York: Seiler, 1911), p. 246.

20. E. L. Thorndike and R. S. Woodworth, "The Influence of Improvement in One Mental Function upon the Efficiency of Other Functions," *The Psychological Review,* 8 (1901), pp. 249–250, 395.

21. Frederic Burk, quoted in Walter H. Drost, *David Snedden and Education for Social Efficiency* (Madison: University of Wisconsin Press, 1967), pp. 58–59, originally in "Review of the Year," *Western Journal of Education,* January 1903, pp. 34–35.

22. Frederic Burk, quoted in W. H. Heck, *Mental Discipline and Educational Values* (New York: Lane, 1909), p. 127 (originally "The Bankruptcy of 'Education,' " *The World's Work,* July 1909).

23. Edward L. Thorndike, *Educational Psychology: Briefer Course* (New York: Teachers College Press, 1914), pp. 268–275.

24. E. L. Thorndike, "Mental Discipline in High School Studies," *The Journal of Educational Psychology,* 15, no. 1 (January 1924), p. 95.

25. Ibid., p. 98.

26. Alexander Meiklejohn, "Is Mental Training a Myth?" *Educational Review,* February 1909, p. 130.

27. In 1916, Harold Rugg defended transfer of training. He found that students of descriptive geometry substantially improved their problem-solving abilities and that formal school subjects developed the "ability to analyze the problem and to organize a method of procedure; to build up ideals, or to organize a method of attack. But it is undoubted that they also make habitual, or automatic, many specific constituents of the complex abilities that function in many complex situations." Rugg later became one of the leaders of the progressive education movement and an outspoken critic of traditional education. See Harold Ordway Rugg, *The Experimental Determination of Mental Discipline in School Studies* (Baltimore: Warwick & York, 1916), p. 116.

28. Pedro Tamesis Orata, *The Theory of Identical Elements: Being a Critique of Thorndike's Theory of Identical Elements and a Re-interpretation of the Problem of Transfer of Training* (Columbus: Ohio State University Press, 1928), pp. 168–169, 171.

29. Ibid., pp. 174–175.

30. Walter B. Kolesnik, *Mental Discipline in Modern Education* (Madison: University of Wisconsin Press, 1958), p. 5.

31. Richard Hofstadter, *Anti-intellectualism in American Life* (New York: Vintage, 1962), p. 349.

32. G. E. Partridge, *Genetic Philosophy of Education: An Epitome of the Published Educational Writings of President G. Stanley Hall of Clark University* (New York: Sturgis & Walton, 1912), pp. 92–93, 99–100.

33. G. Stanley Hall, "The Contents of Children's Minds," *Readings in the History of Psychology,* ed. Wayne Dennis (New York: Appleton-Century-Crofts, 1948), pp. 258–259, 275.

34. Brian Gill and Stephen Schlossman, " 'A Sin Against Childhood': Progressive Education and the Crusade to Abolish Homework, 1897–1941," *American Journal of Education,* November 1996, p. 34.

35. G. Stanley Hall, "Child Study and Its Relation to Education," *The Forum,* 29 (August 1900), p. 691, reprinted in *Health, Growth, and Heredity: G. Stanley Hall on Natural Education,* eds. Charles E. Strickland and Charles Burgess (New York: Teachers College Press, 1965), pp. 79–80.

36. O. T. Corson, "Educational Extremes," *National Educational Association Proceedings,* 1897, p. 150; quoted in Edward A. Krug, *The Shaping of the American High School: 1880–1920* (Madison: University of Wisconsin Press, 1964), p. 111.

37. G. Stanley Hall, "New Departures in Education," *The North American Review,* 140 (February 1885), p. 145.

38. G. Stanley Hall, *Adolescence: Its Psychology, and Its Relations to Physiology, Anthropology, Sociology, Sex, Crime, Religion and Education,* vol. 2 (New York: Appleton, 1904), pp. 456–459.

39. G. Stanley Hall, *Educational Problems,* vol. 2 (New York: Appleton, 1911), p. 618.

40. G. Stanley Hall, "Educational Values," *Journal of Education,* December 27, 1894, p. 424.

41. G. Stanley Hall, "The Ideal School As Based on Child Study," in *Health, Growth, and Heredity: G. Stanley Hall on Natural Education,* eds. Strickland and Burgess, pp. 115–116.

42. Ibid., pp. 116–117.

43. Hall, *Adolescence,* vol. 2, pp. 569, 583, 646.

44. G. Stanley Hall, "The High School as the People's College," in *Health, Growth, and Heredity,* eds. Strickland and Burgess, p. 139.

45. Hall, *Educational Problems,* p. 618.

46. G. Stanley Hall, "How Far Is the Present High-School and Early College Training Adapted to the Nature and Needs of Adolescents?" *The School Review,* December 1901, pp. 649–665; for Eliot's response, see pp. 665–671.

47. Albion Small, "Some Demands of Sociology upon Pedagogy," *American Journal of Sociology,* 2, no. 6 (May 1897), pp. 839–841, 848.

48. Ibid., p. 851.

49. Marvin Lazerson and W. Norton Grubb, eds., *American Education and Vocationalism: A Documentary History 1870–1970* (New York: Teachers College Press, 1974), pp. 69–75. See also Krug, *The Shaping of the American High School,* pp. 218–221.

50. John Marrinn, "Vocational Education for the Rural School," *Educational Review,* June 1913, p. 39.

51. Sol Cohen, "The Industrial Education Movement, 1906–17," *American Quarterly,* 20 (Spring 1968), p. 96.

52. Annual Message of the President, December 3, 1907; quoted in Krug, *The Shaping of the American High School,* p. 225.

53. U.S. Bureau of Education, *Report of the Committee of the National Council of Education on Economy of Time in Education,* Bulletin No. 38, 1913 (Washington, D.C.: U.S. Government Printing Office, 1913), pp. 11–13, 32–34, 35–37. The chairman of the Committee on Economy of Time in Education was James H. Baker, the dissenting member of the Committee of Ten who had argued against the Ten's emphasis on mental discipline and in favor of the power of knowledge.

54. Nicholas Murray Butler, "Vocational Education: An Address" (1913), p. 6, quoted in Cohen, "The Industrial Education Movement," p. 99.

55. Edward A. Ross, *Social Control: A Survey of the Foundations of Order,* rev. ed. (New York: Macmillan, 1916; first published 1901), pp. 174–179; Lester Frank Ward, *Applied Sociology* (New York: Ginn, 1906), p. 95.

56. Ross, *Social Control,* pp. 174–179.

57. See Drost, *David Snedden and Education for Social Efficiency.*

58. David Snedden, "Current Problems of Aim in Physics Teaching," *School and Society,* November 30, 1918, pp. 631–635.

59. David Samuel Snedden, "The Schools of the Rank and File," Addresses Delivered Before the Eighth Annual Meeting of the Alumni Association of Leland Stanford Junior University, May 29, 1900, in Hanna Archives of the Hoover Institution Library, pp. 23–36.

60. David Snedden, "New Problems in Secondary Education," *The School Review,* March 1916, p. 183; see also David Snedden, "Liberal Education Without Latin," *The School Review,* October 1918, pp. 576–599.

61. David Snedden, "Increasing the Efficiency of Education," *The Journal of Education,* July 17, 1913, pp. 62–63; David Snedden, "Proposed Revision of Secondary School Subjects Looking to More Effective Education in Personal Culture and Good Citizenship," *School and Society,* February 8, 1919, p. 161; David Snedden, "The Waning Powers of Art," *The American Journal of Sociology,* May 1917, pp. 805, 808.

62. David Snedden, "Teaching of History in Secondary Schools," *The History Teacher's Magazine,* November 1914, pp. 277–282.

63. George L. Burr, "What History Shall We Teach?" *The History Teacher's Magazine,* November 1914, pp. 283, 286. See also David Snedden, "History and Other Social Sciences in the Education of Youths Twelve to Eighteen Years of Age," *School and Society,* March 10, 1917, pp. 271–281.

64. Snedden, "Liberal Education Without Latin," pp. 576–599; Charles N. Moore, Letter, *School and Society,* November 23, 1918, pp. 622–623.

65. David Snedden, Letter, *School and Society,* December 14, 1918, p. 714.

66. David Snedden, *Vocational Education* (New York: Macmillan, 1923), p. 95.

67. See the exchange between Snedden and Dewey: David Snedden, "Vocational Education," and John Dewey, "Education vs. Trade-Training, Dr. Dewey's Reply," *The New Republic,* May 15, 1915, pp. 41–43.

68. H. Gordon Hullfish, "Looking Backward with Snedden," *Educational Review,* February 1924, p. 69.

69. Snedden, *Vocational Education,* p. 76.

70. Charles W. Eliot, "The Fundamental Assumptions in the Report of the Committee of Ten," *Educational Review,* November 1905, pp. 330–331.

71. Charles W. Eliot, "Industrial Education as an Essential Factor in Our National Prosperity," quoted in *Charles W. Eliot and Popular Education,* ed. Edward A. Krug (New York: Teachers College Press, 1961), pp. 19–20.

Chapter 3: The Age of the Experts

1. H. B. Wilson, "Socializing the School," *Educational Administration and Supervision,* February 1918, pp. 88–94.

2. Yale Kramer, "Freud and the Culture Wars," *The Public Interest,* 124 (Summer 1996), p. 38.

3. Edward Bok, "A National Crime at the Feet of American Parents," *The Ladies' Home Journal,* January 1900, p. 16; Edward Bok, "The First Blow," *The Ladies' Home Journal,* October 1900, p. 16. See also Brian Gill and Stephen Schlossman, " 'A Sin Against Childhood': Progressive Education and the Crusade to Abolish Homework," *American Journal of Education,* November 1996, pp. 27–66.

4. Junius L. Meriam, "Fundamentals in the Elementary School Curriculum," *National Education Association Proceedings,* 1909, pp. 169–175.

5. William H. Elson and Frank P. Bachman, "Different Courses for Elementary Schools," *Educational Review,* April 1910, p. 358.

6. Ibid., p. 359. See also William H. Elson, "The Technical High School of Cleveland," *The School Review,* June 1908, pp. 353–359.

7. William C. Bagley, editorial, *School and Home Education,* March 1915, pp. 238–241.

8. Ibid.

9. William Hughes Mearns, "Our Medieval High Schools: Shall We Educate Children for the Twelfth or the Twentieth Century?" *The Saturday Evening Post,* March 2, 1912, pp. 18–19.

10. William D. Lewis, "The High School and the Boy," *The Saturday Evening Post,* April 6, 1912, pp. 8–11; William D. Lewis, *Democracy's High School* (Boston: Houghton Mifflin, 1914), pp. 54, 65–73.

11. James E. Russell, "The Trend in American Education," *Educational Review,* June 1906, p. 35.

12. Ellwood P. Cubberley, *Changing Conceptions of Education* (New York: Houghton Mifflin, 1909), pp. 16–20.

13. Ibid., pp. 56–58.

14. Ibid., p. 15.

15. Ellwood P. Cubberley, "Does the Present Trend Toward Vocational Education Threaten Liberal Culture?" *The School Review,* September 1911, p. 458.

16. Ibid., pp. 460–462.

17. Cubberley, *Changing Conceptions of Education,* pp. 44, 61–63. Historian Lawrence A. Cremin called this book "a typical progressive tract of the era"; see Lawrence A. Cremin, *The Transformation of the School: Progressivism in American Education, 1876–1957* (New York: Knopf, 1961), p. 68.

18. Cubberly, ibid., pp. 66–68.

19. Ellwood P. Cubberley, *Public School Administration: A Statement of the Fundamental Principles Underlying the Organization and Administration of Public Education* (Boston: Houghton Mifflin, 1916), pp. 278–281, 283–284, 306–317.

20. Charles A. Ellwood, "The Sociological Basis of the Science of Education," *Education,* November 1911, p. 137.
21. National Center for Education Statistics, *Digest of Education Statistics 1995* (Washington, D.C.: U.S. Department of Education, 1996), p. 68.
22. Editorial, *Education,* October 1911, pp. 118–119.
23. Louis W. Rapeer, "College Entrance Requirements: The Judgment of Educators," *School and Society,* January 8, 1916, pp. 45–48; "College Entrance Requirements: The Elimination of the Non-English Languages and the Non-Arithmetical Mathematics," *School and Society,* April 15, 1916, pp. 549–556.
24. Charles Hughes Johnston, "Curriculum Adjustments in Modern High Schools," *The School Review,* November 1914, 577–590.
25. Ibid.
26. Charles Hughes Johnston, "What Is Curriculum Differentiation?" *Educational Administration and Supervision,* January 1916, pp. 49–57.
27. William L. Felter, "On Reconstructing the Curriculum in Secondary Schools," *Educational Review,* June 1914, pp. 46–47.
28. David Tyack and Elisabeth Hansot, *Managers of Virtue: Public School Leadership in America, 1820–1980* (New York: Basic Books), 1982, p. 165; see also David B. Tyack, *The One Best System: A History of American Urban Education* (Cambridge, Mass.: Harvard University Press, 1974), p. 137.
29. "The Texas Survey," *The School Review,* October 1924, p. 565.
30. Ellwood P. Cubberley, *School Organization and Administration: A Concrete Study Based on the Salt Lake City School Survey* (Yonkers-on-Hudson, N.Y.: World Book, 1917), p. v.
31. Ibid., pp. 7, 112–113.
32. Ibid., pp. 136, 191.
33. Ibid., pp. 7, 119–123, 126–127, 132, 141, 171–193.
34. Ibid., pp. 121, 212.
35. John Franklin Bobbitt, "The Elimination of Waste in Education," *The Elementary School Teacher,* February 1912, p. 263; J. F. Bobbitt, "High-School Costs," *The School Review,* October 1915, pp. 505–534.
36. J. F. Bobbitt, *The San Antonio Public School System: A Survey* (San Antonio: San Antonio School Board, 1915), pp. 9–15, 26–27.
37. Ibid., pp. 26–27.
38. Ibid., p. 29.
39. Ibid., pp. 28–29, 37–39.
40. Ibid., pp. 16–21.
41. Cubberley, *Public School Administration,* pp. 325–326, 336.
42. U.S. Bureau of Education, *Negro Education: A Study of the Private and*

Higher Schools for Colored People in the United States ("Prepared in cooperation with the Phelps-Stokes Fund under the direction of Thomas Jesse Jones, specialist in the education of racial groups, Bureau of Education"), Bulletin, no. 38 (1916) (Washington, D.C.: U.S. Government Printing Office, 1917).

43. Ibid., pp. 36–37.
44. U.S. Bureau of Education, *Negro Education: A Study of the Private and Higher Schools for Colored People in the United States,* Bulletin, no. 39 (1916) (Washington, D.C.: U.S. Government Printing Office, 1917), p. 13.
45. U.S. Bureau of Education, *Negro Education,* no. 38, pp. 7, 9, 28, 33.
46. Ibid., pp. 9, 11–13, 25, 35, 42–43. See also James D. Anderson, *The Education of Blacks in the South, 1860–1935* (Chapel Hill: University of North Carolina Press, 1988), pp. 186–237.
47. *Negro Education,* ibid., p. 35. For descriptions of the academic curriculum in public and private high schools for blacks in the South, see Anderson, *The Education of Blacks in the South, 1860–1935,* p. 199. Many northern philanthropists, a primary audience for Jones's report, believed that private schools were an impediment to the development of a sound public school system. See Eric Anderson and Alfred A. Moss, Jr., *Dangerous Donations: Northern Philanthropy and Southern Black Education, 1902–1930* (Columbia, Mo.: University of Missouri Press, 1999), pp. 88–89.
48. W. E. B. Du Bois, "Negro Education," *The Crisis,* February 1918, pp. 173–178.
49. In 1921, Du Bois wrote that Jones, a white man, wanted to make himself the "arbiter and patron of the Negro race in America." The Jones report "took the stand that Negro education directed by Negroes was a failure and that Negro education to succeed must be directed by white people." Its true object, he asserted, was to make sure that the white South and white philanthropies continued to control black education. See W. E. B. Du Bois, "Thomas Jesse Jones," *The Crisis,* October 1921, pp. 252–256.
50. William H. Maxwell, "Efficiency of Schools and Systems," *National Education Association Proceedings,* 1915, p. 395.
51. Ibid., pp. 397–398.
52. William H. Maxwell, "On a Certain Arrogance in Educational Theorists," *Educational Review,* February 1914, pp. 165–182.
53. Ibid.
54. Ibid.
55. Jurgen Herbst, *The Once and Future School: Three Hundred and Fifty Years of American Secondary Education* (New York: Routledge, 1996), pp. 127–130.

56. Andrew F. West, "Is There a Democracy of Studies?" *The Atlantic Monthly,* December 1899, pp. 821–827.

57. Charles W. Eliot, "The Case Against Compulsory Latin," *The Atlantic Monthly,* March 1917, pp. 356–359; Charles W. Eliot, "The Changes Needed in American Secondary Education," paper read at the Second Pan-American Scientific Congress, Washington, D.C., December 27, 1915–January 8, 1916, reprinted in Charles W. Eliot, *A Late Harvest: Miscellaneous Papers Written Between Eighty and Ninety* (Freeport, N.Y.: Books for Libraries Press, 1971; originally published 1924).

58. Abraham Flexner, "A Modern School," *American Review of Reviews,* 53 (1916), pp. 465–474; Abraham Flexner, "Parents and Schools," *The Atlantic Monthly,* July 1916, pp. 25–33; Ross L. Finney, *The American Public School: A Genetic Study of Principles, Practices, and Present Problems* (New York: Macmillan, 1923), p. 261.

59. Paul Shorey, "The Case for the Classics," *The School Review,* November 1910, pp. 587–589. See also Paul Shorey, "Hippias Paidagogos," *The School Review,* January 1909, pp. 1–9.

60. Ibid., pp. 590, 598.

61. Ibid., pp. 610, 613.

62. Paul Shorey, "The Assault on Humanism," *The Atlantic Monthly* (June–July 1917), pp. 793–801; Paul Shorey, *The Assault on Humanism* (Boston: Atlantic Monthly Press, 1917), pp. 73–76.

63. Paul Shorey, " 'The Modern School,' " *Education,* May 1918, p. 684.

64. "Enrollment in High-School Courses in Missouri," *School and Society,* March 20, 1915, pp. 414–415.

65. *U.S. Commissioner of Education, Report, 1916–1917,* vol. 2 (Washington, D.C.: U.S. Government Printing Office, 1917), p. 14; American Classical League, *The Classical Investigation* (Princeton, N.J.: Princeton University Press, 1924), p. 16. In 1910, 84 percent of all high school students studied a foreign language.

66. David Snedden and W. C. Bagley, "Fundamental Distinctions Between Liberal and Vocational Education," *National Education Association Proceedings,* 1914, pp. 164, 167–168, 170.

67. Ibid.

68. Ibid.

69. Marvin Lazerson and W. Norton Grubb, eds., *American Education and Vocationalism: A Documentary History, 1870–1970* (New York: Teachers College Press, 1974), p. 124.

70. National Education Association, *Cardinal Principles of Secondary Education: A Report of the Commission on the Reorganization of Secondary Ed-*

ucation, appointed by the National Education Association, Bulletin No. 35 (Washington, D.C.: Bureau of Education, 1918), pp. 2–3.

71. Ibid., p. 5. See also Edward A. Krug, *The Shaping of the American High School, 1880–1920* (Madison: University of Wisconsin Press, 1964), pp. 384–385.

72. National Education Association, *Cardinal Principles,* p. 3.

73. Ibid., pp. 6–7, 16.

74. Ibid., p. 8.

75. Krug, *The Shaping of the American High School,* p. 336.

76. U.S. Bureau of Education, *The Problem of Mathematics in Secondary Education* (Washington, D.C.: U.S. Government Printing Office, 1920), pp. 17–20.

77. Ibid., p. 15.

78. Krug, *The Shaping of the American High School,* pp. 349–352; Samuel Tenenbaum, *William Heard Kilpatrick: Trail Blazer in Education* (New York: Harper, 1951), pp. 102–107.

79. Thomas H. Briggs, "Secondary Education," *U.S. Commissioner of Education Report,* Vol. 1 (Washington, D.C.: U.S. Bureau of Education, 1914–15), p. 120.

80. U.S. Bureau of Education, *The Social Studies in Secondary Education* (Washington, D.C.: U.S. Government Printing Office, 1916), p. 37.

81. "Social Studies in Secondary Schools: Preliminary Recommendation by the Committee of the National Education Association," *The History Teacher's Magazine,* December 1913, pp. 291–292. Originally printed by the U.S. Bureau of Education, 1913, Bulletin no. 41. See also Michael Bruce Lybarger, "Origins of the Social Studies Curriculum: 1865–1916," Ph.D. dissertation, University of Wisconsin, Madison, 1981; Michael B. Lybarger, "Need as Ideology: A Look at the Early Social Studies," *The Formation of the School Subjects: The Struggle for Creating an American Institution,* ed. Thomas S. Popkewitz (New York: Falmer Press, 1987), pp. 176–189.

82. U.S. Bureau of Education, *The Social Studies in Secondary Education,* pp. 9–11.

83. Lawrence A. Cremin, "The Revolution in American Secondary Education, 1893–1918," *Teachers College Record,* March 1955, p. 307.

Chapter 4: IQ Testing: "This Brutal Pessimism"

1. Ross L. Finney, *The American Public School: A Genetic Study of Principles, Practices, and Present Problems* (New York: Macmillan, 1923), p. 279. See also Ellwood P. Cubberley, *Public Education in the United States: A Study and Interpretation of American Educational History* (New York: Houghton Mifflin, 1916), p. 446. Clarence J. Karier, "Testing for Order and Control in the Corporate Liberal State," *Roots of Crisis: American Education in the Twentieth Century* (Chicago: Rand McNally, 1973), pp. 108–137.
2. Geraldine Joncich, *The Sane Positivist: A Biography of Edward L. Thorndike* (Middletown, Conn.: Wesleyan University Press, 1968), p. 311; Edward L. Thorndike, "Measurement in Education," *The Twenty-first Yearbook of the National Society for the Study of Education* (Bloomington, Ill.: Public School Publishing, 1922), p. 1; Edward L. Thorndike, "Intelligence and Its Uses," *Harper's*, 140 (June 1920), p. 227.
3. Thorndike, ibid., pp. 234–235.
4. Raymond E. Fancher, *The Intelligence Men: Makers of the IQ Controversy* (New York: Norton, 1985), p. 37.
5. Ibid., pp. 63, 74.
6. Ibid., p. 78; Alfred Binet, *Modern Ideas About Children*, tr. Suzanne Heisler (Menlo Park, Cal.: Suzanne Heisler, 1984), p. 106.
7. Henry J. Goddard, *The Kallikak Family: A Study in the Heredity of Feeblemindedness* (New York: Macmillan, 1912); Stephen Jay Gould, *The Mismeasure of Man* (New York: Norton, 1981), p. 168.
8. Mark H. Haller, *Eugenics: Hereditarian Attitudes in American Thought* (New Brunswick, N.J.: Rutgers University Press, 1963), p. 5. See also Margaret Sanger, *Pivot of Civilization* (New York, 1922).
9. Lewis M. Terman, *The Measurement of Intelligence: An Explanation of and a Complete Guide for the Use of the Stanford Revision and Extension of the Binet-Simon Intelligence Scale* (Boston: Houghton Mifflin, 1916), pp. 16–17.
10. Ibid., pp. 91–92.
11. Daniel J. Kevles, "Testing the Army's Intelligence: Psychologists and the Military in World War I," *Journal of American History*, 55 (December 1968), pp. 565–581.
12. Guy Montrose Whipple, "The Use of Mental Tests in the Schools," *The Fifteenth Yearbook of the National Society for the Study of Education*, pt. 1 (Chicago: University of Chicago Press, 1916), pp. 153–154.
13. Lewis M. Terman, *The Intelligence of School Children: How Children Dif-*

fer in Ability, The Use of Mental Tests in School Grading and the Proper Education of Exceptional Children (Boston: Houghton Mifflin, 1919), pp. 157–158, 268–269. See also Lewis M. Terman et al., *Intelligence Tests and School Reorganization* (Yonkers, N.Y.: World Book, 1923), p. 15.

14. Terman, *The Intelligence of School Children*, pp. 1, 10–11. The concept of "intelligence quotient" was established by German psychologist William Stern; see Fancher, *The Intelligence Men*, pp. 102–103.

15. Guy M. Whipple, "The National Intelligence Tests," *The Journal of Educational Research*, 4, no. 1 (June 1921), p. 16; Lewis M. Terman, "The Use of Intelligence Tests in the Grading of School Children," *Journal of Educational Research*, January 1920, p. 20; Paul Davis Chapman, *Schools as Sorters: Lewis M. Terman, Applied Psychology, and the Intelligence Testing Movement, 1890–1930* (New York: New York University Press, 1988), pp. 1, 147.

16. Gould, *The Mismeasure of Man*, p. 177.

17. Terman, *The Intelligence of School Children*, pp. 89–91, 268–269.

18. Ibid., p. 91.

19. Terman, *Intelligence Tests and School Reorganization*, pp. 16–21, 27.

20. Ibid., pp. 21, 27.

21. Ibid., p. 21; Terman, "The Conservation of Talent," *School and Society*, March 1924, p. 364.

22. Fred L. Holmes, "The Menace of the Open Door," *Overland Monthly*, February 1922, pp. 27–29. See also Roy L. Garis, *Immigration Restriction: A Study of the Opposition to and Regulation of Immigration into the United States* (New York: Macmillan, 1927).

23. Arthur Sweeney, "Mental Tests for Immigrants," *North American Review*, May 1922, p. 611.

24. Lothrop Stoddard, *The Revolt Against Civilization: The Menace of the Under Man* (New York: Scribner's, 1922), pp. 42, 262.

25. Cornelia James Cannon, "American Misgivings," *The Atlantic Monthly*, February 1922, pp. 145–157.

26. Robert M. Yerkes, "Testing the Human Mind," *The Atlantic Monthly*, March 1923, pp. 358–370.

27. Ibid., p. 370.

28. Carl C. Brigham, *A Study of American Intelligence* (Princeton, N.J.: Princeton University Press, 1923), p. vii.

29. Ibid., pp. xvii–xviii. Madison Grant, *The Passing of the Great Race; or, The Racial Basis of European History* (New York: Scribner's, 1916); William Z. Ripley, *The Races of Europe: A Sociological Study* (New York: D. Appleton, 1899).

30. Grant, *The Passing of the Great Race*, p. 14.

31. Haller, *Eugenics,* p. 73. See also Leon J. Kamin, *The Science and Politics of I.Q.* (Potomac, Md.: Erlbaum, 1974), p. 19.

32. Brigham, *A Study of American Intelligence,* p. 159.

33. Ibid., p. 57.

34. Ibid., pp. 110–112.

35. Ibid., pp. 192–193, 188, quoting Lewis M. Terman, *The Measurement of Intelligence* (Boston: Houghton Mifflin, 1916), p. 362.

36. Ibid., p. 210.

37. Yerkes, "Testing the Human Mind," pp. 362–363.

38. Lewis M. Terman, "Mental Growth and the I.Q.," *Journal of Educational Psychology,* September–October 1921, pp. 325–326.

39. William C. Bagley, "Educational Determinism: Or Democracy and the I.Q.," *School and Society,* April 8, 1922, pp. 373–375, 379.

40. Ibid., pp. 380, 382.

41. Ibid., p. 384. See also M. R. Trabue, "Some Pitfalls in the Administrative Use of Intelligence Tests," *Journal of Educational Research,* June 1922, pp. 1–11; Guy M. Whipple, "Educational Determinism: Discussion of Professor Bagley's Address at Chicago," *School and Society,* June 3, 1922, p. 601.

42. Lewis M. Terman, "The Psychological Determinist; or Democracy and the I.Q.," *The Journal of Educational Research,* June 1922, pp. 57–62.

43. Walter Lippmann, "The Mental Age of Americans," *The New Republic,* October 25, 1922, p. 213.

44. Walter Lippmann, "The Mystery of the 'A' Men," *The New Republic,* November 1, 1922, pp. 246–248.

45. Walter Lippmann, "The Reliability of Intelligence Tests," *The New Republic,* November 8, 1922, p. 277; Walter Lippmann, "The Abuse of the Tests," *The New Republic,* November 15, 1922, pp. 297–298.

46. Walter Lippmann, "A Future for the Tests," *The New Republic,* November 29, 1922, pp. 9–10.

47. Lewis M. Terman, "The Great Conspiracy: Or The Impulse Imperious of Intelligence Testers, Psychoanalyzed and Exposed by Mr. Lippmann," *The New Republic,* December 27, 1922, pp. 116–120.

48. Walter Lippmann, "The Great Confusion: A Reply to Mr. Terman," *The New Republic,* January 3, 1923, pp. 145–146.

49. John Dewey, "Mediocrity and Individuality," *The New Republic,* December 6, 1922, pp. 35–37.

50. John Dewey, "Individuality, Equality and Superiority," *The New Republic,* December 13, 1922, pp. 61–63.

51. Herbert B. Alexander, "A Comparison of the Ranks of American States in

Army Alpha and in Social-Economic Status," *School and Society,* September 30, 1922, pp. 388–392.

52. Walter Lippmann, "In Defense of Education," *The Century Magazine,* May 1923, pp. 95–103.

53. William C. Bagley, "Professor Terman's Determinism: A Rejoinder," *Journal of Educational Research,* December 1922, pp. 371–385.

54. Ibid.

55. Ibid., pp. 384–385.

56. William C. Bagley, "The Army Tests and Pro-Nordic Propaganda," *Educational Review,* April 1924, p. 184. Bagley, unfortunately, was not entirely immune to the racism of his era. He began his analysis of white-black score differences with this phrase: "While no one can seriously doubt the general superiority of the whites over the negroes in native intelligence, the Army tests show clearly the tremendous influence of good schools in stimulating the growth of intelligence and the corresponding handicap imposed by poor schools" (p. 184). The internal logic of his argument should have led him to delete the first half of the sentence.

57. Lewis M. Terman, "The Possibilities and Limitations of Training," *Journal of Educational Research,* December 1924, pp. 337–340.

58. The best single description of American nativism is John Higham, *Strangers in the Land: Patterns of American Nativism, 1860–1925* (New Brunswick, N.J.: Rutgers University Press, 1955).

59. Warren K. Layton, "The Group Intelligence Testing Program of the Detroit Public Schools," in *Intelligence Tests and Their Use: The Twenty-First Yearbook of the National Society for the Study of Education,* pt. 1 (Bloomington, Ill.: Public School Publishing, 1922), p. 123; Lewis M. Terman, "The Mental Test as a Psychological Method," *Psychological Review,* March 1924, p. 115.

60. W. S. Deffenbaugh, "Uses of Intelligence and Achievement Tests in 215 Cities," *City School Leaflet,* no. 20 (Washington, D.C.: U.S. Bureau of Education, 1925).

61. Michael V. O'Shea, *The Child: His Nature and His Needs* (Valparaiso, Ind.: Children's Foundation, 1924); Eugene Randolph Smith, *Education Moves Ahead: A Survey of Progressive Methods* (Boston: Atlantic Monthly Press, 1924), pp. 72–78.

62. I. L. Kandel, *Examinations and Their Substitutes in the United States* (New York: Carnegie Foundation for the Advancement of Education, 1936), pp. 105–132.

63. Claude M. Fuess, *The College Board: Its First Fifty Years* (New York: College Entrance Examination Board, 1967), pp. 104–113.

64. Henry H. Goddard, "Feeblemindedness: A Question of Definition," *Journal of Psycho-Asthenics,* 33 (1928), pp. 222–225 (for this reference, I am indebted to Gould, *The Mismeasure of Man,* pp. 172–174).

65. Carl C. Brigham, "Intelligence Tests of Immigrant Groups," *Psychological Review,* March 1930, pp. 164–165.

66. Lee J. Cronbach, "Five Decades of Public Controversy over Mental Testing," *American Psychologist,* January 1975, p. 9.

67. Chapman, *Schools as Sorters,* p. 193.

68. Ernest R. Hilgard, "Lewis Madison Terman," *American Journal of Psychology,* September 1957, p. 478; Henry L. Minton, *Lewis M. Terman: Pioneer in Psychological Testing* (New York: New York University Press, 1988), p. 240.

69. Richard J. Herrnstein and Charles A. Murray's *The Bell Curve* rekindled the nature-nurture debate in 1994 by emphasizing the importance of IQ in modern life. But they did not offer any means of establishing with certainty the balance between heredity and environment for any particular individual because no such technology existed; see Richard J. Herrnstein and Charles A. Murray, *The Bell Curve: Intelligence and Class Structure in American Life* (New York: Free Press, 1994). See also Charles Murray, "IQ and Economic Success," *The Public Interest,* Summer 1997, pp. 21–35.

70. Terman, *The Intelligence of School Children,* pp. 10–14.

Chapter 5: Instead of the Academic Curriculum

1. John Franklin Bobbitt, *The Curriculum* (Boston: Houghton Mifflin, 1918), pp. 3–5.

2. Ibid.

3. Ibid., pp. 42–44, 48–49.

4. Ibid., pp. 68–69, 238–243, 255–260.

5. W. W. Charters, *Curriculum Construction* (New York: Macmillan, 1923), pp. 4, 13–14.

6. Ibid., p. 35.

7. Ibid., pp. 44–46.

8. Ibid., pp. 21–22, 94–102.

9. John Franklin Bobbitt, *How to Make a Curriculum* (Boston: Houghton Mifflin, 1924), pp. 2, 7–8.

10. Ibid., pp. 8–9, 11–15, 20–25, 256–260, 267–272. See also John Franklin Bobbitt, *Curriculum Investigations* (Chicago: University of Chicago Press, 1926), for lists of functional activities in every subject area.

11. Edward A. Krug, *The Shaping of the American High School, 1920–1941,* (Madison: University of Wisconsin Press, 1972), p. 30.
12. *The Émile of Jean Jacques Rousseau,* tr. and ed. William Boyd (New York: Teachers College Press, 1971), p. 18.
13. Ibid., pp. 41–42, 50–52.
14. John Dewey and Evelyn Dewey, *Schools of Tomorrow,* rev. ed. (New York: Dutton, 1962; first published 1915), pp. 1–2, 45.
15. Max Eastman, "John Dewey," *The Atlantic Monthly,* December 1941, pp. 671, 678.
16. Katherine Camp Mayhew and Anna Camp Edwards, *The Dewey School: The Laboratory School of the University of Chicago, 1896–1903* (New York: Appleton-Century, 1936), pp. 96–113, 118, 127–137, 156–181, 185–199, 206–218, 240–241.
17. Ibid., pp. 6, 20–22.
18. John Dewey, "The Child and the Curriculum," in *Dewey on Education,* ed. Martin S. Dworkin (New York: Teachers College Press, 1959), p. 97.
19. Ibid.
20. Mayhew and Edwards, *The Dewey School,* pp. 390, 35.
21. Ibid., pp. 8–10, 35.
22. Ibid., p. 22.
23. Dewey and Dewey, *Schools of Tomorrow,* pp. 1–12.
24. Ibid., chaps. 8, 10; Diane Ravitch, *The Great School Wars: New York City, 1805–1973* (New York: Basic Books, 1974), pp. 219–230.
25. Lawrence A. Cremin, *The Transformation of the School: Progressivism in American Education, 1876–1957* (New York: Knopf, 1961), pp. 147–153.
26. Dewey and Dewey, *Schools of Tomorrow,* pp. 14–30.
27. Dewey and Dewey, ibid., pp. 31–32.
28. Junius L. Meriam, *Child Life and the Curriculum* (Yonkers, N.Y.: World Book, 1920), pp. 137, 144, 160, 163–165.
29. Ibid., pp. 343–345, 487–502.
30. Patricia Albjerg Graham, *Progressive Education: From Arcady to Academe* (New York: Teachers College Press, 1967).
31. Samuel Tenenbaum, *William Heard Kilpatrick: Trail Blazer in Education* (New York: Harper, 1951), pp. 63, 185.
32. Ibid., pp. 75–78.
33. William H. Kilpatrick, "The Project Method," *Teachers College Record,* September 1918, p. 320.
34. Ibid., pp. 323, 329–330.
35. Tenenbaum, *William Heard Kilpatrick,* pp. 143, 169, 68.
36. William Heard Kilpatrick, *Foundations of Method: Informal Talks on Teaching* (New York: Macmillan, 1925), pp. 108–109, 128–129.

37. Ibid., pp. 106–107, 148–149, 274–278.
38. Ibid., pp. 102, 105, 141.
39. Ibid., pp. 135–137, 141.
40. Ibid., pp. vii–viii.
41. John J. Tigert, "The Need of Bridging the Gap Between Our Knowledge of Education and Our Educational Practice," in *The Child: His Nature and His Needs,* ed. Michael V. O'Shea (Valparaiso, Ind.: Children's Foundation, 1924), pp. 331–337.
42. Abraham Flexner, *I Remember: The Autobiography of Abraham Flexner* (New York: Simon and Schuster, 1940), pp. 251–252.
43. James S. Tippett et al., *Curriculum Making in an Elementary School* (Boston: Ginn, 1927), pp. 198–219. The best, most comprehensive discussion of the Lincoln School is Peter Lehman Buttenweiser, "The Lincoln School and Its Times, 1917–1948," Ed.D. dissertation, Teachers College, Columbia University, 1969.
44. Caroline B. Zachry, *Illustrations of English Work in the Junior High School* (New York: Teachers College Press, 1925), pp. 8, 41, 45–47.
45. B. J. R. Stolper and Henry C. Fenn, *Integration at Work: Six Greek Cities: An Experience with Social Studies, Literature, and Art in the Modern High School* (New York: Teachers College Press, 1939); B. J. R. Stolper, "Something New Under the Sun?" *Progressive Education,* November 1934, pp. 386–392.
46. Cremin, *The Transformation of the School,* p. 280. This discussion of the influence of the Lincoln School relies on Peter Buttenweiser, "The Lincoln School and Its Times, 1917–1948," pp. 145–162.
47. Zachry, *Illustrations of English Work,* pp. 54–56.
48. Stuart A. Courtis, "Current Practices in Curriculum-Revision in Public Elementary Schools," in *The Foundations and Technique of Curriculum-Construction: The Twenty-Sixth Yearbook of the National Society for the Study of Education,* pt. 1, ed. Harold Rugg (Bloomington, Ill.: Public School Publishing, 1926), p. 133; George S. Counts, "Current Practices in Curriculum-Making in Public High Schools," in ibid., pp. 138–139.
49. Carleton Washburne, "The Philosophy of the Winnetka Curriculum," in ibid., pp. 219–220.
50. Carleton W. Washburne and Sidney P. Marland, Jr., *Winnetka: The History and Significance of an Educational Experiment* (Englewood Cliffs, N.J.: Prentice Hall, 1963).
51. Harold Rugg, *That Men May Understand: An American in the Long Armistice* (New York: Doubleday, 1941), p. 295.
52. Harold Rugg, "Curriculum-Making: Points of Emphasis," in *26th NSSE Yearbook,* pt. 2, pp. 147–149; see also Rugg, "A Preface to the Reconstruc-

tion of the American School Curriculum," *Teachers College Record,* March 1926, p. 604.

53. W. C. Bagley, "Supplementary Statement," in *26th NSSE Yearbook,* pt. 2, pp. 29–37.

54. Ibid.

55. Harold Rugg and Ann Shumaker, *The Child-Centered School: An Appraisal of the New Education* (Yonkers-on-Hudson, N.Y.: World Book, 1928), pp. iv–viii, 33, 60, 112–115, 322–323.

56. Ibid., pp. iv–viii, 60, 125, 131–135.

57. Ibid., pp. 314–324.

58. Rugg, *That Men May Understand,* pp. 305–306.

59. E. M. Sipple, "A Unit-Activities Curriculum in the Public Schools of Burlington, Iowa," *26th NSSE Yearbook,* pt. 1, pp. 207–217.

60. Jesse H. Newlon and A. L. Threlkeld, "The Denver Curriculum-Revision Program," *26th NSSE Yearbook,* pt. 1, pp. 229–240.

61. George S. Counts, *The Senior High School Curriculum* (Chicago: University of Chicago Press, 1926), pp. 12–13. Counts identified eighteen different curricula in Los Angeles, but a decade earlier Charles Hughes Johnston claimed that city had forty-eight (see page 101). The difference between them was a matter of definition, rather than principle.

62. Boyd H. Bode, "The New Education, Ten Years After: Apprenticeship or Freedom?" *The New Republic,* June 4, 1930, pp. 61–64.

63. John Dewey, "Individuality and Experience," *Journal of the Barnes Foundation,* January 1926, pp. 1–6; also John Dewey, *John Dewey: The Later Works, 1925–1953,* vol. 2: *1925–1927,* ed. Jo Ann Boydston (Carbondale, Ill.: Southern Illinois University Press, 1984), pp. 58–59.

64. John Dewey, "Progressive Education and the Science of Education," in *Dewey on Education,* ed. Martin S. Dworkin (New York: Teachers College Press, 1959), pp. 113–126.

65. Ibid.

Chapter 6: On the Social Frontier

1. John Dewey, *Democracy and Education: An Introduction to the Philosophy of Education* (New York: Macmillan, 1916), p. 92.

2. C. A. Bowers, *The Progressive Educator and the Depression: The Radical Years* (New York: Random House, 1969), p. 87; Harold Rugg, "A Preface to the Reconstruction of the American School Curriculum," *Teachers College Record,* March 1926, p. 614. According to Cremin, the Kilpatrick discussion group met regularly until 1934, intermittently from 1934 to 1938,

and then regularly for several more years; see Lawrence A. Cremin, *The Transformation of the School: Progressivism in American Education, 1876–1957* (New York: Knopf, 1961), p. 228.

3. John Dewey, *John Dewey: The Later Works, 1925–1953*, vol. 3: *1927–1928*, ed. Jo Ann Boydston (Carbondale, Ill.: Southern Illinois University Press, 1984), pp. 207, 217–218, 220. Originally published in *The New Republic:* "I. Leningrad Gives the Clue," November 14, 1928; "II. A Country in a State of Flux," November 21, 1928; "III. A New World in the Making," November 28, 1928; "IV. What Are the Russian Schools Doing?" December 5, 1928; "New Schools for a New Era," December 12, 1928; "VI. The Great Experiment and the Future," December 19, 1928.

4. Ibid., pp. 213, 222.

5. Ibid., pp. 219, 228–229.

6. Ibid., pp. 229–231.

7. Ibid., pp. 229, 233, 236.

8. Ibid., pp. 233–234.

9. Ibid., pp. 238–239.

10. Ibid., p. 243; Samuel Tenenbaum, *William Heard Kilpatrick: Trail Blazer in Education* (New York: Harper, 1951), p. 268. For reference to Krupskaya, see George Counts, *The Soviet Challenge to America* (New York: John Day, 1931), p. x. The American philosopher David Sidorsky later noted that the Soviet government had purged the membership of the Soviet Academy of Sciences in the same year Dewey visited; see David Sidorsky, "Introduction," in *John Dewey: The Later Works, 1925–1953*, p. xxxii.

11. John Dewey, *John Dewey: The Later Works, 1925–1953*, p. 244.

12. Ibid., pp. 246, 238.

13. Tenenbaum, *William Heard Kilpatrick*, pp. 264–266.

14. Ibid. George Counts later described S. T. Shatzsky as "a remarkable personality who had been influenced by Jane Addams and John Dewey and who after the revolution was appointed head of the First Experimental Station in People's Education in Moscow"; see George S. Counts, *The Challenge of Soviet Education* (New York: McGraw-Hill, 1957), p. 20.

15. Tenenbaum, ibid., pp. 263–269. George S. Counts, in *The Challenge of Soviet Education*, wrote that Lunacharsky was removed from office in 1928 and that Schatzsky died in 1934 (pp. 20, 62). In "A Humble Autobiography," Counts reported that Pinkevich died in a forced-labor camp in 1939 (see *Leaders in American Education*, Seventieth Yearbook of the National Society for the Study of Education, pt. 2, 1971, p. 162).

16. Tenenbaum, *William Heard Kilpatrick*, pp. 264–269. See also "Teachers College in the News," *Teachers College Record*, February 1930, pp.

492–493 (a reprint of the article from the *New York Sun,* December 16, 1929).

17. George S. Counts, *A Ford Crosses Soviet Russia* (Boston: Stratford, 1930), pp. 153, 170–171.

18. George S. Counts, *The American Road to Culture: A Social Interpretation of Education in the United States* (New York: John Day, 1930), pp. 175–176.

19. George Counts, *The Soviet Challenge to America,* pp. 4–5, 7, 11–13.

20. Ibid., pp. x, 37–39, 42, 50.

21. Ibid., pp. 69, 75, 77.

22. Ibid., p. 316.

23. Ibid., pp. 306–307, 314–315.

24. George S. Counts et al., *Bolshevism, Fascism, and Capitalism: An Account of Three Economic Systems* (New Haven, Conn.: Yale University Press, 1932), pp. 23, 29, 32–33. For the liquidation of the kulaks, see Nicholas Werth, "A State Against Its People: Violence, Repression, and Terror in the Soviet Union," in *The Black Book of Communism: Crimes, Terror, Repression,* ed. Stéphane Courtois et al. (Cambridge, Mass.: Harvard University Press, 1999), pp. 146–158.

25. Arthur M. Schlesinger, Jr., *The Crisis of the Old Order: 1919–1933* (Boston: Houghton Mifflin, 1957), pp. 184–203, 248–252.

26. George S. Counts, "Dare Progressive Education Be Progressive?" *Progressive Education,* April 1932, pp. 258–259.

27. Ibid., pp. 261–263.

28. "Comments on Dr. Counts' Challenge," *Progressive Education,* April 1932, p. 264; Elizabeth Moos, "Steps Toward the American Dream," ibid., pp. 264–265; Ellen Windom Warren Geer, "The Courage to Keep an Open Mind," ibid., pp. 265–267; Nellie M. Seeds, "Educating for Social Change," ibid., pp. 267–269; Elsie Ripley Clapp, "Learning and Indoctrinating," ibid., pp. 269–272; Paul R. Hanna, "The Need for Teacher Training," ibid., pp. 273–274; Allan Hulsizer, "The Rural Problem," ibid., pp. 274–276.

29. George S. Counts, *Dare the School Build a New Social Order?* (New York: John Day, 1932), pp. 34, 45–47.

30. C. A. Bowers, *The Progressive Educator,* p. 23.

31. Lawrence A. Cremin, *The Transformation of the School,* p. 231; William H. Kilpatrick, ed., *The Educational Frontier* (New York: Appleton-Century, 1933), pp. 69, 291.

32. Kilpatrick, ibid., pp. 163–170.

33. Ibid., pp. 173–174, 189.

34. Ibid., pp. 176, 184.

35. Ibid., pp. 184, 186, 190–191.
36. Ibid., p. 291.
37. American Historical Association, *A Charter for the Social Sciences in the Schools,* Report of the Commission on the Social Studies, pt. 1, drafted by Charles Beard (New York: Scribner's, 1932), pp. 44, 55, 100, 105–106.
38. Progressive Education Association, Committee on Social and Economic Problems, *A Call to the Teachers of the Nation* (New York: John Day, 1933), pp. 6, 11, 19–21, 23–24, 26. Counts was assisted in the writing by other radical progressives, including historian Merle Curti and philosopher Sidney Hook of New York University, who was at that time a Communist.
39. C. A. Bowers, *The Progressive Educator,* p. 41.
40. James Truslow Adams, "Can Teachers Bring About the New Society?" *Progressive Education,* 10 (October 1933), pp. 310–314.
41. W. E. B. Du Bois, "Curriculum Revision," address to Georgia State Teachers Convention, April 12, 1935, Du Bois Papers, Park Johnson Archives, Fisk University, quoted in Kenneth James King, *Pan-Africanism and Education: A Study of Race Philanthropy and Education in the Southern States of America and East Africa* (New York: Oxford University Press, 1971), p. 257.
42. William Heard Kilpatrick, *Education and the Social Crisis: A Proposed Program* (New York: Liveright, 1932), pp. 22–27, 52–57.
43. Ibid., pp. 52–57, 60–61.
44. Harold Rugg, *The Great Technology: Social Chaos and the Public Mind* (New York: John Day, 1933), pp. 67, 99–101, 199–203, 254; see also Harold Rugg, *American Life and the School Curriculum* (New York: Ginn, 1936), p. 224.
45. Harold Rugg, *Foundations for American Education* (Yonkers, N.Y.: World Book, 1947), pp. 526–630.
46. I. L. Kandel, "Education and Social Disorder," *Teachers College Record,* February 1933, pp. 359–367.
47. Ibid.
48. Ibid.
49. Report of a Committee, submitted to the Council of the American Historical Association, approved December 1926, "History and Other Social Studies in the Schools," *The Historical Outlook,* March 1927, p. 111; A. C. Krey, "Thirty Years After the Committee of Seven," *The Historical Outlook,* February 1929, p. 65.
50. American Historical Association, Commission on the Social Studies in the Schools, *Conclusions and Recommendations of the Commission* (New York: Scribner's, 1934), pp. 16–17, 34–35, 30, 37.

51. Boyd H. Bode, "Editorial Comment," *Phi Delta Kappan,* November 1934, pp. 1, 7.

52. "Orientation," *The Social Frontier,* October 1934, p. 3.

53. Broadus Mitchell, "The Choice Before Us," *The Social Frontier,* November 1934, p. 16.

54. William Heard Kilpatrick, "Educational Ideals and the Profit Motive," *The Social Frontier,* November 1934, pp. 9–13.

55. Merle Curti, "Our Revolutionary Tradition," *The Social Frontier,* December 1934, pp. 10–13.

56. "The Roosevelt That Might Have Been," *The Social Frontier,* December 1934, pp. 7–8.

57. "Freedom in a Collectivist Society," *The Social Frontier,* April 1935, p. 10.

58. Harry D. Gideonse, "Non-Partisan Education for Political Intelligence," *The Social Frontier,* January 1935, p. 18.

59. John Dewey, "The Teacher and His World," *The Social Frontier,* January 1935, p. 7.

60. Boyd H. Bode, "Education and Social Reconstruction," *The Social Frontier,* January 1935, pp. 21–22.

61. Jesse Newlon, "The Great Educational Illusion," *The Social Frontier,* March 1935, p. 16.

62. "On the Battle Line," *The Social Frontier,* October 1935, p. 23.

63. Counts, *The American Road to Culture,* pp. 115, 135.

64. Charles H. Judd, *Education and Social Progress* (New York: Harcourt, Brace, 1934), pp. 268, 226.

65. Richard H. Pells, *Radical Visions and American Dreams: Culture and Social Thought in the Depression Years* (Middletown, Conn.: Wesleyan University Press, 1973), p. 115.

66. William C. Bagley, "The Soviets Proceed to the Liquidation of American Educational Theory," *School and Society,* January 4, 1933, pp. 62–63.

67. John Dewey, *John Dewey: The Later Works, 1925–1953,* vol. 2: *1935–1937,* ed. Jo Ann Boydston (Carbondale, Ill.: Southern Illinois University Press, 1987), "Summary of Findings," p. 323; from Agnes E. Meyer, *The Washington Post,* December 1937, in ibid., pp. 331–335.

68. "Toward a United Front," *The Social Frontier,* January 1936, p. 103; Daniel Bell, *Marxian Socialism in the United States* (Princeton, N.J.: Princeton University Press, 1967), pp. 142–145; William H. Kilpatrick, "High Marxism Defined and Rejected," *The Social Frontier,* June 1936, pp. 272–274; Jesse H. Newlon, "How Reactionary Is Roosevelt?" *The Social Frontier,* May 1938, pp. 243–244.

69. George S. Counts, *The Prospects of American Democracy* (New York: John Day, 1938), pp. 143–144.

70. George S. Counts, "Whose Twilight?" *The Social Frontier,* February 1939, pp. 135–140; George S. Counts, "A Humble Autobiography," *Leaders in American Education,* Seventieth Yearbook of the National Society for the Study of Education, pt. 2 (Chicago: University of Chicago Press, 1971), p. 164.

71. George S. Counts, "A Liberal Looks at Life," *The Social Frontier,* May 15, 1941, pp. 231–232. For his later work on the Soviet Union, see Boris Petrovich Esipov, *"I Want to Be like Stalin,"* tr. George S. Counts and Nucia P. Lodge (New York: Day, 1947); George S. Counts and Nucia Lodge, *The Country of the Blind: The Soviet System of Mind Control* (Boston: Houghton Mifflin, 1949); George S. Counts, *The Challenge of Soviet Education.*

72. Counts, *The Prospects of American Democracy,* pp. 304–313.

Chapter 7: The Public Schools Respond

1. Hollis L. Caswell, *Curriculum Improvement in Public School Systems* (New York: Teachers College Press, 1950), p. 18; Yale Kramer, "Freud and the Culture Wars," *The Public Interest,* 124 (Summer 1996), pp. 37–51.

2. Herbert B. Bruner, "Present Status of the Curriculum," *Curriculum Making in Current Practice* (Evanston, Ill.: School of Education, Northwestern University, 1932), pp. 6–8, 12–20.

3. Hollis L. Caswell and Doak S. Campbell, *Curriculum Development* (New York: American Book Company, 1935), pp. 1–22; Harold C. Hand and Will French, "Analysis of the Present Status in Curriculum Thinking," *The Changing Curriculum* (New York: Appleton-Century, 1937), pp. 1–31.

4. Diane Ravitch, *The Troubled Crusade: American Education, 1945–1980* (New York: Basic Books, 1983), pp. 52–54. This discussion relies on sections of this earlier work.

5. Charles W. Knudsen, "Critical Analysis of Curriculum Development in State and County School Systems," in *The Changing Curriculum,* Joint Committee on Curriculum of the Department of Supervisors of the National Education Association and the Society for Curriculum Study (New York: Appleton-Century, 1937), pp. 182–184.

6. Ibid., p. 192; Caswell and Campbell, *Curriculum Development,* pp. 173–184; J. Paul Leonard, "Is the Virginia Curriculum Working?" *Harvard Educational Review,* January 1937, pp. 66–71.

7. From the 1890s to the 1920s, many elementary school teachers were trained in the pedagogical methods of Johann Friedrich Herbart, a German

philosopher whose American disciples believed in correlation across different subject fields, especially history, literature, and geography. See especially the writings of Frank McMurry and Charles McMurry. See also Mary Louise Seguel, *The Curriculum Field: Its Formative Years* (New York: Teachers College Press, 1966), pp. 16–46.

8. Eileen Kathryn Rice, *The Superintendency and the Implementation of Progressive Practices in the Ann Arbor Elementary Schools from 1921–1942* (Ann Arbor: University of Michigan Social Foundations of Education Monograph Series, Number 8, 1978), pp. 43, 124.

9. California State Department of Education, *Teachers' Guide to Child Development: Manual for Kindergarten and Primary Teachers* (Sacramento, Calif.: State Printing Office, 1930), pp. 18–23.

10. Ibid., pp. 20–25.

11. William H. Kilpatrick, "Definition of the Activity Movement To-Day," *The Activity Movement: The Thirty-third Yearbook of the National Society for the Study of Education.* pt. 2, ed. Guy Montrose Whipple (Bloomington, Ill.: Public School Publishing, 1934), p. 63.

12. Alice V. Keliher, "The Orientation of Measurement in the Activity Program," ibid., pp. 157–158.

13. Boyd H. Bode, ibid., pp. 79–80.

14. William C. Bagley, ibid., pp. 77–78. (For Isaac Kandel's reaction to the activity movement, see p. 317 in Chapter 8.)

15. John Dewey, ibid., pp. 85–86.

16. William H. Kilpatrick, ibid., pp. 201–202.

17. Helen Hay Heyl, ibid., pp. 116–117; Robert H. Lane, ibid., p. 120; Margaret Gustin and Margaret L. Hayes, *Activities in the Public School* (Chapel Hill: University of North Carolina Press, 1934).

18. Albert L. Hartman, ibid., pp. 110–111.

19. Dessalee Ryan Dudley, ibid., pp. 106–108.

20. E. E. Oberholtzer, ibid., pp. 136–142.

21. Maude McBroom, ibid., pp. 132–135.

22. John J. Loftus, "The Activity Program in New York Elementary Schools," *The Journal of Educational Sociology,* October 1943, pp. 67–70; J. Wayne Wrightstone, "Evaluation of an Activity Program," ibid., pp. 117–120; William A. McCall, John P. Herring, and John J. Loftus, "Measuring the Amount of Activity Education in Activity and Control Schools in New York City," *Teachers College Record,* December 1937, pp. 230–240; William A. McCall, John P. Herring, and John J. Loftus, "Measuring Achievement in Activity and Control Schools in New York City," *Teachers College Record,* February 1938, pp. 423–432; J. W. Wrightstone et al., "Measuring Intellectual and Dynamic Factors in Activity and Control Schools in New York

City," *Teachers College Record,* December 1938, p. 242; Arthur T. Jersild, et al., "An Evaluation of Aspects of the Activity Program in the New York City Public Elementary Schools," *Journal of Experimental Education,* December 1939, p. 172.

23. Benjamin Fine, "New York's Six-Year Progressive Education Experiment," *The American Mercury,* June 1941, pp. 677–685.

24. John J. Loftus, "New York City's Large-Scale Experimentation with an Activity Program," *Progressive Education,* February 1940, pp. 116, 122. Loftus pointed out that the magnitude of the project and the lack of additional resources were enormous obstacles to its success. Arthur T. Jersild, Bernard Goldman, and Catherine L. Jersild, "Studies of Elementary School Classes in Action: I. A Comparative Study of the Daily Occupations of Pupils in 'Activity' and 'Non-Activity' Schools," *Journal of Experimental Education,* June 1941, pp. 207–299; Arthur T. Jersild, Bernard Goldman, Catherine L. Jersild, and John J. Loftus, "Studies of Elementary School Classes in Action: II. Pupil Participation and Aspects of Pupil-Teacher Relationships," *Journal of Experimental Education,* December 1941, p. 119. In the experimental classes, a small number of children in every classroom "tended to monopolize a large proportion of the discussion." This happened most often when children were directing the work of the class, instead of the teacher. It was especially troublesome since one of the purposes of the activity program was "to promote democratic procedures in the classroom."

25. Larry Cuban, *How Teachers Taught: Constancy and Change in American Classrooms* (New York: Teachers College Press, 1993), second edition, pp. 61–71; Arthur Zilversmit, *Changing Schools: Progressive Education Theory and Practice, 1930–1960* (Chicago: University of Chicago, 1993), p. 84.

26. William A. McCall and John J. Loftus, "America's Largest City Experiments with a Crucial Educational Problem," *Teachers College Record,* April 1937, p. 602.

27. Eugene Randolph Smith, *Education Moves Ahead* (Boston: Atlantic Monthly Press, 1924), pp. 34–44; William Scott Gray, *Summary of Investigations Relating to Reading* (Chicago: University of Chicago Press, 1925), p. 27.

28. Smith, ibid., pp. 34–44.

29. "Spot," from William S. Gray, Dorothy Baruch, and Elizabeth Rider Montgomery, *We Look and See* (New York: Scott, Foresman, 1946), reprinted in *Fun with Dick and Jane: A Commemorative Collection of Stories* (San Francisco: CollinsPublishers, 1996), pp. 8–9.

30. Charles Eliot Norton, ed., 4th book, *The Heart of Oak Books* (Boston: Heath, 1898), pp. ix–x.
31. James Fleming Hosic, "The Contents of School Reading Books," *School and Society,* February 7, 1920, pp. 179–180.
32. R. P. Carroll, "The Influence of the Content of Our School Readers," *School and Society,* November 10, 1923, pp. 561–562.
33. Alice M. Ide and Walda Oberg, "The Content of Present Day Readers As Compared with Children's Interests and Reading Objectives," *Elementary English Review,* March 1931, p. 67.
34. "Educators Frown on Old Fairy Tales," *The New York Times,* November 24, 1929, p. 28; "Teachers College in the News," *Teachers College Record,* February 1930, pp. 493–494.
35. Agnes G. Gunderson, "Types of Reading Matter Contained in Readers Published over a Period of Twenty Years," *Educational Method,* 17 (February 1938), pp. 228–230; Agnes G. Gunderson, "Twenty Years of Readers," *American School Board Journal,* July 1937, p. 97.
36. William S. Gray, "Growth of Interest and Appreciation in Reading," *The Elementary English Review,* April 1940, p. 143.
37. "New Course of Study in History for the Elementary Schools of Philadelphia," *The History Teacher's Magazine,* 8 (1917), p. 277.
38. John A. Hockett, "Facing Realities in Elementary School Social Studies," *California Journal of Elementary Education,* February 1936, pp. 136–147.
39. Paul R. Hanna, "Social Studies in the Virginia Curriculum," *Progressive Education,* January–February 1934, pp. 129–134.
40. Paul R. Hanna, "Romance or Reality: A Curriculum Problem," *Progressive Education,* May 1935, pp. 318–323.
41. Henry Harap, "Trends in the Early Elementary Curriculum," *Childhood Education,* October 1937, pp. 53–54. See also Mary Harden and Clara Scranton, "Present Trends and Current Practices in the Teaching of the Social Studies in the Elementary School," *The Historical Outlook,* April 1933, pp. 201–210; Grace E. Storm, *The Social Studies in the Primary Grades* (Chicago: Lyons and Carnahan, 1931), pp. vii–x; "In Search of a Scope and Sequence for Social Studies: Report of the National Council for the Social Studies Task Force on Scope and Sequence," *Social Education,* April 1984, p. 254; Diane Ravitch, "Tot Sociology: Or What Happened to History in the Grade Schools," *The American Scholar,* Summer 1987, pp. 343–354.
42. Jesse H. Newlon, "Key Problems in Achieving an Integrated Program in Education," *National Education Association Proceedings,* 69 (1931), pp. 716–720.

43. Ibid.; Jesse H. Newlon, "The Status of the New School," *Teachers College Record,* April 1931, p. 609.

44. L. Thomas Hopkins, *Integration: Its Meaning and Application* (New York: Appleton-Century, 1937), p. 197; see *Teachers College Record,* February 1936: a special issue on "integration" at the Lincoln School.

45. Hopkins, ibid., pp. 198, 200–201.

46. Ibid., p. 254.

47. Ibid., pp. 22–26.

48. Ibid., pp. 201–209; Howard E. Wilson, *The Fusion of Social Studies in Junior High Schools: A Critical Analysis* (Cambridge, Mass.: Harvard University Press, 1933), pp. 9, 185–187.

49. Hopkins, *Integration,* pp. 217–233.

50. National Association of Secondary School Principals, *Issues of Secondary Education* (National Education Association, 1934), pp. 203–218.

51. F. R. Wegner and Harry Langworthy, Jr., "Roslyn, N.Y., Moves Toward Integration," *The Clearing House,* October 1936, pp. 84–87; "Joy & Happiness Schools," *Time,* March 21, 1938, p. 32.

52. Prudence Bostwick, "A High School Core Program," *Curriculum Journal,* May 1938, pp. 204–207; T. D. Rice, "A High School Core Program," *Curriculum Journal,* May 1938, pp. 201–203; C. L. Cushman, "Conference Appraises Denver Secondary Program," *Curriculum Journal,* November 1938, p. 317.

53. Samuel Everett, "An Experiment in Community School Education," *Educational Record,* October 1937, pp. 532–547.

54. Roberta LaBrant Green, "Developing a Modern Curriculum in a Small Town," *Progressive Education,* March 1936, pp. 189–197.

55. "Active Learning in a High School of North Carolina," *Progressive Education,* December 1938, pp. 629–633.

56. Ethel P. Andrus, "General Procedure at Abraham Lincoln High School, Los Angeles," *The Clearing House,* February 1935, pp. 334–339.

57. Harold Spears, *The Emerging High-School Curriculum and Its Direction* (New York: American Book Company, 1940), pp. 10, 179–187, 303–320.

58. Harold Spears, *Secondary Education in American Life* (New York: American Book Company, 1941), pp. 371–375. Spears was later the principal of the high school in Highland Park, Illinois.

59. Lavonne Hanna, "The Plan of the Core Curriculum in Tulsa," *Curriculum Journal,* December 1939, pp. 350–352; Lavonne Hanna, "The Operation of the Core Curriculum in Tulsa," *Curriculum Journal,* February 1940, pp. 66–68.

60. Paul R. Pierce, "Major Steps in Reorganizing a High-School Curriculum," *School Review,* November 1936, pp. 655–666; Paul R. Pierce, "Curriculum

Organization in a Chicago High School," *Curriculum Journal,* April 1937, pp. 156–160.

61. Miles E. Cary, "Purposeful Activities in the McKinley Senior High School, Honolulu," *Education,* January 1933, pp. 261–268.

62. Ibid.

63. Glenn Kendall, "The Norris Community Program," *Curriculum Journal,* March 1939, pp. 108–110; see also Spears, *The Emerging High-School Curriculum,* pp. 163–178.

64. William P. Patterson, "Curriculum Improvement in a Junior High School, 1935–1939: A Professional Project to Initiate and Guide the Developing of a Continuous Curriculum Improvement Program in the State Street Junior High School in Hackensack, New Jersey," unpublished Ed.D. dissertation, Teachers College, Columbia University, 1940, pp. 48, 159; George H. Geyer, "A Secondary School Program in Transition," Ed.D. dissertation, Teachers College, Columbia University, 1940.

65. N. C. Turpen, "Cooperative Curricular Improvement: To Formulate a Plan for Securing Community Understanding, Cooperation, and Support in Making Basic Program Changes in the High Schools of Alabama," Ed.D. dissertation, Teachers College, Columbia University, 1941, pp. 22–31, 107–111, 129–130; Ravitch, *The Troubled Crusade,* pp. 54–57.

66. William R. Odell, "Two Approaches to High School Curriculum Revision," *Curriculum Journal,* March 1940, pp. 115–118.

67. Knudsen, "Critical Analysis of Curriculum Development," pp. 214–220.

68. Harl R. Douglass, "The Education of Black Youth for Modern America: A Critical Summary," *The Journal of Negro Education,* July 1940, pp. 541–543, 545–546.

69. Ibid.

70. Katharine Whiteside Taylor, *Do Adolescents Need Parents?* (New York: Appleton-Century, 1938), pp. 12–13, 5, 92, 193; this book was written on behalf of the Progressive Education Association's Commission on Human Relations.

71. Ibid., pp. 163, 171–173.

72. V. T. Thayer, Caroline B. Zachry, and Ruth Kotinsky, *Reorganizing Secondary Education* (New York: Appleton-Century, 1939), pp. 7–11, 19, 34–37, 57.

73. Caroline B. Zachry, *Emotion and Conduct in Adolescence* (New York: Appleton-Century, 1940), pp. 1, 135, 352–394, 408–410; this book was written on behalf of the Progressive Education Association's Commission on Secondary School Curriculum.

74. Progressive Education Association, *Science in General Education* (New York: Appleton-Century, 1938), pp. 13, 454–457.

75. Progressive Education Association, *The Social Studies in General Education* (New York: Appleton-Century, 1940), pp. 2–9.

76. Lloyd N. Morrisett, "The Curriculum and Life: An Indictment of High-School Courses That Evade Reality," *The Clearing House,* September 1936, pp. 3–10.

77. Ibid.

78. Edward A. Krug, *The Shaping of the American High School: 1920–1941* (Madison: University of Wisconsin Press, 1972), pp. 318–319; Harry E. Gross, "Designs for Living and Learning," *Progressive Education,* January 1938, pp. 10–11; "We Want a New Education," *Progressive Education,* November 1938, pp. 565–566.

79. Harl R. Douglass, *Secondary Education for Youth in Modern America* (Washington, D.C.: American Council on Education, 1937), pp. vii, 29–30, 20, 96.

80. Education Policies Commission, *The Purposes of Education in American Democracy* (Washington, D.C.: National Education Association, 1938), pp. 47–48, 147.

81. B. L. Dodds, *That All May Learn* (Washington, D.C.: National Education Association, 1939), pp. 13–14, 33, 37–38, 54, 69–70, 122–127, 133.

82. Ibid.

83. American Youth Commission, *What the High Schools Ought to Teach* (Washington, D.C.: American Council on Education, 1940), pp. 7, 21–31. The committee that wrote this report included five professors of education, three city superintendents, a high school principal, and the director of a private vocational school.

84. Wilford M. Aikin, *The Story of the Eight-Year Study* (New York: Harper, 1942), pp. 110–115.

85. W. Lloyd Warner, Robert Havighurst, and Martin Loeb, *Who Shall Be Educated?* (New York: Harper & Bros., 1944), pp. 49–50; as quoted in David L. Angus and Jeffrey E. Mirel, *The Failed Promise of the American High School, 1890–1995* (New York: Teachers College Press, 1999), p. 97.

Chapter 8: Dissidents and Critics

1. Eunice Fuller Barnard, " 'Learning-By-Doing' Confidently Takes Stock," *The New York Times Magazine,* February 27, 1938, pp. 9, 20–21. The movement was also the subject of a cover story in *Time;* "Progressives' Progress," *Time,* October 31, 1938, pp. 31–35.

2. I. L. Kandel, *William Chandler Bagley: Stalwart Educator* (New York: Teachers College, 1961), p. 6.

3. William Chandler Bagley, *Classroom Management: Its Principles and Technique* (New York: Macmillan, 1907), pp. 3, 14, 226–227.

4. Samuel Tenenbaum, *William Heard Kilpatrick: Trail Blazer in Education* (New York: Harper, 1951), p. 224.

5. P. W. L. Cox, "Progressive Education Gets Another Scolding," *Educational Method*, May 1933, pp. 495–499 (with reply by Bagley).

6. William C. Bagley, "Education: The National Problem," *The New Republic,* December 17, 1919, pp. 87–92; William C. Bagley, "Federal Aid for Public Schools," *National Education Association Proceedings,* 1921, p. 618; William C. Bagley, "Academic Freedom," *Educational Administration and Supervision,* March 1935, pp. 161–165; William C. Bagley, "Teachers' Rights, Academic Freedom, and the Teaching of Controversial Issues," *Teachers College Record,* November 1938, pp. 99–108; William C. Bagley, *Education and Emergent Man: A Theory of Education with Particular Application to Public Education in the United States* (New York: Nelson, 1934), p. 131.

7. Bagley, *Education and Emergent Man,* ibid., pp. 144–146.

8. Ibid., pp. 71–72.

9. William C. Bagley, "Is Subject-Matter Obsolete?" *Educational Administration and Supervision,* September 1935, pp. 403, 409–410.

10. Bagley, *Education and Emergent Man,* pp. 74–76, 90.

11. Ibid., pp. 192–196.

12. Ibid., pp. 192–196.

13. Michael J. Demiashkevich, *The Activity School: New Tendencies in Educational Method in Western Europe* (New York: Little and Ives, 1926), pp. 131–132.

14. Ibid., pp. 138–142, 150.

15. M. J. Demiashkevich, "Education for the Unchanging in Civilization," *The Kadelphian Review,* March 1933, pp. 292–293.

16. Ibid., pp. 297–299.

17. M. J. Demiashkevich, "Some Doubts About the Activity Movement," *Harvard Teachers Record,* October 1933, pp. 170–178.

18. Michael Demiashkevich, *An Introduction to the Philosophy of Education* (New York: American Book Company, 1935), pp. 5–6, 22–23, 118–122.

19. Ibid., p. 139.

20. Ibid., pp. 406–411.

21. William C. Bagley, "An Essentialist's Platform for the Advancement of American Education," *Educational Administration and Supervision,* April 1938, pp. 241–256. Bagley initially resisted the idea of inviting Robert Hutchins, the president of the University of Chicago, to join the Essentialist Committee, calling him "a reactionary type"; Bagley also wanted to ex-

clude "subject-matter scholars some of whom lack acquaintance with the problems of the lower schools and are wholly insensitive to the difficulties that are encountered by those who work in the field of universal non-selective education," as well as "those whose opposition to Progressivism is largely conditioned by the fact that many Progressives are known as social and economic radicals." Hutchins was invited to join the Essentialists, but he declined, partly because he didn't like the title of the organization (he suggested "The Association for Education") and partly because he thought its aims were too vague. See letter from William C. Bagley to F. Alden Shaw, November 22, 1937, and letter from Robert M. Hutchins to Michael Demiashkevich, February 7, 1938, Papers of Michael Demiashkevich, Special Collections, Vanderbilt Library, Nashville, Tenn.

22. Eunice Fuller Barnard, "Study Row Stirred by 'Essentialists,' " *The New York Times,* March 2, 1938, p. 8; " 'Essentialist' Group Urges Pupils Be Coddled Less and Taught More," *Newsweek,* March 14, 1938; "Progressives' Progress," *Time,* October 31, 1938, pp. 31–35; F. Alden Shaw, "The Essentialist Challenge to American Education," *School and Society,* April 1971, pp. 210–214. The other members of the original Essentialist Committee, in addition to Bagley and Demiashkevich, were Guy M. Whipple, a prominent educational psychologist; Walter H. Ryle, president of Northeast Missouri State Teachers College; F. Alden Shaw, headmaster of the Detroit Country Day School; Louis Shores, director of the Peabody College Library; and M. L. Shane, professor of modern languages at Peabody College.

23. S. A. Courtis, "The Fascist Menace in Education," *The University of Michigan School of Education Bulletin,* January 1939, pp. 51–53. Gurney Chambers, "Michael John Demiashkevich and the Essentialist Committee for the Advancement of American Education," *History of Education Quarterly,* Spring 1969, pp. 46–56.

24. Demiashkevich believed that his hostility to progressive education and communism prevented him from getting hired at prestigious institutions. An editor of *The Social Frontier* wrote a scathing, *ad hominem* review of Demiashkevich's *Introduction to the Philosophy of Education,* calling it "red-baiting" and part of a "fascist trend." Demiashkevich considered the writer to be a Communist pretending to be a liberal, but Bagley warned him not to print his reply. See Mordecai Grossman, "The Greeks Had a Word for It," *The Social Frontier,* December 1935, pp. 91–92. Reply, Michael Demiashkevich, "A Social Frontiersman Sees Red," undated, in Michael Demiashkevich Papers, Special Collections, Vanderbilt University, Nashville, Tenn.; letter from William C. Bagley to Michael Demiashkevich, December 23, 1935, Demiashkevich Papers, Special Collections,

Vanderbilt University. Demiashkevich complained to his New York publisher that William Heard Kilpatrick had blocked any possibility of his appointment to the faculty at Teachers College and that his book had been excluded from the Teachers College Library by faculty "Liberals" who had placed it on the *index librorum prohibitorum*. Letter from Michael Demiashkevich to W. W. Livengood, American Book Company, November 25, 1936, Michael Demiashkevich Papers.

25. Samuel Tenenbaum, *William Heard Kilpatrick,* pp. 241–242. In contrast to Kilpatrick, Harold Rugg spoke warmly of Bagley despite his differences with him; he described Bagley as a "brake on what he always thought was the too rapidly turning wheel of educational innovation" but added, "My hat is off to a loyal friend, an untiring fighter for what he believed in, a stanch defender of the community of culture, one who practiced democracy as he preached it, and—a rarity in American education during his lifetime—a master of the English paragraph!"—not a bad send-off from a longtime adversary. See Harold Rugg, *Foundations for American Education* (Yonkers, N.Y.: World Book, 1947), p. 607.

26. Harry S. Ashmore, *Unseasonable Truths: The Life of Robert Maynard Hutchins* (Boston: Little, Brown, 1989), pp. xv, 98–103; Robert Maynard Hutchins, *Education for Freedom* (Baton Rouge: Louisiana State University Press, 1943), pp. 12–13.

27. Robert Maynard Hutchins, "The Outlook for Public Education," in *No Friendly Voice* (Chicago: University of Chicago Press, 1936), pp. 107–108.

28. Robert Maynard Hutchins, "The Sheep Look Up," in *No Friendly Voice,* pp. 127–130 (a speech in Los Angeles to the Modern Forum, November 25, 1935).

29. Ibid., pp. 130–131.

30. Robert Maynard Hutchins, *The Higher Learning in America* (New Brunswick, N.J.: Transaction, 1995; first published 1936), pp. 6, 31–32, 56.

31. Ibid., pp. 59–63.

32. Ibid., p. 66.

33. Ibid., pp. 65–69.

34. Ibid., pp. 70–71.

35. Ibid., pp. 78–81.

36. Ibid., pp. 86–87.

37. John Dewey, "Rationality in Education," *The Social Frontier,* December 1936, pp. 71–73; "President Hutchins' Proposals to Remake Higher Education," *The Social Frontier,* January 1937, pp. 103–104. See also Robert M. Hutchins, "Grammar, Rhetoric, and Mr. Dewey," *The Social Frontier,* February 1937, pp. 137–139; John Dewey, " 'The Higher Learning in America,' " *The Social Frontier,* March 1937, pp. 167–169.

38. Eunice Fuller Barnard, "A Teachers' Teacher Tells What Education Is," *The New York Times,* March 21, 1937, p. 5.

39. Ashmore, *Unseasonable Truths,* pp. 125, 128–129; Robert B. Westbrook, *John Dewey and American Democracy* (Ithaca, N.Y.: Cornell University Press, 1991), pp. 445–449.

40. Mortimer Adler, *Philosopher at Large* (New York: Macmillan, 1977), pp. 184–185, 188–189.

41. Ibid.; Sidney Hook, "The New Medievalism," *The New Republic,* October 28, 1940, pp. 602–606.

42. *The Authoritarian Attempt to Capture Education,* Papers from the Second Conference on the Scientific Spirit and Democratic Faith (New York: Kings Crown Press, 1945), pp. v–vii.

43. *The Authoritarian Attempt,* pp. 5–8.

44. Ibid.

45. Ibid., pp. 13–14.

46. Edward A. Krug, *The Shaping of the American High School, 1920–1941* (Madison: University of Wisconsin Press, 1972), pp. 303–306.

47. John Dewey, *Experience and Education* (New York: Collier-Macmillan, 1963; first published 1938), p. 85.

48. Ibid., pp. 85, 71, 78, 82, 86.

49. Ibid., pp. 64–65.

50. Ibid., pp. 17, 61.

51. Ibid., p. 90.

52. Boyd H. Bode, *Progressive Education at the Crossroads* (New York: Newsom & Company, 1938), pp. 40, 70–71, 63.

53. Ibid., pp. 63, 68, 96, 86, 100.

54. Howard Mumford Jones, "Betrayal in American Education," *Scribner's,* June 1933, pp. 360–361.

55. Ibid.

56. Ibid., p. 362.

57. Carl Joachim Friedrich, "This Progressive Education," *The Atlantic Monthly,* October 1934, pp. 421–426.

58. Walter Lippmann, "Education Without Culture," *The Commonweal,* January 17, 1941, pp. 322–325.

59. See Diane Ravitch, *The Troubled Crusade: American Education, 1945–1980* (New York: Basic Books, 1983), pp. 88–91; Harold Rugg, *That Men May Understand* (New York: Doubleday, 1941), pp. 160–166.

60. Augustin G. Rudd, "Our 'Reconstructed' Educational System," *Nation's Business,* April 1940, pp. 27–28, 93–94; C. A. Bowers, "Social Reconstructionism: Views from the Left and the Right, 1932–1942," *History of Education Quarterly,* Spring 1970, pp. 42–47; Robert W. Iversen, *The*

Communists and the Schools (New York: Harcourt, Brace, 1959), pp. 243, 250.

61. O. K. Armstrong, "Treason in the Textbooks," *The American Legion Magazine,* September 1940, pp. 8–9, 51, 70–72.

62. Rugg, *That Men May Understand,* pp. 1–35; Bowers, "Social Reconstructionism," p. 42.

63. William W. Brickman, "I. L. Kandel—International Scholar and Educator," *The Educational Forum,* May 1951, pp. 389–412; Lawrence A. Cremin, "Isaac Leon Kandel: A Biographical Memoir" (Stanford: National Academy of Education, 1966).

64. I. L. Kandel, "The Influence of Dewey Abroad," *Teachers College Record,* December 1929, pp. 239–244. Erwin W. Pollack, "Isaac Leon Kandel: A Pioneer in Comparative and International Education," unpublished Ph.D. dissertation, Loyola University of Chicago, 1989, p. 14 (from the papers of William Fletcher Russell, Special Collections, Milbank Memorial Library, Teachers College). George Z. F. Bereday, "Memorial to Isaac Kandel, 1881–1965," *Comparative Education,* June 1966, p. 149.

65. I. L. Kandel, "Our Adolescent Education," *Educational Administration and Supervision,* November 1932, pp. 561, 564–565.

66. Ibid.

67. Ibid., pp. 568–571.

68. Pollack, "Isaac Leon Kandel," p. 10.

69. I. L. Kandel, "Alice in Cloud-Cuckoo-Land," *Teachers College Record,* May 1933, pp. 627–634.

70. Isaac L. Kandel, *The Dilemma of Democracy* (Cambridge, Mass.: Harvard University Press, 1934), pp. 71–72.

71. Ben D. Wood, "Making Use of the Objective Examination as a Phase of Teacher Selection," *Harvard Educational Review,* May 1940, p. 281; M. Ernest Townsend, "An Experiment in the Professional Examination of Teachers," *School and Society,* October 21, 1939, p. 539.

72. Wood, "Making Use of the Objective Examination," p. 278. Walter A. Anderson, "The National Teacher Examinations—A Criticism," *Childhood Education,* December 1941, p. 179; Ben D. Wood, "National Teacher Examinations . . . A Reply to Dr. Anderson," *Childhood Education,* January 1942, pp. 227–230.

73. I. L. Kandel, "The Teacher's Right to Be Ignorant," *School and Society,* June 22, 1940, pp. 753–755.

74. I. L. Kandel, *The Cult of Uncertainty* (New York: Macmillan, 1943), p. 6. See also I. L. Kandel, "Education and Social Disorder," *Teachers College Record,* February 1933, pp. 359–367; Kandel, "Alice in Cloud-Cuckoo-Land," pp. 627–634; Willystine Goodsell, "The New Education As It Is: A

Reply to Professor Kandel," *Teachers College Record,* April 1933, pp. 539–551.

75. Kandel, *The Cult of Uncertainty,* pp. 19–20, 24–25.
76. I. L. Kandel, "Prejudice the Garden Toward Roses?" *The American Scholar,* Winter 1938–39, pp. 72–82.
77. Kandel, *The Cult of Uncertainty,* pp. 109–110.

Chapter 9: The Great Meltdown

1. Lawrence A. Cremin, *The Transformation of the School: Progressivism in American Education, 1876–1957* (New York: Knopf, 1961), pp. 328–329. Also, Diane Ravitch, *The Troubled Crusade: American Education, 1945–1980* (New York: Basic Books, 1983), pp. 43–80.
2. David L. Angus and Jeffrey E. Mirel, *The Failed Promise of the American High School, 1890–1995* (New York: Teachers College Press, 1999), pp. 66–67.
3. Educational Policies Commission, *Education for All American Youth* (Washington, D.C.: National Education Association, 1944), pp. 142–143, 151–153.
4. Ibid., pp. 234–240.
5. National Association of Secondary School Principals, *Planning for American Youth: An Educational Program for Youth of Secondary-School Age* (Washington, D.C.: NASSP, 1944), p. 174.
6. U.S. Office of Education, *Life Adjustment Education for Every Youth* (Washington, D.C.: U.S. Government Printing Office, n.d.), p. 15. See also Ravitch, *The Troubled Crusade,* pp. 64–67.
7. U.S. Office of Education, ibid., p. 22.
8. Homer Boroughs, Jr., "Mathematics in Life Adjustment Education," *Life Adjustment in Action,* ed. Franklin R. Zeran (New York: Chartwell House, 1953), p. 208.
9. Harl R. Douglass, "The New Movement in Secondary Education for Life Adjustment," *Secondary Education,* February–March 1949, pp. 1–3.
10. National Commission on Life Adjustment Education for Youth, *Vitalizing Secondary Education* (Washington, D.C.: U.S. Office of Education, Bulletin no. 3, 1951), pp. 34–35.
11. Galen Jones and Raymond W. Gregory, *Life Adjustment Education for Every Youth* (Washington, D.C.: Federal Security Agency, 1948), pp. 15–16, 22, 49–53; National Commission on Life Adjustment Education for Youth, ibid., p. 35.
12. National Center for Education Statistics, *120 Years of American Educa-*

tion: A Statistical Portrait (Washington, D.C.: U.S. Department of Education, 1993), p. 55.

13. Charles Prosser, *Secondary Education and Life* (Cambridge, Mass.: Harvard University Press, 1939), p. 86; Educational Policies Commission, *Education for All American Youth,* pp. 7–8.

14. *120 Years of American Education: A Statistical Portrait,* p. 55; National Center for Education Statistics, *Digest of Education Statistics, 1995* (Washington, D.C.: U.S. Department of Education, 1995), p. 68. The war years caused a temporary enrollment decline as young people entered the armed forces or the civilian workforce, but by 1950 enrollment of this age group had rebounded to 76 percent. See also Angus and Mirel, *The Failed Promise of the American High School.*

15. U.S. Office of Education, *How High Schools Organize Activity Programs* (Washington, D.C.: U.S. Office of Education, Bulletin no. 19, 1951); Commission on Life Adjustment Education for Youth, *Look for the Person in the Student* (Washington, D.C.: Federal Security Agency, Office of Education, c. 1950), Benjamin C. Willis Papers, Hoover Institution Library, Box 309.

16. Harl R. Douglass, *Secondary Education for Life Adjustment of American Youth* (New York: Ronald Press, 1952), pp. 81–83; Harold Alberty, *Reorganizing the High-School Curriculum* (New York: Macmillan, 1947), pp. 65–67.

17. Commission on Life Adjustment Education for Youth, *A Look Ahead in Secondary Education* (Washington, D.C.: U.S. Office of Education, 1954), pp. 9–24; Franklin R. Zeran, "Life Adjustment Education in Action, 1944–1952," in Zeran, *Life Adjustment in Action,* p. 45.

18. Grace S. Wright, *Core Curriculum in Public High Schools* (Washington, D.C.: U.S. Office of Education, Bulletin no. 5, 1950), p. 3.

19. Douglass, *Secondary Education for Life Adjustment of American Youth,* p. v; William T. Gruhn and Harl R. Douglass, *The Modern Junior High School,* 2d ed. (New York: Ronald Press, 1956; first published 1947), p. 61.

20. Eileen Kathryn Rice, *The Superintendency and the Implementation of Progressive Practices in the Ann Arbor Elementary Schools from 1921–1942* (Ann Arbor: University of Michigan Social Foundations of Education Monograph Series, no. 8, 1978), p. 126.

21. Helen G. Trager and Marian Radke, "Will Your New Program Work?" *NEA Journal,* December 1948, pp. 612–614, cited in Kenneth D. Benne and Bozidar Muntyan, eds., *Human Relations in Curriculum Change* (New York: Dryden Press, 1951), pp. 287–288; Alberty, *Reorganizing the High-School Curriculum,* pp. 13–15, 144–145; Margaret Rouse, "Present Status of the Elementary School Curriculum," *Texas Outlook,* February 1947, p. 16.

22. C. A. Bowers, *The Progressive Educator and the Depression: The Radical Years* (New York: Random House, 1969), pp. 234–239; Kurt Lewin, "Techniques of Changing Culture," in Benne and Muntyan, *Human Relations in Curriculum Change,* pp. 56; "Introduction," ibid, 66–67; Herbert A. Thelen, "Theory of Group Dynamics," pp. 86–87; Charles E. Hendry, Ronald Lippitt, and Alvin Zander, "What Is Role-Playing?," pp. 239–240. The Benne and Muntyan collection of documents about group development was prepared at the request of the superintendent of public instruction in Illinois and used by the Illinois Secondary School Curriculum Program.

23. In Benne and Muntyan, *Human Relations in Curriculum Change,* pp. 294–295; Kenneth D. Benne, "Democratic Ethics and Human Engineering," *Progressive Education,* May 1949, p. 204.

24. Benne, "Democratic Ethics and Human Engineering," p. 207.

25. Hollis Caswell, *Curriculum Improvement in Public School Systems* (New York: Teachers College Press, 1950), p. 79.

26. Ibid., pp. 48–49.

27. Alice Miel, *Changing the Curriculum: A Social Process* (New York: Appleton-Century-Crofts, 1946), pp. 10, 40, 42–43.

28. Ibid., pp. 42–43.

29. Ibid., pp. 42–46.

30. Caswell, *Curriculum Improvement,* pp. 51–65.

31. Ibid., pp. 115, 153, 233–239.

32. Ibid., p. 331.

33. Ibid., pp. 260–262.

34. Ibid., pp. 258–262; Miles E. Cary, "The Fight over 'Common Learnings' in Minneapolis," *Progressive Education,* May 1951, pp. 205–211.

35. David Riesman, *The Lonely Crowd,* rev. ed. (New Haven: Yale University Press, 1961; first published 1950), pp. 59–65.

36. Ibid.

37. For criticism of the schools' secularism, see Bernard Iddings Bell, *Crisis in Education* (New York: Whittlesey House, 1949).

38. For more on these groups, see Ravitch, *The Troubled Crusade,* pp. 104–109.

39. Mortimer Smith, *And Madly Teach* (Chicago: Regnery, 1949), p. 24.

40. Harry J. Fuller, "The Emperor's New Clothes, or *Prius Dementat,*" *Scientific Monthly,* January 1951, p. 32.

41. Albert Lynd, *Quackery in the Public Schools* (Boston: Little, Brown, 1953), p. 188.

42. Arthur Bestor, Jr., *Educational Wastelands: The Retreat from Learning in Our Public Schools* (Urbana: University of Illinois Press, 1985; first published 1953), pp. 47, 64.

43. Lynd, *Quackery in the Public Schools,* p. 37.

44. Bestor, *Educational Wastelands,* pp. 101–103.

45. Archibald W. Anderson, "The Cloak of Respectability: The Attackers and Their Methods," *Progressive Education,* January 1952, p. 69; Ernest O. Melby, "American Education Is in Danger," *ADL Bulletin,* May 1951, pp. 1, 6; Robert A. Skaife, "The Sound and the Fury," *Phi Delta Kappan,* June 1953, pp. 357–386. See also *Public Education Under Criticism,* eds. C. Winfield Scott and Clyde M. Hill (New York: Prentice-Hall, 1954).

46. Benjamin Fine, "Administrators Bring into the Open Many Questions of Public vs. Private Schools," *The New York Times,* April 13, 1952, p. E9.

47. Lynd, *Quackery in the Public Schools,* pp. 5–11.

48. Bestor, *Educational Wastelands,* pp. 44–46.

49. Anderson, "The Cloak of Respectability," pp. 68–69.

50. Ibid.

51. A. H. Lauchner, "How Can the Junior High School Curriculum Be Improved?" *Bulletin 35,* National Association of Secondary-School Principals, March 1951, pp. 296–304.

52. Ibid.

53. George H. Henry, "Can Your Child Really Read?" *Harper's,* January 1946, pp. 72–76.

54. Carl A. Jessen, *Offerings and Registrations in High-School Subjects, 1933–34* (Washington, D.C.: U.S. Office of Education, 1938), pp. 28–29; Kenneth E. Brown, *Offerings and Enrollments in Science and Mathematics in Public High Schools* (Washington, D.C.: U.S. Department of Health, Education and Welfare, 1956), p. 16; Douglass, *Secondary Education for Life Adjustment of American Youth,* p. 190.

55. Jessen, *Offerings and Registrations in High-School Subjects,* pp. 28–29; Brown, *Offerings and Enrollments in Science and Mathematics,* p. 16.

56. Douglass, *Secondary Education for Life Adjustment of American Youth,* pp. 164–165.

57. Ibid., pp. 170–173.

58. Brown, *Offerings and Enrollments in Science and Mathematics,* pp. 2–4.

59. National Education Association, "Ten Criticisms of Public Education," *Research Bulletin,* 35, no. 4 (December 1957), pp. 134–174.

60. Rudolf Flesch, *Why Johnny Can't Read—And What You Can Do About It* (New York: Harper, 1955).

61. Ibid., pp. 17, 84–85.

62. Jeanne S. Chall, *Learning to Read: The Great Debate* (New York: McGraw-Hill, 1967), pp. 3, 7.

63. Ibid., pp. 278–285.

64. Ibid., pp. 13–15.

65. Ibid., pp. 83, 131, 149–150, 311.
66. Mitford M. Mathews, *Teaching to Read, Historically Considered* (Chicago: University of Chicago Press, 1966), pp. 77–81. The quotes are from a lecture delivered by Mann in 1841.
67. Joseph Mayer Rice, *The Public School System of the United States* (New York: Century, 1892); William A. Mowry, *Recollections of a New England Educator, 1838–1908* (New York: Burdett, 1908), p. 20.
68. Mathews, *Teaching to Read*, pp. 128–129, 134–139, 143. See also Cremin, *The Transformation of the School*, pp. 128–135.
69. John Dewey, "The Primary-Education Fetich," in *John Dewey: The Early Works, 1882–1898* (Carbondale, Ill.: Southern Illinois University Press, 1972), pp. 256–257, 259–261; originally published in *Forum* 25 (May 1898), pp. 315–328.
70. G. Stanley Hall, *Educational Problems*, vol. 2 (New York: Appleton, 1911), pp. 409, 414, 443, 618.
71. U.S. Office of Education, *The Place of Subjects in the Curriculum* (Washington, D.C.: U.S. Office of Education, Bulletin no. 12, 1949); U.S. Office of Education, *How Children Learn to Read* (Washington, D.C.: U.S. Office of Education, Bulletin no. 7, 1952), pp. 4–5.
72. Mathews, *Teaching to Read*, p. 190.
73. Chall, *Learning to Read*, p. 159.
74. Cremin, *The Transformation of the School*, p. 269.
75. Robert A. Divine, *The* Sputnik *Challenge* (New York: Oxford, 1993), p. 17, 159–160. *Life* magazine, at that time the most influential weekly in the nation, ran a five-part series in the spring of 1958 on the troubled state of American education.
76. Hyman B. Rickover, *Education and Freedom* (New York: Dutton, 1959), pp. 24, 31.
77. James G. Hershberg, *James B. Conant: Harvard to Hiroshima and the Making of the Nuclear Age* (New York: Knopf, 1993), p. 708.
78. James Bryant Conant, *The American High School Today* (New York: McGraw-Hill, 1959), p. 40.
79. Ibid., p. 47.
80. Ibid., pp. 58–59, 78, 92–94.

Chapter 10: The Sixties

1. National Center for Education Statistics, *Digest of Education Statistics 1995* (Washington, D.C.: U.S. Department of Education, 1995), p. 108.
2. Edgar Z. Friedenberg, *The Vanishing Adolescent* (New York: Beacon Press,

1959); Paul Goodman, *Growing Up Absurd* (New York: Random House, 1960). James S. Coleman, *The Adolescent Society: The Social Life of the Teenager and Its Impact on Education* (New York: Free Press, 1961), p. 9.

3. Ibid., pp. 167–172, 250–255, 265.

4. Ibid., pp. 16–17, 118–123. Adolescent pregnancy peaked in 1957; when girls became pregnant, they tended to drop out of school and get married. Maris Vinovskis, *An 'Epidemic' of Adolescent Pregnancy? Some Historical and Policy Considerations* (New York: Oxford, 1988).

5. Philip E. Jacob, *Changing Values in College: An Exploratory Study of the Impact of College Teaching* (New York: Harper, 1957), pp. 1–5.

6. Gerald Grant, *The World We Created at Hamilton High* (Cambridge, Mass.: Harvard University Press, 1988), pp. 13–19.

7. Reed Sarratt, *The Ordeal of Desegregation: The First Decade* (New York: Harper & Row, 1966), p. 359.

8. Ibid.

9. Horace Mann Bond, *Black American Scholars: A Study of Their Beginnings* (Detroit: Balamp, 1972), pp. 60–65; Vanessa Siddle Walker, *Their Highest Potential: An African American School Community in the Segregated South* (Durham: University of North Carolina Press, 1996); Thomas Sowell, "Black Excellence: The Case of Dunbar High School," *The Public Interest,* Spring 1974, pp. 5–12; Faustine Childress Jones, *A Traditional Model of Educational Excellence: Dunbar High School of Little Rock, Arkansas* (Washington, D.C.: Howard University Press, 1981); Jacqueline Jordan Irvine and Michele Foster, eds., *Growing Up African American in Catholic Schools* (New York: Teachers College Press, 1996).

10. Edward E. Redcay, *County Training Schools and Public Secondary Education for Negroes in the South* (Washington, D.C.: Slater Fund, 1935), pp. 20, 59, 86; National Center for Education Statistics, *Digest of Education Statistics, 1995* (Washington, D.C.: U.S. Department of Education, 1995), p. 17.

11. Gerald D. Jaynes and Robin M. Williams, Jr., *A Common Destiny: Blacks and American Society* (Washington, D.C.: National Academy Press, 1989), p. 59; Stephan Thernstrom and Abigail Thernstrom, *America in Black and White: One Nation, Indivisible* (New York: Simon & Schuster, 1997), p. 37; John Hope Franklin and Alfred A. Moss, Jr., *From Slavery to Freedom,* 6th ed. (New York: Knopf, 1988), p. 361.

12. Carleton Washburne, *Louisiana Looks at Its Schools: A Summary Report of the Louisiana Educational Survey* (Baton Rouge: Louisiana Educational Survey Commission, 1942), pp. 108–109. (See chapter on "The Negro Public Schools" by Charles S. Johnson.)

13. Ibid., pp. 109, 113–114.

14. Thernstrom and Thernstrom, *America in Black and White*, pp. 79–80.
15. David B. Tyack, *The One Best System: A History of American Urban Education* (Cambridge, Mass.: Harvard University Press, 1974), pp. 217–229.
16. Jeffrey E. Mirel, *The Rise and Fall of an Urban School System: Detroit, 1907–1981* (Ann Arbor: University of Michigan Press, 1993), pp. 186–202, 252–253, 300–335.
17. James B. Conant, *Slums and Suburbs: A Commentary on Schools in Metropolitan Areas* (New York: McGraw-Hill, 1961), pp. 1–2, 40.
18. Ibid., pp. 36, 48.
19. Charles E. Silberman, *Crisis in Black and White* (New York: Random House, 1964), pp. 252–254, 266–267.
20. Kenneth B. Clark, *Dark Ghetto: Dilemmas of Social Power* (New York: Harper & Row, 1965), pp. 111–112, 117.
21. Ibid., pp. 121–125, 134–136.
22. Ibid., pp. 126–127.
23. Ibid., pp. 129–133.
24. Ibid., pp. 131, 133.
25. Ibid., pp. 138, 140, 148.
26. Ibid., pp. 117–118.
27. Mirel, *The Rise and Fall of an Urban School System*, p. 333.
28. Grant, *The World We Created at Hamilton High*, pp. 54–63.
29. Ibid., pp. 4, 53, 61–65, 67.
30. A. S. Neill, *Summerhill: A Radical Approach to Child Rearing* (New York: Hart, 1960), pp. 57–58, 114.
31. *Summerhill: For and Against* (New York: Hart, 1970), pp. 7–8, 17.
32. Neill, *Summerhill*, pp. 3–5, 25, 29.
33. Ibid., pp. 22, 36, 43, 45, 208, 214; Jonathan Croall, *Neill of Summerhill: The Permanent Rebel* (New York: Pantheon, 1983), p. 280.
34. Neill, ibid., pp. 26–27.
35. John Holt, *How Children Fail* (New York: Pitman, 1964), pp. 49, 62, 125.
36. Ibid., pp. 155–157, 174–180.
37. Neil Postman and Charles Weingartner, *Teaching as a Subversive Activity* (New York: Delacorte, 1969), pp. 137–139. A decade later, Postman recanted his radical views in *Teaching as a Conserving Activity* (New York: Delacorte Press, 1979).
38. Carl Rogers, *Freedom to Learn* (Columbus, Ohio: Merrill, 1969), pp. 303–307.
39. Allen Graubard, *Free the Children: Radical Reform and the Free School Movement* (New York: Random House, 1972), pp. 40–41.
40. Thomas Powers, *Diana: The Making of a Terrorist* (Boston: Houghton

Mifflin, 1971), pp. 64–67. See also Todd Gitlin, *The Sixties: Years of Hope, Days of Rage* (New York: Bantam, 1993; first published 1987).

41. Graubard, *Free the Children,* p. 299; Henry Resnik, "Parkway: A School Without Walls," in *High School,* eds. Ronald Gross and Paul Osterman (New York: Simon and Schuster, 1971), pp. 248–262.

42. Joseph Featherstone, "Schools for Children," *The New Republic,* August 19, 1967, pp. 17–21; Joseph Featherstone, "How Children Learn," *The New Republic,* September 2, 1967, pp. 17–21; "Teaching Children to Think," *The New Republic,* September 9, 1967, pp. 15–25.

43. Charles E. Silberman, *Crisis in the Classroom: The Remaking of American Education* (New York: Random House, 1970), pp. 10–11, 207–208, 324, 340–356.

44. James D. Koerner, "The Greening of the Schools," in *Reactions to Silberman's* Crisis in the Classroom, ed. A. Harry Passow (Worthington, Ohio: Jones, 1971), pp. 13–18.

45. Amitai Etzioni, "Review of *Crisis in the Classroom,*" *Harvard Educational Review,* February 1971, pp. 87–98 (reprinted in Passow, *Reactions to Silberman's* Crisis in the Classroom, pp. 90–102).

46. George B. Leonard, *Education and Ecstasy* (New York: Delacorte, 1968), pp. 15, 17, 120, 141–150, 194.

47. Ivan Illich, *Deschooling Society* (New York: Harper & Row, 1971), pp. 8, 12–19, 49–50, 68, 72, 87, 96. Jonathan Kozol, the urban school reformer, proclaimed that *Deschooling Society* "may well be the most important book that has been published in the United States in twenty years." (Kozol himself preferred nonpublic free schools to deschooling.) Kozol's statement appeared on the jacket of the paperback edition of *Deschooling Society* published by Harrow Books in 1972.

48. Joseph Featherstone, "Tempering a Fad," *The New Republic,* September 25, 1971, pp. 17–21.

49. Roland S. Barth, *Open Education and the American School* (New York: Agathon, 1972), pp. 109–112, 138–142.

50. Ibid., pp. 147–156.

51. Joseph Featherstone, Foreword to Barth, ibid., p. x.

52. Donald A. Myers and Daniel L. Duke, "Status in New York State," *Open Education Re-examined* (Lexington, Mass.: Heath, 1973), p. 63; Donald A. Myers, "Why Open Education Died," *Journal of Research and Development in Education,* Fall 1974, pp. 60–67. See also Roland S. Barth, "Beyond Open Education," *Phi Delta Kappan,* February 1977, pp. 489–492.

53. Lisa D. Delpit, *Other People's Children: Cultural Conflicts in the Classroom* (New York: New Press, 1995), pp. 12–17 (originally published as

"Skills and Other Dilemmas of a Progressive Black Educator," *Harvard Educational Review,* November 1986, pp. 379–385).

54. College Entrance Examination Board, *On Further Examination* (New York: CEEB, 1977), pp. 26–31.

55. Ibid.; see also David L. Angus and Jeffrey E. Mirel, *The Failed Promise of the American High School, 1890–1995* (New York: Teachers College Press, 1999).

56. President's Commission on Foreign Language and International Studies, *Strength Through Wisdom: A Critique of U.S. Capability* (Washington, D.C.: U.S. Government Printing Office, 1979), p. 6; National Science Foundation and U.S. Department of Education, *Science and Engineering Education for the 1980s and Beyond* (Washington, D.C.: U.S. Government Printing Office, 1980), pp. 3, 46–48.

57. Clifford Adelman, "Devaluation, Diffusion, and the College Connection: A Study of High School Transcripts, 1964–1981," Paper prepared for the National Commission on Excellence in Education (Washington, D.C.: U.S. Department of Education, 1983), pp. 1, 3, 18–22.

58. William B. Fetters, George H. Brown, and Jeffrey A. Owings, *High School Seniors: A Comparative Study of the Classes of 1972 and 1980* (Washington, D.C.: National Center for Education Statistics, 1984), pp. 5–8. Using different methods, the Adelman study concluded that 42.5 percent of graduates were in the general track, while the Fetters, Brown, and Owings study placed the figure at 38 percent.

59. David Angus and Jeffrey Mirel, "Rhetoric and Reality: The High School Curriculum," in *Learning from the Past: What History Teaches Us About School Reform,* ed. Diane Ravitch and Maris Vinovskis (Baltimore: Johns Hopkins Press, 1995), p. 302; Diane Ravitch, *National Standards in American Education: A Citizen's Guide* (Washington, D.C.: Brookings Institution, 1995), chap. 3; Mirel, *The Rise and Fall of an Urban School System,* chap. 6.

60. Robert A. Johnson et al., *Trends in the Incidence of Drug Use in the United States, 1919–1992* (Washington, D.C.: U.S. Department of Health and Human Services, Substance Abuse and Mental Health Services Administration, 1996), pp. 32–37. See also Edward A. Wynne and Kevin Ryan, *Reclaiming Our Schools: Teaching Character, Academics, and Discipline* (Upper Saddle River, N.J.: Prentice-Hall, 1997), chap. 1.

Chapter 11: In Search of Standards

1. Carol R. Richards and Pat Ordovensky, "Quality Public Education: An Endangered American Dream," *Rochester Times-Union,* April 24, 1980; Jessica Tuchman Mathews, "Decline in Education: (I) The Evidence," *The Washington Post,* October 13, 1981.

2. Bill Honig, *Last Chance for Our Children* (Reading, Mass.: Addison-Wesley, 1985), pp. 43–44.

3. Berman, Weiler Associates, "Improving Student Performance in California: Recommendations for the California Roundtable" (Berkeley, Calif.: California Business Roundtable, 1982), pp. 2–8.

4. Philip A. Cusick, *The Egalitarian Ideal and the American High School: Studies of Three Schools* (New York: Longman, 1983), pp. 39, 69, 122–123.

5. Southern Regional Education Board, *The Need for Quality* (Atlanta: SREB, 1981), pp. 16–20.

6. For SAT scores, see the annual national reports on college-bound seniors published by the College Entrance Examination Board of New York. For the numbers of high-scoring students, see those reports and Rex Jackson, *An Examination of Declining Numbers of High-Scoring SAT Candidates* (New York: The College Board, 1976), pp. 1–3. In 1995, 88,643 students scored over 600 on the verbal SAT (8.3 percent of test-takers), and 229,618 students scored over 600 on the mathematical portion (21.5 percent).

   In 1996, the College Board "recentered" SAT scores. The national average for the verbal SAT, which would have been 428 on the old scale in 1998, was then reported as 505; the mathematics average, which was 488 on the old scale, became 512. For a review of student achievement, see Lawrence A. Stedman, "An Assessment of the Contemporary Debate over U.S. Achievement," *Brookings Papers on Education Policy 1998,* ed. Diane Ravitch (Washington, D.C.: Brookings Institution, 1998), pp. 53–85.

   In 1976, Jeanne Chall of Harvard University reported that the content of widely used high school textbooks had been reduced by as much as two grade levels in the two previous decades. See Jeanne Chall, with S. S. Conrad and S. H. Harris, *An Analysis of Textbooks in Relation to Declining SAT Scores* (New York: College Board, 1976). In 1996, Donald P. Hayes, Loreen T. Wolfer, and Michael F. Wolfe of Cornell University found that the *"entire distribution of verbal scores, from top to bottom, shifted to lower levels"* because of textbook simplification (italics in original). They based this conclusion on a computer-generated word analysis of eight hundred textbooks published between 1919 and 1991. They held that reduced verbal challenge in textbooks at every grade level had caused "a cumulating knowledge deficit," because students were exposed to fewer words and shorter sentences and were less likely to encounter uncommon words. Reading levels were reduced after World War I and again after World War II. By the mid-1990s, the average literature textbook for high school seniors was simpler than the average seventh- or eighth-grade reader published before World War II. See Donald P. Hayes, Loreen T. Wolfer, and Michael F. Wolfe, "Schoolbook Simplification and Its Relation to the Decline in SAT-Verbal Scores," *American Educational Research Journal,* Summer 1996, pp. 489–508.

7. National Center for Education Statistics, *The Condition of Education, 1995* (Washington, D.C.: U.S. Department of Education, 1995), p. 42; National Center for Education Statistics, *The 1994 High School Transcript Study Tabulations: Comparative Data on Credits Earned and Demographics for 1994, 1990, 1987, and 1982 High School Graduates* (Washington, D.C.: U.S. Department of Education, 1998), p. A13.

8. National Center for Education Statistics, *Remedial Education at Higher Education Institutions in Fall 1995* (Washington, D.C.: U.S. Department of Education, 1996), p. 34; Stephan Thernstrom and Abigail Thernstrom, *America in Black and White: One Nation, Indivisible* (New York: Simon & Schuster, 1997), p. 392.

9. National Commission on Excellence in Education, *A Nation at Risk: The Imperative for Educational Reform* (Washington, D.C.: U.S. Government Printing Office, 1983), p. 5.

10. Ibid., p. 7.

11. Ibid., p. 8.

12. Ibid., pp. 18–23.

13. *The Nation Responds* (Washington, D.C.: U.S. Department of Education, 1984).

14. Paul E. Peterson, "Did the Education Commissions Say Anything?" *The Brookings Review,* Winter 1983, pp. 3–11; Lawrence C. Stedman and Marshall S. Smith, "Recent Reform Proposals for American Education," *Contemporary Education Review,* Fall 1983, pp. 85–104. See also David C. Berliner and Bruce J. Biddle, *The Manufactured Crisis: Myths, Fraud, and the Attack on America's Public Schools* (New York: Addison-Wesley, 1995) and Maris Vinovskis, *The Road to Charlottesville: The 1989 Education Summit* (Washington, D.C.: National Education Goals Panel, 1999).

15. Eva C. Galambos, *Teacher Preparation: The Anatomy of a College Degree* (Atlanta, Ga.: Southern Regional Education Board, 1985), pp. 3, 8, 15, 18.

16. Frederic Mitchell and Michael Schwinden, *Profiles of the Education of*

Teachers and Proposals for Reform (Tempe, Ariz.: Arizona State University, 1984), pp. 91–107; Rita Kramer, *Ed School Follies* (New York: Free Press, 1991).

17. J. S. Coleman et al., *Equality of Educational Opportunity* (Washington, D.C.: U.S. Office of Education, 1966); Christopher Jencks et al., *Inequality: A Reassessment of the Effects of Family and Schooling in America* (New York: Basic Books, 1972); Jack Rosenthal, "School Expert Calls Integration Vital Aid," *The New York Times,* March 9, 1970, p. 1; Jim Leeson, "Some Basic Beliefs Challenged," *Southern Education Report,* May 1967.

18. John B. Carroll, "A Model of School Learning," *Teachers College Record,* May 1963, pp. 723–733.

19. Benjamin S. Bloom, *Human Characteristics and School Learning* (New York: McGraw-Hill, 1976), pp. ix–x, 70–71, 208–211.

20. Ronald R. Edmonds, "Effective Education for Minority Pupils: Brown Confounded or Confirmed," in *Shades of Brown: New Perspectives on School Desegregation,* ed. Derrick Bell (New York: Teachers College Press, 1980), p. 121.

21. James S. Coleman, "Recent Trends in School Integration," *Educational Researcher,* June 1975, pp. 3–12; James S. Coleman, "School Desegregation and Schultze's Law," presentation at the Department of Health, Education and Welfare, December 1, 1978 (personal files of James S. Coleman).

22. James S. Coleman, Sally Kilgore, and Thomas Hoffer, *Public and Private Schools* (New York: Basic Books, 1982); Diane Ravitch, "The Meaning of the New Coleman Report," *Phi Delta Kappan,* June 1981; see also Diane Ravitch, "The Coleman Reports and American Education," in *Social Theory and Social Policy: Essays in Honor of James S. Coleman,* ed. Aage B. Sørensen and Seymour Spilerman (Westport, Conn.: Praeger, 1993), pp. 129–141.

23. Theodore R. Sizer, *Horace's Compromise: The Dilemma of the American High School* (Boston: Houghton Mifflin, 1983), pp. 6, 214–217.

24. Ibid., p. 110. Contrary to the educational progressives of the 1920s who had insisted that children should learn the basic skills incidentally, while engaged in activities, Sizer insisted that schools should focus *"exclusively"* (his italics) on the basic skills of literacy, numeracy, and civic understanding for those students who had not yet mastered them.

25. James Traub, *Better By Design? A Consumer's Guide to Schoolwide Reform* (Washington, D.C.: Thomas B. Fordham, 1999), p. 30; Deborah Meier, *The Power of Their Ideas* (Boston: Beacon, 1995).

26. E. D. Hirsch, Jr., *Cultural Literacy: What Every American Needs to Know* (Boston: Houghton Mifflin, 1987), p. xiii.

27. I. L. Kandel, *The Cult of Uncertainty* (New York: Macmillan, 1943),

p. 109; Hirsch, *Cultural Literacy,* p. 135; E. D. Hirsch, Jr., Joseph Kett, and James Trefill, *The Dictionary of Cultural Literacy* (Boston: Houghton Mifflin, 1988). See also, E. D. Hirsch, Jr., *The Schools We Need: And Why We Don't Have Them* (New York: Doubleday, 1996).

28. Hirsch, *Cultural Literacy;* Carleton Washburne, "The Philosophy of the Winnetka Curriculum," *The Foundations and Technique of Curriculum-Construction: The Twenty-Sixth Yearbook of the National Society for the Study of Education,* pt. 1 (Bloomington, Ill.: Public School Publishing, 1926), pp. 219–220.

29. By 1995, 67 percent of children aged five to seventeen were white, 15 percent were black, 13 percent were Hispanic, and 5 percent were Asian/Pacific Islander, American Indian or Alaskan Native. Federal statistical agencies predicted that the numbers of nonwhite children would grow at a faster rate than those of white children. See National Center for Education Statistics, *The Social Context of Education* (Washington, D.C.: U.S. Department of Education, 1997), pp. 5–6.

30. Eleanor P. Wolf, *Trial and Error: The Detroit School Segregation Case* (Detroit: Wayne State University Press, 1981), p. 16; Jeffrey Mirel, *The Rise and Fall of an Urban School System: Detroit, 1907–81* (Ann Arbor: University of Michigan Press, 1993), pp. 298, 307; Carole Kismaric and Marvin Heiferman, *Growing Up with Dick and Jane* (New York: HarperCollins, 1996), pp. 96–100; Donna M. Gollick, Frank H. Klassen, and Joost Yff, *Multicultural Education and Ethnic Studies in the United States* (Washington, D.C.: American Association of Colleges for Teacher Education and ERIC Clearinghouse on Teacher Education, 1976).

31. Frances FitzGerald, *America Revised: History Schoolbooks in the Twentieth Century* (Boston: Atlantic–Little, Brown, 1979), pp. 7–11.

32. California State Board of Education, *History–Social Science Framework for California Public Schools* (Sacramento: California State Department of Education, 1988), pp. 5, 56.

33. New York State Department of Education, "A Curriculum of Inclusion" (Albany, N.Y.: Commissioner's Task Force on Minorities, 1989), pp. 34, 37; Joseph Berger, "Professors' Theories on Race Stir Turmoil at City College," *The New York Times,* April 20, 1990, p. B1; Jacques Steinberg, "CUNY Professor Criticizes Jews," *The New York Times,* August 6, 1991, p. B3.

34. Robert K. Landers, "Conflict over Multicultural Education," *Congressional Quarterly's Editorial Research Reports,* November 30, 1990, pp. 682–695; *African-American Baseline Essays* (Portland: Portland Public Schools, 1989).

35. Arthur Schlesinger, Jr., "When Ethnic Studies Are Un-American," *The*

Wall Street Journal, April 23, 1990; "Text of Statement by 'Scholars in Defense of History,' " *Education Week,* August 1, 1990.

36. New York State Social Studies Review and Development Committee, *One Nation, Many Peoples: A Declaration of Cultural Interdependence* (Albany, N.Y.: State Education Department, 1991), dissent by Arthur Schlesinger, Jr.

37. Paul Gray, "Whose America?" *Time,* July 8, 1991, pp. 12–17; Andrew Sullivan, "Racism 101," *The New Republic,* November 26, 1990, pp. 19–21.

38. David Nicholson, " 'Afrocentrism' and the Tribalization of America," *The Washington Post,* September 23, 1990, p. B1.

39. Henry Louis Gates, Jr., "Whose Culture Is It, Anyway," *The New York Times,* May 4, 1991; Henry Louis Gates, Jr., "Black Demagogues and Pseudo-Scholars," *The New York Times,* July 20, 1992, p. A13. Orlando Patterson, "Black Like All of Us," *The Washington Post,* February 7, 1993, p. C2.

40. Debra Viadero, "Battle over Multicultural Education Rises in Intensity," *Education Week,* November 28, 1990, pp. 1, 11–13; Carol Chmelynski, "Schools See Benefits of 'Multicultural' Curriculum," *School Board News,* October 23, 1990, p. 8; National Association of State Boards of Education, "NASBE Releases Recommendations on Multicultural Education," press release, October 1991; Sandra Stotsky, *Losing Our Language: How Multicultural Classroom Instruction Is Undermining Our Children's Ability to Read, Write, and Reason* (New York: The Free Press, 1999).

41. Barbara Lerner, "Self-Esteem and Excellence: The Choice and the Paradox," *The American Educator,* Winter 1985, pp. 10–16.

42. Barbara Lerner, "Self-Esteem and Excellence: The Choice and the Paradox," *The American Educator,* Summer 1996, pp. 9–13, 41–42.

43. Arthur G. Powell, Eleanor Farrar, and David K. Cohen, *The Shopping Mall High School: Winners and Losers in the Educational Marketplace* (Boston: Houghton Mifflin, 1985), pp. 3–6.

44. Ibid., pp. 4, 62, 188–189.

45. Andrew M. Mecca, Neil J. Smelser, and John Vasconcellos, eds., *The Social Importance of Self-Esteem* (Berkeley: University of California Press, 1989), p. xiv.

46. Neil J. Smelser, "Self-Esteem and Social Problems: An Introduction," ibid., pp. 15–17; Martin V. Covington, "Self-Esteem and Failure in School: Analysis and Policy Implications," ibid., pp. 78–79, 82. See also John Leo, "The Trouble with Self-Esteem," *U.S. News & World Report,* April 2, 1990, p. 16.

47. William Damon, *Greater Expectations: Overcoming the Culture of Indulgence in Our Homes and Schools* (New York: Free Press, 1995), pp. 68–80.

48. Brad J. Bushman and Roy F. Baumeister, "Threatened Egotism, Narcissism, Self-Esteem, and Direct and Displaced Aggression: Does Self-Love or Self-Hate Lead to Violence?" *Journal of Personality and Social Psychology,* July 1998, pp. 219–229; Adam Rogers, "You're OK, I'm Terrific: 'Self-Esteem' Backfires," *Newsweek,* July 13, 1998, p. 69.

49. Harold W. Stevenson, Shin-Ying Lee, and James W. Stigler, "Mathematics Achievement of Chinese, Japanese, and American Children," *Science,* February 14, 1986, pp. 693–699; Harold W. Stevenson, Chuansheng Chen, and Shin-Ying Lee, "Mathematics Achievement of Chinese, Japanese, and American Children: Ten Years Later," *Science,* January 1, 1993, pp. 54–55; Harold W. Stevenson, "Learning from Asian Schools," *Scientific American,* December 1992, pp. 75–76; Harold W. Stevenson and James W. Stigler, *The Learning Gap: Why Our Schools Are Failing and What We Can Learn from Japanese and Chinese Education* (New York: Summit, 1992).

50. Albert Shanker, "A Question of Fairness," *The New York Times,* March 29, 1992; "National Standards and Exams," *The New York Times,* March 1, 1992.

51. Albert Shanker, "The Education Summit: Peak or Pique?" *The New York Times,* September 17, 1989.

52. Albert Shanker, "Cortines Sets Standards," *The New York Times,* May 8, 1994; Albert Shanker, "Making Standards Count," *The American Educator,* Fall 1994, pp. 14–19; Albert Shanker, "Coming to Terms on 'World-Class Standards,' " *Education Week,* June 17, 1992.

53. Diane Ravitch, *National Standards in American Education: A Citizen's Guide* (Washington, D.C.: Brookings Institution, 1995).

54. Lynne V. Cheney, "The End of History," *The Wall Street Journal,* October 20, 1994.

55. Guy Gugliotta, "Up in Arms About the 'American Experience,' " *The Washington Post,* October 28, 1994, p. A3; Tamara Henry, "History by Rote Considered a Dated Approach," *USA Today,* October 26, 1994, p. 1.

56. "Up in Arms about the 'American Experience,' " ibid.; "Now a History for the Rest of Us," *Los Angeles Times,* October 27, 1994, p. A10; "A Blueprint of History for American Students," *San Francisco Chronicle,* October 29, 1994, p. A22; "Revising History," *St. Louis Post-Dispatch,* October 31, 1994, p. B6; "Maligning the History Standards," *The New York Times,* February 13, 1995, p. A18; Carol Gluck, "History According to Whom?" *The New York Times,* November 19, 1994; Theodore K. Rabb, "Whose History? Where Critics of the New Standards Flunk Out," *The Washington Post,* December 11, 1994.

57. John Elson, "History, the Sequel," *Time,* November 7, 1994, p. 64; Charles Krauthammer, "History Hijacked," *The Washington Post,* November 4, 1994; LynNell Hancock, "Red, White—And Blue," *Newsweek,* November

7, 1994, p. 54. Scores of articles were written about the history standards; a good summary is Kenneth Jost, "Teaching History," *The CQ Researcher,* September 29, 1995, pp. 849–872. For a spirited defense of the standards by their writers, see Gary B. Nash, Charlotte Crabtree, and Ross E. Dunn, *History on Trial: Culture Wars and the Teaching of the Past* (New York: Knopf, 1997).

58. Congressional Record, Senate, January 18, 1995, S1025–1035, S1038–1040; Albert Shanker, "The History Standards," *The New York Times,* November 6, 1994; Albert Shanker, "Debating the Standards," *The New York Times,* January 29, 1995.

59. Statement by Richard W. Riley, U.S. Department of Education, September 4, 1994.

60. John Patrick Diggins, "Historical Blindness," *The New York Times,* November 19, 1994; Sheldon M. Stern, "Beyond the Rhetoric: An Historian's View of the 'National' Standards for United States History," *Journal of Education,* vol. 176, November 3, 1994, pp. 69–70.

61. Walter A. McDougall, "Whose History? Whose Standards?" *Commentary,* May 1995, pp. 36, 42. See also Diane Ravitch, "The Controversy over National History Standards," *The American Academy of Arts and Sciences Bulletin,* January–February 1998, pp. 14–28.

62. Council for Basic Education, *History in the Making: An Independent Review of the Voluntary National History Standards* (Washington, D.C.: Council for Basic Education, 1996), pp. 2–9. Some critics were still dissatisfied: see John Patrick Diggins, "History Standards Got It Wrong Again," *The New York Times,* May 15, 1996; Walter A. McDougall, "What Johnny Still Won't Know about History," *Commentary,* July 1996, pp. 32–36.

63. See Ravitch, *National Standards in American Education.*

64. National Council of Teachers of English and International Reading Association, *Standards for the English Language Arts* (Urbana, Ill., and Newark, Del.: NCTE and IRA, 1996).

65. J. Martin Rochester, "The Decline of Literacy," *Education Week,* May 15, 1996; Dick Feagler, "Educators in Dire Need of English 101 Course," *The Plain Dealer* (Cleveland), March 13, 1996.

66. "How Not to Write English," *The New York Times,* March 14, 1996; Albert Shanker, "What Standards?" *The New York Times,* April 7, 1996.

67. Bruce R. Vogeli, "The Rise and Fall of the 'New Math,' " Inaugural Lecture, Teachers College, Columbia University, 1976, pp. 4, 17.

68. Ibid., p. 17; Morris Kline, *Why Johnny Can't Add: The Failure of the New Math* (New York: St. Martin's Press, 1973).

69. *Curriculum and Evaluation Standards for School Mathematics* (Reston, Va.: National Council of Teachers of Mathematics, 1989), p. 66.

70. *Creating a Climate for Change: Math Leads the Way—Perspectives on Math Reform* (New York: Public Agenda, 1993), p. 8.

71. Marianne M. Jennings, "Rain-Forest Algebra and MTV Geometry," *The Textbook Letter,* November–December 1996; John Leo, "That So-Called Pythagoras," *U.S. News & World Report,* May 26, 1997; Lynne Cheney, "Creative Math, or Just 'Fuzzy Math' "? *The New York Times,* August 11, 1997; Romesh Ratnesar, "This Is Math?" *Time,* August 24, 1997; Tom Loveless, "The Second Great Math Rebellion," *Education Week,* October 15, 1997, November 5, 1997, November 12, 1997, December 3, 1997; Jacques Steinberg, "California Goes to War Over Math Instruction," *The New York Times,* November 27, 1997; Martin Gardner, "The New New Math," *The New York Review of Books,* September 24, 1998.

72. California State Board of Education, *The California Mathematics Academic Content Standards for Grades K–12* (1998); Richard Lee Colvin, "State Endorses Back-to-Basics Math Standards," *Los Angeles Times,* December 2, 1997; Richard Lee Colvin, "Math Changes Reflect Broader Schools Debate," *Los Angeles Times,* December 5, 1997.

73. Lauren B. Resnick and Leopold E. Klopfer, eds., *Toward the Thinking Curriculum: Current Cognitive Research* (Alexandria, Va.: Association for Supervision and Curriculum Development, 1989), pp. 4–5.

74. Paul Cobb, "Constructivism in Mathematics and Science Education," *Educational Researcher,* October 1994, p. 4.

75. Rosalind Driver et al., "Constructing Scientific Knowledge in the Classroom," *Educational Researcher,* October 1994, p. 5; D. C. Phillips, "The Good, the Bad, and the Ugly: The Many Faces of Constructivism," *Educational Researcher,* October 1995, p. 5.

76. Frank Smith, *Understanding Reading: A Psycholinguistic Analysis of Reading and Learning to Read* (New York: Holt, Rinehart, and Winston, 1971), p. 2; Frank Smith, *Psycholinguistics and Reading* (New York: Holt, Rinehart, and Winston, 1973).

77. Ken Goodman, *What's Whole in Whole Language?* (Portsmouth, N.H.: Heinemann, 1986), pp. 26, 37–39, 40. See also, Kenneth S. Goodman and Yetta M. Goodman, "Learning to Read Is Natural," in *Theory and Practice of Early Reading,* vol. 1, ed. Lauren S. Resnick and Phyllis A. Weaver (Hillsdale, N.J.: Erlbaum, 1979); Kenneth S. Goodman, "Reading: A Psycholinguistic Guessing Game," in *Theoretical Models and Processes of Reading,* ed. H. Singer and R. B. Ruddell (Newark, Del.: International Reading Association, 1976), pp. 497–508; Frank Smith, "Learning to Read: The Never-Ending Debate," *Phi Delta Kappan,* February 1992, p. 439.

78. Goodman, *What's Whole in Whole Language?,* pp. 25, 37–38.

79. National Academy of Education, *Becoming a Nation of Readers* (Washington, D.C.: U.S. Department of Education, 1985), p. 43; Jane L. Davidson, ed., *Counterpoint and Beyond: A Response to* Becoming a Nation of Readers (Urbana, Ill.: National Council of Teachers of English, 1988); also see Kenneth Goodman, "Afterword," pp. 107–108.

80. Nicholas Lemann, "The Reading Wars," *The Atlantic Monthly,* November 1997, pp. 128–134.

81. *English-Language Arts Framework* (Sacramento: California State Department of Education, 1987), p. 1.

82. John O'Neil, " 'Whole Language': New View of Literacy Gains in Influence," *ASCD Update,* January 1989, pp. 1, 6–7.

83. Robert Rothman, "From a 'Great Debate' to a Full-Scale War: Dispute over Teaching Reading Heats Up," *Education Week,* March 21, 1990, pp. 1, 10–11.

84. Marilyn Jager Adams, *Beginning to Read: Thinking and Learning About Print* (Washington, D.C.: U.S. Department of Education, 1990), pp. 7, 125; Connie Weaver, "Weighing Claims of 'Phonics First' Advocates," *Education Week,* March 28, 1990, pp. 32–33.

85. Kenneth S. Goodman, "Gurus, Professors, and the Politics of Phonics," *Reading Today,* December 1992–January 1993, pp. 8–9, 32; Smith, "Learning to Read," p. 4. See also Michael C. McKenna, Steven A. Stahl, and David Reinking, "A Critical Commentary on Research, Politics, and Whole Language," *Journal of Reading Behavior,* 26, no. 2 (1994), pp. 211–233.

86. State-by-state rankings of NAEP scores were an innovation that started in 1992; see National Center for Education Statistics, *NAEP 1994 Reading Report Card for the Nation and the States: Findings from the National Assessment of Educational Progress and Trial State Assessments* (Washington, D.C.: U.S. Department of Education, 1996), pp. 56–57, 145, 153. In California, 41 percent of white students in fourth grade scored "below basic," as did 69 percent of black students and 78 percent of Hispanic students. Forty-six percent of the children of college graduates in fourth grade registered "below basic," compared to 32 percent nationally.

87. LynNell Hancock and Pat Wingert, "If You Can Read This," *Newsweek,* May 13, 1996; James Collins, "How Johnny Should Read," *Time,* October 27, 1997; Joan Beck, "Phonics Programs Proven to Be the Easiest Way to Teach Reading," *Chicago Tribune,* October 23, 1997.

88. Bill Honig, *How Should We Teach Our Children to Read? The Role of Skills in a Comprehensive Reading Program—A Balanced Approach* (San Francisco: Far West Laboratory for Educational Research and Development,

1996), p. 7; California State Department of Education, *English-Language Arts Content Standards for California Public Schools* (Sacramento: California State Department of Education, 1998).

89. Jeanne S. Chall, *Learning to Read: The Great Debate* (New York: McGraw-Hill, 1967), pp. 307–308.

90. In 1992, 38 percent of fourth-graders scored "below basic" in reading, as did 40 percent in 1994 and 38 percent in 1998; see National Center for Education Statistics, *NAEP 1998 Reading Report Card for the Nation and the States* (Washington, D.C.: U.S. Department of Education, 1999), pp. 20, 71.

91. Catherine E. Snow, M. Susan Burn, and Peg Griffin, eds., *Preventing Reading Difficulties in Young Children* (Washington, D.C.: National Academy Press, 1998), p. 7; G. Reid Lyon and Louisa C. Moats, "Critical Conceptual and Methodological Considerations in Reading Intervention Research," *Journal of Learning Disabilities,* November–December 1997, pp. 578–588; G. Reid Lyon, "Why Kids Can't Read," Testimony to Committee on Education and the Workforce, U.S. House of Representatives, July 10, 1997.

92. *Every Child Reading: An Action Plan of the Learning First Alliance* (Washington, D.C.: American Federation of Teachers, 1998); Louisa Moats, *Teaching Reading IS Rocket Science* (Washington, D.C.: American Federation of Teachers, 1999); Jonathan Fox, "English Teachers Step Up Struggle Against Phonics," *Education Daily,* December 17, 1999, pp. 1, 3–4.

93. National Center for Education Statistics, *The 1994 High School Transcript Study Tabulations,* 1998.

94. Jean Johnson and John Immerwahr, *First Things First: What Americans Expect from the Public Schools* (New York: Public Agenda, 1994); Jean Johnson, *Assignment Incomplete: The Unfinished Business of Education Reform* (New York: Public Agenda, 1995), p. 20; Jean Johnson and Steve Farkas, *Getting By: What American Teenagers Really Think About Their Schools* (New York: Public Agenda, 1997); Steve Farkas and Jean Johnson, *Different Drummers: How Teachers of Teachers View Public Education* (New York: Public Agenda, 1997), p. 9; Steve Farkas and Jean Johnson, *Time to Move On: African-American and White Parents Set an Agenda for Public Schools* (New York: Public Agenda, 1998), p. 31.

Conclusion

1. James Traub, "What No School Can Do," *The New York Times Magazine,* January 16, 2000, pp. 52–57, 68, 81, 90–91.

2. James S. Coleman, *The Asymmetric Society* (Syracuse, N.Y.: Syracuse University Press, 1982), pp. 126–127, 130, 133–137.
3. National Center for Education Statistics, *120 Years of American Education: A Statistical Portrait* (Washington, D.C.: U.S. Department of Education, 1993), p. 56; National Center for Education Statistics, *Common Core of Data, School Universe, 1996–97* (Washington, D.C.: U.S. Department of Education, 1998).
4. John Dewey, "My Pedagogic Creed," in *Dewey on Education,* ed. Martin S. Dworkin (New York: Teachers College Press, 1959), pp. 30–32.
5. Gerald W. Bracey, "Why Can't They Be like We Were?" *Phi Delta Kappan,* October 1991, pp. 111–112. A member of the Princeton, New Jersey, school board objected to a proposal for an academic charter school on these grounds: "Now I want to ask you, who is going to collect your garbage?"; Neil MacFarquhar, "Public, but Independent Schools Are Inspiring Hope and Hostility," *The New York Times,* December 27, 1996, p. A1.
6. Historians of education disagree about the extent to which progressive education actually was implemented in American public schools. The leading historian of American education, Lawrence A. Cremin, called his history of the progressive education movement *The Transformation of the School.* Cremin maintained that progressivism had left an indelible, irreversible imprint on the schools. Diane Ravitch, in the present work and in *The Troubled Crusade: American Education, 1945–1980,* agreed with Cremin. David L. Angus and Jeffrey E. Mirel contended that American high schools had been transformed by progressive ideas in ways that had created a culture of low expectations. Other historians of education, however, notably Larry Cuban (*How Teachers Taught*) and Arthur Zilversmit (*Changing Schools*), claimed that the influence of progressivism on the nation's public schools had been minimal or nil.

   The differences in their views can be attributed to their definitions of progressivism. Cuban and Zilversmit identified progressive education with the child-centered, socially conscious, intellectually stimulating environment that Dewey had advocated. They rightly concluded that this ideal version of progressivism had not been institutionalized in American public schools. Cremin, the present author, and Angus and Mirel defined progressivism as a many-sided movement that included disparate and even contradictory currents. Seen this way, progressivism was parent not only to the social democratic vision of John Dewey but to industrial education, IQ testing, curricular differentiation, social reformism, child-centered schooling, life adjustment education, and other variations of progressive themes that influenced the public schools in important ways.

   See Lawrence A. Cremin, *The Transformation of the School: Progres-*

sivism in American Education, 1876–1957 (New York: Knopf, 1961); Diane Ravitch, *The Troubled Crusade: American Education, 1945–1980* (New York: Basic Books, 1983); David L. Angus and Jeffrey E. Mirel, *The Failed Promise of the American High School, 1890–1995* (New York: Teachers College Press, 1999); Larry Cuban, *How Teachers Taught: Constancy and Change in American Classrooms, 1880–1990* (New York: Teachers College Press, 1993); Arthur Zilversmit, *Changing Schools: Progressive Education Theory and Practice, 1930–1960* (Chicago: University of Chicago Press, 1993).

7. National Center for Education Statistics, *Teacher Quality: A Report on the Preparation and Qualifications of Public School Teachers* (Washington, D.C.: U.S. Department of Education, 1999), pp. 11–12.

Select Bibliography

*In writing this book, I focused on primary sources in the education liter-*ature; references to those sources may be found in the notes to each chapter.

I also relied on the work of many fine historians. The most useful histories of education I consulted (in the order of their publication) were Lawrence A. Cremin, *The Transformation of the School: Progressivism in American Education, 1876–1957* (New York: Knopf, 1961); Raymond E. Callahan, *Education and the Cult of Efficiency* (Chicago: University of Chicago Press, 1962); Patricia Albjerg Graham, *Progressive Education: From Arcady to Academe* (New York: Teachers College Press, 1967); Edward A. Krug, *The Shaping of the American High School, 1880–1920* (Madison: University of Wisconsin, 1964) and *The Shaping of the American High School, 1920–1941* (Madison: University of Wisconsin, 1972); Marvin Lazerson, *Origins of the Urban School: Public Education in Massachusetts, 1870–1915* (Cambridge, Mass.: Harvard University Press, 1971); David Tyack, *The One Best System: A History of American Urban Education* (Cambridge: Harvard University Press, 1974); David Tyack and Elisabeth Hansot, *Managers of Virtue: Public School Leadership in America, 1820–1980* (New York: Basic Books, 1982); Herbert M. Kliebard, *The Struggle for the American Cur-*

riculum, 1893–1958 (Boston: Routledge & Kegan Paul, 1986); Robert L. Hampel, *The Last Little Citadel: American High Schools Since 1940* (Boston: Houghton Mifflin, 1986); David Tyack and Larry Cuban, *Tinkering Toward Utopia: A Century of Public School Reform* (Cambridge: Harvard University Press, 1995); Jurgen Herbst, *The Once and Future School: Three Hundred and Fifty Years of American Secondary Education* (New York: Routledge, 1996); Herbert M. Kliebard, *Schooled to Work: Vocationalism and the American Curriculum, 1876–1946* (New York: Teachers College Press, 1999); David L. Angus and Jeffrey E. Mirel, *The Failed Promise of the American High School, 1890–1995* (New York: Teachers College Press, 1999).

Among the sources that were valuable in gauging what was happening in the schools were Philip A. Cusick, *The Egalitarian Ideal and the American High School: Studies of Three Schools* (New York: Longman, 1983); Gerald Grant, *The World We Created at Hamilton High* (Cambridge: Harvard University Press, 1988); Arthur G. Powell, Eleanor Farrar, and David K. Cohen, *The Shopping Mall High School: Winners and Losers in the Educational Marketplace* (Boston: Houghton Mifflin, 1985); Arthur Zilversmit, *Changing Schools: Progressive Education Theory and Practice, 1930–1960* (Chicago: University of Chicago, 1993); Larry Cuban, *How Teachers Taught: Constancy and Change in American Classrooms, 1880–1990* (New York: Teachers College Press, 1993); Jeffrey Mirel, *The Rise and Fall of an Urban School System: Detroit, 1907–1981* (Ann Arbor: University of Michigan, 1993).

Some general histories, not specifically devoted to education, offered excellent coverage of education issues, not least because their authors were unaffiliated with any pedagogical school of thought. Among these were Richard Hofstadter, *Anti-Intellectualism in American Life* (New York: Knopf, 1963); Robert Divine, *The* Sputnik *Challenge* (New York: Oxford, 1993); and James G. Hershberg, *James B. Conant: Harvard to Hiroshima and the Making of the Nuclear Age* (New York: Knopf, 1993).

Up-to-date biographies are needed for William T. Harris, William C. Bagley, and Isaac Kandel. Two recent books about John Dewey provided helpful background: Alan Ryan, *John Dewey and the High Tide of*

American Liberalism (New York: Norton, 1995) and Robert B. West-brook, *John Dewey and American Democracy* (Ithaca: Cornell University Press, 1991). For a perspective on William Heard Kilpatrick that differs from the one presented in these pages, see John A. Beineke, *And There Were Giants in the Land: The Life of William Heard Kilpatrick* (New York: Peter Lang, 1998).

For their thoughtful assessments of the education of African Americans, I relied on Horace Mann Bond, *The Education of the Negro in the American Social Order* (New York: Prentice-Hall, 1934); Henry Allen Bullock, *A History of Negro Education in the South: From 1619 to the Present* (Cambridge: Harvard University Press, 1967); Kenneth James King, *Pan-Africanism and Education: A Study of Race Philanthropy and Education in the Southern States of America and East Africa* (New York: Oxford, 1971); James D. Anderson, *The Education of Blacks in the South, 1860–1935* (Chapel Hill: University of North Carolina Press, 1988); Vanessa Siddle Walker, *Their Highest Potential: An African American School Community in the Segregated South* (Durham: University of North Carolina Press, 1996); and Eric Anderson and Alfred A. Moss, *Dangerous Donations: Northern Philanthropy and Southern Black Education, 1902–1930* (Columbia: University of Missouri Press, 1999).

The transcript studies produced by the National Center for Education Statistics at the U.S. Department of Education since 1982 are extremely important as descriptions of the courses that high school students took, even though one never knows what sort of content is covered by labels such as "English" or "social studies." Valuable too are periodic reports from the National Assessment Governing Board about student performance on the federally funded National Assessment of Educational Progress, which has been the only reliable measure of achievement since testing of national samples of students began in the early 1970s.

Acknowledgments

*I am grateful to the public schools of Houston, Texas, where I was edu-*cated from 1943 to 1956. Along with my seven brothers and sisters, I attended Montrose Elementary School, switched to Sutton Elementary School after my family moved across town, then Albert Sidney Johnston Junior High School and San Jacinto High School. I treasure the memory of wonderful teachers (particularly my English and homeroom teacher, Mrs. Ruby Ratliff), though I also recall the large number of classmates who were guided into non-academic programs, as well as the policy of *de jure* racial segregation that prevented me from meeting children of other racial backgrounds.

My own children grew up in New York City, where they attended a private progressive school that was academically rigorous and pedagogically venturesome. My sons' teachers included a legendary, inspiring teacher of Shakespeare, a teacher who was a one-man department of classical languages, history teachers who knew how to bring the past to life, and many others who dreamed up projects that fired their students' minds and imaginations. If I could wave a magic wand, this is what I would want for all children.

I had many helpers over the dozen years in which this book was researched and written. I thank the following people who worked at various times as research assistants: Eileen Sclan, Joyce Kong, Tim Counihan, Thalassa Curtis, Hilary Landorf, Melinda Ganeles, and Kelly Walsh.

I thank my dear friend May Shayne, who gathered materials from the Demiashkevich Collection at the Vanderbilt Archives but did not live to see the results of her assistance. Thanks also to the archivists at the Paul Hanna Collection at the Hoover Institution; David Ment of special collections at Teachers College, Columbia University; the New York Public Library; and the New York University Library.

For their comments on early drafts of the manuscript, I am indebted to Jeffrey Mirel, Chester Finn, Jr., Maris Vinovskis, Joseph Viteritti, Michael Ravitch, and Paul Zoch.

I owe special thanks to the late Lawrence A. Cremin, my mentor at Teachers College, a great teacher and a model for other historians.

The writing of this book was generously supported by the Spencer Foundation and the John M. Olin Foundation.

I am grateful to Lynn Chu of Writers Representatives, and I thank Alice Mayhew and Roger Labrie of Simon & Schuster for their energetic efforts to ready the manuscript for publication.

Index

535

About the Author

Diane Ravitch is one of the nation's foremost historians of education and a leading education policy analyst. Her landmark books deeply influenced the national discussion of education standards in the 1980s and 1990s. She is a graduate of the Houston public schools, Wellesley College, and Columbia University. She has been a professor at Teachers College, Columbia University, and at New York University. She served in the U.S. Department of Education as assistant secretary in charge of education research and currently holds the Brown Chair in Education Studies at the Brookings Institution and edits *Brookings Papers on Education Policy*. She lives in Brooklyn, New York.